Psychology

Psychology

Pythagoras to Present

John C. Malone

A Bradford Book
The MIT Press
Cambridge, Massachusetts
London, England

MIT Press books may be purchased at special quantity discounts for business or sales promotional use. For information, please email special_sales@mitpress.mit.edu or write to Special Sales Department, The MIT Press, 55 Hayward Street, Cambridge, MA 02142.

This book was set in Palatino on 3B2 by Asco Typesetters, Hong Kong.
Printed and bound in the United States of America.

Library of Congress Cataloging-in-Publication Data

Malone, John C.
Psychology : Pythagoras to present / John C. Malone.
    p. cm.
Includes bibliographical references and index (p.   ).
ISBN 978-0-262-01296-6 (hardcover : alk. paper) 1. Psychology—History. I. Title.
BF81.M35 2009
150.9—dc22   2008034947

10 9 8 7 6 5 4 3 2 1

Contents

Preface and Acknowledgments

What is real? Do we live in the three-dimensional world that Isaac Newton envisioned? Does time flow like a river? Why is the sky blue? Are human beings aggressive because of their heredity? Do we see with our eyes or through our eyes? Are we born with complete knowledge that is gradually awakened during our lifetime? Is artificial intelligence really intelligent? Do we have free will? How should we deal with depression? How should we raise and educate children? How should we deal with crime? Is what we call the "mind" just another word for the "brain?"

These are all psychological questions, and they, along with many similar questions, deal with the most interesting issues in life. In several decades as an academic psychologist, I have thought about such things and interacted with countless students who shared this interest. Many times I have encountered students who arrive at my university with top scores in mathematics and science and with advanced placement credits in scientific subjects. The hard sciences come easily for them, they report, but psychology is "interesting," and, though they aim for medical or dental school, they major in psychology.

We all grow up in a society that teaches us that our minds and bodies are different in kind and that our minds see, hear, smell, and touch because sensory receptors in our eyes, ears, noses, and skin make copies of a real external world and create a mental copy. This doctrine comes to us from deep in antiquity, from Pythagoras and Plato. It has appeal and thus forms the main basis for Western thought. However, even so fundamental an account has faced credible opposition over the centuries, and we shortchange ourselves if we don't know about such alternatives.

We also miss out if we don't realize that a lot of good advice comes from the writings of the best thinkers of the past. Pythagoras, Thales,

Plato, Protagoras, Aristotle, Diogenes, and Epictetus all offered tried and tested advice on the leading of our lives and the treatment of psychopathology. But so did Berkeley, Hume, John Stuart Mill, Herbart, Wundt, James, Freud, Skinner, and Bem.

I have researched the history of psychology for decades, consulting original sources when I could and impeccable translations when necessary. I wrote and rewrote, revised and condensed, finishing with this book, of which I am proud. The content is accurate and, I believe, useful to an intelligent modern reader. I only wish that it could have been three times as long, but practical considerations preclude that.

I thank my mentors and fellow students for their conversations long ago at Duke University. In particular, I owe much to John Staddon, who taught me what it means to be a scholar and who has helped me over the years in more ways than I can ever repay. I also thank the many colleagues and students who have influenced me (and still do) at The University of Tennessee, Knoxville. I especially thank Gordon Burghardt, who has always been an inspiration and a model and who has encouraged me countless times.

Of course, I am grateful that my manuscript was received by Tom Stone, at The MIT Press, who first suggested that I write a "book" rather than a "textbook." I can't thank him enough and I only wish that someone had suggested that ten years earlier.

Finally, I thank my best friend and the person with whom I agree most on things in general, my wife, Carlene Valdata Malone.

Psychology

1   History, Psychology, and Science

If I have seen further, it is by standing on the shoulders of giants. (Isaac Newton, in Ferris 1988, p. 362)

Bernard of Chartres used to say that we are like dwarfs on the shoulders of giants. (John of Salisbury, 1159, in Ferris 1988, p. 41)

Gell-Mann...remarked...that if he had seen further than others, it is because he was surrounded by dwarfs. (In Ferris 1988, p. 310)

Progress, far from consisting in change, depends on retentiveness....Those who cannot remember the past are condemned to fulfill it. (Santayana 1905)

The Relevance of History

Pythagoras was one of the most influential people who ever lived, according to an authoritative commentator (Russell 1945), since he strongly influenced Plato, who was perhaps *the* most influential writer of all time. Plato's works strongly shaped the thinking of early Christians, especially St. Augustine, as well as the thought of countless others, including Sigmund Freud. Platonic thinking has so permeated Western thought as to be taken for granted, and a sketch of twentieth-century psychology shows that Plato is strikingly modern, though he died in 347 B.C. Aristotle also lived over two thousand years ago, yet a sympathetic modern interpreter of B. F. Skinner's psychology suggested that Aristotle understood Skinner's doctrines better than did the famed behaviorist himself (Rachlin 1994).

Further, at about the turn of the twentieth century, James Rowland Angell and John Dewey both noted that the new "functionalism" that had developed in America was a return to Aristotle's views, and sixty years later the novelist Ayn Rand described Aristotle as the source of the values that made America great. Aristotle also taught a doctrine that 2,000 years later would be called "self-actualization" by Goldstein, Maslow, Rogers, and others. Even Jean Piaget's conception of the mind of the very young child is precisely Aristotle's, a view very different from that of conventional psychology.

And Aristotle is only one individual in the long history of thought that has preceded modern psychology. Plato was even more influential— he greatly influenced Freud, as well as countless others. Both of these Greeks of antiquity are worth knowing, as are many other ancient and not-so-ancient thinkers—not just because we should know the precursors of modern views but because these ideas are frequently *better* than modern ones. That is why history is relevant.

Presentism: History as Justification for the Present
Those who dispute that conclusion include those who argue that our predecessors, surely including the ancient Greeks, knew nothing of the science and technology of the twentieth century, which represents the culmination of advances in our knowledge of physics, chemistry, and biology over the centuries. According to this view, the gain in knowledge has progressed continuously, sometimes quickly and sometimes slowly, but change has virtually always meant *improvement*, and the current state of affairs is the best that has ever existed. This seems clear in the natural sciences, where it is absurd to compare current knowledge of particle physics or astronomy with the state of knowledge of the nineteenth century, to say nothing of comparisons with that of the ancient Greeks.

This point of view is *presentism*, and it values history only as an arrow pointing to an ever-better future, so that knowledge of history is helpful only insofar as it shows which way the arrow points. Since current knowledge incorporates all that is of value in the past, it is better to know the present well than to wallow in the scrap heap of outmoded and discarded ideas. Authors who embrace this view often boast that their reference list contains no entries more than ten or twenty years old.

Presentism is compelling when applied to well-developed disciplines that can now point to clear technical advances. Thus, having no access to anything like the Stanford linear accelerator, Descartes was unlikely to progress far in the analysis of subatomic particles, and we may safely ignore his views on that subject. Presentism is still plausible, though less convincing, when applied to the biological sciences, where our conceptions of the nature of life have not greatly changed over the past several thousand years. But what of psychology at the turn of the twenty-first century?

An overview based on a consensus of popular textbook presentations would run pretty much as follows:

1. Psychology is the study of mind and behavior, which are two different things.

2. The mind is almost synonymous with the brain. The mind is composed of faculties, or powers, such as attention, memory, and reason, and these faculties are localized in specific brain centers or distributed in specific neural networks.

3. The senses, such as vision, are directly analogous to input channels —sensory information enters and is "processed." Seeing and hearing are somehow brought about by nerve cells in the brain.

4. The mind/brain is profitably viewed as a "wonderful computer."

It is almost impossible to entertain the idea that this is the best conception of psychology that has ever existed. In fact, it is not greatly different from Plato's psychology!

There is a lot that is good in Plato, but it's not his psychology, and we can do better if we try. It *is* difficult, because the mind/brain/ computer viewpoint is pervasive and actually remolds history, as presentist writers compose new histories by selecting material that contributes to the appearance of an unbroken ascent to the currently popular model. Thus, writers find "anticipations" of modern views in the thought of the ancients, and Aristotle is portrayed as an empiricist/associationist, hardly distinguishable from the simple associationists of the early twentieth century!

What to Expect in This Book

A Note on Historiography
During the second half of the twentieth century, many authors pointed out that extant histories of psychology (and other disciplines) were deeply flawed. Just as histories of nations had been strongly slanted to conform to the biases of jingoist authors, histories of psychology were biased. There was great wringing of hands and attempts to right the wrongs that had been done to Wundt, to Fechner, and even to Watson and Skinner. And there was acknowledging of the difficulty in writing

history, since the actors were long gone and documentation of their work was scattered or completely unavailable. The reader was to bear in mind that the writing of a history is a creative act, so that the writer's personal history must be taken into account.

One may disagree strongly with that argument! Such subjective factors may be the case in writing political histories, but they are of no concern to us. The fact is that the subjects of our history are indeed long gone, but they left writings that are authentic beyond any doubting, even when we consider writers who lived in ancient Greece. In a later chapter, we will read a brief poem that has been attributed to Plato and, in any event, was translated by Percy Shelly. There is no telling whether that is authentic. We will also read a passage from the *Theaetetus* concerning the nature of our experience and we may rest absolutely assured that Plato wrote it! We may be similarly sure that Aristotle wrote or dictated *De Anima* and *Nichomachean Ethics*. If we read those original sources, assuming fair translation, we can know that we are getting the author's account firsthand. We may interpret it differently than intended by the author, but that is possible with any account, including the one you are reading now.

Had psychologists read Wundt in the original, rather than relying on obviously misleading translation, there would have been no need to correct so many mistaken conclusions regarding his theories. Everything in this book derives from original sources or impeccable secondary sources—but here are my biases.

The Author's Biases: Guiding Themes
This is a history of *ideas*, more than of people, and we will see that several main themes run through the past 2,500 years. These are as follows:

• *The nature of mind*—is it different in kind from matter, or are both matter and mind merely aspects of some underlying reality? Perhaps mind is all that exists and matter is illusion. Or perhaps mind is illusory. Each of these views had its defenders and continues to have defenders today.

• *Statics and dynamics*—is psychology best viewed as a process, as activity? Or may it be better treated as interactions among things? For example, is sensation best seen as the taking in of copies of objects or as an activity we perform?

- *The nature of knowledge/belief*—what can we know and how do we know it? Is all knowledge and belief the product of sense experience, or are we born with innate knowledge? Perhaps we are born with mental categories that determine how we will construe the world.

- *What is the self?*—Is the self a stable entity that is born, lives, and dies, or is it a constantly changing thing, so that we are not the same "self" in youth and in old age?

- *The question of ethics*—what is the best way to lead our lives, and what is the goal of life? Should we seek happiness, or is there a better goal, as the Epicureans and Stoics believed?

- *The nature of will*—what is free will, and is it only an illusion? How do we account for our voluntary, "willed" acts?

Many other questions will arise, needless to say, but those are the important ones. They are the questions that are important to psychology, as opposed to those of interest only to philosophy or to history. Also important to psychology is the nature of explanation and the definition of science, a topic that we will consider very briefly.

A Note on Science and Explanation

Early in the twentieth century a group of Austrian philosophers attempted to establish the definitive "philosophy of science," laying out the rules by which science progresses and delineating science from nonscience. Their efforts exerted a great influence during the first half of the century, but by the end of the century, it was widely agreed that their contribution was of questionable value. The philosophers of the "Vienna Circle" had produced *Logical Positivism*, which we should not confuse with the positivism of the nineteenth century.

Positivism
This is the view that our descriptions and explanations of phenomena must be anchored in sense experience. In its simplest form, it demands that our accounts be "sensible"; we must be able to refer our audience to happenings that are describable in sensory terms. For example, *phlogiston* was a substance proposed by two German chemists, Johann Becher and Georg Stahl, in the eighteenth century to account for what we call combustibility. The problem with phlogiston was that it was supposed to be a substance, but one that had no effects on our senses

and was thus undetectable. However, its supposed existence could make sense of many chemical phenomena, as well as rusting, burning, and the like, and research based on the phlogiston theory may have transformed alchemy into chemistry.

Historians of science nonetheless treat the phlogiston theory as an unprofitable diversion and an impediment to the proper chemistry that was introduced by Lavoisier. And phlogiston was surely not a concept compatible with the new positivism. August Comte wrote a six-volume treatise, *Philosophe Positive*,[1] that described a progression in science from theocratic to metaphysical to positive. Theocratic accounts invoke the supernatural, whether fire and rain gods or the Judeo/ Christian God, to account for the existence of nature and the course of events. Comte saw metaphysical explanations as an improvement, though still unsatisfactory. They refer to "things beyond the appearances"—Plato's Forms, Kant's noumena, and Descartes's intuitions—which refer to agents that are incomprehensible, since they transcend the senses. The positivists will have none of this, correctly charging that metaphysics is (literally) nonsense.

Comte was only one of a long line of thinkers, from Francis Bacon through Ernst Mach and B. F. Skinner, who made a simple and powerful argument. That is, if we wish to explain something, we must stick with the sensory experiences that define that thing, and if we devise a theory that relies on unobservable, "nonsensical" agents, we are far astray. Ernst Mach, an Austrian physicist and positivist, who is frequently misunderstood, was a modern positivist. He argued against non-sensory constructs such as the atom and the electron, so he was routinely criticized for disallowing things that were commonly accepted. However, if you look into the history of the concept of the electron, you will find that Mach may have had a point. The electron apparently does not exist as a *thing*, and we mislead ourselves if we believe in a subatomic world of tiny solar systems, with nuclei and electrons as sun and planets.

Objectivity

This is, of course, the most frequently cited characteristic of science, and it is sad to be charged with failure to be "objective." But what is objectivity? We are told that to be "objective" is to be impartial– unbiased, and we know, as did Aristotle, Francis Bacon, and many others, that we are always biased. The trick is to be properly biased, which must mean to be biased as are other people. Objectivity, as reflected in agreement among observers, has its problems, however. There have been many opinions shared by many people over many centuries that we regard as obvious nonsense. Many still believe in astrology, magic, and learning while asleep, so consensus need have nothing to do with objectivity and the essence of science. Maybe verifiability is the hallmark of science and "objectivity."

Verifiability

Edmund Halley had plans to calculate the distance of the planet Venus from the earth by observing its transit time[2] from two widely separated spots on earth. This was a fine idea in 1716, but the opportunity for such observations comes only rarely. In the case of Venus, the next opportunities would be in 1761 and 1769, by which time Halley would be over a hundred years old if he were living at all. All he could do is urge others to do the work.

And what kind of a criterion is verifiability? It specifies that an objective statement concerns an observation that can be repeated by the same observer or by someone else. For example, the action of sulfuric acid on marble is capable of objective description—I may observe it repeatedly or we may observe it. Notice that this way of defining "verifiable" makes clear that it is essentially the same as *intersubjective*, or equivalent to *public knowledge*. Agreement by more than one observer is a simple case of verification and, as we know, verification is not enough!

Peirce and Popper: Refutability

Karl Popper (1963) argued persuasively that verification is a poor criterion for "objectivity" or "scientific meaningfulness," using an argument similar to that made by physicist and philosopher Charles Sanders Peirce in 1878. That is, if one were truly to verify something, say the relation between thunder and lightning, one must make enough observations of thunder–lightning to be confident of the relationship. But how large must that sample be?

As Peirce pointed out, there is no large enough number of observations that we can make to assure certainty, given the number of potentially observable instances that have occurred over the millennia, each of which might have provided a counterinstance. This holds for observations and for experiments of whatever kind, and Peirce suggested that conducting an experiment to determine whether some part of nature is orderly or not is equivalent to putting a spoonful of saccharine into the ocean in order to sweeten it.

In the same vein, Popper argued that *refutability* is the hallmark of scientific statements, since nothing can be truly verified, for the same reasons given by Peirce. But statements can be shown false, given a single counterinstance. I need only one case of an object falling in a vacuum and accelerating faster than thirty-two feet per second, and a "law" is broken. Refutability, not verifiability, is the criterion for objectivity, or the guide to deciding whether statements or questions are meaningful or vain.

Meaningful Questions   By meaningful questions, Peirce and Popper meant those that we can hope to answer decisively. Such questions must be cast in such form that refutation is possible. We cannot ask, to use an example from Peirce, whether the taking of the communion is really properly interpreted by the Catholic Church or by Protestant denominations: is the taking of the sacraments really the taking of the body and the blood of Christ, or is it symbolic? What experiments could be performed and what observations could be made to settle the issue? None that we can conceive; hence, the question is not meaningful. By the same token, Popper was inspired to adopt the criterion of refutability when he was struck by the apparent *irrefutability* of Freudian theory, compared with the refutability of Einstein's theory of relativity.

Many common questions are meaningless—unanswerable because there are no observations that could allow their refutation. "Are humans basically good or evil?" "Are all things in the process of self-actualization?" *Good* is an undefined—or vaguely defined—attribute, and self-actualization is a name for the fact that things change over time. Could any observations answer either question? What of astrology, an ancient discipline as popular now as it was three thousand years ago? Can an astrological prediction be tested—shown to clearly be wrong? Or are the predictions sufficiently vague that a believer can find confirmation in them?

When believers overzealously seek confirmation of predictions made in chemistry, physics, or biology, the case is different. Consider the almost-daily discovery of cures for cancer and the demonstrations of cold fusion in the late 1980s. In the case of "the cancer cure of the moment" and cold fusion, accepted criteria for testability and falsifiability settle the questions for most researchers. In astrology, such issues can never be settled. That is why astrology is not science—we might wonder whether much of psychology is in a similar state. For an insightful and refreshing discussion of explanation in psychology and in science in general, see Machado and Silva (2007).

Progress in Science

Boring and the Zeitgeist

Many accounts for the progress of science emphasize the influence of the times in which advances occur. Thus, Newton attributed his success to his predecessors, such as Galileo and Kepler, who provided the "shoulders of giants" on which he stood. Freud's insights on unconscious motivation were amply supported in Fechner's writings, and his theories of biological drives and energy were held earlier by his teacher, Ernst Brücke, in whose laboratory Freud worked during his student years. Where would Darwin have been if there were not ideas of evolution in the air all around him? His grandfather, Erasmus, as well as Malthus and Wallace, more than paved the way; given the zeitgeist of the early nineteenth century, someone was bound to propose a plausible theory of evolution by midcentury. If not Darwin, someone else would have played the part.

Edwin G. Boring (shown in figure 1.1), whose views (1950) on the history of psychology exerted tremendous influence during the twentieth century, was a prime exponent of the zeitgeist (Hegel's "spirit of the times") interpretation of the progress of science. According to this view, progress is an accretion, the building up of facts and the evolution of theories, so that Newtons, Faradays, Freuds, and Madam Curies are inevitable, given their precedents. This is the point of view taken for granted by the public at large and by the traditional philosophy of science, whose job it is to pass on the "received view." It is the way that all of us are taught to see the progress of science, both in high school courses and in college. And this view has to be at least roughly true, since we have seen progress over the centuries, at least in technology. But did this all happen gradually, as a function of the zeitgeist?

Kuhn's Revolutions

Kuhn wrote of the moment, in 1947, when, while reading Aristotle, he made his own great insight.

Figure 1.1
Boring. Courtesy of the Archives of the History of American Psychology, University of
Akron.

Over the last thirty years, "The Structure of Scientific Revolutions" has sold
over a million copies, an astonishing number for a work of serious scholarship.

"I'm much fonder of my critics...than my fans."

Kuhn even tried to take back the word "paradigm," suggesting instead "exemplar." (All four quotations are from Gladwell 1996, p. 32)

Thomas Kuhn, with a Ph.D. in physics, published an unlikely best
seller, *The Structure of Scientific Revolutions* (1962), for a series of monographs called the International Encyclopedia of Unified Science. Philosophers had made science, the most exciting of disciplines, dull and
plodding—the zeitgeist raises enthusiasm in few. Kuhn showed that
the progress of science is not the slow accretion of accomplishments by
one generation that lays a foundation for the next. Instead, it is a series
of "intellectually violent revolutions," separated by peaceful interludes.
The fact that he specifically excluded psychology and other social

sciences need not concern us—his book stirred sociology and psychology as much as it did the natural sciences, where it clearly applied.

The influential little book proposed that science was a social enterprise characterized by *revolution*, not evolution. Far from an orderly accumulation of facts that add to a universally shared view of reality, Kuhn argued that science shows revolutionary struggles, leading to fundamental changes in the way that whole sciences are construed. Later viewpoints are not necessarily more "scientific" than earlier ones, and there is nothing essentially unscientific about Aristotelian dynamics, phlogistic chemistry, or the thermodynamics of caloric. These worldviews were simply replaced by other worldviews, following a sequence that probably has more to do with the *sociology of science* than with "science versus pseudoscience."

Kuhn examined the circumstances surrounding some of the acknowledged "turning points" in the history of science, those associated with Copernicus, Newton, Lavoisier, and Einstein. In each of these cases, the scientific community eventually rejected a set of time-honored beliefs and adopted a new set. A marked discontinuity in thinking occurred in each case—*revolution*—rather than a gradual evolution in thinking as findings "accumulated."

Kuhn used the term *paradigm* to refer to a set of beliefs shared by virtually all workers in a scientific field. Newton's mechanics serves as a familiar example—a paradigm that treats space, time, and mass as absolutes and that successfully accounts for an amazing variety of phenomena, ranging from the motion of a projectile to the falling of leaves to the orbiting of planets. This paradigm, that treats the universe as dead, purposeless matter obeying universal mechanical laws, replaced the mechanics of Aristotle, which envisioned the universe as filled with purpose and composed of "essential natures." With Newton's triumph, we no longer saw plants as "trying" to grow and stones as falling due to their "jubilance" in returning to earth.

A paradigm includes all the beliefs that are taught to professionals in a field, and no one ignorant of the paradigm can be taken seriously as a scientist. Newtonian physics, Darwinian evolution, and the astronomy of Copernicus were all paradigms, as were their predecessors, the physics of Aristotle and the chemistry of the phlogiston theory. But, as Kuhn described paradigms, it is clear that there have been none in psychology, since no general framework of interpretation has been universally accepted. While philosophers of Newton's time might question the fundamental status of time, no physicists did, and, while some question the details of evolutionary theory, no biologist questions the theory in general aspects. No such state of affairs has existed in psychology.

The History of Paradigms   Given a paradigm, *normal science* never involves real discoveries; rather, research is concentrated on *puzzle solving*, or showing how more and more phenomena of interest can be explained within the framework of the paradigm. The scientists of the Enlightenment of the eighteenth and nineteenth centuries were not trying to discover new phenomena—they were trying to fit all phenomena into the mechanical space/mass/time framework that Newton had used to explain the motion of bodies. Does the fall of a stone exemplify the same laws shown in the flight of an arrow or of a comet? Are the bodies of animals *and* of humans merely complicated clockwork mechanisms? All efforts aimed to show that the laws at hand could encompass all reality.

The normal science paradigm chugs on for years or for centuries, with ordinary puzzle solving sometimes bothered by *anomalies*, or findings that seem foreign to the paradigm. In physics, the finding that heavier objects do not fall faster in a vacuum was a difficult anomaly for Aristotelian physicists.[3] When anomalies become numerous enough or serious enough, the paradigm is modified to deal with them. This blurs the paradigm, of course, and, in the classic example, the geocentric theory of Ptolemy[4] endured for over a thousand years because Ptolemy had modified it so much with added eccentrics and epicycles. It thus accounted for otherwise anomalous observations of heavenly bodies, but everyone knew that it was so bizarre that it could represent no conceivable reality.

Kuhn proposed that the final stage is that of *crisis*, where the paradigm is defended by the old generation of scientists, if only because it is in that paradigm that their reputation and prestige are invested. Younger scientists lack that baggage and so join their senior dissenters who have brought about the crisis. All of this finally leads to the dissolution of the paradigm and its replacement by a new one. Aristotelian physics would never have left unless Newton's paradigm had been there to replace it.

Do Revolutions Really Occur?   Kuhn saw science as a social enterprise that advances through the violent overthrow of one paradigm by another. Russell Hanson (1958/1965) proposed a similar theory but emphasized the way that people conceive things, so that the change from Aristotelian to Galilean physics is a "Gestalt shift," or a new perspective on the world.[5] Hence, his view was revolutionary, like Kuhn's, but occurring at the level of individual scientists. Others, like the philosopher Laudan, combined the evolutionary and the revolutionary accounts, really no trick, showing that great individuals were more important than Boring allowed and softening the disruptive influence of revolutions in science.[6] But thank heaven for Thomas Kuhn, whether he exaggerated his case or not. Finally there was something *interesting* in the philosophy of science!

Is Science Possible?

An unintended effect of Kuhn's book was its appeal to cranks, who would publish manuscripts that the authors felt were "paradigmatic," while "the postmodernists used his book to suggest what he never believed: that his scientific paradigms were as faddish and ephemeral as trends in art" (Gladwell 1996, p. 32).

Kuhn had emphasized social/cultural influences on science, providing a welcome revision of the logical positivist "introductory chapter" model. However, in the late twentieth century, the social/cultural aspects of science were stressed to an extreme degree by humanists who might be called "postmodernists." They argue that science is wholly a social enterprise, as are art and literature, and that there is no such thing as objective truth.

This is a position that is difficult for many people to understand, let alone accept. In particular, chemists, physicists, and other physical scientists may have more difficulty in comprehending it than do their colleagues in the humanities. One writer tried to help by translating postmodern thought into words that are understandable to scientists. A biological anthropologist and anatomist named Cartmill (see figure 1.2) offered this simplified description:

First, objective reality is a myth. There is no "other" out there to be objectified. All others are part of the self. All so-called realities are subjective, and all of them are constructs. The ones that find widespread acceptance are consensual arrangements, party platforms, socially hammered out to satisfy a variety of pragmatic and political aims. Facts are arranged and negotiated, not discovered. Second, since different reality constructs are incommensurate with each other and potentially infinite in number, observation and experiment can never force us to choose one to the exclusion of all others. It follows from this that

Figure 1.2
Cartmill. Personal collection.

any claim to know something about a real world is at bottom a power grab, a bid to eliminate cultural and political diversity by dictating the terms and content of everybody's discourses. Therefore, scientists' claims to knowledge are really political claims, dressed up as detached objectivity. (Cartmill 1991)

Cartmill went on to discuss the views of Jean Baudrillard, "France's leading philosopher of post-modernism," who accuses the science of biochemistry and molecular genetics of promoting a social and political program, in that DNA's power of control promotes a neo-capitalist cybernetic social order.

Such an astounding proposal is actually only the extreme of very reasonable views, and they are held by advocates who are unaware that less extreme contextualist views have been held by many others, such as Wundt, Meade, Kantor, and Skinner. Those authors were not advocating the abandonment of science; they promoted merely a change from the primitive mechanical science of the Enlightenment. This seems to have been realized by Cartmill, who was not totally opposed to all forms of this view.

He proposed that scientists deal with postmodern critics by emphasizing technology. We may never be able to answer questions like "Do
we really understand thermodynamics, and how can we be sure?" But
what of the question, "Do we really know how to make automobiles,
or are we just kidding ourselves?" The answer here is that we *do*
know, and the ancient Greeks did not. This supposes that advances in
technology must correspond in some way to advances in understanding of reality, a case that is not necessarily easy to make. Perhaps
a wiser method for dealing with the recent crop of "pop" critics
of science is Cartmill's proposal that all students (and postmodernists) dissect a human body, "which is one of the great transforming
experiences."

2 Science and Psychology in Ancient Greece

For by convention color exists, by convention bitter, by convention sweet, but in reality atoms and void, says Democritus.... The qualities of things exist merely by convention; in nature there is nothing but atoms and void space. (Galen, in Nahm 1964, p. 160)

He (Protagoras) said that man is the measure of all things, meaning simply that that which seems to each man also assuredly is. If this is so, it follows that the same thing both is and is not, and is bad and good. (Aristotle, in Nahm 1964, p. 226)

The Two Strains in Ancient Greek Thought

It is not always recognized that there were two clear strains in early Greek thought—the naturalist scientific and the mystical scientific. The philosophers of Miletus, beginning with Thales, were the naturalists. They showed that mind and body are not necessarily natural divisions of reality—it is possible, even "natural," to see all reality composed of one substance, not two. To a lesser extent, the philosophers of the Greek colony of Elea, in what is now Italy, were also naturalists. However, while they agreed that mind and matter were one, they taught that truth was discernible only through reason, not through bare sense experience.

These two groups were the naturalistic strain in Greek thought, and they are usually given appropriate attention by philosophers and by historians of psychology. However, differences in the opinions of Milesians and Eleatics in the sixth century B.C. were negligible when the teachings of either group were compared with those of the Pythagoreans, who combined the dualism and mysticism of Eastern religion with the science of the Greeks.

Figure 2.1
Pythagoras. Courtesy of the National Library of Medicine, National Institutes of Health.

Pythagoras

The dualism, which separates matter and mind, body and soul, God and the world, won however a place in Greek philosophy even at this early period, when Pythagoreanism arrayed Orphic mysticism in a cloak of science. (Zeller 1883/1964, p. 41)

For a thousand years scientist–mystics followed the teachings of Pythagoras (see figure 2.1), whose ideas had immense and lasting influence, aside from that exerted on his followers. It may seem odd that science and mysticism coalesced for long, but that has frequently happened in history. Even Isaac Newton, perhaps the most important figure in the development of Western science, was obsessed with alchemy and religious mysticism—John Maynard Keynes, having gone through a trunk of Newton's papers that he bought at auction, was shocked at what he found and called Newton "the last of the magicians" (Ferris 1988, p. 104).

Pythagoras lived through the sixth century B.C. and probably died in 495 B.C. He was influenced by the Milesian philosophers, especially Anaximander and Anaximenes, and was probably a student of the latter. The chief source of information about Pythagoras and other presocratic thinkers is Kathleen Freeman (1947), who based her work on the nineteenth-century classic work of Diels. It is impossible to determine exactly what Pythagoras taught and what his followers contributed. He purposely left no writings and demanded secrecy from his disciples.

He taught advanced material to those he admitted as Students (called "Esoterics") and presented only rough outlines to those called Auditors. Records could thus arise from either group, making it difficult to sort the essential from the trivial. Even Heraclitus, who was almost a contemporary, seriously misunderstood him. Kathleen Freeman noted that sifting the genuine precepts of Pythagoras from later modifications and counterfeits and correctly interpreting their meaning "was even in ancient times a thankless task" (1953, p. 256). The secrecy of the Pythagoreans was legendary and continued long after Pythagoras's death. In one case, a woman follower named Timycha (ca. 300 B.C.) bit off her tongue and spat it out at the tyrant Dionysius of Syracuse, Sicily, rather than reveal Pythagorean mysteries (Menage 1690/1984).

The Pythagoreans

According to the historian Iamblichus, writing in the fourth century A.D., there were 218 men and 17 women in history clearly identifiable as practicing Pythagoreans. These would be well-known people, so the total number of Pythagoreans was far greater. One of the last to call himself a Pythagorean was Lycon of Tarentum in the late third century A.D. That means that the teachings of Pythagoras, a mixture of religious and mathematical beliefs, had persisted for almost a thousand years.

Because of that mixture, Bertrand Russell (1945) called him a combination of "Einstein and Mrs. Eddy" (the latter being the founder of Christian Science). Pythagoras himself was "one of the most important men that ever lived," according to Russell. This is because some of his beliefs were adopted by Plato two centuries later and then were passed on through the millennia to our time.

It was Pythagoras who coined the word "philosophy." He was born on the island of Samos in Ionia, the Greek colonies in western Asia Minor, and moved as an adult to Croton, one of a number of Greek colonies in what is now southern Italy. He influenced contemporaries at the nearby colony of Elea, Xenophanes and Parmenides, and he influenced Plato.

Religious Views Pythagoras's religious teachings were a modification of Orphism, the worship of nature that was always the real religion of the ancient Greeks; the pantheon of gods (Zeus, Apollo, Athena, and so on) represented only the official religion, not the religion of the people. After all, those gods were difficult to admire, let alone worship, since they were essentially humans who were immortal and who possessed magic powers. Religions that hope to be popular do better if they promise adherents an attractive afterlife, impart the ability to work magic, include secret "mysteries" known only to insiders, and feature sacrifices and barbaric fertility festivals.

That was Orphism, also called the cult of Bacchus or of Dionysus (see figure 2.2).[1] The cult of Bacchus arose in the fertility rituals of agricultural and savage people living in Thrace, north of Greece. Orpheus was a Thracian bard, perhaps an actual individual, but very likely mythical, who is supposed to have spread a form of this religion to the Greeks in a version palatable to them.

According to one of many versions of the myth, Bacchus/Dionysus was born the son of Zeus and his daughter Persephone. He was killed by the titans (e.g., Chronos, Oceanus, Prometheus), who tore him apart and ate him.[2] Luckily, the goddess Athena rescued the heart and gave it to Zeus, who ate it and produced from it a new Dionysus. Zeus, understandably angered, destroyed the titans with thunderbolts. From their ashes, including Dionysus-as-digested, came humanity. Here is an early version of the idea of death and rebirth that is part of many religions, as well as the belief that people are partly earth-born (the titans were considered nondivine) and partly divine.

In practice, devotees would seek ecstasy in dancing by torchlight on mountaintops, arousing "enthusiasm," or communion with the god. Eventually, the sacrificial goat would seem to be Dionysus himself, and it would be attacked, torn to pieces, and eaten, reenacting the acts of the titans. Orphism was predominately feminine, and many husbands hesitated to interfere with these celebrations.

The Pythagoreans did not accept these barbaric aspects of Orphism, and in fact they were usually vegetarians who forbade animal sacrifice and emphasized the importance of intellectual over sensual pleasures. However, they did accept some of the theology of Orphism and they

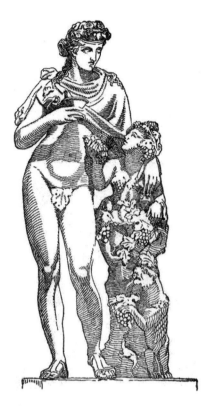

Figure 2.2
Dionysus. Courtesy of http://karenswhimsy.com.

certainly accepted its ascetic aspects. Aside from enthusiastic gatherings, orphics were concerned with purification of their bodies to render them fit to progress in the next world. They tended to follow fixed customs, and they valued self-control, loyalty, silence, and obedience. Such virtue readies the soul for the next life.

The Air Is Full of Souls Not only did the many members of the cult of Dionysus/Bacchus believe in souls but they believed in the transmigration of souls, or metempsychosis. Depending on the good or evil done during a lifetime, a man might be reborn as a man, a woman, a horse, a dog, an insect, or another animal. Proper living meant upward transmigration, the endpoint being life in a star.

One corollary of the doctrine of metempsychosis is the possibility that a stray soul could enter any body. Pythagoreans believed that the air itself was full of souls; the constant motion of dust particles seen in a shaft of light (Brownian movement) was evidence for that. These souls can affect our dreams and send omens to both humans and animals (Freeman 1953, p. 253).

Themistoclea   Interestingly, a woman may have supplied the ethical portion of the Pythagorean philosophy. According to Menage (1690/ 1984), Themistoclea (Theoclea/Aristoclea) may have been the sister of Pythagoras. She was priestess of Apollo at the famous oracle at Delphi, where questions put to the god, accompanied by offerings, were answered through the priestess. It appears that in this way Pythagoras received many of the ethical principles that he espoused. Themistoclea is also the first recorded woman to be called a philosopher, a title made possible by Pythagoras's coining the term "philosophy"—the love of truth for its own sake, rather than for some immediate practical purpose.

The Music of the Spheres   The Pythagoreans are best known for their doctrine that the key to reality lies in number. Everything had a number that "explained" it—the soul was 4, as was health, the earth was 2, the sun was 1, justice was 4 or 9, and even number itself had a number: 10. Ratios, consonances (symphonies), and harmonies were everywhere. Even the planets in their orbits made music, "the music of the spheres," which we don't hear because we are so accustomed to it (though Pythagoras claimed to hear it, according to Freeman 1953, p. 82). It is in music that the power of number showed itself most clearly. Imagine quantifying something that mysterious!

Suppose you pluck a string (line AE in the following display) that produces a tone that we call "f":

A———B———C———D———E

While it sounds, you clamp the string at three fourths of its length (at B). When this shorter segment (BE) is plucked, it makes a pleasing "consonant" sound, probably because of a sharing of harmonics (see the clear and authoritative discussion of this subject in Handel's classic 1989 text). Every third harmonic of the higher frequency (three fourths of the string—300 Hz, 600 Hz, 900 Hz, 1200 Hz…) matches every fourth harmonic of the sound produced by the previous vibration of the whole string (400 Hz, 800 Hz, 1200 Hz…). When the ratio of the lengths of the two vibrating strings is composed of small whole numbers, the number of matches of harmonics is greatest, and more "consonance" results. This 4:3 ratio produces a "fourth," or an increase in pitch of four steps (f, g, a, b).

Pythagoras also found that when the string was clamped so as to form a ratio of 3:2, a pleasing sound was produced. This would be the case if, after BE was plucked, a clamp was placed at C, two thirds of the previous length, and the string again plucked. This is a "fifth" (an increase in pitch of five steps—b, c, d, e, f) and likewise probably depends on matching harmonics for its pleasing sound. Finally, when he plucked AE and clamped the string at C, producing a ratio of 2:1, plucking CE (or AC) produced a consonant sound raised an octave, or eight steps (as in f, g, a, b, c, d, e, f).[3]

What is so impressive about that? Consider the ratios that produce pleasing sounds: 1:1, 4:3, 3:2, and 2:1. And consider this:

1. The two consonant ratios, the fourth (4:3) and the fifth (3:2), span eight steps, or an octave (2:1), which is also consonant. Therefore, Pythagoras discovered concord in number and music.

2. A tone, a fourth, a fifth, and an octave are produced by the ratios 1:1, 4:3, 3:2, and 2:1. As fractions, these become 1/1, 4/3, 3/2, and 2/1. The lowest common denominator is 6, producing 6/6, 8/6, 9/6, and 12/6. Finally, the numerators form two pairs, 6/8 and 9/12, which, expressed as fractions, are equal! You may have also noticed that the ratios $1/1 \times 4/3 \times 3/2 = 2/1$. Hence, unity (equality) is produced from disparity.

One of the three daughters of Pythagoras, Arignote, wrote many works on philosophical topics and on the mysteries of Ceres (the goddess of growth) and Bacchus. About number, she wrote:

... the eternal essence of number is the most providential cause of the whole heaven, earth, and the region in between. Likewise it is the root of the continued existence of gods and daimones, as well as that of divine men. (Menage 1690/1984)

This illustrates the heart of Pythagorean philosophy that began a tradition that lived on through Plato and Descartes to modern theories that stress formal, mathematical answers to questions. Bertrand Russell wisely noted that mathematics is the "chief source of belief in eternal and exact truth" and in a world of ideal relations beyond the reach of sensory experience (1945, p. 37). The influence of mathematics, emphasizing intuition and reason over sensory experience and appearances, was both profound and unfortunate, in Russell's view. However, that emphasis led the Pythagoreans to hold that even the soul is a "harmony."

The Nature of Reality   Geometry was very important to the Pythagoreans, and the famous theorem of Pythagoras is only one of his contributions.[4] He also saw geometry as the basis for reality. Pythagoras proposed a geometrical atomism that was adopted in its entirety by Plato in the *Timaeus*, predictably enough, based on number.

The four elements later attributed to Empedocles were given specific geometrical forms so that earth was assumed to be composed of tiny cubes, six-sided figures. Fire, prickly as it is, was made of tiny tetrahedrons, four-sided pyramidal figures, while water is so slippery because of atoms shaped as icosahedrons, twenty-sided figures very nearly spherical. Air was composed of octohedrons, or eight-sided particles.

In addition, the Pythagoreans believed in a cosmology that featured earth as a planet, not as the center of the universe, and in "counter earth," which was logically necessary in order to bring the number of heavenly bodies to ten, which was regarded as a sacred number. In their view, the total number of such bodies comprised Earth, the moon, the sun, Mercury, Venus, Mars, Jupiter, Saturn, the fixed stars, and counter earth. Following their mathematical interpretation of the universe, the unit of measure was the earth and the "wheel of stars" was nine times the size of earth, the orbit of the moon was eighteen times the size of earth, and the "wheel" of the sun was twenty-seven times the size of earth.

Interestingly, they believed that time was not fixed and that different sized bodies make different "bends" of time (Freeman 1953, p. 253). This shows that Kant's much later pronouncement, shared by virtually everyone, that time is a fixed part of our framework for experience was not shared by all ancient thinkers. They also believed in a set of "opposites," part of an eternal conflict that is united by/as harmonia. The opposites had to total ten, a sacred number, and were as follows:

limited/unlimited

odd/even

one/many

right/left

male/female

rest/motion

straight/curved

light/darkness

good/bad

square/oblong

Pythagoreans stressed the constant changes and conflicts in the world and the ideal state of harmonia. This applied to their views on health, since that too is a harmony, achieved largely through diet. Pythagoras believed that all food has pharmacological effects and should be treated as drugs; the drug effect is apparent in the case of wine, where the effect is extreme, but other foods also have effects.

Pythagorean Precepts   Pythagoreans constituted a cult, for whom the opinions of Pythagoras were Truth. Countless bits of wisdom were attributed to him, and followers memorized as many as they could. Critics, such as Heraclitus, charged that they measured wisdom merely in terms of the number of allegorical precepts that a person had memorized. Some examples from Freeman (1953, p. 255) of these precepts are:

- "Do not poke the fire with a sword." (Or irritate the angered person.)
- "Do not eat beans." (Since they appear to hold a tiny embryo . . .)
- "Shoe the right foot first."
- "Do not speak without a light."
- "Do not have intercourse with a woman wearing gold."

Theano   Pythagoras died in a fire in the home of one of his daughters, and his school continued under the apparently capable direction of his wife and pupil, Theano. She is the most famous of the many women who were Pythagoreans, and she left a fragment, *On Piety*, that clarifies the relation of number and matter. According to Theano, number is not the origin of matter, as some proposed; rather, it is the determining and ordering principle in nature (Waithe 1987).

Beginnings of Scientific Psychology in Greece

Becoming and Being

From the mysticism and dualism of the Pythagoreans, we now turn to the naturalism and monism that was far more typically Greek (Zeller

1883/1964, p. 34). Two chief themes that define modern psychology have defined thought through the centuries. They don't correspond well to the familiar distinctions between rationalism and empiricism. The real distinction lies in the relative emphasis placed on statics versus dynamics; philosophers traditionally refer to being versus becoming (Nahm 1964).

Thinkers, both ancient and modern, who stress statics (or "being") tend to be rationalists, who give little or no credence to the evidence of the senses. For them, experience is an illusion and real knowledge comes only through exercise of the power of reason. For some ancients, this amounted to communication with the gods or reminiscences of previous lives. For moderns, it is more often seen as cognitive or mental processing, though it also characterizes mystic and other views that posit a higher reality beyond the world of ordinary sense experience. The Pythagoreans clearly belong to this group, as do the philosophers of Elea. Most importantly, this is the view of Plato and those many subsequent thinkers who followed his path.

Those who stress dynamics (or "becoming") may also value reason, but for them far more importance is attached to the information of the senses. The world that we experience is no illusion, but it is a world of constant change, and much effort is required to sort out general principles that accurately describe its operation. The philosophers of Miletus held this view, as did Heraclitus and Aristotle, as well as the many subsequent philosophers for whom there is only one world—there is no distinction between the perceived and the "real" world.

Milesian Naturalists and Eleatic Rationalists

Do the earliest Greek thinkers really have anything to do with our understanding of psychology? One eminent source (Brett/Peters 1965, p. 37) wrote:

To those who think of psychology exclusively in terms of rats in mazes, neurotics in the consulting room, intelligence tests, and brass instruments, it cannot seem anything but odd to start the story of psychology with the early Greek cosmologists.

He then went on to show how basic ideas of Freud and many others were appreciated by the ancients. Early philosophers are often described as concerned solely with the physical world, and we are told that only with Socrates and the Sophists did consideration of the human psyche begin. This is false—the earliest Greek thinkers were materialist monists, a view that has clear and important implications for psychology as we will see below.

The Materialist Monists of Miletus

The city of Miletus lies on the coast of Asia Minor and was a center for commerce and industry in the sixth century B.C. Many writers have speculated on the reasons that this was the site for the first human thoughts that we would call "philosophical." That is, the Milesians were the first to show serious concern for matters that were not obviously utilitarian.

The Egyptians, Babylonians, Persians, and other civilizations had devised calenders, made astronomical observations, invented writing, and accomplished many building projects that seem amazing even today. However, these activities were invariably carried out in the service of practical matters, such as agriculture, navigation, commerce, and industry. The Milesians were not impractical; Thales himself was a paradigm of military and engineering achievement. But he and his fellows also showed concern for useless knowledge that concerned the nature of things independent of likely practical application.

The Milesians were the first to seriously wonder about the nature of reality—the question "What is real?" is the question of ontology. They asked questions about the origin and nature of knowledge—"What can we know and how do we know it?" is the question of epistemology. They wondered what ways of living are best if one is to find happiness, thus asking questions of ethics. And in all of this they speculated on the nature of mind, beginning the study of what we call psychology.

The first psychological thought that deserves our attention comes from Thales and his Milesian colleagues. They provided an interesting and plausible explanation for reality in general and for the relation between mind and body.

Thales and the First Scientific Statement

Some say that soul is diffused throughout the whole universe; and it may have been this which led Thales to think that all things are full of gods. (Aristotle, *De Anima*, 1.2, 405a19)

Thales (636–545) was one of the "seven sages" of ancient Greece, as listed by later historians and commentators. A total of twenty-seven people appeared in various "lists of the seven," but only Thales and a few others (e.g., Solon and Bias) appeared on every list. As an engineer, Thales altered the course of a mighty river (the Halys) while serving on a military expedition for Croesus, the king of Lydia. He invented the manhole, predicted an eclipse on May 28, 585 B.C., cornered the market on olive presses after predicting a rich harvest, and experimented with static electricity, which he viewed as related to lightning. The prediction of the (solar) eclipse was possible because of his knowledge of Babylonian observations that led to what was called the Saros—a period of eighteen years and eleven days separating solar eclipses.

He is also credited with accurately measuring the height of a pyramid, no mean feat in the days before geometry. He did it by standing by the pyramid in the sunshine until his shadow was equal in length to his height. Then he measured the shadow cast by the pyramid which would be, of course, equal to the pyramid's height.

The "first scientific statement" was something like, "water is best," or "water is the physis." By physis is meant the substance that is the basis for all existence and that accounts for phenomena through constant change—largely, through condensation and rarefication. As the Greeks viewed matters, understanding/explanation of phenomena was largely a problem of determining what material was involved. A burning feeling is explained when one sees that a flame has touched the skin and one knows that "flame material" produces such effects.

The suggestion that water is the basic constituent of reality is reasonable, given that water clearly takes on three forms: solid, liquid, and gas. It seems no great leap to infer that perhaps water may condense to firmer stuff than ice and thus form earth and rock. As water rarefies, it evaporates, forming visible steam, and this may be a step toward the final category of reality, fire. Anyone who has held a hand over a boiling kettle may feel the truth of this.

Anaximander and the Infinite   Anaximander was a contemporary of Thales, a respected astronomer and geographer, and—unlike Thales—he was a writer. Anaximander was the first prose-writing Greek, though all of his works were lost except the following single sentence:

The beginning of that which is, is the boundless but whence that which is arises, thither must it return again of necessity; for the things give satisfaction and reparation to one another for their injustice, as is appointed according to the ordering of time. (Zeller 1964, p. 43)

What does this mean? The most reasonable interpretation, although there are others, is that it concerns Anaximander's thoughts on reality.

If water were the physis, how may we account for the conflict of contraries, the fact that the other forms of matter—air, fire, and earth—are destroyed by it? Water extinguishes fire and dissolves earth, so how can it be a form of fire or earth? The same holds for any of the four elements of reality. Thus, Anaximander (610–545 B.C.) proposed that the physis is something other than earth, air, fire, and water that is constantly changing form.

He called it various names: infinite, unbounded, and indefinite. But whatever it was, it included us. It was uncreated, indestructible, and constantly "moving."[5] Different substances are produced by this movement. Warmth and Cold "separate out" first and together form the Moist, from which comes Earth and Air and the Circle of Fire that surrounds the earth. Anaximander was really the author of the doctrine of constant change.

Anaximenes and the Breathing Universe

Just as our souls, which are made of air, hold us together, so does breath and air encompass the world. (Zeller 1964, p. 46)

Anaximenes (fl. 585–528 B.C.) was a student of Anaximander and perhaps of Parmenides (Nahm 1964, p. 43) and proposed that the physis is not the infinite, but air. Seeing air as the principle of life (the pneuma means "air," "spirit," or "breath"), Anaximenes viewed both the macrocosm, the universe, and animate beings as alive.

He proposed that condensations and rarefactions of air account for the world of appearances, an adaptation of the proposals of Thales and Anaximander. Perhaps more important, he proposed a physical explanation for the rainbow, as the effect of the sun's rays on thick clouds. He also proposed natural explanations for eclipses and recognized that the moon derives its light from the sun. Many of his explanations were grossly incorrect, but only a century or two before, "Homer" had reflected the common view of the time when he treated the rainbow, Iris, as a person.

The Microcosm and the Macrocosm Like the other Greeks of his
time, Thales was a naturalist. Naturalism, in this context, treats all phenomena as occurrences in nature, all explainable in the same terms. We
are part of nature, and the universe as a whole, the macrocosm, may be
viewed as an enlargement of the individual human (the microcosm), or
vice versa. We are each a little part of nature, and nature itself is an extension, so to speak, of us.

Hylozoism or Hylopsychism or Vitalism If we are a part of nature
and nature is nothing but constant transformations in water, or whatever physis, then what is mind and what is consciousness? Are we
reduced to mindless mechanisms? Where is mind?

The answer for the Milesians is that mind is distributed through the
universe, and it is not "unnatural." Greeks of this period saw nature as
animate and psychology (and theology) as part of physics. Before the
fifth century B.C., the only thinkers who believed that mind and matter
were separate were the Pythagoreans, who were regarded (rightly) as
mystics.

The virtue of this view is that humans are seen as part of the natural
universe, and thus their passions and thoughts are subject to laws. As
the universe is lawful and may be predicted to an extent, the human
psyche is lawful and may also be mastered. For these ancients, habit,
climate, and diet were the key to the control of the psyche (Brett/
Peters 1912/1965). The alternative is that of the Pythagoreans and the
dualists who followed. For them, mind and body are different in kind
and the mind is, essentially, beyond understanding or control. Clearly,
the material monist view is the optimistic one, though, oddly enough,
it is almost always interpreted as pessimistic!

Heraclitus: Becoming

[H]is works, like those of all of the philosophers before Plato, are known only
through quotations, largely made by Plato or Aristotle for the sake of refutation. (Russell 1945, p. 45)

In fact, Heraclitus left 130 fragments, but they do little good, since he
was an eminently nasty and contemptuous man, who purposely wrote
as obscurely as possible so that he would not be understood. Consider
the following excerpts (Nahm 1964, pp. 96–97); the first is the famous
pronouncement that is usually expressed, "we don't step twice into
the same river":

In the same rivers we step and do not step; we are and we are not.

Life and death, and walking and sleeping, and youth and old age, are the same; for the latter change and are the former, and the former change back to the latter.

Good and bad are the same.

Heraclitus (544–484 B.C.) lived in Ephesus, just up the road from Miletus and the most powerful city in Ionia after the Persians took Miletus. He adopted Anaximander's conflict of contraries as basic, but he emphasized it more than did Anaximander.

According to Diogenes Laertius,[6] "fire is the element, all things are exchange for fire and come into being by rarefaction and condensation; but of this he [Heraclitus] gives no clear explanation. All things come into being by conflict of opposites, and the sum of things flows like a stream." Like his predecessors, Anaximander and Anaximenes, he believed in periodic destruction and rebirth of the universe. Meanwhile, nature is nothing but change, as the earth–water–fire cycle continues. As the sea exhales moisture, the earth exhales as well, and this upward path returns earth to water and water to fire, a reverse of the downward path, where we can see water raining out of the fiery sky. Air was not mentioned.

Heraclitus speculated on mind as well as a part of physics. Most important to him was the conflict between fire and water—dry and wet. The object of self-mastery is to keep the soul dry, presumably because of the superior nature of fire. However, the soul prefers to be moist. Like the Pythagoreans, Heraclitus saw souls all around us, but they weren't the personal entities that Pythagoras assumed. Heraclitus was a materialist, and mind was only one kind of matter—fire. The following excerpt comes from Sextus Empiricus:

The natural philosopher is of the opinion that what surrounds us is rational and endowed with consciousness...we become intelligent when we get this divine reason by breathing it in, and in sleep we are forgetful. (Nahm 1964, p. 97)

Though we "breathe it in," the rationality around us is really fire, and when we sleep, the rationality in us (our fire) dims. The "fire" in us communes with the fire that surrounds our bodies. This is a form of empiricism for which Empedocles is better known: the doctrine that like knows like was also assumed by many others of the ancients.

Given the works of the Milesians, Heraclitus added little but an impetus to the philosophers of Elea to refute him. However, in proposing that fire and change were the only realities, was he anticipating modern conceptions that posit energy as fundamental? The intentional obscurity of his writings ensures that we will never know the answer to that question.

Eleatic No-Changers: "Unnatural Philosophers"

The Milesians and Heraclitus interpreted experience as phenomena of the senses, characterized by constant change. Our knowledge of the world can come only from seeking patterns in the flux. The philosophers of Elea disputed this interpretation in what seems a bizarre way, so that Aristotle called them the "unnatural philosophers." They were Xenophanes, Parmenides, and Zeno. Zeller (1883/1964, p. 67) noted this concerning them:

It was not without justification that Plato and Aristotle called the Eleatics the "interrupters of the course of the world" and the "unnatural scientists." Nevertheless the philosophy of Parmenides was of great significance for posterity.

Xenophanes the Rhapsodist   Xenophanes (570–475 B.C.) was a colorful character, a wandering rhapsodist[7] who eventually became a poet himself. Unlike most philosophers, he did not come from a wealthy family. He left Colophon in Ionia after the Persian invasion; he was twenty-five when he left, and he wandered for sixty-seven years. He attacked the official view of the gods, as represented anthropomorphically in his day. He wrote:

But mortals suppose that the gods are born (as they themselves are), and that they wear man's clothing and have human voice and body.... But if cattle or lions had hands, so as to paint with their hands and produce works of art as men do, they would paint their gods and give them bodies in form like their own. (Nahm 1964, p. 84)

This was precisely Spinoza's argument two millennia later, and, like Spinoza, Xenophanes believed that the Deity was everywhere and *everything*.

The All-One is without beginning and end and is always similar to itself and thus unchangeable. It is organically inseparable from the world, not comparable to humans in form or in thought, remains motionless and does not move from place to place. In fact, Xenophanes thought it demeaning for a god to "be somewhere else" and "to come when called."

He wrote, "It (being) always abides in the same place, not moved at all, nor is it fitting that it should move from one place to another." His pantheism features a god "all eye, all ear and all thought; effortlessly it swings the All with the strength of its mind" (Nahm 1964, p. 85). From this point of view, reality, the All-One, is not knowable through sense experience and, in fact, sense experience is wholly illusion. In particular, all movement and change of other kinds are illusions.

If god, which is all reality, does not move from place to place, then movement is just apparent. Here is a rationalism that is not based on dualism and the afterlife, as was the case with the Pythagoreans. Xenophanes was a monist like the Milesians, but he was by no means a naturalist and he was not an empiricist.

Parmenides: Immortality   Parmenides (540–470 B.C.) came from a noble and rich family in Elea and wrote an excellent constitution for that city, but was talked out of politics and into philosophy by the Pythagorean Ameinias (Zeller 1883/1964, p. 85). He became a follower of Xenophanes and, like him, expressed his views in poetry. His poem On Nature is divided into two parts, The Way of Truth and The Way of Opinion. In the second part he gives the opinion of mortals, explaining all as transformations of fire and earth, which Aristotle believed was his attempt to account for phenomena. More recent opinion holds that Parmenides was simply acquainting disciples with the Pythagorean philosophy, so that they could better refute it. His argument in the first part, The Way of Truth, is not straightforward:

It must be that that, which may be spoken of and thought of, is what is; for it is possible for it to be, but it is impossible for nothing to be. This I bid you think on. (Nahm 1964, p. 93)

"Nothing" does not exist!

Regarding the Milesian doctrine that reality consists of different manifestations of a physis, whether water, air, or the infinite, so that, for example, air condenses to water or earth and rarefies to fire, Parmenides asks why air appears to be other substances. He accepts a belief common among Greeks that thought is similar to what is known and argues that thought, not the senses, knows the invariant. If they are not air and air is the physis, the variants are nonexistent. Similarly, Heraclitus's world of change is a world of illusion.

It is/being is the only reality, and anything else is nonexistent. *It is* could not have been created, nor can it be destroyed—being cannot come from nonbeing, nor can it become nonbeing. *It is* is finite on all sides, like the bulk of a well-rounded sphere, equally balanced from the center in every direction. There is no empty space, and motion is therefore impossible. And even a corpse has sensations; as a monist, Parmenides is willing to allow sensation to all matter.

Reality is a homogeneous, motionless, timeless sphere devoid of perceptual characteristics? Bizarre as that seems, it is at least partly reasonable concerning the illusory nature of time. According to Parmenides, anything that can be thought—exists—and anything that ever existed still exists. All this follows from the assumption that time is an illusion, and we will see the same argument proposed by Saint Augustine centuries later.

Parmenides was attacked for the seeming absurdity of his views—rationalism is in many ways absurd (since it is nonsense), and it is only through reason, not experience, that Parmenides's conclusions can be entertained at all. The Eleatic philosophy was in need of defense and its defenders were Melissus of Samos and Zeno of Elea. Melissus was a general from the island of Samos who defeated an Athenian fleet when Samos revolted in 441 B.C. He also expanded Parmenides's sphere to infinity, since a lesser-sized sphere has boundaries and thus nothing must surround it. "Nothing" was, of course, unacceptable. But only Zeno will concern us here, since he was far more influential.

Zeno: What Was the Purpose of His Famous Paradoxes? Zeno of Elea was a favorite disciple of Parmenides and a handsome man who flourished[8] in the mid fifth century B.C. He lectured in Athens when forty and later was accused of plotting against the tyrant Nearchus of Elea. He was tortured to death without implicating his accomplices, and, like the Pythagorean woman Timycha a century later, is said to have bitten off his tongue and spat it at his persecutor.

His purpose was to defend Parmenides's rationalist philosophy against detractors, and he did so in such a way that Aristotle called him the inventor of dialectic (Zeller 1883/1964). The targets of his forty deductions, in which he began with opponents' postulates and showed them to result in contradictions, were the Pythagoreans. He criticized their atomism, their belief in empty space, and their belief (shared by the Milesians) that motion and other change are basic aspects of reality.

Some of his deductions were shown faulty by Aristotle, while others persisted as paradoxes until modern times.

Empiricism and common experience tell us that the world is a multitude of things and that they are always changing. Is that illusion? Does the rational method of the Eleatics show that matters are different? Zeno asked whether the "many" is finite or infinite. It would seem that the number must be finite, yet any pair can have another between them and so on, leaving the number infinitely great.[9] If there are many things, are they infinitely small (like the atomon), which is invisible with no mass, extension, or bulk? How do many such "nothings" add to produce a "something?" One grain of millet falling makes no sound. How can a million grains make a sound? How can a million "nothings" make a "something"?

Yet, if the unit has some magnitude, then it is divisible. The divisions must also be divisible, and so on to infinity. Thus, the unit must be infinitely large, since it is infinitely divisible. Hence, there cannot be many things, since they would have to be, but could not be, infinitely small or infinitely large.

There cannot be empty space, since if everything is in space, that means in something. Hence, space must have an end or limit, and it must itself be in something, and so on. This appears to be the first historical example of an infinite regress (Nahm 1964, p. 98). If everything is actually the All-One, then nothing moves and what we perceive as movement is illusion. This conclusion is defended by Zeno's most famous arguments.

First, consider the problem of the moving arrow. The arrow must either be moving at a place where it is or where it is not. It cannot be moving in a place where it is, or it would not be there. It cannot be moving in a place where it is not, since it is not there. Hence, it cannot be moving. The paradox of the arrow involves the question of instantaneous velocity and was not soluble until the development of the calculus two thousand years later (we will see Newton's solution and Berkeley's critique). Similarly, an arrow fired at a wall never reaches it, since it must first traverse half the distance, then half of the remainder, and so on, leaving an infinite series of halves.

Aristotle pointed out the fallacy in this argument, which also applies to the problem of Achilles's race with the tortoise. The problem is stated as if distance is infinitely divisible, but time is composed of a fixed number of instants. In fact, time is infinitely divisible, and an infinite series of instants suffices to cross an infinite series of points. If both time and space are viewed as composed of a finite number of parts, the problem is also solved.

The Eleatic Contribution

The Eleatics show us, interestingly, that it is possible to be a material monist and yet believe in a reality beyond sensation. However, they were indeed "unnatural," since they deprecated the information gained through the senses and emphasized the importance of reason.

Reason leads to odd conclusions for the Eleatics and for many subsequent thinkers. Parmenides's questioning the reality of time and thus suggesting that everything that ever existed exists now has obvious implications for immortality and was adopted by Saint Augustine. Zeno's arguments show that logic can make the world provided by the senses seem a strange place, perhaps no stranger than the "reality" of Parmenides.

The Pluralists

The natural science of the Milesians was opposed by the "unnatural science" of the rationalists of Elea, but both groups were materialist monists. A view competing with both of them was the pluralism of Empedocles and Anaxagoras.

Empedocles

Empedocles (493–433) was a physician of Agrigentum in Sicily who revived a woman who had been dead for a month and who reportedly jumped into Mount Etna to show that he was a god. Contemptuous toward his fellows, he asked, "But why do I harp on these things, as if it were any great matter that I should surpass mortal, perishable man" (Russell 1945, p. 56)? He proposed a theory of evolution which featured a time in which every conceivable kind of organism existed, multiheaded oxen with human faces, fish with feathers, individual organs and limbs that wandered about. Though he evidently did not have "natural selection" as survival due to fitness in mind, only those variants survived that exist now.

He believed in transmigration of souls, saying, "Wretches, utter wretches, keep your hands from beans" (Russell 1945, p. 57), and he anticipated Plato's famous allegory of the cave. He was a scientist/ mystic who wanted to transcend nature; he was a dualist who believed in a higher spirit world yet had no need for a mind! Thought was carried on by the blood, and perception was entirely mechanical. The "spirit" he assumed in each of us was wholly unnecessary, except to partake in reincarnations.[10]

Part of his mysticism was a remarkable theory of substance that is beyond the scope of this summary. However, one feature is very relevant because of its great influence on subsequent psychology—he championed the four elements that became the bases for the temperaments of Galen and countless others.

In addition, we know or sense things that are made of the same material that constitutes the sense organ: like knows like. This extremely popular conception explains vision as the contact of fire (light) with the "fire in our eyes," the gleam in a living thing's eye. Touch depends on contact of earth with earth; audition occurs when the air in our ear contacts outer air; taste and smell require contact of water in us and from without. Plato and many others adopted this theory, and it is not a bad one. The relations of likeness and unlikeness also determine desires and aversions.

Anaxagoras and Mind

Anaxagoras (500–428 B.C.) was the first philosopher to live in Athens, and it was he who made the greatest error of his age. To his credit, though born wealthy, he avoided politics and devoted himself to pure research. Like Empedocles and the Milesians, Anaxagoras believed that space was filled with matter and that phenomena were changes in the composition of matter. For Empedocles, it was changes in earth, air, fire, and water, and for Anaxagoras it was "seeds."

According to Anaxagoras, reality is a mechanical compound of tiny bits of many qualitatively different substances—gold, bone, feathers, and so on. Everything, however small, has pieces of every kind, and what we call something (e.g., fire, snow) depends on the preponderance of some particles. Most importantly, some particles are parts of mind or nous, the moving and controlling force in the universe, the source of animation in living things, and the basis for soul and reason in humans.

However, unlike the Pythagoreans and other dualists (Plato, for example), Anaxagoras did not view mind as better and higher than other matter—it was just another form of material. Mind was essential in his cosmogeny, where it acted as a giant centrifuge to separate out other matter, but that is of little relevance here. What is relevant is the introduction of a perfect and "unnatural" substance—mind/nous—to materialism. Aristotle commented (Nahm 1964, p. 144) appropriately:

Anaxagoras uses mind as a device by which to construct the universe, and when he is at a loss for the cause why anything necessarily is, then he drags this in . . .

Ancient Medicine

Life is short, the art long, opportunity fleeting, experiment treacherous, judgment difficult. (Hippocrates, in Bartlett 1992, p. 71)

Crito, I owe a cock to Asclepius; will you remember to pay the debt? (Plato, *Phaedo*, In Kaufmann 1963, p. 161)

Plato compared two forms of medicine that were current in his day. One, the "old way," was that used by the heroes of Homer's tales and by the poor. A sick person might drink a powerful potion or undergo bleeding or consult a priest—there would be a cure or not, and if not, the patient would die and be at an end of trouble. The second method, however, might never actually cure the patient, but life might be extended for decades, with the patient a burden to everyone, constantly tending himself. This is the method of Hippocrates, and it conforms to the material monists' view that we are part of nature and that health results when bodily processes are harmonious.

Hippocrates—*On Regimen*
Hippocrates (469–399) was born on the island of Kos, off the coast of modern Turkey (ancient Ionia). He was the most famous physician of ancient times and described his views on medicine in a treatise called *On Regimen*.

He wrote (Brett/Peters 1965, p. 55) that man is the particular known through the universal—this is another expression of the microcosm and macrocosm viewpoint. As the universe is a composite of elements, so are we, and health is a relation among our elements. Activity and nutrition alter this relation, as does environment—climate, seasons, winds, and locales. Hence, treatment involves adjustment of food, exercise, and environment. A skilled physician is one who can detect slight changes in health and prescribe the appropriate adjustment.

The basic elements that comprise us are based on the principles of fire and water, as Heraclitus had argued. Fire is the arranger, the former, the vital and intellectual principle, which is weak in youth and in old age. Water is prevalent in infancy and is the basis for the humors and the nourishment of the body. If environment, food, or exercise change, the fire–water balance may be disrupted and disease occurs. Individuals may also be naturally inclined toward an imbalance leading to sickness.

The body humors arise from the fire–water principles:

Cold–earth–phlegm

Dry–air–yellow bile

Hot–fire–blood

Moist–water–black bile

These are the things that actually get out of balance. This theory of humors was adopted by many but is usually associated with Galen, physician to Roman Emperor Marcus Aurelius in the second century A.D. It remained popular for many centuries.

As father of medicine and author of the famous oath bearing his name, Hippocrates argued for what he thought to be the "concrete" study of health and disease. He specifically denounced what he called "occult" treatments (Brett/Peters 1965, p. 54), especially those associated with temple medicine, the other main approach to medicine. It too survived for many centuries, even longer than did Hippocrates's humors. And it parallels current practices in important ways that should attract our notice.

The Greek Asklepeia

In the ancient world medicine was practiced by specialists who eventually formed a priesthood. In Greece these people practiced in temples devoted to Asklepios, an actual practicing physician who was deified as a god of medicine. The treatment was described by Ellenberger (1956, pp. 293–294).

Like modern health spas, the Asklepeia were located in beautiful spots. Before going, the patient heard reports about the cures that occurred there and doubtless rehearsed them during the travel to the temple. Upon arriving, the patient was "purified," a procedure including fasting, drinking sacred water, and other rites, about which little is now known.

The crucial part of the treatment was the night spent in the sanctuary, called the incubation, during which the patient lay on the ground, dressed in a purple-striped gown and sometimes wearing a crown. The underground room in which this occurred was called the abaton, and its walls bore inscriptions describing the miracles that occurred there. In later times patients lay on a couch called a kline, and from this comes our word "clinic," referring to a hospital with beds.

Ancient authors claimed that things happened to the patients during the night in the abaton and that the cures were thus effected. The patient could experience apparitions, oracles, visions, or dreams. An "apparition" occurred when an awake patient saw the figure of Asklepios or the patient might hear a voice, feel a wind, or see a blinding light. An "oracle" was a dream in which a god or a priest told a patient what to do, and a "vision" was a dream featuring a prophecy about the patient's near future. What the ancient authors called a "dream proper" was a dream which itself brought the cure. It did not need to be interpreted for the patient—its occurrence was enough.

This seems to have no counterpart in modern psychotherapy, but Ellenberger suggested that it may. First, a Swiss Jungian, O. A. Meier, attributed a similar concept to a student of Mesmer named Kieser, who believed that such cures occur when "the inner feeling of the disease becomes personified and expresses itself in symbols." This explanation is probably similar to what might be offered in the fifth century B.C.

The ancient Greek patient on the kline, in the abaton of the temple of Asklepios, could certainly experience the same transformation of disease into dream. It seems clear that temple medicine depended heavily on the patients' faith that cures were to be had. The posh psychotherapy consulting room, the wonderful reputation of the therapist, and the framed certificates and degrees from famous universities on the wall all must serve the same function that the trappings of the temple served in the cures of long ago.

Democritus and Protagoras: Two Directions

In the fourth and fifth centuries B.C., two main interpretations of the relation of mind and body were clearly formulated, and they have remained in pretty much their original form through the millennia. Their first clear renditions appeared in the teachings of Democritus and Protagoras. The issue was the nature of epistemology, or the question of the origin and nature of knowledge.

The Atomism of Democritus

One influential attempt to deal with this problem is associated with Democritus, probably born in 460 B.C. and a student of Leucippus, of whom no writings survived (Kaufman 1961, p. 58). Democritus was born in Abdera, also the birthplace of Protagoras, the Sophist whose views were so different. Democritus may well have been influenced by Pythagorean teachers and wrote a work of his own entitled "Pythagoras" (Nahm 1964, p. 163). He was apparently knowledgeable in many areas, from physics to ethics to education.

Anaxagoras, who proposed an infinity of "seeds," held that they vary infinitely in quality, or the nature of their being. Leucippus and Democritus saw their atoms as all qualitatively identical. They differed in size, shape, and density, but not in the material comprising them. Unique among the ancients, they also postulated the existence of the void; atoms circulate in empty space, nonbeing. The notion of emptiness is still difficult to accept, and it is only recently that the existence of an "ether" to fill space and propagate light waves and other radiation has been abandoned.

When Democritus proposed that reality is largely empty space, he flew in the face of learned opinion in his time, as well as the opinion of centuries to come.

Atomism and the Psyche   According to Nahm (1964, pp. 165–166),

His opinions are these. The first principles of the universe are atoms and empty space; everything else is merely thought to exist. . . . The qualities of things exist merely by convention; in nature there is nothing but atoms and void space.

The end of action is tranquility, which is not identical with pleasure . . . undisturbed by any fear or . . . any other emotion. This he calls well-being and many other names.

For Democritus, things come into existence and cease to exist as atoms comprising them coagulate and disperse. All change arises from the redistributing of atoms in space. The number of possible worlds is infinite, since the number of atoms of various shapes and sizes is infinite and their constant movement means that reality constantly changes.

The soul is likewise composed of atoms, but these are more swiftly moving than are body atoms. If the soul atoms escape and disperse, we die, and this is a constant danger. Luckily, the air around us is filled with these rapidly moving atoms, and if we keep inhaling, we can replenish any soul atoms that may have escaped (recall the Pythagoreans'

belief that the air was filled with souls). When we die, "the pressure of
the atmosphere dominates and the atoms can no longer enter to ward
off expulsion because breath has ceased."[11]

The Maxims of Democritus   Democritus left us with an epistemology
that has survived over two thousand years, the expression "Birds of a
feather flock together," and a long list of maxims that seem as relevant
now as they must have then (Nahm 1964, pp. 200–202):

- It is hard to be governed by a worse man.
- He that always yields to money could never be just.
- Fools learn by misfortune.
- One should accept favors with the expectation of returning them
manyfold.

The Epistemology of Atomism   For the atomists, knowledge arises
because objects are constantly giving off copies of themselves (eidolae,
simulcra). Objects vibrate, as the atoms of which they are constituted
constantly move, sending delicate hollow frames of different shape
and organization that remain coherent because "birds of a feather flock
together" (Nahm 1964, p. 189). They are real particles, not just reflected
light, and they may mold the air that travels to our eyes.[12]

These copies or representatives literally pass through us and, on the
way, they are detected by our special psychic (soul) atoms. Since
the soul atoms are finer and more closely packed than are body atoms,
they act as a sieve, "straining" the copy atoms and detecting their pattern. For the atomists, we see, hear, smell, and touch because we take
part of the substance of the things we sense into our bodies.[13] In many
versions of this theory, we respond to representations in a "like knows
like" manner.

Atoms are all made of the same material—"being"—and are indestructible, but they vary greatly in shape and size, as well as in arrangement, proportion, and motion. While there is no color in nature,
the shape of atoms and their arrangements give us color, so that white
is smooth and black is rough.

Flavors depend specifically on the shapes of atoms and "sweet"
arises from large, spherical atoms and sour from large, rough, angular
atoms. Though specific sense organs are most affected by atoms producing sound, light, and other sensations, it is the body as a whole

that senses, since soul atoms are of a kind and are distributed through the body (Nahm 1964, p. 192). This is known as the representational theory of perception and of knowledge and it implies that our sensing is seldom accurate.

Clearly, we do not consciously sense atoms, so our experience does not correspond to Democritus's "reality" of atoms and void. And the copies of the things we sense may be distorted in transit, and thus what we sense is often not true, or "trueborne." The repetition of the same kinds of stimulation can also produce self-generated responding, so that we may sense in the absence of sense objects by generating familiar patterns, just as Hebb (1949) proposed in his famous doctrine of reverberating circuits as a model for brain function. However, self-generation may not exactly correspond to original stimulation, and thus error may arise from this self-generated "bastard" knowledge. It is through confirmation—"agreement and disagreement" of past and subsequent experiences—that we distinguish truth and error, at least insofar as that can be done.

Twenty-five Hundred Years Later The representational theory was crude and, needless to say, we no longer accept it. Or do we? How do we deal with the same problem today? For example, how do we see?

We are told that this process has been thoroughly worked out. We know that light strikes objects and is reflected from them onto our retinas. A copy of the (inverted) object forms on the retina, and optic nerve fibers fire. The transmission of neural impulses passes to the lateral geniculate body of the thalamus and is sent from there to the occipital (visual) cortex. The copy of the object that is first cast on the retina is duplicated several times in the thalamus and presumably is duplicated in the cortex. That is how we see!

However, let us consider that for a moment. A copy of the object falls on the retina, more copies form in the thalamus, and finally we have copies in the cortex. Is this an improvement, or just a restatement of the ancient representational theory? It is not literally a restatement; we have not mentioned psychic atoms, but in fact we have them as well. Instead of psychic atoms, or soul atoms, we prefer terms like "higher neural centers," "mind," "cognitive processing mechanisms," and so on. But we mean the same thing. We find that we use up the whole nervous system and have no more than what we began with—a copy. And we have no clue as to how anything is actually seen.

This problem is part and parcel of the static view of things, which assumes that there are *things* and there is *us*. We gain knowledge of the things somehow, and the only way that such knowledge can occur is if the things that we know directly contact us. Philosophers call this view epistemological dualism; there are subjects (such as ourselves) who know objects (the things that we sense), and the subject and object are two different things. How could it be otherwise?

Remember that there is one awful problem with this static view of things. That is, copies are made and remade, but nothing is seen or heard or smelled or felt or tasted. A camera or a tape recorder can do what the copy theory says that we do. Those devices lack only "psychic atoms." Is such a theory worth much?

One seeming solution lies in giving a personality to the psychic atoms. "I" am that personality, and I live approximately an inch behind the bridge of my nose. "I" may be thought of as a little "person in our heads," and it is that little person who does the seeing, hearing, and so on. This is a fine explanation as long as we don't care about the workings of the little person.

One option is to forget the whole problem and leave it to philosophers, the clergy, and mystics. Or we could wait for brain researchers to find the magic neurons that do the seeing and hearing. However, that would be no help, as William James realized in 1890 (chapter 6). If a "magic arch-neuron" were found, that would not explain anything, since the magic neuron would itself be composed of molecules and any one or more of them might hold the magic. We might better consider an alternative to the representational theory.

Protagoras and an Alternative to Rationalism
The fact is that the static view that relies on the subject/object distinction and that cannot explain seeing and hearing is not the only way of looking at things. An alternative was proposed while Democritus was alive, and it has been passed on in various versions down to the present.

That alternative stresses dynamics (processes) rather than statics (things), and it was first proposed by the Sophist philosopher Protagoras. His proposal seems strange, since it is unlike the familiar story that we have been taught since early childhood. Yet it is worth considering in view of the fact that the representational theory leaves out everything that is really important.

We will find that essentially the same view was held by Aristotle, Thomas Aquinas, Brentano, James, Holt, Kantor, and Sartre. But the representational theory has had much more influence, partly because of the great influence of Plato. Democritus greatly influenced both Socrates and Plato, and Plato was accused by several ancient authors of plagiarizing him. Protagoras's view was discussed only as an error to be refuted.

Sophists were professional teachers; they taught for a fee, and what they taught was practical. Protagoras even offered a money-back guarantee if the student did not think he had received his money's worth. The subjects were rhetoric (the art of public speaking), dialectic (the art of reasoning), politic (the art of government), and eristic (the art of making the worse appear to be the better case). Obviously, the line separating the latter two is a fuzzy one.

The Relativity of Knowledge   Protagoras was an extreme empiricist, meaning that he believed that all of our knowledge comes only from experience and, since our experience is personal, unique, and changes as we age, there are at least as many "worlds" as there are individuals! Actually, like his fellow native of Abdera, Democritus, he did believe that some knowledge is innate. That is, we all have a sense of reverence and of right; anyone lacking these is subhuman and should be put to death (Freeman 1953, p. 347). Other than that, there is no certain knowledge, as Protagoras put it in a famous quotation that Plato said was the opening sentence of his book *Truth*:

"Of all things the measure is Man, of the things that are, that they are, and of the things that are not, that they are not." (Kaufmann 1963, p. 72)

As William James wrote much later, when we go, the "world" goes with us. The earth opens, the sky falls, the mountains crumble, and all things end their existence. This is because what is "real" is the product of our personal experience! We actually have a part in determining what is real. This departure from the rational emphasis of Democritus and all earlier Greek thinkers, especially the Eleatics, was radical. As Nahm (1964, p. 227) wrote, "The importance of this contrast between Protagoras' and Democritus' theory of knowledge may scarcely be overemphasized."

The reason that each of our worlds is unique[14] lies in the fact that experience is what shapes the world, and experience is not exactly what

Democritus thought it to be. Protagoras did not accept the view that a "real world" sends off copies in the form of atoms that affect some mysterious "psychic atoms" within us. He realized that this really begged the question; instead of the copy theory, Protagoras stressed activity as the basis of reality, in that way agreeing with Heraclitus. Experience is a succession of perpetual transitions, taking the form of interchanges with our environment. Such interchanges are dialectic relationships.

The Nature of Perception Perception for Protagoras was an interchange. For example, when we see an object, such as an orange, we do not receive copies of it, as the representational theory holds. The orange really has no existence apart from our perceiving it. Things exist only while someone is perceiving them (Freeman 1953, p. 349), as Berkeley and Hume would argue two thousand years later. The orange and the eye are two "realities," and seeing the orange is two processes; the eye gives the orange its form and color and the orange gives the eye its perception. Seeing-the-orange is a single event, an interchange between the eye and the orange. It is not the effect of an object on a subject, viewed as two distinct entities (Brett/Peters 1912/1965, p. 62).

The Recoil Argument If, as Protagoras taught, all knowledge is relative and the individual is the "measure of all things," is every opinion true? Or, is every opinion at least as true as every other? This is clearly the conclusion drawn by ancient critics of Protagoras, including Plato, and by later writers who point to the "recoil argument" as evidence that Protagoras cannot be correct (Freeman 1953, p. 350). The argument is simple: since every opinion is true, so is the opinion "every opinion is false." If that is a true statement, what do we have? One imagines a world filled with disputing lawyers, endlessly debating, getting no closer to truth and aiming only to persuade listeners. And all of this done purely for pay. Was that what Protagoras had in mind?

In the nineteenth century an American philosophy developed that assumed that truth exists in degrees. Thus, Newton's physics is true, but quantum theory is truer. The relative truth of a statement depends on its pragmatic (or practical) utility. Protagoras appears to have held a similar view, unsurprising, since the Sophists were nothing if not pragmatic.

According to both Diels (Freeman 1953, pp. 348–350) and Russell (1945, p. 77), Protagoras taught that opinions are all true, but some are "healthier," "more desirable," and "better" than others. One of the founders of pragmatism, F. C. S. Schiller, habitually called himself a disciple of Protagoras (Russell 1945, p. 78). Records are not available that would allow further consideration of this, but what little we have suggests that pragmatism may have originated long ago.

Sophistry   As precursor to Aristotle, one would expect that Protagoras would have been venerated by later historians, but he was not. Part of the reason for this was no doubt the charging of fees for instruction that was practiced by the Sophists. Neither Plato nor Aristotle needed to charge their students, since both were wealthy and the Greeks clearly disdained members of the crafts who worked for a fee.

A more important reason was the reputation for argumentation as an end in itself that was associated with the Sophists. The Sophists of eristic, especially, were concerned with winning disputes with no care for the right or wrong, the truth or falsity, of the issues involved. Protagoras did not really belong in that group.

All Sophists were not as wise as Protagoras; Gorgias, for example, seems to epitomize pointless rhetoric. Consider a fragment of his argument showing that nature does not exist:

... (if) the non-existent exists, it will at one and the same time exist and not exist; for in so far as it is conceived as non-existent it will not exist, but in so far as it is non-existent it will again exist... Furthermore, the existent does not exist either. For if the existent exists, it is either eternal or created or at once both eternal and created; but, as we shall prove, it is neither eternal nor created nor both; therefore the existent does not exist.... From which it follows that nothing exists. (Nahm 1964, pp. 247–250)

Protagoras, unlike the Milesians and Eleatics, was not concerned with the physis; his concern, like the other Sophists, was centered on practical concerns and epistemology—human affairs. This concern was central to Socrates as well, which is why he is often considered the last of the Sophists.

Athens in Socrates's Time

In the late fifth century b.c. Darius I of Persia demanded tribute from the Greek city-states, leading to the Persian Wars. In 490 b.c. the Persians were defeated at Marathon but were victorious in the famous battle at Thermopylae, where 300 Spartans and 700 Thespians faced an estimated 200,000 Persians. In 480 b.c. Xerxes I burned Athens, but a series of Greek victories followed, as the Athenian fleet destroyed the Persian navy at Salmis and a Greek confederation under Spartan command defeated the Persians in Cyprus in 466 B.C. The Persians were forced then to recognize the independence of the Greek states.

Athens had led the confederation of Greeks to victory over the Persians and continued receiving monies from Sparta and the other cities even after the war. In 432 B.C. a number of Greek cities rose up against Athens, protesting the vassal status that had been imposed upon them during the Persian Wars, and a new war raged until 404 B.C. This Peloponnesian War led to the ultimate defeat of Athens by a league of cities led by Sparta and Corinth, and it was then that the "thirty tyrants" were briefly placed in charge of Athens by the victors.

Socrates

Who Was Socrates?
It is difficult to be certain about many details of Socrates and his life—accounts by two of his students differ greatly. One student was Xenophon, a general and none-too-bright man who described Socrates as dull and commonplace and not deserving of being put to death as he was. Russell (1945, p. 82) distrusted this account, since "A stupid man's report of what a clever man says is never accurate." The second account comes from Plato, of course, who used Socrates as the spokesman in many of his thirty-five dialogues.[15]

Socrates was the son of a sculptor, Sophronicus, and a midwife, Phaenarete. The date of his birth, according to Zeller (1964), was apparently the 6th of Thargelion (May–June). He was a stonemason and carver and was very poor, constantly reproached by his wife, Xanthippe, for neglect of his family. He was completely self-taught as a philosopher and must have become dissatisfied with natural philosophy, such as that of the Milesians and Eleatics, since he lost interest in it early in life. He attended lectures by the Sophists and even recommended pupils to them. It was their emphasis on human affairs, especially on epistemology and ethics, that Socrates shared.

Socrates and Alcibiades   Alcibiades was a colorful, gifted, and well-born politician and soldier who was a small boy when his father was killed while commanding the Athenian army. He was a distant relative of Pericles, who ruled Athens during the "golden age" of the mid fifth century B.C. Pericles became his guardian but had little time to spare for him, so he became a disciple of Socrates, who appreciated his quick wit and handsome appearance.

Alcibiades and Socrates served in the army, and in 432 B.C. Socrates saved his student's life, defending him while he was wounded— Alcibiades returned the favor years later, in a battle at Delium, north of Athens. However, overall, Socrates's example and his ethical teachings appear to have been lost on Alcibiades. Though he was impressed by Socrates's moral strength, Alcibiades was unscrupulous, extravagant, self-centered, treacherous, and without self-discipline.

By the age of thirty, the lessons of Socrates were lost to him, and he concentrated on demonstrating courage in battle and on polishing his speaking in the Assembly (Ecclesia). In 420 B.C. he became general, and, after abortive attempts to form successful alliances against Sparta, he managed to convince the people to send a major expedition against Syracuse, on Sicily, in 415 B.C. That began what became an amazing career.

He was co-commander of the expedition, but, just before the time to sail, there was a panic produced by the mutilation of busts of Hermes, messenger of Zeus and patron of those who use the roads, which were set up throughout the city. Alcibiades was accused of this crime and forced by political enemies to sail with the charge still over his head, despite his protestations that an inquiry be made.

Soon after arriving in Sicily, he was recalled for trial—he escaped and fled to Sparta and later learned that he had been condemned to death in his absence. He advised that Sparta send a general to aid Syracuse against Athens and that Decelea, near Athens, be fortified. Having thus betrayed Athens and ensured the destruction of its expedition, he seduced the wife of Sparta's King Agis II, who was with his army at Decelea.

In 412 B.C. he stirred revolt among Athens' allies in Ionia (western Asia Minor) and attempted to ingratiate himself with the Persian governor of Sardis. Then, incredibly, he was invited to return to the Athenian fleet, where he was desperately needed. He did so and in 411 and 410 B.C. destroyed the Spartan navy and its supporting Persian army. In 409 B.C. he led the Athenians in the capture of Byzantium. He returned a hero to Athens in 407 B.C. and was put in full charge of the war against Sparta and its allies.

Shortly thereafter he was deposed by political enemies and moved to a castle in Thrace, northeast of Greece, where he remained a disturbing influence. When the Spartans surprised the Athenians and destroyed their fleet, the war ended and Alcibiades had no safe place to go. He fled to Phrygia in northwestern Asia Minor, taking refuge with the Persian governor, who had him murdered when requested to do so by Sparta.

Alcibiades was an amazing man, but he was by no one's standard a virtuous person. When the democratic government returned to power in 403 B.C., it was the example of Alcibiades that helped condemn Socrates. This was after Sparta was defeated at Munychia and the thirty tyrants were removed. The charge brought in 399 B.C. was that of corrupting the youth of Athens. Alcibiades was prime example of this alleged malignant influence.

The Philosophy of Socrates Claiming to know nothing, Socrates questioned the citizens of Athens in an effort to arouse them and lead them to examine their life and its meaning. As Zeller put it:[16]

All that he could do was to set men in unrest and bring them into embarrassment. He often produced this result by pretending to receive instruction from others, whose mental inferiority was revealed in the course of the conversation. This procedure was keenly felt by those who suffered from it.

His wisdom, he felt, lay only in his knowledge of his ignorance, and his goal was to show others that they too were ignorant—this to pave the way for self-examination that might lead to truth and virtue.

For Socrates, knowledge and virtue were inseparable—happiness lies only in doing that which is good, and to do good requires that we know what is good. No one willingly does evil, and the fact that evil deeds are done shows only that people are ignorant. Happiness, self-sufficiency, and truly virtuous conduct come only from knowledge of truth (the good), and that comes from self-examination and contemplation, not from adherence to traditional beliefs. For Socrates, this self-examination and search for virtue took precedence over trivial things, such as pleasures of the body, clothes, and the like. He was known for his simple life and poverty, to which he subjected his wife, Xanthippe, and his children.

Athens was democratic to a fault during much of Socrates's life, and even judges and generals were elected or chosen by lot. Socrates argued for education and competence rather than equal opportunity (that is, chance in this case). Who is best fit to mend a shoe or build a ship or heal the sick, one who is trained and experienced or one who is democratically elected? He urged the young men who had been chosen to be generals and finance directors to educate themselves in their new occupations. So doing required a demonstration of the fellow's incompetence and made him no friends. Finally, "it was decided that it was easier to silence him by means of the hemlock[17] than to cure the evils of which he complained (Russell 1945, p. 84).

The Death of Socrates   Socrates was tried and sentenced to death by the democratic government that replaced the thirty tyrants Sparta had installed after their victory over Athens. According to Plato, he would not have been convicted if only 30 of the 501 judges had voted differently. Juries always had an odd number of members, to avoid tied votes, and the balloting for Socrates came out surprisingly favorably—221 for acquittal and 280 against. Why was he killed?

In cases where the accused was condemned, the prosecution and defense each proposed a penalty and the jury had to choose between them. In this case the prosecution proposed death and Socrates was expected to propose a fine or exile. Instead he proposed that he be given free meals in the Prytaneum, where the Council of the Assembly met, a privilege granted to heroes of the Olympic Games and public benefactors. Finally he offered to pay a fine, but the vote for death was 360 to 141. After an unusual delay and a chance to escape, he drank the poison and died.

The Contribution of Socrates   The dialectic method used by Socrates and by Plato was borrowed from Zeno and Protagoras and guaranteed that topics in empirical science would not arise. Such a method, which begins with a question like "What is good (or truth, or justice, or friendship)?" and proceeds through an interchange of questions and answers is only useful to clarify the ways in which we use words.

As Russell (1945, p. 92) noted, conclusions reached are merely linguistic, not discoveries in ethics. In all of the dialogues, it is clear that Socrates/Plato has a conclusion in mind which is supposed to be "discovered" by the slave boy, who finds that he "knew the Pythagorean theorem all along," or by the mathematician Theaetetus, who "knew all along" that knowledge is more than perception.

These demonstrations of uncovering innate knowledge in the "discoverers" depend upon Socrates's acting as a "midwife" (like his mother). However, this midwife appears to be creating the baby, as well as delivering it. As Russell (1945, p. 92) noted, the leading questions asked by Socrates in these dialogues would not be allowed by any judge. And the dialectic method would show its limitations if the questions were more than those of linguistic usage—it would do poorly with subjects like determining the truth of the germ theory of disease!

Socrates and "Good"   Socrates's life was devoted to the search for knowledge as a basis for ethics. One always does what is right or "good" if one has the knowledge of right and of good. However, Socrates had no real metaphysics—no theory of the ultimate nature of reality. And he had no anthropology—no real theory of the nature of humanity. That being the case, what is the criterion for good?

Eduard Zeller, in the 1892 edition of his 1883 classic work on the Greek philosophers, suggested that the criterion of truth and goodness for Socrates was actually the criterion of usefulness and pragmatic success. (Interestingly, this suggestion is missing in the 1928 edition of the Zeller book, edited by Wilhelm Nestle.) However, if "good" is a pragmatic matter, Socrates was even more similar to the Sophists than has been generally recognized.

3   Statics and Dynamics in Ancient Greece

A thing, then, that every soul pursues as the end of all her actions, dimly divining its existence, but perplexed and unable to grasp its nature with the same clearness and assurance as in dealing with other things, and so missing whatever value those other things might have. (Cornford 1964, p. 216)

Plato and Ancient Cognitive Psychology

Plato (427–347 B.C.; see figure 3.1) was the son of Ariston and Peristione, both of whom came from distinguished families. He was named "Aristocles," after his grandfather but was a skilled wrestler as a youth, given the nickname "Plato" because of his broad shoulders and chest (Zeller 1964, p. 133). It is likely that he served in the Athenian cavalry as a youth. He knew Socrates, who was influential in Athens when Plato was a child, and his change from poet to philosopher must certainly have been due to Socrates's influence.

Athens had been defeated by the alliance led by Sparta in the Peloponnesian War when Plato was a young man and a government of rich citizens, the Oligarchs, or thirty tyrants, was installed, sponsored by Sparta. Athenians welcomed this government, blaming the previous democratic government for creating conditions that caused the war and for misconduct of the war once it began. The thirty men who comprised this government included many friends and relatives of Plato, and they assumed that he would support them. Plato described his feelings at the time in a letter written late in his life:

No wonder that, young as I was, I imagined they would bring the state under their management from an iniquitous to a right way of life.... It was not long before I saw these men make the former constitution seem like a paradise. (Cornford 1964, pp. xxvii–xviii)

Figure 3.1
Plato. Courtesy of the Archives of the History of American Psychology, University of Akron.

When the thirty tyrants were ousted and democracy restored, Socrates was quickly tried, condemned, and sentenced to death. This affected Plato and other students of Socrates deeply; it may account in part for Plato's writing *The Republic*. He burned the tragedies he had written earlier. While Plato's was no "republic" to be sure (the German translation is *Die Stadt*, "the city," and is more accurate), it is a proposal for government that is rational, rather than one run by the mob or by the rich or by the power hungry. Ironically, it is a city in which Socrates could never have lived, since there was no place for a troublesome gadfly (Kaufman 1961, p. 93). Plato's thoughts on the events of the time (ca. 400 B.C.) and his political aspirations continued in the same letter:

In these unquiet times much was still going on that might move one to disgust.... Unfortunately, however, some of the men in power brought my friend Socrates to trial on an abominable charge, the very last that could be made against Socrates—the charge of impiety.

Cornford went on to suggest that Plato had "not yet seen" that to get things done one must "put up with associates not to his liking, lay aside ideal aspirations, and stoop to opportunism and compromise" (p. xvii). Plato would hardly have considered such an option.

Plato's plan following the death of Socrates was succinctly described by Cornford, in a way that underscores its oddness:

After his death, a few of his closest friends, including Plato... resolved to defend his memory and to continue his work. Plato chose to do this by writing imaginary conversations, showing how very far Socrates had been from "demoralizing young men." (p. xix)

Through almost all of his dialogues, Plato spoke through his teacher, Socrates. In most cases it is impossible to discern whether it is Socrates or Plato whose views we are reading. Plato attributes all to Socrates, who left no written records of his teachings.

The Academy Lasted 916 Years

Plato's school, the Academy, was so named because of its location in the grove of Academus (a legendary hero) located about a mile northwest of Athens. He established it in 387 B.C., modeled after the Pythagorean schools that he had visited in Italy after the death of Socrates. On the way home from Italy, he stopped at Aegina, which was at war with Athens; he was taken to the slave market to be sold. Luckily for him, he was ransomed by Anniceris, a friend and Cyrenaic.[1] When Anniceris refused to be repaid the money, Plato used that sum to buy the land for the Academy (Zeller 1964, pp. 129–135).

Since the Cyrenaics were Sophists, in effect, Platonic philosophy thus received its first boost from those who sympathized with Protagoras. Nevertheless, the purpose of the Academy was to train students to attend to the immutable framework underlying reality, to be sensitive to being, rather than becoming, to use his words (Russell 1959, p. 57).

No fees were charged for admission, students stayed for varying periods, and not only Greeks but also many foreigners attended.

However, the school did produce many of the statesmen and military leaders of Athens. Discussions and lectures began early in the morning, and pupils lived in small houses scattered around the garden that was the Academy. Plato himself invented a loud whistling alarm clock that summoned the students to class (Zeller 1964, p. 137). The Academy lasted over 900 years, until it was closed by the Christian Emperor Justinian in A.D. 529.

Two Sources of Knowledge: The Essence of Platonism

Plato distinguished between opinion and knowledge, the former arising from sensation and the latter from reason. Opinion, or "belief," comes from the senses and is decidedly inferior. It is often illusory and relative, like the tepid water that feels warm when the hand is cold and cold when the hand is warm. Another name for such inferior, maybe dream-like stuff is doxa, and Plato illustrates its indeterminate nature by comparing it with a child's puzzle:

A man who was not a man
seeing and not seeing
A bird that was not a bird
perched on a bough that was not a bough
pelted and did not pelt it
with a stone that was not a stone.
(Cornford 1945, p. 188)

Thus, we misinterpret the sight of a eunuch throwing a piece of pumice at a bat perched on a reed.

Knowledge, on the other hand, is unchanging, absolute, and eternal. It exists as Forms, sometimes called "ideas," that Plato viewed as existing in some other place. They include absolute ideals of good and evil, right, wrong, beauty, ugliness, dirt, and all relationships and class terms. What exactly populates the world of Forms is somewhat debatable, partly because Plato changed his opinion so many times over the decades of writing the dialogues.

What Are the Forms?   Do the Forms correspond only to the good, so that justice and cleanliness are Forms and injustice and dirtiness are corruptions of that perfection? Doesn't Plato call the highest level of knowledge the "Good," and doesn't that mean beautiful, clean, and just, and whatever else is pure and noble? Or does "justice" correspond to one form and "injustice" to another? Do bad and worthless things find their ideal representation in the world of Forms? It is clear that this latter interpretation is the correct one, at least from Plato's perspective through his writings.

Eduard Zeller (1964) is a standard source for accurate interpretations of Greek philosophers, referred to by those who wish to avoid the layers of interpretations accrued in the textbooks in philosophy and psychology over the generations. Regarding the range of Forms, Zeller wrote (pp. 148–149):

The ideas are for him not mere things of thought...but realities. There are ideas of everything possible: not merely of things, but of qualities too, and relations and activities; not only of natural things, but of the products of art, and not only of valuable things but of bad and worthless things.

Rather than a corruption of beauty and injustice, ugliness and injustice are fundamental ideas, representations of Forms in heaven. The same conclusion is reached by Sir David Ross, who has specialized in the study of Platonic Forms. He wrote:

[H]e says "According to this argument is the beautiful any more and the not-beautiful any less a reality?," and the answer that is expected and is forthcoming is "No... [regarding] 'evil,' or 'ugly'..." It *might* be possible for a theory of ideas to dispense with the Idea of evil and with Ideas of its species.... But there is nothing to show that Plato ever took this line. (Ross 1951, pp. 43, 168–169)

The Neoplatonists and church fathers of five centuries later would interpret the doctrine of Forms differently, so that it became the heaven of religion and home of only the Good and the beautiful, with the phenomena of sense pitifully imperfect, dirty, and unjust. However, that was not Plato's view.

He illustrated levels of knowledge by pairing them with corresponding activities of mind (Cornford 1964, p. 221). For Plato, imagining and belief, below the line, are doxa, or opinion, and thinking and knowledge are activities that deal with truth. This is illustrated by the divided line.[2]

Picture a line divided into four segments: AB, BC, CD, and DE, such that their lengths are ordered short to long, so that AB < BC < CD < DE. AB and BC represent the light and power of the sun, giving us Conjecture (AB) and Belief (BC). This refers to the two types of uncertain knowledge, or Opinion—images of shadow and reflection (AB) or of objects and animals (BC). Both represent the uncertain and changing world of the senses—Doxa.

CD and DE represent Knowledge—the influence and offspring of the Good. CD, longer than AB or BC, corresponds to mathematical thought, abstract cubes, globes, and other logical constructions. DE, the longest line and largest portion of possible knowledge, is the realm of the Forms—perfect beauty, justice, and all other ideals.

Functions of the Forms   Zeller (1964, p. 149) noted three roles for the Ideas—ontological, teleological, and logical. In the first role they represent real being, the objective reality that is unchanging and eternal, just as Parmenides had described it. Appearances have their realities only because of participation in the Ideas. The Ideas/Forms are reality.

Second, they have a teleological function in that they lend a purpose to existence, that being to recognize or realize the Forms behind things, analogous to the artist's effort to abstract the essence or "idea" of a pastoral scene. Their third, logical, aspect lies in their bringing a classificatory scheme to lend order to a world that is otherwise chaos. This is the aspect of Form that Plato emphasized more and more as he grew older, though he never abandoned the first two.

Reminiscence–Anamnesis

The way to happiness is to know what is good and what is good is the truth. Hence, the goal of life is the pursuit of truth, and that means knowing the Forms. Piercing the veil of appearances is difficult and is possible only for "highly gifted natures, after a long course of intellectual discipline and practical experience" (Cornford 1964, p. xxix). The "knowing" itself is a sort of remembering—recalling knowledge that one had before birth but that became clouded by subsequent sensory experience and the opinion (inferior knowledge) that sensation brings.

Plato described the amnesia that occurs in Hades that obliterates memories of past lives. After a somewhat constrained choice of a new identity—varieties of men, women, and animal—the souls were bound by the threads of necessity, making their choice of new identity irreversible. Their memories of past life fade after crossing the "plain of Forgetfulness," leading to the river of "Unmindfulness," from which they must drink. Then, in the midst of thunderstorm and earthquake during the night, they are "driven upwards in all manner of ways to their birth, like stars shooting" (Jowett 1873, p. 397). Small wonder that all memory is lost!

Actually, reminiscence is only one part of what Plato calls reason. The other two parts are memory and dialectic. "Dialectic," as Plato used the term, referred to a simple question and answer series, continued until it was possible to get a grasp on the logos of the Form involved. Logos here means only "account," not the lawfulness of the universe. The clearest argument for this rationalist view appears in the dialogue, *Theaetetus*, though it is evident throughout Plato's writings. The question revolves around the issue of whether the senses provide true knowledge. Is knowledge all derived from perception, or must one go beyond the "veil of appearances?"

Is Knowledge Merely Perception?

Plato clearly opposed the epistemology of Protagoras, which he attacked directly in several dialogues. The excerpt below is taken from the *Theaetetus*, named after a famous mathematician who had been killed in battle at Corinth. In this dialogue, he is cast in an imaginary conversation with Socrates. As is typical in Plato's dialogues, an argument for the case that he will refute is first made, followed by the refutation, ostensibly appearing as an insight by the individual being questioned by Socrates. Lines spoken by Socrates are identified by S and those of Theaetetus by T (Rand 1912, pp. 11–26):

S: When anything, which affects me, exists for me and no other person, is it not perceived by me and no other?

T: That is evident.

S: Then my sensation is true for me since it is inseparable from my existence. As Protagoras says, I am judge both of the existence of what is for me and the non-existence of what is not.

T: That seems to be the case.

. . .

S: Right noble, then, was your decision that knowledge was nothing else than perception. Homer and Heraclitus with their crew, who say that all things flow and are in a state of motion, and the all-wise Protagoras with his view that man is the measure of all things, and Theaetetus, who concludes from these theories that knowledge is sensation, are all of one accord. Is that not true, O Theaetetus? Shall we call this result the young child at whose birth I have assisted? Or what do you say?

T: Then it must be so, Socrates.

This conclusion is reached after a host of arguments supporting Protagoras and the relativity of knowledge. Not only does sensation differ among individuals, but the same person senses differently when drowsy and alert or when healthy and sick. Even dreams may seem real, and at any moment we find ourselves unable to determine for certain whether we are perceiving or dreaming! All of the evidence supports Protagoras, as well as the Milesians, Heraclitus, and Empedocles, who stressed constant change—"becoming," rather than "being." In the imaginary conversation, Theaetetus accepts this view as one that he has held all along. And that view is the true one.

But Theaetetus (and thus, Protagoras) is "correct" only briefly; Theaetetus soon sees the light, though the reader may judge to what extent his conclusion was forced by Socrates:

S: If some one were to put this question to you, With what does a man see white and black colours and with what does he hear high and low tones? you would say, I think, with his eyes and ears.

T: I should.

S: …Reflect, is it more correct to say that it is with the eyes that we see or through them, and that it is with the ears or through them that we hear?

T: I think "through" is better, Socrates.

"Aha!" Is that a stroke of insight or what? Could a counselor in a court of law ask such leading questions as does Socrates? Bearing that in mind, we may now see Theaetetus "discover" truth:

S: and would you be willing to allow that what you perceive through one faculty you cannot perceive through another? You cannot, that is, hear through the eye as we hear through the ear?

T: I grant that readily.

…

S: That is well said. And what faculty will reveal to you the common elements not only of sensible qualities, but of all things…

T: You allude to being and not being, likeness, and unlikeness, the same and the other, and unity also, and other numbers applicable to things, and you evidently wish to know through what bodily instrument the soul perceives odd and even and all that is akin to them.

What Socrates "alludes to" here is the knowledge of ideal categories. As the dialogue continues, it is increasingly evident that the originality of Theaetetus's conclusions is suspect:

S: You follow me surpassingly well, Theaetetus; that is just what I want.

T: Verily, Socrates, I cannot tell what to say, if not that these things unlike sensible objects seem to need no special organ, but that the soul contemplates the common elements of all things through itself.

S: You are beautiful, Theaetetus, and not ill-favored...For that was my opinion too, and I was anxious for you to agree with me...

T: Clearly not, Socrates; indeed it is now quite evident that knowledge and sensation are different.

What Can the Senses Tell Us?

As is clear, Plato depreciated the role of the senses in gaining knowledge. Opinion, or inferior knowledge, is explained in terms of the representational theory of perception, much as it was proposed by Democritus. He proposed in the dialogue, *Timaeus*, that particles from objects strike us and we come to "know" the objects when the particles correspond to the same kinds of particles in our bodies. The four kinds of particles are the four elements of reality proposed by Empedocles.

As Theaetetus "discovered," real knowledge is within us; we were born with it and need only "remember" it. Prior to birth, souls exist in the world of Forms (essences, ideas), where the perfect (ideal) instance of every kind of thing and relationship is present and is known to us. The world (or dimension) of Forms must exist, reasoned Plato (e.g., in *The Republic*), since we have knowledge of many things in their perfect Forms, which certainly do not exist on earth. We can imagine perfectly straight lines without ever seeing one, as is the case with a perfect horse, tree, sunset, instance of justice, and so on.

The belief that "real" reality is hidden and that it is not what our senses present to us has been a persisting theme for thousands of years, in both religions and philosophies. Plato's version of "truth beyond the veil of appearances" is derived from the popular theory of Pythagoras, presented in Plato's *Timaeus*. But how can we know reality, if not through sensory experience? For Plato, as for most Greeks before him, knowing this reality is equivalent to knowing what is the "good," and is thus the basis for ethics and thus the key to happiness.

The Allegory of the Cave Ancient authors attributed the allegory of the cave to Empedocles, but it could as well have been proposed by Parmenides, Zeno, Pythagoras, or any other rationalist. As Plato presented it, the world of sense experience is as unreliable a sign of truth as would be shadows thrown on the wall of a cave. Imagine humanity as a figure chained in a cave, with a view of a wall in front. Behind the figure there burns a fire and between the fire and the human figure's back march a procession of shapes and objects. The light from the fire casts shadows of the procession's objects on the wall facing the chained figure, and the figure imagines that what is seen is real—it is the only reality perceivable by the figure.

This is meant as analogous to the human condition, in which the ever-changing world of sights and sounds is mistaken for the real world of Forms. How can we escape the chains that keep us in the cave and emerge into the sunlight to experience reality as it actually is? Book VII of *The Republic* reveals how this escape is possible.

One must study and understand those subjects that involve abstractions. These include arithmetic, plane and solid geometry, astronomy, and harmonics. Astronomy is important only as it concerns the movement of solid bodies, and harmonics is the study of harmony. While these subjects have practical applications, their real worth is in leading the soul out of the ephemeral world of the senses and into the unchanging world of the mind. Thus we pass from darkness into light and come to understand the idea of the Good.

The Three Parts of Soul and Society

No one knows how long the ancient Greeks had believed in a three-part psyche, but surely the several writers who were "Homer" referred to nous, thymos, and menos as three aspects of the soul, and that was centuries before Plato's time. Like earlier Greeks, Plato accepted the microcosm/macrocosm principle and proposed a soul that is constituted like a nation. This is *The Republic*, a proposal for a city that is an enlargement of the individual. The astonishing similarity between details of Freud's psychodynamic theory and Plato's theory of personality as presented in this work has been noted often.[3]

Elsewhere,[4] Plato compared the soul's three parts to a charioteer and his two winged horses. The charioteer, as the leader, represents the rational aspect of the individual, and that corresponds in the Republic to the higher class of guardians—the rulers of an ideal state. The white winged horse is characterized by courage, humility, control, reverence, and temperance—it is the "spirited" or "passionate" horse. But the dark horse is proud, insolent, deaf, wanton, and pleasure seeking. The two horses represent the spirited and appetitive aspects of individuals, and these correspond to the Republic's lower order of guardians—the military class—and to the "herd" portions of the state.

Plato and Adjustment The individual soul is well-adjusted when there is a proper balance among the three parts. One might think that the appetites, savage and capable of any infamy, even incest, should be restrained as much as possible. However, this is not "balance," as Plato sees it, and harmonia requires the appetites. Interestingly, this aspect of the soul "frisks" while the rational part sleeps, and its aim includes the begetting of children, an aim that may be expressed in other ways, such as in art or poetry. Hence, Plato described what would later be called "sublimation." The dark horse of desire is apt to emerge during sleep:[5]

the wild beast in our nature, gorged with meat and drink, starts up and walks about naked . . . and there is no conceivable folly or crime, however shameless or unnatural—not excepting incest or parricide—of which such a nature may not be guilty. (Jowett, p. 330)

Two millennia later, Freud shared that view: "The good are those who content themselves with dreaming what the wicked actually do"(1913, p. 493).

Plato proposed a program of education to supply the three kinds of citizens who would live in this city. Their roles must be well-defined, since this is a city governed by people, not laws—in fact, the Republic had no laws! However, this city would run smoothly, unlike the existing states, which resemble a person doctoring a disorder by trying any new remedy that comes along (Jowett 1873, p. 138). In what must be the fairest system of education yet proposed, all children received the same schooling to the age of twenty. Early education began with physical education—gymnastics, weightlifting, and so on, followed by six years of training in music,[6] so that the soul may learn harmony and rhythm and grace. The students were twenty years old when the first "Great Elimination" occurred. This series of tests lasted over several days and was aimed at discovering every strength and every weakness. Most examinees failed and became the workers, businesspeople, artists, and crafters—the people who worked with their hands or in business and who comprised what Plato called the herd.

After a further ten years of education, another Great Elimination is held and most of the thirty-year-old examinees are winnowed out to form the lower class of guardians, the auxiliaries, or soldiers. For them, life is a Spartan one, eating simple food, owning nothing, having no husbands or wives, and communally raising children. They are the soldiers, expected to give their lives at any moment for the defense of the city. These superior people were expected to live what Adeimantos, one of the discussants, noticed was an uninviting life, yet they had the means to take over governing themselves. Why shouldn't they do so?

Evidently the myth of the metals—gold, silver, and iron—is to act as a mystical sanction for the arrangement of classes. All humans are made from earth, but the metals in them differ. The masses have only iron and the few have gold. But the guardian-soldiers are silver (Jowett, p. 125).

This is the royal lie, necessary to maintain the separation of the levels of society. Three points should be noted concerning this passage. First, the reference to males must be an artifact of translation, since it is clear throughout *The Republic* that women are treated no differently from men and that women may serve in any of the three levels of society (see especially Book V).

Second, the reference to "God" concerns no Olympic god, but a living god that watches over us and promises us personal immortality. Such a religion is essential if the state is to be strong. The "will" of such a god enforces the social order, and an attractive afterlife makes it possible to willingly sacrifice one's life for the good of the state. Plato favored the censoring of depressing religious material, such as the doctrine that Hades is a depressing place. An afterlife in which we are pale and lifeless and require blood offerings to lend us strength to speak is unappealing.

Third, it is clear that this is no hereditary government, since the son or daughter of a ruler could descend to the herd or the auxiliaries and the child of a herdsman or a soldier could ascend to the ruling class. All were not equal, but all had equal opportunity. And one rises by performance in the Eliminations, not through the hypocrisy of voting. "This is a democracy of the schools, a hundred times more honest and more effective than a democracy of the polls" (Durant 1954).

The rulers, or higher-order guardians, were the highest and the smallest group, men and women who had actually become philosophers and kings. After the second great elimination, they had received five more years of education concerning the highest abstractions— were they then fit to rule? Such philosophers are often rascals of no use to anyone, despite their wisdom, so a final test remains.

At the age of thirty-five, they are cast into the herd with no favor or advantage and must make a success of themselves during the next fifteen years. Those who do so are officially rulers and thereafter divide their time between governing and philosophy.

Government and Human Nature The ideal state, Plato's republic, may well never exist on earth, but only as a form in heaven, though Plato tried to teach such politics to Dion, son of the tyrant of Syracuse. What we see in fact, Plato observed, is a tiresome cycle of four degenerate Forms of government that often follow a fixed order. One seemingly good government is a government by ability, where an aristocracy of superior people rule benevolently.

However, an aristocratic government, even if it is an aristocracy of ability rather than birth, degenerates into the timocratic or honor-worshiping military government when the warrior class prevails over the wisdom-loving class. This is ascendance of the spirited, the auxiliaries, and the same imbalance in the individual results in a person who is valiant but contentious and overambitious.

In time, the timocracy degenerates into oligarchy, or rule by the rich few, after the quest for honor turns to love of money. In the oligarchic individual, the desires (appetites) have overcome the reasoning and spirited parts. The oligarchy lasts until the poor multitudes revolt against the rich few and institute the next form of government, the democracy, or rule by the people. The oligarch individual is overly influenced by desire, mainly the desire for money. The democratic individual is even more ruled by desire, not only for money, but for many unnecessary things.

There is a very good case against rule by the people and Plato raises it, pointing out that an excess of liberty turns the population into a mob. As the people "run from the smoke into the fire," they fall prey to the argument that they need a Protector to restore law and order. The Protector, whose slogans always refer to being for the people, as opposed to those who are enemies of the people, quickly establishes the last form of government, the tyranny, as he becomes absolute ruler.

The tyrant enslaves the people but is himself enslaved by his desires, which are even more unreasonable and unnecessary than is the case for the democratic individual. Plato pitied the tyrant, slave to fear, want, every sort of misery, and all kinds of wickedness. All four Forms of government are bad, and the individuals corresponding to them are "maladjusted." But the order of happiness corresponding to each

personality type runs in descending order from democratic to oligarchic to aristocratic to tyranny.

Plato and Freud
While Plato was often accused by the ancients of plagiarism, Sigmund
Freud could well be accused of the same in his adaptations of Plato's
work. This would give Freud's ideas great antiquity, given that they
parallel Plato's and that Plato's were not original. There is no difficulty
here, but it is strange to realize this and know that Freud claimed originality for his basic concepts and always held that he was uninformed
of earlier philosophical and psychological views. In his *History of Psychoanalysis,* he conceded that Arthur Schopenhauer had in the eighteenth century anticipated his ideas on repression, but he wrote that,
"I am again indebted for having made a discovery to not being a wide
reader"(Freud 1917, p. 3) Indeed.

But the parallels between Plato and Freud are striking, and they re-
mind us that "new" ideas are often of ancient origin. Their longevity
means that we should pay them heed. Klein (1970) detailed the many
similarities between the views of Plato and Freud and noted Freud's
reluctance to see any similarities with earlier views. This reluctance on
Freud's part has been reported by many others.

The only nonmedical courses that Freud took in medical school were
six taught by Franz Brentano between 1874 and 1876.[7] Ernest Jones,
Freud's biographer, also reported that Brentano recommended Freud
as translator of a set of essays by John Stuart Mill. Freud did the translation, including one essay on Plato! And in 1899 Freud wrote a letter
in which he said that he was reading Burckhardt's *History of Greek Civilization,* "which is providing me with unexpected parallels" (Klein
1970, p. 60).

Hence, from the 1870s to 1899 Freud had every opportunity to absorb Plato's basic ideas, and it is disingenuous of him to claim that his
knowledge was "very fragmentary." Yet, there is no reference to Plato
until the fourth edition of *Traumdeutung* (translated as "The Meaning
of Dreams") in 1914, fourteen years after the first edition.

Parallels between Plato and Freud   First, and most obvious, no
reader can consider Plato's three-part soul without comparing it to
the intrapsychic forces of Freud's last years. But that three-part division preceded Plato, at least roughly, as the menos, thymos, and nous,
and it reappeared frequently over the centuries, as the "passions,"

"will," and "reason." However, there are more specific similarities than that.

Second, consider the emphasis on adjustment. It is true that all the ancient Greeks believed in "harmonia," but Plato's harmony existed among the three parts of the psyche. As in the state, the auxiliaries may be unhappy, but the good of the whole was what counted. Similarly, the gratification of the appetites, or Freud's *Es*/id must often be denied for the good of the whole. This doesn't mean that reason must always rule—Freud did not encourage overintellectualization, and Plato taught that the appetites and passions must be given some leeway.

Third, for Plato and for Freud, adjustment does not come easily and requires a long and difficult education—Plato's schooling or Freud's analysis—before harmony may be achieved. Sensory experience, as we may be conscious of it, is of little import—it is the meaningless froth on the surface of the ocean. Both Plato and Freud deprecated conscious experience, and Plato's views on hidden meanings are apparent in the *Theaetetus* selection and in many other dialogues where unknown "knowledge" is brought to light in the process of dialectic.

Fourth, both saw the appetites as largely sexual forces that could be expressed directly or sublimated through art, music, or other endeavors. Plato divided Eros into the profane type that leads to children and the sacred kind, expressed as love for the Forms as eternal truths. Motives may be functions not only of appetite and reason but also of the passions, so we seek honor and glory and avoid censure and shame.

Fifth, both saw the appetites "frisking" during sleep, committing all manner of hideous crimes through dreams. The quote above from Plato could well have come straight from Freud's writings in 1915. Finally, the auxiliaries, as soldiers for the state, were not expected to know the truth of the highest philosophy, but they were to have "correct belief." This is to say that the rulers supplied a code of conduct that was correct and was to be obeyed but which was not necessarily understood by the soldiers. It is hard to imagine a better description of the superego as internalization of the rules of society than as the holder of "correct belief."

Freud's popularity during the twentieth century may owe a good deal to the fact that his basic tenets have survived a long time. Remember, it was well-known in ancient times that Plato was a frequent plagiarizer, so these ideas are surely older than the fourth century B.C.

The World in Aristotle's Time

Prior to Aristotle's time, Greece had existed as free city-states, a condition that ended when Philip II of Macedonia and his son, Alexander the Great, conquered and dominated Greece.

In 334 B.C. Alexander invaded Persian territories with 30,000 infantry and 5,000 cavalry, including 5,000 Greek mercenaries. In ten years he conquered Asia Minor, Syria, Egypt, Babylonia, Persia, and other lands as far to the east as the Punjab in India. He destroyed the Persian Empire, the greatest that the world had known (in Russell's opinion, 1945, p. 218), in three battles.

His life was so remarkable that he may well have believed that his mother, Olympias, had had relations with a god. His men persuaded him to stop their eastward march into India, and they returned to Babylon in 800 ships in 327 B.C., where Alexander died four years later at age thirty-two.

During the period of the Macedonian occupation, as for many years past, Greek civilization was largely urban—rich commercial cities surrounded by agricultural land, often with barbarian populations. The cities did not require a rural population of the same blood and with equal political rights (Russell 1945, p. 220). It was this kind of society in which Aristotle lived and worked and in which he made his astonishing contributions to human knowledge. And Alexander was his patron.

Aristotle

A further problem respecting the attributes of the soul is whether they all belong to body and soul together or whether any of them are peculiar to the soul alone—a difficult question but unavoidable. (Wheelwright 1935, p. 67)

Aristotle (384–322 B.C.; see figure 3.2) was born in Stagira, an Ionian colony in Macedonia. His family moved to Pella, the capital, where his father, Nichomachus, served as physician to the king, Amyntas II. Aristotle became a friend of Amyntas's son, Philip, a friendship that later led to Aristotle's tutoring of Philip's son, Alexander, who conquered the known world as Alexander the Great (see figure 3.3). As Alexander was invading Asia, Aristotle founded a school in a park named for Apollo Lyceus (enlightener or wolf slayer), and, for that reason, the school was known as the Lyceum. He taught there for eleven

Figure 3.2
Aristotle. Courtesy of the Archives of the History of American Psychology, University of Akron.

years, strolling with pupils on the park grounds; hence, his school was called "peripatetic," from the verb "to walk about."

Alexander's Macedonian armies had been occupying Greece for some years when he died in 323 B.C.; he saw himself as a promoter of Greek (Hellenic) culture to the rest of the world, and indeed he was. However, many Greeks resented the rule of the Macedonians, and, when Alexander died, Aristotle, his pupil and subsequent recipient of the equivalent of millions of dollars in support from him, was accused of irreligion. Aristotle refused to allow Athens to repeat its crime against Socrates and retired to his late mother's country estate, where he died a year later.

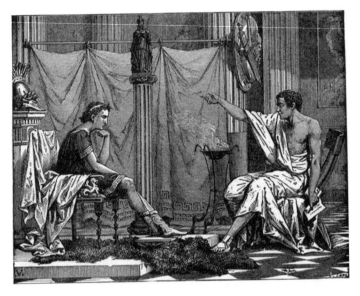

Figure 3.3
Alexander. Courtesy of http://karenswhimsy.com.

Aristotle's influence over the thought of the next two thousand years was profound and often criticized[8] as an impediment to the development of Western science. In fact, much of the "Aristotelianism" that was so influential later would have disgusted Aristotle himself. For our purposes, he was a genius who contributed a complete treatment of what constitutes an explanation, who wrote the first psychology book (actually three books) and from 400 to 1,000 other books (Zeller 1964), and who inspired the later work of Aquinas, Brentano, Dewey, Kantor, and James. These thinkers carried on Aristotle's stress on dynamics, or processes, as opposed to his teacher's stress on statics, or things.

Where Is the Magic?

The Pythagoreans and Plato conceived the world as a machine composed of atoms and the body as a lifeless vessel necessary to house and to empower the immortal soul. The soul was the very definition of magic, capable of knowing the truth inherent in it because of its past existences and intermissions in the world of Forms. This magical entity was similar in its chief features to the "ghosts" in all of the machines that have been proposed by mind/body dualists from ancient times through Descartes and through the mechanical and computational models of the centuries since. The essentially lifeless machinery of the body is a mere housing for a magical mind—at least, according to this extremely popular theory.

Can we do without this magic? No, we cannot. The fact is that the universe is partly magical, and we can only choose where to draw the line separating the magic and the inert machinery. Pythagoras, Plato, and the information processors chose to concentrate the magic in a "soul," or "mind,"—or ghost. That is a method that worked in the physical sciences from Galileo on. However, another division of magic and "natural" had great appeal for many centuries, and it still does. If we are unconcerned with the development of modern science, we may even prefer it to the method of concentrated magic.

Like the monists of Miletus and Elea, Aristotle preferred to distribute the "magic" through nature. Different substances were different because of specific "essences," or "natures," that gave them their properties, and living things were different because they were organic, a name that Aristotle coined. Plants, animals, and humans have lower or higher "souls" as the defining aspect of their being. This is best understood by considering Aristotle's treatment of causality.

Aristotle and Causality

Aristotle's "doctrine of the four causes" is far more interesting than most discussions of the nature of explanation. He proposed that an explanation of any phenomenon had to include specification of four causes: the material cause, formal cause, efficient cause, and final cause. A commonly used illustration—and extremely poor example—lies in the "explanation" for the existence of a statue.[9] The material cause was the stone, the formal cause was the plan of the sculptor, the efficient cause was the sculptor himself, and the final cause, or purpose of the thing, was to decorate a room. We think of causes in a narrower way today; the efficient cause, or agent, is what we typically mean by "cause."

But what if we consider something more interesting than a statue? Aristotle's point does not really apply to artificial things, like a statue—his is a view of nature in general, not artificial things, which are nature secondhand. For example, why does smoke rise? Why are people different in temperament and ability? Why do stones fly through the air when we throw them? Why do objects accelerate as they fall? Why do they fall in the first place? These are the sorts of things that Aristotle considered in his discussion of causality.

What is the efficient cause when there is no sculptor? What is the final cause when purposes less trivial than interior decoration are involved? Why does smoke rise? What is the efficient cause in that case? Aristotle often conceived the efficient cause of a phenomenon as an indwelling agent—an essence in the material that directs it toward its appointed end, telos, or final cause. Smoke rises because it is its "nature" (in the scheme of things) to rise. Eventually all of the smoke everywhere will be up where it belongs.

This "essential nature," or "purpose within," was called its entelechy. Stones fall for a similar reason; they belong at the center of the earth and it is their entelechy to fall. They accelerate on their way because of an aspect of their entelechy, what was later called "jubilance" (Butterfield 1965, p. 18). After all, as they fall, they are nearer and nearer "home."

The universe is unwinding toward an appointed end, and everything is constantly becoming more of what it is supposed to be. Everything, living and nonliving, is thus actualizing as Goldstein, Maslow, and Rogers suggested in the twentieth century and as German philosophers of the nineteenth century believed.

The prototype for this teleological view is Aristotle's doctrine of the four causes. Matter has essences, "natures," and things happen "naturally." We will see that this vitalist doctrine posed problems for many centuries, since it is incompatible with what became Western science, yet it provides good accounts for many events that we observe daily.

However, for practical purposes, Aristotle's essences and natures were treated as the "metals" were treated in Plato's Republic. This implied that one's station in life was determined by one's essence or nature, and that depended largely on one's parents—Aristotle did not share Plato's egalitarian views.

Hence, if your father was a cobbler and your mother a grocer, it was apparent that your nature was that of a tradesperson. The child of a famous general or a society woman would have a different nature. Any attempt to evaluate people so as to change their position in society was, for Aristotle, meddling with the "natural" course of things. For many centuries Aristotle's doctrine of essences was used to justify the rigid arrangement of society by social class as the "natural" order. The equality of opportunity of Plato was not a feature of Aristotle's thinking.

De Anima

De Anima is a collection of Aristotle's writings that deal with psychological matters; it begins with long critiques of his predecessors. This is fortunate, since many of them left no written record, and critical reviews by Aristotle (and Plato) are often all that we know of the works of thinkers such as Thales.

The Latin translators who chose the title clearly did so because anima means soul in Latin. However, the reader of this work is left with the impression that Aristotle did not treat anima as soul, at least as we use the word "soul." For him, anima is not the soul of theology, nor is it the separate "mind" that Plato and common sense assumed.

It is clear that Aristotle did not accept the representational theory of perception and that he, like Protagoras, stressed dynamics, activity, and process. What is anima?

- It is inseparable from the body; it is not something in the body.
- It is not a static thing; it is a shaping force.
- It is a sum of life functions.
- It is a way in which bodies may have life.
- It is the functioning of a body with organs.
- If the eye were an animal, seeing would be its soul.

Note also that *De Anima* is a collection of works that may have been written over twenty or more years. This explains some contradictory statements that resulted from Aristotle's switch from being a disciple of Plato to an independent thinker. Despite these caveats, we may be assured that the ideas involved are Aristotle's, "pretty nearly in the form under which it came from his own mind and was given originally either to his own disciples or to the world" (Wheelwright 1935, p. xxiii).

Does the Soul Require the Body? Aristotle began with the same question that was asked by Descartes almost two thousand years later: What is the relation of soul and body (Wheelwright 1935, p. 67)?

A further problem respecting the attributes of the soul is whether they all belong to body and soul together or whether any of them are peculiar to the soul alone—a difficult question but unavoidable.

He points out that in "a majority of cases" the soul neither acts nor is acted upon independent of the body. This is surely true of anger, courage, desire, and all sensation, such as vision and touch.

Thinking may seem to occur independent of the body, yet, Aristotle suggested, much (perhaps all) thought consists of imagery, and that requires the body. How can one conceive a visual or auditory or tactual image without experience with the corresponding sense organs of the body? Is there anything, any functions or characteristics, that is peculiar to the soul alone?

If there are no unique aspects of the soul, then it does not have independent existence. For Aristotle, this makes the soul comparable to the straightness of a line. A line may be straight and have many other properties—length, width, color, and what it touches, for example. However, straightness by itself has none of these properties, existing only as an aspect of lines. Soul is, by the same token, an aspect of body:

Similarly, we may take it that the affections of the soul—angry passion and gentleness, fear, pity, courage, and even joy, love, and hate—always involve body; for their occurrence is accompanied by some specific affection of the body. (Wheelwright 1935, pp. 67–69)

Body and Soul as Matter and Form   A house may be treated as bricks, stones, and timbers or as a shelter from heat, cold, and storm. Or it may be both—a form or plan (*eidos*) embodied in the material and directing to certain ends. Matter and form for Plato were separate things; objects of daily life and cases of truth and beauty were instances of ideal Forms that existed in a world of ideals.

Aristotle saw matter and form as inseparable. When we refer to "substance," we mean either matter, in itself not a "this," or the shape and form of something that allows us to distinguish it from other things. Or we mean both. Aristotle saw the situation as potential made actual:

By matter we mean potentiality, by form actuality.... Soul, therefore, must be substance in the sense that it is the form (*eidos*) of a natural body endowed with the capacity of life. Substance in this sense is actuality (*entelecheia*); and soul, therefore, is the actuality of body as just defined ... (Wheelwright 1935, pp. 73–74)

So, are soul and body identical? Such a question is as superfluous as asking whether wax and the imprint on it are identical or whether the material of a thing is identical with the thing of which it is the material. An eye and seeing are matter and form, and if the eye could not see, it would no longer be an eye; like a carved or etched likeness, it would be an eye in name only. The relation is the same when we consider "our whole conscious life" and "the whole sentient body as such" (Wheelwright 1935, pp. 73–75).

Is the Mind Only Its Objects?
Protagoras proposed that all mind was reducible to sensation, while Democritus and Plato (and uneducated common sense) saw mind as fundamentally different. Aristotle's position was clear and presages the act psychology of Brentano and the radical empiricism of James:

Accordingly, the intellectual faculty, like the sensitive, has no other intrinsic nature than that of being a certain capacity; from which it follows that "mind" (*nous*, as we may call this aspect of the soul—I mean its thinking and judging aspect—has no actual existence before it thinks . . . the mind is "potentially," so to speak, identical with its objects, but is not actually identical with any of them until it thinks . . . (Wheelwright 1935, pp. 94–95)

Aristotle's views on life after death provided difficulties for later Christian writers, especially Thomas Aquinas. Aristotle believed that what survives death loses the power of sensation and, thus, memory and thought—hardly an appealing hereafter:

But we have no recollection of the activity of mind in a pure state; for when mind is in that state it is not affected by impressions; while conversely, the impressionable side of mind is perishable. (Wheelwright 1935, p. 97)

What is "mind in a pure state?" He was referring to the condition of mind as it exists before birth or as it does after death. Without the body and its sense organs, there is no sensory experience and no memory! What is left is not very appealing as basis for an afterlife.

Whether this interpretation of Aristotle is correct may seem moot, but it was a momentous issue to the Christian thinkers of the Middle Ages as we will see.

Aristotle and Motivation   Plato's position on motivation was similar to that of Freud as we have seen. Motivation was differently treated by Aristotle, and his interpretation, taken superficially, resembles the associationist theories of the nineteenth century, though it is a mistake to identify Aristotle as a real associationist. Sensation is what James much later called "knowledge by acquaintance," and pleasure and pain arise because there are objects out there that are "natural" or "unnatural," which is to say, good and evil:

Indeed, to feel pleasure and pain is nothing else than to respond with our general sensibility to good and evil as such, and this is what constitutes desire and avoidance. (Wheelwright 1935, pp. 98–99)

This passage summarizes Aristotle's views on the simplest bases for motivation, which follow from his emphasis on essences, or "natures," of things. Some things are good for us, and we react to them with pleasure; other things are evil, and we react with aversion (Zeller 1964, pp. 206–207). This is true even in the "animal soul," which is capable of only vegetative and sensory functioning.

Since we remember, in the sense that we continue to sense things that are absent and to date them as past, we are constantly imagining (via phantasma) sensations and their accompanying pleasures and pains. If we approach that which conjures up past pleasure and try to stay away from that which reminds us of pain, we are motivated by simple hedonist gears. For Aristotle, such reactions to phantasma are desires and aversions.

Those seeking predecessors for recent theories find associationism and hedonism in Aristotle, a meaningless finding for two reasons. First, these trivial aspects of Aristotle's theory are hardly conspicuous in his thinking—surely the conception of entelechy and the metaphysical and epistemological monism[10] distinguishes Aristotle more than the mention of commonplaces, such as associationism and hedonism. Second, it is difficult to identify anyone, past or present, who does not believe that associations play a part in daily life, if only to explain active recall, as Aristotle suggested.

Aristotle Was No Associationist

Men who have good memories are not the same as those who are good at recollecting, in fact generally speaking the slow-witted have better memories, but the quick-witted and those who learn easily are better at recollecting. (Diamond 1974, p. 250)

Recollection and memory are very different, and associationism applies only to the former. Even Plato cannot avoid mention of association by similarity and contiguity of particulars and forms, so some classify him as an associationist (Herrnstein and Boring 1965, p. 327; Leahey 1992, p. 55)! However, associationism is a theory of mind that posits elements, such as sensations and ideas, and explains experience as compounds of these elements. David Hume, George Berkeley, James

Mill, and Edwin Guthrie were associationists. Plato and Aristotle were not.

On the other hand, everyone who has ever considered the way in which we recall things—when we are actively trying—notices that we tend to go through a chain of ideas (images or whatever) that are connected because they occurred together in the past or because they are similar or because they are connected in some other way. We may not notice that we are doing this, but indeed we are. When I misplace my keys, I mentally trace my activity, beginning with the last time that I recall having them. "Then I closed the car door, shut the garage door, walked to the house, stopped to feed the birds." Such sequences are common in life, but hardly the paradigm for all mental activity!

Marjorie Grene (1963, p. 261) said that Aristotle's theory of memory and recollection deserves more attention than is usually given it "for its contrast both to Plato and to the point of view of modern associationist theories of mind like that of Hume." Here is what Aristotle wrote "On Memory and Recollection" (Diamond 1974, pp. 250–252).

He believed that memory is common to humans and many animals and that it is akin to perception—"that part of the soul to which imagination belongs." And, of course, "only animals which perceive time remember" (Diamond 1974, p. 250). Memory is a modification of the soul, as the effects of perception are retained, all processes retaining the potential/actual theme of Aristotle's theory.

"Memorizing preserves the memory of something by constant reminding. This is nothing but the repeated contemplation of an object as a likeness, and not independently." How can we perceive things not present? "But surely this can and does occur. Just as the picture painted on the panel is at once a picture and a likeness . . . and for this reason sometimes we do not know, when such stimuli occur in our soul from an earlier perception, whether the phenomenon is due to perception, and we are in doubt whether it is memory or not" (Aristotle, 450 b11, in Grene 1963, p. 166).

Nicomachean Ethics

Hedonism, or the view that motivation is wholly explained as striving for pleasure and avoiding pain, says only that we seek some things and are repelled by others. Unless pleasure and pain are defined more clearly than they ever have been, everyone remains a hedonist by definition, including Socrates and Plato, who scorned most bodily pleasures, seeking "happiness in knowledge of the good." Aristotle was no more a hedonist than they.

Pleasure and pain have little to do with happiness—even a slave or a child could experience "pleasure." But happiness is something that appears in "a pattern of life" (Rachlin 1994), not in moments of pleasure. Consider what we mean by happiness, asked Aristotle, and we find as many definitions as we do for the verb "is." For example, is happiness to be found in knowing and doing the "good," as the Platonists proposed? How many "goods" are there, and how many degrees of each good? There must be an infinity of each of them, and the Platonists thus tell us little, aside from the fact that vulgar pleasures are not good. But there is no one Platonic "good" of which some things partake. There are many goods.

In Book 1 of the *Nicomachean Ethics*,[11] Aristotle concluded that happiness comes from doing good, but "good" depends on the capabilities of the individual. We cannot expect the level of goodness in the actions of a child that we expect in the adult. In a way, he proposed that there is a "highest and best use" for each of us, a potential to be actualized, and the closer we approach that ideal, the happier we may be.

One Swallow Does Not Make a Spring

Happiness cannot occur in a moment of pleasure but only over appreciable periods of time, and Aristotle wrote:

> But we must add the words "in a complete life." For as one swallow or one day does not make a spring, so one day or a short time does not make a man blessed or happy . . . (*Nichomachean Ethics* in Loomis 1943, p. 92)

As is the case for many virtues and so-called "states of mind," such as courage, honesty, love, pain, contentment, and happiness, one swallow or one day is not enough. Happiness arises in the satisfactions that come from consistent noble action—doing "the highest and best" that one can over a long time, perhaps a lifetime, and certainly over many years. One honest act does not define honesty, nor does a single virtuous act define virtue and happiness.

Patterns of Actions

Honesty, love, virtue, and happiness are among many terms that are extremely difficult to define—the best that we can do is follow Aristotle's definitions. That is, "love" and "happiness," to use two common examples, are not really emotions or even states of mind. They refer instead to activities extended over appreciable spans of time. "Love" is reflected in what one says and does over time, and it persists during sleep and while engaged in replacing a fuel injector. Similarly, "happiness" is a pattern of moral activity over time, not a fleeting experience that even a child might feel. A child may know pleasure but cannot know happiness.

Make a Habit of Virtue

Moral virtue on the other hand is the outcome of habit, and accordingly its name, *ethike*, is derived by a slight variation from *ethos*, habit. From this fact it is clear that moral virtue is not implanted in us by nature; for nothing that exists by nature can be transformed by habit. (Loomis 1943, p. 101)

That was Aristotle's point in Book II, where he defined morality as a potential to be actualized, beginning with habitual action in childhood. The greater pleasures, those that may bring real happiness, require a relinquishing of what are commonly called pleasures—the activities that come from food, drink, sex, sloth, and the lot—and children lack the wherewithal to do this. Therefore, they must be compelled to do the "good" and moral actions at first, though they may feel it to be unpleasant. Morality, the key to happiness, is a potential in everyone which, like other potentials, may never be realized or develop at all without help, which may be coercion.

Habit and the Actualization of Moral Capacity

Since moral acts are pleasant, but not of the "violent" sort of pleasure, their habitual repetition under compulsion will eventually establish them. The subtler but higher pleasure they bring will eventually take effect, and compulsion will no longer be required. For example, we teach the child the "natural/good" degree of attention to be paid to food. Two vices lie in the extremes of gluttony and starving oneself—the mean is the virtue, what constitutes sensible eating. Proper courage is a mean between the extremes of cowardice and reckless abandon. The practice of that mean must be made habitual.

As this occurs, we see that the index for good and moral behavior is the pleasure that is produced, and the higher/less "violent" pleasures need their chance to occur. With time, the occurrence of actions, as choices over time, changes our character. That is to say, it leads us to

behave in a continuously more moral way and thus allows us to experience more happiness.

Aristotle believed in free will (as Zeller 1964) insisted and in Book 3
emphasized the importance of "willed choices," rather than reliance on
natural virtue. A person who is naturally virtuous finds pleasure in
doing good and has some degree of happiness. However, voluntary
(willed) virtuous acts bring more happiness, since their occurrence
means that some vulgar pleasure has probably been forgone, and that
makes the act more virtuous and thus brings more happiness.

If one is naturally brave, there is some happiness in the commission
of acts reflecting that natural virtue. However, the person who is afraid
and must choose to do the brave act is the better for it. In foregoing the
immediate small pleasure of fleeing from danger, one gains the greater
pleasure of willing to do the right thing. In time, the right thing will
become the habitual thing.

The Highest Pleasures
The highest pleasures require the use of one's highest capacities—in
humans this is the exercise of reason in contemplating the highest
abstractions of the universe. Only the most blessed few are capable of
experiencing such pleasures. For most, these pleasures are unachievable, and so it is best for them to achieve whatever high level of moral
conduct as their conception of the "good" allows. For some, this may
restrict virtue to the attainment of "honor," defined as approval from
one's peers. For others, virtue may be limited by athletic achievement
or by military success, or by fashioning art—whatever one's "nature"
defines as the limits of one's comprehension of "good."

Free Will
In humans the highest level of soul, reason (nous), allows voluntary
action (free will) as a function of desire (reaction to good) and reason.
Zeller, the authority here, believed that Aristotle was clear in uncondi-
tionally supposing freedom of will. Desire and reason decide on final
aims, the process is voluntary, and individuals are therefore account-
able for their actions (Zeller 1964, p. 208). He wrote that there is "nothing more precise in Aristotle."

Also precise is Aristotle's conviction that people differ in their ability
to reason and thus in their capacity for virtuous action. Some people
are more admirable than are others, just as some oaks grow more lux-
uriently than do others. Russell (1945, chapter XX) pointed out that

Aristotle had very different ideas about justice than we do—his philosophy calls for it, since people are not created equal.

A son or a slave is property, and a father or master may dispense justice as seen fit—there can be no injustice to one's own property. One cannot even be friends with a slave, since a slave is a tool, not a person, unless the slave aspect is ignored. Everyone deserves respect and love according to worth, so that the inferior should love, obey, and respect the superior far more than the superior need love and respect them. Thus, wives, children, subjects, and slaves should have more respect and love for husbands, parents, monarchs, and masters than those superiors have for them.

This flows from Aristotle's physics—matter has form inextricably bound to it, and form exists in many kinds and degrees of perfection. The lout will not understand astronomy whatever his education, and he should properly be subservient to the educated (and therefore educable) man. Human equality was a Pythagorean and Platonic tenet, and it would be a key Christian belief, of course. However, it was not Aristotle's belief.

The *Nichomachean Ethics* tells us to find happiness through a pattern of life characterized by moral choices. These choices, or virtuous acts, are dependent on our vision of the "good," so that older, wiser people are capable of more virtue. Since virtue is the essential condition for happiness, the wise are thus the happiest.

Ayn Rand's "Objectivism"

Ayn (as in "mine") Rand (1906–1982) was a Russian–American author of novels such as *The Fountainhead* and *Atlas Shrugged* (1943 and 1957, respectively), based on a philosophy which she saw as similar only to Aristotle's. All other philosophies she attacked, literally to the end—her last piece was *Philosophy: Who Needs It?*, published posthumously by Bobbs-Merrill (1982). The following is from an address she gave to the graduating class of the United States Military Academy at West Point on March 6, 1974. She had just finished reciting the evil effects of some philosophies. If philosophy is evil, why study it? She answered:

Not all philosophies are evil, though too many of them are, particularly in modern history. On the other hand, at the root of every civilized achievement, such as science, technology, progress, freedom—at the root of every value we enjoy today, including the birth of this country—you will find the achievement of one man, who lived over two thousand years ago: Aristotle.

However, she believed that we have turned from Aristotle, and this was mainly the achievement of the humanities, cause of a large part of our current problems:

Now observe the breach between the physical sciences and the humanities. Although the progress of physical science is slowing down (by reason of a flawed epistemology, among other things), the momentum of the Aristotelian past is so great that science is still moving forward, while the humanities are bankrupt. Spatially, science is reaching beyond the solar system—while, temporally, the humanities are sliding back into the primeval ooze. Science is landing men on the moon and monitoring radio emissions from other galaxies—while astrology is the growing fashion here on earth; while courses on astrology and black magic are given in colleges; while horoscopes are sent galloping over the airwaves of a great scientific achievement, television. (Rand, p. 97)

During the 1960s and 1970s, she acquired something of a cult following and established a training institute in New York City. Readers who were college students in those days probably are familiar with Rand's novels, though it may have occurred to few that she rejected all philosophies but Aristotle's. What would Aristotle say about Rand as an Aristotelian?

The characters of her novels are superior and productive people who are self-actualized and who know right and wrong when they see it. Aristotle certainly did believe in gradations among people, and he believed that right and wrong are objective things. These admirable people are contrasted with the worthless parasites and the incompetent that comprise almost all of society. Her heroic characters are conscious of things, never just "conscious"; so their souls are one with their objects (their work is their life) as Aristotle prescribed. No abstract or otherworldly ideas mediate their view of reality.

Aristotle in fact did oppose mediation by ideas (or copies), so when Rand's characters perceive a concrete world of things, they are perceiving as Aristotle stipulated. And he was surely an elitist who would have concurred with Rand's judgments on the relative worth of individuals. Hence, if Aristotle's views are restricted to epistemology and ethics, Ayn Rand may be a twentieth-century exemplar.

4   From Aristotle to the Enlightenment: Pagan Psychologies Give Way to Christianity

If someone handed over your body to any person who met you, you would be vexed; but that you hand over your mind to any person that comes along, so that, if he reviles you, it is disturbed and troubled—are you not ashamed of that? (Epictetus, in Kaufman 1961, volume 1, pp. 557, 561)

After Aristotle: The Hellenistic Age

When Alexander died in 323 B.C., he left two sons, an infant and one unborn. They were in no position to succeed him, and three of his commanders divided the world among them after considerable conflict. Antigonus Monothalmus took Europe, Ptolemy took Egypt, and Seleussus eventually took Asia.

They held their lands as military dictatorships supported by their shares of the Macedonian army and by Greek mercenaries. Greek became the language of literature and culture and remained so until the Islamic conquest almost a thousand years later. The world was not peaceful.

Earlier, when the Greek city-states had been free, there was disorder, but the Macedonian disorder was intolerable. The Romans, when they came, were stupid and brutal compared to the Greeks, but they maintained order and they owned Greece, Africa, and Asia by the late second century B.C.

During these turbulent times, people turned to philosophies for advice on how best to endure. Eventually, Christianity supplanted them all and absorbed many of their appealing aspects.

Rivals of the Academy and the Lyceum

Even during the lifetimes of Plato and Aristotle, other philosophies were attracting adherents in Athens. These philosophers had no

Figure 4.1
Diogenes. Courtesy of http://karenswhimsy.com.

interest in the science of the presocratics and of Aristotle and no faith in the ideal world of Plato. They aimed to ease the pains of life by advising students on how best to live it. All four schools were influenced by the model of Socrates.

The Cynics

It is easy to see how a student of Socrates, who "knew nothing," could question conventional wisdom, customs, and practices as did Antisthenes (440–370 B.C.), a rich old man who had lost all faith in the possibility of knowing truth.

Somehow that realization led Antisthenes to give up his fortune and preach asceticism on the streets. He lectured against government, private property, marriage, and religion and urged a return to nature. He attracted followers, among them the son of a criminal who Antisthenes tried to drive off with a stick. However, he could not drive off Diogenes (see figure 4.1), who made the views of his teacher famous and whose habits led to the naming of the school.

Diogenes's father was imprisoned for defacing the coinage, and the son's goal seemed to be to deface the world (Russell 1945). He opposed all custom and convention as false—all offices and ranks, patriotism, mourning the dead, wisdom, riches, and happiness. He lived as a dog, and thus the name Cynic was used, based on the Greek word for "dog." He is said to have lived in a tub, but it appears likely that he actually lived in a large pitcher, such as those used in primitive burials.

He is also said to have responded to Alexander's offer of assistance by asking only that the conqueror of the world "stand out of my light." In many stories he is portrayed as wandering with a lantern looking for "an honest man." In another case he, possessing only a bowl out of which to eat, finds a poor child who had nothing—not even a bowl. Of course, Diogenes reacted by breaking his own bowl. If he had given it to the child, he would only have done a disservice by providing something that could later be lost.

Like Antisthenes, Diogenes preached virtue, which at the time meant what we mean by "tranquility." Virtue comes with the liberation from desire and emotion—it is the freedom that comes with indifference to changes in fortune. Perhaps surprising, lectures by the Cynics extolling poverty, doing without, and eating only simple food were very popular among members of the upper classes, especially in Alexandria. Very likely such messages assuaged whatever guilt they might have had about having wealth when so many were poor. According to the Cynics, it was the poor who were better off!

The Cynics' stress on liberation from desire and emotion was later adopted by the Stoics, who refined and modified the "poverty is virtue" doctrine in such a way that many Roman emperors and empresses could be virtuous but wealthy.

The Skeptics

The Cynics were moralists, who criticized the practices of society, but the original Skeptics were similar to the Sophists in stressing relativism and denial of absolute truth. The founder of the school was Pyrrho (360–270 B.C.), a former soldier in Alexander's army. He taught that we don't and cannot know absolute truth and that consequently there is no truly rational ground for choice. Hence, it is proper to conform to whatever is customary in one's society, since no one has a handle on truth and falsity or on right and wrong.

Among the Skeptics, Timon (d. 235 B.C.) stands out because of the similarity of his skepticism to that of David Hume in the eighteenth century (though Hume had nothing good to say about these skeptics). According to the few fragments that are extant, he did not doubt the phenomena that form our experience; it was only the certainty of the truth of them that he doubted. This is, as we will see, similar to Hume's moderate position.

To find peace, it is necessary to know three things: the nature of things, the proper attitude toward them, and the benefits which that attitude brings. As far as the first, we cannot know things as they are but only as they appear to us. Hence, our attitude must be that everything is uncertain, provisional. We can never say, "That is so," but can only say that it seems so. This attitude brings us ataraxia, or tranquility, in that no objective good or evil exists and so all is subjective and should not disturb us. This is the benefit brought by the skeptical attitude.

Later Skeptics seemed more like the lesser Sophists, and, in an irony of ironies, they took over the Academy, the institution founded on the premise that Truth is knowable and is the only good! However, it is possible to read Plato's dialogues as skeptical treatises, as did Arcesilaus, who died in 240 B.C.

In almost all dialogues, Socrates was the discussant and he continually professed to know nothing. Most dialogues reach no firm conclusion, implying that there is none to be reached. Some dialogues, such as *Theaetetus*, make much of showing that both sides of a question are valid. Finally, Plato's dialogues might easily give the impression that the question and answer of dialectic is the whole point, rather than merely a means to arrive at truth. Is it any wonder that the Skeptics saw Socrates as one of them?

Arcesilaus taught that one should not maintain a thesis, only refute others—it is cleverness that is important, not the truth of the matter, since there is no truth that we can know. He and his successor Carneades (fl. 150 B.C.) would frequently give lectures a week apart in which the thesis defended in the first lecture was refuted and a contradictory thesis presented in the second.

It is interesting that this utter skepticism, that was criticized by Hume in the eighteenth century, was accurately described and critiqued by Plato in *The Republic*—Book VI gives a description of and condemnation of the academic who panders to the mob. This was not the model for the philosopher kings of the ideal state—rather, it is the model for the rascals who gave philosophy a bad name before Plato's time.

Epicureanism as Therapy

We all think of Epicureans as pleasure-savoring sensualists, not as hardy ascetics, but the classical followers of Epicurus were hardly hedonists. Our misapprehension was shared by notable ancients, however, and Epictetus said of Epicurus, "This is the life of which you declare yourself worthy—eating, drinking, copulation, evacuation, and snoring" (Russell 1945, p. 241). But that is far from the truth!

Epicurus (342–270 B.C.) was born to a poor family on Samos, the island off the coast of Asia Minor where Pythagoras was born centuries earlier, and was taught by a pupil of Democritus named Nausiphanes, nicknamed "the mollusk." Of Epicurus's 300 books, none survive, though many fragments of his creed remain, such as forty of the most important articles, famous in antiquity as Principal Doctrines (reprinted in Kaufman 1961, pp. 549–553).

Epicurus's doctrine concerned the pursuit of ataraxia, or tranquility, and that required a pursuit of the proper pleasures that come with the satisfying of certain desires. These are necessary and lead to pain when they aren't satisfied; such desires as hunger and thirst are necessary desires. However, there are also unnecessary or illusory desires, "vain fancies," desire for rare and expensive food and wine, wishes for fame and power. These are desires that can never be sated and bring only pain. Ataraxia involves savoring pleasures that are easily gotten by use of the senses and the eating of simple food and drink. Epicurus himself lived on bread and water, with cheese on holidays. His twenty-ninth principal doctrine reads (Kaufman 1961, p. 552):

Of our desires some are natural and necessary; others are natural, but not necessary; others, again, are neither natural nor necessary, but are due to illusory opinion.

Fulfilling necessary desires requires little and leads to tranquility. Trying to fulfill the unnatural and/or unnecessary is a never-ending and frustrating task. Among the most common of the unnecessary desires are those concerning sex. As he put it, "sexual intercourse has never done anyone good" (Russell 1945, p. 245).

Fear No Pain, Pursue No Pleasure   Live on bread and water, avoid sexual intercourse, and have no aspirations for wealth, power, honor, or fame if you wish to be an Epicurean. And by avoiding pain, he meant giving no thought to it, having no fear of it—after all, it really isn't anything to fear. His doctrine number four tells us "Continuous pain does not last long in the flesh; on the contrary, pain if extreme, is present a very short time." Thus, intense pain will be brief and therefore of little concern. Even in long illness there will probably be "an excess of pleasure over pain in the flesh." If pain is mild, we can handle it through mental discipline.

How to Have No Fear of Death   The second barrier to ataraxia comes from fear of death and fear produced by religions. As far as religion, Epicurus was prepared to believe that the gods do exist—why else would they be believed in? However, because they are wise they no doubt follow his precepts and abstain from public life and thus have no concern for humans. So, we have nothing to fear from the gods.

And why fear death? Epicurus was a thoroughgoing materialist and an atomist, who accepted the theory of Democritus, who had lived only a century earlier. Soul atoms are evidenced as breath and heat—the "pneuma" of Democritus—and death means the dispersal of all of our atoms, soul atoms included. His second precept reads, "Death isn't anything to us; for the body, when it has been resolved into its elements, has no feeling, and that which has no feeling isn't anything to us" (Kaufmann 1963, p. 549).

His philosophy survived for six centuries after his death but was eclipsed by another that became the creed of Rome and that has survived as an inspiration to leaders of the twentieth century. That was the philosophy of Stoicism, an adaptation of the philosophy of Heraclitus and some of the ethic of the Cynics and Epicureans.

The Stoics
Stoics were originally called Zenonians, after Zeno of Citium, in Cyprus, a Phoenician–Semitic who lived from 334–262 B.C. Zeno was repelled by Platonic dualism (Zeller 1964, p. 230) but admired Heraclitus, from whom his cosmology came, and Socrates, Antisthenes, and Diogenes, who inspired his ethics. Unlike Plato and like the early Milesians, Zeno favored scientific research, since virtue required knowledge.

The Stoic Universe   The cosmology of Zeno himself was only one of many variations that Stoics held over the centuries. However, the basic theme was the same for most, and it gave comfort to believers during a historical period in which comfort was sorely needed. Aspects of it survived in the views of Plotinus and even in those of Saint Augustine.

For Zeno, reality was embodied in a world soul, a universal reason which was ultimately fire. This world soul was evidenced in the cohesion of inorganic matter, or hexis, in the growth of plants, and in the rational aspect of animals and humans. Nature is ultimately reason, and all minds are part of the one—a view that hearkens back to the Milesian naturalists in treating the part (the microcosm) as a part of the whole (the macrocosm).

In the beginning, god transformed part of his fiery vapor into air, which changed in part to water, earth, and fire. After the present world period, all will change back to fiery vapor; then, after a period, the process repeats, yielding a never-ending succession of universes. Strangely, each new universe is a precise duplicate of the last, which is to say that the same sequence of events repeats endlessly. For Zeno, every minute detail of daily life has happened in past universes and it will happen in future ones. The sequence of events in the universe and in our lives is fixed inevitably—determined to the smallest detail.

Believing that, two conclusions follow immediately. First, all nature is of one piece and the Stoics were material monists, just as were the Milesians. What is real is always substance; there is no spirit in the Stoic universe. Second, if all is determined, down to the most minute event, there is little point in complaining when life doesn't go as we wish.

Stoicism and Knowledge Regarding the first point, the soul is indeed a fragment of the divine fire or world soul, a fact that allows us to act virtuously, though the mechanism by which this occurs is difficult to understand. As far as knowledge goes, the soul has two functions, knowing and feeling; knowing is clearly "good" and consists of three types of reasoning.

"Feeling" includes the emotions of pleasure, lust, anxiety, and fear and is bad—in fact, it is the ultimate evil. Will, we will see, becomes for the Stoic a feature of reason. Knowing includes central reason, inner reason, and outer reason. Central reason refers, in a funny way, to innate ideas. However, it specifically refers to a tabula rasa, the "blank slate" of extreme empiricism, upon which sense experience writes. However, the Stoics of the third century B.C. had the wisdom to notice that this implies innate ideas, since the writing on the slate reflects properties of the slate itself, the "potential knowledge" of Aristotle, as well as properties of the stimulation.

All minds are part of the one universal mind, and reasoning means to be "possessed by reason," since nature is full of it. In fact, "nature" and "reason" are synonymous, and instinct is no more than the manifestation of universal reason in an unconscious form. If animals operate wholly or largely by instinct, then they are wholly or largely rational.

For humans there is a common body of ideas knowable by the senses, which act by apprehending presentations, true presentations being "marked." Interestingly, the senses were seen as "reaching out" for sensations, so that vision was conceived as depending on cones extending out from the eyes, much like beams from two parallel flashlights. Very close objects are blurry because much of the object falls outside the narrow end of the cones.

Objects of sensation, or representations, are "so constituted that they compel us to give assent to them, in that they are connected with consciousness" (Zeller 1964, p. 232). In a way, this is an example of the "like knows like" principle, since it is rational force that gives qualities to matter and we know it by means of our share of the rational force.

Inner reason is what we take to be "reasoning," the conscious processes of judgment and choice. Outer reason, interestingly enough, refers to the power of speech, viewed as a form of reasoning. Reason, in all its forms, is always correct—it's infallible unless it is corrupted.

Emotion as the Source of All Error: Stoic Counseling   Plato believed that emotion must be controlled by reason, and Aristotle advocated that emotion be "moderated." Not so the Stoics, who viewed emotion as aberration, corruption, disease, hallmark of insanity, enemy of reason, and unnatural. One does not try to "moderate" disease and evil— one must eradicate it.

Virtue is a struggle to eliminate emotion and attain apathia (Zeller 1964, p. 239). This "apathy" isn't ambitionless lethargy—it is a "cultivated indifference" that raises one above the muck of emotion. In a way, it is an early form of the "mental health view" (Klein 1970, p. 215):

> Their chief concern was to foster an inner life of rugged personal integrity that would be immune to the lusts, hungers, and cravings associated with pleasure-seeking impulsiveness.... They were apathetic with respect to the pleasures of the table, the thrills of becoming wealthy or famous, and the joys of gratified desire...cultivation of virtue...called for the suppression of desire and emotion by disciplined thinking and willing.

Stoics acted as counselors and therapists, a topic treated by at least one author (Fuller 1945) in addition to Klein.

To gain a healthy and "autonomous" personality, one must become indifferent to wealth, poverty, disease, imprisonment, power, honor, health, and life and death. That is what is meant by "virtue," and virtue is attainable only with knowledge that transforms one from a fool to a virtuous person. All humans are originally fools, but once wisdom is gained, one's virtue cannot be taken away by anyone or anything—except by insanity, which is a loss of contact with nature.

Stoics welcomed injustice and cruelty as opportunities to cultivate virtue by remaining indifferent to calamity. One must even devalue one's own life, and Zeno, along with many others, voluntarily ended life when conditions seemed to warrant it. The common method, used by Zeno, was voluntary starvation. The right-thinking Stoic must be ever prepared to end life if it seems appropriate or "the natural thing to do."

The Paradox of the Stoic Will   The Stoics remained over the centuries the most fatalistic of fatalists, the most determined determinists. As Marcus Aurelius put it (*Meditations*, in Eliot 1909, p. 275):

Whatever may happen to thee, it was prepared for thee from all eternity; and the implication of causes was from all eternity spinning the thread of thy being, and of that which is incident to it.

Stoic writings abound with similar pronouncements that express a faith in a predetermination of all events that happen anywhere. In fact, this predetermination includes all human affairs and actions, and will is no exception. Yet, it is will that is the basis for virtue—one must cultivate the ability to remain calm when others break down.

Epictetus was a slave of a freedman of the emperor Nero and a much-quoted Stoic author who draws a somber parallel between collecting shells and collecting other things (Kaufman 1961, p. 257). If your ship lands briefly and you go gathering shells, you may be required to leave them when the ship leaves. It is the same with "a little wife and child" that you may have to give up "and run to the ship, without even turning around to look back."

Never say about anything, "I have lost it," but only "I have given it back." Is your child dead? It has been given back. Is your wife dead? She has been given back.... If you make it your will that your children and your wife and your friends should live forever, you are silly.

When a child dies, the parents wail and moan. However, it isn't the death that is distressful, since it does not distress others—it is the parents' judgment that is distressing. The writings of Epictetus and other Stoics are filled with admonishments against emotion and with arguments for training oneself to will restraint and right thinking. How can that be done if will is as determined as everything else that happens? No one knows.

Brett (Brett/Peters 1912/1955, pp. 157–158) viewed the problem as insoluble, writing that, "Into the morass of difficulties thus caused there is no need to plunge" and "they failed to explain the possibility of freedom, but they succeeded in being free." Zeller, the nineteenth-century authority on the classic philosophers, had similar difficulties, since the Stoic doctrine of "inviolable necessity" had to include the will. Russell (1945, p. 266) considered one explanation.

The way that a Stoic, whose views were those of Zeno, might defend the position is as follows. First, god, the soul of the universe, is free but decided to act according to fixed general laws. The laws chosen are good in general, but not in every case. This allows for cases of unmitigated evil as the exceptional cases, leaving much apparent evil as actually part of a greater good. Second, humans are (or have) part of this fire that is god, and when we act virtuously, that is, in accordance with what must be, this will of ours is part of god's, which is free.

As is clear, this argument does not bear close inspection, and the Stoics may as well leave will as free. In fact, all that free will appears capable of is suppressing emotion and accepting the inevitable. We must do what is fated: *Volentum fata ducunt, nolentum trahunt.*[1] The difference between human and beast is only that while all must obey, only humans can know that they must obey. And that is known only after foolishness and insanity are overcome so that feeling can be properly expunged.

Best-Known Stoics While Stoicism shared key features with Cynicism, there was one important difference that gave an immense advantage to the Stoics. That is, while both philosophies forbade the love of possessions, position, power, good food, and other luxuries, Stoicism did not forbid riches and power, as long as one did not have feelings about such things. It was the feeling aroused that was the evil, and many Stoics were the richest and most powerful people on earth. Many Roman emperors and prominent figures, such as Cicero, were Stoics.

Lucius Annaeus Seneca (4 B.C.–A.D. 65) was a Spaniard and tutor of the emperor Nero. He may have corresponded with the apostle Paul and was believed by early Church Fathers to have become Christian.

In any event, he was quoted and paraphrased in early Christian writings.

Seneca is interesting largely in his illustration of living one's principles. He was accused by Nero of participating in a plot and allowed to commit suicide rather than be executed. Seneca asked for time to straighten his affairs and, denied it, told his family, "Never mind, I leave you what is of far more value than earthly riches, the example of a virtuous life" (Russell 1945, p. 260). He then opened his veins and bled to death while dictating to his secretaries. Such Stoicism was not confined to males, however.

Arria the Elder was a Roman Stoic who died in A.D. 42 and whose husband, Caeccina Paetus, was condemned to death by suicide for suspected participation in a plot against the emperor. According to Pliny the Younger, "when the time came for him to die, the heroic Arria plunged a dagger into her own breast, saying, 'It does not hurt, my Paetus'" (Kersey 1989).

Epictetus, already quoted above, was a Greek and a one-time slave in Rome, born in the middle of the first century A.D. According to Eliot (1937, p. 116), "Few teachers of morals in any age are so bracing and invigorating ... the tonic quality of his utterances has been recognized ever since his own day by pagan and Christian alike."

Marcus Aurelius Antoninus (121–180) was a great admirer of Epictetus and quoted him frequently. His *Meditations* (he called it "Reflections") was a set of twelve books, partly a diary, which were written in Greek. He was the adopted son of Emperor Antoninus Pius and himself served as emperor from 161–180. Many of his writings were done while he was on military duty defending the northern borders of the empire. While authorities (e.g., Zeller 1964, p. 292) don't regard him as a great philosopher, his writings have touched many and convey well the Stoic point of view. Consider this quotation (Eliot 1937, p. 268), one of many counseling us on dealing with the troubles of life: "Today I have got out of all trouble, or rather I have cast out all trouble, for it was not outside, but within and in my opinions."

It was painful for the emperor to order the persecution of the Christians during his reign. According to Eliot (1937, p. 192), military reverses and pestilence during his reign "threw the populace into a panic, and led them to demand the sacrifice of the Christians, whom they regarded as bringing down the anger of the gods. He seemed to have shared in the panic and sanctioned a cruel persecution." For Eliot, this symbolizes the last gasp of resistance to Christianity as the act of "the last, and one of the loftiest, of the pagan moralists."

The Late Roman World

Rome officially fell on August 28, 476, a ludicrous fact that could be improved upon only if the hour of the day were given. Thousand-year empires[2] don't expire so quickly, and just as Rome was not built in a day, it did not end in a day. Its lengthy demise during the second through the fifth centuries was described as especially unpleasant by those who lived during those times.

In 165 returning legions from the east brought plague, perhaps smallpox, that seriously depopulated the empire, and in 167 the Marcommani launched the first full-scale barbarian attack on Rome. Plague and the legions annihilated them by 172. Plague remained, killing 2,000 per day in Rome by 189. A later "pandemic" was described in 255 by the Bishop of Carthage—it spread from Africa through Europe, devastating Alexandria and leading to many conversions to Christianity.

This was the Western world in the third century A.D., and Neoplatonism was a product of that world. It merged with Christianity, which was to become dominant in the fourth century.

Plotinus and Neoplatonism

The Stoics had identified Nature with God, but Plotinus regards it as the lowest sphere, something emanating from the Soul when it forgets to look upward towards nous. (*Enneads,* IV, 8, 1, in Russell 1945, p. 290)

Plotinus (205–269) lived his philosophy, which is to say that he was extremely ascetic, slept and ate minimally, ate no meat, remained celibate, gave away his fortune, freed his slaves, and otherwise pursued the Cynic ideal of freedom from possessions and thus from needs. He is supposed to have experienced ecstatic union with God on four occasions. His works were compiled and published after his death by Porphyry,[3] arranged as six *Enneads*, or groups of nine treatises.

The philosophy of Plotinus appeals only to a certain taste; it is worth considering if only because it had a great influence on the thought of Augustine and, thus, on the thought of the early Middle Ages. Surprisingly, it also influenced Charles S. Peirce, the clear-thinking founder of American pragmatism in the late nineteenth century (Brent 1993).

Plotinus as "Neoplatonist"

Plato died 552 years before the birth of Plotinus, a time span equal to that separating our time from the mid-fifteenth century. Thus, Plato was clearly an "ancient" in the time of Plotinus, and his ideas may not have been well preserved. Whether or not that is the case, his teachings totally lacked one aspect of Plato's thought and that was Plato's concern with the practical matters of ethics and virtue.

The Republic, as well as other dialogues, is filled with concern for "doing the right thing" in common circumstances. Plato's emphasis on the unchanging truth of the world of Forms was "as justification for effort...(an) answer to those who saw in life nothing but a ceaseless change that made effort vain" (Brett/Peters 1965).

For Plotinus, the world of Forms was the *only* real world, and our existence is a shadow, a state from which to flee. He advocated constant meditation, not action, so that the soul can remain as much as possible in the mystical spiritual world, where it isn't subject to change, has no memory, self-consciousness, or reflection. It does nothing but directly behold The One.

The Soul of Plotinus

The soul isn't matter, it is the part of us belonging to a higher degree of being—descended from The One—and its association with the body is degrading. Since it is part of the ultimate reality, The One, it is more correct to say that "The body is in the soul," rather than vice versa. The soul may perceive, reflect, or contemplate, representing a change from occupation with sensation to contemplation of itself.

Its highest function is the pure activity of thought, which is occupation with the eternal and changeless, out of time and without memory. The soul is then at rest, essentially unconscious—contemplating The One. It appears that the conception of the Eleatics, Xenophanes and Parmenides, was alive and prospering 700 years after their time.

Reality According to Plotinus

The One is ultimate Being, "God," from which derives nous, which for Plotinus was thought—as a perfect set of ideas, in the sense that Plato's reality was in a set of such ideas. In this way, the One/God/Being, which is unity itself,[4] can generate the plurality of things. As Plotinus saw it, the material world was created by soul as a copy of the ideal world. In so copying, soul is itself corrupted a bit and the copy can bear only the slightest resemblance to the ideal world. He refused to sit for a portrait, saying that it would amount to a "shadow of a shadow"—a copy of his body, which is itself a copy (Brett/Peters 1965).

Plotinus on Time and Memory   Plotinus did indeed show what Brett (Brett/Peters 1965, p. 210) called "a penetrating insight," when he argued that all explanations of memory as sensory aftereffect were fundamentally wrong. Memory isn't of stored impressions; it is the soul's power to know its former activities. Some of these aren't sensations; they are prior thoughts, and we often remember something that "did not happen," except as an activity of the soul. And if consciousness, the activity of the soul, is thus seen as basic, memory and time become secondary (Brett/Peters 1965, p. 210):

Memory is simply consciousness viewed in extension: it is self consciousness expanded into a time series. All consciousness is in a sense self consciousness: it is the self that makes unity and unity is the essence of consciousness. Memory stems the flow of things, puts an end to the flux of the material world.

Plotinus entertained other unusual views, including the possibility that objects look smaller at a distance because they lose magnitude over distance: "What wonder, then, if size be like sound—reduced when the form reaches us but faintly ... stripped, so to speak, of magnitude as of all other quality" (Diamond 1974, p. 110).

We will see that Plotinus's interpretation of memory and time was used in answering critics of early Christian doctrine. We must not credit Plotinus too much, since what seems an insight was only a corollary of a mystical worldview.

The Late Roman World of Aurelius Augustine

Constantine sanctioned Christianity via the Edict of Milan in 313, evidently because many of his soldiers were Christian. This edict not only legalized Christianity but created heresy, so that well-meaning believers could find themselves in danger of excommunication.

During the lifetime of Augustine, the early Church clashed with the State when a Macedonian rebellion angered the Emperor, Theodosius, who ordered 3,000 rebels massacred at Thessalonica. Bishop Ambrose of Milan forced the emperor to do public penance on December 25 of 390, an unheard of demonstration of the power of the new Church.

The legions were withdrawn from Britain to protect Rome itself, but Alaric and the Visigoths sacked the city in 410. Curiously, it was at this time that the invading Huns introduced the wearing of trousers, quickly replacing the Roman togas because of advantages in maneuvering on horseback. In 430 it was only the plague that stopped the Huns at Prague, and the same year the Vandals besieged the North African city of Hippo, where its bishop, Aurelius Augustine, died. Augustine was a colorful man, church authority for 800 years, but a better psychologist than theologian.

Augustine's Revival of Plato

Tolle Lege, Tolle Lege

The world for Saint Augustine is the place of countless voices, voices of nature calling to the soul...none more than all these is the voice of God whose eternal presence is an eternal appeal to the human will. (Brett/Peters 1965, p. 217)

"Take up and read," said the child's voice to Aurelius Augustine in the garden of Bishop Ambrose in Milan. That was the moment of his conversion to Christianity, after a life of debauchery and repeated "failures of will." He was born in North Africa in 354 and died there in 430 as Bishop of Hippo, even as the Vandals were besieging the Roman city. He studied law at Carthage, had a mistress at the age of sixteen, whom he kept for ten years, and became a Manichean[5] for a time. He traveled to Rome and to Milan, skeptical of Christianity but attracted to Plotinus and Neoplatonism.

His parents arranged a suitable marriage for him, feeling that it would be best in furthering his career, and he was sad to see his mistress packed off to Africa, vowing that she would never know another man. However, since the marriage could not take place for two years, owing to the bride's youth, Augustine took another mistress for the interim. Little wonder that he later considered himself a monster of iniquity. This was the time during which he prayed for "chastity and continence, only not yet" (*Confessions*, Book 8, chapter 7).

His mother, Monica (later Saint Monica, as in "Santa Monica"), tried hard to convert him, but it took the child's voice and what Augustine read to do the deed. He "took up and read" a bible that opened to Paul's Epistle to the Romans, a strange book indeed.

The Early Church

Christianity grew in popularity in the Roman Empire, having changed from a reformed Judaism to an independent movement that finally gained official favor in Rome. The promise of immortality was far more appealing than Neoplatonism, which, "being based on difficult arguments, could not become widely popular" (Russell 1945, p. 331). In 379, the Emperor Theodosius gave full support to the Catholic Church, and Christianity, sanctioned by Constantine in 313, became the official religion of Rome. Even the Goths, who sacked Rome in 410, were Christians.

During the fourth century, three men stood out as the "Doctors" of the Church.[6] Saint Ambrose was largely a politician who fought for the power of church over state, Saint Jerome was responsible for the Latin Bible and for the development of asceticism and monasticism, and Saint Augustine worked out the theology of the Church and remained the authority on that subject for at least 800 years.

And that authority was real. The Church "was vigorous, able, guided by men prepared to sacrifice everything personal in its interests, and with a policy so far-sighted that it brought victory for the next thousand years" (Russell 1945, p. 335). The civil government, on the other hand, was like civil governments before and since: "the State was feeble, incompetent, governed by unprincipled self-seekers, and totally without any policy beyond that of momentary expedients."

The Church was also a haven in a world filled with constant upheaval and warfare, as the Empire slowly dissolved. In an oft-quoted letter, Jerome wrote in 396 (Russell 1945, p. 343):

I shudder when I think of the catastrophes of our time. For twenty years and more the blood of Romans has been shed daily between Constantinople and the Julian Alps.... The Roman world is falling: yet we hold up our heads instead of bowing them.

That was fourteen years before the sack of Rome by Alaric. The sack, in 410, led many to charge that the adoption of Christianity meant that the old gods had deserted them and that was the reason for their misfortunes. In *The City of God*, Augustine pointed out that Rome may have been sacked, but at least the Visigoths were Christians! That may seem small comfort, but it meant that they respected churches and that those who fled to them were thus protected. The Romans had never respected temples of whatever kind, and thus the pursued had no sanctuary.

The perceived imminent destruction of the world, or the end of organized society, was a theme that carried for centuries, into the Middle Ages, and in large part accounted for the appeal of Augustine's thought, just as it accounted for the appeal of Neoplatonism in other, secular, forms.

Augustine's Theology

Paul's Epistle to the Romans greatly influenced Augustine, who read every line with the closest attention, leading to his emphasis on the *elect* and on predestination. All inherit original sin, and thus all deserve eternal damnation. Without baptism, all (even infants) suffer eternal torment in hell. And infants deserve it—casual observation shows that they are not only sinful but are monsters of iniquity. He even reconstructed his own infancy, based on later observations of infants (*Confessions*, in Diamond 1974, p. 470). However, certain people, the elect, are chosen to go to heaven. All that is open to interpretation, as we will see.

Augustine's Psychology

Promoting sin and guilt may itself be a sufficient contribution to psychology, but Augustine contributed more concrete things. First, he argued persuasively for the fundamental trustworthiness of subjective experience and for the position that truth may arise from faith/revelation and from belief/introspection.

Second, he argued strongly for the existence of a "self" independent of sense experience—this clearly places him with the Platonists, as opposed to the Aristotelians. Third, he argued for a sophisticated interpretation of faculties, such that they are interdependent. Finally, Augustine countered critics of the doctrine of creation by following Plotinus and interpreting time in a subjective (and interesting) way.

The Indubitability of Private Experience   It is taken for granted that a saint of the Catholic Church accepts divine revelation as prime source of knowledge, but Augustine was of a scientific bent and believed that our subjective experience was no illusion. When we consider our experience, we find three things that we cannot doubt. From this we conclude that true knowledge is available from introspection, not just from revelation. The following, from *The City of God*, makes this point in a way that now seems amusing (*The City of God*, Book XI, chapter XXVI, in Kaufman 1961, pp. 601–602):

... For we both are, and know that we are, and delight in our being, and our knowledge of it. Moreover, in these three things no true-seeming illusion disturbs us ... I am not at all afraid of the arguments of the Academicians, who say, What if you are deceived? For if I am deceived, I am ...

I exist, I know it, and I love my being. If I am mistaken in this belief—and I don't really exist—then I "love false things," a being that does not exist. Even if I doubt my real existence, I must admit that there is a doubter. But is that self that exists an independent thing, or merely a by-product of my body's functions?

The Independence of the Self   Aristotle had viewed the self/psyche as inseparable from the body, as the form and the functioning of the body. Likewise, the Milesians and Eleatics, as well as Heraclitus, were monists, for whom mind and body were inseparable. Only the Pythagoreans and their "issue"—Plato and the Neoplatonists—assumed that there was a basic distinction between mind and matter. Augustine, as a Christian, was not about to doubt the independent existence of the self. His argument appears in a piece titled "On the Trinity" (in Rand 1912, pp. 132–135). He there asked the question, "Is the mind equal to its contents?" This, the position of Aristotle and of the material monists, could not be tolerated, and he presented his argument against it.

He proposed that the error made by his targets was in failing to note that mind knows itself—he refers to the certainty with which we know, remember, and love our being. Now, for Augustine, to know something meant to know its substance, and mind therefore knows its own substance when it knows itself. But mind is certain that it isn't air, fire, water, or function, since it would feel "different" when thinking of one of those things. If mind were really fire or function, we would think of fire or function as immediate and real, not as imaginary and absent.

In fact, anticipating the Turing machine,[7] Augustine argued that mind cannot be made of anything else, since it cannot think of itself as anything else. And it cannot think of that which *itself* is, either, any more than the Turing machine can read its own tape. Like Plato and the Platonists, Augustine insists that mind is its own substance—it is what remains after all of its objects are removed.

Memory as Source of Knowledge   Like Plato, Augustine interpreted the gaining of knowledge as a reminiscence. However, he did not believe that this was a recovery of that which has been forgotten—it is a coming-to-consciousness of "that eternal thought which is ours through the unity of our nature and God's being...the Self is the exhaustless mine from which the jewels of thought are raised into the light: all that we find is found in our own minds" (Brett/Peters 1965, p. 220). And how do we find it? Gaining of knowledge (or, better, becoming conscious of it) requires both our effort and the grace of God.

Memory is strictly a spiritual activity, and memory is always of *ourselves*, not of things. Some memory is sensual, and other is intellectual—in all cases it is present, but not conscious—memory is the making us conscious of what we know. When individual items or aspects of the room are lit, we aren't really "retrieving" them but "illuminating" them.

In the course of his discussions of memory in the *Confessions*, Augustine commented on characteristics of good memory—it appears that he recognized what were later called "laws of memory" as well as did twentieth-century memory researchers. Augustine wrote that the most important factor is the exercise of the mind's activity in the first place—what William James was to stress as the chief determinant of memory—the initial attention exerted.

Then he mentioned intensity of original impressions, repetition, order, and revision (organization). And, naturally, memory involves the awakening of one idea by another. This is remarkable, since Augustine was writing in the fifth century—or are such things immediately evident to anyone who considers the question of recollection, as did Aristotle and so many others?

Faculty Psychology and the Pelagian Heresy
Augustine argued cogently against the existence of separate faculties of understanding, will, memory, and whatever, much as William James and others did in the late nineteenth century. This became important in the quelling of a powerful heresy during his time.

A priest named Morgan (Pelagius) of Wales was a liberal who taught that one could act virtuously through one's own moral effort/ free will and that, along with orthodoxy, would guarantee a place in heaven. Individual free will and willpower can overcome sin—sinning is always a voluntary act!

By "willing" to live virtuously or to sin, we deserve the rewards or punishments that God provides in the next world. Many accepted this doctrine, both in the East and the West, and it was only through Augustine's efforts that Pelagianism was eventually declared heretical.

Final condemnation of the Pelagians and semi-Pelagians occurred at the Council of Orange in 529.[8]

Augustine's opposition to the Pelagians lay in this emphasis on free will, a position incompatible with Augustine's teaching that no one can abstain from sin through willpower; it is only the grace of God that allows anyone to be virtuous. Certain people have been chosen by God for salvation—they are the elect. No reason can be offered to justify God's method here; His ways are often incomprehensible to us, but what is clear is that will has nothing to do with it.

Augustine derived this interpretation from a careful reading of Paul's epistle to the Romans. Even a casual reading of that text shows that early Christians, including Paul, preached predestination and the futility of efforts to gain salvation. This view was adopted much later by John Calvin but has not been held by the Catholic Church since the thirteenth century. Though it may be heretical as theology, as a psychological doctrine it has great merit as we will see below.

Related to that point of view, Augustine opposed the division of mind into independent faculties. It appears to fit well with his opposition to free will as an independent agent. In the passage below, he argues that mind isn't separable into faculties by pointing out that each of them assumes the existence of all the others as parts of it. For example, my use of free will takes for granted that I have the faculties of sensation, perception, judgment, memory, and so on (Rand 1912, pp. 135–137):

> Since, then, these three, memory, understanding, will, aren't three lives, but one life; nor three minds, but one mind; it follows certainly that neither are they three substances, but one substance.... For I remember that I have memory, and understanding, and will; and I understand that I understand, and will, and remember; and that I will that I will, and remember, and understand; and I remember together my whole memory, and understanding, and will...what I don't know, I neither remember nor will.

Consider what this means for the practices of the Church at that time. If, as Morgan/Pelagius held, free will is independent, then anyone, however feeble understanding and memory be, still has "free will" to accept the Truth when exposed to it. If this is the case, then a denial of orthodox truth is also done as a matter of free will and implies evil presence. All kinds of methods may be employed to combat that evil!

If, however, faculties tend to go together and weak understanding is apt to be accompanied by weak memory and will, then many people will simply lack the wherewithal to understand revealed truth when it is before them. In such a case, where the capacity is absent, there is no point in blaming an individual or condemning an evil.

From a modern perspective, the "grace" that Augustine believed was required for salvation may plausibly be interpreted as heredity—has a person's genes (grace of God) enabled a nervous system that has the capacity to understand God's message? This is the interpretation of the foremost authorities (Brett/Peters 1965 and Zeller 1964). Both oppose the later opinion of Russell (1945, p. 365), who treated Augustine as promoter of a "ferocious doctrine."

There Is No Time

Behold, I answer to him who asks, "What was God doing before He made heaven and earth?" I answer not, as a certain person is reported to have done facetiously (avoiding the pressure of the question), "He was preparing hell," said he, "for those who pry into mysteries." (*Confessions*, Book XI, chapter XIV, in Kaufman 1963, p. 588)

Augustine attempted to answer all critics of the faith, including those who asked what occupied God before he created the universe. According to the argument, creation is good and any delay in creating it is therefore bad. Since there was a definite moment of creation (actually, six days), the period antedating that was empty and bad. The question is, why was there a beginning? The answer is that before the creation of humanity there *was* no time, hence no "before." Consider how puzzling is time, as Augustine did in chapter 15 of the *Confessions*: "What, then, is time? If no one ask of me, I know; if I wish to explain to him who asks, I know not…"

Suppose that we think of a long time in the past or in the future—Augustine suggests a hundred years. In what sense is that long that does not exist? The past is gone, it isn't "long," and the future does not exist with any duration either. Past and future are what Thomas Hobbes would call "figures of speech," but that wouldn't happen until the seventeenth century. So we might say that "it has been long," but was it long when already past or when still present? Can any time have duration? What is time as it passes? This is a question answered by Wilhelm Wundt and by William James in the late nineteenth century. Augustine did about as well (Kaufman 1963, 590–591):

Let us therefore see, O human soul, whether present time can be long…. Is a hundred years when present a long time? … but the present has no space.

Where, therefore, is the time which we may call long? . . . then does the present
time cry out in the words above that it cannot be long.

There was no "then." There is no time as far as God is concerned;
time is subjective—the creation of the soul. Consider the implications
for immortality. If time is a feature of the mind and not an independent
dimension, "life after death" becomes as meaningless as the question of
God's activity before the creation. There was no "before" and there is
no "after," except as part of the activity of the soul.

It is interesting to note that, despite his rationalism and theological
concerns, Augustine had great respect for science in general and for
the importance of observations in particular. His conclusions regarding
the subjectivity of time arose in part out of his observations of rhythm.
He saw that we are limited in our ability to apprehend a passage of
music as a whole, or even as a very large segment (cf. Handel 1989).

Aquinas and the Revival of Aristotle

The Middle Ages
Until the twelfth century, when their power waned, the Arabs preserved and translated the accumulated wisdom of the West. For
pagans and heretics, such as the bulk of the population of Egypt, who
contested the divinity of Christ, Arab conquest was a blessing. The
Arabs tolerated any religion that had "a holy book" and required only
that tribute be paid by non-Islamic subjects.

Aided by pagan and heretic philosophers fleeing persecution, Arab
thinkers became the authorities on Greek philosophy, especially Aristotle's, which they favored. The Arabs had conquered Syria by 636,
and Persia by 650, thereby gaining access to much of Aristotle's work.
Aristotle was preferred to Plato in these regions, and the Arabs, fortunately, benefited from that.

Medieval Education
Universities were founded at Salerno, Bologna, and Paris by the
twelfth century, noted for medicine, law, and theology, respectively.
In 1167 Oxford was founded, and Cambridge followed in 1200. Since
Latin was used in instruction, students could attend different universities throughout Europe. The medieval curriculum in liberal arts comprised the trivium, or baccalaureate, consisting of grammar, logic, and
rhetoric.

A master's degree required completion of the quadrivium, that being arithmetic, music, geometry, and astronomy. Together, the trivium and the quadrivium included what were called the seven liberal arts.[9] Further study was required for degrees in law, theology, or medicine. A graduate could teach with a master's degree and a license issued by a university or a cathedral church.

Church schools started far earlier, and a notable example was the school begun by Saint Benedict at Monte Cassino in the year 540. The Benedictines are the oldest of the monastic orders and were responsible for the production of thousands of saints and clerics.[10] The Dominican order, put in charge of the inquisition in 1233, was not founded until 1215.[11]

In only the previous century Spain was recaptured from the Arabs, as was Sicily, and Greek science was restored to the West. This was largely the writings of Aristotle, as passed from the Syrians, but the Arabs unwittingly mixed that with Neoplatonism to form a bizarre whole. The first writer of philosophy in Arabic was Kindi (d. ca. 873), who translated parts of Plotinus's mystical *Enneads*, which was published as the theology of Aristotle (Russell 1945, p. 423). Two others, known in the West as Averroës and Avicenna, though themselves not original, exerted great influence on the thought of the great apologist, Thomas Aquinas.

Avicenna

Abu Ali Al-Hosain ibn Abdallah ibn Sina (980–1037) was a Persian physician and philosopher perhaps better known as Avicenna (see figure 4.2). He was a great influence in the West for centuries after his death He was evidently allowed to indulge a passion for wine and women even in a strict Islamic society by maintaining friendships with powerful princes who valued his medical abilities.

A child prodigy, Avicenna knew the Koran by heart at ten and was well read in philosophy, law, and mathematics when he began the study of medicine at sixteen. By eighteen he was famous as a physician. He described himself as dominated by an insatiable thirst for knowledge (Downs 1982).

He produced perhaps 160 books on a wide range of subjects and was called Prince of All Learning, Prince of Physicians, and Father of Geology in the Moslem world. His monumental work, *The Canon*, comprises his medical work and was authoritative in the West from the

Figure 4.2
Avicenna. Courtesy of the National Library of Medicine, National Institutes of Health.

twelfth to the seventeenth centuries—it is still consulted occasionally in the Moslem East.

The Canon of Avicenna

The Canon was widely accepted among physicians, in part due to Avicenna's skill as a classifier and encyclopedist. Divided into five books, it covers the theory of medicine, the simpler drugs, special pathology and therapeutics, general diseases, and pharmacology. Approximately 700 drugs were described. Diabetes, anthrax, and parasitic worms were well described—and fifteen qualities of pain are described!

Religious beliefs prevented dissection, and surgery was considered an inferior art, to be carried on by those of inferior rank—barbers, executioners, and bathhouse keepers. This assignment of surgery to nonphysicians was transmitted to Europe along with *The Canon* and remained the practice into the eighteenth century. A beneficial innovation of Avicenna's lay in the use of a red-hot iron, instead of a knife.

The iron was exceedingly painful, needless to say, but it killed bacteria and saved the lives of many who would have surely died of infection. Antiseptic practice was otherwise unknown, and surgery by cautery was generally abandoned by the sixteenth century as a cruel and brutal practice. Death from infection increased, of course.

For us, he was the master Muslim Aristotelian, who supplied the model of the soul to the West, first to Albertus Magnus, who repeated a fundamental error in design. Then it passed to Thomas Aquinas, who simplified and perfected it, producing the synthesis of Christian doctrine and of the best science of the time—Aristotle's.

Avicenna's "Powers"

Avicenna followed Aristotle in dividing the psyche into vegetative, animal, and rational divisions. The vegetative soul was that part that we hold in common with other living things that are capable of generation (production–birth), augmentation (growth), and nutrition. The animal or sensitive soul is more interesting—in fact, it is the most interesting aspect of Avicenna's soul.

This *anima sensibilis* or *vitalis* is composed of three main parts: appetites, interior senses, and exterior senses. The *vis appetitiva* corresponds to desire and aversion, the *vis concupiscibilis* and the *vis irascibilis*. The former is the representation of desire, viewed as "expansiveness" and the latter as aversion, viewed as contraction.[12] While this power commanded movement, actually execution was left to an unnamed motive power that could well be called "animal will."

The second part of the animal/sensitive soul is external sense, composed of the traditional five senses and adding four aspects of touch: temperature, wetness/dryness, texture, and hardness.

Finally, the animal soul features the inner senses. The common sense is used as Aristotle used it, to refer to the fact that some objects of sensation, such as length and width and number, can be apprehended by two or more senses. Second is the *vis formativa*, or the power of primary retention. This is the power to unite the series of images that is the world outside us and uniting them into a permanent object.

It could be called a creative imagination, but retention seems better. In the language of more recent times, this is the integrator that unites the world of discrete stimulations of receptors. A third power of the animal soul is the *vis cogitava*, or the power to form abstractions and to form associations. Along with that goes *memoria*, the simple storage and recollection of memories.

The final aspect of the animal soul is *vis aestimativa*, or "estimation," referring to the instincts of animals and the prejudices of humans. Avicenna used this to explain reactions between animal predators and prey, as well as the tendency of a man to "know" that a child is to be treated gently.

Avicenna's Error?

All of this, if not strictly and slavishly borrowed from Aristotle, is at least compatible with Aristotle's writings. However, Avicenna's treatment of the rational soul is otherwise, and one can only conclude that the Neoplatonism that tainted so much also found its way into Avicenna's thinking. He proposed that the rational soul has two parts, the *intellectus contemplativus* and the *intellectus activius*. Nothing is wrong with the contemplative intellect, viewed as a sort of potential "knowing," just as Aristotle thought of potential knowing.

However, the active intellect is Plato's separate soul/knower! It is pure actuality, separated form, a separate independent reality, and very definitely not merely the form of the body. It is an agent that is free of the body, a gratuitous addition to the Aristotelian soul that shows how far was Avicenna from an understanding of his subject.

However, the faculty psychology that Avicenna described became the basis for Thomas Aquinas and thus part of the foundation of Catholic philosophy.

Averroës and Accurate Interpretation of Aristotle

Abu al-Walid Muhammad ibn Ahmad ibn Muhammad ibn Rushd was called Averroës by medieval European scholars and was the chief reason that Aristotle's works were recovered in the twelfth century. He lived from 1126 to 1198, born to a distinguished family of jurists in Moslem Spain. He was thoroughly versed in the Qur'an, Islamic scripture, Hadith, traditions, and fiqh, or law, trained in medicine, and rose to be chief judge (qadi) of Qurtubah (Cordoba).

His great impact lies in his correct interpretation of Aristotle's views on the afterlife. The rational soul may be imperishable, but it is also unimpressionable, lacking sensation, imagination, and thinking, since the body and its sense organs cease to exist. This means that there is no survival of the individual personality, and that presented a terrible problem for the Church.

Albertus Magnus and Thomas Aquinas

In 1879 Pope Leo XII commended the study of Aquinas' philosophy in an encyclical, *Aeterni Patris*. The encyclical praises the saint in the highest terms: "as far as man is concerned, reason can now hardly rise higher than she rose, borne up in the flight of Thomas; and faith can hardly gain more helps from reason than those which Thomas gave her." (Kaufmann 1963, p. 585)

Thomas Aquinas (1225–1274), the "Angelic Doctor," was the leading light of Catholic thought in his time and has remained that over the centuries. He was canonized in 1323 by Pope John XXII, and in 1879 Pope Leo XIII recommended that his philosophy be made the basis for instruction in all Catholic schools. A recent champion of his views was the French philosopher Etienne Gilson (1884–1978). As Gilson put it, "Personally, I don't say of Thomas that he was right, but that he is right" (Kaufman 1963, pp. 585–586). His philosophy, "Thomism," is the philosophy of the Catholic Church, and it is Aristotle modified in such a way as to be compatible with Catholic doctrine.

Originality in Aquinas?

Thomas Aquinas considered himself a theologian, not a philosopher. Hence, he wouldn't claim to be a psychologist. His psychology is properly presented as a slightly modified version of the faculty psychology of Avicenna. However, the adaptation of Avicenna was actually the work of Albert the Great, who knew a good rendering of Aristotle when he saw it. Albert's psychology, though it differs in small ways, is Avicenna's. Aquinas adopted it in large part.

However, Albert's reconciliation of Aristotle and Christian immortality was not satisfactory. Soul was interpreted as the form of the body, but also as substance that was separable and thus capable of independent existence (Brett/Peters 1965, pp. 280–288). This would be satisfactory to Plato, but surely not to Aristotle. The reconciliation was really Thomas Aquinas's contribution. Aristotle was The Philosopher, as Thomas called him, and he accepted Aristotle's opinions concerning logic, physics, astronomy, biology, psychology, metaphysics, and ethics (Kaufman 1961, p. 586). Much of his work took the form of the disputation.

The Medieval Disputation

By the thirteenth century, philosophical/theological questions were often treated through *disputatio*, a popular teaching device. A master (professor) would announce a date for the disputation of a question or thesis so that other faculty of the university could attend. On that day classes were canceled and the faculty, along with their bachelors and students, were "visitors" at the site of the disputation. The master directed the disputation, but the respondent, or defender of the thesis, was his bachelor, who was equivalent to a modern graduate student and for whom this was a part of his training.

The visiting masters and bachelors and, occasionally, students presented questions and objections to the thesis, directed to the bachelor, who answered all arguments. If the bachelor experienced difficulties, the master stepped in to assist, but the bachelor was expected to sustain the argument without help. The objections were received in no special order, but only as they were raised, and the disputation continued until all objections and questions had been countered and answered.

The disorganized notes that were kept of the proceedings were then worked over by the master, who put them into a clear form. The objections raised were listed, followed by arguments in favor of the thesis. This was followed by the "answer" (*respondio*), in which the master expressed his views, and by separate answers to each objection that had been raised. This "determined" the truth of the matter and could only be done by a master.

The Adaptation of Avicenna's Faculty Psychology by Aquinas

The psychology of Aquinas was based on faculties, much like the framework proposed by Avicenna. The *Vegetative Soul* was treated in the same way, and the *Sensitive/Animal Soul* was similar to Avicenna's. Aquinas proposed the five *external senses* that thereafter were commonly accepted, and he, like Avicenna, proposed several *interior senses*: imagination, estimation, memory, common sense, and *cogitava*. There was no *vis formativa* sense, but, in general, Avicenna'a faculties were very similar. The great difference came in the treatment of the animal appetites and the rational soul.

The Animal Appetites   Avicenna treated the "animal will" as did later writers, as a "concupiscible" (approach/expand) and an "irascible" (withdraw/contract) pair of opposites. Aquinas took a different and puzzling tack—he proposed that concupiscible appetites included things like joy, sorrow, love, and desire, while the irascible appetites appeared in hope, despair, courage, fear, and anger. How does one label these dispositions? How do joy, sorrow, and love, form a category, as opposed to hope, despair, fear, and courage?

The answer lay in the so-called *Cardinal Virtues* of Aquinas (in Kaufman 1963, pp. 622–623). These are *Prudence, Justice, Temperance,* and *Fortitude.* The concupisciple appetites refer to the second two—those that require *temperance*—self-control and discipline, while the irascible appetites refer to those requiring *fortitude.* When a visiting student from the Pontifical Institute of St. Thomas Aquinas in Rome pointed that out to me, the division made by Aquinas became clear.

The Rational Soul   For Aquinas, the rational soul includes *free will,* the intellectual appetite, as opposed to the animal appetites. It also includes the *intellect,* composed of possible/passive/potential reason and "nous," actualized reason—the latter needs a body with organs to operate, and therein lies a tale.

The Struggle with the Averroëists: *Summa Theologica*
St. Thomas carried out hundreds of disputations, collected as his *Quaestiones Disputatae.* For psychology the most interesting of those concern his struggle with Averroës, the Spanish–Arabian commentator on Aristotle who was of wide influence and who was typically referred to by the churchmen as "the Commentator." Aristotle himself was referred to as "the Philosopher."

Aquinas's difficulty lay in the fact that Averroës understood Aristotle all too well and his interpretations were probably more accurate than those of Aquinas, at least in the view of writers like Bertrand Russell. Averroës and some of his Christian adherents, such as Siger of Brabant, held that Aristotle's philosophy precluded an afterlife in which the soul survived with any faculties that required the use of bodily organs. While the potential for vision and memory might endure, no actual seeing or remembering could occur without a body through which that potential must be actualized.

Aristotle clearly taught that, without the body, the soul may exist only as nous, lacking powers that require bodily organs. Whether nous is imperishable then becomes moot, since immortality without memory or sensation does not fit our vision of an afterlife.

Summa Theologica was Thomas Aquinas's masterpiece, the reconciliation of faith and reason, of Catholic doctrine and Aristotle. It was a book intended for novices; his *Summa Contra Gentiles* was a more sophisticated work, meant for use in dealing with philosophically advanced pagans. Using the excellent translation of Aristotle that he obtained from his friend, William of Moerbeke (taken from the Greek, rather than Arabic), Aquinas considered those problems that were the most difficult to resolve.

The question becomes that of the nature of mind and of its relation to body, and Thomas attempted to answer it. The passage below was written in the thirteenth century and translated from Latin by Rand (1912, pp. 138–142). The issue is whether we have one soul or several, and this is of interest since we and other animals have nutritive and sensitive souls and these perish with the body. Is there a separate "human" soul that survives death, even though Aristotle stressed the unity of the soul? And is that soul personal, or just a part of the universal soul?

Do We Have a Personal Afterlife?   The scholastic style used by Aquinas is as he presented it. As was his custom, he followed the question with an answer that he considered wrong, followed by supporting arguments for that answer. Then he responded, producing counter-arguments demolishing that position, and ended with what he believed to be the correct answer. Remember, Thomas's works became official Catholic doctrine in 1897 (Rand 1912, pp. 138–142):

QUESTION LXXVI. RATIONALITY THE ESSENTIAL FORM IN MAN

Article 3. Are there besides the Rational Soul in Man, other Souls different in Essence?

...II. If it be said that the sensitive soul of man is imperishable there is opposed to such a view, the declaration of Aristotle...that what is perishable differs in kind from that which is imperishable. But the sensitive soul in the horse, lion, and other animals is perishable. If therefore it were imperishable in man, then the sensitive soul in man and brute wouldn't be of the same kind.... But this is incongruous...

III. Aristotle says "the embryo is first animal, and then man".... But this wouldn't be possible if the sensitive soul had the same essence as the rational...

(b) I reply that Plato postulated...in one body different souls, distinguished likewise by their organs, to which he attributed diverse vital functions...

Aristotle refutes...this view so far as it concerns those powers of the soul which in their activities employ bodily organs.... His reason is that in the case of those animals which though cut in two still live, the different operations of the soul in any one part are still found, such as feeling and desire...

Thus, plants are more perfect than inanimate objects; animals again rank above plants; and man in turn rises above the beasts.... In like manner the rational

soul contains within its powers, both what belongs to the sensitive soul of the brutes, and likewise to the nutritive soul of the plant...
(c) I.... If the soul be thus capable only of being sensitive, it is perishable; but if it has with the sensitive nature also rationality, it is imperishable... it is impossible to dissociate incorruptibility from the rational.
...
III. The embryo has at first only a sensitive soul. If this be superseded, it receives a more perfect one, which is both sensitive and rational.

Thus, at some point a rational and sensitive soul is traded in for the sensitive soul of the infant. Aquinas used Aristotle's principle of the unity of the soul, as the form of the body, and the doctrine that lower functions are contained within the higher. When the rational soul is received, it incorporates the sensitive and the vegetative souls and all participate in the afterlife.

Nonetheless, that soul that survives death may have vegetative, sensitive, and rational capacities, but without a body, it has no sensation, no images, no memory, and therefore no individual personality. It exists only as form, but form is only potential without matter. The body is required to actualize the potential of the sensitive and vegetative aspects of the soul. How can Aquinas deal with that? Brett, authority here, and Zeller as well (Brett/Peters, Zeller 1883/1964) agreed that what is required is the literal resurrection of the body so that the potential sensing and remembering can be made actual.

Reason versus Will   In *Summa Theologica* Aquinas addressed the old problem of the relation of reason and will. In recent times that question has been asked in different form—as the relative contribution of rationality and irrationality to personality, this a key aspect of Freudian theory. In the seventeenth century it characterized Hume's seemingly contradictory conclusions—skepticism and a faith in the reality of the world. For Kant, reason and will were the topics of two of his main works. Aquinas characteristically began the consideration of question LXXXII, "The superiority of reason to will," by presenting a seemingly ironclad argument for the position that he opposed. Thus (Rand 1912, pp. 145–146):

I. The final cause or the good is the object of the will. But the final cause is the first and highest of causes. The will, therefore, is the first and highest of the faculties.
II. Natural objects ascend from the imperfect to the perfect. Thus also in the faculties of the soul, the order of progress is from the senses to the reason,

which is superior. But the natural process is from an act of mind to an act of will. The will is therefore superior to and more perfect than the intellect.

That seems clear enough—and in essential agreement with the Pelagians a millennium earlier. However, since Augustine managed to have the Pelagians declared heretical and since Thomas often referred approvingly to Augustine, this cannot be the end of it. Aquinas's next sentence points out that Aristotle gives (10 *Ethics*, 7) reason the first place among faculties. Since Thomas must show how this has to be correct, he begins with his traditional "I answer ..."

The answer is complex and illustrates the subtleties of Aquinas's thinking. He argues that faculties may be considered either absolutely or relatively. Considered absolutely (isolatedly), reason is superior to will, since the object of reason is the "very idea of desirable good." The will may be directed toward a desirable good, but the idea of that good is dependent upon reason, since reason knows the idea. Since will must depend on reason in this case, reason is "more noble, and more sublime."

But relatively/comparatively, will may sometimes "stand higher" than intellect. Intellect knows things that are comprehensible, but the will acts toward "the object as it is in itself." This doesn't necessarily mean that the object is comprehended as reason comprehends. In cases of reaction to good and evil, the reaction is that of the will—the comparable reaction of the intellect is to judge things as true or false.

Hence, on occasion, the will may react with horror and aversion to an evil that is incomprehensible to the intellect. Aquinas makes clear that which is very unclear in Hume, writing 500 years later (see chapter 7). That is, we can react to things in ways that we cannot understand rationally.

Perhaps illustrating that kind of irrational "understanding" that comes from revelation was the experience of Thomas Aquinas on December 6, 1273. He was saying mass in Naples and was somehow enlightened, leading to his famous statement, "I can do no more; such things have been revealed to me that all I have written seems as straw, and I now await the end of my life" (Ferris 1988, p. 64). No one knows what was revealed to him, and he died the following year.

5   The Enlightenment

The diligent achievement of the ancients is still in our possession; they make their own past present to our times, and we ourselves wax dumb.... Notable miracle! The dead live, the living are buried in their stead. (Walter Map, in Ross and McLaughlin 1949, pp. 602–603)

Aristotelianism and the Enlightenment: The Authority of the Ancients

Aristotle described the universe as not only orderly but as filled with purpose. Objects were defined in terms of their natures, essences that made them what they were and explained their activities. This was the most influential interpretation of nature for over two thousand years after his death. It is not surprising that Aristotle's views persisted so long in biology, since his acorn-to-oak-tree teleology makes a lot of sense when applied to living things. Don't children seem to "unfold" as they mature, and doesn't the puppy seem to contain the dog that it will "naturally" become?

However, it is less obvious why Aristotelian science survived so long in physics and chemistry, where things seem more stable. But perhaps that stability is characteristic of the "nature" of inorganic things. Consider first chemistry, where the influence of what has been called Aristotelian thinking—the belief in essences—seems clearest. Bear in mind that Aristotle would not have endorsed much of this.

Chemistry: Phlogiston as Aristotelian Essence
As late as 1800, leading chemists such as Joseph Priestly were certain that water was an element, as was air, and that combustion involved the release of phlogiston. The phlogiston doctrine was surely

Aristotelian; combustibility was viewed as a property of some kinds of matter, and that property existed as a literal essence—phlogiston.

As the "fire element," phlogiston joined water, earth, and air as the four constituents of reality proposed by the ancients. And, from an Aristotelian appeal-to-common-experience argument, phlogiston should exist. When things burn, they appear to become smaller—as if something (phlogiston) is removed as they are "reduced to ashes." And as a thing burns, doesn't it appear that something is struggling to escape from it? Don't we hear it hissing from the wood as it burns in our fireplace?

German chemists Becher and Stahl knew that the reduction in mass was only apparent and that burning actually causes a net increase in weight. Thus phlogiston, which escapes when something burns, has a bizarre Aristotelian "nature" to account for the increase in weight. It has "negative weight," or levity, so that losing phlogiston actually makes a body gain weight! Does combustion mean the addition of oxygen, as we have been taught, or could it be the loss of phlogiston?

Physics: Aristotelian Mechanics—Appealing

The earlier revolution wrought by Galileo and Newton was directed against a theory of mechanics that derived from the physics of Aristotle. It is not a bad theory and, if observations of physical occurrences are the data to be explained, it serves quite well. To refute it required Galileo to imagine circumstances that do not exist in experience: the frictionless surfaces and weightless pulleys of elementary physics textbooks. However, what if we stick to real-life observations? Consider a few examples, and see that Aristotelian mechanics is appealing.

Force and Velocity   First, the Aristotelian physics of Galileo's time held that a constant force applied to an object produces a constant velocity, assuming that resistance remains constant. Doesn't that make sense? How would one falsify it in an age when scientists had to use their own pulse rate as a stopwatch? For Aristotle, there were two kinds of motion: natural and violent. Natural motion was any movement directed toward the center of the earth; this owed to the "nature" of heavy objects and required no further explanation. All other motion was "violent" and required application of force. As long as force was applied, motion continued, and it continued at constant velocity unless resistance (from the air, ground, and so on) changed.

What's wrong with that? If I apply constant force (F) to a constant mass (M), given that friction does not change, I should observe a constant velocity. It appears true in daily life, and so it was believed for millennia. It took the genius bordering on madness of Isaac Newton to show that constant force, mass, and resistance leads to *acceleration*, expressed in his second law of motion as $F = MA$ or $A = F/M$.

Aristotle also believed, sensibly enough, that velocity increases as force remains constant and as resistance decreases. In a vacuum there is no resistance and velocity would thus be unlimited—infinite—and for this reason Aristotle believed that a vacuum is impossible. This is a belief shared by thinkers from Thales to Einstein, and Galileo held it. However, we now know, since Newton told us in his first and second laws, that this is not the case.

Weight and Rate of Fall   One of Aristotle's principles that gained notoriety concerned the effect of weight on free fall. "Weight" refers to the attractive force exerted on an object by the earth, which is another way of describing what Aristotle would call a part of the object's "essence." All heavy terrestrial bodies move naturally toward the center of the universe; for Aristotle, that was the earth.[1] Since "heavy" means the tendency of an object to fall, a heavier object should fall faster—what else can "heavier" mean?

On earth it is awfully difficult to answer such a question. In fact, in 1612 Coresio dropped objects from the Tower of Pisa and the heavier object reached the ground first. It took the thought experiments of Galileo to show that the rate of acceleration of falling bodies is independent of weight or mass, given that air resistance is not a factor (Ferris 1988, pp. 90–94).

Consider a cannon ball weighing thirty pounds falling from the Tower of Pisa. If a fifteen-pound ball is dropped at the same time, will it fall more slowly? Coresio would say yes, for the good reasons above. Imagine the situation as did Galileo.

Suppose the thirty-pound ball is cut in half, and the two fifteen-pound halves joined as a sort of dumbbell—no one would predict that it would now fall more slowly, as might be predicted if the two halves were entirely separate. But what is the minimum "connection" that keeps them from being separate? What if the bar joining the pieces were made thinner until it was just a thread? When does the object change from a heavy whole to lighter halves? Looking at the question in this way led Galileo to conclude that rate of fall could not depend on weight.

Kepler, Galileo, and Newton: The Enlightenment

With Galileo, Newton, Descartes, and many others, the universe seemed at last understandable. It was a great machine, and therefore it became less mysterious than was the universe of the Scholastics, which was understood only by God. T. V. Smith and Marjorie Grene (1940, p. 5) expressed this view:

Galileo declared and succeeding scientists like Boyle and Newton agreed with him, that nature was written in mathematical letters. They agreed, that is, that mathematics is not only to be used as an instrument in physics but that the physical world really *is* the mechanical–mathematical system physics describes...

The demonstration of this great discovery should serve to counter the skepticism that was sweeping Europe, as the teachings of the Church seemed less and less plausible as descriptions of reality.

The Rise of Skepticism

Since the beginnings of history, most people have believed in magic and the supernatural. This was the appeal of Orphism in ancient Greece, and it was the appeal of Neoplatonism and of astrology. During the Middle Ages, the power and influence of the Church held such beliefs in check, since the Church had authority over the supernatural and could enforce belief if necessary.

What happened when science began to be successful? It meant a diminishing in the authority of the dogma of the Church, since revelation was often contradictory to science. For the Scholastics, the earth would always be the center of the universe, because it had to be.

In the period 1450–1465 Cosimo de'Medici, first of the line of rulers of powerful Florence, acquired an incomplete manuscript of the infamous *Corpus Hermeticum*, the book of magic and spells that was supposed to have originated in ancient Egypt. It had not been translated, except for a small part. Medici's secretary was Marsilio Ficino, and he was ordered to translate the *Corpus* immediately. Medici was to die the next year and may have had intimations of it; thus, he hoped that this book of magic could help in some way.

Ficino, like many educated persons, really did believe in magic—God and the universe were seen as one, a harmony that was expressed in music and in mathematics. The magic spells were like keys that brought one "into tune" with the universe—as Ficino wrote, "When I sing a song to the sun it is not because I expect the sun to change its course but I expect to put myself into a different cast of mind in relation to the sun."[2]

A reaction to widespread skepticism and devotion to magic was the rise of philosophies to combat the Skeptics and show that reason and sense experience can lead to certain knowledge. The writings of Bacon, Hobbes, Descartes, and Locke are sprinkled with references to the Skeptics, and how this or that argument "answers the skeptics" (Locke) or "cannot be shaken by the skeptics" (Descartes).

The Enlightenment and Psychology

Galileo's Separation of Physics and Psychology

In 1623 Galileo published *The Assayer*, in which he threw the Aristotelian essences out of the physical world, leaving them in a limbo or in individual psyches. The full repercussions of this would not be clear for at least a century. Galileo asserted that material bodies have shapes, occur in different numbers, and move slowly or rapidly. These would later be called primary qualities, and they are the properties of things that are assumed to be part of the things themselves. Whether they are observed by us or by any other creature, those properties exist and constitute what Galileo meant by the natural world that he urged we investigate.

What of colors and scents and sounds, and tastes and touches? What of the warmth of the fire and the green of the grass? All such things are "mere names," he wrote, and really not understandable. All such secondary qualities, as they would later be called, are not part of the natural world and one can only "pass this over in silence."

This was the first clear delineation of the understandable world of physics and the mysterious "world of the mind." In the natural world, observations correspond to things that actually exist. In the experienced world, observations may have no counterpart in physical nature. Psychology may never be treated "scientifically," in the sense that Galileo understood science (Gregory 1987, p. 282).

Figure 5.1
Francis Bacon. Courtesy of the National Library of Medicine, National Institutes of Health.

Francis Bacon: A Philosopher King?

It is given to us to calculate, to weigh, to measure, to observe; this is natural philosophy; almost all the rest is chimera. (Kaufman 1961, p. 2)

Francis Bacon (depicted in figure 5.1) was born in London, son of Sir Nicholas Bacon, Keeper of the Great Seal for the first twenty years of Elizabeth's reign. His mother was Lady Anne Cooke, daughter of the chief tutor of King Edward VI and sister-in-law of Lord Burghley, Lord Treasurer of England. She was herself a linguist and a theologian, who often corresponded in Greek. Interestingly, she took over her son's education, at least until the age of twelve, when he was sent to Cambridge.

After three years at Trinity College, Cambridge, Bacon was sick of the Scholastics and their cult of "interpreted Aristotle." He was offered a post with the ambassador to France, which he accepted and kept until his father died in 1579. The death was a surprise and left him penniless. He practiced law for a time and in 1583 was elected to parliament representing Taunton, a post to which he was repeatedly reelected.

A Government of Laws, Not People

The Earl of Essex was a powerful friend, who gave Bacon an estate at Twickenham (Durant 1954, p. 109), a gift that would ensure lifelong gratitude in most recipients, but not in Bacon. Essex arranged a conspiracy to imprison Elizabeth a few years later, and Bacon wrote letter after letter urging him to abandon the plan. Nonetheless, Essex tried, failed, and was imprisoned. Bacon pleaded for his release, and he was temporarily freed. Incredibly, he then raised an army of sorts and attempted to incite revolution in London, actions that angered Bacon, who had in the meantime been appointed a prosecutor. Essex was arrested, prosecuted by Bacon, convicted, and executed.

In 1606 Bacon was appointed Solicitor-General, in 1613 Attorney-General, and in 1618 Lord Chancellor, the highest civilian post in the country. However, a few years later his fortunes changed much for the worse. In 1621, a week after he was named Viscount St. Albans, already knighted as Baron Verulam in 1618, he was accused of accepting bribes, pled guilty, and was fined £40,000 plus an indeterminate sentence in the Tower of London. Those penalties were dropped after four days in the Tower, but a final sentence, disqualification from holding public office, remained.

Knowledge Is Power

Bacon was the great promoter of empirical science during the early seventeenth century. He argued for science based on observation, not authority or reason, and he did so in an appealing and charming way. In promoting science, he saw himself as arguing for reason as an alternative to the authority given to the ancients and to the faith based on revelation. Science and religion were two different things, and what is certain to faith is nonsense to science. However, that is fine, as far as Bacon was concerned, and he remained a religious man: "I had rather believe all the fables in the legend, and the Talmud, and the Alcoran, than that this universal frame is without a mind" (*Oxford Dictionary of Quotations*, 3rd ed., p. 25). Science is separate, and its goal is the mastery of nature. Bacon urged his contemporaries to make discoveries and improve life; consider the effects of gunpowder, printing, and the compass, which have "changed the whole face and state of things throughout the world" (*Oxford Dictionary of Quotations*, p. 28).

Bacon wrote *The Great Instauration* as a reconstruction of philosophy to turn it from the sterile rationalism of the Scholastics to the inductive empiricism of his science. *Novum Organum* explained how this can be done, and *The New Atlantis* described a society in which science makes its proper contribution. The government of this advanced society includes no politicians, and there are no parties, conventions, speeches, lies, or elections.

Only those of high scientific repute join the government, and that government is composed of technicians, architects, astronomers, geologists, physicians, chemists, and even sociologists and psychologists. However, those in the government govern strangely, aiming to control nature: "The End of Our Foundation is the Knowledge of Causes and secret motions of things, and the enlarging of the bounds of human empire, to the effecting of all things possible" (*The New Atlantis*, Cambridge Press, 1900, p. 34).

Bacon and Induction: Critics Were Wrong

Bacon's great contribution was to argue eloquently for the method of induction, whereby instances are observed and classified and empirical generalizations made. Thus, order is found in nature and, that being done, one may form hypotheses to "explain" the order that is found. Many writers criticized Bacon for failing to appreciate the importance of hypotheses formed in advance of observation, pointing out that what constitutes an observed "instance" is itself the product of such a hypothesis.

This is a very tiresome argument that is raised even by Bertrand Russell (1945, pp. 543–545) and that has been taken up by almost every writer since. Durant (1954, p. 133) noted this error was common. That is, it is apparently easy to view Bacon as anticipating logical positivism, of treating phenomena as perfectly objective things that all can agree on and that all see. That is hardly fair in Bacon's case and reveals a failure to actually read his work, particularly *Novum Organun*, the new "Method" meant to replace Aristotle's logic as applied by the Scholastics.

Bacon emphasized the necessity of a means of classification of observations, so that we avoid "simple enumeration," which could lead to an endless and useless mass of material. One "lights a candle" with preliminary observations and experiments; that can mean only that observations are guided, as any reader of Bacon must conclude. The passage was preceded by a discussion of deficiencies in meditation and in logic as paths to knowledge (*Novum Organum*, lxxxii, in Burtt 1939, p. 57).

Spiders, Ants, and Bees
In yet another illustration of method, Bacon compared the ways of seeking knowledge with the behavior of insects. The ant appears to mindlessly gather items without order, in the manner of simple empiricism. The spider gathers nothing; rather it spins everything out of itself, in the manner of a rationalist, such as the Neoplatonists, who seek truth in contemplation, or the Scholastics, who defer to ancient authority. The proper method is shown by the bee, who not only gathers, but arranges (and selects what it gathers!).

The Two Ways to Seek Knowledge
Bacon described two methods of seeking knowledge that were common in his day and are common today. His point is best made by reference to recent issues.

Consider three examples of interpretation that seem well supported by observation. Then consider how useful they really are. First, children learn language with almost inconceivable rapidity, or so it seems to many observers who study the development of language. They propose that children are innately prepared to learn grammar and effectively possess a "language acquisition device."

Second, all humans and animals seem guided by the seeking of pleasures and the avoidance of pain. It seems obvious that hedonism is thus the basis for all motivation. Third, we seem to be able to keep track of about six or seven items at a time—for example, the digits in a phone number. That means that we have a short-term memory store of a half dozen, more or less. Now consider aphorism number xix from *Novum Organum*:

There are and can be only two ways of searching into and discovering truth. The one flies from the senses and particulars to the most general axioms, and from these principles, the truth of which it takes for settled and immovable, proceeds to judgment and to the discovery of middle axioms. And this way is now in fashion.

This way seems *ever* in fashion, since the "mind longs to spring up to positions of higher generality, that it may find rest there; and so after a little while wearies of experiment" (aphorism xx).

The three examples above all exemplify this quick and easy scanning of data and leaping to an explanation that satisfies us. However, it is not the best explanation, and that is certain. Psychology is replete with theories that represent this inferior method of pursuing knowledge—in fact, any theory that can be summed up in a few words ("instinct," "cognition," "processing," "conditioning," "reinforcement," "brain centers") is apt to be of this kind.

The proper method "derives axioms from the senses and particulars, rising by a gradual and unbroken ascent, so that it arrives at the most general axioms last of all. This is the true way, but as yet untried." (aphorism xix) Bacon's study of heat was meant as an illustration of this method. Robert Boyle claimed that he did indeed follow Bacon's method as we will see below.

The alternative and the proper method is to pass from the observations through the making of further observations and the discovering of middle axioms. Finally, our patience will be rewarded and we will discover the highest axioms. This sure strategy is less appealing to most of us, who want the answer, *now*, even if it is a bad answer.

Two Kinds of Experiments

The two kinds of investigation were characterized as two ways of doing experiments. *Experimenta lucifera* were experiments that "cast light" and consisted of manipulating things and noting consequences. For example, what is the effect of intensive early training on the development of language use in children? Once enough experiments of this type have been done and we thus know something about the process of learning language, we can do *experimenta fructifera*, those which "bear fruit." This would mean that we have learned enough through observation and simple manipulation to allow hypotheses that are more than vague generalizations. We will then have no reason to refer to "language acquisition devices."

The Idols

To clear our heads and observe nature wisely, we must do our fact-gathering *lucifera* experiments and we must beware of what Bacon called the "idols" that prejudice our observations. The idols of the tribe refer to biases that arise because we are human and we suppose that our way of perceiving is the only way. We live in a world of colors and of sounds, and that is what we take to be reality. However, dogs and many humans do not share our world of colors; they live in a world of shades of gray. The world of sounds is vastly different for dogs, as any owner of an ultrasonic whistle knows. And the sun seems to rise in the east and set in the west, but it is we who are doing the moving (relatively speaking), not the sun.

Idols of the marketplace are misconceptions that are due to the careless and loose use of words. All of us use the word "truth" and "the self," but do we mean the same things when we use them? We may assume that "they" know what is really meant by such terms—that there is a body of experts somewhere who have the definitions down pat, just as the meter is defined by the standard in Paris. However, there are many groups of experts, and each has its own set of definitions. We cannot get far if we are using disparate definitions of the same terms.

Bacon's idols of the den are misconceptions held by our families or by whatever small social group surrounds us. Our family units and circles of friends may lead us to have such prejudices, and those will blind us to whatever virtues may be possessed by individual candidates of whatever party.

Finally, and most damaging, are the idols of the theater, the dogmas of scientific, religious, and philosophical authorities, so called because they are presented to us as if they were on a stage in a theatrical production. Many absurd ideas have been introduced with the words, "modern science has shown," and we believe it—otherwise, we are ignoring the wisdom of modern science.

Bacon's Influence

Practicing what he preached, Bacon was on his way by carriage from London to Highgate in March of 1626. He was wondering how long meat might be kept if spoiling were prevented by packing it in snow. He stopped and performed such an experiment on a chicken and in so doing was seized by chills and forced to a nearby house. He died on April 9.

In addition to his emphasis on science, Bacon was a great contributor to popular psychology—he could be called the founder of social psychology (Durant 1954, p. 122). He proposed in *The Advancement of Learning* that inquiry be made into the shapers of the mind—custom, exercise, habit, education, example, imitation, emulation, company, friendship, praise, reproof, exhortation, reputation, laws, books, studies, and so on. This study too is part of science, as far as Bacon was concerned.

Did scientists follow Bacon's advice? There is much dispute about that, and the consensus is that Bacon's mainly inductive model was not really the model that succeeded. Bacon illustrated his method of selective classification and organizing to understand the phenomena of heat.

Thomas Hobbes: All Intelligence Is Artificial

For seeing life is but a motion of limbs, why may we not say that all *automata* (engines that move themselves by springs and wheels as doth a watch) have an artificial life? (*Leviathan*, 1651, Introduction)

Thomas Hobbes was born (prematurely) in 1588, along with his twin, "fear." His mother was frightened by the invading Spanish Armada, sent by Philip II, during Thomas's birth. She could not know that the armada would be quickly defeated and dispersed by such captains as Howard, Drake, and Hawkins. Hobbes attributed aspects of his adult personality to that experience, but it did not shorten his life or limit his productivity. As Russell (1945, p. 548) wrote of Hobbes, "I cannot discover that he wrote any large books after the age of eighty-seven."

Hobbes's father was a poor and ignorant country vicar, but a well-to-do tradesman uncle helped him prepare for the university. He received the same sort of scholastic education at Oxford that Francis Bacon received at Cambridge, and, like Bacon, he carried away a dislike for universities.

In 1608 he began a lifelong association with the family of Lord Cavendish, as his son's tutor, companion, and, later, secretary. Hobbes knew Bacon but seemed unaffected by his views and became interested in science and psychology only when he was around forty. He visited Galileo in Italy in 1634.

Thereafter he became concerned with the conflicts between King Charles I and Parliament that later led to the civil war and the beheading of the king. During the war, Hobbes was in Paris, where he spent eleven years associating with the intellectuals there, many of whom were displaced royalists like himself. And he tutored the Prince of Wales, later to become King Charles II after the restoration.

Leviathan

During this period, Hobbes was anxious to improve government by analyzing the principles that determine the behavior of individual humans and of the aggregate of humans, the state. He published *Leviathan* in 1651 as part of a larger work, but his fame rests largely on it alone. For Hobbes, a devout believer in science and reason, there was need for improvement in government, and, like Plato, he turned to the individual as the microcosm corresponding to the state as macrocosm.

Hobbes was convinced that the proper government was an absolute monarchy, and he opposed democracy for some of the same reasons that Plato opposed it. The state is a machine just as is the individual, and the parts of both of these types of mechanism show a clear and natural correspondence.

Hobbes fully accepted the mechanistic implications of the new science of Kepler, Galileo, and Descartes, as his interchanges with Descartes over the *Meditations* clearly show. Life is "motion of limbs," so machines have life—albeit it an artificial one. And, as atoms comprise matter that comprises machines and living things, the humans that make up a state function as invisible parts of that greater whole.

If it is natural to view one's own body as machinery—the heart a spring, the nerves strings, and the joints wheels, with sensation and imagination produced by movement of atoms, then why not view a sovereign's counselors as a sort of memory? Why not view the laws of a nation as equivalent to reason in the individual? For Hobbes, memory and reason in the individual are products of "industry"—education and practice, just as the skill of the counselor or the wisdom of the law comes from human training and experience. Hobbes would say that they arise "by art," meaning that they are human produced, artificial.

Hobbes's Psychology

Our Conscious Experience   Aristotle saw conscious experience as imagery, meaning relations with objects of sensation. Plato and the Platonists saw it as a barrier, a screen, a veil of appearances, blocking out the real world beyond. Hobbes, interested in explaining experience so that he could explain politics, described what he called the train of thoughts. First, what are thoughts? "All fancies are motions within us, relics of those made in the sense" (1939, chapter III). Thoughts are "relics," remains, leftovers, residues, mementos, souvenirs.[3] Whatever is an idea was present earlier as sensation. This does not mean that thoughts resemble the objects that produced the original sensation.

Objects affect us either immediately, as in the case of taste and touch, or mediately, as in seeing, hearing, and smelling. The sense organ is pressed, and this pressure is transmitted as motion via nerves or "other strings and membranes of the body" to the brain and heart. Those organs exert a counterpressure directed outward, thus making the source of the sensation seem external. We react outward when we sense; we do not passively absorb stimulation. All of this "motion" appears to us as "fancy, the same waking as dreaming." When we press, rub, or strike the eye, Hobbes noted, it makes us fancy a light, and pressing the ear causes noise. "So do the bodies also we see or hear, produce the same by their strong though unobserved action."

Sensations, or fancies, are thus secondary qualities, a term coined by Robert Boyle, Hobbes's contemporary. As thoughts occur in trains, their appearance is not "altogether so casual" as it seems to be. A thought appeared in the past as sensation (and as prior thought), and it was then followed by some other sensation or thought. That is what will happen the next time that the thought appears—it will be followed by whatever followed it in the past. And that is the truth.

However, sometimes the earlier sensation, say the sight of a seagull, was succeeded by one thing—a summer sunset, and on other times by other things—fishing boats and so on. What will succeed that, or any idea, this time? Hobbes wrote, "only this is certain, it shall be something that succeeded the same before, at one time or another."

Unguided Thought and Regulated Thought   Thought goes on constantly, even when we are paying no mind, are not trying to remember something, and are not reasoning explicitly. This "mental discourse" may be unguided, without design, wherein there is no passionate thought and the thoughts wander,...as in a dream." This is life for those with no company and with no cares about anything. Yet, we may "ofttimes perceive the way of it," as in his example of a "discourse during our present civil war."

...what could seem more impertinent than to ask, as one did, what was the value of a Roman penny?... For the thought of the war introduced the thought of the delivering up of the king to his enemies; the thought of that brought in the thought of the delivering up of Christ; and that again the thought of the thirty pence which was the price of that treason . . . all this in a moment of time; for thought is quick. (Burtt 1939, p. 137)

Thus, even thought that seems completely random can be seen to have "a way to it"; it is a train of association by contiguity in time and space. In this case, merely substitute King Charles I for Christ and some one of his enemies as the betrayer, Judas.

Regulated thought comes in two kinds. Regulated thought either seeks causes for an observed effect or imagines effects that may issue from a given "cause"; we "imagine what we can do with it once we have it." In the first case, either man or beast can react to hunger pangs with thoughts of hours since feeding, as well as innumerable other effect-to-cause cases. However, in Hobbes's opinion, only humans can think from causes to possible effects—this being curiosity, which he saw as absent in animals.

Reason, Prudence, and Memory   Since thought is ordered, the relics/ thoughts that make up the train are signs, or "Signes," as Hobbes wrote. A person with much experience can act prudently, since the future is predictable to such an individual. Many thoughts now present will act as cues, or signs based on "a like past. . . . As he that foresees what will become of a criminal, re-cons what he has seen follow on the like crime before . . . the crime, the officer, the prison, the judge, and the gallows" (1651/1939, p. 139). Naturally, the more frequent has a course of things been observed, the more certain is the sign.

The Future as Fiction   Hobbes's "mental train" is a stamped-in copy of an objective world that chugs by—all that one needs is the five senses to record it. The stamped in sequence need not resemble the real-world sequence, of course; Hobbes stressed that experience is mainly of secondary qualities, produced in the observer.

Prudence, recall from memory, and other faculties amount to no more than replays of this recorded sequence. That being the case, only that which has been "recorded" can be "replayed," and this means that words like infinity and time cannot be conceived. "When we say anything is infinite, we signify only that we are not able to conceive the ends, the bounds of the things named; having no conception of the thing, but only of our own inability" (1651/1939, p. 140).

And what of time: past, present, and future? Examine experience and we find that they are illusory, "The present only has a being in nature; things past have a being in the memory only, but things to come have no being at all; the future being but a fiction of the mind, applying the sequels of actions passed [sic], to the actions that are present" (1651/1939, p. 139). Augustine had 1,200 years earlier argued for the subjective nature of time, Kant would do so two centuries later, and William James followed suit in 1890. Hobbes mentions it as a matter of fact, one of the most obvious conclusions drawn from a consideration of the "mental train" that is our experience.

Speech and Concepts
Speech transfers our mental discourse into verbal form, "or the train of our thoughts into a train of words." Basically, words serve to mark things so that they are remembered and to signify relationships among things. However, words are also the source of greatest possible danger when used improperly. One may, first of all, register one's thoughts wrongly, by inconsistently relating specific words to specific thoughts. In so doing, we may deceive ourselves, by registering with a word that which we never conceived. Does my word "infinity" really correspond to a thought?

Nature is never mistaken, closed Hobbes, "and as men abound in copiousness of language, so they become more wise, or more mad, than ordinary" (Burtt,1939, p. 143). Hobbes's concern was shared by later, even twentieth-century philosophers and psychologists who warned against the misleading use of metaphor and other figurative language (Burtt, 1939, pp. 145–147).

Hobbes warns of saying that "faith is 'infused'," as if faith were a fluid or other substance that could be transported. Related to that is the giving of names of bodies to names and speeches. These cases of reification assign a permanence to qualities or states of things; they assign a "thingness" to activities. Modern examples of this fallacy are terms like personality, character, intelligence, learning, motivation, cognition, and other activities, processes, or states that we treat as if they may be poured like a fluid or otherwise treated as things, though they do not really refer to discrete entities. B. F. Skinner, among others, would make the same point centuries later.

Hobbes and Motivation
Hobbes was a hedonist, though he made no great issue of it, taking for granted that pleasure and pain are constant accompaniments of our

activities. Animals are characterized by two sorts of motions, as he put it, the vital motions and the voluntary motions. The first refers to processes of digestion, circulation, respiration, and other aspects of the scholastic vegetative soul. Voluntary motion, on the other hand, is another name for the passions and refers to movement that is initiated internally by means of "fancies in the mind."

Voluntary action is either appetite (desire) or aversion—approaching or withdrawing—and the objects that provoke such actions are what we call "good" and "evil." From approach and withdrawal, Hobbes proposed a list of simple passions, derivative from desire and aversion. Those are appetite, desire, love, aversion, hate, joy, and grief. They gain different names depending on four things: the likelihood of obtaining what is desired, the nature of the object loved or hated, the consideration of many of them together, and, finally, from the alternation or succession of them. He gave many examples, such as:

- hope is appetite with opinion of attaining.
- curiosity is the desire to know, and why.[4]
- religion is fear of invisible power... imagined from tales publicly allowed.
- superstition is fear of invisible power... imagined from tales not allowed.

Hobbes and Will

Hobbes described many more derivatives of desire and aversion, corresponding to dozens of "passions." He viewed experience as a constantly changing combination of thoughts and passions, rising and falling, alternating, and coming and going. The sum of desires, aversions, hopes, and fears continues until action is taken or decided to be impossible, and this is what Hobbes called deliberation. And "it is called *de-liberation* because it is a putting an end to the *liberty* we had of doing, or omitting, according to our own appetite or aversion" (1651/1939, p. 154). This occurs in beasts as well, since the succession of appetites, aversions, hopes, and fears is no less than in man—"and therefore beasts also deliberate."

This leads to one simple interpretation of will that interprets volition as a passive and derivative process. Hobbes put it well, as he argued against Augustine, Aquinas, and the Scholastics, who posited a faculty of will:

The definition of the will given commonly by the Schools, that it is a *rational appetite*, is not good. For if it were, then there could be no voluntary act against

Primus inaccessum qui per tot sæcula rerum
Eruit è tetris longæ caliginis umbris.
Mysta sagax, Natura, tuus, sic cernitur Orbi

Figure 5.2
Descartes. Courtesy of the National Library of Medicine, National Institutes of Health.

reason. For a *voluntary act* is that which proceedeth from the will, and no other.... Will, therefore, *is the last appetite in deliberating.*

Descartes's Rebuttal of Skepticism

The Chancellor Bacon had shown the road which science might follow.... But then Descartes appeared and did just the contrary of what he should have done: instead of studying nature, he wished to divine her.... This best of mathematicians made only romances in philosophy. (Voltaire, quoted in Durant 1926/1954, p. 234)

Descartes's Life

René Descartes (depicted in figure 5.2) was born in 1596, the son of a counselor for the parliament of Brittany. On his father's death, Descartes inherited estates, which he later sold, investing the proceeds, which left him an income sufficient to live on the rest of his life. He had been schooled at the Jesuit College at La Flêche, where the library, reputation, and surroundings attracted David Hume, who spent several years there a century later.

However, the school produced the same aversion to Aristotle and to the Scholastics that their educations at Cambridge and Oxford produced in Bacon and Hobbes. Like Bacon, Descartes placed his faith in science, and, like Hobbes, he had faith in reason, though reason was not the product of "industry" as Hobbes believed.

Descartes never married but had a daughter who died at five, an event he called "the greatest sorrow"[5] of his life. He dressed well and always wore a sword or a swordbelt (Haldane 1905); he worked short hours and read little. Some suggested that he pretended to work less than he actually did (Russell 1945, p. 560). He left France to spend twenty years in Holland and took few books with him, but among those he took were the Bible and Thomas Aquinas. According to Elisabeth Haldane (1905), most of what one could call his "library" consisted of books that he had been given as presents, so it appears that he was not much of a reader.

As a student he had been sickly and so was allowed to remain in bed through the morning, a practice that he continued through life, until his move to Stockholm in 1649. To gain peace from pre-noon visitors, he joined the Dutch Protestant army of Maurice of Nassau, engaged in the Thirty Years' War, serving from 1617 to 1619. He then moved to join the Catholic army of Maximilian of Bavaria and spent the winter of 1619 to 1620 in the city of Neuburg, near Ulm, where he had the experiences described in his *Discourse on Method*.

Soldiering and Mathematics: The First November 10

On November 10, 1618, Descartes was examining a mathematical puzzle posted on a wall in Breda, Holland. He had not learned Dutch and asked a passerby to translate—that was Isaac Beeckman, a doctor and mathematician from Middleburg who had come to Breda to help in his uncle's butcher business and to seek a wife. That chance meeting began a friendship of many years.

Beeckman instructed him in the combining of physics and mathematics—the study of falling bodies, mechanics, geometry, and hydraulics. At Beeckman's request, Descartes wrote a treatise on music, dated

December 31, 1618. In 1630 Beeckman claimed to have originated Descartes's ideas, leading Descartes to testily reply that "one knows that I am accustomed to instructing myself even with ants and worms, and one will think that is how I used you" (Vrooman 1970, p. 50). That was a dispute to come much later and to last only briefly. His relationship with Beeckman was almost always cordial and there is no doubt that the older man influenced Descartes greatly. Beeckman envisioned the uniting of the sciences, a goal that was to occupy Descartes for life.

Dreaming Near Ulm

In November 1619, Descartes was housed for the winter in the town of Neuburg, on the Danube near Ulm, deep in Bavaria between Stuttgart and Munich. He had just returned from the coronation of the Emperor Ferdinand at Frankfurt and had spent the previous twenty months with his mathematical friend, Isaac Beeckman. Ulm was a center for mathematical studies and home of Johann Faulhaber, the most famous mathematician in the country and a member of the Rosicrucians, outlaws in both Holland and France.

Faulhaber had just published a book on arithmetic and algebra and (mockingly) asked Descartes to solve a problem. Descartes, irritated, solved all the problems that Faulhaber could pose and even aided the master in solving problems posed by a rival in Nüremberg, Peter Roten (Haldane 1905, pp. 62–63). This experience, similar to the months spent with Beeckman, was very exciting for Descartes.

Because of this, his biographer described him as "greatly overstimulated."[6] At twenty-three, he was concerned about how to best spend his life, and his experiences soldiering were not promising to date. He was showing himself to be unusually skilled at mathematics and other forms of "philosophy," but it was not clear that this should be his vocation. He retired for the winter in a rented house where, because of these circumstances, he had a memorable experience that changed his life.

He recorded on X Novembris, 1619, that the foundations of the Admirable Science and of his vocation were revealed in a set of dreams that he considered supernatural. He described the dreams in the greatest detail, and many subsequent readers, including Freud, have considered their significance. This all happened after a day of meditation in a heated room and perhaps even in the stove.[7] Descartes, who analyzed the dreams as they occurred, interpreted them as telling him that his life should be devoted to uniting the humanities and sciences.

August Comte found it annoying to find at the origin of modern philosophy a "cerebral episode," which could easily be diagnosed as pathological (Maritain 1946, p. 11). Descartes was definitely interested in the Rosicrucians at the time and had spent much time with Professor Faulhaber of Ulm, a mathematician and ardent Rosicrucian.[8] Hence, his mental state could have been suspect.

Rules for the Direction of Our Intelligence

It was probably in 1628, just before his move to Holland and nine years after his idea for the new method, that Descartes wrote a set of rules to guide thinking—his attempt to educate his readers. The piece was not published until 1701, a half-century after his death, and what was published was a copy left in Holland; the original was irretrievably lost. It is here that Descartes referred to "simple natures," and similar reference is found nowhere else in his work, though all else in the *Rules* appears later in other works. Hence, this is his one clear reference to what amount to the primary qualities of Boyle.

According to Descartes, there were to be thirty-six rules—twelve describing the new method, twelve showing mathematical applications, and twelve applied to general philosophy. But the text ends after number XXI, and the last three of those are presented without discussion. In the later *Discourse on the Method*, we are left with four only. In the *Rules*, Descartes first defined his most important terms, one of which is intuitions. These are often conceived of as innate ideas, though he definitely did not view them that way. Here is what he said and what a modern commentator wrote. Both concern what we may know with certainty, which is to say, clearly and distinctly.

What May We Know as "Clear and Distinct"?
The only two sources of knowledge are *intuition* and *deduction* (Rule III). Intuitions are clear and distinct and hard to come by for some people. Descartes remarked on this in his *Principles of Philosophy, Principle XLV*:

There are indeed a great many persons who, through their whole lifetime, never perceive anything in a way necessary for judging of it properly; for the knowledge upon which we can establish a certain and indubitable judgment must be not only clear, but also distinct. I call that clear which is present and manifest to the mind giving attention to it ... but the distinct is that which is so precise and different from all other objects as to comprehend in itself only what is clear. (Haldane and Ross 1911, p. 237)

Descartes considered the example of an investigator reasoning out the properties of light rays, based on what is known concerning light (Rule III). The point of the illustration is to urge that the method of deduction must sometimes rely on empirical knowledge gained from specialists, as is the case when we wonder what happens to light rays as they enter a denser or less dense medium—reason fails us there, and only observation suffices. However, this has nothing to do with *clear and distinct* ideas, since sensory observations never have that characteristic—never, unless they refer to intuitive knowledge: "By *intuition* I understand, not the fluctuating testimony of the senses" (Haldane and Ross 1911, p. 7). He expressed doubt about the reality of sensation in general, especially what were later called by Boyle "secondary qualities." He concluded that for such ideas, "it is not necessary that I should assign any author besides myself... because they exhibit so little reality that I can not even distinguish the object represented from nonbeing" (*Meditation III*).

Empirical phenomena that are clear and distinct are *simple natures*;... the cognition of which is so clear and distinct that they cannot be analyzed by the mind into others more distinctly known. Such are figure, extension, motion, number, and so on; all others we conceive to be in some way compounded out of these. (Rule XII) (Haldane and Ross 1911, pp. 40–41)

Discourse on Method
Discourse on the Method of Rightly Conducting the Reason and Seeking for Truth in the Sciences was originally published with three illustrative essays on optics, physics, and geometry, and they will be described below. The work was published anonymously, as Descartes insisted, by Jan Maire of Leiden in 1637. This was Descartes's first published work, at the age of forty-one.[9] The original French edition was succeeded by a Latin version published by Louis Elzevir.[10] Descartes's anonymity was lost when Mersenne revealed to everyone that Descartes had authored it. Descartes's income from the book was 400 copies of it.

The most famous passage in the book deals with the four rules of method that he found to be "quite sufficient":

The first of these was to accept nothing as true which I did not clearly recognize to be so... and to accept... nothing more than what was presented to my mind so clearly and distinctly that I could have no occasion to doubt it.

The second was to divide up each of the difficulties which I examined into as many parts as possible....

The third was to carry on my reflections in due order, commencing with objects that were the most simple and easy to understand....

The last was in all cases to make enumerations so complete and reviews so general that I should be certain of having omitted nothing (Haldane and Ross 1911, p. 92).

The six parts of this work were meant to accompany the three essays (on optics, physics, and geometry) that illustrated applications. However, his science was lacking, and the essays were soon dated anyway, so that the *Discourse* was left on its own. In it Descartes considered the sciences, discussed rules of method, derived rules of morality, proved the existence of God and the soul, and considered questions regarding physics, circulation, medicine, and the man/beast distinction. Finally, he suggested ways to advance knowledge and explained why he wrote this treatise.

In the course of this he summarized his lost book, "The World," discussed dissection and Harvey's recent demonstration of the circulation of the blood, wrote of automata and the obvious machine nature of the body, and compared animals to clocks.

Descartes's Mathematics and Science

Since he arrived in Holland in 1618, Descartes had ceaselessly written and experimented in algebra, geometry, physics, and optics. His aim was to show the mathematical unity of all the sciences and, as shown in his *Rules for the Direction of the Mind*, the *Discourse on Method*, and accompanying essays, mathematics was synonymous with science, and any discipline that was a science was subject to order and measurement. One of his first tasks was applying his method to space, after which he would analyze motion, as Galileo was doing at the same time.

"La Geometrie" was an essay accompanying the *Discourse*, but it was surely the first conceived. He had worked on the application of algebra to geometry since his early twenties; by 1628 he had developed the method of drawing tangents to curves, and even before that he considered a new form of notation.

He introduced the modern notation for powers, which at the time used the letters R, Q, and C for root, square, and cube. He suggested also using alphabet letters to stand for variables, so that $x + 4x^2 - 7x^3$ would replace the old notation, which was $1R + 4Q - 7C$ (Vrooman

1970, p. 118). Descartes's contribution has been incorporated into all of the texts on analytic geometry of our day, and all appreciate his invention of Cartesian coordinates, the familiar x–y axes of life.

"Les Meteores" is Descartes's physics. Here again he applied his method, illustrating the principles of the *Discourse* and making the universe a mechanical place, free of mysticism. He treated meteorology, avalanches, and even parahelia, false suns that appeared over Rome in 1629 (Vrooman 1970, p. 124–125). He explained them as he did the rainbow, as due to refraction, not reflection as the Aristotelian view held. However, the essay is as noted for its errors as for its achievements. For example, Descartes knew nothing of electricity and did not connect lightning and thunder. Yet, his writing on storms and tempests was useful, and it was incorporated into a standard work on navigation (Fournier's).

Another essay was Descartes's optics, or "La Dioptrique," concerning the "science of miracles." Knowledge of optics allowed one to produce the same illusions that magicians produced with the help of demons, or so Descartes wrote. He proposed a machine for grinding telescopic lenses and considered the nature of light and color. Light is a movement in bodies which are luminous, and refraction shows light affected like a bouncing ball. Thus, as is true of all of his physics, light affects us by being transmitted through matter and striking our receptors.

In fact, all the universe operates by "impact"; there is no action at a distance, as Newton proposed, and Cartesians of the later seventeenth and early eighteenth centuries criticized Newton and his followers for resorting to such magic. Descartes was the first to propose that color has something to do with the speed of actions meeting the eye. He had dissected animal eyes and suggested lenses to treat various visual problems.

Descartes quickly assumed scientific authority in France. This provided the pulpit for his philosophy, published in 1641 in Latin, and intended as a scientific proof of the basic tenets of religion. This was titled *Meditations of First Philosophy*.

Descartes's *Meditations*

This famous work was published in its second edition in Amsterdam in 1642 by Louis Elzevir, with the objections and replies that were missing in the first edition published in France. Descartes wrote these six meditations as a sort of autobiography and a means to serving the highest purpose. He attached a letter "to the most wise and illustrious the dean and doctors of the sacred faculty of theology in Paris."

He claimed that his "excellent motive" was to prove the existence of God and the soul's immortality so that infidels, who cannot believe through faith, may be persuaded through reason. It is in the *Meditations* that Descartes tried to state his case most clearly, though it is stated also in the *Discourse on Method* and in *Principles of Philosophy* (parts IV and VI–XII, respectively).

Descartes pretended to be filled with doubt about the certainty of everything, so as to determine what is left as clear and distinct and thus true. People view themselves as bodies which can be seen with their eyes and which therefore seem most real, while the idea of the soul and of God is "clearly" less distinct. Echoing Plato and the Platonists, at least on this particular, Descartes tried to describe what he meant by "doubting" and "knowing" and "clearness" and "distinctness."

In the first meditation he explained doubting and the possibility that an evil genius may be deceiving him—of what can he be certain? His body may change and all that he sees and hears and feels may be illusion. In fact, there is no way to be certain that he is not dreaming at any given moment.[11]

Depending on whether one reads the first or the second edition, the famous statement echoing Augustine has assured Descartes's place in history—"Je pense, donc je suis," or "Cogito ergo sum." The fact that doubting can occur assures a doubter and a mind,[12] the certain truth from which he began to explain all of nature. In the second meditation the soul is verified as clear and distinct and immortal. Here we find Descartes even considering the possibility that he exists only when thinking: "I am—I exist: this is certain; but how often?"

Descartes concluded that he existed even when dreamlessly asleep and that this "thinking thing" has faculties: it doubts, understands (conceives), affirms, denies, wills, refuses, imagines, and perceives.

God is conceived as clear perfection in the third meditation, and the idea of Him must mean a source, or else the idea would exist only in the mind of Descartes, who would therefore be perfect and all powerful! Hence God exists and, in the fourth meditation, Descartes argued that He does not deceive us, since that would be an imperfection, impossible in a perfect being. The fifth and sixth meditations elaborate arguments for God and discuss imagination versus understanding.

Perhaps the best thing about this work is that objections to it were solicited by Mersenne and published in the Elziver second edition, along with replies by Descartes. They add something that the bare Latin original lacks.

Replies to Hobbes's Criticisms of His *Meditations*

Thomas Hobbes, out of favor in England where Cromwell was in power, was in Paris at the time of publication of Descartes's work. He was asked by the publisher to join several other critics and to list his objections to the main points of the *Meditations*. These were published as accompaniment to that work, along with replies by Descartes.

The following excerpts were chosen because Descartes expressed himself in a less formal manner than is the case in most of his writings. The replies are those of Descartes and are the only writings that I know that bring Descartes to life—as a likable person with wit and temper. The objections were written by Hobbes, whose work is always entertaining. The following quotations and paraphrases derive from the translation of Haldane and Ross 1934, pp. 60–78.

Are We Asleep or Awake?   Hobbes's First Objection begins by noting that Meditation I makes it obvious "that we have no criterion for distinguishing dreaming from waking and from what the senses truly tell us...and therefore...we shall be justified in doubting whether or not anything exists." However, Hobbes then noted, Plato and many others considered the uncertainty of sense data and everyone knows that dreaming and waking may be difficult to distinguish. Thus, Hobbes concluded, "I should have been glad if our author, so distinguished in the handling of modern speculations, had refrained from publishing these matters of ancient lore."

Descartes replied that he was not trying to "retail" these ideas as new, but merely wanted to prepare the readers' minds for considering intellectual from corporeal matters.

A Clear Idea of God?   The fifth of Hobbes's objections concerns the interesting question of what exactly is meant by the word "idea." In particular, what is meant by "clear ideas," such as the idea of God? One can imagine a person or a physical object easily enough, but when we imagine an angel, the object is a "fair winged child," or whatever, and we are quite certain that this is not what angels are like. This being the case, how can we have a clear and distinct idea of God, as Descartes claims that we do? As Hobbes put it:

It is the same way with the most holy name of God; we have no image, no idea corresponding to it. Hence we are forbidden to worship God in the form of an image, lest we should think we can conceive Him who is inconceivable.

Hobbes compared knowledge of God with the blind person's conception of fire. Though blind, one can feel oneself growing warm and infer that the warmth is caused by something.

When that cause is called "fire" by someone else, the blind person may conclude that she has a knowledge of fire, though there is no image of it. Similarly, our "idea" of God can be no more than a conclusion drawn from other experiences, so that we conceive of an eternal and all-powerful being and one "merely gives a name to the object of his faith or reasoning and calls it God."

However, Descartes claimed an "idea of God in our soul" as the starting point of his reasonings, so Hobbes objected that "he should have explained this idea of God better, and he should have deduced from it not only God's existence, but also the creation of the world."

Hobbes seemed to be asking a lot, and his question reflected the common misunderstanding shown when someone says that the body is clearly and distinctly perceived but the idea of God is not clear. This shows failure to understand what Descartes meant by "clear and distinct," since perceptions, such as those of one's body, are never clear and distinct.

Descartes's answer is worth quoting:

REPLY

Here the meaning assigned to the term idea is merely that of images depicted in the corporeal imagination; and, that being agreed on, it is easy for my critic to prove that there is no proper idea of Angel or of God. But I have, everywhere, from time to time, and principally in this place, shown that I take the term idea to stand for whatever the mind directly perceives ... I employed this term because it was the term currently employed by philosophers for the forms of perception of the Divine mind, though we can discover no imagery in God; besides I had no other more suitable term.

An Idea of the Soul?   Is there an idea of the soul? That is Hobbes's seventh question and the object of strong disagreement between the two men. In the following centuries, both Hume and Kant would agree with Hobbes—there is no idea corresponding to the soul.

OBJECTION VII

...We only infer by means of the reason that there is something internal in the human body, which imparts to it its animal motion, and by means of which it feels and moves; and this, whatever it be, we name the soul, without employing any idea.

We know God and we know the soul, Descartes replied, but our ideas of those things are not images nor are they describable in sensory terms. One cannot help recall Plato's Forms, likewise indescribable unless talent and effort is invested.

Passions of the Soul: We Are Machines

The work titled *Passions of the Soul* was written and published in French in the winter of 1645–46, only four years before his death. It was the last work he published—he was reluctant, as always, to publish, and the publisher, Louis Elziver, was hardly eager, since all of Descartes's publishers complained about the small sales of his books. It was Chanut, French ambassador to Sweden, and others who urged it through, and the final copies were probably received by Descartes in Sweden before his death. Here, more clearly than elsewhere, he argued for the "human machine" with the supernatural soul.

Living and Dead Bodies

Descartes compared a human body and a watch (*Passions* article VI, in Haldane and Ross 1911), much as Hobbes was comparing humans and machines during the same period. Descartes had done quite a number of dissections and was struck by the obvious mechanism of the body, just as is anyone who performs dissection. Descartes was also impressed by the mechanical statues that were the rage in the gardens of the nobility during this period. Engineers had devised not only hydraulic statues of Greek deities, such as Diana and Neptune, but even mechanical ducks that swam and excreted pellets!

He referred when young to a so-called "Palace of Marvels" and a curious magnetized automaton that is not mentioned in later writings.[13] Dissection and the mechanical amusements fit the larger theme of universal mechanism that Descartes, Newton, and a host of lesser savants were popularizing. For Descartes, the "human machine" was a given, but his previous conclusions required also a soul that was of different substance.

Why Mind and Body?

The argument for the fundamental distinction between mind and body was obviously not original with Descartes—but Descartes was different. For one thing, he did not always make the distinction, and in early writings he described matter as having an "active principle, love, charity, and harmony" (Haldane 1905, p. 50).

As he wrote to the clerics at Paris when he published the Meditations, his argument for God and for the soul was a reasoned one, not a statement of faith, and this was unique, at least since Aquinas's attempt to convince intelligent "gentiles." In several of his writings Descartes argued for the mind/body distinction on grounds that only *cogito* is clearly and distinctly perceived, while all that pertains to body is uncertain. Mind cannot be doubted, but matter can be.

Retaining the ancients' concept of substance, he referred to matter as extended substance, meaning that it occupies space. It also obeys mechanical principles (natural law), moves, generates heat, and does not think. Animals are constructed solely of extended substance.

Mind, the thinking aspect of the soul, is nonextended substance, is free, occupies no space, and is never experienced as sensation, any more than is God. Mind thinks and experiences in two ways: as actions and passions (article XVII). Actions are "desires" of the soul, including will, and aspects of reason (such as doubting, conceiving, affirming, denying, imagining, and refusing). All of these were supposed to be independent of the body.

The passions, on the other hand, required the body and include all of the senses and emotions. The senses were enumerated in the usual way, with vision by far the most important, and the emotions were conventional also (wonder, love, hatred, aversion, joy, and sadness). Animals experience the passions as well, though they were supposed to lack the active part of the soul and their chances for an afterlife were slim indeed. Note again that all sensation lacks distinctness, since it depends on the body.

Evidence That the World Is Not Merely Sensation

Descartes realized that sensation is unreliable and dependent on the condition of the perceiver; nonetheless, as undependable as sensation is, we may know that there is indeed real extended substance at the root of it. He illustrated this by noting that wax has a specific taste, color, texture, and smell and that it makes no sound when we strike it with a rod. However, if it is heated, all of these properties change. Yet, despite the ringing sound that now is made when it is struck and the difference in appearance and taste, we still know that it is the same piece of wax. This owes to innate ideas of substance that do not depend on specific sensory evidence.

Perhaps a more important reason for his assuming the dualism of mind and body appears in a reply to one of Hobbes's objections in the second edition of the *Meditations*. Descartes wrote: "On the other hand, both logicians and as a rule all men are wont to say that all substances are of two kinds, spiritual and corporeal" (Kaufman 1963, p. 79).

Will and Understanding

The relation between the passions and desires (the passions and actions) of the mind, or thinking part of the soul, are clear when we consider the will and the understanding (*Principles of Philosophy*, XXXII). The understanding is what we might call "thought" and requires two sources—innate ideas and the passions, including sensation, memory, imagination, and all other body activities. This is the source of all error. Thought also has access to innate ideas, existing as potential to which form is given—these include "ideas" of self, God, perfection, substance, quality, infinity, unity, and perhaps others.

As thought throws out ideas of sensation, and imagination, mixed with glimmers of innate ideas, will freely chooses to assent, dissent, attend, or ignore. A "wise" person will choose to attend to clear ideas and remains free of error. A fool has a foolish will that attends to sensory ideas as if they were clear and complains that the idea of God is vague!

The Machine of Our Body

A thinned version of the blood pumped from the heart fills the cavities in the skull and is released when tiny tubes are opened by tiny valves. Descartes frequently referred to his essay on optics and the nerves and muscles that he saw operating the eye—these were the basis for his interpretation of the body machine in general. These animal spirits flow into the muscles and swell them, causing contraction (and elongation of antagonists).

The sensory nerves may be viewed as bell ropes that are pulled or vibrated or cut and so cause sensations of color, warmth, and pain. Even humidity causes specific patterns of release of animal spirits and the accompanying sensations. Specific pores in the brain correspond to specific sensory memories, and the "swishing" of animal spirits to them triggers those memories. Attention means that the spirits are still, and imagining and dreaming, like sensing, mean that the spirits are active.

Sleep comes when the sensory "lines" loosen and the valves shut, draining the spirits from the head. Worn paths account for memory and habit, and some paths come preworn, as is the case when we interpret a retinal image and pupil size as "a far object." Other preset connections show just how much a machine the body is:

If someone quickly thrusts his hand against our eyes as if to strike us, even though we know him to be our friend, that he only does it in fun, and that he will take great care not to hurt us, we have all the same trouble in preventing ourselves from closing them.... (*Passions*, article XIII)

In the same work, Descartes proposed a biological basis for the development of habits. In article XVI he remarked that "the machine of our body" is formed such that movement of the animal spirits causes them to open some pores and paths more than others. And nerve paths joined to sense organs may be opened frequently, allowing easier passage of spirits. Together, "movements that we make without our will contributing thereto" are habits that are no different in kind from the movements of a watch.

Experience may also change a bird dog's natural reaction to the sight of game and the sound of a gun, and it may change our reaction to food:

Thus when we unexpectedly meet with something very foul in food that we are eating with relish, the surprise that this event gives us may so change the disposition of our brain, that we can no longer see any such food without horror, while we formerly ate it with pleasure...and the same thing is noticed in brutes.... (article L)

Writers referred to such aversions long before Descartes's time, but the significance of classical conditioning and learned aversions would not be recognized until the twentieth century.

A Thought on Descartes's Mind/Body Separation

Descartes was condemned in his day and thereafter for his mind/body dualism. Some criticisms were (and are) frivolous; for example, he had proposed the pineal body as the point of interaction between mind and body. The pineal was the only organ that he could find that did not occur as a pair, bilaterally symmetrical, like the arms, legs, eyes, teeth, and most internal organs, including brain structures.

In Descartes's mechanical person, the pineal acted almost as a valve, directing animal spirits from the ventricles through the tubes (nerves) to inflate the muscles. Through the pineal, the body affected the soul and vice versa, recalling that the body could run just fine without the soul.

Now, pineal means "shaped like a pine cone," and the pineal body serves some function in governing diurnal cycles—the third eye on the top of some reptiles' heads projects to the pineal. He chose the pineal because he believed it occurred only in humans and only humans have souls. In this respect, he clearly was wrong. However, that is of little matter—whatever organ he may have proposed as the point of interaction of mind and body would have been equally wrong. Let's forget the pineal body.

What of the mind/body distinction itself, apart from the problem of interaction? That is the distinction of common sense, the same common sense that supposes that demons and gods cause fire, rain, and drought. It is also the position taken by the ancient dualists, Pythagoras and Plato and their myriad descendants and followers, including many religious and mystical writers, such as Plotinus and Augustine.

Ancient scientists, on the other hand, were apt to be monists, who disregarded or denied mind/body dualism. This includes the Milesians and Eleatics, both of which were materialist monists, and Aristotle and his followers over the centuries. Averroes and Aquinas are included in that group, and the latter's theology can easily be seen to be more congenial to science than that of Augustine, which it replaced.

Given this affinity between monism and science, how can Descartes, who was beyond any doubt a scientist, go to such lengths to argue for the substantial difference between mind and body? The answer is not hard to find and also explains Galileo's position, as well as that of many subsequent and contemporary scientists. In short, Descartes (and Galileo) wanted to explain the universe as a neat mechanism, involving matter, local motion, and forces that were transmitted by impulse only. It was a universe from which all Aristotelian essences had been expunged—matter was matter, whether a person's arm or a block of wood. The only difference was density and composition of corpuscles. Everything that was not matter was outside their explanatory scheme and should be considered outside nature. The Aristotelians had mixed the natural and the unnatural, and the contribution of the Enlightenment was to unmix them.

Christina of Sweden

Descartes's wishes to be left in peace were thwarted through his life, but never more so than when he was put into correspondence with Queen Christina of Sweden. This was the doing of the French ambassador, Chanut, and led to Descartes's premature death.

Christina was the daughter of Gustavus Adolphus, considered the greatest Swedish king, who was a champion of Protestantism and who brought Sweden into the Thirty Years' War. Gustavus died when Christina was five, and she became queen in 1644, at the age of eighteen. Described as eccentric, she "thought that, as a sovereign, she had the right to waste the time of great men" (Russell 1945, p. 560) and sent questions to Descartes on the nature of love. Raised in the company of men and shielded from the influence of women, she was raised to lead Sweden, powerful after its part in the Thirty Years' War.

However, she was interested in philosophy—aware of the revolution that was the Enlightenment, she wanted instruction from the best teachers available. She wondered about the answers to questions such as, "What is the nature of love?," "How do we develop a love of God from natural knowledge?," and "Which is worse, excess love or hate?"

Descartes sent her a treatise on love, as well as his writings on the "passions of the soul," which evidently impressed her, since she asked him to come to her court. After some time he agreed, and she sent a warship to transport him to what he described as a "land of bears, in the midst of rocks and ice" (Kersey 1989, p. 76). He arrived in September of 1649 to find that Christina wanted instruction but could spare time only at five in the morning, when she was fresh and undisturbed.

The winter was the worst that Scandinavia had seen in a very long time, and Chanut became seriously ill. Descartes cared for him, and that, along with the unaccustomed early rising and the cold, resulted in Descartes's death by pneumonia in February 1650. Chanut recovered, and Christina abdicated in 1654, having named her cousin, Charles X Gustavus, as her successor. She never married, converted to Catholicism, and moved to Rome, where she died in 1689, poor and unknown.

A Message from LaMettrie: Is Mind Necessary?

Article XL of *The Passions* includes the following statement:

The passions incite the mind to will the things to which they prepare the body, so that the sentiment of fear incites it to will to fly; that of courage to will to fight, and so on of the rest.

We might well wonder with Julian Offray de La Mettrie (1709–1751) if "mind" really has any part in such a sequence—it appears superfluous, as the following variation shows: "The passions incite the body, so that the sentiment of fear incites it to fly; that of courage to fight, and so on of the rest." It was easy to conclude, as did La Mettrie, that Descartes's body/machine needed no "nonextended substance" and that Descartes's introduction of mind was "but a trick of skill, a ruse of style, to make theologians swallow a poison, hidden in the shade of an analogy which strikes everybody else and which they alone fail to notice."[14] Julian de la Mettrie admired the mechanistic aspect of Descartes and assumed that the "unextended substance," the mind that could operate independent of the body, was only "a trick of skill" intended to deceive.

La Mettrie echoed Aristotle when he asked for one small change in Descartes's machine—let matter have feeling:

Since all the faculties of the soul depend to such a degree on the proper organization of the brain and of the whole body, that apparently they are but this organization itself, the soul is clearly an enlightened machine...a few more wheels, a few more springs than in the most perfect animals. (*L'Homme Machine*, 1748, trans. Bussey and Calkins)

Like most presocratic Greeks, and like Aristotle, Aquinas, and Hobbes, La Mettrie was unwilling to posit a spiritual substance that was independent of matter—this materialist position was similar to that expressed in Dewey's paper on the reflex arc concept (1896). "Taking nothing for granted," La Mettrie cited evidence showing that mind and body are inextricably linked and that an independent soul is a chimera. He was a physician, as may be guessed by a reader of his evidence.

First, the flesh of all animals, including humans, palpitates after death, and muscles separated from the body contract when stimulated. Intestines, removed from the body, may continue peristaltic movement for a long time. An injection of hot water may reanimate the heart and muscles after movement has ceased. A frog's or toad's heart may be kept beating for an hour if it is placed on a hot table or chair. Men whose hearts have been cut out while alive have leapt several times, just as beheaded chickens, kittens, and puppies may walk about for a considerable time. In all of these gruesome cases, life/vitality appears to be distributed through a body as an aspect of biological material, and this animation shows itself when body parts are stimulated or the body is left heartless or headless.

A second class of evidence comes from the obvious effects of the body on the mind. A fever convinced La Mettrie that thought is wholly dependent on bodily processes, and other examples abound.

This identity of mind with organized matter produces an old and venerable ethical tradition, and La Mettrie cited Pythagoras as its originator. All ethics reduces to bodily care, and this is a function of temperance: "it is the source of all virtues, as intemperance is the source of all vices."[15] The picture of the Enlightenment human–machine was summarized well by La Mettrie:

To be a machine, to feel to think, to know how to distinguish good from bad, as well as blue from yellow, in a word, to be born with an intelligence and a sure moral instinct, and to be but an animal, are therefore characters which are no more contradictory, than to be an ape or a parrot and to be able to give oneself pleasure. (Herrnstein and Boring 1965, p. 278)

However, this machine is not the dead mechanism of Descartes or of Plato. It is a machine with feeling, closer to the vision of Aristotle and of Aquinas.

6   British Empiricism and Kant: What Is *Reality?*

...at no time in his life would Locke admit his debt to Hobbes...it may...have been due to the fact that the word "Hobbist" came to be a pejorative one...and Locke was forever anxious to avoid a bad name. (Cranston 1957, pp. 19, 21)

Locke and the New Way of Ideas

The Oxford Scholar

When Locke (see figure 6.1) was nineteen, he participated in the political machinations that were necessary for admission (called "election") to Oxford, enlisting the help of his father and of powerful friends, some of whom were generals of Oliver Cromwell, ruler, as Lord Protector, of England. His first publication was a pair of hymns in praise of Cromwell in 1654 on the occasion of the defeat of the Dutch.

The classical education of Westminster was continued at Oxford, where students arose at five for chapel, ate breakfast at six and then studied logic, metaphysics, and classical languages until dinner at noon. Two hours of work followed, and supper was taken at seven. Conversation with each other or with tutors was always in Latin, and the B.A. degree was awarded only after surviving a Disputation, in which a thesis had to be maintained or attacked before an audience, much as was the practice in the time of Thomas Aquinas.

At the same time, the influence of the Puritans was so great that all Oxford men of Locke's generation had to hear at least two sermons a day and remember them. Each Sunday between six and nine each student had to go to some "person of known ability and piety" to summarize the sermons they had heard (Cranston 1957, p. 31).

Figure 6.1
Locke. Courtesy of the Archives of the History of American Psychology, University of
Akron.

Locke the Physician

At Oxford, Locke escaped the normal requirement to take holy orders
in order to remain at the University by soliciting a letter from the King
himself, received by the dean on November 14, 1666. Locke had a master's degree and had hoped to gain a Doctor of Medicine degree without the bother of going to all the lectures required for the degree of
Bachelor of Medicine. He had been working with David Thomas, a
renowned physician, and had shown himself quite handy. On Locke's
request, the chancellor of Christ Church College of Oxford had
announced that Locke be exempted from the bachelor's requirements,
but that had been ignored by the medical faculty. Having acquired a
master's, one could remain only by becoming an ecclesiastic or a physician. The King's letter allowed Locke to remain without becoming
either.

Later Locke tried to gain an honorary D.M.; several such degrees were to be given in November of 1670, on the occasion of the visit of the Prince of Orange, and Lord Shaftesbury, Anthony Ashley Cooper, wrote a letter requesting the degree for Locke. John Fell was still Dean of Christ Church, and he objected, as did others. Lord Shaftesbury was miffed, but Locke received no D.M. during his life (Cranston 1957, p. 139). Nonetheless, he sought University chairs of medicine and frequently treated patients.

His most important patient was Anthony Ashley Cooper,[1] first Earl of Shaftesbury, the diminutive nobleman whose household Locke joined. Lord Ashley had suffered a fall that left internal injuries which he treated with therapeutic waters. However, in May of 1668 he became seriously ill due to a "supporting hydatid cyst of the liver" (Cranston 1957, p. 113). Locke consulted the best doctors in the country, including the Puritan Sydenham, and then hired a surgeon barber to open Ashley's abdomen. Locke inserted a silver tube to drain the abscess, and Ashley was restored to health. He wore a silver, then a gold, drain tube for the rest of his life and could not have been more grateful to his "physician."

The Origins of the *Essay*

Locke corresponded with a number of people, one being Gabriel Towerson, who raised the issue of the possible existence of the "Law of Nature," not to be confused with what came to be called the "laws of nature" in the twentieth century. The Law of Nature is the moral law—the right and wrong—that the Creator has made "evident to and compelling to every rational being." The Stoics believed in such a law, as did the medievals and many of Locke's time. It requires little "reflection" to see that Descartes believed in such knowledge, since it must exist in creatures who have clear and distinct ideas of a Deity.

It is difficult to believe that the Law of Nature was key to the divine right of kings in the minds of many thinkers of the time. In fact, acquaintances of Locke, Robert Sanderson and James Tyrrell, collaborated in 1661 in editing a book written by Tyrrell's grandfather, James Ussher, Archbishop of Armagh. The book was titled, "The Power Communicated by God to the Prince and the Obedience Required of the Subject." According to Cranston (1957, p. 66), "its contents fulfill the promise made in the title." In Locke's England, the divine right of kings was closely tied to the belief in innate ideas, hence the interest in "Natural Law."

In 1660 Locke argued that the Law of Nature exists, since God exists and made laws governing everything, including human conduct. However, Locke concluded that our knowledge of the Law is not innate, as Descartes would have it—rather, it is derived from sensory experience. His arguments are more convincing regarding the sensory basis of all knowledge—empiricism—than they are concerning the Law of Nature. But this would come decades later in his famous *Essay*.

Reading Descartes

Locke began reading Descartes in the late 1660s and found that he "relished" philosophical studies. In particular, he found that he often disagreed with Descartes but that he could always understand him, "from whence he was encouraged to think that his not having understood others had, possibly, not proceeded altogether from a defect in his understanding" (Lady Masham, in Cranston 1957, p. 100). Locke's reading was restricted to the *Meditations* and to the *Discourse*, once the latter was available in Latin.

The *Essay Concerning Human Understanding*

Locke's masterpiece was the "essay" that runs to more pages than one expects of an essay, since it was written over a twenty-year period and comprises four volumes! It was intended as the work of "an underlabourer in clearing the ground a little and removing some of the rubbish that lies in the way to knowledge."[2]

What is knowledge and what can we know for certain? This was Locke's question, and it is clear that it is the same as Descartes's question. Their answers were similar. Since Locke read Descartes, and not the other way around, any influence of one on the other has to be that of Descartes on Locke. This was the case and has been documented by Mrs. C. S. Johnson (Cranston 1957, p. 265).

The New Way of Ideas Locke began consideration of the limits of human understanding by examining the nature and source of knowledge. Seemingly contradicting Descartes, he proposed that all knowledge comes from one source—"I imagine that all knowledge is founded on and ultimately derives itself from sense, or something analogous to it, which may be called sensation." That is, of course, the very definition of empiricism and the reason that Locke is identified with that view.

If we consider our experience, wrote Locke, we see that it has a content, and that content is divisible into ideas. What we know are ideas, and an idea is defined as any content that can be the object of our attention. He gives examples ranging from ants to apples to elephants to an army; each of these corresponds to an idea. This characterization of experience deserves comment.

First, this is a purely mediational point of view—we never experience things directly, as Aristotle would have it, but only through the "intervention of ideas." Hence, this is a view similar to that of Democritus and the other representationalist theories. The assumption that knowledge is a *representation* of some outer reality that is not directly knowable is a key assumption of most rationalist theories—yet, Locke is the father of English Empiricism!

He is empiricist in that he argued, through much of the *Essay*, that all knowledge comes from experience. Sensation acts to fill the "empty cabinet" or to write on the "tabula rasa—blank slate." Locke was adamant on this point and offered evidence that knowledge is acquired from experience, not innate universals awakened by sense, as Descartes held. This is clear in chapter II: "No Innate Principles in the Mind."

This may be shown in four main ways. First, even those "earliest truths" that we know do not require innate knowledge. The ideas of objects in space and time and of geometry are acquired over months and years of experience in a world that is laid out in time and space. Related to that is the fact that universal agreement on such matters does not require the possession of shared universal ideas. Locke rightly pointed out that any alternative is preferable to the positing of innate ideas, since that conclusion stops thought on the matter, as in the case of ethics and "Natural Law."

A third argument against innate ideas is the common observation that children and idiots lack them. Locke found it absurd to suggest that children really do have inborn ideas of "right and wrong" and of the Pythagorean theorem, but that experience is necessary to awaken them. That was the position of Plato, of course, and of all the Neoplatonists, including those of Locke's day.

A final argument for the empirical origin of knowledge and against innate ideas lies in the development of reason in children. Locke suggested that there is a clear progression from simple sensing ("see the blue ball"), to abstracting ("blue" as a concept), learning sameness and difference, naming, and reasoning. This gradual development is there for any observer to see and makes unnecessary the succession of "aha" experiences that accompany the awakening of innate ideas.

Distinction between Primary and Secondary Qualities Locke's friend Boyle had proposed a distinction between experiences that are caused by objects and those that are produced by the observer, and so had Galileo, Hobbes, Descartes, and others. Locke followed their lead and distinguished primary and secondary qualities. His definition of primary qualities is worth quoting (Burtt 1939, p. 265): "Take a grain of wheat, divide it into two parts: each part still has *solidity*, *extension*, *figure*, and *mobility* . . ."

Qualities are powers of objects to produce ideas in us. Primary qualities are those that produce ideas in us that resemble the objects involved. When we speak of solidity, form, number, size, and motion, we refer to real things that exist independent of us. They are the "common sensibles of Plato and Aristotle." We know of such qualities because we live in a mechanical world of particles and "imperceptible particles" given off by objects strike us, affecting us "by impulse." These particles are suited to us as to "essences and archetypes" in our bodies that "answer to them." The "nerves . . . convey them from without to their audience in the brain, the mind's presence-room (as I may so call it)" (*Essay*, Book II, chapter III, part 1, in Kaufman 1961, p. 198).

Can one be an empiricist and thus argue for the sensory basis of all knowledge, yet believe in such primary qualities? Locke could and took for granted that the cherry may lose its color, smell, odor, texture, and all other sensory attributes, yet there remains a *"je ne sais quoi"* that is the substance of the cherry. Any reader of Locke can see that he was not the sort of person who could doubt the existence of material reality. If a listener could not understand how he can know that substance exists, solid stuff, Locke answered:

If any one asks me, *what this solidity is*, I send him to his senses to inform him: let him put a flint or a football between his hands, and then endeavor to join them, and he will know. If he thinks that this is not a sufficient explanation of solidity . . . I promise to tell him what it is . . . when he tells me what thinking is, or wherein it consists; or explains to me what extension or motion is . . . (*Essay*, Book II, chapter IV, part 6, in Kaufman 1961, p. 201)

Descartes had to rely on a benevolent God to guarantee reality, and Locke would not seriously dispute that conclusion. However, Locke used simpler appeals against the argument that all may be a dream, and that "reasoning and arguments are of no use, truth and knowledge nothing." Can such a critic contend that there is not "a very manifest difference between dreaming of being in the fire, and being actually in it" (*Essay*, Book IV, chapter II, part 14, in Kaufman 1961, p. 227).

Secondary Qualities   Galileo had defined science in 1625 and explicitly ruled out colors, sounds, heat and cold, and other secondary qualities, as Boyle had named them.[3] Hobbes and Descartes had recognized secondary qualities as well, and Locke could hardly have been unaware of their views. Yet, oddly, it is his name that is most often associated with the distinction between primary and secondary qualities.

Secondary qualities produce ideas that do not resemble their causes, as Locke defines them—since they are partly produced by "particles in our senses." We feel pain when steel divides our flesh only because God arranged such a relation between an idea and an object. Color is an idea produced by particle motion affecting the particles in our senses, and, like all secondary qualities, the "texture and motion of primary qualities," along with the action of particles in our senses, produce the idea.

Like primary qualities, which produce ideas of mass, number, movement, and so on because of imperceptible particles that strike us, secondary qualities also produce their effects "by impulse." However, it is the pattern, the "texture and motion" of the particles, that is important. This seems little different from attributing color to the frequency and wavelength of light that is in fact the major physical correlate of color.

But we never know the objects "as they are." Locke made official that basic empiricist belief—that the basis of knowledge is sensation and sensation is a function of the perceiver. Objects have the power to produce ideas in us—their qualities—and we know those ideas, never the things themselves. "Why say that warmth is in the fire and pain is not?" Both ideas are in us, and they are there as particular ideas, not as general ideas (universals or innate ideas) that are awakened by sensation. That point is illustrated well by Locke's answer to a question posed in 1690 by a friend in Ireland. We could not be certain that Locke's answer was correct until the twentieth century.

Molyneux's Question: Can The Blind "Receive" Sight?

Locke was at pains to show that we do not come with universal, "innate" ideas that are awakened by sensory experience. Locke dealt with this issue in answer to a query from a friend in Dublin, the astronomer and philosopher William Molyneux, who wrote:

Suppose a man born blind, and now adult, and taught by his touch to distinguish between a cube and a sphere (be) made to see: (would he be able) by his sight, before he touched them... distinguish and tell which was the globe and which was the cube? (Locke 1690, Book 11, Ch. 9, Sect. 8)

Locke's answer was no, on grounds that ideas are specific—they do not awaken universal ideas, such as those of form (globe and cube). Such ideas are built from experience and, if the experience is solely tactual, then there will be no knowledge of visual form. Molyneux corresponded frequently with Locke and asked such a question, no doubt, because his wife was blind, and there was no good information on the restoration of vision after long blindness. Since Locke's time, we have gained a lot of information corroborating his opinion.

Hebb, in his classic *Organization of Behavior*, published in 1949, summarized the data collected by the German Von Senden, who published in 1932 an account of the effects of newly acquired vision in adults. Gregory and Sacks provide more recent accounts (Gregory 1963, 1987; Sacks 1993). The pattern of findings is as described by Hebb:

Investigators (of vision following operation for congenital cataract) are unanimous in reporting that the perception of a square, circle, or triangle, or of sphere or cube, is very poor. To see one of these as a whole object, with distinctive characteristics immediately evident, is not possible for a long period. The most intelligent and best-motivated patient has to seek corners painstakingly even to distinguish a triangle from a circle. There is for weeks a practically zero capacity to learn names for such figures, even when tactual recognition is prompt and complete. (1949, p. 28)

Even when learning had occurred, it did not readily generalize to new situations. One patient who had learned to identify a white cardboard square could no longer do so when it was turned around, so that its yellow back was presented. Other patients, who had learned to identify an egg, a potato, and a sugar cube in ordinary white light could no longer do so when the objects appeared in colored light.

Hebb suggested that a similar learning process takes place in each of our infancies, agreeing with Locke's position, at least in general.

Richard Gregory has described other cases of this kind, usually corroborating Hebb's account but occasionally supporting the "universal ideas" position, albeit weakly.

However, in 1993 the eminent neurologist and writer Oliver Sacks provided a detailed account of a man's gaining of vision after forty years of blindness. The title of the article, "To See and Not To See," prepares the reader for what might be called the latest word on the issue. The patient was at first agnosic—did not recognize objects—so indeed there were no universal ideas to call up. Sacks noted that "there were no visual memories to support a perception, there was no world of experience and meaning awaiting him. He saw, but what he saw had no coherence. His retina and optic nerve were active, transmitting impulses, but his brain could make no sense of them" (Sacks 1993, p. 61). Locke was right.

Reflection: The Second Source of Ideas

In addition to sensation, there is a second source of our ideas and that is reflection, or the mind's operations upon its ideas. This includes thinking, willing, doubting, believing, knowing, and reasoning—all faculties of the mind and all somehow derived from sensation. Locke wrote that "in bare naked Perception, the Mind is for the most part only passive" (Book II, ix.1). However, the mind becomes active mighty quickly, it appears, so that "if not taken notice of, there is no perception" (Book II, ix.3). Perception is thus the first faculty of the mind and corresponds to what occurs when one "sees, hears, feels, &c., or thinks."

Locke proposed a very active mind when he discussed reflection— "thinking . . . wherein the mind is active; where it, with some degree of voluntary attention, considers any thing" (Book II, ix.1). After perception, the mind may reflect through memory, discernment (judging same or different), comparing, compounding, naming, and abstraction. The senses begin by letting in the light.

Words, Definitions, and Ideas

These operations of the mind—reflection—create new ideas and thus new knowledge, as the simple ideas of the senses become the complex ideas of thought. Locke believed that words merely label ideas and that simple ideas are those that cannot really be defined but whose meanings can only be taught by example. Showing a child a picture of a pear along with the word is only to give an ostensive definition, no definition at all in Locke's mind.

Words with meaning, that can be defined by presenting other words, are those representing complex ideas, products of reflection. Words like "incest" and "adultery" (Locke's examples) may be understood by one who has never witnessed either but who is familiar with the simple ideas of which the complexes are composed.

Many complex words are meaningful, as established by convention, and such meaning may be unequivocal and precise. However, other words are not so precisely definable and form the large class of vague words that are used by rascals for purposes of persuasion. Such words are "duty" and "honor," and they also deceive those who are led to believe in some real essences—the "essence" of duty and honor.

Such vague terms destroy the "instruments of knowledge and communication." "He that hath names without ideas, wants meaning in his words, and speaks only empty sounds." Such a person lacks the "materials of true knowledge in his understanding and hath instead thereof chimeras" (Book III, x.8). Critics were later to accuse Locke himself of such misuse of language when considering the use to which he put the noun, "idea." Some even accused him of tacitly accepting Descartes's doctrine of innate ideas.

Reflection, Willing, Pleasure, and Pain: Locke on Motivation

Reflection gives us the ideas of perception ("I am seeing something") and of willing ("I am wanting or intending something or some act"). Pleasures and pains accompany almost all of our ideas, both of sensation and reflection. By pleasure and pain he meant "whatever delights or molests us; whether it arises from the thoughts of our minds, or anything operating on our bodies (Book II, chapter 7, in Kaufman 1961, p. 202). The degrees of pleasure and pain may be called satisfaction, delight, pleasure, happiness, or uneasiness, trouble, pain, torment, misery, anguish, or other things. Without this color added to our ideas by the "infinite wise Author of our being,"

we should have no reason to prefer one thought or action to another, negligence to attention, or motion to rest . . . and pass . . . time only in a lazy, lethargic dream. (Book II, chapter VII, in Kaufman 1961, pp. 202–203)

Pleasure and pain thus become the attractive power of ideas and determine that we pay attention to them. Some of these ideas are those of action, and we thus are moved to act. This is hedonism—the doctrine that our actions are guided by pleasures and pains—and it may therefore appear that Locke was a "Hobbist" as far as free will goes. That is, free will is a nonentity, since will is merely a "name for the last appetite preceding action," as Hobbes put it.

In fact, Locke was congratulated by friends for shunning the "Hobbist" doctrine of automatism and similarly avoiding the "free will" position. Locke believed that the question of free will was a fool's issue (he was right) and that all that we can know is that reflection gives us the idea of will as a product of its work on the simple ideas. We do not know whether the will is free of determinants. Hence, the free-will issue is "a long agitated but unreasonable problem" (Cranston 1957, p. 379).

This Sort of Madness
Locke's only treatment of the association of ideas concerns prejudice, madness, unreasonableness, and flawed thinking—he wrote that "I shall be pardoned for calling it by so harsh a name as Madness, when it is considered that opposition to Reason deserves that Name, and is really Madness" (Book II, chapter 33).

When our ideas correspond to the true order of the world sequence, the "connexions" are natural. However, when they arise out of chance pairing or unwise education, the connexions (associations) are unnatural and lead to much mischief. Locke offers the common example of the ghost and goblin stories that are told to children to ensure that they will fear the dark and the musician who cannot help but hum a tune once the opening notes sound.

A person feels injured by another and constantly thinks of the injury and the offending person, cementing them together and thus raising hatred from what might have been a simple slight. Another person suffers great pain during a surgical operation that provides a cure. Despite gratitude to the operator (physician), the patient so associates pain and physician that the sight of the latter cannot be tolerated.

Locke thought that time would loosen the bond of association and that often that was the only treatment. As he wrote:

…why time cures some disorders in the mind, which reason cannot.… The death of a child, that was the daily delight of his mother's eyes, and joy of her soul, rends from her heart the whole comfort of her life, and gives her all the torment imaginable…some…spend their lives in mourning, and carry an incurable sorrow to their graves. (Book II, chapter XXXIII)

But such is *not* the usual case for Locke, just as it was not for Hobbes. Believers in a material world who treat the mind as a mirror need no laws of association, apart from the contiguity in time and space that is characteristic of the world's events.

Locke construed the mind as an independent entity, almost as independent as the mind of Descartes. It came without innate ideas, but faculties that comprised reflection fully served that function. Real empiricism and associationism were yet to come.

Locke's Later Life and Lady Masham

Locke returned to England in 1688 after several years in France and Holland. With a new government that was favorably disposed toward him, Locke became Commissioner of Appeals and then Commissioner of Trade and Plantages.

In an opinion written for the Board of Trade in 1697, he proposed what seems vicious treatment of the poor, though he saw it as charitable. He urged that any male between fourteen and fifty found begging near a seaport was to be held at hard labor until one of His Majesty's ships came by so that he could then be pressed into lifelong naval service.

The workhouses in which he urged that paupers be kept and where their children were to learn the virtues of labor and of religion were the models for the institutions that appeared in Dickens's portrayals of the life of the poor in England. The pauper children were to have their "bellies kept full of bread" alone as normal diet and they were to be given watery gruel only when the weather was very cold. Since the same fire that heats a room could heat the gruel, the expense would be minimal. With such strict control over expenses and elimination of frills, the cost of keeping a pauper child to adulthood would be entirely offset by the labor contributed by the child.

Locke suffered from asthma all of his life and so moved to the country, twenty miles from London, in 1691. He moved into the estate of Sir Francis Masham and Lady Masham, Damaris Cudworth, who Locke had known for nine years and with whom he carried on a long correspondence. She was the daughter of the Cambridge Platonist Ralph Cudworth and was herself converted from that view to Lockian empiricism.

She and Locke had earlier exchanged love letters as "Philander" and "Philoclea." Presumably they didn't marry because Locke was fifty and she was twenty-four when they met. When he moved in, to spend the next thirteen years, he brought upwards of 5,000 books and rooms of furniture. He occupied a prime two, and later three, rooms of the estate, which at that time had a moat and several lakes, providing a pleasant, if quiet, environment for him. He remained there until his death in October 1704 in a chair with Demaris at his side.[4]

She defended Locke's views against the Platonists, even criticizing a book by one of them, John Norris, that was dedicated to her. And Norris was associated with Mary Astell, likewise a Platonist, whose 400-page *The Christian Religion* was an attempt to refute Locke point for point in the old scholastic manner. In 1690 Lady Masham published *Discourse Concerning the Love of God*, where she charged Norris with promoting "theories of love for pure abstract forms" and thus turning attention from real-world problems. She also ridiculed Mary Astell's proposal that ethics depends on pure (Platonic) ideas. Masham defended Locke even after his death and her biography of Locke was published after her own death.

George Berkeley: Reality as Mental Context

Looking backward, we can see that Berkeley was entirely correct. (Berlinski 1995, p. 114)

On January 29, 1729, a ship that had begun its voyage at Gravesend on the Thames reached Newport, Rhode Island, carrying Dean George Berkeley (pronounced Barkley). Berkeley was a newly married clergyman of forty-five who had come to the colonies to buy land for a college in the Bermudas. He had worked on the most ambitious educational plan since Plato's *Republic*.[5] Berkeley had planned the project for five years and hoped that it would serve as a source of instruction for "English youth" and for "a number of young American savages, in Christian religion, practical mathematics, and other liberal arts and sciences."[6] He had raised five thousand pounds from private donors, and Prime Minister Robert Walpole had assured him another twenty thousand.

The mission to America ended in disappointment when Walpole diverted the funds for his college to the more pressing needs of a princess's marriage. His house in Newport still stands, and proceeds from the sale of ninety-six acres of land were donated to Yale University, as were 1,000 books.[7] He exerted a great personal influence on Samuel

Figure 6.2
Calkins. Courtesy of the Archives of the History of American Psychology, University of
Akron.

Johnson, an Episcopal missionary and Yale tutor, who later became the
first president of King's College, later renamed Columbia University.

Berkeley returned to England in 1731 and published *The Analyst* in
1734, an attack on materialism through the destruction of the conceptual bases for the calculus, as conceived by Newton. Queen Caroline
arranged that he be appointed Bishop of Cloyne in Ireland, resulting
in twenty years helping the Irish and in fighting policies that promoted
"the flourishing of our Protestant gentry, exclusive of the bulk of the
natives" (Calkins 1929, p. xvii, see figure 6.2). His writing during that
period is marked with the eccentricity of his promotion of tarwater, a
cure, he believed, for many ailments that he had learned from the
Indians of America.

In 1752 he moved to Oxford, an ideal place for a scholar, he felt,
where his son George was a student. He asked to resign his bishopric,
but George II refused, saying that he would die a bishop. Shortly thereafter he did just that, while sitting by the fire drinking tea in his house
on Holywell Street. His wife was reading aloud from Paul's first letter
to the Corinthians, and Berkeley's last words were a comment on that
piece of scripture.

Berkeley's philosophy had an enormous impact on thought, and that impact continues to this day. Hume adapted the epistemology of Berkeley so skillfully as to remain one of the most influential of philosophers. However, Berkeley's analysis of sensation and perception remained his. It was pure psychology, and that influence is still clear in modern theory and research. It all began as a reaction to Locke and a remedy for Locke's problem.

Berkeley's Correcting of Locke's Empiricism: We Can Never Know the World

This I cannot comprehend, for how can I know that the picture of anything is like that thing, when I never see that which it represents? (Locke, quoted by Aaron 1931)

Aaron followed the quotation above with, "Locke, no doubt failed to realise how devastating this criticism would prove to be in the subsequent history of philosophy. (As Berkeley saw, no representative theory of perception or of knowledge can withstand it)." Locke's quotation came from a critique of Malebranch included in a posthumous collection, and it appears certain that young George Berkeley read it no later than 1708, a year before his famous "New Theory of Vision" was published.

Berkeley (1687–1758) eventually became an Anglican bishop, and as a young man he was alarmed by the evident materialism of Locke's view. Locke's representational view held that our experience is no more than copies produced by a material world as it passes by and affects our senses. Berkeley found this view repulsive and suggested that Locke had made an odd and obvious error in his reasoning.

As subsequent events showed, Berkeley was correct. The story begins with his *An Essay Towards a New Theory of Vision*, published in 1709 when George Berkeley was twenty-two years old. To understand his achievement, a work of genius, considering the prevailing views of the time, we must consider also what might be called "The Old Theory of Vision."

Berkeley's "New Theory:" Distance Is Not Visible

Berkeley treated perception in his New Theory of Vision, proposing what later adopters called the context theory. The shape and size of objects, as well as their distance from us, are not directly perceived.

Instead, our experience depends upon the context of our ideas. A given retinal image, along with feelings of eye position (convergence/divergence) and accommodation (change in the shape of the lens), along with sensations of touch, "means" that an object is of such and such size and is at such and such a distance from us.

This opposes the "old theory," which was the nativist theory of Descartes that suggested that space perception is based on cues such as those dependent on imaginary lines extending from the eyes to objects. We judge the angle formed by the lines, their length (the intensity of light rays), and the diffusion of light rays; this, with an image read off the retina by the mind, is interpreted as depth.

Obviously, it is a materialist theory that construes us as machines that can calculate angles and judge the intensity of light rays, as well as their dispersion. Descartes saw no difficulty in this, since the soul actually does the judging as it reads the image formed on the pineal body. Space filled with objects is given and is known by the soul.

However, Berkeley argued otherwise; perception cannot be based on cues that we do not discern, that are not in experience. Who calculates angles as Descartes supposed? No one but geometers, like Descartes.

In vain shall all the *Mathematicians* in the World tell me, that I perceive certain *Lines* and *Angles* which introduce into my Mind the various *Ideas* of *Distance*: so long as my self am conscious of no such thing. (1709, in Herrnstein and Boring 1965, p. 120)

How do we perceive distance, or "outness," as Berkeley called it? It is a matter of customary contexts of associations. As he wrote in 1709:

A Man no more Sees and Feels the same Thing, than he Hears and Feels the same Thing.... They may, indeed, grow Greater, or Smaller, more Confused, or more Clear, or more Faint. But they do not, cannot Approach, or even seem to Approach, or Recede from us. (Berkeley 1732, no. 50)

Thus, the shape and size of objects, as well as their distance from us, are not directly perceived. Instead, our experience depends upon the customary context of our sensations. Consider an example given by William James (1890), who accepted this theory, as did many others. Hold up your index finger before your face at a distance of a foot or so and focus on it with both eyes. Continue to do this and close one eye, but keep that eye aimed at the finger. Now maintain that position and open the eye. You will see that the finger appears to move closer; why should that be?

The answer is simple. When we close an eye, the eyeball rotates outward slightly, though we believe that it remains trained on the finger, where we left it. When we open the eye, the eyeball returns to the finger, thus rotating slightly inward. In ordinary experience, when we are gazing at a target and our eyes rotate inward, it is because the object is approaching us.

Focus on the finger and move it slowly toward your nose and you will feel the movement of the eyeballs inward; this is referred to as convergence. Thus, the finger appears to move toward us because the retinal image is accompanied by sensations of convergence that ordinarily mean that an object is approaching. However, the experience is in us; it is our eyes' movement, and we are fooled.

A similar explanation applies in assessing the lengths of vertical and horizontal lines. If you draw a two-foot horizontal line on a blackboard facing a group of viewers and ask them to tell you when a vertical line, raised bisecting the horizontal, is equally long, you'll be in for a surprise. Cast it as an exercise in "manipulation of images," suggesting that the viewers mentally rotate the vertical and "compare" it with the horizontal. Once all have agreed that the vertical is as long as the horizontal, measure it off and you will be amazed to see it underestimated by perhaps thirty percent! Sometimes there is not enough blackboard left to complete the vertical line. Bartenders and servers know that a tall, narrow glass will lead to less drinking than will a short, wide glass, since we routinely overestimate verticals by twenty percent to thirty percent (Wansink and Van Ittersum 2003).

Locke's Error: Belief in Something Unknowable by Mind?

Imagine headlines that announced the discovery of the existence of a substance that is widely believed in but which is completely unknowable by the human mind. People of Berkeley's day did believe in such a substance, and, amazingly, great thinkers like Descartes and Locke were among the believers. However, belief in something "independent of and unknowable by mind" can only produce confusion. That is why Berkeley tried to stamp out this mystical belief in matter. What better way to stem the tide of materialism?

If one argues that all knowledge comes from the senses, as empiricists do, then one cannot also hold that we have innate "archetypes" that let us know primary qualities. If all knowledge is the product of our senses, then all that we can know are secondary qualities, dependent on us. We cannot even view secondary qualities as modified products of primary qualities, as Locke did; color is not apprehension of patterning of "imperceptible particles," any more than mass is apprehension of the particles themselves.

We have only sensory experience, not experience of particles—to say this is only to say what we mean by "empiricism." If we take away the taste and color and texture and all other "secondary qualities" from the cherry, we are not left with Locke's *"Je ne sais quoi."* If we take away its secondary qualities, we take away the cherry!

A World of Pure Experience   This expression was used almost two centuries later by William James, but it provides a fair description of Berkeley's proposal. If all that we experience is sensory, then all is dependent on us—all subjective! The world becomes only a plausible hypothesis, no more than the sum of our individual experiences. This is subjective idealism; what is real is ultimately mental (our experience), and it is particular to each individual.

When a tree falls in the forest, does it make a sound? Well, what is a sound? It is something that is heard; it is a part of the experience of some living thing. A falling tree may produce movement of air (or earth or water) which would produce "sound" if a hearer were present, but otherwise there would be no sound.

Sounds, smells, tastes, light and dark, colors, and objects are aspects of experience and thus exist only in the experiencer. Even the movements of air, earth, and water that occur when the tree falls, exist (are known) only if an observer experiences them.

Samuel Johnson was an essayist and author of a famous dictionary who scoffed at Berkeley's critique of materialism. Referring to the theory, he kicked a large stone, saying, "I refute it thus." He thought that he had shown that the world was "real," by which he meant "material" and thus more than a conglomeration of sensory experiences. But, of course, he showed no such thing. The sensations arising from his display were, like the visual sensations accompanying them, no more than sensations.

Berkeley's Associationism   If we have only our experience as the basis for reality, then we must be an associationist, or so Berkeley thought. Recall that Locke and Hobbes believed that we were copiers and that our experience mirrored the succession of real-world events. Thus, the only "association" involved is association by contiguity in time and space. If we cannot rely on the existence of any such world sequence, how do we account for the order of our thoughts?

Berkeley suggested that ideas are ordered not only by their contiguity in space and time (when last experienced) but also because of their similarity and causal relationships. He included a special case of contiguity which he called coexistence, to include things that change together over a range, like frequencies of thunder and of lightning.

The Analyst

It is easy for physicists and chemists, even mathematicians, to believe that their work is more solid and more "natural" than whatever is done by the humanist, theologian, or other "unnatural" scholar. According to this reasoning, the psychologist should always defer to the physiologist, who should bow to the chemist, who should admire the physicist. Such deference is commonly expected, and psychologists may seem to defer not only to natural scientists, where there is a precedent for deferral, but even to engineers and computer technicians.

Berkeley pointed out the foolishness in such "natural science worship" when he defended theology against the mathematics of Newton and Halley. He published *The Analyst* in 1734, destroying the foundations of the calculus, which had been invented independently by Newton and Leibniz only half a century earlier. In doing so, he left a lesson that we should not fail to learn.

He was responding to a critic of his conception of matter and space who pointed out that one could not take Berkeley seriously, since if he were correct, it led one "to suspect that even mathematics may not be very sound at the bottom" (Fraser 1901, p. 4), and, surely, mathematics is sound, is it not, especially when contrasted with the humanities, including religion? However, when a mathematician criticized religion, it became so much the worse for mathematics. A circulated opinion held that a poet of the time, Sir Samuel Garth, was impervious to Christianity when on his deathbed, since Sir Edmund Halley, famous mathematician and astronomer, had convinced him that this religion was an imposture, because its professed revelation of God was incomprehensible (Fraser 1901, p. 4).

Hearing of this, Berkeley, who was recovering from an illness and temporarily unable to read, found himself "for amusement" passing his mornings in "thinking of certain mathematical matters, which may possibly produce something." It produced *The Analyst* and a flurry of papers and pamphlets for and against Berkeley's arguments that continued for almost a decade. Berkeley's aim is clear in his introduction, addressed to Halley, who was at the time considered second in science only to his close friend, Isaac Newton. Berkeley began as follows:

A DISCOURSE ADDRESSED TO AN INFIDEL MATHEMATICIAN
Whereas then it is supposed that you apprehend more distinctly, consider more closely, infer more justly, and conclude more accurately than other men, and that you are therefore less religious because more judicious, I shall claim the privilege of a Free-thinker; and take the liberty to inquire into the object, principles, and method of demonstration admitted by the mathematicians of the present age, with the same freedom that you presume to treat the principles and mysteries of Religion; to the end that all men may see what right you have to lead, or what encouragement others have to follow you. (Fraser 1901, pp. 17–18)

Berkeley's examination is forty-three pages long and shows that a bishop may be a very skilled mathematician. The heart of his argument was summarized by the mathematicians Davis and Hersh (1981) and concerns the calculation of instantaneous velocity. For example, as an object falls, its velocity and position constantly change as a function of time. It follows that every intermediate velocity is achieved for an instant only, and it becomes a problem to determine that instant or to calculate velocity at some other instant.

Newton, in his earliest writings on the calculus, called the position function the "fluent" and the velocity function the "fluxion." One calculates the fluent using the equation: $s = 16t^2$, where s represents distance and t represents time in seconds; this is the familiar equation applicable to falling bodies ($s = 1/2gt^2$), and it may be used to calculate average velocity by finding s and dividing by t.

However, what of instantaneous velocity? This became intelligible only after the invention of the calculus. Integral calculus involves the summation of infinite series of such "instants" while differential calculus derives properties of a function at single instances. Consider the instantaneous velocity of an object one second after falling, that is, during the period from $t = 1$ and $t = 1 + dt$, where dt is an infinitesimally small increment of time.

The instantaneous velocity must refer to distance over time and thus is ds/dt, both infinitesimally small values. We simply use the equation $s = 16t^2$ with the two values of t to find ds, the difference between s when t is 1 and when it is $1 + dt$:

$$ds = 16(1 + dt)^2 - 16$$
$$= 16(1 + 2dt + dt^2) - 16$$
$$= 16 + 32dt + 16dt^2 - 16$$
$$= 32dt + 16dt^2.$$

Instantaneous velocity is then ds/dt, so that

$$ds/dt = (32dt + 16dt^2)/dt$$
$$= 32 + 16dt.$$

The answer that Newton wanted was 32 ft/sec, and the 16dt term was dropped. And why not drop it? It represents an infinitesimally small quantity, since dt represents vanishingly small increments. Is the method legitimate? Berkeley said no; he referred to Newton's fluxions (dt):

...and what are these fluxions? The velocities of evanescent increments. And what are these evanescent increments? They are neither finite quantities, nor quantities infinitely small, nor yet nothing. May we not call them the ghosts of departed quantities? (Fraser 1901, p. 44)

Two modern mathematicians (Davis and Hersh 1981, p. 245) assess the effect of Berkeley's critique as follows:

Berkeley's logic could not be answered; nevertheless, mathematicians went on using infinitesimals for another century, and with great success. Indeed, physicists and engineers have never stopped using them.

David Hume: The Culmination of Empiricism

[Q]uite apart from any influence, it is the existence of such brilliant writers and thinkers as David Hume that makes the history of philosophy worth studying. (Kaufman 1961, p. 308)

Kaufmann was not alone in his admiration for Hume (depicted in figure 6.3), a brilliant thinker and a charming writer. Adam Smith, the political economist and author of *Wealth of Nations*, called Hume "our most excellent and never to be forgotten friend...approaching as nearly to the idea of a perfectly wise and virtuous man as perhaps the nature of human frailty will permit."[8]

Figure 6.3
Hume. Portrait by Allan Ramsey. Courtesy of the Scottish National Portrait Gallery.

Treatise, Essays, and Enquiry
In 1748 he published *Philosophical Essays Concerning Human Understanding*, which contained the *Enquiry Concerning Human Understanding*, a much-revised version of the first volume of the treatise. The revision leaves out a lot of the material of the original, and some authorities claim that Kant, Hume's almost-contemporary critic, might better have read the treatise than its revised abridgement. But Hume clearly preferred the later version, since he made known through advertisement that the treatise was "a juvenile work," and that the *Enquiry* "may alone be regarded as containing his philosophical sentiments and principles" (in Kaufman 1961, p. 318). The *Enquiry* may then be considered the work that made his reputation as England's[9] greatest philosopher.

What Is Experience?

Locke's "New Way of Ideas" left the mind as the product of experience with a real, physical world that informed us through "impulse," as imperceptible particles were transmitted to us. Berkeley had pointed out what Locke seemed to know, which was that the physical world is unknowable and, in the last analysis, we have only our ideas. These are reliable only as long as God makes them so, since all of our knowledge is only our own experience and the world outside us exists only by grace of the Deity.

Hume accepted Berkeley's analysis in large part. Experience is indeed content, and objects are compounds of familiar elements. However, Hume was not really a subjective idealist in the sense that Berkeley was. For Hume, we have assurances that a real world exists independently of us, but it is not God who maintains it, and it is not through reason that we know it.

Impressions and Ideas

This is a distinction central to Hume's thesis—there are two distinctly different contents of mind and it is crucial that they be kept distinguished. Impressions, often called "sensations" by Hume, which include "all of our more lively perceptions, when we hear, or see, or feel, or love, or hate, or desire, or will" (in Burtt 1939, p. 593). Impressions occur as the pain of excessive heat, the pleasure of warmth, the taste of pudding, or the feeling of voluntary movement of an arm. Impressions also correspond to what we call "real," and it is difficult to refute the witness, who "saw it all happen."

A different kind of perception, to use Hume's word, occurs when we recall a sensation or anticipate it. Sometimes we anticipate or remember so strongly that we almost feel or see the object, but unless we are mad, these perceptions, or ideas, are never mistaken for impressions: "All the colors of poetry, however splendid, can never paint natural objects in such a manner as to make the description be taken for a real landscape. The most lively thought is still inferior to the dullest sensation" (Hume, in Burtt, pp. 592–593). Ideas are the images of memory, anticipation, thinking, and reasoning. Both impressions and ideas come as simples and complexes.

All Familiars and Reflection   As did Hobbes, Locke, and Berkeley before him, Hume argued that all elements of experience are familiars,

however unnatural they may seem. The gold mountain is a composite of ideas of gold and of mountains, just as the idea of wings and horses gives us Pegasus. Reflection molds the elements of experience into the composites of complex ideas.

Reflection is not the set of faculties that Locke added to the empty cabinet—it includes only four aspects: augmenting, transposing, combining, and diminishing. Simple impressions are those that are indivisible and strong, like the red in the coat of a soldier or the note of a fife. Simple impressions produce simple ideas, as memory images or as anticipations, and include sensation, emotion, and will—such feelings are not reducible to others. Complex impressions, like the sight of a soldier, produce complex ideas, like the memory image of the soldier.

However, the augmenting, transposing, combining, and diminishing of ideas via reflection may produce problems and ideas without meaning, since the complex ideas produced may have no counterpart in impressions. The complex ideas of infinity, God, nature, self, and cause are ideas only—they have no corresponding impressions and hence are jargon only.

Add to this the constant process of association that Hume adopted from Berkeley. Ideas are associated by contiguity in time and space, similarity, and causality—a process of attraction of impressions and ideas analogous to gravitation and part of the "original qualities of human nature." No wonder that so many of our ideas are "false compounds" and that there is so much "jargon to banish":

First, when we analyze our thoughts or ideas, however compounded or sublime, we always find that they resolve themselves into such simple ideas as were copied from a precedent feeling or sentiment.... The idea of God, as meaning an infinitely intelligent, wise, and good Being, arises from reflecting on the operations of our own mind, and augmenting, without limit, those qualities of goodness and wisdom... (Hume, in Burtt 1939, p. 594)

Consider Hume's analysis of the origins of knowledge:

Sources of Ideas for Hume

Simple Impressions ——————⇒ Simple Ideas

Complex Impressions ——————⇒ Complex Ideas ("True")

Reflection: augmenting, combining -⇒ Complex Ideas (Many False)
transposing, diminishing   ⇑

Association: contiguity, similarity, causality* ————⇑

Hume's point is that many complex ideas exist, like the gold mountain and the winged horse, that have no counterpart in sensation; there are no corresponding impressions for them, and they are thus meaningless. Two of these false compound ideas are that of causality and that of the self.

Humean Causality: Good-Bye to Certainty

Hume went to great length to show that all that we know of causes and effects comes from our experience or in recounting of the experience of others. We cannot know in advance that fire burns or that water drowns or that snow melts or that iron is heavier than wood. All knowledge is the product of experience.

This is illustrated in our idea of causality itself—if that idea is a chimera, with no basis in experience, then all the "laws" of science, religion, and whatever are only tentative. Yet, that is the case, and a moment's consideration shows that there is no impression or set of impressions that correspond to causality. Think of any instance— thunder and lightning, colliding billiard balls, a paper cut and pain— and see that the only relation involved is succession in time.

In all of these cases, an antecedent is followed by a consequent and that is that. We need no more than the law of association by contiguity in time and space; A is followed by B, and if the sequence is reliable, we call it "cause and effect." That is Humean causality, and it is the way we have treated causality since Hume. It means that we know only our own experience—solipsism—"alone self." What is the self?

There Is No Impression for the Idea of Self

Impressions are lively, strong, and reliable. They are thus all that we can be sure is real. When we examine the idea of self, we find, as William James would in 1890, that it is a complex idea partly of our own manufacture. Kant, Hume's powerful critic, would agree that "there is no impression for the self" (*Treatise*, part IV, section VI).

If the self is a unitary entity that is born and lives and dies, there should be some feelings uniquely associated with it. Otherwise, the self is something that is inferred from the perceptions that we do have, much as Hobbes suggested that the smell, warmth, and crackling noises lead the blind to infer a fire as cause, even though there is no direct visual experience of the fire. If that is similar to our experiencing of the self, then the self is a complex idea with no basis in sensation.

Consider your experience and appreciate Hume's point. However you picture "me," it is a picture with a brief history, isn't it? You are the same "me" that you were yesterday, and even last month—but how about last year? Are you the same "self" that you were five years ago? What is it that we experience when we consider our "self"? Is it any more than specific sensations, and could we even consider our "self" without them? Hume thought not:

> For my part, when I enter most intimately into what I call *myself*, I always stumble on some particular perception or other, of heat or cold ... and were all my perceptions remov'd by death, and cou'd I neither think, nor feel, nor see, nor love, nor hate after the dissolution of my body, I shou'd be entirely annihilated, nor do I conceive what is farther requisite to make me a perfect nonentity. (*Treatise*, part IV, section VI)

Hume seems correct, and this being the case, we might well wonder from where do we get the absurd notion that we are a "self" independent of percepts of sight and sound and touch and smell and emotion. Hume tells us that is the same process that leads us to attribute identities to the objects of sense.

Because we cannot distinguish a single, persisting object from a series of different, but related objects, we call them the same, though we have an odd feeling that they are not the same:

> In order to justify to ourselves this absurdity, we often feign some new and unintelligible principle, that connects the objects together, and prevents their interruption and variation. Thus we feign the continued existence of the perceptions of our senses, to remove the interruption; and run into the notion of a *soul*, and *self*, and *substance*, to disguise the variation. (*Treatise*, part IV, section VI)

The question of the nature of knowledge and of the self is an old one, and it has not gone away. The interested reader may examine William James's classic, *The Principles of Psychology*, to find the same argument, most clearly in his chapter X, "The Consciousness of Self."

Hume on General Ideas

The further we are removed from impressions, those reliable and lively perceptions, the more prone we are to being misled by jargon and complex ideas that have no meaning. The lack of meaning owes to the fact that the ideas correspond to no impressions and only one remedy remains—a visit to the library:

When we run over libraries, persuaded by these principles, what havoc must we make? If we take in our hand any volume: of divinity or school metaphysics, for instance; let us ask, *Does it contain any abstract reasoning concerning quantity or number?* No. *Does it contain any experimental reasoning concerning matter of fact and existence?* No. Commit it then to the flames: for it can contain nothing but sophistry and illusion. (*Enquiry*, section XII, part III, in Burtt 1939, p. 689)

Hume on Morality, Motivation, and Emotion

We all recognize right and wrong, good and bad. Shocking crimes are recognized universally as evil. Hume was certain that morality was not the product of reason, as Hobbes had believed; reason only allows us to recognize the goodness and badness that exist whether reason knows it or not. This means that morality is not merely idea, the product of rational thought. After consideration of countless cases of good and bad, Hume concluded:

Thus the course of the argument leads us to conclude, that since vice and virtue are not discoverable merely by reason, or the comparison of ideas, it must be by means of some impression or sentiment they occasion, that we are able to mark the difference betwixt them.... Morality, therefore, is more properly felt than judg'd of.[10]

Attraction/repulsion, love/hate, pleasure/pain, contentedness/uneasiness are impressions—sensations as fundamental and "given" as is C sharp or red. They are determined by the human constitution. But Hume was also certain that moral reactions were not in response to the "Law of Nature," God's law that was the foundation of morality for Locke.

Hume against Skepticism! What?

Hume criticized skepticism, first as advanced by Descartes, then as presented by Berkeley. Finally he attacked the "utter" skepticism of some ancient Greeks and of many writers of his own time. Hume was no skeptic—he was simply skeptical that reason could provide certainty. Space forbids long excerpts, but one passage is particularly instructive: recall the paradoxical nature of matter and space—is matter infinitely divisible?

...how shall this question be determined? By experience, surely; as all other questions of a like nature. But here experience is, and must be entirely silent.

The mind never has anything present to it but the perceptions, and cannot possibly reach any experience of their connexion with objects…nothing can be more sceptical…some of the paradoxical conclusions of geometry or the science of quantity. (Kaufman 1961, pp. 404–414)

What Hume meant in the last sentence is worth our fullest consideration because we frequently are confronted with such questions—for example, how do we account for telepathy or for the amazing rapidity with which children learn language? Both questions deal with things that do not actually exist or occur. Hume was referring to paradoxes of the sort proposed by Zeno of Elea and used as proof that the evidence of our senses has nothing to do with reality.

"Matter can and cannot be infinitely divisible," is a contradiction that illustrates this limitation of ours. It is a problem that transcends our reasoning powers. Paradoxes raised by the Skeptics are only paradoxical because they refer to "abstract" or "general" ideas rather than to our experience. Such general ideas are best abandoned. Hume believed that we don't have to explain phenomena that don't occur as a part of our experience.

Kant's Reaction: Psychology Is Not Enough

Hume, by his criticism of the concept of causality, awakened him from his dogmatic slumbers—so at least he says, but the awakening was only temporary, and he soon invented a soporific which enabled him to sleep again. (Russell, in Egner 1958, p. 70)

Immanuel Kant[11] (depicted in figure 6.4) spent all of his long life in Königsberg, then a city in East Prussia and later the Soviet city of Kaliningrad, site of a large naval base. It is true that he never traveled more than a few miles from Königsberg, but he argued in his *Anthropology* of 1798/1978 that the city was so cosmopolitan that there was no danger of his developing a parochial outlook. His earliest writings dealt with astronomy, and his philosophical works, *Critique of Pure Reason*, *Critique of Practical Reason*, and *Critique of Judgment*, did not appear until 1781, 1788, and 1790, respectively.

Where Was Hume's Error? Was It an Error?

Kant read Hume's *Enquiry Concerning Human Understanding*, the brief version of his *Treatise* that did not include many of the supporting arguments contained only in the latter. Nonetheless, he was able to un-

Figure 6.4
Kant. Courtesy of the Archives of the History of American Psychology, University of Akron.

derstand readily that Hume's case was sound, and, in fact, Kant agreed with most of what Hume had concluded. It is clear from Kant's frequent references that he not only admired and respected Hume but seemed to genuinely like him. For example, in his *Anthropology*, Kant referred to "the sensitive and gentle Hume."

Like Hume, Kant believed that all that we can know is our experience and that the soul is not felt as an entity but only as an idea in consciousness. However, Hume showed that we can have no knowledge of causality other than as reliable contiguity of impressions and ideas; nor can we know anything with absolute certainty, since our experience has no ascertainable source. Kant was unwilling to accept such radical conclusions, and he was too wise to accept the "convictions" of common sense that were offered as antidotes to Hume by the Scottish School. After some twelve years of thought and study, Kant's reply was ready, and the writing of the *Critique of Pure Reason* took only a few months.

For Hume all of our knowledge was constructed of impressions and ideas associated by contiguity in time and space and by similarity. In every case we start from simple or complex impressions (sensations) that undergo modification in the imagination so that they may be augmented, diminished, or combined. The resulting complex ideas are true and reliable insofar as they correspond to some antecedent impressions.

We may think of the gold mountain as a complex idea, but there is no complex impression that corresponds, unless we have actually experienced a gold mountain. To refute "this our doctrine," Hume wrote, produce the idea for which there is no corresponding impression or set of impressions from which to construct it. The implication was that anything conceivable could be explained by reference to impressions (sensations), associations in space and time, and augmenting, diminishing, and combining.

For Kant, Hume's generation of experience, and thus, the world, through association assumed that there exist a priori synthetic truths. That is, we must have knowledge of nature in advance of experience.

What Is Implied by Associationism?
We need not even consider the serious problem of defining "similarity" as a principle of association; consider only the law of association by contiguity, including causality as very reliable contiguity. The objects that you now see around you are compounds of sensations that you call objects because they do occur together as compounds. The rain that I hear outside my window is actually a set of auditory impressions that have often appeared as part of a compound of sights, sounds, feelings of wetness, and odors; its existence is, as far as I can know, only my experience, and I apprehend it only because I have experienced it before.

Like all of my knowledge, it is a compound of sensations and ideas joined by contiguity in time and space. As we know, and as Hume stressed, we think of the world as external and never as within us; what is important is that our world is built as the consequence of our experience.

Kant seized on the most basic assumption of Hume's associationism, that connections form among elements appearing close in time and space, and pointed out that this evidences a priori synthetic knowledge, the knowledge of time and space. Not only does association by contiguity assume time and space, but the very possibility of sensory experience itself requires that time and space be known in advance. All knowledge may derive from experience, but experience itself requires knowledge before it is possible.

Consider what we mean by "space," and imagine no space. We can readily conceive of large spaces, small spaces, divided spaces, and so on, but we cannot conceive of no space. Space is thus the external sense, the form of outer sense, without which experience is impossible. If we conceive a sensation, we may view it as within us or outside us, but it is someplace in space. Time is similarly a precondition for experience.

Our conception of a sensation requires something that begins and ends; the conception of an object requires relative permanence (in time). As Augustine concluded for very different reasons long before Kant, time is real for us, since we cannot have experience without it. Kant referred to time as the internal sense; like space, it is a precondition for experience.

Both depend on the "subjective constitution of our mind, apart from which they cannot be predicated of anything whatever." They are objective with respect to our sensibility, meaning that, for us, they are real and objective. Other kinds of beings with other sensibilities may not frame experience in space and time, but we must, and no experience could yield the ideas of time and space because no experience is possible without time and space a priori.

Transcendental Idealism

Kant was (perhaps unfairly) challenging Hume's "appeal to experience as the basis for all knowledge" by demanding inclusion of the conditions necessary for experience. Kant called our knowledge of time and space "Anschauungen," meaning "points of view," though the translation is usually intuitions. An intuition is therefore a way in which we cast experience because we come equipped to do so. This means that intuitions are transcendental or beyond sensory experience; they are also beyond or prior to reason.

The existence of things, their number, their properties, and causal relations among them are therefore determined by *our* makeup, not because that is the way things "really are." If we wear inverting prisms, we see the world as inverted, but not because that's the way it "really is."

Empirical Intuitions

How did Kant deal with sensation, specifically? In his terms, sensation occurs as an empirical intuition with a "phenomenon" as its object. The "intuition of phenomena" includes both a priori and a posteriori aspects: form and matter, respectively. The fact that we see, for example, means that we have an a priori capacity to see; that is the form of seeing.

When we see something specific, such as form or color, that is the "matter" of seeing. Hypothetically, seeing can be conceived as "pure," rather than the seeing of something. This form-without-matter or "pure intuition" still leaves extension in space and form as an a priori pure intuition.

Phenomena and Noumena

Our a priori Anschauungen, or intuitions, generate our empirical world. The knowledge of that world is real and "objective," bearing in mind that this holds only with regard to our experience. We can rely on the laws of science and make predictions with confidence, since, as a student of mine put it, "our minds will continue to structure experience in the same ways." In that sense, we know objective truth, and Hume is refuted.

Kant believed that his predecessors had mistakenly believed that they were dealing with the world as it really is—that is, with things in themselves. His critical philosophy was concerned with the limits of human knowledge, limited as it is by our intuitions. Kant put it well in his *Prolegomena to Any Future Metaphysics*:

This complete (though to its originator unexpected) solution of Hume's problem rescues for the pure concepts of the understanding their *a priori* origin, and for the universal laws of nature their validity, as laws of the understanding, yet in such a way as to limit their use to experience...not by deriving them from experience, but by deriving experience from them. (Kaufman 1961, p. 571)

If we can know nature only as phenomena (objects of empirical intuitions), how can we know that anything real exists beyond or underlying phenomena? Kant went to great lengths arguing that we cannot in any way know anything about "noumena," or the "things in themselves"—reality independent of our sensory experience. Such "things" are unknowable, do not exist in space/time, are not substance, and are not describable in terms of our categories. Why postulate noumena in the first place? Why leave our "island of truth," as Kant asked, to misuse the "pure understanding," the source of all truth, considering things that are beyond it?

There really is no good reason, but Kant advanced three reasons for proposing noumena, or things in themselves:

1. It is logical, given phenomena, that something produce them.

2. Our "apperceptions" (clear percepts) seem united, though empirical intuitions corresponding to several senses may be involved. Do we see and hear a cannon because the soul unites the separate sensations, as Socrates suggested in Plato's Theatetus? The unity of perception suggests a correlate in the world of noumena.

3. Our world of phenomena is the product of our particular form of sensibility. Kant could not prove that ours is the only form of intuition/sensibility, so perhaps another race of beings is able to experience things that we do not. Maybe what are noumena for us would be phenomena for them. Since Kant believed that all the planets are populated, this is more reasonable than it may seem at first.

The Categorical Imperative

Kant's views on ethics appear in *The Fundamental Principles of the Metaphysic of Ethics* (1785/1938), a work preparatory to *The Critique of Practical Reason* (1788), in which he proposed the famous concept of the categorical imperative, the only basis for moral action. The point of view emphasizes duty, urges suppression of emotion, and is otherwise similar to the views of the Stoics. In Kant's terms, there are two kinds of moral command, the "hypothetical imperative" and the "categorical imperative." The first commands us to do something (such as help the unfortunate) because of the results produced or the good feelings we will have.

Such an act is moral (good), however, only if it is done without consideration of the outcome for us or for others. Each act must be considered as it might apply to a wider field than any particular instance. In fact, we should "Act as if the maxim of your action by your will were to become a universal law of nature" (1785/1938, p. 38). Consider this example from Kant (1785/1938, p. 39):

A person who is wearied with life because of a series of misfortunes that has reduced him to despair still possesses sufficient reason to be able to ask himself, whether it may not be contrary to his duty to himself to take his life…he will soon see that a nature, whose law it would be to destroy life by the very feeling which is meant to stimulate the promotion of life, would contradict itself and therefore not persist as nature.

In other cases, the goodness of an act depends on the lack of feelings associated with it. If we help the poor because it is objectively correct, that is good, but if we do so because it makes us feel good, there is no morality involved. The goodness is in an attitude of doing one's duty, not in considering the results of an act. It is clear that there is some merit in the view that many so-called good deeds are self-serving; it takes little reflection to see that the golden rule, "do unto others," is largely self-serving too, and that is why Kant rejected it.

Logical Positivism and Kant's Transcendentalism
In 1934 the logical positivist A. J. Ayer was twenty-four years old and published a critique of Kant in the journal *Mind*. In it he presented the position of logical positivism with respect to transcendental (or metaphysical) theories.

Kant's entire response to Hume—his epistemology—is a metaphysical enquiry, concerned as it is with whatever underlies or transcends phenomena. Ayer argued that "even to ask whether there is a reality underlying the world of phenomena is to formulate a bogus question," and that anything said about such a reality is a "piece of nonsense." Ayer showed that metaphysics is vain and that there is no remedy for its defects. Whatever methods or form of reasoning is used by the metaphysician, "he succeeds in saying nothing."

Whorf: Language, Time, and Space

Benjamin Lee Whorf was an amateur linguist and an engineer who worked full time for the Hartford Insurance Company. His job allowed lots of travel, and he pursued his avocation, the study of American Indian languages. He coded several of these languages for the first time, and he made observations on the significance of the grammatical forms that he found in some of them. In particular, his analysis of the Hopi language casts doubt on Kant's conviction that all humans, owing to the way in which they must structure the world, assume time and space as givens. The Hopis have an Aristotelian way of looking at things, but here are Whorf's conclusions regarding time and space (1956, pp. 57–58):

I find it gratuitous to assume that a Hopi who knows only the Hopi language and the cultural ideas of his own society has the same notions, often supposed to be intuitions, of time and space that we have, and are generally assumed to be universal. In particular, he has no general notion or intuition of TIME as a smooth flowing continuum.

This followed a careful examination of a language in which the verbs have no tenses. Is such a language practical or even possible? How can one communicate, even with oneself, with no reference to "yesterday," or "last week," or "later today?" Evidently, it is possible, but we haven't the space to discuss it fully. In a word, the Hopi concept of time is included in changes in things from "time to time," as we would say. So I am now different from the last time you saw me (our "yesterday"), and the time that passed is represented in my changed status.

7   Scottish and English Practical Psychology

Also, Reid was incredibly unfortunate in the quality of most of his followers in the Scottish school; their dogmatism and even downright stupidity did Reid no good. (Todd, 1989)

Hume had reduced all philosophy and science to subparts of psychology. Our knowledge of what we call reality is the product of our association of impressions and imagination (reflection), which augments, diminishes, and transposes our impressions. No one could fault his reasoning. In Britain he came to be widely admired, especially by Thomas Reid, his contemporary, and later by Thomas Brown and John Stuart Mill.

But Reid could not tolerate Hume's conclusions and appealed to what he called "common sense" in his attempt to refute him. Reid's followers in Scotland later rejected such a God-given faculty and returned to the sophisticated associationism of Berkeley and Hume. However, Reid prevailed in the end, since his Scottish philosophy of common sense did find a home in America, where it prospered.

Who Dares Oppose the Copy Theory?

Reid was the conspicuous scholar of his day to accept the premises of empiricism but to reject the doctrine of mediation by ideas that was the prevailing view since Locke. He was an epistemological realist, a tough thing to be in the eighteenth century.

Reid's Background and Philosophy of Common Sense
Reid became professor of philosophy at King's College, Aberdeen, in 1751 and later succeeded Adam Smith, Hume's old friend, as professor of moral philosophy at the University of Glasgow. At Aberdeen he was

a regent, who took charge of a group of students after their first year of learning Greek. He taught his class all their subjects, these being natural science, mathematics, logic, metaphysics, political philosophy, and ethics.

The problem for Reid was that he was a Protestant minister and professor entrusted to instill what were accepted as established virtues in his pupils. Yet, he "respected Hume as the greatest metaphysician of the age" and he had "lernt more from his writings in matters of this kind than from all others put together." He read Hume's *Treatise* "over and over with great care" (Gallie 1989). The problem was that, from Reid's point of view, Hume's reasonings led inevitably to skepticism, an unsatisfactory conclusion. Yet there was no flaw in them, given the premises with which he began. It was thus the premises that Reid questioned.

Reid's Refutation of "Hume"

[I] was not a little surprised to find that, it leans with its whole weight upon a hypothesis, which is ancient indeed.... The ancient hypothesis, of which I could find no solid proof...is that what we perceive is not external reality, "but only images and pictures imprinted upon the mind, which are called impressions and ideas." (Klein 1970, p. 645)

Reid's attacks were aimed at the theory of ideas, the view that experience is mediated by ideas (sensations, perceptions, impressions) and that it is therefore indirect—thus, truth cannot be assured. This was the view of Plato and of all of the Platonists that followed over the centuries and of Democritus and all those who accepted the copy theory of perception. It was the view of Descartes, Hobbes, and, of course, Locke. It was not exactly the view of Berkeley or of Hume, though their idealism and apparent skepticism placed them in the same category.

To qualify for attack by Reid, one had to espouse the theory of ideas as a theory of "slippage," so that untrusty sense organs copy a real world but do not copy it accurately. The reason that Hume and perhaps Berkeley do not qualify is that they did not take for granted a real external world independent of our experience of it. Indeed, the world can be no more than our experience, so "slippage," or misrepresentation, is meaningless. Reid did not fully grasp this, and if he had, he might have dismissed Hume and Berkeley out of hand. But he lumped all who proposed that ideas are the basis for our experience and made Hume chief target.

He charged that Hume had forced moral judgments to degenerate to "autobiographical statements about one's own feelings of approbation or disapprobation" Todd (1989, p. 4). This was because reason was incapable of determining the certainty of anything but individual experience. For Hume this did not mean that we have no assurance of an external reality, only that this assurance cannot be based on reason. Hume had reduced metaphysics, including morals, to epistemology and had reduced epistemology to associationism. In all this lies a fundamental error, Reid believed, and it goes back to the beginnings of Hume's reasonings.

Common Sense and the Unprovable

Reid's *Inquiry into the Human Mind on the Principles of Common Sense* was published in 1764, and a second volume, *Essays on the Intellectual Powers of Man* appeared after his death. Reid's thesis was that experience is more than sense experience and that common sense acts as a part of the "original constitution of the mind" and that it is the "will of Him who made us" that we know the real external world. There are five criteria for demonstrating common sense and thus debunking the theory of ideas.

First is the criterion of self-evidence, according to which some things are recognized by everyone and carry their own illumination—the "inner light" of Plato or the clarity of Descartes. The remaining criteria are universal acceptance, irresistibility, unprovability, and confirmability. Irresistible beliefs include the belief in a natural world, freedom of choice, and the like.

First principles are "unprovable," since they are fundamental—this is similar to Kant's argument for the transcendental nature of space, time, and matter. However, Reid's unprovable first principles come from inductive observation of people's behavior and opinions in everyday life. Basic truths, such as the reliability of sensation and the existence of an external world, are accepted by everyone who understands the statement, and it is only the double talk of philosophers who make what is true and familiar seem strange and uncertain.

Reid is frustrating to the serious reader, who has difficulty deciding whether he meant common sense as a faculty or as a synonym for "intelligence." His followers had the same difficulty, as Reid's disciple and successor, Dugald Stewart (depicted in figure 7.1), wrote, "The phrase Common Sense...has occasionally been employed without a due attention to precision" (quoted in Klein 1970, p. 642).

Figure 7.1
Stewart. Courtesy of the Archives of the History of American Psychology, University of Akron.

Common sense is a name for the fact that we are constitutionally compelled to view ourselves as the same person that we were last month, that we must separate the external world from the perceiving individual (the world is not "just my ideas"), that we believe that other intelligent organisms exist (you, for example), and that "the future course of nature will resemble the past" (Stewart, from Klein 1970, p. 643). Anyone who called such beliefs into question in the world of practical concerns would "expose himself universally to the charge of insanity" (Ibid).

An eminent clinical psychologist and historian, Donald B. Klein, noted that Reid's view conforms to that of psychiatry and that expressions of Humean skepticism would be interpreted as being "out of touch with reality." Descartes too, in expressing doubt about his personal existence, would be diagnosed as psychotic.

Misunderstanding Hume?

In questioning the certainty of perception, Hume seemed to Reid to be questioning reliance on the senses altogether:

Common sense, the consent of ages and nations, of the learned and the un-learned, gives the lie to Hume. I resolve not to believe my senses. I break my nose on a post, step into a kennel, and am committed to a madhouse. (Boring 1950, p. 191)

Who can seriously doubt the reliability of sensory experience? We don't doubt the accuracy of eyewitness testimony, do we? And thus Reid critiqued Hume, who allegedly told us to doubt the senses in daily activities. How could anyone so misinterpret Hume? How could Hume advocate ignoring our senses, since that is all that we have and impressions usually do not fail us? No wonder that Reid was so merci-lessly criticized by everyone since Kant. He was the educated spokes-man for popular opinion, and therein lies his popular success and his scholarly failure.

The Nature of Perception

Reid was adamant in his insistence that perception is not mediated by ideas, and he put this most clearly in his fourth oration, given in 1762. Having traced the history of the theory from the ancients to Locke, Reid excused Locke but condemned Hume (Todd 1989, p. 77). Reid charged that Hume's "philosophical madness" and "ravings" crystal-lize in the doctrine that "apprehension and judgment are of the same genus," which is to say that imagination, memory, and sensation differ only in degree. True enough, wrote Hume, impressions and ideas are different in intensity, and it is possible that they be confused if an im-pression is weak and an idea is strong.

Not so for Reid. Perception of a real object is fundamentally different from apprehension of memories or imaginations, and this is clear un-less one is misled by the theory of ideas. Perception always refers to an object external to consciousness and involves a conviction in addition to sensation. Reid asked the reader to consider the smelling of a rose, an act of perception with three discernible aspects.

Smelling the Rose

In an "appeal to the reader's thoughts," and no doubt to common sense, Reid asked us to see that perception of an external object is an act beginning with the "clear and distinct" notion of an object. This notion, or perception, is caused by the smell of a rose or some other sensation, which occurs "in me." However, it refers immediately and surely to an outside quality in an object, and that reference is what Reid meant by "perception." Part of the perception is the conviction ("common sense") that the external object exists and that it is known immediately, not through any sort of inference or reasoning.

Reid and the Faculties
As a matter of fact, the common sense that separates sensation and perception became only a facet of a constitution that gives us thirty powers of mind, or faculties. These come in two kinds, active and intellectual. The active faculties consist of what are commonly called motives and traits, such as pity, duty, love of children, need for property, self-preservation, hunger, imitation, need for power, self-esteem, gratitude, and fourteen others. The intellectual faculties include perception, reasoning, judgment, memory, conception, and the moral sense. Reid's list of faculties has often been identified as that used by the phrenologists of the nineteenth and twentieth centuries, but that is not really the case.

The Problem with Children
Reid discussed cases where the faculty of perception fails us—for example, a lunatic who believes that he is made of glass is not perceiving correctly. What of children who often seem to confuse reality and fantasy? Reid raised a serious problem for himself in discussing that topic:

> But whether children, from the time that they begin to use their senses, make a distinction between things which are only conceived or imagined, and things which really exist, may be doubted. Until we are able to make this distinction, we cannot properly be said to believe or to disbelieve the existence of anything. (Rand 1912, pp. 361–373)

The logic here is not difficult to fault and may invite a criticism that is fatal to Reid's case.

Hume and Berkeley argued that our perception of an external world is the product of experience with compounds of sensations. According to this view, the concept of "external reality" can exist only after some life experience, and this is why children confuse reality and imagination more often than do adults. An object becomes real as it displays properties common to other real objects. A real stone does not vanish when we refuse to think about it. That being the case, it is clear that learning the difference between "real" and "imaginary," or to say the same thing, "existent" and "nonexistent," is well explained by the Humean point of view. In fact, the explanation of that distinction and how it comes to be is the chief thesis of that point of view.

Dugald Stewart, Disciple

For the first fifty years or so of the American republic, if any philosophy at all was taught in any American academy it was generally the Scottish philosophy, and the texts were the works of Reid or Stewart or texts derived directly from them. (Todd 1989, p. 2)

Dugald Stewart (1753–1828) was the son of a mathematics professor at Edinburgh and became professor of moral philosophy at the same university, a post that he held from 1785–1820. He was Reid's disciple and popularizer, who published the three volumes of his *Elements of the Philosophy of the Human Mind* in 1792, in 1814, and in 1827.

His writings were full of grist for popular audiences, these being times when "science" was popular among the members of the privileged class and lecture halls were easily filled by audiences eager to hear of the latest discoveries in science, even "moral science." Stewart and his fellows found an especially receptive audience in America, newly independent and seeking staffers for its universities.

The Influence of the Scottish School in America

Granville Stanley Hall was the "great founder" of psychological institutions at the turn of the twentieth century—the early laboratories, associations, journals, and even institutions were largely his doing. He spoke in 1894 about the popularity and influence of the Scottish Common Sense philosophy in the first half of the nineteenth century (Martin 1961, chapter 1). According to Hall, American professors "drew back" from Berkeley and Hume, finding Reid and Stewart offering a "safer way" for them.

Philosophies that assumed that humans have a sense of morality, that we directly experience a real world, and that we have free will were welcome in the fundamentalist religious circles of America. And that clergy, who ran the colleges and universities, found that the Scots' use of association and "desire, will, and feeling was lucidity itself and fitted our practical country" (Martin 1961, p. 3). Indeed, the Scottish philosophy was more popular in America than it was in Scotland (Martin 1961, pp. 4–5).

Scottish Educators in America

John Witherspoon graduated from the University of Aberdeen and became president of the new College of New Jersey, later Princeton University, in 1768. Thereafter, he was provost at the University of Pennsylvania. He lectured for twenty-five years on Scottish Common Sense philosophy and, through him, multitudes were influenced. His students included 13 college presidents, 114 clergymen, 20 senators, 24 members of the House, 13 governors, and 3 Supreme Court Justices.

Thomas Jefferson knew and respected Dugald Stewart, whom he called one "of the ablest metaphysicians living, by which I mean investigators of the thinking faculty of man" (Martin 1961, p. 8). Jefferson also asked Stewart for help in finding foreign teachers for the University of Virginia.

Later Scots introduced the opinions of Reid and Stewart to other universities. At Harvard, it was Levi Frisbie who brought Scottish Common Sense in 1817, and President Thomas Clap instilled it at Yale in the late eighteenth century, through his course in Moral Philosophy. Stewart impressed Emerson and Thoreau at Harvard, where he was particularly appealing, as he was to many professors at smaller universities. In 1825 the Pennsylvania Academy of Fine Arts obtained a portrait of Stewart and gave a copy to the corresponding academy in South Carolina.

What was this philosophy that was so American and so fit for our youth? If we survey the contents of Dugald Stewart's *Outlines of Moral Philosophy*, we will see just what was "self prescribed by a society that desired the very latest in sedation" (Martin 1961, p. 54) and we will find a few surprising good ideas that are usually credited to others.

Stewart's *Outlines of Moral Philosophy*: The Powers of the Scottish Mind

This work was first published in 1793 and was in its nineteenth edition in 1897, the edition now commonly available. The book begins with the most lavish praise for "Lord Bacon," who ushered in "one of the most important eras in the history of science" (Stewart 1793/1897, pp. 3–4). This noble achievement was the promotion of the method of induction, as an analysis and a synthesis, and was mighty impressive to Stewart, who seemed to understand Bacon more clearly than did many of that great empiricist's critics.

Stewart, like Reid and others, believed that mind may not be spoken of unless it is recognized that certain powers are inherent in it. He divided these into Intellectual Powers, of which there are at least ten, and Active and Moral Powers, of which there are at least five main divisions. Let us briefly examine these powers and see wherein lay the appeal of Stewart's work.

Intellectual Powers

The following listing is a paraphrasing of Stewart's definitions of the faculties that constitute the mind:

- Consciousness refers to the immediate knowledge of our sensations and thoughts and of the present operations of the mind. It is consciousness and memory that provides the conviction of personal identity.

- External Perception is the direct apprehension of the external world as real, not as mediated by ideas.

Stewart believed that we directly perceive what others called "primary qualities" via signs that are seldom accompanied by pleasure and pain and "we acquire an habitual inattention to them in early infancy which is not to be surmounted in our maturer years."

This is the cardinal thesis of the Scottish Common Sense School and opposes the "Ideal" theory of Hume and particularly of Descartes and Locke, who believed that our sensory knowledge is always of secondary qualities. This was particularly obnoxious to Reid, in that they too believed in a material world of primary qualities but argued that it was not directly knowable by us. For them the world is "placed beyond the reach of our faculties; beyond which it is impossible for us to ascertain anything." Mediation by ideas is false and repugnant, since, "If the Ideal Theory be admitted, the foregoing argument against the existence of matter is conclusive; but the theory is unsupported by evidence, and is even inconceivable" (Stewart 1793/1897, pp. 11–13).

- Attention is indeed a mental power, an "act or exertion of the mind" to fix things in memory and to be used to explain other things.

- Conception is the power to represent to oneself sensations that were formerly conscious and external objects formerly perceived.

Interestingly, Stewart noted that "It is commonly understood that conception is accompanied with no belief in the existence of its objects; but various considerations render this opinion somewhat doubtful" (p. 15). However, if that is the case, and if imagined objects may be accompanied by belief in their existence, then where is Reid's "Conviction" that was the basis for the realism of the Scottish School and which guaranteed that our sensations were perceptions of reality and not just chimera? Amazingly, this was not clear to Stewart, who ever saw himself as Reid's disciple.

• Abstraction is the work of the power of attention, which can attend to aspects of particular perceptions and ignore others.

Thus, we form the ideas of objects and classes of things, such as humans, truth, and the variables of algebra. However, these derive from particulars and do not imply some essences. There are no Platonic Forms or innate ideas in this Scottish philosophy.

• Association of Ideas occurs in too many ways to enumerate, such as resemblance, analogy, contrariety, space, time, cause and effect, premises and conclusion, and others.

This describes the train of our thoughts to a large extent and relates to the operation of the will. We cannot call up a particular thought, but once it is present it may "solicit our notice." And if a "crowd" of ideas is present, our attention may choose and select and even detain a particular thought, thereby stopping the train. This is the most interesting part of our "constitution."

Stewart went on to emphasize the influence of habit in the ordering of associations and the impact that this has on morality. It is association that leads to many of our actions, so that good and bad associations lead to good and bad actions. "Early to bed and early to rise" is an associated chain of words that can strongly influence a basic set of actions. More will be said on that account later in this chapter, but one interesting instance Stewart cited has to do with effects of literature, music, and drama on our moral behavior. Watching plays, listening to music, and reading novels

gives no exercise to our active habits. . . . In the contemplation of imaginary sufferings, we stop short at the impression and whatever benevolent dispositions we may feel, we have no opportunity of carrying them into action. (Martin 1961, p. 99)

The watching of plays and the reading of novels bring to mind situations that should call for action, but we acquire the habit of not reacting. When we face the real thing and real injustice or suffering calls for action, will we fail to respond due to an acquired immobility?

Nativism That Has a Familiar Ring

Nativism was popular in the psychology of the late twentieth century, and readers of that literature cannot help but see its reflection, perhaps in simpler form, in Stewart's writings. When we read "God-given Common Sense," we need only to substitute "hereditary endowment." Consider a few more of these faculties.

Stewart viewed Memory, Imagination, Judgment, and Reasoning as faculties that are actually aspects of our God-given Common Sense, hallmark of the Scottish School. It was taken for granted that "coeval with the first operations of the intellect" we have intuitions regarding our personal identity, an existing material world, and natural laws governing it. All reasoning is intuitive or deductive (precisely the view of Descartes), and Stewart cited Locke in support of the proposition that statements like "the material world exists" are known intuitively, with no need of intervening ideas, as in a chain of reasonings. Other things are known through deduction, where intervening ideas form a chain that is our reasoning, shown clearly in the syllogism.

Even learning, construed as the capacity to form habits, is part of our God-given heritage. Powers formed by Habit are innumerable and are called such things as "Quickness, Acuteness, Penetration, Presence of Mind, Good Sense, Sagacity, Comprehension, Profoundness," and many others. These all depend for their development on the varied conditions of life to which one is exposed, particularly regarding education or the business in which one engages.

Auxiliary Faculties and Principles include language use, which assumes the existence of "natural signs," consisting of certain facial expressions, body gestures, and tones of voice. Imitation is of similarly great importance, not only in the education of children but in all of our lives. Imitation is also the cause of the "contagious nature of insanity, of convulsions, of hysteric disorders, of panics, and . . . of the cures pretended to be effected by means of animal magnetism" (ibid., p. 28).

Active and Moral Powers

These include appetites, desires, affections, and the moral sense. Appetites number three: hunger, thirst, and sex, each of which is a periodic and satiable need. Desires are of many kinds, and Stewart mentioned only the "most remarkable." They include what others later called "instincts," "needs," and "motives."

The desire for knowledge, or "curiosity," is part of our constitution, as is the social instinct, which grows with the pleasures gained from society. The need for esteem is part of our original nature, and so is the desire for power, which is treated as "efficacy" in dealing with the world. From the desire for power arise the desires for property, knowledge, wealth, liberty, self-control, and the like. We also have the desire for superiority, a "malevolent" part of our nature, which supports all manner of malevolent secondary desires by association.

Affections include all feelings of emotion, which divide into benevolent (love, pity, admiration, and so on) and malevolent (hatred, revenge, jealousy, envy, and so on). Some benevolent feelings are originals and ultimates, but most are combinations of ultimates. In the case of malevolent feelings, all are "grafted on by error and criminal habits," except one. That one is resentment, which is instinctive in the case of personal danger and deliberate in cases where experience is necessary in order to discern that one has been wronged. In all cases, the term "passions" may be substituted for "affections."

Self Love Makes Us Human
Self Love is an affection that is the product of foresight and control that is peculiar to humans and which allows us to form the notion of happiness and to thus seek it. It is absent in animals, which cannot conceive happiness or the future, and it allows humans to overcome their animal natures and to attend to better things: It is resentment that appears as the manifestation of Self Love (ibid., p. 44).

Knowing Right and Wrong: Agreeing With Hume?
The Moral Faculty is an original and not resolvable sense of duty that is expressed in all languages, involves emotions evoked by instances of right and wrong, and is not the product of education and fashion. Indeed, Stewart quoted Rochefoucault (ibid., p. 44), who remarked that even "Hypocrisy itself is an homage which vice renders to virtue." The moral sense was important to Stewart and received extended discussion.

Perception of right and wrong leads to clear emotions best classified as fundamental reactions, appearing also as the perception of merit and demerit. All of this constitutes a moral obligation not due to reason but to our natural perception of right and wrong. We received essentially the same opinion from Hume.

Figure 7.2
Brown. Courtesy of the National Library of Medicine, National Institutes of Health.

Stewart and Free Will

Our free will is an aspect of a mind that nature intended us to direct outward, so we seldom attend to it. It is only this inattention that makes plausible the absurd notion that mind is unnecessary and that all is material.

Stewart criticized the British Empiricists, especially Locke, who agreed with the Scots in general but was chiefly responsible for the infernal doctrine of ideas and the inevitable path to Hume that was blazed by that doctrine. Stewart's viewpoint was eagerly adopted by the founders of America and absorbed into the fabric of American culture. It was compatible with the fundamentalist Protestant religions of the American colonies and with the frontier-conquering spirit. However, at home, in Scotland, it was too simpleminded for most.

Thomas Brown: The Subtle Scot

Thomas Brown (1778–1820; see figure 7.2) earned a medical degree from Edinburgh University when he was twenty-five and was a fairly good amateur poet. But his goal was to serve on the philosophy faculty at a university, a goal he eventually attained. He published a treatise on Hume's philosophy, particularly as it applies to causality, as it appears in powerful causes. This was sufficient to gain him a post assisting Stewart, who suffered poor health, and to later gain his own post.

He was twenty-six when the Hume piece was published, and during the period of his tenure at Edinburgh he delivered lectures that were extremely popular and were published as a set of 100 after his premature death: the *Lectures on the Philosophy of the Human Mind* (1820). In those lectures he showed every evidence of being a "Humean" rather than a member of the Scottish School. The only puzzling aspect of his view was the constant reluctance to be an associationist—like Reid, he preferred the term suggestion, and that was an important choice of terms that owed to his avocation as a poet.

Brown's Reinterpretation of the Tale of the Rose

Reid had proposed that the smell of a rose illustrates the God-given faculty that transforms the sensation to the conviction that it arises from an external cause. Brown interpreted the matter as Hume might have (Herrnstein and Boring 1965, p. 178):

[The] complex process that takes place in the mind, when we ascribe the various classes of our sensations to their various external objects ... imply, as Dr. Reid contends, a peculiar mental power ... or just the result of a more general power.

The more general power is association, and the "conviction" of Dr. Reid implies that the sensor has already developed the concept of existence of external objects, and that requires, in this case, experience with roses. "If I had never seen a rose" and had no experience with sensations of resistance and extension, I would have a sensation which I might attribute to a cause of some sort, but how could I attribute it to a rose or to any other external object?

More specifically, Brown argued that sight, smell, and hearing are not sufficient to gain this concept and that what we call a "real" object must include a context of sensations that features muscular resistance and exertion, as well as extension in space. A real object resists our movements and the more that it resists, the more real it is. The process begins with the infant's first grasp, when resistance is met and movement is interrupted.

Suggestion as Opposed to Association

"Suggestion" seems a close synonym for "association," and it should seem mysterious that Brown purposely referred to the process of suggestion—what's in a word? The answer lies in his avocation as a poet, where simile and metaphor are so important and the "sky smiles," the "forest frowns," and the "whiteness of untrodden snow" suggests the "innocence of the unpolluted heart" (Klein 1970, pp. 674–695). Such suggested relations are hardly associations, in the sense that my reciting of the Lord's Prayer or the alphabet is a demonstration of associative thought.

Thus, when Brown proposed that the primary laws of association be contiguity, resemblance, and contrast, he was restricting their application to ordinary associations of ordinary memory. More interesting mental activity does not proceed thus, as poetry shows us, but is described by other laws, the secondary laws of association as they have been called since his time. However, he called them laws of suggestion. Secondary in name only, these are far more powerful in determining our mental activity.

Secondary Laws of Suggestion/Association

Suggestion by analogy that can relate a falling apple to "falling" moons and planets is what lifts humankind from its "original imbecility." This is clearly the most important form of suggestion and shows why so-called "trains of association" cannot be traced back to their origins. It is not only the branching of an associative tree that makes tracing difficult; it is the frequent work of suggestion by analogy that does it.

When analogy is based on emotional congruity, suggestion becomes yet more difficult to trace. The quiet of the cathedral suggests eternity, a topic more difficult to contemplate while eating breakfast. A lovely spring morning suggests the freshness and energy of youth by arousing the same emotional feeling. This may also cover projection, so that we see our surroundings gloomy or bright, depending on our momentary emotional state—like suggests like.

Other secondary laws include duration, so that the "longer we dwell" on objects, the more we rely on our memory of them. They also include liveliness, frequency and recency, and what could be called context specificity. "The song, which we have never heard but from one person, can scarcely be heard again by us, without recalling that person to our memory" (Lecture II in Diamond 1974, pp. 290–292).

To this list that grows long we add the influence of habit, as exemplified in the professional peculiarities that determine that an engineer views a landscape differently from a farmer and that the two experience different suggestions. Together, these modifiers of primary laws render the course of thought utterly unpredictable (Diamond 1974, p. 292). However, the secondary laws do explain why a simple $A \rightarrow B \rightarrow C \rightarrow D$ will never be sufficient—there are too many other determinants of suggestion.

Tom Brown's Father

We speak daily of ourselves and others as "selves" that endure from birth to death as continuous entities. However, do we remain the "same self?" Perhaps the self is itself a complex idea that changes rather than an impression that remains from childhood to old age. As evidence, consider the great changes that may occur in one's "personality" as the years pass:

We quit our country . . . and after an absence of many years we return. . . . We eagerly seek him . . . who first led us into knowledge. . . . We find him sunk, perhaps, in the imbecility of idiotism, unable to recognize us,—ignorant alike of the past and of the future. . . . When we observe all this . . . do we use only a metaphor of little meaning when we say of him that he has become a different person . . . ? (In James 1890, volume 1, note p. 371)

The assumed identity of the self from day to day and birth to death finds a parallel in the life of a pair of socks, from the same source:

"Sir John Cutler had a pair of black worsted stockings, which his maid darned so often with silk that they became at last a pair of silk stockings."

And we change in ways that make us wholly different, though we cling to the conviction that something in us never changes. As Hume pointed out, we just can't help doing it.

Other Early Commentators on Associationism

What Is Associationism?

The bare mention of association does not make one an associationist. Thus, Aristotle mentioned that active recollection, as opposed to mere "remembering," often involves a string of associations, where the links are determined by contiguity, similarity, and contrast. Was Aristotle thus an associationist? Hardly—in describing Aristotle's entelechy-filled world of events occurring "naturally" and the soul identical with what it thinks, the process of trying to remember a name through a chain of associations is pretty small stuff.

In fact, Augustine mentioned associationism more and put more stock in it than did Aristotle, yet he is seldom mentioned as an associationist. That is because other salient aspects of Augustine's psychology overshadow his associationism. In the case of Aristotle, his monistic epistemology seems strange and difficult to most readers, so any hint of the familiar is eagerly grasped. Aristotle the epistemologist eludes us, but Aristotle the associationist does not.

One thing is certain, and that is the fact that there is no historical figure or contemporary person who was not or is not an associationist when it comes to *recollection*. Consider three thinkers of the eighteenth century who really were associationist and contributors to the new "moral science."

Francis Hutcheson

Hutcheson's interest lay in morality, and he saw the principle of association, given short shrift by Locke, as the basis for differences in esthetic judgments. He proposed that esthetic judgments are so diverse because of the effects produced by the association of ideas:

Associations of Ideas make Objects pleasant, and delightful, which are not naturally apt to give any such Pleasures; and the same way, the casual Conjunctions of Ideas may give a Disgust.... Thus Swine, Serpents of all Kinds, and some Insects really beautiful enough, are beheld with Aversion by many People, who have got some accidental Ideas associated to them. (Diamond 1974, pp. 282–284)

For example, the idea of the beauty of trees and forests—groves, trees, woods—arises from many often unnoticed sources. Trees are beautiful, and their shade is often welcome, as is the fact that they can shield us from observation. They provide solitude and thus attract the religious, the melancholy, the pensive, and the amorous. We even think of divinity, since the "heathen priests" placed their fictional deities there. Hutcheson noted that the faint light in Gothic churches has gained an aura of divinity, since the churches are only used in religious exercises.

Hutcheson thus proposed the basis for the great diversity of human esthetic judgments and emotional reactions, but he was careful to add one proviso, perhaps for Hume's benefit. He stressed that despite all of this diversity in judgments, we all share the same "internal sense of beauty," and many things delight and repel us all.

John Gay: Functional Autonomy of Motives?

The "Reverend Mr. Gay" was the first to apply associationism to moral judgments, and this was done in an anonymous piece published in 1731—it is only the fact that it aroused David Hartley's notice that Gay was identified at all. It was Gay who noticed that what was called association by others could account for what his fellows were calling "instinct."

People easily imagine that they have innate ideas, because of "forgetting how they came by them," and instincts like the love of money and power, as well as love of honor, order, and other things that seem so common as to be innate. "Yet, The case is really this" (quotes from Diamond 1974, pp. 588–591), wrote Gay. First we "perceive or imagine real Good (fitness to promote our happiness) in things that we love and approve of." Those things and pleasure become so associated that they never occur one without the other, and this remains the case even after the basis for the connection "is quite forgot."

How many Men are there in the World who have as strong a taste for Money as others have for virtue; who count so much Money, so much Happiness; nay, even sell their Happiness for Money; or to speak more properly, make the having Money, without any Design or Thought of using it, their ultimate End? . . .

They sell their happiness for money?[1] Gay's interpretation of acquired motivation makes recent renditions seem lame by comparison —consider that this excerpt is only a scrap from a longer and an anonymous piece.[2] His immediate effect was to spur on David Hartley, who published his version of the human association machine almost two centuries before Clark Hull would offer his remarkably similar interpretation.

David Hartley

Evidently knowing nothing of Hume, but impressed with Newton's mechanics and John Gay's thoughts on association (in Rand 1912, p. 313), the physician David Hartley (1705–1757) proposed the first thoroughgoing associationism, arranged as a neural/mental parallelism excerpts (from Rand 1912, pp. 313–330). As a physician, Hartley saw how vibrations of the sort that Newton described in nature could be duplicated in the nervous system, much like the representative theory proposed by Democritus two millennia earlier. Such vibrations could leave a residue in the nerves, in the form of "miniature vibrations" (*vibratiates* and *vibratiuncles*) that serve to code memory. Our experience is a train of sensations, with simultaneous compounds representing objects and successive associations forming the train of thought.

He laid out a series of Propositions in which sequencing of stimulus-produced sensations (A, B, C, etc.) determines parallel nerve activity. Such activity (a, b, c, etc.) remains as *vibratiates* and *vibratiuncles* in the nerves themselves, thus representing the original sequence as a set of memories. These memories become associated via contiguity, so that the occurrence of the first member (a) sets off the occurrence of the rest (b, c, etc.). This may happen as well if only the first part of the external stimulus series occurs, so that A → a, b, c, etc.). This is the case when we say "A, B, C," and our nervous system echoes "d, e, f…"

The subject, the manner of presentation, and the principles involved are strikingly similar to twentieth-century treatments. Consider Hartley's Proposition III from the work published in 1749:[3]

Prop. III—The Sensations remain in the Mind for a short time after the sensible Objects are removed.

This is very evident in the sensations impressed on the eye. Thus, to use Sir Isaac Newton's words, "If a burning coal be nimbly moved round in a circle, with gyrations continually repeated, the whole circle will appear like fire."

Hartley's subsequent propositions detail a mechanical associationism according to which the sequence of stimuli in the world stamp an imprint on the human association machine.

The Mental Mechanics of James Mill

James Mill (1773–1836) was educated as a Protestant minister but made his living as a writer, historian, and, finally, employee of the East India Company. He was a close friend of Jeremy Bentham and with him founded the political philosophy of utilitarianism. His famous son, John Stuart Mill, was intentionally raised to be a genius, which he in fact became, excelling his father in both philosophy and political theory.

James was the son of a petty tradesman at Northwater Bridge in the county of Angus in Scotland. As a boy, his abilities were brought to the attention of Sir John Stuart, one of the Barons of the Exchequer, and Mill was "in consequence, sent to the University of Edinburgh at the expense of a fund established by Lady Jane Stuart (the wife of Sir John Stuart) and some other ladies for educating young men for the Scottish Church. He went there through the usual course of study, and was licensed as a Preacher, but never followed the profession; having satisfied himself that he could not believe the doctrines of that or any other Church."[4]

He tutored for a few years, living with various families in Scotland, and then moved to London to make his living as an author, a precarious occupation he followed until 1819, when he was appointed to India House. He was then 46 and had published a year earlier a massive volume, *The History of British India*. Prior to that time he had married and had nine children and "a considerable part of almost every day was employed in the instruction of his children" (John Stuart Mill, in Lerner 1961, p. 13).

James Mill did his great mass of writing at a table facing his son, who was experiencing education at his father's hands. The child had, by the age of eight, read in Greek *Aesop's Fables*, all of Herodotus, Xenophon, Memorials of Socrates, and many of Plato's dialogues, including the *Theaetetus*, which he could not understand at age seven, reading it in Greek. At age eight he began reading Greek poets, beginning with the *Iliad*, and started Latin, which he taught his younger sister as he progressed. All along, he was learning arithmetic, history, and other subjects.

The older Mill is of special interest to us because he was the first (discounting the less clear and coherent work of Dugald Stewart) to write an extremely plain and lucid account showing how associationism explains interesting aspects of our daily experience. This was accomplished in his masterpiece, *Analysis of the Phenomena of the Human Mind*, written over a series of six summer vacations. Mill's associationism was popular and easily comprehended; it therefore came to represent empiricism and associationism in general. Thus, years later when the Gestaltists attacked the theories of Wundt and Titchener, it was really the "mental mechanics" of Mill, generic empiricism and associationism, that was the target.

What Is Our Experience?

Mill evidently knew nothing of Kant but would have no doubt dismissed his a priori "intuitions" as irrelevant. He was certainly familiar with the Scottish philosophy of Reid and Stewart, and he mentioned the pleasure that he felt recalling a lecture by Stewart. However, he had no use for the faculties of mind that his Scottish colleagues promoted. Let us consider James's views, which are clear, refreshing, and useful, just as is a fairly modern counterpart, the learning theory of Edwin Guthrie (e.g., 1952). First, what is our experience? Mill tells us that it is simpler than we might have supposed (1829, p. 70): Following Locke's simple treatment of "idea" as whatever is the object of thought, rather than Hume's analysis to irreducible constituents of experience, Mill shows that he does not use sensation and idea precisely as Hume used impression and idea:

I see a horse: that is a sensation. Immediately I think of his master: that is an idea. The idea of his master makes me think of his office; he is a minister of state: that is another idea ... (1829, pp. 70–71)

Hume's sensations (or impressions) were clear and lively, as are our sensations, but Hume could not know that they were produced by an object. For James Mill, this is not a problem to be long considered; objects produce our sensations, and how they do so is a "problem for physical philosophy" (1829, p. 71). Our ideas are copies of sensations, not the objects that produce them. Both sensations and ideas are defined as Locke defined "ideas"—whatever may be the mind's object. Mill (1829, pp. 71–72) followed David Hartley in distinguishing synchronous and successive associations:

Of the order established among the objects of nature, by which we mean the objects of our senses, two remarkable cases are all which here we are called upon to notice; the SYNCHRONOUS ORDER and the SUCCESSIVE ORDER.

Following Thomas Brown, synchronous associations are treated as "real" objects when associated with the ideas of muscular contraction and ideas of touch that suggest extension in space.

What Determines the Strength of Association?
Our ideas are linked by contiguity—closeness in time and space—that reflects the order of our sensations, produced somehow by an outside world. Mill was not in the least skeptical of the existence of external reality. Ideas that occur synchronously or successively with great frequency are more strongly associated. Hence, the sight, touch, smell, and taste of a ripe apple is experienced so often as just such a complex that the elements seem indissolubly joined—they "coalesce." And the alphabet we learned as a child is composed of letters that are joined in rigid sequence—again the effect of frequency.

Other compounds are joined also by vividness, by which Mill meant recency and pleasant, painful, or otherwise emotional aspects. Vividness also separates sensations from ideas, so that the former are usually more "vivid." We will see uses for vividness as relative recency or remoteness in time and as emotional content.

Mind Is All in the Ideas

James Mill explained all of the phenomena of the human mind as the outcomes of passive compounding of ideas, beginning with simple ones that join to form "complex" ideas, which themselves combine until we reach the highest-order idea, that of "Every Thing." From Hartley he borrowed the term "duplex idea" to refer to a compound of complex ideas, but we will speak only of more or less complex associations. An interesting example lies in the analysis of a seemingly simple idea, that of "weight."

"By association, merely" weight may be shown to contain many ideas, as shown below:

How Many Ideas in "Weight?"

"WEIGHT" ... means → Resistance → Will

→ Muscle Contraction

→ Direction → Place

→ Extension → Space

→ Motion → Time

→ Space

Rather than begin with intuitions of time, space, and substance, as did Kant, or with faculties, as did Reid, Mill put all of the power in the ideas. There *are* no mental powers or faculties. Rather than a faculty of discrimination, there are different sensations. Rather than a faculty of attention, we need only recognize that some sensations and ideas are more interesting than are others; again, the power is in the ideas. We consider below ways in which mental powers and faculties may be treated as aspects of the content of experience, rather than as autonomous powers.

The Founder of Psychosomatic Medicine?

Experience begins with sensation, and James Mill added the "alimentary sense" to the standard five and attached special importance to the last—sensations arising from the viscera within the body. Such sensations usually go unnoticed but play a large part in our moods. He described a case in which one learns of the death of his son. The words of the messenger are scarcely heard, but through association they bring thoughts of the son:

It is my son that is before me, suffering, acting, speaking...and kindled the affections, have been as little heeded, as the respiration which has been accelerated, while the ideas were received. (Mill, 1829, chapter 3)

The important factor is the presence of sensations from internal organs that add color to our experience but that are seldom appreciated as sensations.

Not only do some of our most important sensations come from within the body, but some ideas are associated with certain conditions within the body. This relation of idea and viscera can account for bodily ills and for the nightmares we sometimes have.

Thus, anxiety, in most people, disorders the digestion. It is no wonder, then, that the internal feelings that accompany indigestion, should excite the ideas which prevail in a state of anxiety...and this is sufficiently confirmed by the horrible dreams to which men are subject from indigestion. (Ibid.)

Stress, anxiety, "disagreeable circumstances" produce disordered agitation in the stomach, intestines, and elsewhere in the viscera. Thus, when overeating or disease produce those same feelings in the body, it is natural that we experience sensations of anxiety. This often occurs for reasons we cannot name, since we don't notice the body sensations. Or, even if we do, we attribute them to their accustomed source and search for the cause of the anxiety that must be causing them. However, often there is no such cause to be found.

Nineteenth-Century Popular Associationism

Carpenter: Mental Physiology
W. B. Carpenter was a physician and physiologist who authored an influential text, *Principles of Human Physiology*. One chapter in both the fourth and fifth editions (1852 and 1855) was entitled "Outline of Psychology," which Carpenter expanded to produce his *Principles of Mental Physiology*, published in 1876. It was one of the sources referred to most often by William James, in his classic *Principles of Psychology*, and it contained an amazing amount of information that is thoroughly modern.[5]

The Training of the Moral Habit

Carpenter's chief thesis was that habit is all important, and that organs "grow to the habitual mode." This applies to muscles, which grow or atrophy according to use, and to the nervous system, which determines character, depending upon the habits established in youth. In both cases, inheritance plays a larger or smaller role as well.

"Man has been said to be a bundle of habits," including intellectual and moral habits; the present is the resultant of the past, so that whatever we learn, think, or do in our youth will come again in later life either as a Nemesis or as an Angel's visit.[6] He recommended that order and regularity be established as early as possible. Even the infant must not be brought out of its bed simply because it is crying. He also recommended what a century later would be called the "extinguishing of crying" in the infant who demands to be held before its nap (p. 354).

Discipline must be established in infancy so that the habit of self-discipline is planted; this is just what Aristotle had suggested. This must begin as external coercion until a habit of duty or obligation is formed as the "internal correlative." Along the same lines, he stressed the importance of modeling by older siblings, who are more influential than parents, the parents being so different from the children as to be unemulated.

Finally, Carpenter (and Alexander Bain) emphasized the training of willpower through exercise, since "will is a habit." However, he went further than Freud was later to do in arguing that the effects of such exercise may be in part inherited. Carpenter believed that all "right habits of thought" in general were hereditary and that if we increase our thinking power, we improve the thinking power of future generations.

Bain and Physiological Psychology

Alexander Bain (1818–1903) founded the journal *Mind* and wrote textbooks that even further influenced the thought of the nineteenth (and twentieth) centuries. His *The Senses and the Intellect* was published in four editions between 1855 and 1879 and was so filled with facts that one wonders how anyone could be so diligent as to compile them all. The final (1879) edition even featured a long appendix, "The Psychology of Aristotle."

A second volume, *The Emotions and the Will*, was published in 1859 and in three later editions through 1899. The two tomes sold poorly at first but became the standard for the next fifty years. Abridged and combined, they appeared as *Mental and Moral Science* in 1868.

Bain was born to the family of a poor weaver in Aberdeen and spent many long hours at the loom as a child (this account is based on Boring 1950). He was on his own by seventeen and mastered geometry, algebra, trigonometry, and "fluxions" before entering Marischal College, then separate from Aberdeen University, at the age of twenty-two. For the next twenty years he continually sought university posts but was unsuccessful. He was hired at Glasgow as professor of mathematics and natural science, but resigned after a year because of low pay and arduous duties.

Most of his time was spent in freelance writing in Scotland and in London, where he became acquainted with John Stuart Mill and assisted in the writing of Mill's *Logic*. In 1860 he was offered the chair of English and logic at Aberdeen, a post he held for the next twenty years. Knowing nothing of English and not enough about logic, he wrote textbooks and manuals on both over the first few years of his appointment. However, his main interest was psychology, and his two masterpieces in the field had been out for a few years.

They were meant to be physiological treatments of psychology. Bain was no physician, but he knew Carpenter personally, used Carpenter's *Human Physiology*, and had taken a postgraduate course in anatomy (Boring 1950, p. 238). This was not the speculative physiology of a Descartes or a Hartley. In large part because of Bain, William James could begin his *Principles* of 1890 with the confident assertion that psychology was essentially physiology.

Activity Is Basic

In *The Senses and the Intellect*, Bain stressed the fact that organisms are typically active, rather than passive, and this is evidenced in ordinary muscle tonus, in the continual activity of the circulatory system and other systems, in the fact that we awaken from sleep, and spontaneously feel energetic. The movement of the infant, when warm and fed, shows also that we are active beings.

Thought Is Always Relative

Relativity is a fundamental law of thought, falling under one of the three primary attributes of thought, the consciousness of difference, or the act of discrimination. The other two major attributes were the consciousness of agreement and the fact of retentiveness. Relativity includes the law of contrast, as well as relations like "parent/child, up/down, north/south, and light/dark, along with an infinity of others" (Bain 1879, p. 9). The attribute of retentiveness turns out to be exhaustively explained by the principle of association by contiguity.

Hence, the leading associationist text of the nineteenth century emphasized both spontaneous activity and relativity. It also emphasized the law of diffusion, such that all stimulation affects the activity of the whole body, much like the strings of a harp resonate to large vibrations occurring around them. A loud noise has, we now know better than did Bain, effects on more than our cerebral cortex—it alters our heart rate, perspiration, pupil constriction, and other indices of sympathetic nervous system arousal. Sokolov (1963) called all of these changes the "orienting response," and it has been offered as an indicant of attention.

The color red or the smell of musk makes us stronger, for example, by altering heart rate and muscle tonus. Other colors and sounds produce other effects, documented by James (1890) in his chapter XXIII, "The Production of Movement." If we open a vein and watch the blood pulse out, it can be made to flow faster at the beat of a drum. The most exciting (to our body) color is red, the exciting taste is sour, and musk is the "dynamogenic" odor.

Bain was also responsible for the first—or one of the first—statements of the theory of ideomotor action to explain voluntary ("willed") behavior. According to this view, voluntary behavior begins as spontaneous or as reflex behavior, so that we pull our finger from a flame because a spinal reflex pulls it for us. Or we orient toward a light because it is moving and thus "captures" us. Once all of these elementary movements occur, a track is left in the nervous system, meaning that the movement will recur more easily in the future.

The "idea" of the movement requires sensation, as we find when attempting to walk or to sign our name while under anesthesia and unable to see our movements (Bain 1879, pp. 328–329). When we think of the sensations of movement, it is difficult not to repeat the movements, and our "recollection is suppressed articulation" (Bain 1879, pp. 338–339). The child acts out while describing, the dog's eyes move while it dreams, and we feel the finger crook as we imagine the feelings that accompany crooking.

Trial-and-Error Learning

Ideas of movements lead to movement, and those ideas are often accompanied by ideas of pleasures and pains—thus arises our self-control. However, the young are often unable to exert such discipline, since they cannot clearly enough envision future pleasures and pains.

For this reason, a bit of punishment is needed (Bain 1879, p. 334). Trial and error learning was emphasized in 1859 in *The Emotions and the Will*.

His views on trial and error were formed when he observed the first few hours of life of two lambs. Their initial movements seemed random, but chance contacts with the mother's skin or nipple quickly organized and directed movement. In a day, the sight of the mother led to behavior directed toward suckling, all the result of trial and error (Boakes 1984, p. 9). Other examples involve human babies removing needles that prick them or acting to gain warmth when cold.

Bain wrote, "when pain co-exists with an accidental alleviating movement, or when pleasure co-exists with a pleasure-sustaining movement, such movements become subject to the control of the respective feelings which they occur in company with" (ibid.).

Bain also pointed out, as if it were the greatest commonplace, that imitation is not chiefly of children imitating adults. Rather it is "notorious" that it is the nurse who imitates the child, at least in matters of speech. He was careful to emphasize that imitation is certainly common, but it is not instinctive. The "associative principle is an indispensable requisite here as elsewhere" (Bain 1879, p. 417); we see no imitation in the youngest infants and we see it develop slowly and gradually when it does appear, especially in the learning of speech.

His chapter on "The Moral Habits" offered practical advice on changing our habits—important matters for both Carpenter and Bain. William James discussed this in his famous chapter "Habit" (1890, pp. 145–146).

All of this practical associationism was less concerned with epistemology than were Berkeley and Hume, just as contemporary applied psychologists are unconcerned with epistemology. However, seemingly subtle questions have powerful practical consequences, as John Stuart Mill, one of the greatest minds of the nineteenth century, well knew. He returned to the question that concerned Hume and Kant—is knowledge all acquired after experience, as Hume contended, or do we come with intuitions?

John Stuart Mill's Theory of Belief

The effect of Mr. Mill's review is the absolute annihilation of all Sir W. Hamilton's doctrines, opinions, of all he has written or taught.... The whole fabric of the Hamiltonian philosophy is not only demolished, but its very stones are ground to powder. (Pattison 1965, p. 562)

As mentioned above, John Stuart Mill (1806–1873) was raised to be a genius, and a genius is what he became. He was tutored by his father, James, so that he was reading Greek at the age of three and Plato at eight. In later life he counted himself fortunate to have been so educated (*Autobiography*, p. 27).

As a young man of twenty-five he was strongly attracted to the brilliant Harriet Taylor, aged twenty-three, a married woman with whom he maintained the closest possible correspondence for twenty years. When her husband died, they eventually married and lived a life of bliss, for seven years. At that time, in France, she died of tuberculosis, probably caught from him—he was devastated (Lerner 1961). After returning briefly to England and serving in Parliament, representing Westminster, he returned to Avignon and spent the last years of his life in a cottage near the grave of Harriet. Her daughter Helen came to live with him and perhaps served the same function that Harriet and his father had served.

He has been judged as one of the foremost intellects who ever lived, but it is clear that he viewed Harriet as more intelligent. It is certain that she collaborated on many of his political pieces, and he expressed his opinion of her in the dedication to *On Liberty*:

To the beloved and deplored memory of her who was the inspirer, and in part the author, of all that is best in my writings—the friend and wife.... Were I but capable of interpreting to the world one half the great thoughts and noble feelings which are buried in her grave, I should be the medium of a greater benefit to it, than is ever likely to arise from anything that I can write. (In Lerner 1961, p. 152)

Another great influence on him was the years he spent, as had his father, working for the East India Company. He rose to the post of Secretary, meaning that he was in charge of all operations in India not clearly military. The company was dismembered by Parliament and the pieces sold to highest bidders and political cronies, at least as Mill described it. His tenure there did him some service in clarifying and properly presenting his writing (ibid., p. 57).

Time for Combat

For John Stuart Mill, philosophy was not an academic discipline, cut off from the other doings of the world. In particular, the conflict between intuitionism, or rationalism, and empiricism had clear practical consequences:

Now, the difference between these two schools of philosophy, that of Intuition, and that of Experience and Association, is not a mere matter of abstract speculation; it is full of practical consequences.... The practical reformer has continually to demand that changes be made in things which are supported by powerful and widely spread feelings.... (*Autobiography*, p. 160)

By "intuitionist" is meant any of the class of theories that assume that we have intuitions/faculties/innate category systems through which we apprehend the world. Kant is the most eminent example of an intuitionist, but Reid and Stewart are exemplars as well. So was Sir William Hamilton, described by Brett as "incredibly erudite" (Brett/Peters 1912/1965, p. 447). Mill's (1865) book, *An Examination of Sir William Hamilton's Philosophy*, provided an elegant empiricist counterargument to the intuitionist theories. To prepare for his argument, consider first his doctrine of mental chemistry presented in his *Logic* (1843).

Mental Chemistry versus Mental Mechanics

Thomas Brown had persuasively argued that a physical object is the sum of sensations of color, texture, form, and muscular resistance, and Mill believed that Brown was correct. However, he found it impossible to sort out the sensations, especially those of muscular resistance. That may be the origin of our conception of matter early in our lives, but it seemed not the current basis for what we call real. This led him later to conclude that such feelings cannot be what lead us to call some objects real and others imaginary.

Down with Intuitions

His alternative to Brown's theory began with his crushing of Hamilton's intuitionism (J. S. Mill 1865, chapter 11). What do we mean when we call one thing a real object and another a mere phantasm, illusion, or image? The line between real and imagined may be hard to draw, as Dugald Stewart pointed out. What we call real cannot depend upon feelings of muscular resistance, since these are swallowed up in the mental chemistry out of which compound ideas are made. The alternative Mill provided is the case for those who believe that knowledge of space and objects in it is not innate but is an acquired product.

We Do Not Perceive Sensations

Sensation itself provides only a minute amount of what we believe that we see, hear, smell, taste, and touch. What we expect to experience has a lot to do with what we do experience; as Mill put it, we make a "heap of inferences." An extreme example of this occurs in séances, where a person readied to see a departed loved one sees just that. What the medium running the séance presents as "the departed loved one" need not be an accurate replica, since the expectation of the subject can make the replica accurate. Is it really the loved one who is seen? Indeed it is, in the same sense that we see loved ones now around us as we believe they "really" are. We see them colored by all of the past experiences with them and with the feelings that we have for them.

Mill noted that a mountain in clear air is judged nearer, since "clearer means nearer"; again, the present sensation is not the determinant of the perception. If we look at a landscape inverted, either because our head is inverted or because we are looking through an astronomical telescope, we notice that the scene appears flat and that colors and contrasts are vivid and striking. That is because when we ordinarily view a landscape, the colors and contrasts are cues for depth and distance, and, as such, they become "absorbed" into the scene. When the scene is inverted, color and contrast lose this function, so the scene is flat and the colors are noticed.

Matter is a name for reliable sources of sensation, as represented in the cloud/context/fringe of past experiences with a given sensory core. The feelings produced seem even more real than the present core of sensations themselves; hence, they "inevitably generate" a belief in matter and a belief that we know matter intuitively. The origin in past sensation, the previous contexts, is forgotten.

Kant Refuted, after a Fashion

Mill thus refuted Kant, in a sense, by insisting that we stick to psychological explanations. Kant's logic led to the conclusion that we require innate intuitions in order to have experience in the first place. Mill argued that this was an unwarranted conclusion. To understand our experience, we must begin with experience, and that comes as sensations in time and space. We do not ponder the origins of time and space; that is a metaphysical and not a psychological enterprise.

Mill's position would be called phenomenological today, and while contemporary phenomenologists would disagree with him on many matters, they would agree that the basis for understanding experience is experience.

8 Darwin and Evolutionary Thinking

I worked on true Baconian principles, and without any theory collected facts on a wholesale scale. (Charles Darwin, in Ferris 1988, p. 233)

... in every generation the inferior would inevitably be killed off and the superior would remain—that is, the fittest would survive. (Alfred Russel Wallace, in Ferris 1988, pp. 242–243)

How extremely stupid of me not to have thought of that. (Thomas Huxley, in Ferris 1988, p. 243)

Origins of Evolutionary Thought

Aristotle believed in a *scala naturae* of fixed species arranged from low to high. It seems well expressed, and endorsed, by John Locke in the seventeenth century:

When we consider the infinite power and wisdom of the Maker, we have reason to think that it is suitable...that the species of creatures should also, by gentle degrees, ascend upwards from us towards His infinite perfection. (Ferris 1988, p. 223)

The worry of many believers in such a continuum of being was the discovery of gaps—"missing links"—in the continuum of being. When such evidence of extinction was found, as in the remains of woolly mammoths, sabre-toothed tigers, and plants that were never seen living by human eyes, *catastrophism* was used to explain it. Just as God had sent the Flood, gigantic geological changes had changed climates, flooded regions, raised mountains, and wiped out whole species in the blink of an eye. Part of this explanation rested on the fact that many of these catastrophes were possible only when the earth was young and could not occur today. Hence, the present was cut from the past, which was left unknowable. But at least extinction was intelligible.

Influences on Darwin

An opponent of this view was Charles Lyell,[1] a Scottish geologist, who saw the theory of catastrophes winnowing a fixed scale of species as "dogma...calculated to foster indolence" (Ferris 1988, p. 225). He proposed *uniformitarianism*, which posited gradual change in life forms due to natural causes that are the same today as when life began. Extinction of species depends on causes similar in kind to those that cause erosion of rock. Uniformitarianism had originally been proposed by Scottish geologist James Hutton, who saw "the ruins of an older world in the structure of our planet" (Ferris 1988, p. 225).

Lyell spent his life traveling and making notes on the constantly changing earth that he saw. His father had been a botanist, and he had studied entomology, so he was sensitive to the "continual flux" of the animate world. And he saw how gradual change, not catastrophe, could affect life forms:

Forests may be as dense and lofty as those of Brazil, and may swarm with quadrupeds, birds, and insects, yet at the end of ten thousand years one layer of black mould, a few inches thick, may be the sole representative of those myriads of trees, leaves, flowers, and fruits. (Ferris 1988, p. 228)

The reason for mentioning Lyell is that the first volume of his book was packed by Charles Darwin (see figure 8.1) for his trip around the world during the period 1831–1836 on H. M. S. Beagle.[2] Darwin had dropped out of medical school and failed to do well in the undemanding theological studies to which he had been consigned in hopes that if he was unfit to be a physician like his father, perhaps he could be a parson. His chance to sail on the Beagle owed to contacts at Cambridge and to the fact that botany may be the field where he could use his unusual powers of observation and collecting.

Darwin was the "collector of dry facts"[3] that were necessary to understand the laws governing the variety of life forms in the world. And he was an observer, as a friend, Dr. Edward Eickstead Lane, wrote in describing walks taken with Darwin:

No object in nature, whether Flower, or Bird, or Insect of any kind, could avoid his loving recognition. He knew about them all...could give you endless information. (Ibid., p. 232)

Darwin described himself as seeing as if through the eyes of Lyell, writing that "I feel as if my books came half out of Sir Charles Lyell's brain" (ibid., 231–232). Throughout his travels he saw evidence for Lyell's thesis—an old world, changing now as it has been for time out

Figure 8.1
Darwin. Courtesy of the Archives of the History of American Psychology, University of Akron.

of mind. He found marine fossils in Chilean mountains twelve thousand feet high and developed a theory of atolls based on volcanic action and erosion, coupled with the slow buildup of coral.

As the earth changed, so could living things. Darwin left England a creationist, like almost everyone else, and returned in five years with some doubts. And he should have had doubts! His grandfather, Erasmus Darwin, had published *Zoonomia* in the 1790s, a fiercely evolutionary book that wondered about the one organism from which all others, of all species, evolved—*"THE GREAT FIRST CAUSE...THE GREAT ARCHITECT! THE CAUSE OF CAUSES! THE PARENT OF PARENTS!"* (Ibid., p. 236).

Erasmus Darwin argued that changes in species over the course of time are due to outside influences and that an animal, once changed, passes on that change to its offspring. This belief in inheritance of acquired characteristics was endorsed also by his grandson.[4]

Thomas Brown and Erasmus Darwin

The associationists of the early nineteenth century were only too ready to accept instinct, as long as it was reasonably defined. Thomas Brown was a member of the Scottish School of Common Sense and critiqued *Zoonomia*, in his "Observations on the Zoonomia of Erasmus Darwin," in 1798. Arguing that instinct is no news, Brown wrote:

Those who defend instinct as a "divine something, a kind of inspiration," are, indeed, worthy of ridicule. But, if by the term instinct be meant *a predisposition to certain actions, when certain sensations exist*, the admission of it is so far from being ridiculous, that, without it, the phenomena of animation cannot possibly be explained. (In Diamond 1974, p. 385)

Lamarck

Charles Darwin's grandfather was only one influence—he also knew well the thesis of Jean Baptiste de Monet,[5] the man most closely associated with the doctrine of the inheritance of acquired characteristics, who in fact took as central that principle which Erasmus Darwin took for granted.[6] Though much of his work was fraught with folly in presentation and interpretation,[7] he correctly emphasized three important things:

1. That species vary under changing environmental influences. Unchanging conditions may produce what appear to be static life forms.

2. That there is a unity underlying species diversity.

3. That species are subject to progressive development. This development as "improvement" owing to effort made Lamarckianism attractive to many.

Following Erasmus Darwin, Lamarck emphasized the passing on of acquired traits through a "law of use and disuse," such that a deer-like animal forced to seek higher and higher foliage for feed gives rise over generations to the giraffe. Similarly, animals that live in darkness, like moles, lose vision and eventually eyes. Other speculation by Lamarck and his colleagues brought biological discussion into disrepute for some years. We will see that Lamarck's belief in the inheritance of acquired characteristics was eventually adopted by Charles Darwin himself and by many others.

Malthus and the *Essay on Population*

A third influence on Darwin had to be the Rev. T. R. Malthus, mathematician and economist, whose *Essay on Population* struck both Darwin and Alfred Russel Wallace with the ideas of struggles and survivals. At the time, the chief intent of Malthus's work was the warning that over-population is attended by famine, since subsistence cannot match the geometrical increase in populations.

This was 1798, published anonymously at a time when the utilitar-ian philosophers, including Adam Smith, Joseph Priestly, and Jeremy Bentham, were promoting the idea of universal peace, liberty, and equality, allowing limitless increases in population. Malthus's thesis did not make the utilitarian paradise as attractive as it had seemed, since the paradise would have no curbs on population. However, it did make one think of struggles among members of the same species for scarce resources. The survivors would live to reproduce.

Finally, Darwin himself claimed that the greatest influence on him was that of Professor John Stevens Henslow of Cambridge. He was expert in botany, entomology, chemistry, minerology, and geology (in Darwin's view; de Beer 1983, p. 36), and Darwin spent much time with him. Henslow seems almost a model for what Darwin himself was to be taken for by later detractors. His strength was his drawing of conclusions from "long-continued minute observations," but Dar-win doubted that "anyone would say that he possessed much original genius" (de Beer 1983, p. 36).

Like Henslow, Darwin was a careful observer, and he became a great collector, especially of beetles. In his autobiography, he wrote:

I will give a proof of my zeal: one day on tearing off some old bark, I saw two rare beetles and seized one in each hand; then I saw a third and new kind, which I could not bear to lose, so that I popped the one which I held in my right hand into my mouth. (de Beer, pp. 34–35)

Darwin's Work

By the end of the Beagle's voyage in 1837 Darwin was recognized as a painstaking naturalist who had worked on barnacles and mammalian fossil forms and had written on geology and reefs. He was thought to be patient, reflective, and prone to ponder before publishing. What he did next is best described by himself:

When on board H. M. S. Beagle, I was much struck with the distribution of the organic beings inhabiting South America, and the geological relations of the present to the past inhabitants. These facts seemed to throw light on the origin of species.... My first note-book was opened in 1837.... After five years' work I drew up some short notes; these I enlarged in 1844.... Mr Wallace, who is now studying the natural history of the Malay Archipelago, has arrived at almost exactly the same general conclusions. (Singer 1959, pp. 301–302)

The *Origin of Species* was published in 1859 and revolutionized biology and other disciplines as well. Darwin surely did not "discover" the concept of evolution, and he was mistaken on many counts, but his was the evidence that sealed the fate of the catastrophists and the fixed scale of nature. After formulating his theory by 1839 and outlining it by 1844 in a 230-page essay, Darwin sat on it for fifteen years while he settled in the country and fathered ten children. He wrote books on his voyage, on reefs, on volcanos, and on seven years' work with barnacles. However, he did not write *The Origin* until he realized that Wallace was going to beat him to it.

One reason for the delay, no longer accepted, was his constant illness. He suffered from intense headaches, vomiting, and heart palpitations and consulted the best physicians in England looking for a cure.[8] He also had himself hypnotized, underwent hydrotherapy, and spent a life described by his son Francis as "one long struggle against the weariness and strain of sickness" (Ferris 1988, p. 240). His illness has never been diagnosed; he may have suffered from severe allergies or from a disease contracted in his travels.

Whatever the disease, it did not prevent his work on other subjects, so the delay must have been due to fear of the consequences of publishing evidence for evolution. Aside from the unreasoning opposition of the church, there was scientific opposition to such views and a disdain for the concept of evolution, "which had long been an enthusiasm of ecstatics and occultists devoted to seances and tales of fairies flitting across the moors at dawn. To advance so amateurish a theory was to invite learned ridicule" (Ferris 1988, p. 241).

Darwin did write up his views—in pencil—in 1842. The 230-page manuscript was only found in 1896, fourteen years after his death. With his wife's death in that year, the family house was vacated, and the earliest formulation of Darwin's theory was found in a cupboard under the stairs (Freeman 1977, p. 1). Darwin was astonished when he received Wallace's paper on June 3, 1858.

It was titled, "On the Tendency of Varieties to Depart Indefinitely from the Original Type," and Wallace sought Darwin's opinions. Wallace was also a collector of plants and insects, was influenced by Lyell's writings, and had read Malthus. While recovering from malaria, he hit on the notion of competition and that the fittest would survive, to use his words (Ferris 1988, p. 243). Darwin was inclined to be magnanimous and let Wallace take the credit, but he was persuaded by Lyell and Hooker to make a joint announcement of his and Wallace's conclusions and to speedily write a brief account for publication. The "abstract," as he called it, was 200,000 words long and finished within a year. That was *The Origin of Species by Means of Natural Selection*.

That book is so detailed as to tire some readers, and Darwin indeed intended to give "a long catalogue of dry facts" (ibid., p. 243). If not for Wallace's letter and the haste that it forced, he would have included many more facts than he did. Was he merely a "kind of machine for grinding general laws out of large collections of facts," as he asked himself? Darwin replied to such critics:

Some of my critics have said, "Oh, he is a good observer, but he has no power of reasoning." I do not think that this can be true, for the Origin of Species is one long argument from the beginning to the end, and it has convinced not a few able men. No one could have written it without having some power of reasoning. (Ibid., p. 244)

Is the Earth Old Enough? William Thomson, Belfast-born mathematician and physicist, whose specialty was heat and whose title was Lord Kelvin, announced in 1868 that the sun could be no more than 500,000,000 years old. Such a brief span seemed insufficient for natural selection to have produced the current diversity of life, so Darwin and many others were driven to accept Lamarckian inheritance of acquired characteristics.

In this way, a few generations could produce a mastiff with an inherited fear of butchers, perhaps acquired by successive generations witnessing animals being slaughtered by butchers. By the same token, a gentleman could be produced after a few generations of savages pass on the mental improvements gained by living in civilization.

After Darwin's death, matters changed and the earth grew much older. Kelvin had based his assessment on the opinions of Hermann Helmholtz, who assumed that the sun's heat was generated by release of energy as its mass was contracted by gravity. Such a process could go on no more than 40,000,000 years, a figure raised to 500,000,000 by Kelvin, assuming that Helmholtz was right regarding the process producing heat.

Kelvin allowed that there "may be laws that we have not discovered," and there were. The discovery of radioactivity by Wilhelm Roentgen led to Cambridge physicist Ernest Rutherford's perfecting of dating through assessment of decay of radioactive materials.[9] He could say with confidence that "this piece of pitchblende is seven hundred million years old," based on the amount of uranium or radium remaining in it.

Rutherford knew that this discovery "thus increases the possible limit of the duration of life on this planet, and allows the time claimed by the geologist and biologist for the process of evolution" (Ferris 1988, p. 249). However, this was after the turn of the twentieth century. During the last decades of the nineteenth century, it was universally agreed that natural selection alone could not explain evolution.

Alfred Wallace: Are Humans Exempt?   Darwin originally had little to say about human evolution, but Wallace did. In 1864 he applied natural selection to human evolution and dealt with two problems that frequently were brought up. First, why do humans seem so far superior in intelligence to even the great apes, and second, why do remains of prehistoric ancestors appear similar in body and form to moderns who discover their remains? Shouldn't their brains have been smaller?

Wallace proposed that humans underwent natural selection long ago and that resulted in an upright posture and present physical characteristics. However, humanity's control over its environment freed it from further pressures of natural selection. Further development occurred through the accumulation of knowledge and technology and through cultural transmission. Such transmission occurs widely among animals, as well, and Wallace emphasized the learning involved in birds' nest building and singing.

Wallace was far better traveled than was Darwin and other evolutionists, and he was impressed by the intelligence of savage peoples, who seemed "little inferior to the average member of our learned societies" (Boakes 1984, p. 6). Their brains lacked only education, just as the European brain lacked cultural education in prehistoric times. The modern human brain seemed to Wallace to have existed in advance of the needs of its owner, and it seemed impossible that it could have developed through small variations subjected to natural selection. This could have occurred only through the intervention of some higher power. Hence, Wallace added a Deity to assist natural selection on humanity's behalf. Such a conclusion could not be allowed to pass uncontested, and Darwin answered in 1871.

Darwinism and the Human/Animal Schism   In that year Darwin published *The Descent of Man*, devoted to showing that the differences between man and beast were not so great as to warrant Wallace's "suprahuman intervention" to account for the human brain. Two chapters aimed to show that reason and higher mental powers exist in animals other than humans and that our status is therefore not unique. Others pointed to instinct in human behavior, a topic that was popular in the late nineteenth century and, following a period of disrepute, resurfaced in the last decades of the twentieth century.

It was Porphyry who, in the third and fourth centuries, was an opponent of the Christian sects of his time; he attacked them because of their eating of flesh, though the animals whose flesh was consumed had souls like their own. Like Darwin many centuries later, Porphyry diminished the distinction between human and animal "mind."

As proof that animals have souls, Porphyry pointed to the same sorts of evidence that Darwin used in his arguments for the existence of animal minds. First, animals have reason, which in those times was divided into "outgoing" or "indwelling." Evidence for outgoing reason lies in the communication among animals, who seem to understand one another, at least at some level. The counterargument that we cannot understand them is moot, wrote Porphyry, since we do not understand humans of other nationalities and languages, but we do not deny them souls on those grounds.

And, in fact, we do understand them to an extent, since we can tell when they are hungry, angry, or fearful. As far as indwelling reason, is it not obvious that animals seem to feel envy and that they have virtues such as courage and industriousness? They have no written laws, but neither did humans at one time, yet humans are supposed to have souls. Finally, like humans, animals are liable to go mad. Is it only prejudice that denies them souls (Brett/Peters 1965)?

Though he was almost certainly unfamiliar with Porphyry's arguments, Darwin agreed and pointed to scores of examples supporting the presence of intelligence in animals—examples suggesting emotional experience, reasoning power, and proto-language. Everyone is familiar with the playful puppy, and Darwin referred to playful ants, pretending to bite and exhibiting clear signs of jolliness. We know also the courageous dog, the faithful horse, and the curious cat—example after example can be brought to show that animals feel happy, sad, dejected, proud, brave, jealous, and so on. Animals show emotion much as we do.

The old saw that animals are guided by instinct and humans by reason was popular in the nineteenth century and seemed beyond any dispute. How can a spider learn to spin a web and how can a pigeon build a nest unless nature has implanted wisdom in advance—as instinct? Doesn't intelligence replace instinct as we pass from lower to higher organisms?

However, Darwin dismissed this view, pointing to the direct, not inverse, relation between instinct and reason. Organisms like the beaver, which learns quickly and is otherwise intelligent, have many instincts, and simple, less reasonable organisms, such as insects, have correspondingly fewer instincts. Reason does not increasingly replace instinct as we pass up the phylogenic scale (for Darwin, there really was no "scale" of higher and lower).

Critics at the time and since were quick to point out that Darwin's case for reason and emotion in animals was not entirely persuasive. Even a century later, the question of mentality in animals was debated.

Herbert Spencer's Evolutionary Associationism

Herbert Spencer was a self-educated writer and civil engineer who made his living as a journalist and became friends with Thomas Huxley, self-described as "Darwin's bulldog." He was also acquainted with Henry Lewes and Marian Evans; it was evidently Spencer's insistence that their relationship be platonic and his introducing her to Lewes that led to her becoming George Eliot, supported in her novel writing by Lewes.

Spencer applied the principle of evolution to all subjects, years before Darwin's *Origin* was published. Darwin's opinion of Spencer seemed mixed admiration and abhorrence. As he wrote,

Herbert Spencer's conversation seemed to me very interesting, but I did not like him particularly... I think that he was extremely egotistical. After reading any of his books I generally feel enthusiastic admiration.... Nevertheless I am not conscious of having profited in my own work by Spencer's writings.... His conclusions never convince me.... Anyhow they have not been of any use to me. (de Beer 1983, p. 64)

By 1855 Spencer had published his *Principles of Psychology*, which, like his other books, applied evolutionary thought to everything. He saw a development of simple to complex in every part of nature, animate and inanimate. In behavior he saw a "correspondence of inner to outer relations," as the world imprints itself on the organism's nervous system, just as rain from a roof makes a ditch in the ground below it. Successively deeper imprints are passed on, Lamarckian style, to successive generations, and the world–organism correspondence grows closer.

The nervous system evolves from simple reflexes to compounds of reflexes, or instincts. Then memory is added and finally reasoning and consciousness. The simple law of association by contiguity is responsible for the whole process, and, if a conscious thought regularly accompanies an action, the action becomes increasingly automatic and eventually occurs without consciousness. Since Lamarckian inheritance was also a feature, an individual who had made piano playing habitual enough would likely pass on "musical ability" to his children.

Spencer also provided an evolutionary interpretation of hedonism. Organisms act to prolong pleasures and to get away from feelings of pain. Pleasures appear to be correlated with beneficial, healthy activities, such as eating and staying warm, while pains are accompaniments of detrimental activities. This is clearly the work of natural selection, wrote Spencer, since individuals who happened to find pleasure in biologically harmful activities would perish, as did the mammal that enjoyed holding its head underwater until it passed out.

In higher animals, including humans, this natural correlation can become less clear. Since humans have resisted natural selection and their environment has changed radically, the connection between emotion and biological benefit is no longer assured, and what humans enjoy is not necessarily good for humanity. Like Bain, Spencer explained learning as trial and error, with selection ("trials") dependent on consequences (Boakes 1984, p. 13).

Promotion of Racism: Maybe Not

Regarding society, Spencer was a proponent of what came to be called *Social Darwinism*, the view that natural selection properly rewards the fittest with success and wealth and weeds out the inferior. He advocated maximum personal liberty and minimal government. Vaccination programs and care for the insane or unable should be stopped, since such measures only preserve the weak and thus promote regression of the human race.

His race theories forbade the mixing of races, since each had acquired a "certain constitutional adaptation to its particular form of life" and mixing them can only lead to maladaptions that correspond to neither of the originals. When asked by a Japanese politician whether Japanese should be allowed to marry foreigners, he urged "By all means, therefore, peremptorily interdict marriages of Japanese with foreigners" (Gossett 1963, p. 151).

Spencer saw the inheritance of acquired characteristics everywhere. He believed that his own hands were small because his ancestors had been schoolmasters who did not engage in manual labor. Germans were often nearsighted, he believed, because of their studiousness during the past few centuries. He even suspected that Quakers were more prone to color blindness and to tone deafness because of their ancestors' avoidance of music and bright colors (Gossett 1963, p. 152). However, his racism was softened by its assumption of malleability that allowed rapid change. He proposed that the Irish immigrants to America had rapidly civilized, losing their "Celtic aspect," evidently in a single generation.

Because races could quickly change in fundamental characteristics due to inheritance of acquired characteristics, Spencer later seemed overly environmentalist in the eyes of the genuine racists. He supervised a vast compilation of volumes by a number of writers on Descriptive Sociology, and eight parts were in print by 1881. The project was not a moneymaker and so was suspended, though he left provisions in his will for its continuance.

There was much evidence in these volumes for nonracist explanations of the practices of primitive peoples, and, happily, its influence was great. According to one estimate (Gossett 1963, p. 153), most people who entered the field of sociology between 1870 and 1890 did so because of the influence of his writings. And, since his support of laissez-faire government made him a darling of the business classes, many of these conservative fans used their influence to ensure that sociology departments were founded in American universities (Gossett 1963, p. 153).

Darwin's Bulldog

Thomas Huxley[10] wrote little on the evolution of intelligence, performed no notable experiments, and proposed no theory to account for the adaptiveness of behavior. However, he took seriously the implications of the belief that animals were complex biological machines and that there is continuity between humans and animals. The inescapable conclusion is that we are "conscious automata," so that consciousness is an epiphenomenon.

Huxley was a doctor's apprentice as a youth and studied enough to win a scholarship to a London hospital, where he passed the first part of the medical examination at the age of twenty in 1845. He gained an appointment as assistant surgeon on H. M. S. Rattlesnake and spent from 1846 to 1850 in the South Pacific, where he studied marine anatomy and sent the results back to England. During several more years, he made his reputation with other papers on marine anatomy and was appointed to the Government School of Mines, later to become the Imperial College of Science and Technology. He spent thirty-five years there but was famous by 1858, both as a comparative anatomist and as a popular speaker.

It appears that Darwin saw in Huxley a valuable ally for the promotion of the doctrine of natural selection, should he agree with it. In 1859, upon reading *The Origin*, Huxley saw the power of the theory and then remarked "How stupid not to have thought of that!" He told Darwin that he would supply the "combativeness" that "may stand you in good stead" (Boakes 1984, p. 17).

In 1860 Huxley did just that, in a highly publicized interchange with Bishop Wilberforce of Oxford at the meeting of the British Association for the Advancement of Science on June 30. Wilberforce, called "Soapy Sam," after his habit of rubbing his hands together as he spoke (Ferris 1988, p. 245), condemned Darwin's theory as "a dishonoring view of nature," and asked Huxley through which of his grandparents he was related to a monkey (or ape, in some accounts). "The Lord hath delivered him into my hands," whispered Huxley to a friend, Benjamin Brodie; then he rose and replied as follows:[11]

A man has no reason to be ashamed of having an ape for his grandfather. If there were an ancestor whom I should feel shame in recalling it would rather be a man—a man of restless and versatile intellect—who, not content with success in his own sphere of activity, plunges into scientific questions with which he has no real acquaintance, only to obscure them by an aimless rhetoric, and distract the attention of his hearers from the real point at issue by eloquent digressions and skilled appeals to religious prejudice.

For ten years thereafter Huxley wrote and spoke in defense of Darwinism, so that Charles himself could remain content in the countryside having children. However, by 1871 overwork and financial strain brought on a breakdown that put Huxley out of action for a year—the year that George Spalding presented his data at the summer meeting of the British Association.

Romanes: Dualism and Lamarckianism

In 1874 Darwin was struck by a letter published in *Nature* and invited the author, George John Romanes, to visit him at home in Kent. Romanes[12] had been a student of physiology and carried out careful work in Scotland on jellyfish and on the nature of reflexes. He was recognized for this work by election to the Royal Society at the age of thirty-one. However, his interest in the evolution of mind was what earned him lasting fame and a bit of notoriety. He proposed, with Darwin's support and approval, to examine evidence for mentality in animals and to determine in what ways minds differ.

Animal Intelligence

He had collected reports of intelligent animal activity from contacts all over the world, and he received Darwin's notes on behavior. Darwin was pleased to see Romanes taking on a task that he viewed as important, and many at the time saw Darwin passing on the mantle to the much younger Scot. Romanes planned to sort out his masses of material by first classifying the observations and then deducing the general principles of a theory of mental evolution. The presentation of the classified observations was published first by itself as *Animal Intelligence* in 1882, a few weeks after Darwin's death. Romanes was afraid that if this book were judged in isolation from the planned theoretical interpretation, it would be considered "but a small improvement upon the works of the anecdote mongers" (Boakes 1984, p. 25). And that is precisely what happened.

Romanes tried to critically evaluate the cases he presented, so that his would not be just another "pop" book describing the wonderful world of animal minds. However, he absolutely trusted sources that he judged competent, so he included stories of communication of complex information among snails. When a bishop and a major general reported the same story, Romanes included their account of a tribunal of rooks judging a miscreant jackdaw.

What Is the Mind?   Aside from the unfortunate character of the first book, Romanes made a positive contribution to the defining of mind, not only in animals but in other humans as well. Only my own mind is available to me as thoughts and feelings—to know the thoughts of others I must rely on what Romanes called the "ambassadors of the mind." Those ambassadors are the behaviors of others, including their vocalizations. It is fair to say that when I infer conscious experience in others I make an objective inference based upon their activities. The sheep bounding across the field must feel something like what we would feel like doing the same thing. The fact that I can make an inference of any kind owes to the fact that I can make a subjective inference about my own mental states. When I judge that certain of my behavior is accompanied by certain mental states, I am justified in making an objective inference and assuming that other organisms feel the same thing under the same circumstances. Given that we can never know the mind of another, it is of course debatable whether we can know our *own* mind so well, but that was not an issue for Romanes and his fellows. The only way that we can access other minds is in this way. Asking for more is "the skeptical demand for impossible evidence."

Romanes also defined mind, or set the criteria for the legitimate inferring of mind, in a way that was adopted by many during the late nineteenth and early twentieth centuries. The question is one that later puzzled Freud—when are we justified in interpreting an organism's action as evidence for mind, or conscious experience? When a dog fetches a stick, or a monkey cracks a nut, or a bird feeds its young, or a worm digs a burrow—are any of these activities evidence for mind? What is mind, or rather, what shall be the criteria for what we call mind?

Romanes proposed that mind and consciousness may be assumed when activity is purposeful—directed toward a goal—and when it improves with experience. In other words, mind requires the ability to learn to reach goals. This eliminates reflex behavior, where goals are routinely achieved, but learning is not a conspicuous feature. Mind means purpose and ability to learn.

The Tree of Development of Mind When Romanes thought of "mind," it was not the conception of mind held by Huxley—an epiphenomenon accompanying the workings of the machine. It was mind in the sense that Descartes thought of it, as an entity utterly separate from body and capable of influencing the activity of the body. His *Mental Evolution in Animals* (1884, two years after Darwin's death) proposed a scale representing the evolution of mind as a set of mental abilities ranging from lower to higher, as a tree with human mind at the top. Such a higher/lower arrangement was not what Darwin would have done and was more in keeping with the views of popular "evolutionists" like Herbert Spencer.

The infant recapitulates, or retraces, the history of mental evolution. At one week the infant has memory, as do worms; at three weeks it has primary instincts, showing surprise and fear, equivalent to the abilities of insect larvae. At ten weeks, the infant can show social feelings, pugnacity, curiosity, and industry, like insects and spiders, and at four months it reaches the level of reptiles, showing recognition of persons, and already having shown affection, jealousy, anger, and play. By the age of a year, the infant is at the level of monkeys and elephants, meaning that it is capable of revenge and rage. The "tree" of mental development is difficult to misinterpret.

Romanes on Instinct   Romanes inferred conscious intent in interpreting the behavior of an animal, even when chance learning was an obvious alternative and his definition of instinct was unusual. Actions of animals that he deemed "instinctive" were those in which something like "inference" or "consciousness" was present or could be present—instinct was teleologically defined, as was mind. He viewed instinct differently from Spencer, who saw it as no more than compound reflexes that are inherited progressively over generations—in a Lamarckian process, habits in individuals becomes habits in the race.

For Romanes, selection and inheritance of acquired characteristics were both important, so that instincts are operated upon by natural selection to produce nonintelligent habits, which are not modified during an individual's lifetime. However, learned behavior may become automatic habit and becomes inheritable. These "secondary instincts" are capable of rapid change, so that even within a few generations a family of English mastiffs can acquire the fear of butchers (Boakes 1984, p. 31).

Romanes did no notable research in comparative psychology. He spent a good part of his time during the last years of his life seeking evidence for Lamarckian inheritance, to counter the "neo-Darwinism" that was gaining favor. According to this view, not endorsed by Darwin most of his life, natural selection operates on variations and no Lamarckian principle operates at all. August Weismann, a German biologist, had argued that heredity depends only on selection acting on the "germ plasm" and modifications occurring during an individual lifetime are not heritable.[13] Neither Spencer nor Romanes supported so exclusive a role for natural selection, nor would Darwin himself, had he lived to see 1884.

Morgan: Monism, Natural Selection, Experiment

As Darwin had chosen Romanes to succeed him, Romanes chose Conwy Lloyd Morgan (1852–1936), who he regarded as "the shrewdest, as well as the most logical critic that we have in the field of Darwinian speculation" (Boakes 1984, p. 32). The relationship between the two began with a note to *Nature* in which Morgan corrected Romanes's interpretation of "scorpion suicide."

Differing with Romanes, but Agreeing as Well

Morgan did not hesitate to differ with other of Romanes's interpretations that inferred human mental characteristics in the special tricks of pet animals. Darwin had earlier advised Romanes to keep a pet monkey and observe it. Romanes did get a monkey but left it to his sister to care for it and perform the drudgery associated with care of an obnoxious pet.

Nonetheless, he interpreted the monkey's successful use of a screw as the discovery of "the principle of the screw," quite a different matter. Concerning Romanes's analysis of the emotions, Morgan wrote, "I feel myself forced at almost every turn to question the validity of his inferences" (Boakes 1984, p. 33). Owing to his father's financial irresponsibility, Morgan was unable to follow the family practice and obtain a law degree at Oxford; after grammar school he was sent to the London School of Mines. Thomas Huxley was there at that time—1869—and Huxley's lectures maintained his interest in biology and evolution, interest that had begun with the reading of Herbert Spencer years before.

On graduation, Morgan hired on as a companion to a family touring America, and during the several months that this took, he read Darwin. He spent a year as a research associate at the School of Mines, but, unfortunately, it was the year that Huxley spent having his "breakdown." After many temporary jobs, Morgan was employed at a small college in South Africa, teaching science, English Literature, and history. In 1884 he was able to return to England to the new college at Bristol as Professor of Geology and Zoology, and it was during the nine years there that he established his reputation.

Revising Spalding

Douglas Spalding (this section after Boakes 1984, pp. 14–16) was an uneducated mender of slate roofs who happened to hear Alexander Bain speak at Aberdeen in 1862 and so became interested in the relative influence of instinct and experience in animal behavior. He later met John Stuart Mill, who we have seen was interested in the same question, at Avignon and was greatly impressed. By 1872 he had carried out a series of experiments, which he described at a meeting at Brighton. Where and how Spalding's work was done remains unknown.

Among other things, Spalding showed that swallows and other birds that were restrained by collars, so that they could not move their wings from the day that they hatched, appeared to fly as well as other birds when the impediments were removed at the age when such birds ordinarily fly. Spalding had shown that some coordinated behaviors are indeed instinctive and that sensory experience or practice is unnecessary for their execution.

Morgan had been invited to reexamine Spalding's findings by an American friend, and, when he did so, he was more struck by the influences of early experience on later behavior than by the instincts that so impressed Spalding. He found that a chick's accuracy of pecking improved a great deal with early experience and that there appeared to be no innate recognition of water. A so-called "instinctive" reaction to hawks was evidenced to other stimuli, such as sudden and loud noise produced by a violin. Hence, the instinctive reaction was not as specific as Spalding felt it to be.

Morgan and Learning   Morgan's best-known experiment probably was that showing rapid learning by chicks of the foul taste of the caterpillar of the cinnabar moth. They quickly learned to avoid such caterpillars, an accomplishment made easier by the distinctive blue and gold bands marking them. In Morgan's view, it was learning because of consequences—successful responses give satisfaction, and those responses are repeated. Unsuccessful ones give no satisfaction and are not repeated.

Morgan knew that such learning had been called trial and error by Bain, and he studied other instances of it, beginning with the escape of a duckling from a pen constructed with newspaper walls. An escape through a hole made in the wall at one spot was followed on the next occasion by an attack on the same spot and another escape.[14]

Tony and the Interpretation of Behavior   Another of Morgan's reports concerned his pet fox terrier, Tony, who learned to open a gate by placing his head between the vertical rails of the fence and under the horizontal latch. The practice began by chance, as Tony often spent time with his head between the rails, looking out at the road. On one occasion, he happened to have his head under the latch and he lifted his head in such a way as to open the gate. After a pause, he ran out through the open gate.

Over a period of three weeks, Tony placed his head between the rails enclosing the latch more and more often and less often between the other rails. After three weeks he could go straight to the latch, open the gate, and leave the yard. An observer like Romanes would be impressed with the mentality thus displayed, but Morgan noticed something else. He pointed out that "even now he always lifts it with the back of his head and not with his muzzle which would be easier for him" (in Boakes 1984, p. 36).

Morgan seems not to have been a master experimenter; however, unlike Romanes, the observations he made were usually repeated over an appreciable period, so that the course of development of an action could be studied. Such a strategy helps to avoid the overgenerous attribution of mentality that occurs so easily when only isolated observations are made.

The Ever-Misinterpreted Canon

Morgan first published his famous canon in 1894 and introduced it publicly at the International Congress of Psychology in 1892. It has commonly been interpreted as an admonition against anthropomorphism, as practiced by Romanes, and an urging for parsimony (the opinion of Boring 1950, p. 474). In one of the forms in which Morgan put it:

In no case may we interpret an action as the outcome of the exercise of a higher psychical faculty, if it can be interpreted as the outcome of one which stands lower in the psychological scale. (In Boakes 1984, p. 40)

Examples of cases to which Morgan referred were those in which a horse was said to understand the principle of the inclined plane when it took a zig-zag course up a steep hill or when a dog was believed to understand geometry when it cut off a rabbit running a predictable path.

Morgan offered "process" as substitute for "faculty" and also offered a scale of faculties/processes, so that "higher" and "lower" have some meaning. Rather than assume a branching tree of functions representing "lower" to "higher," Morgan inexplicably proposed a loose linear scale, similar to that of Spencer in 1855. That means that the only way to describe mentality is as a continuum with more or less of the same thing—whatever that might be called.

The lowest level is that of simple associations, and Morgan proposed two basic kinds—associations among sense impressions and those among actions and outcomes.[15] This corresponds to the learned taste aversions that he had studied and experiments such as rabbits' escapes through newspaper walls and Tony's escapes through the latched gate.

Morgan then described perception of relations, the separation between human and animal capabilities. Tony was unable to return a nine-inch stick when he had to bring it through a six-inch space between fence posts, though that would have shown perception of relations, as long as it was clear that trial and error was not involved. Counting was also mentioned as a case of perceptual learning, and probably Morgan would have considered cases of relational learning later presented by the Gestaltists under the heading of "transposition."

Higher-level processes, found in no animal, appeared as perception of abstract relationships: "counting," not dependent on particular objects, or "matching to sample," or choosing the object intermediate in size from a set of three objects. Such abstraction is required for the thought that is independent of its objects and so allows flashes of insight that elude animals and other concrete thinkers, or so Morgan thought.

If an organism is capable of these functions, then it is both a human and probably not a schoolchild or a peasant. Such a being may even be capable of the concept of self, though the child and peasant may well not have such a concept and the animal surely does not. So wrote Morgan in 1894. Overlaying this scale were faculties such as communication, memory, and others that appeared in higher or lower forms depending on the species in question. Animals could communicate, Morgan felt, to the extent that they could indicate fear or draw attention to some object—simple associations that have nothing to do with relationships or abstractions.

What the Canon Really Meant   Lloyd Morgan (1894) was by no means opposed to the practice of anthropomorphizing. He explicitly proposed that comparative psychology must involve a "doubly inductive process," including the observer and the observed.

The two inductions involved are actually the subjective induction concerning the observer's states of consciousness and the objective induction from observed behavior in others. Thus far, there is really no difference between Morgan's and Romanes's subjective inference of one's own mentality and the observation of the "ambassadors of the mind" in the behavior of others that allows objective inference of other mental states.

However, Morgan was less charitable than was Romanes in assigning mentality to animals, and his famous canon follows from a consideration of ways in which minds may vary. They may differ in what he called the method of levels, the method of uniform reduction, or the method of variation.

If the method of levels applied, we would find that snails, dogs, and humans differ in simple possession of faculties. It is conceivable that snails can only sense, that dogs can sense and perceive, and that humans can sense, perceive, and reason. In an ascending series of species, higher faculties are added onto lower ones. The most absurd aspect of this possibility is that it treats each mental power as a full-blown, present-or-absent entity, so that the sensing of the snail, dog, and human are identical and new faculties are simply added. Scratch the method of levels.

If the method of uniform reduction were the case, all animate creatures would have all possible mental powers and faculties, but in differing degrees, according to their station. Humans would have a lot of abstractive power, while earthworms would be capable of less abstraction. Similarly, the memory of the baboon would exceed that of the butterfly, but even the butterfly would have the faculty of perception and a sense of self. This too seems an unlikely mode by which minds might differ.

This leaves only the method of variation, the only reasonable possibility in Morgan's view. The three faculties may vary nonuniformly, so that one organism, say the dog, has more of the faculty of sensation than does the human or the snail but less perception and abstraction than the human has. Perhaps in visual acuity, olfaction, and audition the dog surpasses the human, who in turn excels in other ways.

Such a reasonable mechanism allows for superiority of animals, especially in sensory and simple association ways, and thus explains phenomena such as the wonderful horse of Herr von Osten, Clever Hans. Hans's wonders lay not in reasoning ability, as first thought, but in sensitivity to subtle cues of breathing and movement inadvertently produced by human onlookers. The clear possibility of suprahuman "lower faculties" in animals means that it is there that we should look for explanations of their behavior, before resorting to "higher psychical functions."

That is the point of Morgan's canon—he explicitly denied that he was invoking a law of parsimony, since simpler explanations are not always better. Many authors who have misinterpreted Morgan have evidently failed to read his works.

Darwin's Contribution[16]

Darwinism became functionalism in American psychology, a view held by many but most closely associated with William James and his student James Rowland Angell, as well as John Dewey. Angell discussed Darwin's influence on psychology and his shortcomings as a psychologist in 1909. The shortcomings apply with equal force to any number of comparative psychologists since, from Romanes to the present.

On the positive side, Darwin always argued for the continuity of mind, from animals to civilized human—differences in range and power, though great, were not differences in kind. In Darwin's time and for decades after, Alfred Wallace would argue that natural selection stopped with humanity and that an unfathomable gulf exists between man and beast. Wallace pointed to other natural discontinuities as evidence: organic/inorganic, organic–sentient and conscious, and sentient–conscious/rational. Further, he argued that music and mathematics represent activities that could have had no adaptive function and hence could not have arisen through selection.

Even in 1909 it was safe to say that most scientists accepted the continuity of mind. Darwin was less successful in demonstrating mind in animals for the same reason that Romanes and Morgan were unsuccessful. One must have a reasonable model of mind to be inferred in animals, and Darwin did not have one.

The Dangers of Darwinism: Sir Francis Galton

Francis Galton (see figure 8.2) was a grandson of Erasmus Darwin and cousin of Charles Darwin. He is usually described as responsible for showing the relevance of statistics for biology and as a short-sighted and superficial thinker whose interests ranged from meteorology to eugenics.

Galton as Psychologist

Sir Francis dabbled in many areas during a long life, publishing one of his best-received books when in his late sixties. He began as a successful young scholar, educated by his father, as was John Stuart Mill. He began the study of medicine at sixteen, excelled in medical studies, and interrupted them only to study mathematics at Cambridge. After an illness that temporarily stopped his education, he received a large inheritance that permanently ended any need for education or degree or occupation.

Galton contributed to meteorology, introducing the word "anticyclone" in 1863. Thereafter, he was mainly concerned with heredity. In

Figure 8.2
Galton. Courtesy of the Archives of the History of American Psychology, University of Akron.

the service of that interest he showed that fingerprints are individual and permanent (early 1890s), introduced composite photographs (1879), classified mental images as visual and auditory, and did many other things. He tried to measure the efficacy of prayer, mapped the distribution of beautiful women in Britain's counties, and measured fidgeting as an estimate of boredom during scientific lectures. He is most known for his attempts to show that the human race is degenerating rapidly. He believed that the prejudices of his youth were true and that men of his station, ancestry, education, tastes, and opinions were superior to other humans. The main works of his life were attempts to justify his prejudices that ever grew stronger.

Hereditary Genius   In 1869 *Hereditary Genius* was published to show that selective breeding can produce "a highly-gifted race of men" and so offset the processes that are "at this very moment working toward the degradation of human nature." He assumed that "high reputation is a pretty accurate test of high ability," and that examination of the English judges from 1660 to 1868, as well as the statesmen and premiers, commanders, writers and scientists, poets, painters, and musicians will show that high ability is inherited.

Galton's survey turned up fewer than 400 men that met his criterion of "extraordinary genius." His point was that a large proportion of these eminent men were interrelated. His conclusion has been quoted often and found an audience in Britain and in America only too ready to agree:

I have no patience with the hypothesis occasionally expressed, and often implied, especially in tales written to teach children to be good, that babies are born pretty much alike, and that the sole agencies in creating differences between boy and boy, and man and man, are steady application and moral effort. (In Sahakian 1968, pp. 263–264)

Just so the schoolboy learns his limits over the years, and so when he is mature, unless "blinded by self conceit," he knows his place: "He is no longer tormented into hopeless efforts . . . but he limits his undertakings to matters below the level of his reach (ibid.).

Darwin read the first fifty pages of this book and, kind as ever, wrote to his cousin that "you have made a convert of an opponent in one sense, for I have always maintained that, excepting fools, men did not differ much in intellect, only in zeal and hard work; and I still think that this is an eminently important difference" (Boakes 1984, p. 46). The sort of evidence that impressed Galton was that of numbers, and he had an obsession with quantification through his life. In 1868 he cited the performances of an extremely select group, those earning honors in mathematics at Cambridge University.

Each year between 400 and 450 boys were examined over eight days, for five and a half hours a day. Each boy understood and was equally prepared for these exams, which they knew provided "the most powerful inducements, namely, those of competition, of honour, and of future wealth" (Sahakian 1968, p. 265).

About 100 would achieve honors in mathematics, and the first forty of those were distinguished by the title of wranglers. It is desirable to be even a low wrangler, and to be the senior wrangler is an honor and a virtual guarantee of success in life. All knew that "the fairness and thoroughness of Cambridge examinations have never had a breath of suspicion cast upon them" (Sahakian 1968, p. 265). Though the examination marks were secret, Galton managed to get hold of several lists of them and scour them for evidence. He found, for example, that one list showed 300 marks for the low man, 1,500 for the lowest wrangler, and 7,500 for the senior wrangler. This meant to Galton that the high-scoring man was capable of solving problems of twenty-five times the difficulty of the low man and five times the difficulty of the low wrangler! Numbers were important to Galton.

Despite differences in motivation, which Galton acknowledged, the difference between the honors students seemed so great as to demand innate differences in ability. And even the low man was a genius compared with the 300 nonhonors students who fell below. Such folks are like the average people who go to public lectures and gain nothing (Sahakian 1968, 266).

Galton and Mental Testing   Galton introduced the association test (1883), in which subjects write down all the associations that come to mind during four seconds following a stimulus word. He analyzed his own associations, used suggestion to make himself a paranoid, and set up an "Anthropometric Laboratory" in 1884 to collect data on human physical and mental characteristics. It was his belief that mental power is directly related to sensory acuity, partly because women had never been successful as wine tasters or piano tuners!

The "Galton whistle" was also described in 1884 as a means of differentiating people, partly by age. He made a whistle from a brass tube less than a tenth of an inch in inner diameter and used a sliding piston calibrated to pitch. He was delighted that older people, who fancied that they heard everything, were surprised and displeased to find that younger companions heard pitches to which they were deaf. Loss of hearing might be expected to accompany general loss in mental power. He tested all of the animals at the zoo and the dogs and cats on the streets of London and in Switzerland. He found cats and small dogs to be most sensitive to high pitches and insects not sensitive at all.

Eugenics and Statistics   Galton strongly favored the selective breeding of humans, given the success in breeding livestock and given what appeared to him to be the progressive degeneration of humankind with unlimited breeding allowed to the inferior.[17] He named the practice of eugenics (1883), and first introduced statistics to biological matters.

The Belgian astronomer Lambert Quetelet had already done statistical studies on what he called the "average man" and in 1848 published *On the Social System and the Laws which Govern it*. This compendium showed the relation of particular head sizes, heights, and other characteristics to those of the average man. Such use of the normal curve had been made earlier by LaPlace and Gauss, but for the purpose of application to games of chance.

It was Quetelet who envisioned the average man as nature's goal and noted that "The average is the most frequent value and nature's large errors are rare" (Boring 1957, p. 477). Galton was obsessed with quantification, setting up scales to measure genius, for example, in units of frequency of occurrence. A progression from A to X marks the "just above average intellect" at A and the "one in a million" man at X. A descending scale, from a to x, classifies the "below average," through "idiots and imbeciles" at f, g, and x. In 1869 Galton expressed his belief that ancient Athenian civilization was as far superior in mental ability to British civilization as Britain was superior to the primitive societies of the late nineteenth century.

The eugenics movement was meant to correct the disastrous degeneration of humanity. Galton, Pearson, and Weldon founded the journal *Biometrika* in 1901, the year Pearson founded his Biometric Laboratory at the University of London. And in 1904 Galton endowed a research fellowship in eugenics at the same university, first awarded to Karl Pearson. The Francis Galton Laboratory for National Eugenics at that university was combined in 1911 with Pearson's older Biometric Laboratory as a laboratory of applied statistics.

With the mathematical aid of J. D. H. Dickson, in 1886 he produced the "index of co-relation," later called "Galton's function," and finally the "coefficient of correlation," so named by F. Y. Edgeworth in 1882.[18]

Blindness Induced by Averaging Data   Singer (1959, p. 552) noted a strange consequence of Galton's attention to statistical groups—it caused him to miss individual cases, where discontinuous variations appear. Thus, he and his followers studied the inheritance of eye color and they experimented with (sweet) peas, phenomena that well illustrate Mendelian inheritance, but the significance of Mendel's work entirely eluded them. This in spite of the fact that Galton noted "blended inheritance" and reported "sports." But they diminished the importance of the individual case, blinded by the appeal of averaged data! This seemed to Singer one of the most extraordinary events of nineteenth-century science.

A Question of Style

Huxley, Morgan, and Galton were three very different personalities and of differing degrees of scientific merit. Boakes (1984, pp. 49–50) detailed the impressions that these men produced in those who knew them. From one point of view, the unfairness of life was once again illustrated.

Morgan ended his career at Bristol University, sadly enough as a vice-chancellor who, like most of that rank, did little to further the study of comparative psychology or anything else. He was unassertive and remained at the fringe of British science at an obscure and provincial university. A visitor, James Mark Baldwin, described Morgan as "contemplatively combing a long beard that was as fine as his logic."

Galton and Huxley were more visible and were described by Beatrice Webb, who was a long-time friend of Herbert Spencer and thereby met most of the luminaries of the day. Her impressions, made in the 1880s, were far more favorable toward the wealthy and well-spoken hereditarian and eugenicist, whose research was frankly aimed at supporting his views on the natural superiority of the privileged male. She felt less kindly toward Huxley, who had been largely responsible for establishing the Imperial College of Science and Technology and ensuring that Darwinism prevailed (Boakes 1984, p. 50):

She found Huxley a disturbing person, with a strain of madness and haunted by melancholy . . . the one who stayed in her mind as the ideal man of science was Francis Galton, with his "perfect physical and mental pose."

Certainly this was an ironic conclusion.

9   Nineteenth-Century Science and Psychology's Rise

A good many times I have been present at gatherings of people who...with considerable gusto have been expressing their incredulity at the illiteracy of scientists. Once or twice I have been provoked and have asked the company how many of them could describe the Second Law of Thermodynamics. The response was cold; it was also negative. (C. P. Snow 1961, p. 512)

The Supremacy of Germany and the Beginnings of Modern Psychology

Psychological research, or psychology as a science, began in German universities during the nineteenth century because Germany was the only place where organized science existed, at least as we came to know it during the twentieth century. Until 1920 there were more psychological research publications in German than in any other language, and German domination extended to the traditional sciences as well (Littman 1979, p. 45). The position of leadership in science that Germany enjoyed owed to its university system and to its ensuring the mixture of research and teaching.

The German educational system featured self-perpetuating laboratories and research groups organized around the most eminent scientists of the time. Thus, leaders like Müller, Weber, Helmholtz, Brücke, and many others worked within the university structure and established research programs that continued over generations. This was not the case elsewhere in Europe or in America.

Further, Germany established the first modern university, at Halle, in 1694. The writings of Descartes and Bacon, printed in German, replaced the Latin scholastic texts still used elsewhere in Europe. The famous practice of *Lehr- und Lernfreiheit*, or freedom of both professors and students to teach and to learn what they wished, was promoted in German universities as early as the early eighteenth century.

In 1807 the Treaty of Tilsit meant that Halle was no longer part of the German states, and a new university was established at Berlin with von Humboldt[1] as director of instruction. Lectures and seminars replaced student recitations, and chairs were established for the most distinguished professors. Key to the system was the close involvement of students with professors, scholarship, and research. This ensured a continuity of scholarly endeavor that was unique at the time.

Education in France and Britain
In contrast, France released the best scientists from the instruction of students, so that they were wholly divorced from educational curricula. Perhaps as bad, the universities were divided into separate schools (faculties) regulated by restrictive bureaucracy. The complete separation of research and teaching left the best scholars and scientists with special privileges as professors at the College de France but with absolutely no influence on education or educational policy at any level. Research and the educational establishment were utterly separate, having a disastrous effect on the training of potential scientists.

The situation in England was even worse. The only real universities in all of England before 1836 were Oxford and Cambridge, and both of them were largely devoted to ecclesiastical training. Particularly at Oxford, eloquent professors defended a form of idealism based on Kant and bitterly resisted the development of science. The establishment of the University of London in 1836 improved matters, but that was, after all, only one university. Scotland and Ireland were far better off, having had universities at Aberdeen, Edinburgh, Glasgow, Belfast, and elsewhere, but in England science was not done at universities—it was the avocation of wealthy and talented amateurs, such as Cavendish, Priestly, Boyle, Darwin, and their like. Others, like James and John Stuart Mill, were not wealthy, but had occupations that afforded the time for scholarship.

Education in America
The situation in the United States was worse even than that. When Edward Thorndike was a student at Wesleyan University in the 1890s, the two physics texts were translations from French originals (Joncich 1968, p. 67). Not only was America behind Europe in higher education, but it had no real universities until 1890. There were, of course, academies and colleges long before that time, but they were closely related to the church and were typically antiscientific. Their philoso-

phy was largely that of the Scottish School of Common Sense, a view which we have seen was not congenial to creative research and scholarship.

Typically, a master's degree had to be obtained from the baccalaureate (undergraduate) institution, and no doctorates were awarded until the 1860s. If one wanted training in science, philosophy, medicine, or even history, the best advice was to go to Germany—and go many did. College in general was not a valued institution in America until almost the twentieth century. During the nineteenth century, interest actually declined; in 1838, one out of 1,200 boys went to college, and by 1869 only one in 2,000 did so (Littman 1979, p. 47). That speaks volumes for the value placed on a college education during that century.

By 1880 there were about 400 American graduate students in master's programs in America and about the same number in graduate doctoral programs in Austria and Germany. When the German-trained people returned, they brought with them the conviction that scholarship and research belonged in universities. Hence, the main features of the model of university education that we accept as "normal" were originally a unique aspect of the German system. Experimental psychology began in Germany because that was where science in general was growing.

Fechner and Psychophysics

I was always open to the ideas of G. T. Fechner and have followed that thinker upon many important points. (Freud 1935)

...the year 1987 was celebrated as a "Fechner Year." In the German-speaking countries alone, three international "Fechner Conferences" were organized (at Leipzig, Passau, and Bonn) and Division 26 of the American Psychological Association hailed Fechner as the "Columbus of the new psychology." (Scheerer 1987, 197–202)

Weber's Discovery

Ernst Weber (1795–1878) was a physiologist and anatomist and professor at Leipzig from the age of twenty-three. He pioneered the investigation of the perception of space on the skin surface and promoted the idea that each sensory nerve fiber serves a specific area on the skin, a "sensory circle." However, he is most remembered for a discovery reported in 1834 (Herrnstein and Boring 1965, pp. 64–66), published in Latin, and concerned with the process of discrimination.

Weber's original interest was in assessing the effect of the muscle sense on the discrimination of weights held in the hands—how much does hefting the weights, thus involving the muscle sense, aid in discriminating, compared with judgments made with the hands held still in front of the subject? Hefting the weights did improve performance, but the more interesting discovery was what is sometimes called Weber's Law. This is what he wrote:

In observing the disparity between things that are compared, we perceive not the difference between the things, but the ratio of this difference to the magnitude of the things compared. (Ibid., p. 64)

If you hold two weights, one of 30 ounces and another of 29, the difference is felt as easily as is the difference between weights of 30 and 29 half-ounces or 30 and 29 drams (a dram is 1/8 of an ounce). Yet the differences in the pairs of weights are an ounce, a half ounce, and an eighth of an ounce.

At the same time, we cannot distinguish weights of 33 and 34 ounces, even though the difference involved is large—eight times the difference in the 30/29 dram discrimination. This is because it is not the absolute values of weights that are important, but the ratio of the disparity and the heavier weight. This ratio is 1/30, so that we can discriminate easily a 29- and a 30-ounce weight but cannot perceive a difference between a 39- and a 40-ounce weight or a 97- and a 100-ounce weight. The ratio in this last case is only 3/100, or 1/33.3. This is less than the minimum 1/30 that Weber found necessary.

Weber noted "that expert and practiced men feel a disparity of weight if it is not less than 1/30 of the heavier weight, and perceive the disparity to be the same if, in place of half ounces, we put drams." What is critical is the ratio of change in stimulation to level of ongoing stimulation. For a given task, that ratio is a constant over wide variations in absolute stimulus values. As Fechner later put it:

$dR/R = K.$

The R refers to the stimulus value, since Reiz means "stimulus," "charm," or "irritate" in German.

Weber showed the ratio to hold for other modalities as well. We can discriminate lengths of lines if they differ by a ratio of 1/100 of the longer line, and trained musicians could discriminate differences in pitch of 1/322. We do not discriminate absolute differences among stimuli; we discriminate ratios, and that is a fact discussed as a part of

Figure 9.1
Fechner. Courtesy of the Archives of the History of American Psychology, University of Akron.

common experience in every psychology textbook written during the last decades of the nineteenth century.

Wundt described the method for determining just noticeable differences (jnds), or Weber ratios. He found the jnd for sensations of light to be 1/100, for muscular sensation to be 1/17, and for pressure, warmth, and sound to be 1/8. These values vary a lot, depending on where pressure is applied to the skin surface, what kind of sound is used, and so on.

Fechner's Remarkable Life

Gustav Fechner (see figure 9.1) was born in 1801 and lived until 1887. He was the second of five children born to a Protestant minister who died when the child was five. Gustav was raised by an uncle. He received an MD from the University of Leipzig, though he never practiced as a physician. He experimented in physics and obtained a lectureship in physics at age twenty-three. By the age of twenty-nine he had forty publications in physics. The next year he devised the first practical method for measuring direct current (DC) and published 175 pieces in physics during subsequent years.

During this period, he did hack work translating texts in physics and chemistry from French—in one case, he translated a household encyclopedia of eight volumes and 9,000 pages. All this was necessary to augment his income, since academics who were not professors were not paid well. Nonetheless, he showed the *sine qua non* of the scholar in his humorous pieces, published under the pen name of "Dr. Mises." When the importance of iodine in the diet was recognized, there was a period when it was touted as the answer to all ills and prescribed for all sorts of maladies. "Dr. Mises" published "Understand that the moon is made of iodine" ("*Beweiss, das der Mond aus Jodine besteht*"). Another considered the comparative anatomy of angels, who are spherical and perceive gravitation as we do light. In all, fourteen of the pieces appeared.

Fechner was appointed a professor of physics at the age of thirty-two and was, in Freud's words, "broken by success" ("*Scheitern am Erfolg*"). From age thirty-three to thirty-nine he was an exhausted man and finally collapsed entirely, living as a secluded invalid for three years. He suffered depression, hypochondria, and visual problems related to earlier research on visual afterimages in which he stared at the sun. The walls of his rooms were painted black, and he spent his time writing poetry and devising riddles.

Just prior to and during this period of depression and invalidism, Fechner became obsessed with the idea of life after death—in 1836 he published *Das Buchlein Über das Leben nach dem Tod* ("The Little Book Concerning Life after Death") in which he proposed three periods of existence, beginning with conception to birth, characterized by sleep, birth to death, characterized by sleeping and waking, and life after death. Logically, the last should be characterized by wakefulness.

After recovering from his depression, he went through a period of elation, promoted a pleasure principle, and became a philosophy professor. At age forty-seven he wrote the first monograph on the psychology of plants—*Nanna, or the Soul of Plants*.[2] In the same year he published *Zend Avesta*, outlining his philosophy of nature.

And his was a philosophy of nature that provided the impetus for the founding of experimental psychology. Fechner's obsession was to show that mind and matter were but two aspects of a single underlying reality. From the day view (*Tageansicht*), the world and all reality was mind, but from the night view (*Nachtansicht*), all was matter. If he could show how mind and matter are translatable one into the other, that would show that they were two aspects of the same thing. Many before and after Fechner held the same view—belief in a metaphysical monism and an epistemological dualism—but they did not share his fanatic ambition to convince others. The answer came to him on the fateful morning of October 22, 1850, while in bed.

The Elements of Psychophysics

Two volumes of data and argument were published as *Elemente der Psychophysik*[3] in 1860, the year that the mind was subjected to measurement, despite Kant's and Herbart's denial of the possibility. For Fechner, the proof of the identity of mind and matter lies in the demonstration that mind may be calibrated—scaled in physical units. This was the purpose of the three original psychophysical methods that were used to collect the data that proved the identity hypothesis.

The methods, familiar to every college student, were the method of ascending and descending limits, used to determine absolute thresholds, and the methods for assessing differential thresholds, the method of right and wrong cases and the method of average error.

Proving the Identity Hypothesis: Ingenuity Itself   The steps Fechner used in his famous argument justifying the legitimacy of his methods are described clearly and in detail in Boring's classic work (Boring 1950). I reproduce it in simplified and (necessarily) interpreted form. It is a clever argument that repays some consideration—it puzzled many people for many decades.

Fechner assumed first that it is impossible to measure sensation (mental events) directly, since there is no basis for assigning numbers to felt sensations. However, we can judge present/absent, equal, or more/less when considering sensations produced by specific stimuli or sets of stimuli. This means that our scaling must deal with confusions, or errors in judgments of present/absent, equal, more/less. The unit of mind must be a unit of error in judgment. And here comes the first trick.

Fechner referred to Weber's Law, not so called by Weber himself, treating it as a great universal law that is key to the measuring of mind. But how could this be? Weber's Law refers only to stimulation, stating that over wide ranges of stimulus values, the amount of change that we can just discriminate, that is just noticeably different, is a constant—$dR/R = K$ has nothing to do with sensation. Or does it?

Fechner seized on the notion that a jnd is a mental entity. Further, he proposed that all jnds, within or among modalities, are subjectively equal. Consider whether that is true. Imagine hefting two weights that are indistinguishable in heaviness, as small increments are gradually added to one weight. Finally, the weights are noticeably different—hold that feeling. Imagine now a pair of tones identical in pitch and heard successively. One tone is increased in frequency until it is noticeably different—what is that "feeling of difference?" Is it the same as the feeling accompanying the lifted weights? Is either feeling the same as the feelings when heavier weights are judged or very different pitches are judged?

Fechner took advantage of the fact that the subjective equality of jnds is a possibility in the minds of most people, but it is a possibility that cannot be directly tested. However, while others debated the plausibility of the phenomenal equality of jnds, Fechner was ready with proof of an unusual and a compelling kind, with more data than could be doubted.

The Form of the Psychophysical Function Fechner's method for scaling sensation was simplicity itself. First we set up Cartesian coordinates, with the vertical axis (y-axis) divided into equal intervals, since that axis corresponds to sensation and sensation is to be measured in jnd units, already assumed to be subjectively equal. Hence, we have an equal-interval vertical scale of sensation.

On the stimulus side, we begin by determining the threshold value for loudness of a tone (that is, air pressure, dB level). For ease of description, let us say that the jnd for the particular stimulus continuum and task that we are using is 1/2, a gigantic value. For any level of stimulus, an increase of 1/2 is necessary to be just noticeably different.

This means that we begin at the value that we found is at threshold level (heard fifty percent or seventy-five percent of the occasions that we present it, depending on how we define "threshold"). To find the first jnd, it follows that we will have to present a new stimulus that is $1\frac{1}{2}$ times as strong as the threshold value, since our jnd is 1/2. That value, 1.5 times the threshold value, produces one unit of sensation, in Fechner's reckoning.

To find the next jnd, we increase the strength of the stimulus until it is just noticeably different from the first jnd value (1.5T). Of course, this value will be $1\frac{1}{2}$ times that value, or 1.5T. We continue, and continue to find that the rate of increase in stimulus strength increases by a ratio—Weber's Ratio—which in this case is 1/2.

The increase is exponential, meaning that it is described by the stimulus value raised to some power. In this case, the power is one and a half. Fechner believed that such plots actually measured sensation and that the amount of sensation produced by each stimulus value had thus been scaled!

Is that legitimate? It is only if the y-axis is really an equal interval scale—if jnds are really subjectively equal. Are they? Fechner produced a strong argument that they are, since the functions that he usually found were not only exponential, but a particular kind of exponential function—they were logarithmic, the "log" being simple base 10. As Fechner put it: S = K log R.

Sensation is related to stimulation according to a function featuring a constant particular to the stimuli and the task used and the log value of the stimulus values used. That is mind measured, if Fechner was right. Consider his proof.

Proof that jnds Are Subjectively Equal   Fechner provided an illustration to convey the significance of what he had done; it was only a simple table of logarithms (excerpted in Herrnstein and Boring 1965, pp. 66–75):

Number	Logarithm
10	1.0000000
11	1.0413927
100	2.0000000
110	2.0413927
1000	3.0000000
1100	3.0413927

Notice that the series on the left is a set of pairs where the increase is 1 and 1/10 (1.1). If the jnd in a psychophysical task were 1/10, that would correspond to the pairs of numbers in that series. Increases of 1, 10, and 100 each produce one jnd, which Fechner maintained were subjectively equal.

Now, the psychophysical functions that he found were log functions, as we have seen, and therein is justification for the assumed equality of jnds as sense magnitudes. The log values in the right column correspond to the numbers in the left column, and look what they show. The difference in log value for each pair is .0413927, even though the difference in absolute magnitudes of stimulation ranges a hundredfold. Ratio increases in stimulation correspond to equal differences in sensation.

Mind and body are identical if it can be shown that one can legitimately translate one into the other—the trick is to translate units of mind into units of physical stimulation. His insight was to use the jnd as the unit of sensation (mind). He found that if we assume that jnds are subjectively equal, we can scale sensation by calculating stimulus values necessary to produce successive jnds. Once we have done that, we have a function that relates mind and body and we can determine the sensory value of any value of stimulus.

However, are jnds subjectively equal? He found that the function he obtained with many stimulus continua and many kinds of task was a simple logarithmic function. Such a function, by definition, involves equal log differences for equal ratio differences. If the log values correspond to sensation and the ratios to stimulation, he appears confirmed—jnds are (subjectively) equal. Or so he concluded.

Unconscious Sensations

Fechner also proposed partial thresholds, a notion not appreciated for a century after his work. This means that stimulation may produce a bodily response, for example, an orienting or change in brain electrical activity, yet be unknown to the individual. In the 1970s and 1980s researchers found that, indeed, brain response to stimulation need not be consciously felt and that different thresholds may be demonstrated for verbal versus motor responses (Bridgeman 1986).

Fechner's psychophysics was criticized by many capable foes during the nineteenth century, yet it remained influential a century after its origin in 1860. S. Smith Stevens created and directed the Institute of Psychophysics at Harvard, and it was he who brought Georg von Bekesy to America, where he conducted his Nobel Prize winning work. Stevens is best known for his promotion of direct scaling, rather than the indirect methods of Fechner. He also was an opponent of parapsychology—the study of "extrasensory perception," or ESP, that waxes and wanes in popularity much as does wholistic medicine and astrology.

S. S. Stevens—Psychophysics and ESP

Stevens reviewed a book on ESP in 1967, where he recounted an amusing and instructive interview with a reporter for the college newspaper. He already testified that he found ESP difficult to consider seriously, since it requires that one "tread the boggy mire of evidence for inputs without sensors." It is a manifestation of human faith, similar to other manifestations: "Creatures in saucers are not likely to stop their visitations upon us as long as they can home in on the glowing beacon of human faith." Believers will not be dissuaded, since, conveniently, "evidence for things hoped for has a persistent way of turning up when faith is threatened."

There are many reasons for discounting the supernatural, Stevens wrote, and he would believe in it when "telepathy, clairvoyance, precognition, or psychokinesis can be produced on demand." As it was, he was indifferent, and his indifference had a long history—going back to the "salad days" at Duke University. Some time during that period, a reporter from *The Harvard Crimson* wandered into his office asking for information about ESP. Stevens recounted what followed:

"What," he asked, "is the Psychology Department doing about it?"
I told him that departments are mere committees and that only people do research.
"Then who at Harvard is doing research on ESP?" he asked.
"No one, so far as I know," I said.
The reporter was indignant that a department of psychology could neglect a subject so revolutionary and challenging, especially a department in the university of William James, William McDougall, and the many other Harvard people who have concerned themselves with the occult.... Harvard has had the makings and tradition of a spook center, if ever there was one.
"Why aren't you working on ESP?" the reporter finally asked.
"Because I am studying a much more interesting phenomenon," I told him.
He shifted his notebook and asked, "What is that?"
"If you put a wire in your ear and fill the ear with salt water," I told him, "you can listen to a radio program without using a loudspeaker."
That did it. The reporter scooped up the details and ran the story in the student paper. The national press then picked it up and gave it space, complete with cartoon strips, and for a brief interlude ESP was knocked out of the headlines.

Stevens went on with a thoughtful explanation for the resistance of psychologists to seriously considering paranormal phenomena. We see "so many tainted experiments" in our own specialty, "so many claims of 'significant' results from insignificant studies," and so many "spurious verdicts" that we hardly need "the further distraction of miraculous demonstrations based on far-out odds in the percipient responses of rare and sensitive subjects." He did not mean that telepathy is impossible, but that we are better off trying to demonstrate the possible. One interpretation is that the so-called conventional senses have not been well enough understood to warrant attention paid to "extra-sensory perception." Along those lines, Stevens spent decades investigating sensory scaling, an investigation that led him to repeal Fechner's Law a century after it was passed.

S. S. Stevens Repeals Fechner's Law

In 1960 Stevens published an article in *Science* titled, "To Honor Fechner and Repeal His Law." This critique, published during the centennial anniversary of Fechner's *Elements*, charged that Fechner's methods were faulty and also that they were unnecessary.

In brief, Stevens proposed that stimuli actually lie on two continua, which he called prothetic and metathetic. Prothetic continua are those in which a change in physical stimulus value may plausibly be viewed as an increase or decrease in sensory effect. Examples of prothetic continua are loudness, pressure (including heaviness), length, warmth, and saturation (purity) of color.

Metathetic continua are those where a change is a difference in kind, not an addition or subtraction of something sensory. For example, the change in wavelength of light over the range 400–600 μ is correlated with differences in experienced color. However, is the change from 400 to 500 μ an "increase in wavelength" that produces "more blue until it becomes green?" That is hardly the case—changes in wavelength are accompanied by changes in kind, not in degree. Pitch is a similar case, and so is angular orientation.

Stevens held that Fechnerian scaling, accomplished indirectly through the use of jnds—units of error—makes sense only if the stimulus continua are prothetic. Subjects then make errors in judgments of more/less/equal along the same dimension. Such methods do not make sense, Stevens argued, for metathetic stimulus continua, since judgments concern differences in kind—absolute differences.

Direct Scaling   Metathetic continua warrant direct, or manifest, scaling methods. Disagreeing with Fechner, Stevens claimed that people can reliably and directly judge sensory magnitudes if only they are given a scale with which to calibrate their judgments. The methods Stevens promoted were not new, since Titchener, Merkel, and others used them at the turn of the twentieth century. However, no one had argued as convincingly as he that subjects can reliably judge ratios of stimulation.

The most popular method, fractionation, was used by Stevens (1936), establishing his sone scale for loudness. Subjects are given some stimulus value of loudness or pitch, or some other dimension. The subject is asked to choose a value that is some fraction, usually half, or to adjust the stimulus itself to half value. Many judgments of many stimulus values are made, and occasional tests are included whereby the subject doubles the given stimulus value.

Does fractionation truly measure sensation? Wendell Garner (1974) found that his subjects' judgments of half loudnesses depended strongly on the range of loudnesses presented. With a standard 90-dB stimulus and comparison stimuli of 55–65, 65–75, and 75–85 dB, half-loudness judgments were close to 60, 70, and 80 dB, respectively. Can we really judge ratios, or are we so context-dependent that the question is moot?

Magnitude estimation is another method championed by Stevens and requires the subject to match a number to perceived magnitudes of stimuli. In early uses of the method, the subject was presented with a standard stimulus and a number—the subject's modulus. A standard loudness might be assigned the value of 10 and the subject told to rate other stimuli in relation to that value. Hence, the subject assigns the first stimulus a value of 8, the second a value of 15, and so on.

Stevens often used nonnumerical scales as indices of perceived magnitudes, and subjects might be instructed to squeeze a hand dynamometer to indicate the value assigned to a standard stimulus (loudness, pitch, or whatever). Satisfactory results came with these methods, and Stevens was convinced that direct scaling was possible—Fechner's indirect methods were unnecessary and less accurate.

Advocates for both Fechnerian indirect and for Stevens direct scaling exist today, but the issue was enlarged after the 1960s, which brought a new era in psychophysics, one that emphasized the motivational aspects of sensation. The new method was signal detection theory, and it changed the face of psychophysics permanently.

Signal Detection Theory

During the early 1950s, Bell Telephone was laying transcontinental telephone lines in America and facing the problems involved in sending signals over very long distances. If a full strength and full content signal were to be sent from Maine to California, the cost of boosting the signal along the way would be prohibitive. Bell engineers found that about half the message could be deleted, yet a listener could easily understand it. For example, an auditory signal presented in bursts of 100 milliseconds on and 100 milliseconds off leaves a normal sounding message, even though signal energy is halved.

In dealing with such problems, signal detection theory came into being (Galanter 1962; Green and Swets 1966), providing a new orientation toward psychophysics. Prior to signal detection theory, it was widely assumed that our sense organs act as detectors, with quite fixed capacities and thresholds. Thus, an audiologist would determine your threshold for loudness by presenting an ascending and descending series of loudnesses, assessing your sensitivity.

The threshold might change from day to day, depending on your alertness and motivation, but that would average out if you were repeatedly tested. The threshold was treated as a separate entity. One of the basic tenets of signal detection theory is that the assumption of a fixed threshold is not useful. So many factors determine what we sense and don't sense that the old concept of a threshold is misleading.

Green and Swets present the history of psychophysics clearly and with authority. The story is too long to include in our survey, but it is well worth the reading!

Helmholtz: The Scientist's Scientist

Whoever, in the pursuit of science, seeks after immediate practical utility, may generally rest assured that he will seek in vain. (Kaplan 1992, *Bartlett's*, 16th ed., p. 18)

No reader of this book will need to ask why I have dedicated it to Helmholtz.... If it be objected that books should not be dedicated to the dead, the answer is that Helmholtz is not dead. The organism can predecease its intellect, and conversely. My dedication asserts Helmholtz's immortality—the kind of immortality that remains the unachievable aspiration of so many of us. (Boring 1942, pp. xi–xii)

Helmholtz (see figure 9.2) was born Hermann Ludwig Ferdinand von Helmholtz in 1821 in Potsdam, Germany. His father was a teacher of philology and philosophy in a gymnasium, the German equivalent of American high school and two years of college. His mother's name was Caroline Penne; she was a descendant of William Penn, the Quaker founder of Pennsylvania.

Figure 9.2
Helmholtz. Courtesy of the Archives of the History of American Psychology, University of Akron.

Helmholtz himself appears to have benefited little from his early formal education, rather from independent reading of whatever science books he could find. His geometry appears to have come from play with blocks while very young, rather than from formal instruction years later. Forced to sit through the lectures on literature, he worked out optical problems out of the teacher's sight (Boring 1950, pp. 297–315).

Learning prose by heart was "torture," and it is said that languages did not come easily to him—he had difficulty with idioms and irregular grammar. Yet, he could memorize poetry and memorized works of Goethe, whole books of the Odyssey, and many odes of Horace, all of which he quoted later in life. And he learned several languages—he could read Arabic fables in the original by the age of twelve (Warren and Warren 1968, p. 3).

Through the help of an influential relative, the surgeon general, Mursinna, Helmholtz won a government medical scholarship for training at the Friedrich-Wilhelm Institute in Berlin. It was agreed that he would serve eight years as an army surgeon after graduation. Helmholtz much preferred physics, but his family's circumstances dictated that he aim for a more practical career.

He became leader of a group whose members would powerfully influence the science of the nineteenth century. The group included Emil du Bois-Reymond,[4] Ernst Brücke,[5] and Karl Ludwig. Later the group was called the Helmholtz school. After spending 1838–1842 at Berlin, Helmholtz submitted a doctoral thesis supporting Müller's hypothesis that nerve fibers originate in cells in ganglia. For the next forty-five years he published at least one major piece every year—and sometimes several—totaling over 200 papers and books.

The Antivitalists

Müller was a vitalist, who believed in a vital force that separated the living and the nonliving. Death meant a loss of vital force and the subsequent dissolution of the body, since the vital part held it together. Most older physiologists of the 1840s believed in vitalism, as formulated by G. E. Stahl, but Helmholtz did not. This vitalist view is clearly in keeping with the Aristotelian notion of essences, which had been purged from physics, but which still held influence in biology.

An early success came from his paper "On the Conservation of Energy," in which he showed vitalism unnecessary. This was so because all heat generated by muscle was explainable if one knew the original condition of the muscle and the end products of metabolism. Only chemistry was involved, no vital force needed to intervene. He applied the law of conservation to physical systems in general, both living and inorganic, presenting an elegant argument in terms of mathematical physics at a meeting of the physical society in Berlin. Despite some dispute regarding priority, Helmholtz received credit for the first precise mathematical expression of the law.

Helmholtz Escapes the Army

Helmholtz's friends were concerned about "the conservation of another force...the mind of Helmholtz himself" (Warren and Warren 1968, p. 6) and determined to get him freed of the remainder of his army obligation. He had served five of the required eight years and, thanks to von Humboldt, was released from the remainder of his term. He immediately took a job as lecturer and assistant in the Academy of

Arts and the Anatomy Museum in Berlin. In 1849, less than a year later, he became associate professor of physiology at Königsberg.

Bringing Light into the Darkness

His next feat, bringing instant world fame, was the invention of the ophthalmoscope, a simple device that allowed one to look into the interior of the living human eye. This had never been done, since ordinarily when one looks into the pupil, the observer's head must block light necessary to illuminate the retina. Helmholtz used a half-silvered mirror to reflect light onto the retina. By the age of thirty he had revolutionized ophthalmology. "Ophthalmology was in darkness, God spoke, let Helmholtz be born—and there was light," expressed the gratitude of a toast-giver at the Ophthalmological Conference in Paris in 1867. And all this came about because he was trying to devise a way to demonstrate to his students that light is reflected out of the eye.

Reaction Time Studies

By 1850 Helmholtz determined, though crudely, the velocity of the neural impulse—or, more accurately, he determined that the impulse had a velocity and was not instantaneous. He extended this research from nerve–muscle preparations to reaction times of human subjects. Thus began mental chronometry, the analysis of reaction time that became popular in the late nineteenth century and was revived during the late twentieth century.

Helmholtz's Research in Vision and Audition

After inventing the ophthalmoscope in 1850, at the age of twenty-nine, he conducted a series of experiments on color vision, as well as experiments on physiological acoustics. He published over forty papers on vision and audition during the 1850s and 1860s. This includes his monumental *Treatise on Physiological Optics* in three volumes, the first in 1856 and the third in 1867, and his work on audition, *Sensations of Tone* (*Tonempfindungen*) in 1863. Translations of these works are still used by students of vision and audition.

He also invented another device during this period—the ophthalmometer, which allowed measurement of the images reflected from the anterior and the posterior surfaces of the lens. This allowed accurate measurement of the curvature of the lens's surfaces, and thus, of the amount of accommodation of the lens; it is still a standard piece of laboratory equipment.

In 1855 he became professor of physiology and anatomy at Bonn and in 1858 became professor of physiology at Heidelberg, where he established his Physiological Institute. There Wilhelm Wundt was assigned as his assistant for two years. Respect, but no deep friendship, developed between the two.

Helmholtz's father and then his wife died in 1859, a year after he arrived at Heidelberg, and he was incapacitated for several months with headaches, fever, sleeplessness, and fainting spells. He recovered, spending his time in research in vision and audition, with his mother-in-law caring for his two children. After a bit more than a year, he married Anna von Mohl, which led to his introduction to the royal family, where he would become a favorite of the future Kaiser and Kaiserin.

At Heidelberg, Helmholtz researched the motions of violin strings, friction in fluids, the Arabic–Persian musical scale, properties of ice, electrical oscillations, and even treatment of hay fever (Warren and Warren 1968, p. 11). And his masterworks on the hearing of tone and the last two volumes of his *Optics* were completed—all this between 1860 and 1869.

He found the epistemological/psychological aspects of his work particularly tiring—for example, the "Perception of Sight" in the *Optics*. He suffered with migraine headaches that would stop his work for at least twenty-four hours. He went to places that offered cures and spent time walking through the Mont Blanc region. When he recovered and had finished the third volume of the *Optics*, he turned more and more to physics and mathematics. Psychology is frustrating, as he wrote to his friend Karl Ludwig:

For the time being I have laid physiological optics and psychology aside. I found that so much philosophizing eventually led to a certain demoralization, and made one's thoughts lax and vague; I must discipline myself awhile by experiment and mathematics, and then come back later to the Theory of Perception. (Warren and Warren 1968, p. 12)

His final psychological work was a paper with N. Baxt in 1871 titled "On the Time Necessary to Bring a Visual Impression to Consciousness," where a tachistoscope was used to show that the duration of exposure necessary for identification of an object depended on brightness, area, complexity, and familiarity. And a postexposure masking field was used to extinguish afterimages. His research on perception ended there, but he had spent perhaps his best years, from thirty to fifty, on that subject. He went to Berlin, where an Institute of Physics was built for him, in 1871.

Later Research

His work from then on involved thermodynamics, chemistry (the electrical nature of bonding), meteorology, and electromagnetic theory, with his student Heinrich Hertz. In 1877 he became rector of the University of Berlin and was elevated to the nobility in 1882 by Wilhem I. In 1888 he became first president of the Physical Technical Institute at Charlottenberg, near Berlin.

Helmholtz had long been friends with Werner von Siemens,[6] called "the German Edison," but unlike Thomas Edison, Siemens had formal technical training, organizational and financial ability, and a great fortune. In 1884 Siemens's son married Helmholtz's daughter, Ellen, and Siemens moved to improve his old friend's position. Teaching took too much of Helmholtz's priceless time, so the Institute and the position of director was created to free him from that and allow time for research.

He traveled to America for the Electrical Congress in Chicago in 1893. On the return trip he evidently suffered one of his fainting spells and fell down a flight of stairs. He recovered from a great loss of blood slowly and in 1894 suffered a cerebral hemorrhage. He remained semi-conscious for two months and died on September 8, 1894.

If John Stuart Mill Were a Scientist

In 1866 (*Optics*, volume 3) Helmholtz published a treatise on vision in which he emphasized the "empirical" viewpoint. He stressed the fact that what we see (or hear, etc.) is not the objective fact that it seems to be; nor need it correspond to the stimulus as coded on the receptive surface, such as the retina. Like John Stuart Mill, whom he praised, Helmholtz believed that we notice only a small part of what may be identified as objective stimulation:

... we are not in the habit of observing our sensations accurately, except as they are useful in allowing us to recognize external objects. On the contrary, we are wont to disregard all those parts of the sensations that are of no importance so far as external objects are concerned.

Instead of noticing all the forms of stimulation constantly falling on the receptors (i.e., all the "sensations," in his terms), we pragmatically select those that aid us in getting around in the world.

Early in our lives we learn that a given retinal image, sensations from our eye muscles, and the consequences when we raise our arm to touch tell us whether an object is near or far. This is not known by the infant, who may therefore try to touch the moon or to the adult who gains vision for the first time and feels that the scene is "touching my eyes" (Gregory 1987; Hebb 1949). However, it is known to those of us who have long ago learned what we may touch and what we may not. In perceiving an object at a distance, we unconsciously respond to the host of cues that we have found to be reliable indices of distance; we make an unconscious inference in Helmholtz's terms.

He cited many examples of such inferences, which are so rapidly made by us so many times a day that we pay them no mind. In some cases they are more evident, as when an amputee "feels" stimulation on a phantom limb. A sensory nerve ending at the stump of the limb may be mechanically stimulated by clothing or dressings, leading to a clear sensation "from" the missing limb. A lifetime of experience prior to the amputation connected the feelings accompanying the firing of that nerve with stimulation on the skin surface of the limb.

Similarly, vision may fade gradually in one eye and yet be noticed only when we close the other eye, as when looking through a telescope. Helmholtz also pointed out that we ignore the fact that most of what we see appears as double images, except for objects at whatever distance we may be focusing at the moment (i.e., the horoptor). If you hold a finger a foot or so in front of your nose and remain focused on it while noticing objects ten or twenty feet away, you will appreciate that the latter appear as double.

Helmholtz likened the influence of unconscious inference to the behavior of a person in a familiar darkened room. One can navigate efficiently, though visual cues are minimal, since the layout of the room is known by past experience. In the same way, we navigate through daily life by unconsciously inferring the presence and location of objects, by noting only a small part of the "objective" stimulation that is present.

He championed the labeled-line theory of sensation, as it was later called. According to this view, there are specific tuned receptors for discrimination of pitch, for example, and if we can discriminate 16,000 pitches (as an unachievable upper limit), then we have 16,000 tuned pitch receptors in the cochlea. These receptors are connected to individual nerve fibers—labeled lines—that project to specific cortical targets. Both this view and its counterpart in color vision, the trichromatic theory, are imperfect but have worked as well as has any competing theory.

Attention as Selective Filter

The process of unconscious inference was an active one, in Helmholtz's view, and his term for it, *Unbuwüsste Schluss*, means "unconconscious conclusion," as occurs when we actively decide something. In 1894 he described findings in section 28 of the *Optics* that convinced him that attention is a voluntary faculty (Warren and Warren 1968, pp. 249–260). The experiments concerned directing attention to parts of a dark visual field subsequently illuminated for a fraction of a second. During that brief period, a display of letters was visible and he tried to read and remember as many as he could.

He found that he could direct his attention to parts of the field, without eye movements, since there was not enough time for them. He could attend to the upper right quadrant or shift attention to the lower left and thus read and retain letters from either area. He wrote:[7]

These observations demonstrated, so it seems to me, that by a voluntary kind of intention, even without eye movements, and without changes of accommodation, one can concentrate attention on the sensation from a particular part of our peripheral nervous system and at the same time exclude attention from all other parts. (Warren and Warren 1968, p. 259)

The question of attention, whether it be voluntary or involuntary, had played an important part in the history of psychology, particularly during the seventeenth and eighteenth centuries. It would remain a central question in the subsequent centuries.

Another German pioneer, Hermann Ebbinghaus, by no means comparable in genius, extended the domain of scientific psychology by showing that the mental faculty of memory could be objectively studied. In so doing, he clarified the role of awareness in cognitive processes. And he wrote textbooks that popularized the New Psychology without pandering to popular tastes and preconceptions.

Ebbinghaus

Psychology has a long past, but only a short history. (*Abriss der Psychology*, 1922)

He was by no means prone to rush into print.[8]

Hermann Ebbinghaus was a merchant's son, born near Bonn, who studied history and philology at Bonn and then attended classes at Halle and Berlin, where his interests turned to philosophy and to science. He served in the army during the Franco–Prussian War and returned to Bonn, where he received a doctorate in philosophy, with a dissertation on the unconscious as formulated by von Hartmann. He then spent seven years in independent study, including two years in Berlin and time in France and in England as a tutor.

He is supposed to have found a copy of Fechner's *Elemente* in a used book store in Paris[9] that inspired him to extend experimental methods beyond those allowed by Wundt. There is no doubt that he was influenced by Fechner, since he dedicated his *Psychologie* to Fechner and wrote "ich hab'es nur von Euch" ("I got it only from you") (in Boring 1950).[10] In 1885 he published *Uber das Gedächtniss*, his famous study of memory that earned him instant fame.[11]

In 1886 he was Ausserordentlich Professor at Berlin, where he remained for eight years, doing no more work on memory—he did publish research on brightness contrast and on Weber's law and brightness. In 1890 he founded the *Zeitschrift für Psychologie und Physiologie der Sinnesorgone*, the first journal in Germany that was not concentrated on Wundt's Leipzig research, as was *Philosophische Studien*.[12] Ebbinghaus had editorial assistance from Helmholtz, Exner, Hering, Lipps, G. E. Müller, and Stumpf—truly the cream of the non-Wundtians of the time.

In 1893 Ebbinghaus published his theory of color vision, and he moved to Breslau in 1894, until moving to Halle in 1905. At Breslau he studied mental capacity in schoolchildren, inventing the Ebbinghaus completion test, an association test that was later widely used and became a part of modern mental testing.

The William James of Germany

By 1897 Ebbinghaus had published the first volume of his immensely successful *Grundzuge der Psychologie*, a general text that has been often compared to James's famous *Principles of Psychology*. This was immediately successful and was revised in 1905, followed by ninety-six pages of the second volume in 1908. He was asked to do a third edition of the first volume, but died unexpectedly of pneumonia in 1909, before that or the completion of the second volume could be accomplished.

Others revised the first volume after his death. His style, like that of William James, was "readable and kindly" (Boring 1950, p. 390), which accounts for its popularity. However, what lives on still is his study of memory.

Ebbinghaus's Contribution: Awareness and Memory

In a truly heroic piece of research, Hermann Ebbinghaus (1885) investigated the course of forgetting due just to the "influence of time or the daily events which fill it." Mimicking Fechner's psychophysical procedures, the inspiration for his work, he listed 2,300 consonant–vowel–consonant (CVC) nonsense syllables (though some words appeared, as he noted). These syllables were chosen so as to have no meaning in German (e.g., DUB, JIK, COZ).

You may notice that many products have since been given CVC names, making them more memorable than was the case in Ebbinghaus's day (e.g., BIZ, DUZ, JIF, FAB). He learned over 1,200 lists of three-letter nonsense syllables, with eight, twelve, or more syllables in each list. During each session, which lasted twenty minutes or so, he read through the lists one by one, at a rate of one syllable per two fifths of a second, repeating each of the lists until he could recite it twice without error. Successive lists were separated by a pause of fifteen seconds, and his measure of memory retention was the savings in time when he relearned the same set (of eight or so) lists after a lapse of time.

This savings method is actually quite ingenious. Suppose that you learn some set of material for an exam and, when faced with the task of recalling it, you go blank. Are you indeed blank—is the effect of your study nil? Similarly, are your forgotten memories of last year or of ten years ago gone without a trace, or is something left? You recall nothing, so how can "what is left" be assessed? Savings in relearning is one way.

The Battle over Color Vision: Newton to Now

Helmholtz, Hering, and their schools disagreed on many issues, chief among them being the proper sense in which the eye may be said to possess and to require a mind with which to see.... The schools' antagonistic interpretations of all of these phenomena grew out of deep and divergent methodological commitments and ultimately out of disparate conceptions of the nature of life and of organic function. (Turner 1994, p. 4)

Newton's Experiments

Isaac Newton had proposed seven primary hues in the visual spectrum. When Newton passed daylight through a prism, he cast it on a paper "about two and twenty foot distant from the prism" (Herrnstein and Boring 1965, p. 8) and asked a friend to mark with a pencil those points where each color seemed most "full and brisk." The seven-note musical scale[13] no doubt led him to seek seven primaries; those seemed to consist of red, orange, yellow, green, blue, indigo, and violet, and those were the hues marked off by his "friend." If the seven primaries are laid around the circumference of a circle, Newton proposed that their mixture produces all seen hues and brightnesses.

Newton proposed that vibrations in the "ether" beat and dash against the eye, just as air beats on the "organs of hearing" to produce sounds. The vibrations that come to us mixed produce sensations of white, while those of greatest "bigness" produce sensations of red and the smallest are felt as blue, if each is present separated from the mixture. Since "bigness" refers to wavelength, he was correct—reds and blues correspond to long and short wavelengths, respectively.

Young Reduces the Number of Primaries
It was 150 years later that Thomas Young was interested in color vision, and Newton's theory of vibrations seemed to make sense to him. However, seven primaries were too many. His trichromatic theory explained color vision as the combined effect of three photoreceptors in the retina, one sensitive to short wavelength/high frequency vibrations (the blue end of the visible spectrum), one sensitive to middle wavelengths (e.g., green), and one sensitive to long wavelength/ low frequency signals (the reds). Stimulation of individual receptors and combinations produces phenomenal colors. Combined stimulation of a red receptor and a green receptor, for example, produces yellow.[14]

Young proposed a small number of fundamental receptors for a very good reason. He knew that visual acuity is approximately the same in monochromatic light and in white light. If that is so, there had to be few receptor types—if there were fifty or a hundred, the narrowing of the wavelength of light presented, as when it is monochromatic (red, or green, etc.) would mean that only a fiftieth or a hundredth of the receptors would be involved. And that should decrease acuity, an effect that does not occur. However, if there were few receptors, say three, then a sizable fraction would be stimulated even in narrowly monochromatic light and acuity would remain good.

Young retained three principal colors, but shortly thereafter he changed their identities to red, green, and violet. Like Newton, he viewed other colors as mixtures of the primaries and seemed to share Newton's hunch that colors mix in a manner analogous to the mixing of sounds.

Colors do indeed mix, but not as do sounds. Trained musicians can decompose and separately identify the sounds that comprise a chord or other compound. But no one, however trained or sensitive, can separately identify the parts of light mixtures. In other words, sounds can never be mixed so as to produce a new pure sound, but lights can be mixed to produce what seems a pure resultant color. One of the most salient examples of such mixture is yellow.[15]

We cannot distinguish a yellow monochromatic light from a yellow that is a mixture of red and green lights. That is because, as Young held, the two yellows are actually the same, at least as they act on our visual equipment. There is no yellow receptor, only the combined action of red and green receptors.

Young found that he could mix lights of three "principal colors" and apparently produce all other colors. It took three lights, not two, and a variety of wavelengths would do—what was necessary was a long-, a medium-, and a short-wavelength light—a "red," a "green," and a "blue." However, any number of reds or greens or blues would do; the primary colors were not a unique set of three.

Helmholtz on Color Mixing: 1852–1855

In 1852 Helmholtz published a short paper on mixing of *Grundfarben*, or primary colors, where his results seemed to contradict Young's thesis.[16] He passed light through a V-shaped slit and through a flint glass prism, producing overlaps in the spectra that included all possible combinations of pairs of colors. He noted that only the mixture of indigo–blue and yellow produced white. Since yellow and blue are conventionally thought to produce green, he was led to specify the basic distinction between additive and subtractive color mixture.

Our retinas are struck by light, and it is the mixtures of lights that additively determine our color perceptions. When we mix paint, however, the color that we see is the remainder of a subtractive process. The pigments reflect to us only what they do not absorb, and that depends on the material composition of the pigments. Subtractive light mixture is a messy business and not helpful in understanding color vision.

Helmholtz also mixed three-component combinations of lights and produced many new colors but few that seemed to him to really match spectral colors. The combinations always seemed washed out and whitish; for example, concerning yellow he wrote that a mixture of red and green "rays"..."never generate so bright and vivid a yellow, as the red rays do" (Turner 1994, p. 96). He rejected Young's theory.

Helmholtz was strongly criticized for this poor research and reasoning by an unknown mathematics teacher named Hermann Grassman, who showed that Newton's color circle required complements for each primary. He also argued that Newton specified color sensation by reference to hue, brightness, and saturation, and that these corresponded to wavelength, intensity, and intensity of intermixed white. Mathematical demonstrations were included, and Helmholtz was stung by the critique.

Clerk Maxwell Steps In

The Scotsman James Clerk Maxwell was twenty-four years old in 1855 and had been experimenting with color for six years. He had read the papers of Helmholtz and of Grassman and in 1855 published a paper in the *Transactions of the Royal Society of Edinburgh* that carried color mixing far beyond Helmholtz.

Maxwell used a rotating color wheel—an inner circle had black and white papers that overlapped so that the proportion of black to white could be adjusted. When the wheel was spun, this altered the shade of gray that appeared. An outer circle featured adjustable areas of three colors, called by Maxwell "vermillion," "ultramarine," and "emerald green"—that is, red, blue, and green. When the wheel spun, observers saw a mixed color that depended on the three primaries and the proportions of them present.

Maxwell usually asked subjects to match these "outer" colors to various grays in the inner circle—he then computed the amounts of the primaries necessary to match a given gray. Occasionally he operated in more straightforward form and matched colors presented on the inner wheel with mixtures of three hues on the outer wheel. His success in matching any color or gray with different proportions of three primaries convinced him that Thomas Young had been correct and that the "theory of three distinct modes of sensation in the retina, each...produced in different degrees by the different rays" was correct (excerpt in Turner 1994, p. 101).

Helmholtz had rejected that theory in 1852, but the young Maxwell tactfully neglected to mention that in his published paper. Maxwell understood Young to mean that every monochromatic light stimulates all three color responses, though to different degrees—we see red when the red receptor is stimulated more strongly than are the green and blue ones. For this reason, we can never know to what spectral value the red receptor is really tuned and we cannot locate the three primary hues on a color circle. We can guess that the values are an extreme red, a green, and blue or violet.

Helmholtz Adopts the "Young–Maxwell Theory"

Helmholtz quickly realized that Maxwell had recognized the power of Young's theory, and he quickly put it to use himself. In the second volume of his famous *Handbook of Physiological Optics*, published in 1860, he applied Young's theory so thoroughly that the view came to be called the "Young–Helmholtz" theory, despite Maxwell's priority.

There are serious shortcomings of that theory, but space precludes discussing them all. However, one has to be mentioned, and that is the general argument of Ewald Hering.

Hering versus Helmholtz

The foreword to Hering's 1872 treatise set out his first and polemically most effective reply to Helmholtz's criticism of the nativist position. It occupied only five pages, yet it was calculated for maximum polemical effect and—always important to Hering—maximum provocation of his opponents. (Turner 1994, p. 121)

Ewald Hering had worked as a pure physiologist in Vienna, collaborating early with Josef Breuer, later to be Freud's mentor, in which Breuer showed the self-regulation of the respiratory function (the Hering/Beuer reflex). Alone, Hering showed in 1870 that inflation of the lungs accelerates cardiac activity and vasoconstriction centers in the brainstem. Such self-regulation was a secondary focus of what was later to be the Hering School.

Breuer influenced him greatly, and the two of them decided that the same nerve fibers of the vagus nerve (the Xth cranial nerve) carry impulses of two kinds—to inhale and to exhale. Thus, nerves may have "multi-form potency" (Turner 1994, p. 121), which could be innervated in different ways and produce a sensation or its opposite. They also found that the vagus did not produce the same effects when it was cut and the stump was stimulated. Hence, mere conduction is not enough, and nerves always act in a context.

For the rest of his life Hering held to the conviction that living things are equilibria of antagonistic processes. He saw this as the naturalistic view and contrasted it with that of Helmholtz, which he described as "spiritualistic" and relying on "psychological platitudes" to explain things that are physiological processes. Oddly, it may seem to modern readers, Hering saw the empiricist/nativist debate as a side issue and of little importance. The real issue was between "spiritualists" and "physiologists"—the spiritualist always limits the realm of the innate, so as to leave more room for the human spirit to operate.

And Helmholtz was a "spiritualist," since he attributed contrast effects and other visual phenomena to "psychological factors," varieties of unconscious inferences. A physiologist would look for physiological explanations, not psychic ones! If he wanted a quarrel with the Helmholtz who had sworn an oath against vitalism years ago, this was the way to do it.

For Hering, every "subjective" light sensation has a "physiological basis in the organ of vision, and cannot arise merely out of false judgments" (Turner 1994, p. 125). He coined the expressions "simultaneous and successive contrast,"[17] referring to the brightness contrast effects that Helmholtz had treated as two separate things, "contrast" and "afterimages."

Contrast was caused by the same physiological processes, in Hering's view, and his choice of terms reflected that. For example, in the retina, "visual substance" breaks down (dissimilates) under the effects of light (a "D stimulus") and builds up (assimilates) in the absence of light. This is an "A process." The rate of dissimilation depends on the strength of the stimulus and the momentary condition of the visual substance—as the D stimulus persists, the rate of breakdown decreases. A rested eye exposed to strong light sees it as intensely bright, but it grows fainter as adaptation occurs.

Hering and many others viewed yellow as a "pure" color—it was difficult to imagine it as a combination of red and green lights as the Young/Helmholtz theory proposed. On that score they were wrong, however, and it is easy to show that yellow is always a mixture of red and green. It is shown with an anomaloscope, a device for presenting two adjacent fields with different light sources illuminating them. One field is yellow, produced by a monochromatic "yellow" light, say of 570 nanometers. The adjacent field is also yellow but produced by a mixture of red and green lights, say 660 nanometers and 520 nanometers. The procedure was described by Gregory in his classic, *Eye and Brain* (1978, pp. 128–130).

An observer adjusts the mixture of red and green lights so as to make a yellow that matches the monochromatic "real" yellow of the adjacent field. The eye is then directed to a bright red light until the eye adapts and the red fades. While the eye is adapted, the gaze is returned to the anomaloscope and the subject is asked whether the two fields still appear to be the same color. The subject will see both fields as green, and they will be the same green. The match is not disturbed by the adaptation to red, and there is no need to mix a different proportion of red and green in the mixture field to match the monochromatic yellow.

The Young–Helmholtz theory and its backers won the day, it would seem, and the discovery of three chromatic photopigments in the 1960s seemed to cinch the case. Cones that showed maximum sensitivity to 445, 535, and 570 nanometers embodied the blue (S), green (M), and red (L) receptors that the Young–Helmholtz theory required.[18] The receptors were there and the color mixing data seemed "close enough."

During the 1950s, Hurvich and Jameson developed a quantitative version of Hering's model that included three inputs from S, M, and L receptors and operated as an opponent-process model (Hurvich and Jameson 1957). Such processes remained largely unknown, however, as did the large effect that color contrast has on our experience of color. Thus, the advent of Edwin Land came as more a surprise than it should have.

Edwin Land Creates a Furor

Recently a jolt has been given to the more complacent by the American inventive genius Edwin Land. (Wandell 1995, p. 287)

Edwin Land was not concerned with what colors matched what mixtures of other colors. He was concerned with what was seen, and color matching data seemed to have little to do with color appearance. He had developed a way of producing low-cost polarizing filters while in his early twenties and black and white instant developing (Polaroid) film before he was thirty. He was planning to produce an instant color film in the 1950s and so was experimenting with color in his laboratory. What he found seemed incredible, both to himself and to his critics—it is described in several sources.[19]

Land repeated the original color mixing experiments of Young and Maxwell with one important difference—he used color transparencies of scenes, rather than pure hues. In a key discovery, he obtained three photographic negatives of the same scene, each taken through a different filter—blue/short wavelength (S), green/medium wavelength (M), or red/long wavelength (L).

They were then converted to positive transparencies and projected through their original filters to provide superimposed pictures on a screen. This is equivalent to projecting a color transparency on a screen—an ordinary Kodachrome transparency gives us all the colors that we ever see, and it does so by passing white light through a mixture of the dyes S, M, and L, just as Young did.

According to lore,[20] one of his projectors failed—the blue (S) one—and no one noticed a change in the colors of the scene. The reds, blues, greens, yellows, oranges, and the rest remained unchanged. Experimenting further, Land found that any two of the three projectors were sufficient to leave a normal scene—whether it be blue and green (S and M), blue and red (S and L), green and red (M and L) made little difference. As long as the two wavelengths used were not too closely spaced, their combination seemed to produce normally colored scenes.

Land even found quite acceptable colors when only one projector, with a red (L) filter, was used and no filter was used on a second projector. What one might expect is nothing but a pink scene with portions of varying saturation, but instead we find green and other colors not physically present; that is, there was no (M) middle-wavelength light present. Land believed that he had shown the three-color "classic" theory to be fatally flawed.

Early color films had used two colors, but no one realized how good they could be. And everyone knew that there had to be more to color vision than Young's three colors, since no mixture of three, or however many, primary colors could produce metallic colors, like gold and silver, or brown, perhaps the commonest color seen in much of the world. What was needed was Land's pointing out the huge effect of contrasts and context, just as Fechner had pointed it out to Helmholtz a century before. It was all in the colored shadows.

This is plain when we consider that Land's effects occur only when the scenes viewed are scenes, not when a color chart or completely unfamiliar display is presented. The colors in a scene appear as complex patterns, producing contrasts and inferences, so that the three colors involved produce a far greater range of colors than when the same three lights appear as a simple pattern of overlapping circles.

Would Helmholtz have been surprised? Hardly.

... puerile, dull, dogmatic, absurd, foolish, and ... the most frontless piece of charlatanry that the age had produced, while the "cunning craniologers" who were beginning to roam the country were seen as quacks, empirics, manipulating impostors, and itinerant mountebanks to be looked upon "as rather knaves than fools." (Cooter 1984, p. 22)

Phrenology's Modern Ghosts

The quotation above refers to phrenology, long regarded as a pseudo-scientific fraud, but initiated by Franz Josef Gall (see figure 10.1), an eminent Viennese physician and anatomist, who was the first to distinguish the white and gray matter of the brain. He gathered masses of data relating "mental and moral" attributes to the shape of people's heads. He proposed twenty-six faculties, or "personality organs," each complete and located in specific sites in the brain. If we have a lot of a trait, such as facility with language, the brain will be highly developed in the corresponding area and will cause the skull to bulge at that point.

The phrenologist, also called craniologist, zoonomist, physiognomist, and other things, could then analyze personality by examining the surface of the skull. Organ number two is Philoprogenitiveness, love of children, and is located at the back of the head, since Gall believed this area to be prominent in women and in apes, both of whom supposedly love children more than do men. Organ number 22 is Individuality, located immediately above the nose, since that is what seemed large in the face of Michelangelo and small in Scottish people! It may seem that phrenology is ridiculed today, but if you attend to newspapers and television, you will see that the general point of view remains popular—we still appear to believe in mental motives and powers (faculties) that are localized in specific brain areas.

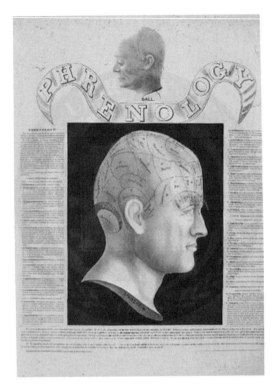

Figure 10.1
Gall. Courtesy of the National Library of Medicine, National Institutes of Health.

Sometimes they are conceived as existing in their entirety in some location—perhaps as "memory units" in the cerebral cortex. "Didn't someone, Penfield, I think, revive memories by stimulating the cortex of patients?" we think. "Scientists Discover Pleasure Centers in the Brain" headlined a Montreal newspaper in the 1950s, and variations on that announcement have appeared frequently in newspapers and magazines since.

You may also have heard of "aggression centers" in the brain. As recently as the late 1960s and the 1970s many people were operated upon by surgeons who believed that there were such centers (see Valenstein 1973). We hear also that there are "feeding and drinking centers" in the brain, and every decade at least two or three "satiety hormones" are reported, each hoped to be the chemical that will turn off our hunger and make us slim. Sometimes it is the "arousal" center that makes news or dopamine that causes "awakenings" of Parkinson-ism patients.[1] In countless cases the spirit of phrenology lives on in the localization of faculties in discrete brain structures or in the amazing effects of a new hormone. The same applies to the fruits of so-called "split brain" research.

Richard Gregory noted that laterality theories, which posit language functions in the left cerebral hemisphere and spatial apprehension in the right, tell an old tale:

One might say that the current interest in "cerebral dominance," with the left hemisphere of the cortex supposedly "analytic" (responsible for skills such as arithmetic and logical thinking) and the right hemisphere "synthetic" or "analogue" (responsible for intuitive and artistic skills), is the dying kick of phrenology. (Gregory 1987, p. 619–620)

In fact, if we add up all of the claims for "centers" of one kind or an-other in the brain, we could list most of the motives and powers pro-posed by the phrenologists. Almost a dozen separate functions have been attributed to one brain structure, the hippocampus, and it isn't even in the cerebral neocortex.[2] Does that support phrenology?

Localization of Function: Finding the Right Names for Functions

Let us examine the evidence and briefly look at the history of research in this area. We will find that specific parts of the brain *do* serve spe-cific functions, as it seems they must, but it will also be clear that these functions are often hard to name. That is, when we list functions like attention, memory, learning, arousal, hunger, aggression, and the like, our list seems not to correspond to the functions built in by the archi-tect of the nervous system.

Happily, recent research seeking the classic "centers" of the phrenol-ogists has brought a new understanding of the characteristics of the nervous system. This allows a revision of the list of centers, thus advancing our knowledge of psychology, as well as of neuroanatomy and physiology.

The biology of the nineteenth century was a mixture of three main views—vitalism, materialism, and phrenology, the popular "science" of the day. The vitalists, such as Johannes Müller, followed Aristotle in distinguishing the organic and inorganic as different in kind, a view opposed by Helmholtz and his materialist fellows, who argued that living things are dependent on ordinary physical/chemical processes, just like the rest of nature. Phrenology appealed to the conception of mind and brain that the public could understand and endorse. They expanded on the ancient doctrine of faculties, already popular in Britain by the early eighteenth century, and tied it to hypothetical brain localization.

The Nineteenth Century

Phrenology

Before 1820 phrenology was regarded with disdain in the Edinburgh Medical and Surgical Journal, London Medical Repository, British Critic, Monthly Critical Gazette, Critical Journal, Literary Journal, the Monthly, Quarterly, Augustan, Eclectic, and Edinburgh reviews, the Gentleman's, New Monthly, Literary Gazette, and Blackwood's magazines, to mention only the most widely circulated. (Cooter 1984, p. 22)

Franz Josef Gall's original purposes were laudable—he criticized the cavalier definitions of mental powers, or "faculties," then in fashion, particularly in France. Gall proposed to survey populations with known defects or excellences of what could be faculties and to examine their brains (indirectly) for differences. For example, he examined the skulls of hundreds of thieves, seeking the locus of the propensity to steal.

Gall described the method he used to collect data:

I assembled a number of persons at my house, drawn from the lowest classes...I gained their confidence and induced them to speak frankly by giving them money and having wine and beer distributed to them. When I saw that they were favorably disposed, I urged them to tell me everything they knew about one another, both their good and their bad qualities, and I carefully examined their heads. This was the origin of the craniological chart which was seized upon so avidly by the public. (Cooter 1984, p. 4)

An ever-credulous (or cynical) popular press and a gullible public were ready to believe that the mind was a group of faculties and that a raised portion of the skull meant that the brain was larger than normal at that location and that whatever faculty was housed there was excessively developed—and why not? Gall's data were extensive and seemed good. People *did* differ in their "faculties" of memory, self-preservation, love of children, combativeness, and so on, and the relation of these traits to features of the skull surface seemed convincing. Gall was no charlatan—he proposed a list of twenty-six faculties and felt that his model of the brain was better than that of folk psychology.

Figure 10.2
Spurzheim. Courtesy of the National Library of Medicine, National Institutes of Health.

Spurzheim and Later Phrenology

Though it began seriously enough with Gall, his student, Johann Gaspar Spurzheim (see figure 10.2), popularized phrenology, and others spread its doctrines throughout England. Phrenology was exceptionally popular in England, and it was even compared to Methodism in its appeal. The similarity of Methodism and phrenology lay in the practice of pointing to one's works and wealth as evidence that one was a member of the elect—this led to much of the entrepreneurship that constituted the "Protestant ethic."

Similarly, evidence for one's election could be gotten by brushing the hair aside and examining the head. Surely, the elect would be identifiable by the favorable distribution of faculties revealed by the phrenologist! Harriet Martineau remarked on why "ignorant persons" were so taken with phrenology:

... they learned that their bodies were a part of the universe, made of substances and governed by laws which it is man's duty to obey. It was a new view to them that by knowledge and self-management, men have their health, and the development of their minds in their own hands. (Cooter 1984, p. 197)

So phrenology was the "delight of the half-educated and half-witted" transformed to a popular religion through the efforts of Spurzheim and of the Scotsman George Combe. Combe's *The Constitution of Man* was on most bookshelves, and readers saw its doctrines as an escape from the tyranny of the nobility and its henchman, the church. Phrenology was the equalizer, as Charles Thorold Wood lectured in 1838:

... [the Queen] does not possess a single faculty more than any of those I am now addressing. The monarch has three lobes—the animal, the moral, and the intellectual—so have you. (Cooter 1984, pp. 184–185)

Spurzheim's Rendition of Gall   Johann Gaspar Spurzheim published *Philosophical Principles of Phrenology* in 1835 and, in volume II of that work, presented a very concise and penetrating summary of philosophy, from the Milesians and Eleatics to his time. His descriptions were surprisingly accurate, given that the great historians of philosophy, Diehls and Zeller, for example, had not yet done their work.

Throughout his summary of the history of philosophy, Spurzheim referred to Thomas Reid, often cited as the philosophical predecessor of the faculty psychology of phrenology. However, Spurzheim was critical of Reid on basic issues, including the independent status of consciousness. Reid felt that consciousness was a "thing in itself," while Spurzheim saw it otherwise.

Consciousness, Perception, and Attention   In Spurzheim's opinion, consciousness is not a special aspect or faculty of mind. Rather, it is "an effect of the activity of one or several mental faculties" (ibid., p. 32). It exists in all of the operations of mind and is almost synonymous with mind, which cannot be thought of without consciousness. There are various kinds of consciousness, and these are to be "specified by philosophy."

Perception was for Reid a very important faculty—it was the God-given assurance that a real world exists independent of us. Spurzheim allows this for the intellectual faculties, adding that there are as many sorts of perceptions as there will turn out to be sorts of intellectual faculties. Then, foreshadowing the opinions that Freud would make famous, Spurzheim speculated on the "perceptions" of the affective faculties—that is, hunger, fear, and the like. He proposed that some faculties, such as these, exist only to procure "impressions that are perceived by other faculties." As he wrote:

> The affective functions are blind and involuntary, and have no knowledge of the objects respectively suited to satisfy their activity... it is still certain that the intellectual faculties alone procure clear consciousness. (Spurzheim 1825, p. 33)

Freud would later refer to "primary and secondary process" to make the same distinction. The fact that Spurzheim felt similarly only shows that the distinction between unconscious motivation and conscious intellect that goes back at least to Plato was still commonly accepted in the early nineteenth century.

Attention was a voluntary act for Reid and a consequence of desire for Hobbes. However, Spurzheim wrote that "attention, in none of its acceptations, is a single faculty; for if it were, he who possesses it in a particular sense should be able to apply it universally" (Spurzheim 1835, p. 35). There is no single entity called attention—there is an infinitely large set of "attentions." One's customary diet—plants or flesh—determines attention to different objects; boys attend to "horses, whips, and drums," while "little girls prefer dolls, ribands" (ibid.). One person may prefer philosophic discussion while another prefers witty conversation. "Sheep never attend to philosophy or theology." As the activation of a faculty, there are as many species of attention as faculties of the mind. Believing he was following Kant, he proposed that perception is the passive knowledge of externals and attention the active form of knowing.

The assumption that there are as many "attentions" as there are faculties applies as well to memory and to will/desire. Each is specific to a faculty, in Spurzheim's view, and hence there are as many memories and wills as there are faculties. Effectively, this reduces will to "the last appetite before action," as Hobbes envisioned it. Indeed, Spurzheim thought that "the exhibition of true will is very rare" (1825, p. 49).

The Faculties   Examples of the actual faculties proposed by Spurzheim, after Gall, follow (1835, volume II, section II). The lack of activity of any of these faculties led to the opposite effects:

ORDER I: Affective faculties or feelings

Genus I—Feelings common to man and animals (total 13)

- Alimentiveness—organ that responds to impressions of hunger and thirst; Disorder—gluttony, drunkenness
- Destructiveness—violent death of animals, to live on their flesh; Disorder—murder, cruelty
- Amativeness—physical love, propagation of species; Disorder—adultery, incest, etc.
- Philoprogenitiveness—preservation of offspring; Disorder—spoiling children, their loss as calamity
- Adhesiveness—attachment to all around us—friendship, marriage, society, habit; Disorder—grief when loss
- Combativeness—courage, defense; Disorder—quarrelsomeness, disputation, attack, anger
- Secretiveness—to conceal; Disorders—lying, hypocrisy
- Acquisitiveness—to acquire that necessary for life; Disorder—theft, usury, fraud

. . .

- Cautiousness—to be cautious and circumspect; Disorders—anxiety, fear, uncertainty, melancholy
- Self Esteem—to esteem oneself; Disorders—pride, disdain

. . .

Genus II—Affective faculties proper to man; Benevolence—benevolence in general; Disorders—benevolence to the undeserving or at the expense of others
- Reverence—to respect what is venerable; Disorders—idolatry, bigotry

. . .

- Marvellousness—Admiration of and belief in supernaturality; Disorders—sorcery, astrology, belief in demons

. . .

- Imitation—imitation, artistic expression; Disorders—buffoonery, grimaces
ORDER II—Intellectual faculties (14 & external senses)
Genus I—External senses, are vision, audition, olfaction, the skin senses, and gustation, as conventionally treated.

. . .

Genus II—Internal senses, or perceptive faculties, which procure knowledge of external objects, their physical qualities, and various relations.

Individuality, Order

Configuration, Calculation

Size, Eventuality

Weight and Resistance Time

Coloring, Tune

Locality, Language

Genus III—Reflective faculties

Comparison, Causality

Faculties as Fundamental   Spurzheim was clear on the priority of faculties. Earlier claims that the faculties were secondary, the product of education, cannot be true. Spurzheim assumed that this "education" was due to pleasures and pains—trial-and-error learning. However, he opposed hedonist explanations. There are as many wants as there are faculties, and the degree of the wants reflects the activity of the faculties. The pleasures attending the satisfaction of these wants are different—compare the pleasure of eating and of reading poetry.

It is pleasure and pain that are secondary, reflecting the activity of faculties. By the same token, attention, understanding, and will cannot be the cause of our faculties—they reflect the activity of faculties. Spurzheim was more than ready to accept the fact that education affects us mightily. He points out that all one need do is consider how different were the Athenians and the Lacedaemonians (Spartans), which is completely attributable as the effect of differences in the constitutions governing the two cities.

However, he felt that the effects of education are often exaggerated, and, in Spurzheim's day, the chief example of this practice was Helvetius, who taught that foxes learn to hunt, birds learn to sing, and human faculties result from education. But, Spurzheim asked (1825, pp. 64–65), why is the progress of art and science so slow—all should improve steadily as the cumulative effect of instruction. Yet, is our art better than that of two thousand years ago? Why do we acknowledge the births of geniuses? Why does each of us have some faculties stronger than others? Education is not the whole story.

Yet, Spurzheim also opposed the doctrine of innate ideas, whereby moral principles are innate and action predestined. That view "lost its authority by degrees, and it was easy to combat it, as it is not conformable to nature" (1825, p. 64). The truth is neither extreme nativism nor extreme empiricism. For Spurzheim, faculties are inherited powers and their activation may occur spontaneously. However, if nature does not supply the faculties, "external wants cannot excite them." (Spurzheim 1825, p. 64)

The Constancy of the Nature of Animals and Humans Spurzheim felt that teaching could not elevate the general level of humankind. If education were the determinant, why are there geniuses? That is, why do some few people seem vastly intelligent? The answer must lie in what Nature provided them. Spurzheim even described animal geniuses, such as the dog who ran outside to bark, drawing the other dogs outside, only to rush in and take the best spot in front of the fire. The other dogs were frequently deceived in this way, yet none ever imitated the practice—the deceiving dog was a "genius." M. Dupont de Nemours's cow could open the gate, but no other cows learned the trick. Instead, they waited impatiently at the gate for the genius cow to do it.

In summary, Spurzheim believed that all faculties are innate but subject to modification of function, depending on circumstances. Second, faculties exist in different degrees, both within individuals and among people. And nature has "stamped a difference upon the sexes; some faculties are more active in women, others in men. Men will never feel like women, and women will never think like men" (1825, p. 80).

George Combe and the Optimism Regarding Phrenology
George Combe (1788–1858) was the Scottish moral philosopher who spread the glad tidings of phrenology to England and America. By 1832 there were twenty-nine phrenological societies in Britain and a host of journals, including the *Phrenological Journal*, edited by Combe from Edinburgh from 1823 to 1847. In his *The Constitution of Man Considered in Relation to External Objects* (1834), he concluded by enumerating the virtues of phrenology and the ancient problems that it would solve.

Phrenology, according to Combe, accomplished for the moral sciences (psychology) what Galileo and Newton had accomplished for astronomy. Combe argued that phrenology had settled the matter of the "number of elementary feelings and intellectual powers" and shown how primitive faculties differ in strength, how different feelings are merely different modes of action of the same faculty, and how the size of different parts of the brain is related to the strength of different faculties.

With the knowledge brought by phrenology, many practical problems can be dealt with effectively and many errors of the past could have been avoided (Combe 1834, p. 199). Criminal law cannot be effective if it ignores the fundamental nature of humanity.

The burning of witches showed, in Combe's opinion, the predominance of the faculties of Destructiveness and Wonder over Intellect and Benevolence. War and other evils depend similarly on the dominance of some faculties over others. This must change—"the mental condition of the people" must change before institutions and cultural practices change. Phrenology was a wonder, and the knowledge of it was preached as the savior of humanity.

Flourens's Critique of Phrenology[3]

In the early nineteenth century Gall's lectures in Vienna stirred interest in localization of function in the cerebrum. However, the claims made by him and Spurzheim for precise localization of complex cognitive functions was widely challenged. A prominent critic was Pierre Flourens (1794–1867), who sweepingly rejected all ideas of localization. Flourens recognized only three major functional regions—the cerebrum, the cerebellum, and the medulla. Within those divisions, functioning was global.

For example, the function of the cerebrum is sensory, and as animals that survive their removal "lose perception, judgment, memory and will . . . therefore the cerebral hemispheres are the sole site of perception and all intellectual abilities" (Brazier 1959, p. 44). However, these abilities are not located in specific areas of the cerebrum.

In an experiment that became famous, he kept a pigeon alive after removal of the cerebral hemispheres. A poor pet, the bird was blind and deaf and constantly appeared asleep, though it moved when poked. In Flourens's opinion, the bird had lost its will and even the "faculty of dreaming." However, its pupils still reacted normally to light and it retained the sense of equilibrium. If the medulla was sectioned, death came quickly, and it was clear to Flourens that here lay the mechanisms for respiration and for life functions in general.

The cerebellum, the last major division of the brain, had motor functions, since he found that its removal caused loss of coordinated movement in birds and mammals. It was the initiation and control of movement that was Flourens's main research interest for many years, so it is ironic that he was rendered paralyzed for a long period before his death.

During the 1820s, the researchers who were carrying out such experiments were accused of "mutilating animals" by Gall. And the search for localization of function was not so easily stopped. Indeed, Gall had placed the faculty of speech in the anterior lobes of the brain, and in the 1860s, thirty years after his death, that opinion seemed to be vindicated.

The tendency to seek and to find structure–function relationships in the brain continued through the middle of the twentieth century, when a revision of strategy occurred. It seemed that the faculties of folk psychology and the Scottish School—attention, sensation, perception, reasoning, and the like—were not the names for the functions that seemed connected with structures. Before considering the revision that occurred in the late twentieth century, consider the substantial developments in what we now call "cognitive neuroscience" that occurred in the nineteenth century.

Nineteenth-Century Science

The science of the nineteenth century, especially in physiology, had a profound effect on the development of psychology later in the century. To most observers, science was showing that the model of British Empiricism that was influential at the turn of that century was essentially correct. As Hartley had proposed and as James Mill had elaborated, the mind is actually a biological entity that acts as an association machine. Consider the evidence for the mechanical nature of organisms, including their brains, and for empiricism—the sensory origins of the mind.

The Neural Impulse
The many thinkers following Descartes and others of the Enlightenment believed that the body was a wonderful machine run by a ghost, the "mind." According to this view, the mind sent its mental instructions to parts of the body instantaneously; magic need not take time!

Given that context, it is amazing that Albrecht von Haller (1708–1777), a Swiss who studied at Tübingen and at Leiden, freed himself from the dogma of the age and proposed irritability as a fundamental property of living tissue. That part of the body is irritable if it contracts when touched and it requires no mediation by the soul. On the other hand, sensitivity is evident when stimulation "transmits the impression of it to the soul." This argument, presented in 1753, prepared the way for the materialist theories to come later in the century (Brazier 1959, pp. 1–58 provides a clear and authoritative account).

Then, once it became clear that messages were sent via electrical impulses, a bit of magic seemed lost. It is true that electricity has an aura of magic about it, but its behavior is quite predictable; "mind" is pure magic. Boring (1950, p. 30) described well the circumstances of this discovery.

Luigi Galvani showed in 1791 that a frog leg kicked when touched by rods of different metals. He first observed a leg with nerve and a piece of spinal cord hung from a piece of iron with a brass hook through the cord. It twitched when electricity discharged nearby, whether due to lightning or to a Leyden jar. He found that he could make the leg kick by touching the nerve and the outside of the leg with wires of different metals if the other ends of the wires were touched together. In so doing, Galvani created the first electric battery, with the frog leg furnishing the wet cell material.

A further (and macabre) demonstration involved a frog's leg hanging by its nerve from a grounded brass hook with its foot touching a silver plate. If the plate were also grounded, the leg would continue kicking indefinitely. In Galvani's opinion, he had demonstrated "animal electricity."

Galvani's interpretation was opposed by the physicist Alessandro Volta (1745–1827), whose work with electricity led Napoleon I to make him a count in 1801. Prior to his work, static electricity was generated with friction machines and "stored" in Leyden jars. He created the first electric battery that could produce a constant flow. This was the voltaic pile, composed of alternate silver and zinc plates separated by brine-soaked cardboard. Stimulation of body parts with current from this source produced muscular contraction—hence the source was outside, not inside the organism—there was no animal electricity, Volta claimed.

The Rate of Neural Conduction

Despite the cogency of Volta's argument, the great physiologist Johannes Müller still saw (as we do) the electricity as animal produced. It was his student Hermann Helmholtz who was the first to measure the rate of conduction of this electricity as it traveled along a nerve.

Müller doubted that the rate of neural conduction could ever be measured but suggested three values, ranging from 150 feet per minute to 5,757,600 million feet per second, a velocity sixty times that of light! The actual velocity varies from 3–400 feet per second, depending on the diameter of the fiber. His student, Hermann Helmholtz, invented the myograph and used it to calculate the velocity of conduction in the frog's leg; this turned out to be 90 feet per second. He also investigated differences in conduction time in human nerves when stimulation occurs on a toe or on a thigh. Based on differences in reaction time (see below), he estimated the conduction velocity to lie between 50 and 100 meters per second. It really doesn't matter what the true values are; what matters is that there *are* values. That is, neural conduction is not infinitely rapid; unlike magic, it takes time (Brazier 1959, p. 14).

Sensory and Motor Nerves

Descartes had assumed that the tubes that carry messages via the animal spirits to the mind were different from the tubes that carry the motor command to the muscles. One of the ancient Alexandrian Greeks, Erasistratus, made a similar assumption, but it was not until the early nineteenth century that the real distinction between sensory and motor nerves was discovered. As was common, controversy over priority ensued.

Sir Charles Bell (1774–1842), England's foremost physiologist and anatomist, was born in Scotland but worked and lectured in London. He typically worked late at night and lectured on his findings to medical students in the morning. His most famous finding was that cutting the posterior (dorsal...back) roots of the spinal cord produced no violent movements but touching the anterior (ventral...front) roots produced convulsions. Clearly the latter had purely motor effects. He published a pamphlet, "Idea of a New Anatomy of the Brain," in 1811 and made 100 copies for friends.

The premier physiologist in France at the time was François Magendie (1783–1855; see figure 10.3), whose discovery was similar, but who published his results in a standard journal in 1822. He noted that when

Figure 10.3
Magendie. Courtesy of the National Library of Medicine, National Institutes of Health.

an animal's posterior/dorsal roots were cut, there was no reaction to stimulation of a limb, but the animal was capable of moving the limb. Sectioning of the anterior/ventral root led to paralysis. Hence, like Bell, Magendie found conduction of the motor impulse is carried in different fibers from those that carried conduction in. One-way conduction in sensory and motor fibers is basic to the principle of reflex action, an important principle for physiology and for psychology.

Reflex Action

Galen (ca. 190) described the pupillary reflex; Descartes proposed a reflex mechanism to account for all animal and most human activity, and the word "reflex" was first used in 1736 by Astruc. The term was meant to indicate "reflected"; the effect of a stimulus is reflected out in the reflex response.

In 1751 Robert Whytt, another Scot, wrote an essay arguing that the spinal cord is independent of "mind"; it is a pure mechanism, as Descartes had suggested. Whytt showed that the heart and intestinal muscles may continue rhythmic contraction and relaxation long after removal from the body.

This view, echoing LaMettrie, was carried on by another Scot, Marshall Hall, who reported to the Royal Society in 1833 that spinal reflexes were unconscious. He described the activity of decapitated newts and snakes with severed spinal cords—in neither case did the animals move unless touched. But move they could.

Oddly, proposals such as that touched off the real debate regarding reflex action—is reflex action independent of consciousness and mind, the action of a mere mechanism? Or, is it still guided by some diminished level of mind/consciousness? Reflexes are purposive, and that implies mentality. The eminent physiologist Pflüger held this position; in his view, consciousness played a part in all neural action, and he referred to a "soul of the spinal cord."

The issue was discussed by William James (1890, chapter 4), who posed it as the problem of continuity of mind and matter. Thus, if we act adaptively because we have mind and the spinal cord acts adaptively without our commanding it, it must have a degree of mind of its own. On the other hand, the spinal cord acts according to several fairly simple mechanical principles, as shown by Sherrington (1906). Maybe the brain is just as mechanical and what we call "mind" is superfluous.

Reflexes of the Brain

During the time when brain structures were being related to sensory and speech functions, a young and brilliant Russian army surgeon demonstrated something interesting about the functions of higher neural centers in the control of lower ones. Ivan Sechenov published a delightful little book, only recently translated into English (1863/1965), *The Reflexes of the Brain*, in which he attempted to show exactly how an utterly mechanical brain and nervous system could account for all of our behavior and experience, including the behavior of a man with an ideally strong will acting according to some high moral impulse and conscious of everything he does!

His analysis is ingenious and rests in part on his demonstration of "central inhibition"—that the stimulation of the brain (of a frog) can inhibit reflex activity controlled by the frog's spinal cord. This finding, unknown to Hughlings Jackson and to Anstie, corroborated their teaching that higher neural centers inhibit lower ones.

Specific Nerve Energies

Johannes Müller's famous *Handbüch der Physiologie* was published between 1833 and 1840. It was composed of eight volumes totaling 750,000 words; 256 pages of the fifth volume were devoted to the doctrine of specific nerve energies. Boring described the issue in this way:

Locke knew that ideas simulate the primary qualities, like intensity, shape, and size, but the secondary qualities, like greenness and shrillness, have only symbolic representation. Greenness and shrillness are vibrations, but in the mind they are sense qualities. (Boring 1950, p. 39)

Müller's point, as authoritative physiologist at Berlin and teacher of three of the four great physiologists of the century, was that Berkeley was correct in his criticism of Locke. We perceive only the state of our nerves, not some outer reality. In proposing that each major sensory nerve has its own quality or "energy," Müller was suggesting that there is either something special about the nerve or about its target.

All sensory nerves are ultimately stimulated by vibrations of various frequencies or by reactions to molecular "keys"; some we call sound, others light, and others touch, smell, or taste, depending on the nerve stimulated. We now assume, of course, that the "energy" is in the cortical target of each nerve, though we have no idea how that is so.

Fritsch and Hitzig

Work concerning the functions of specific parts of the brain was rare and difficult before the 1840s, when anesthetics such as chloroform and nitrous oxide were discovered. Prior to that time, surgery was extremely traumatic and painful, needless to say, and many of the early biological discoveries were made at the cost of the agonies of the organisms that were under study.

Some of the findings in the eighteenth and nineteenth centuries came as the result of battlefield examinations of soldiers—not because they were being used as subjects, but because their injuries often gave the attending physicians information about the function of the injured organs. A salient example occurred in 1870 during the war between Prussia and Denmark when two German physicians, Fritsch and Hitzig, discovered that an area of the cerebral cortex just forward of the central sulcus produced movement of limbs when it was touched. This discovery of the "motor cortex" was replicated and extended in subsequent experiments with dogs. David Ferrier, a British physiologist, later mapped the area, showing how specific muscle groups are represented in the area. This is the "motor homunculus" that appears in textbooks.

Shortly thereafter, in 1874, an American physician named Bartholomew chanced on a patient named Mary Rafferty. She suffered from an ulcerous wound that left part of her brain exposed. In his examination, Bartholomew discovered that the area of the cerebral cortex just to the rear of the central sulcus is the brain center for touch. Adjacent to the "map" of the body that Ferrier had drawn to account for movement was the corresponding "map" for touch. Everything seemed to be falling into place.

Merzenich and a New Twist
In the 1980s M. M. Merzenich discovered that the receptive fields in the somatosensory cortex of the postcentral gyrus are surprisingly malleable. For example, after amputation of a finger, the cortical receptive field for that finger is "invaded" by the receptive fields for the neighboring digits. This totally unexpected malleability of the sensory cortex—the "map" of the body surface—changed our view of the cortex as a set of fixed maps influenced by "association" cortex.

Sherrington and Integrative Action
Just after the turn of the century, the great British physiologist Sir Charles Sherrington presented the Silliman lectures at Yale and published his masterpiece, *The Integrative Action of the Nervous System*. Sherrington did not emphasize the importance of the synapse or the reflex itself; indeed, he purposely did not mention "reflex" in his title (Swazey 1969). However, the major impact of his work lies in the evidence he amassed for the existence of the synapse, a term which he coined. The neglect of the more important conception of integrative action was a pity, as Pribram (1971) agreed.

During the late nineteenth century, there was still a sizable body of physiologists and neuroanatomists, including Golgi, who doubted the existence of the synapse and who opposed the neuron theory. Though it may seem amazing to us now, they believed that the nervous system was one long and continuous whole; there were no gaps or "synapses" dividing it. Sherrington showed that this "reticularist" view was mistaken by laying out the differences between conduction in a nerve trunk and in a reflex arc; needless to say, the concept of the reflex means nothing without the concept of the synapse.

Broca's "Language Center": Lesson in Interpretation

Müller believed that vision, olfaction, and touch were dependent upon specific structures, though he was unsure whether it was nerve or target that was responsible. The search for brain targets subserving specific functions appeared to take a giant leap forward in 1861 when Pierre-Paul Broca discovered what appeared to be the "speech center." A patient described as otherwise normal was unable to articulate language, though he could understand it. He was called "Tan," since "tan-tan" were the only syllables he could utter. For years he had been paralyzed on the right side, evidently due to a series of strokes (to which we refer later).

He was referred to Broca for treatment of an infected bedsore and soon died. Upon autopsy he was found to have a lesion in the left hemisphere of the lower frontal lobe just forward of the temporal lobe (the inferior posterior frontal lobe)—an area scarcely four centimeters square. For a century this area was known as the speech center—its function turned out to be not what it seemed to Broca.

Reassessing Broca's Finding   It now appears that Broca found what he had been trained to expect to find when he discovered "Broca's area," the language/speech center. In 1861 Broca reported that his patient, who had suffered a stroke, was essentially normal except for his loss of the ability to speak. Karl Pribram is an eminent neurosurgeon and psychologist who believes that patients showing "Broca's aphasia" may suffer from more general disabilities than the loss of the ability to speak. His investigation shows that Broca did indeed find what he was expecting to find. Pribram (1971) wrote:

Broca had been taught that language was a function of the frontal lobes; his teachers derived their doctrine from the phrenologists who had reasoned that man's high forehead and his linguistic ability were two of his most distinguishing features; ergo they might well be related. Broca reasoned that the only place where his aphasic patient's lesion overlapped the frontal cortex was in the posterior inferior portion. Hence Broca's area.

Broca's patients had suffered strokes that involved the middle cerebral artery; this produces widespread damage, but it was the damage to the frontal cortex, Broca's area, that Broca noted. Is the area the seat of speech? Pribram suggests that it is not:

Evidence against Broca's claim is simply that excision of Broca's area in man's brain, and damage to this area, has been inflicted without causing any severe linguistic disturbance... Presumably therefore all of the lobotomies performed for psychosurgical reasons (over 10,000) injured Broca's area to some extent. Yet not a single report of aphasia due to lobotomy occurred. (Pribram 1971, p. 357)

In two catatonic patients who had not spoken in over twenty years, removal of Broca's area produced fluent speech that remained.

Is Broca's area the speech center? Pribram went on to argue that since its removal does not impair speech and may even improve it, it is not necessary for speech production. Nonetheless, it is possible that an intact and malfunctioning Broca's area may interfere with the motor production of speech. This, however, is a bit different from the conventional definition of "speech center." Penfield's "memories" suffered a related fate.

Penfield's Memories

Wilder Penfield was a Canadian neurosurgeon who operated on a variety of patients, including epileptics. In many cases of epilepsy, anti-epileptic drugs are ineffective and the sufferer is left undergoing embarrassing and life-threatening seizures, with no recourse other than a dangerous operation as a remedy. The operation includes the removal of portions of cerebral cortex that electroencephalogram analysis has suggested are responsible for the seizures. In the course of the operation the patient is awake, while the neurosurgeon probes for the offending tissue. If signs of a seizure can be evoked, the cortical area is destroyed (e.g., by burning it with DC through the electrode or by aspiration).

In the course of these procedures in the late 1950s, Penfield found that his stimulations, especially in the parietal and temporal cortex, often aroused vivid memories in his patients, complete with color and sound. Often an incident from many years ago seemed to be relived, described by the patient as though it were being played on a videocassette. Penfield's discovery was described in countless introductory psychology books, and it seemed to add to the mounting evidence that the phrenologists, though wrong in detail, were correct in general. The brain seemed to be composed of many parts, and each part has an

Figure 10.4
Lashley. Courtesy of the Archives of the History of American Psychology, University of Akron.

obvious and unique function. Penfield found stored memories, or so it seemed. We will return to this issue.

Lashley and the Engram

In a powerful display of faith in the precise localization of function in the brain, a young Karl Lashley (Lashley is shown in figure 10.4) offered to trace the neural connections in the frog brain and thus determine how the frog brain worked. He had found some discarded slides of sections of the frog brain, and the neural connections seemed to him to be traceable. He was shocked to learn that the stain used was extremely selective and that the tissue he saw was therefore a very small fraction of the total.

Despite his discouragement, he spent a substantial part of the rest of his life trying to accomplish that mission. His findings had a profound and lasting influence on the search for brain–behavior relations (Thompson and Robinson 1979). In 1929 he published a monograph,

Brain Mechanisms and Intelligence, detailing his findings concerning the effects of brain lesions on the ability of rats to learn mazes. He used three mazes, with one, three, or eight blind alleys. His procedure consisted of operations in which he destroyed greater or lesser portions of the cerebral cortex of his rat subjects, followed by tests of their ability to learn the mazes. What he essentially found was that quite a bit of the cortex had to be destroyed before any deficit was found and, surprisingly, that it did not matter from what part of the cortex tissue was destroyed.

Thus, such and such a deficit would be found on the most difficult maze with destruction of fifty percent of the cortex. However, it did not seem to matter what fifty percent was destroyed, as long as the primary projection areas were spared. A rat that had one large lesion comprising half its cortex would perform similarly to a rat that had twenty small lesions scattered over the cortex. What was important was only the percentage destroyed, not its location.

This means that the cortex is equipotential; any part can carry out the function of any other part, within limits. The degree of the deficit did increase with the size of the lesion, however, which led Lashley to propose the principle of mass action. This means that cortical tissue may be equipotential but that its efficiency depends on the amount which is remaining—the mass of cortex available is important.

The 1929 report was very discouraging to researchers aiming to show localization of function in the brain. If the particular locus of brain damage is not crucial, then how can specific memories be stored in specific places? Whether the memory trace (or engram) consists of neural circuits, concentrations of proteins such as RNA, or presence of neurotransmitters, the location of the lesions should be very important.

Lashley continued his search for a great many years, a search that he described in 1950 ("In Search of the Engram"). After his 1929 monograph he tried slicing the cortices of his subjects, so that their brains resembled sliced hams, only to find no deficits in learning tasks. He destroyed the linkage between the sensory and the motor areas and even lesioned the cerebellum. The cerebellum influences motor behavior, and, since other lesions had little effect, maybe the engrams required to learn mazes were stored there. But even those subjects, whose movements were hampered and who crawled, rolled, and squirmed along the alley, came to the choice points and rolled down the correct alley.

He concluded that since learning requires that the effects of experience be somehow stored, learning is impossible. His search for the engram had convinced him that memories are not stored, at least not in specific locations. If they were, how could one account for the finding of equipotentiality? He seriously considered the possibility that memory depended on DC electrical fields on the surface of the cortex, a theory held by Pavlov and the Gestaltists. Research showed that this theory was untenable.

Lashley's Legacy   Other data corroborate Lashley's basic findings, and two authoritative reviewers (Pribram 1971; Thompson and Robinson 1977) agree that his findings were legitimate. Instances of serious brain damage producing little deterioration in performance abound. For example, Chow and Leiman (1970) destroyed three-quarters of the visual cortex of cats and at the same time cut more than three-quarters through their optic nerves. Such an operation would reduce the animal's vision to near nil, one would think, and it does cause disruption of a previously learned visual discrimination.

However, the cats relearned the discrimination as quickly as they had originally learned it! Other data show the discrimination performance of cats and other animals to be passable after even greater destruction of the visual pathway. It seems that a few hundred visual cortical cells is sufficient for the learning of fairly difficult visual discriminations.

Is Your Brain Really Necessary?

That was the title of a piece appearing in *Science* (Lewin 1980). It describes the findings of a British neurologist, John Lorber, at the University of Sheffield in the United Kingdom. Lorber's research involves hydrocephalics, whose brain ventricles accumulate an excess of cerebrospinal fluid. When this occurs in an infant or young child, the skull expands to make room for the excess fluid. But in older children and adults, the skull is not malleable and the fluid crushes the forebrain against the inside of the skull. In many instances great brain damage occurs, accompanied by grave disturbances in function. However, in a great many cases, there is no obvious deficit, even though the brain damage is extreme. As Lorber put it:

There's a young student at this university, who has an IQ of 126, has gained a first-class honors degree in mathematics, and is socially completely normal.

And yet the boy has virtually no brain.... When we did a brain scan on him, we saw that instead of the normal 4.5-centimeter thickness of brain tissue between the ventricles and the cortical surface, there was just a thin layer of mantle measuring a millimeter or so. His cranium is filled mainly with cerebro-spinal fluid. (Lorber quoted in Lewin 1980, p. 1232)

The eminent British neuroanatomist, Patrick Wall, at University College, London, commented that "Scores of similar accounts litter the medical literature, and they go back a long way." He praised Lorber for compiling a remarkable set of data, rather than relying on mere anecdotal accounts. Wall wondered how we may account for such findings.

How indeed may we account for them? If Lorber is right and if Lashley's search means anything, then we must at least question the old supposition that the cerebral cortex is the seat of all intelligent behavior and particularly that it is the repository for precisely localized memories. But what of Penfield's famous findings?

Penfield Reconsidered

Penfield was no doubt sincere in his belief that he had found the anatomical substrate for memory, but Valenstein (1973) showed that more recent evidence paints a somewhat different picture. Fedio and Van Buren (1971), at what was then the National Institute for the Study of Neurological Disease and Stroke, point out that many surgeons use precisely the procedure used by Penfield, yet no one seems to have found revived memories as he reported. Such patients often do report seeing flashes of light or hearing brief sounds, suggesting another interpretation for Penfield's finding.

Imagine yourself as a patient under the conditions experienced by his patients. You are undergoing a brain operation and, while you were under anesthesia, the surgeon has cut through the scalp, the skull, and the dura under the skull. You are now sitting there awake and the surgeon is touching your brain with a stimulating electrode! It is surely fair to say that you might be a little "on edge" or "reactive" under such circumstances.

Suppose now that during the stimulation you see a flash of light or hear a sound, just as you might see flashes and hear "bells ring" when something strikes you in the head. You say, "I heard something," and the surgeon asks what it was. Was it like a train whistle? Yes, it was, and you add, "I can see the station, and there is my mother," and so on. With a little prodding, completely inadvertently done by the surgeon, a patient may well tell many stories under such circumstances. Does this amount to the revival of memories? In a sense it does, but the stimulation of the brain surface appears to arouse only light flashes and brief auditory sensations. The elaborations of these are aroused by the questions of the surgeon in the context of a highly reactive subject.

Penfield was entirely well meaning, and no reader of his autobiography, *No Man Alone* (1977), could believe that he was intentionally perpetuating a fraud. He found what his education had led him to expect, and one cannot blame him for believing that he found it. However, others did not find it, and the reason for their failure is clear.

Motivation and Emotion

Thou shalt not sit
With statisticians nor commit
A social science

(Auden 1946, st. 27)

Probably the best-known discoveries in physiological psychology occurred in the area of motivation and emotion; this includes the discovery of what some called "reward" and "punishment" centers, feeding centers, aggression centers, and the like. The story involves the limbic system, particularly the hypothalamus.

If the brain were an apple, its core would be the limbic system, old cortex arranged essentially the same in us as it is in dogs, rabbits, and rats. Limbic means "border" and refers to the brain tissue bordering the midline of the brain. The hypothalamus, a cluster of cell bodies about as large as the tip of your thumb, is a crucial part of this system and controls the autonomic nervous system.

The autonomic nervous system is subdivided into the sympathetic and the parasympathetic branches. The division was suggested by two Viennese neurologists, Karplus and Kreidl, in 1909, and subsequent research has supported their view. They suggested that the anterior (forward) portion of the hypothalamus controls parasympathetic activity; this includes conservative functions such as sleep, sexual activity, feeding, and other "vegetative" functions.

On the other hand, the posterior (rearward) hypothalamus controls aggression, flight, and other activities that use up energy in the interests of survival. The posterior hypothalamus increases sympathetic activity, which means that heart rate increases, blood is shunted from the viscera to the muscles, the lungs exchange gases more rapidly, and the affected organism is more able to fight for its life or to flee. And Karplus and Kreidl were correct, as many studies since have shown. The hypothalamus seems to be a center for motivation and emotion, and in a sense it is.

Papez's Circuit

In 1936 a neuroanatomist, James Papez, made a bizarre proposal, based wholly on anatomical evidence and reasonable assumptions about the nervous system and emotion. Until that time, what was later called the limbic system was known as the "rhinencephalon," meaning "smell brain." In humans and in other creatures it was believed to subserve the sense of smell. Oddly, however, this "core" of the brain was strikingly similar in the parts involved and in their organization, as one traced an ascending series of animals from rat, through rabbit, dog, and ape to humankind. Additionally, the limbic cortex is proportionally larger in humans! Since olfaction is certainly far more important to a rat or a rabbit than it is to us, why should our limbic structures be proportionally larger?

Papez proposed that the limbic cortex does not serve olfaction; because of its location, it more likely serves emotion. Countless lesion and stimulation studies done before and after Papez's proposal support his suggestion; some will be considered below. His reasoning was based on the size and the location of the limbic area—consider his reasoning.

We now know that stimulation of the brainstem reticular formation (Moruzzi and Magoun 1949; Hebb 1955) produces nonspecific arousal of the entire forebrain. The reticular formation passes through the limbic area and could easily set off activity in the "Papez circuit." Neural activity beginning in the reticular formation could activate cells in the hippocampus, which would be transmitted via the fornix to the mammillary bodies of the hypothalamus. The mammilothalamic tract then carries the message to the anterior nuclei of the thalamus, which are "intrinsic" nuclei, meaning that they communicate largely with the rest of the thalamus, and thus with the rest of the forebrain. They project directly to the cingulate cortex and thus can easily cause general arousal.

So what happens when we are emotionally aroused? Perhaps the object that causes the arousing has its effects in the primary projection areas of the cortex (e.g., the visual and auditory cortex) and at the same time produces activity in the brainstem reticular formation, as was suggested by Hebb in 1955. The activation of the reticular system is communicated to the hippocampus and from there, via the Papez circuit, it reaches the anterior nuclei of the thalamus.

The experience of emotion depends on the limbic system, including the hypothalamus, which produces sympathetic autonomic activity. (The term "sympathetic" refers to the fact that such energizing is general, causing the affected systems—the circulatory and respiratory systems, for example—to act together, or "in sympathy.") Along with this, appropriate brainstem approach/avoidance mechanisms are triggered (Glickman and Schiff 1967; Valenstein 1973) and fight/flee behaviors are generated in the skeletal muscles. Thus, we have the conscious appreciation of the stimulating event, as well as the activation of the sympathetic nervous system. Together, these account for both the experience and the expression of emotion.

The Hypothalamus

During the twentieth century, mounds of evidence accumulated that tie in the limbic system with what appear to be instances of emotional behavior. In addition, one small part of this system, the hypothalamus, has been implicated in so many behaviors that the tiny organ has taken on the role of the major center for motivation. We will briefly trace the history of research concerned with the functions of the hypothalamus; it tells us some very important things about the presuppositions of researchers in motivation and emotion.

The hypothalamus became popularly accepted as the center for motivation with the work of Walter Hess, a Swiss who studied the effects of electrical stimulation of the hypothalamus in cats. This work led to a Nobel Prize in 1949. After stimulating in 4,500 sites in 480 cats, Hess concluded that he could produce hunger, fear, or rage, depending upon the specific sites stimulated. The hypothalamus seemed to be the center controlling common and important motives.

In 1942 Hetherington and Ranson found what came to be called the "satiety center" in the hypothalamus. When they destroyed the ventromedial nuclei (VM) of that organ, their rat subjects ate voraciously, gained huge amounts of weight, and became what Schachter later called "creatures of nightmares." The rats sometimes doubled their body weights after the operation, evidently because the VM tell rats (and humans) when to stop eating. When the VM are destroyed, the "satiety signal" is lost, and, as subsequent research showed, rats, cats, dogs, porpoises, and sparrows eat far more than normal. So the story went.

Naturally, if there is a brain center that tells us when to stop eating, there must be one to tell us to eat, one would think. In 1951 Anand and Brobeck at Yale University found the "feeding center." While attempting to insert stimulating electrodes into the amygdala of rats (the amygdala is covered below), they inadvertently destroyed the lateral nuclei (LH) of the hypothalamus and found that their subjects died after the operation. The cause of death was aphagia; the rats refused to eat and spat out food that was forced in their mouths.

Interestingly, Karl Pribram (1971) noted that many rats died before the operation; the researchers expected to find changes in feeding behavior as a result of damage to the amygdala and therefore prepared an unpalatable preparation of axle grease and sawdust to see if the operated rats would eat it. The rats found it so tasty that they ate enough of it to die before the operation could be performed!

Thus, the hypothalamus seemed to control both eating and not eating. If the VM "satiety" center were damaged, hyperphagia, or gross overeating, occurred. If the LH were destroyed, eating ceased. Reasonably enough, when the VM was stimulated, eating ceased, and stimulation of the LH produced eating. Here were the feeding and satiety centers, and everyone accepted them. The only question was what new centers would be discovered to account for new behaviors? No wonder Hess won the Nobel Prize.

Feeding and Satiety Centers: Another Look   The functions of the nuclei of the hypothalamus in the regulation of feeding have become far clearer since the early work of Hetherington and Ranson and of Anand and Brobeck. Few would now argue that the VM is the "satiety center" and the far LH the "feeding center." This is because it is now evident that stimulation and destruction of these regions have more general effects than had been assumed. Additionally, it is now fairly certain that effects produced through manipulation of VM or LH are actually produced through effects on fiber tracts that pass through these areas. A landmark paper written by a social psychologist (Schachter 1970), of all people, drew attention to recent research on the hypothalamus and to the change in our view of brain function that was called for.

Reevaluation of LH and VM Function   A great deal of evidence indicates that the effects of VM and LH lesions are more general than had been believed and that the ordinary functions of the two structures are inhibitory and excitatory, respectively. Destruction of the VM removes an inhibitory influence and leads to increased responsiveness to strong external cues. Stimulation of the VM seems aversive and certainly does not increase responsiveness.

The LH appears excitatory, so that stimulation of it appears in some ways to act as does destruction of the VM. Such stimulation can maintain lever pressing, produce feeding, cause stalking of prey, and result in other activities that seem describable as "outer directed." Destruction of the LH causes decreased responsiveness to external stimuli and even to one's own body. Operated cats will remain immobile, even when placed in uncomfortable positions, and will ignore stimuli that would ordinarily elicit strong reactions. This sensory neglect is a powerful general effect, yet, as Carlson (1991) noted, the lateral hypothalamus was called the "feeding center" for approximately two decades! Therein lies a lesson for us.

Cognitive Neuroscience and "Brain Centers"

Space limitations prevent a more thorough discussion of late-twentieth-century research regarding the amygdala and aggression, "reward/pleasure" centers, and related matters. Suffice to say that the conclusions described above hold—the search for simple "centers" for ill-described faculties and motives shows that structures serve more general functions than originally supposed. For an excellent and authoritative, albeit dated, summary, see Valenstein (1973).

Of course there is localization of function in the brain! However, that doesn't mean that our experience is a conglomeration of elementary sensations from the activities of individual receptors. And it does not mean that there are discrete structures storing our memories, causing our moods and emotions, and producing our drives. Beginning in the 1960s, the psychological categories used by brain researchers began to leave the realm of common sense "faculties and motives." The brain became more complicated, but more intelligent.

11   The New Psychology: Wundt, Würzburg, and Müller

The only thing new in the world is the history you don't know. (Harry S Truman, in Kaplan 1992, p. 655)

... Wundt as portrayed today in many texts and courses is largely fictional and often bears little resemblance to the actual historical figure.... (Blumenthal 1975, p. 1081)

The lack of graduate programs in psychology, as well as in other fields, led many students from around the world to Germany, where the educational system was advanced and institutionalized. American students returned home and set up laboratories and degree programs that were self-conscious copies of German models. However, what was copied was altered; for example, Wundt's Leipzig laboratory (figure 11.1 shows Wundt's laboratory, and figure 11.2 shows his journal) was a popular model, but, despite the large number of Americans who worked under his direction, Wundt's fundamental ideas were not transplanted accurately. In fact, it is likely that most of these students did not know or understand Wundt's views.

We begin with Wundt's antithesis, Johann Herbart, who was a skillful proponent of mathematical psychology, though he did not favor experiment—his was the older, rationalistic psychology that the "New Psychology" of the nineteenth century fought to replace. Writers as various as Wundt and William James attacked him; hence, he served a useful function as representative of the old that must be cleared for the New Psychology that Wundt represented.

Herbart and the Psychology That Wundt Opposed

He exhibited the not uncommon case in science in which inadequate data are treated with elaborate mathematics, the precision of which creates the illusion

Figure 11.1
Wundt lab. Courtesy of the Archives of the History of American Psychology, University of Akron.

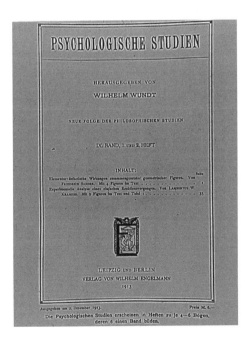

Figure 11.2
Wundt's journal. Courtesy of the Archives of the History of American Psychology, University of Akron.

that the original data are as exact as the method of treatment. (Boring 1950, p. 260)

Herbart's Principal Views

Herbart saw psychology as a science (*Wissenschaft*), and so was the first writer to do so. However, science was not limited to experimental science, as we tend to limit it—it included the nonexperimental, and psychology was classified as part of that. Psychology was science, but experiment was impossible, he believed. It is empirical, since its subject matter is the observation of experience—its goal is the mathematical characterization and explanation of experience.

The War of the Ideas

Herbart went to great lengths to argue that the mind is unitary and that it cannot be analyzed to parts. Yet, he then proposed that ideas are constantly interacting and that they vary in strength as the result of the interaction. This apparent contradiction is resolved when we realize that he opposed the division of mind into faculties, a practice that was very popular in Europe at the time that he was working. When he divided consciousness into ideas, he viewed this as in keeping with the unitary nature of mind—it is that unitary nature that produces all of the interactions among ideas.

Herbart proposed that ideas actually have three properties—quality, strength, and duration. Quality is that property that makes one idea different in kind from another, as the quality "red" makes an idea different from another that has the quality "loud."

Herbart did not believe that psychology had any need for physiology, but the body is not irrelevant. Whether an idea becomes conscious depends on body condition to some extent. The body may block the arousal of an idea—this is repression (*Druck*) as occurs in sleep. The body may also facilitate the arousal of an idea, as when intoxication or passion brings ideas to mind. This he called *Resonanz*. Ideas may also cause movement if practice unites thought and action, and feelings may produce bodily movement.

Herbart typically labeled ideas a, b, and so on, and in general they were called *Vorstellungen*,[1] or "presentations, appearances." Every idea has a fixed quality, and it is different from other ideas—there is no blending of one idea to another—they are discrete and individual things. Their strength (*Kraft*), however, may vary indefinitely and refers to the insistence or clearness of an idea.

Each idea struggles to preserve itself and achieve "complete liberty," rather than its opposite, "complete inhibition." Other ideas try to inhibit one another, and the "metaphysical reason why opposed ideas resist one another is the unity of the soul of which they are the self-preservations" (Boring 1950, p. 255). Even when it is completely inhibited, the idea is not destroyed but remains intact. It passes from "reality" to "tendency." (This seems Freudian, and it is. Freud was probably not influenced by Herbart, but Fechner was, and Freud was influenced by Fechner.)

Herbart represented the reality/tendency distinction by inventing the notion of the threshold, or limen of consciousness. Strong ideas remain above the threshold and are clear, while the weak and/or inhibited ideas are below the threshold and thus unconscious. At any moment there is a competition among ideas, since strength, and thus consciousness, depends on congruence with other ideas.

Thus, ideas that are below threshold may enter consciousness only when the ideas that are conscious change their composition so that they are consonant with the idea seeking entry.[2] Once conscious, the idea is apperceived, that being the raising of an idea to consciousness and the assimilating of it into the ideas already there, the apperceiving mass. Apperception was a term borrowed from Leibniz and applied by Herbart to education.

Ideas do not always war—sometimes there is no opposition among them and they join, producing fusion. Tones may unite to produce a fusion "buzz," and red and green may fuse to yellow. When sights and sounds join, they become a complication, since they come from different senses. Apperception, fusion, complication, assimilation, and even *Vorstellung* were all terms that were taken over by Wundt, who strongly opposed Herbart on many grounds.

Herbart's Mathematical Psychology

Kant, as well as common sense, held that the mind—consciousness—was beyond science since it was beyond mathematics. The physical world has dimensions in space and time, but our experience has only the dimension of time; there are no lengths or widths or heights or masses when it comes to sensations and ideas. There is nothing to measure and thus no possible applications of mathematics. Given the prevalence of that view both during and after his time, Herbart was widely criticized for his contentions that the mind was quantifiable. On one occasion he answered these critics in a lecture before a skeptical audience—the arguments have a decidedly modern ring (excerpt in Diamond 1974, pp. 673–678).

He began by suggesting that, were Socrates to return and see the successes wrought by mathematics in architecture, artillery, astronomy, physics, and elsewhere, he would ask why we do not apply it even more widely, especially toward the understanding of ourselves. What would we answer? We would have to say that our reluctance is due to habit—no one has "ever heard of applying mathematics except to objects which are either spatial in themselves, or can at least be spatially represented." That includes forces that increase and decrease with distance. But how can one measure the mind (Diamond 1974, p. 674)?

What yardstick can we use to measure and compare our mental experiences, the changes taking place in our ideas, feelings, and desires? Our thoughts are swifter than lightning—how shall we observe and describe their path? Human fancies are as flighty as the winds, our moods as uncertain as the weather—who can find measures for them, to bring them under the rule of mathematical laws? Where measurement is not possible, neither is calculation; consequently, it is not possible to use mathematics in psychological investigation. So goes the syllogism which is put together by clinging to habit and adding an untruth.

What is the untruth? Herbart claims that it is the belief that we can only calculate after having taken measurements! "Quite the contrary!" Our hypothetical laws relating magnitudes, even if known incorrect, can serve as the basis for calculation. Indeed, we must operate with laws that we know to be wrong if we are ever to find laws that are true. We must try different hypotheses—guesses at laws—until we find ones that work. Herbart went on:

> Kepler tried out the ellipse...; Newton likewise tried out whether gravitation, inversely as the square of the distance, would suffice to keep the moon in its path around the earth; if this assumption had not sufficed he would have tried another power, such as the cube or the fourth or the fifth power of the distance.... (In Diamond 1974, p. 674)

Critics also objected that mathematics requires quantities, but that psychology offers only states and activities differing greatly in qualities. However, Herbart noted that true qualities of things are completely hidden from us and when we think that we are perceiving qualities of things, their basis is only *quantitative*. Different tones, for example, are produced by different frequencies of vibration. And, however many different qualities one thinks can be discerned in the mind, it is certain that there are also an infinite number of quantitative differences—ideas are stronger, weaker, clearer, dimmer, quicker, slower, more numerous or less so. We ceaselessly waver between more and less.

What of free will? Herbart's opinion is worth the quote:

Other objections to quantification exist because of prejudices that we want dearly to keep. "What shall I say about freedom? First, that I am tired of talking about it.... Keep your freedom, because it does not really exist in the sense which you give to the word." (In Diamond 1974, p. 675)

What does mental life offer for measurement? Only two magnitudes—"the strength of individual ideas, and the degree of inhibition among them." Calculation of those two magnitudes is simple, he believed, but complications arise when we consider the "degree of connectedness" between the ideas. Then a fourth factor enters, namely, the number of connected ideas, arranged as long or short chains and as complete or incomplete connections. The last occurs when a chain involves one idea connected to a second, the second to a third, and the third to a fourth, all to different degrees, but the first and third, second and fourth, and so on, are not connected at all.

Also ideas of space and time depend on these connections, and not in supposed basic forms of sensibility. Mathematics must be applied—it is "the ruling science of our time. Its conquests grow daily, though without any clamor. If we do not have mathematics with us, we will one day have it against us" (Diamond 1974, p. 675).

Wundt

In the hands of introspective psychologists, such mental processes as sensations, images, and simple feelings were often treated as static bits of consciousness and thus given over to a false elementism for which Wundt is held responsible and against which the new movements...have reacted. (Blumenthal 1985, p. 341)

Wundt's Remarkable Life

Recent writers, like Bringmann (Bringmann et al. 1980) and Blumenthal, have shown that Wundt's views were misrepresented for decades and form the basis for the standard treatment in introductory psychology books. Should we care? Well, if psychology is to have a history, might it not be comforting to know that it is at least approximately accurate concerning events of little more than a century ago? If we cannot rely on at least that much accuracy, then any attempt to trace our history is futile.

Like Helmholtz, Lotze, and many others before and since, Wundt determined to obtain a medical degree so that he could earn a living. Unlike the case in most countries, German medical schools were truly academic, so that graduates were not merely technicians. Research was encouraged and, in his first year (1853), Wundt published a report on the sodium chloride content of urine. His medical research continued through his second year, and in his third year he published a piece concerning the effects of sectioning the vagus[3] on respiration. His medical training was complete in 1855 when he was twenty-three years old.

In 1856 he worked with Müller at Berlin, then returned to Heidelberg the same year and officially received his medical degree. From 1857 to 1864 he worked as a dozent, or part-time lecturer, in physiology. He published three papers in physiology during 1856 and 1857 and his first book in 1858, at age twenty-six—*Lectures on Muscle Movement*.[4] After seventeen years at Heidelberg and a year at Zurich, his interests shifted to psychology. In 1875 he accepted a chair of philosophy at Leipzig.

The Leipzig Laboratory

In 1875 Wundt established a laboratory, which was recognized by the University in 1883. The "Institute of Experimental Psychology" was listed in the university catalog in 1894. The Leipzig laboratory's traditional date of founding is 1879, the date of the first student publication, and it became a model for others—Kiesow set one up in Italy, at Turin, and Theophilus Boreas established the Athens laboratory in 1899. A replica laboratory was built in Moscow in 1912 and in Tokyo in 1920. The Tokyo lab was burned by student radicals in the 1960s. The buildings that housed the original laboratory remained intact until the night of December 4, 1943, when a group of British and American bombers blew it off the face of the earth, along with much of Leipzig.

The city of Leipzig attempted to buy Wundt's library after the Second World War but could not afford it. Wundt's heirs auctioned the 15,840-volume library, refusing bids by Harvard and Yale, since they were adamant in their refusal to deal with Americans. The library was bought for Tohuku University in Japan by their agent, Professor Tanenari Chiba.

Wundt supervised over 180 doctoral students during the more than three decades that the lab operated. They included his first assistant, Oswald Külpe, later to found the Würzburg School, and his second assistant, James McKeen Cattell, pioneer in intelligence testing in America. Another pioneer was Lightner Witmer, also a student of Wundt and the founder of the first psychological clinic in America, at the University of Pennsylvania.

Two more famous students were Edward Titchener, founder of structuralism and mainstay of the Cornell University department, and Granville Stanley Hall, founder of four of the first ten American laboratories. Hall also founded the psychological laboratory at Clark University, the American Psychological Association, and the first American psychological journals—and he brought Freud and Jung to America in 1909.

Hothersall (2004, p. 130) notes that another student of Wundt's was the most famous person in the world, according to two newspaper polls taken in the 1930s. That was Hugo Eckener, who had done his dissertation on the topic of attention and distraction and was later the commander of the Graf Zeppelin, an airship that made several round-the-world voyages and was an object of wonder and admiration by the public.[5] Finally, an ingenious student in Wundt's lab was George Stratton, known for his work on the effects of distorting prisms on visual perception. That serves as example of the far-reaching effects of Wundt's Leipzig laboratory research.

Two Examples of Leipzig Research and Its Aftermath

Stratton (1897) found, while at Johns Hopkins University, that humans adapt quickly to distorting lenses that invert the visual field and that reverse it left to right. Stratton's original experiment lasted eight days, and he served as his own subject. The subject of distorting lenses was of interest to Wundt, who described findings on the subject in the fourth edition of his *Outlines* in 1902. Stratton had worked with others on the sense of touch while at Leipzig, but others had studied aspects of vision, including space perception.

Wundt described the effects of wearing glasses that make straight lines look curved. Subjects wear the glasses until adaptation occurs—that is, the straight lines no longer appear curved, though the image on the retina is not. When the glasses are removed, straight lines appeared curved in the opposite direction. Wundt recognized that the image on the retina comes to act as the sign for whatever is established by the observer's actions, touch, and kinesthesis—exactly as Berkeley claimed in the eighteenth century and Helmholtz claimed in the 1860s.

If ")" comes to be seen as a straight vertical line because the glasses produce that image, but touch tells us "that is straight," then ")" comes to mean straight. When the glasses are removed, what is presented as a straight line will be seen as "(" since "straight" has already been identified as ")."

In the 1960s, Richard Held of MIT carried out experiments on the effects of deprivation of vision in infancy and effects of movement in determining visual perception (Held and Rekosh 1963). His group also replicated Wundt's 1902 findings. Their subjects wore distorting lenses under one of two conditions: either while moving around on foot in a room with pictures of spheres of various sizes covering the walls or while wheeled in a wheelchair.

After this experience, subjects removed the glasses and adjusted a line (an adjustable wire) until it looked straight. As Wundt would predict, those subjects who actively moved in the "sphere room" while wearing the distorting lens adjusted the line so that it was actually curved. There was no such effect for the wheelchair group, and other researchers replicated this finding. Wundt's participation in such research—the influence of experience on perception—was clear but seldom noted.

The Time-Order Error

In Wundt's time, medical students published research findings, and one of his projects cast light on the problem that arose at the Greenwich Observatory in 1795. Observers tracking the movement of stars had to coordinate the change in position of a star with the ticking of a clock. Judging the simultaneous occurrence of a star crossing a wire in the eyepiece with a clock's tick proved difficult, and there were famous errors.

What determines the making of such judgments? In 1861 a young Wundt was the expert on that subject and published an early report on anachronistic perception, as James (1890, p. 411) called it, or subjective time displacement, as Wundt called it. His method involved a circular scale with an index hand that moved across it, like the sweep second hand moves across the scale of a clock. Once every revolution a bell rang, and the point at which that happened could be set and reset. The speed of the moving hand could be changed, but one revolution per second was typical.

Subjects always misjudged by a half second or more—usually, as a "negative error." This means that they placed the arrow 500 milliseconds or more before the actual bell ringing. Manipulations in the speed of rotation of the wheel, or its acceleration and deceleration, show that the error may be increased.

The hand moves quickly, its tip describing a circle in a second or so. At some point, the bell rings and the subject specifies where the hand pointed on the scale when the bell rang. The subject watches and hears many revolutions—"a single revolution is never enough" (James 1890, p. 413). First, a general region of the scale is isolated, and gradually the bell is linked to a specific point on the scale. If we mark and choose a false position on the scale, we can "hear the bell" at that point, so long as it is not too far removed from the true point. Whatever the procedure, the outcome has been corroborated many times—we cannot attend to two stimuli simultaneously, at least when one is visual and the other auditory.

What Categories of Research Were Done in Wundt's Leipzig Lab?
So, if you imagine Wundt's laboratory as a scene filled with people giving introspective reports, you will be far from accurate. Boring (1950, p. 332) and, more recently, Blumenthal (1975) and Danziger (1980) categorized the work done at Leipzig, showing that introspective reports were scarcely evident. Boring's report is undocumented, while Blumenthal examined 180 actual published reports emanating from Wundt's research group and published in *Philosophische Studien* between 1883 and 1903. Only four were found by Blumenthal, while Boring's account reports none. Consider first Boring's account.

One third of the work concerned sensation, most of which involved vision: six studies were done on the psychophysics of light and the retina (1884–1902), three on the psychophysics of color (1891–1898), peripheral vision (1889–1890), color blindness (1892), the Purkinje effect,[6] and negative afterimages. Six, including Edward Titchener's research, involved binocular vision (1892–1901), apparent size (1889), and illusions. Studies of vision occupied a quarter of the effort of Wundt's group.

Work in audition was carried out from 1883–1891, including the study of beats and other combination tones (1892–1901) and fusions. Research on touch included localization and discrimination, including Margaret Washburn's work from 1895–1902, not completed at Leipzig. Kiesow carried out studies of taste from 1894–1898.

There were studies of the time sense and estimation of temporal intervals (1881–1896) and reaction time studies, using the Donders subtractive procedure, accounting for one sixth of the total. Another tenth was devoted to studies of attention, a tenth concerned with feeling and fluctuations of attention (as caused by rhythmic musical patterns), as well as examination of effects of stimulation from several senses, called complication experiments, and the question of prior entry, the effect on stimuli of preceding stimuli.

The range of auditory attention was examined in 1884, as was the fluctuation of attention when weak stimuli, such as a faintly ticking clock, are used (the subject of Hugo Eckener's work). Some studies were carried out in the 1890s concerned with feeling, following Wundt's theory of emotion, to be described below. And there were a few scattered works on association, but that subject, like the introspective report, was rare indeed. Wundt's program was a well-rounded investigation of topics that would be later classified as "sensation and perception."

Wundt's System: Fundamentals

For Wundt, "experimentalism was always secondary to philosophical views" (Boring 1950, p. 332), and his philosophy held psychology to be the science of experience (*Erfahrungswissenschaft*). Experience isn't "inner," since it doesn't come inner or outer—it is "*anschaulich*," or what we would call "phenomenal."

One method of studying experience is self-observation, which is not introspection (*"innere Wahrnehmung"*); it is done "without implying anything about a mental eye that turns about and looks into the mind" (Boring 1950, p. 322), since experience is not inside—it is just there. All sciences study experience, but psychology deals with immediate experience, uninterpreted and not translated into some theory of reality, such as Newton's physics embodies.

Ideas Are Not Stored and Retrieved

It follows from his emphasis on immediate experience that there is no unconscious bin where ideas go until they are summoned back to consciousness. That was the despised doctrine of Herbart, and Wundt had none of it. As he wrote in 1894,

[chronometric investigations] taught me to recognize that the concept of "reproduced" ideas is one of the many forms of self-deception which has become fixed in our language to create a picture of something that does not exist in reality. I learned to understand the "idea" as a process which is no less changing and transient than a feeling or act of will. (Blumenthal 1985, p. 34)

Is There a Self?

Wundt, like Hume and Kant long before him, pointed out that there is no phenomenal self. That is, there is no "me," aside from all of the changing perceptions of light and dark and sound and touch. If we begin with experience, we do not begin with a feeling of self. What is the feeling of self that we do have from moment to moment, which flickers on and off and dies out when we are unconscious?

That feeling—or the addition of feeling/emotion to sensation—is what Wundt meant by apperception, a term that was very important to him but which was, ironically, most closely associated with Herbart, whose views Wundt disparaged. We might think of apperception as voluntary, active attention, as when we strain to hear a faint ticking or to remember a face or a name.

The opposite of apperception, or apperceptive attention, is what James (1890, chapter 11) said the Germans called "*Zerstreutheit*," a sort of fuzzy absentmindedness. When one stays too long in the library, a point may be reached where time stops and our attention melts away—scatters. That is *Zerstreutheit*, and it is the opposite of focused attention, or apperception.

Methods: Experiment and Geschichte

The research methods of the Leipzig laboratory were restricted to psychophysics, attention, and the other areas mentioned. Notice that there is no mention of "thinking" or "motivation" or "judgment" or "language" or "social psychology." That is because one of Wundt's most fundamental beliefs was that such complicated human phenomena are not profitably studied in a laboratory or with individual subjects. Such things are understandable only through the method of *Geschichte*, meaning "story," or "history," and this aspect of his work is called his *Völkerpsychologie*, or "cultural psychology."[7]

He wrote his *Völkerpsychologie* after 1900 in ten volumes, most still awaiting translation. Two volumes deal with language, two with myth and religion, and one each with society, art, law, culture, and history.[8] We must agree that a real understanding of what are usually called cognitive processes, or "thinking," must indeed consider a field wider than that of the individual. That was Wundt's conviction, and we will see that it led to conflict with well-meaning followers who tried to extend laboratory methods to higher mental processes and, in doing so, incurred Wundt's censure.

Wundt's Interpretation of Conscious Experience

The aim of *Beschreibung* (literally, "description"), the name given to the reporting of conscious experience, was analysis to what Wundt called "part-contents." This was a poor method, in his view, and accounted for only two percent of his research. It was a poor method because consciousness was like a river, constantly changing; hence, it is impossible to consider isolated bits of it. He opposed the analysis to "elements," and in fact used the term *Elemente* in only one chapter title.

Insofar as one could artificially abstract an element, it would be the *Vorstellung*, or "appearance" or "conception." It could be analyzed to three parts, image, feeling, and impulse. The image part of the *Vorstellung* could vary in quality (e.g., color, pitch, smell) and intensity. Other aspects, like duration and clearness, were dependent on personal experience and cultural factors—they were subject to treatment as cultural psychology. Feeling was the emotional or affective aspect of experience, and it varied along three dimensions, specified by Wundt's tridimensional theory of emotion.

These dimensions were pleasantness, tension, and arousal, ranging from pleasant–unpleasant, relaxed–tense, and depressed–excited. When Wundt referred to "feelings" like pleasure and unpleasure ("Lust" and "Unlust"), he meant the feelings that attach to experience as we normally live our lives. Hence, listening to a Wagner piece may give us feelings of pleasure, feelings of tension as a note is held and relaxation as it ends, and feelings of arousal or depression. These are constantly changing from second to second. Real "emotions," like sadness and anger and joy, are always larger things, dependent on many things, and thus treatable only by the methods of *Völkerpsychologie*.

Wundt Was Not an Introspectionist

Boring's classic textbook (1929/1950) was a source for many writers (including this one), and some readers believed that it presented Wundt as an introspectionist and associationist, a sort of "James Mill who conducted research." Those who were misled by this could have found the real Wundt in any number of translated selections in books of readings, even when the translators, like Titchener or Judd, either did not understand Wundt or, more likely, viewed one aspect of his wide-ranging interests as the only important part of his work. In any case, in the 1980s, Blumenthal tried to set the record straight for those who needed it (Blumenthal 1985, pp. 28–29). For instance, he clarified what Wundt meant by "self-observation," or *Selbstbeobachtung*:

Wundt defined Selbsbeobachtung as the scientific study of mental processes (perception, memory, emotion, attention etc.) by means of objective techniques such as reaction-time measurements, counts of word associations, or discriminative responses to stimuli. Wundt contrasted those techniques with, and soundly dismissed, innere Wahrnehmung or sometimes reine (pure) Selbstbeobachtung—subjective descriptions and interpretations of one's private experiences—when used as raw data in psychological experiments. Wundt (1874, p. 4) argues that experimental psychology necessarily involves the separation of the observer from the thing being observed.

Blumenthal was critical of the sloppy scholarship of the many writers who described a Wundt who never existed:

In light of these facts, it is ironic that later historical accounts of Wundt, using out-of-context translations and simple mistranslations, led to his being caricatured as the father of the introspectionist school.

Wundt's Critique of the Doctrine of Association
Wundt distinguished between *apperception*, or active and voluntary attention, and association by contiguity or similarity, which had been practiced for centuries in England, Scotland, and America. Apperception was very important to him—easily the most important concept in his psychology—while association was hardly worth mentioning.

Külpe's *Grundriss* (1893/1909) included interpretations of Wundt's position on associationism and apperception. As Külpe put it:

Lastly, Wundt has distinguished between associative and apperceptive connections. The former are the result of given relations between ideas, e.g., their contiguity in space or immediate succession in time; the latter require a comparative and selective activity of the subject, i.e., the aid of apperception. (p. 189)

We will see that this is far different from the practice of Titchener and other introspectionists, though they attributed their inspiration to Wundt. Only recently has attention been called to Wundt's actual views on apperception, association, and other topics.

Wundt's Unique Version of "Associationism" Wundt's son, Max, was a philosopher at Tübingen University in 1944 when he commented on his father's position regarding associationism:

Whoever in particular ascribes to my father such a conception could not have read his books. In fact, he had formed his scientific views of mental processes in reaction against a true elementistic psychology, namely against that of Herbart, which was dominant in those days. (Blumenthal 1985, p. 33)

Wundt proposed what he called laws of psychic causality to describe the contents of experience and the relations among these contents. Recall that experience was for him a process, a stream, and that the *Vorstellung* was by no means a static thing. He argued frequently against atomistic associationism, both as represented by the British and by Herbart.

Laws of Psychic Causality   Wundt's "associations" are "structural integrations, creative syntheses, fusions, perceptual patternings." The river of experience is governed by laws, just as is a river of water, but the laws are not laws of association. In 1896 Wundt's description of these laws was translated by Judd.[9] The laws of interest are what Wundt called the laws of creative synthesis or resultants: these consist of fusions, assimilations, complications, and memorial associations.[10]

Bear in mind that this treatment was meant to explain ordinary experience as mental complexes—the elements, as we might call them, were sometimes called *Gebilde*, meaning "creation" or "construction." Bizarrely, Titchener and Judd translated it as "composite"! (Wundt 1922, p. 107; 1907, p. 99) Wundt also referred to *Gesamtvorstellung*, meaning "whole or total appearance." This was translated as "aggregate of ideas." Small wonder that Wundt has been misunderstood and cast as an associationist.

The Laws of Resultants, or Creative Synthesis
Wundt believed that successive associations, like those that bind together the successive letters of the alphabet for us, are only one type and are the "loosest" kind. More important are simultaneous compounds, or resultants.

The first of these that he described are fusions, where the elements are completely lost in the compound. This is what James Mill called instances of "coalescence," and occur in the "clang," which is composed of tones, but none are discernible. The whole is made of parts but is different from the sum of the parts. Fusions also appear as chords and as spatial illusions. When we watch a flickering light and the frequency of flickering is increased, a point is reached where the light appears steady. That is the critical frequency at fusion and varies with illumination and other factors.

Assimilations refer to complexes in which one part is influenced by other parts, whether in memory or simultaneously present. For example, animal cries and the sounds of rushing water or of wind or machinery can sound like words "almost at will." Who hasn't momentarily "heard" the message of the whirring ventilation system or that of the wind? Listen carefully to the nearest electric motor, fan, or compressor right now, and you can make it speak to you.[11] John Stuart Mill's theory of belief and Helmholtz's unconscious inference rely on assimilation, though Wundt was forever anxious to stress the fundamental difference between his views and theirs. This lay in Wundt's emphasis on apperception as an active attentional process and Mill's and Helmholtz's relatively passive portrayal of attention. Similarly, we often "fill in" meaning to the words that we hear or read, so that we frequently misunderstand. The filling in is assimilation (adding verbal material to presented verbal material; Meringer and Mayer 1895; Blumenthal 1985, p. 31).

In addition to such auditory assimilations, there are many assimilations of feelings, referring to all of what we call esthetic experiences. Such things are difficult to study, thought Wundt, since present and past aspects tend to unite, forming an unanalyzable "single, unitary, total feeling" (Wundt 1907, p. 107).

Assimilation is common in vision as well, illustrated in the many spatial illusions. It is assimilation that accounts for Berkeley's perception of distance—"the knowing of one idea by virtue of another idea." Thus, assimilation adds to the binocular image the third dimension of depth,[12] and it determines whether we see a scene as normal (that is, in relief) or reversed (in intaglio).

We will see a solid or a hollow hemisphere depending upon whether the eye fixates first on the center or the periphery. Wundt believed that we always move our eyes from the nearer to the more distant and the sensations accompanying this movement act as cues for depth. If we fixate first on the periphery and move our eyes inward, we see the hemisphere as in intaglio, depressed into the surface of the scene. If we fixate first on the center, the hemisphere is seen in relief, extending toward us.

The same applies to the Necker cube and to Mach's book. Whichever line segment we fixate on first is interpreted as nearest, and if that is the edge of Mach's book, we next fixate on the spine of the book, which we interpret as farther away, and hence "see" a book that is open toward us. Fixate first on the spine and the book is seen as open away from us.

Assimilation applies to many other visual phenomena and illusions. The interrupted line appears longer because of the increased "eye energy" required to scan it. Wundt placed great stock in the effect of the amount of activity involved in seeing. The more activity or effort, the longer or farther away we "see" something. The vertical line seems much longer than the horizontal because of the work done in scanning from low to high.

Draw a three-inch horizontal line right now and mark its center. Then draw (freehand) a three-inch vertical line from that center point. You will see that the vertical line appears much longer than the horizontal. Try covering part of the top of the vertical line until it appears more nearly equal to the horizontal. You may be surprised at how much of the line must be removed to produce that effect.

Visual assimilations always involve sensations of eye movement and thus border on complications, or compounds involving two or more senses. When we speak, we experience an auditory/motor/visual complication, and when we read, the compound is visual/ auditory/ motor. Sometimes the parts of the complication are hard to identify— they are "obscure affective tones"—for example, a rough surface, a dagger point, or two knife blades thrusting at one another but never quite touching, which give us a feeling of "all-overishness," to use William James's term. Wundt's most charming example of complication was "holding a screaming child."

Successive Associations: Not Chains
The stream of experience rarely constitutes an associational series— Wundt proposed that it is only when normal apperception is disturbed, as in the flight of ideas of the insane, that ideas pass in chains. Normally, the sequence is limited to two "apperceptive acts." "In the great majority of cases, the association thus formed is limited to two successive ideational or affective processes connected, in the manner described, through assimilations or complications. New sense impressions or some apperceptive combinations...may then connect themselves with the second member of the association.... In normal cases such serial associations, that is, associations with more than two members, hardly ever appear." (Wundt 1922; Herrnstein and Boring 1965, p. 405)

Sensation is immediately acted upon by apperception—active and voluntary attention—so that the sound of a whistle brings me the sights and sounds of a train, for example. The compound is then protracted and splits as apperception selects an aspect and assimilation elaborates on it. Rather than a chain of successive elements, it seems more like a kaleidoscope, constantly changing in many aspects at once (Herrnstein and Boring 1965, from a questionable translation by Judd).

Wundt emphasized that experience is not a sum of elements and that ideas do not have power in themselves. Apperceptive synthesis creates *Gesamtvorstellungen* (whole appearances), and creative synthesis (assimilation) then acts on it. If apperception fails to act, then something is wrong, and associational series may occur frequently.

Such abnormal trains of association, free of apperception's influence (the influence of selective attention), were viewed by Wundt's student, Emil Kraepelin, as aspects of what is now called schizophrenia. This interpretation is still current and has grown in popularity.

Wundt and Will
Despite the emphasis on voluntary, selective attention in experience, and the resulting feeling of free will, the will is not utterly "free" in the sense that Descartes or Plato viewed it as free. However, it is also not determined in a straightforward way. An understanding of will requires more than laboratory research—it depends upon culture and is thus part of *Völkerpsychologie*:[13]

What we call free will is part of a more general conscious nexus, of which the individual mind constitutes only one link. The general direction of the individual will is, you see, determined by the collective will of the community in which its possessor lives.

Külpe and the Errant Würzburg School
There was not a word on thought, and thereby hangs the tale of Külpe's life. (Boring 1950, p. 401)

Wundt had always declared that experimental psychology cannot deal with the higher mental processes and that only *Völkerpsychologie* applies to subjects like judgment, language, and reasoning. However, some of his students disagreed, and his assistant, Külpe, determined to apply experimental methods to the "higher processes." Wundt, predictably, railed against the "mock experiments" that Külpe's group performed.

Oswald Külpe (1862–1915) was born in Candau in Latvia, a part of Russia close to East Prussia. In 1881 he went to Leipzig to study history but was attracted to Wundt's laboratory, where he worked for a year.

Still interested in history, he spent a semester at Berlin, home of great historians like Diels. Undecided between philosophy and psychology with Wundt or history, his initial interest, he went from Berlin to the laboratory of Georg Elias Müller at Göttingen, skilled experimentalist and archrival of Wundt. Külpe spent three semesters with G. E. Müller and even began a dissertation on feeling, a theoretical piece that he finished and published later at Leipzig.

Külpe's Positivistic Attitude

Külpe and others in Wundt's group, particularly Edward Titchener, were greatly influenced by the positivism promoted in Germany by the physicist Ernst Mach and the philosopher Richard Avenarius. Both Mach and Avenarius criticized theory which referred to unobservable entities, the existence of which was doubtful. For example, Mach questioned the reality of the electron, since it was unknown to experience.[14]

For Külpe, positivism meant that psychology should concern itself only with what is experienced—that has to be the basis for all knowledge and theory. Hence, when writing his book, he would not refer to higher mental processes at all, unless there was something to say about them. Wundt might speak of will and apperception and mental stages revealed in reaction time experiments, but there was no conscious experience of such things and thus no warrant for mentioning them.

His *Fundamentals* dealt with sensation—in fact, that filled the first third of it. Another tenth described memory, including a little Ebbinghaus and a lot of British associationism. Feeling occupied another tenth of the book, as did fusion and colligation, Külpe's term for combinations in time and space, including space perception and reaction time data. According to Boring, his criticism of the subtractive procedure in mental chronometry "is supposed to have been its death-knell" (Boring 1950, p. 400).

As Boring concluded his description of Külpe's book, he noted, "There is not a word on thought, and thereby hangs the tale of Külpe's life" (Boring 1950, p. 401). Twenty years later Külpe wrote a second book meant to replace the *Fundamentals*. He died before it was finished, and Bühler arranged to have it published posthumously. It was based on Külpe's lectures during the past few years, and, amazingly, like the textbook of 1893, it had no chapter on thought! According to Bühler, the lectures did not deal with thought.

The Würzburg Research
Fortunately, a collection of translations of the original published work of this group was provided by the Mandlers (1964), on which the following description is based. The work began officially in 1901, with the report by Mayer and Orth, and continued until at least 1907, with Karl Bühler's conclusion—or so it turned out to be.

The Course of Thought   "Dr. Marbe has set us the task..." began a paper by A. Mayer and J. Orth titled "The Qualitative Investigation of Associations." They went on to explain that Karl Marbe had set them the task of examining the associations that arise when the subject reacts with a spoken word to a word called out to him. There were four subjects, including Mayer and Orth, a procedure common in the introspective experiments of the time. The experimenter would call out "Ready" and then a one-syllable noun, beginning a stopwatch at the same time. The subject was to respond with an association, much as was done in Wundt's laboratory, where Wundt himself provided the record short reaction time when he responded with "Blitzen" (lightning) to the word "Donner" (thunder).

These were monosyllables, like "tree," "child," and "house" (*Baum*, *Kind*, and *Haus*), and, unlike in Wundt's procedure, these subjects were asked to describe any intervening conscious processes. You might imagine that the word "tree" would bring the image of a pine tree or a Christmas tree and the image would be clear to the subject, who would respond "pine" or "Christmas" and describe appropriate imagery. However, that was not the case.

Subjects almost invariably reported that there was no reportable intervening conscious process, though there was an imageless "feeling" of some kind, perhaps best described as a disposition. Karl Marbe called this a *Bewusstseinslage*, translated as a "disposition of consciousness," an "orientation of consciousness," or a "conscious attitude." Whatever it was, it was indescribable.

How It Feels to Make a Judgment   A second study was carried out by Marbe himself, also in 1901, entitled "Psychology of Judgments." Marbe summarized the then-recent history of opinion concerning the making of judgments whereby Brentano viewed the process as a "recognition/denial" phenomenon or a matter of association. Wundt, on the other hand never saw discrimination as anything but "segmentation," that being a function of apperception, not association.

Marbe's experiment required subjects to discriminate differences in held weights. As in Mayer and Orth's study, subjects were to strain to detect "intervening conscious processes," and again there was nothing there to report. There were only the *Bewusstseinslagen*. Interestingly, Marbe concluded that judgment always depends on knowledge obtained from previous experience, usually in a specific culture—hence, he wrote, "judgment" cannot possibly exist in consciousness. In so concluding, Marbe was conceding that Wundt was correct—thought does not belong in the laboratory. This marked the end of Marbe's participation in the laboratory.

Messer's Degrees of Bewusstseinslagen   The *Bewusstseinslage* became a familiar occurrence in the Würzburg lab, illustrated by August Messer, who in 1906 published *Experimental-Psychological Investigations of Thinking* (*Experimental-psychologische Untersuchungen über das Denken*).

He pointed out that *Bewusstseinlagen* had become frequent in subjects' protocols and was abbreviated as *Bsl*. Using the "*Ausfragemethode*," the question-asking method, subjects frequently described their experience as "*Bsl*," a concept with which they were familiar before the experiment and which they had no hesitation to invoke.

Messer proposed that the *Bsl* be viewed not as an indescribable element of thought, appearing with the describable images and feelings, but as thought itself. Thought is an indescribable orientation of consciousness which can nonetheless be categorized into gradations. At the highest level, a *Bsl* feels like a disposition of comprehension, as in a word meaning that is not clear. The second gradation has "meaning," but no words attached. In all, Messer described over thirty levels of "dispositions," or gradations of *Bsl*!

Ach and Einstellung   Another prominent Würzburger was Narziss Ach, whose most famous piece appeared in 1905, applying "systematic self observation" to the reaction experiment. This was done in several ways—for example, a subject might be instructed to flex his right forefinger when a white card was presented and to flex a thumb or a left forefinger when a red card was presented. In other versions, the stimulus and response items might both be verbal—"give the name of a river," for example. What was found when subjects were asked to describe "intervening conscious processes?" What else could it be but indescribable *Bewusstseinslagen*?

Ach noted that instructions often influence "apperception," including the *Bewusstseinslagen*, and called these determined apperceptions *Einstellung*, which literally means "set," or "tune in."[15] Many American psychologists adopted either the German term or referred to "set" or "predispositions."

Bühler and the End of the Würzburg School   Karl Bühler published in 1907, using the "method of systematic self-observation" and a variant of the *Ausfragemethode* in which complex questions were asked and the subjects were to describe, afterward, the "intervening conscious processes." Actual questions that were asked included:

- "Was the theorem of Pythagoras known to the medievals?"
- "Why are manhole covers round?"
- "Why are women's shoes more expensive, the smaller the size?"

The questions were meant to occasion thought—for example, it is clear that the ancients knew of the Pythagorean theorem, but the knowledge of the ancients was lost for centuries, as we have seen. Can I think of when the medievals might have learned Greek geometry?

In the course of retrospective reporting of conscious states, Bühler's subjects seemed to report three main classes of *Bewusstseinslagen*. The first was the rule orientation,[16] in which thought is rule directed without any clear rule in awareness. The second category was the intention, where there is a knowing/intending of meaning without any specific meaning in mind. Third is the relational orientation, where the orientation is toward relations, but they are, again, not in awareness.

Wundt Was Not Amused

It must be aggravating and disheartening to watch one who managed your laboratory for eight years leave and carry out a research program that is contrary to everything that you believe and have taught. Plus, as a former student, his views are apt to carry the authority of your reputation!

That is no doubt why Wundt reacted so strongly in bitterly condemning the Würzburg program (in a sixty-page article in *Philosophische Studien*, 1907, pp. 301–360). Thought is not amenable to the methods of experimental psychology—it requires *Völkerpsychologie*. The Würzburg reports are of no value for obvious reasons. First, they describe the findings of "mock experiments," that might have the appearance of experimental method, but in fact do not. The use of "systematic self-observation" has no application when the *Ausfragemethode* is used.

Külpe's group was confusing attention, which for Wundt was an active analyzing and synthesizing thing, with consciousness. That means that the apperceiver is trying to describe its acts of apperception, and all that it can come up with, naturally, is some vague feeling of disposition or activity.

Whether Wundt was right is a matter for debate, but it seems telling to notice that the Würzburg program melted away when Külpe left for Bonn. And it is true that Külpe never did much thereafter, and he never wrote that "chapter on thought" that had eluded him. On the other hand, Wundt worked until his death at age eighty-eight, lecturing to audiences of 600 well into his eighties. And it took a world war and the destruction of Germany to stop his research program.

The Legacy of Würzburg

There was not a word on thought, and thereby hangs the tale of Külpe's life. (Boring 1950, p. 401)

But the chapter on thought was missing! Bühler said that Külpe had not been lecturing on the topic. (Boring 1950, p. 407)

What had happened? The first quotation above refers to Külpe's introductory textbook of 1894, prior to the work of the Würzburgers. The second refers to a posthumously published book composed of Külpe's notes arranged by Bühler. The two books appeared twenty years apart and were substantially different, but neither featured a chapter on thought. What had happened?

In 1912 Külpe did publish a paper on thought, summarizing the work at Würzburg and drawing what conclusions could be drawn. However, few found it satisfying. The problem was that the discovery of imageless elements was interpreted as a negative discovery—insofar as *Bewüsstseinlagen* exist, the study of consciousness is futile. The study of thought lies essentially outside the reach of introspection, as Wundt had maintained for many years.

Edward Titchener would call such things "conscious attitudes." And, against all odds, he would defend the method of introspection against all challengers, including Wundt! In the next chapter we will see how Titchener dealt with imageless thought and even how he dominated psychology for a considerable period.

Wundt's Legacy and the Leipzig Laboratory after 1920
Wundt's work continued for a decade after the dissolution of the Würzburg School, and even in 1912, at the age of eighty, he was lecturing to audiences of 650 students and visiting scholars. His last years were spent on his *Völkerpsychologie*, or cultural psychology, which had more influence than is recognized. His experimental methods were carried off and continued by students such as Cattell and Judd, while Titchener, like Külpe, used methods that Wundt harshly criticized.

What Happened to the Völkerpsychologie. The first volume of his *Völkerpsychologie* was influential for its treatment of "*Sprachpsychologie*," or psycholinguistics—linguists divided into groups that supported either his views on language or those of the Herbartian linguist Hermann Paul (Blumenthal 1970). Paul favored taxonomic analysis, viewing language as sets of elements chained by associations into words and larger groups. Wundt's opposition to this view led to a running battle that lasted for forty years, from 1880 until 1920.

Wundt adopted a generative view of language, whereby a germinal mental impression unfolds via a constructive mental process based on the selective action of apperception. The unity of the sentence that results reflects the unity of the original germinal mental impression, so the sentence may be expressed in many ways. He invented the tree diagram (Wundt 1900) that was later widely used by linguists. Such diagrams show sentence parts that are produced by selective attentional focusing. The initial "germinal" impression is divided into two—the subject/predicate division, each of which may be further subdivided before an actual sentence is uttered.

For the articulate, such processes are not part of conscious awareness, but Wundt noted that the process may be infinitely creative. In 1900 Wundt offered examples, such as "Caesar crossed the Rubicon," "The Rubicon was crossed by Caesar," "When at the Rubicon, Caesar crossed," and so on. Clearly, Wundt's views were more similar to the transformational grammars of Noam Chomsky than to those of associationists of the nineteenth or the twentieth century.

The rest of the volumes on cultural psychology, dealing with art, mythology, religion, law, and morals, have received less notice.

G. E. Muller: Wundt's Rival
Georg Elias Müller was not the physiologist and the philosopher that Wundt was—he was an experimenter and tough-minded scientist, whose influence on the "new" psychology was second only to Wundt's. Photographs always portray him as a serious and even menacing man, and, in fact, he believed that a strong influence on the formation of his character resulted from his voluntary service in the Prussian infantry in 1870 during the Prusso–Danish War.[17] That experience shook him loose from earlier and softer interests and dedicated him to exactness and rigor.

Following military service, he studied at Leipzig under Moritz Drobisch, a Herbartian who was then defending Herbart's theory against attack by Wundt. The chief bone of contention, aside from the fact that Herbartianism was not really experimental, was Herbart's adherence to the British empiricist interpretation of attention as a secondary and relatively passive process. This was far different from and incompatible with the central role Wundt gave attention—as the active and selective agent, apperception.

Müller left for Göttingen in the early 1870s to study with Rudolph Lotze. There he was first exposed to truly experimental psychology and wrote a doctoral dissertation in 1873 titled *An Analysis of Sensory Attention*. His interpretation of attention was in keeping with his Herbartian past and ensured a lifelong dispute with Wundt.

This became the pattern for his later work, as he refined and developed the earlier work of Fechner, Ebbinghaus, Cattell, and Wundt on psychophysics, memory, reaction time, and spatial localization, respectively. He extended Hering's work in color vision and Mary Calkins's on the learning of paired associates.

He was fond of physiological reductionism, even suggesting that attention is importantly controlled by changes in concentrations of blood in different parts of the brain. Heightened blood supply could, he felt, produce greater cortical activity at affected locations and lead to an overflow of energy that produces "voluntary" movement.

Müller as Individual and as Teacher
Stern as he appeared and vociferous a critic as he was, it is surprising to learn from colleagues and students that he was a shy person with

no interest in the honors that he won (Katz 1935, pp. 377–380). One student, Erich Jaensch, described him as an inspiration and a "bulwark against liberalism, laxity, and cultural decadence, as well as a positive force for intellectual discipline."[18]

Müller never allowed himself to go to bed before midnight or to arise later than six o'clock, according to a friend, Edouard Claparede. Müller needed all of the self-discipline and dedication that he could muster, since Göttingen University gave him little assistance. It was not until 1887 that he was given research space, and it was four years later that token funding was provided for his laboratory. Stories circulated that funds for research often came from his personal salary. Nonetheless, in 1892 his laboratory was described by an American visitor as perhaps the "best for research work in all Germany."

Müller's Research

Müller was most interested in psychophysics, his idea of the model for correct science, and it was the model for his research in other areas. Katz wrote in 1935 that it is possible that Müller was the last lecturer in any German university to deliver a course of three-hour lectures on psychophysics, "and indeed few would have held forth on such a dry subject with so much force and impressiveness" (Blumenthal 1985, p. 56).

His first assistant at Göttingen was Friedrich Schumann, who had just received a Ph.D. in physics and was very skillful at designing and building experimental apparatus. He was a key figure in establishing psychology as a "brass instrument" discipline (Blumenthal 1985, p. 58), both during the fourteen years he assisted Müller and ten subsequent years at Berlin (Boring 1950, p. 374). Müller and Schumann published in 1889 on the psychophysics of judgments of lifted weights, concluding that heavier/lighter judgments depended on muscular anticipation, a finding that would have pleased Helmholtz.

In 1885 Ebbinghaus had published his classic study of memory, and in 1887 Müller and Schumann began a series of memory experiments using Ebbinghaus's methods. The results were published in 1893, including the rules for forming nonsense syllables. Unlike Ebbinghaus's practice, the subject and the experimenter were never the same person, and Müller pointed out the weakness of Ebbinghaus's solitary method.

Alfons Pilzecker had arrived at Göttingen in 1886 and stayed for over fourteen years. He finished a dissertation on attention under Müller, and in 1893 the two began a continuation of the memory research. Another student of Müller, Adolph Jost, had contributed Jost's law, holding that when two associations are of equal strength, a repetition strengthens the older more than the younger. Müller and Pilzecker published in 1900, showing the significance of reaction times as indicants of the strength of associations. That monograph and the work with Schumann determined the course of research in memory for decades to come.

They first showed the effects of proactive and retroactive interference and of spaced versus distributed practice. They used the paired-associate method first suggested by Mary Calkins and examined effects of motivation—the "intention to learn."

Müller invented the venerable "memory drum," a horizontal drum with verbal items on its surface, rotated behind a screen, so that one item at a time was exposed in a small window facing the subject. When pairs of items were used, as in paired-associate learning, an electrically controlled clock began when the first item appeared and stopped when the subject's response activiated a voice key.

Müller's last project on memory filled three volumes and was titled *Analysis of the Processes of Memory and Mental Representation* (Blumenthal 1985, p. 57), published during 1911–1913. Along with more standard summaries of previous work, he included a detailed case study of a famous mnemonist named Rückle, whose feats are listed in the flyer included in David Katz's 1948 book.

Müller the Proto-Gestaltist

Müller was by no means a Gestaltist, but he typically considered the effects of attention on memory performance. Still feuding with Wundt, he avoided the word "attention," referring instead to "attitude," "determining tendency," and "set" (Külpe spent three semesters with Müller). He particularly liked the term *Anlage* to refer to such effects. And before the turn of the century, Müller favored the learning of verbal materials as "wholes," rather than parts, because of the beneficial effects of configurational properties, or *Gestaltqualitäten*, that organize and stabilize memory.

However, that does not make one a Gestaltist, and Müller always saw wholes as compounds, in the manner of Herbart. When groups of elements have additional configurational properties, he called them *Komplexqualitaten*. In the early twentieth century, students of Müller became interested in these matters, including David Katz, who was his assistant from 1907 to 1918, Friedrich Schumann, Geza Revesz, and Edgar Rubin.

Katz had gotten his doctorate in 1906 and in 1909 published his paper on the phenomenology of color, distinguishing volumic color, surface color, and film color.[19] Rubin came from Copenhagen in 1912 and spent two years getting a degree under Müller. His book discussing figure–ground relations was published in Göttingen and later became closely identified with the Gestalt movement, in spite of its source.

Other students of Müller include Lillien J. Martin, a student from 1894 to 1898, and Victor Henri, a student of Binet, both of whom worked in psychophysics. Narziss Ach, of the Würzburg School, was his first official assistant, from 1901 to 1904, and ultimately replaced him (Boring 1950, p. 377). Eleanor A. McC. Gamble from Wellesley was a student in 1906–1907 and published a classic monograph on the method of reconstruction for the gauging of memory.

Müller retired in 1921, and by 1930 he had completed a two-volume work on color vision, but it included introspective data that were by that time anathema to most workers in vision. He died in 1934, having been the first experimental psychologist in the modern sense of the term.

12 Early-Twentieth-Century Psychology: Titchener and Freud

The death of no other psychologist could so alter the psychological picture in America...clear-cut opposition between behaviorism and its allies on the one hand, and something else, on the other, remains clear only when the opposition is between behaviorism and Titchener, mental tests and Titchener, or applied psychology and Titchener. (Boring 1927, p. 489)

The transplanting of psychology from Germany to America led almost at once to a conflict concerning its status as a pure or as an applied discipline. Is psychology really science, or should it be devoted solely to "helping troubled people?" Secondarily, it was even uncertain whether psychology could *ever* be an independent science or whether it should remain a division of philosophy.

American Psychology: Science or Therapy?

In the beginning, it was Edward Titchener (see figure 12.1) who stood most strongly for psychology as an independent and a nonapplied science. His interpretation of the New Psychology from Germany was dominant in the first American laboratories, and he did everything that he could to ensure that its dominance would continue. Though the facts now may seem otherwise, there is every reason to believe that he thought that he was carrying on Wundt's vision for psychology and that the stages of his career and development paralleled Wundt's.

E. B. Titchener and Structuralism

Despite his best intentions to the contrary, it only took one student, Edward Titchener, to present Wundt's system altered beyond recognition and to leave Wundt's name attached to ideas that he never had and

Figure 12.1
Titchener. Courtesy of the Archives of the History of American Psychology, University of
Akron.

that he rejected as strongly as he rejected the Würzburg program.
Wundt, as we have seen, was not an introspectionist, nor did he endorse analyzing experience into elements. In fact, we saw that he was
quite opposed to the practice of introspection, the *"verfehlte Methode"*
(false method).

Titchener's Definition of the New Psychology

However, that was evidently not Edward Titchener's impression—
even though he had translated much of Wundt's writings. For Titchener, the New Psychology meant introspection and analysis, for the
simple reason that every science must begin with a morphology—the
study of "what" is to be explained. Biology had to begin with taxonomic classification of organisms and the identification of bodily
organs before it could even consider studying "how" organisms and
organs work. Physiology is the study of the functioning of an anatomy,
and that must *follow* the anatomical work.

That is the "what," and for psychology that means a cataloging of
mental content—the content of consciousness. Once that is done, we

may worry about how that content comes to be organized the way it is—perhaps through laws of association or in some other way. That will be the study of the "how," and psychology is nowhere near ready for that enterprise, Titchener thought.

When anatomy and physiology are well enough understood, biologists can consider the "why" questions, and in theoretical biology those are bound to be questions for evolutionary theory. When psychology has answered its basic "what/how" questions, it may then progress to its "why" questions, all concerned with the brain and nervous system. Titchener had years of experience in physiology, and that no doubt left him in awe of the nervous system, in which he placed all answers to "why" questions. Other factors in his education molded him in other ways, as we will see below.

Titchener's Life

E. B. Titchener was a scholarly prodigy born in 1867 in Chichester in southern England of a venerable family that was without money at that time, requiring him to win scholarships to Malvern College and then to Brasenose College of Oxford University. He studied philosophy for four years at Oxford, and it appears that British associationism and empiricism led him to be interested in Wundt and the New Psychology.

However, that psychology was physiological, and so he translated all of the third edition of Wundt's *Physiologische Psychologie* and took it to Leipzig, only to learn that the fourth edition was coming out soon. On Wundt's advice, Titchener spent a fifth year at Oxford studying physiology, as a research student with Sir John Scott Burden-Sanderson.

He was skillful in language; when Burden-Sanderson gave him a paper in Dutch to read for a report to be given in a week, Titchener said that he didn't know Dutch. "Learn it," said Burden-Sanderson, and he did. Ten papers in physiology resulted from this year's work with Burden-Sanderson, so his first published work was in biology.

He then spent the years 1890–1892 at Leipzig, earning a Ph.D. in psychology under Wundt. His work at Leipzig was in mental chronometry, all the rage at the time, and his first published psychological research was on reaction time. For his dissertation research, he studied the binocular effects of monocular stimulation. Upon returning to England, he found that there were no jobs for physiological psychologists, and, after teaching biology at Oxford during the summer of

Figure 12.2
Washburn. Courtesy of the Archives of the History of American Psychology, University of Akron.

1892, he moved to Cornell University, where an old Leipzig Wundtian, Frank Angell, was leaving his laboratory and moving to Stanford.

He remained the picture of a nineteenth-century aristocratic Oxford scholar. Rather than bowing to the pragmatism and egalitarian sentiment of the turn of the century, he remained aloof from the common herd. This isolated him at Cornell, "though his theatrical teaching style attracted a great many students" (Blumenthal 1985, p. 71). Blumenthal attributed his anachronistic habits to his background in an old English family and his Oxford education. He would not accept a dinner invitation from Cornell's president unless it was hand-delivered by a coachman. He spoke precisely and elaborately and customarily wore academic robes! He was a man to impress some and to arouse skepticism in others, like Margaret Floy Washburn (see figure 12.2), his student and the first woman to be awarded a doctorate in psychology.

Cornell There were few textbooks in America, so he translated Külpe, Wundt's *Human and Animal Psychology*, and parts of *Physiological Psychology*, and he wrote his own *Outline of Psychology* (1896) and

Primer of Psychology (1898). His main work, *A Textbook of Psychology*, was first published in 1896 and went through sixteen printings by 1899. It was revised several times between 1909 and 1928. At first he worked on his own laboratory experiments, then directed students' work. By 1900 his students included Margaret Floy Washburn, Walter Pillsbury, and Madison Bentley and more than thirty published studies had come from his laboratory.

His lectures were "trenchant and powerful" (Heidbreder 1933, p. 117) and immensely popular. Edwin Boring, a onetime assistant and student of Titchener, described the lectures as he remembered them in 1927 (pp. 489–506). How did he interact with his graduate students? They "saw him at the house and not often" (ibid.). Professors who had been at Cornell for many years had never seen Titchener, so detached was he, and they could not even come to his lectures to see him, since the lecture room was full of sophomores and no one else was admitted!

Structuralism

Titchener called his system "structuralism," a name that Wundt would *never* have used, and opposed it to "functionalism," a name he applied to psychologists influenced by Darwinism and the emphasis on adaptive activity. Functionalism was fundamentally flawed, Titchener thought, since it demanded explanations referring to purpose and goals. That teleological hallmark was a return to philosophy and would draw us back into that philosophical morass from which we were just escaping! Functionalists were also prematurely considering "why" questions, before answering the "what" and the "how." Titchener insisted that we begin with the "what"—the structure of the mind as revealed in consciousness.

The Mind   Physics deals with independent experience, with experience "altogether independent of any particular person." That refers to experience of a world that we assume is there whether we are or not and in which certain things are constant. From that point of view, physical space is constant, the same always and everywhere, and its unit is the centimeter. Viewed independently, time is also constant, and its unit is the second.

However, Titchener continued, psychological facts and laws refer to *dependent* experience, and those laws do not correspond to the laws of physics. The two lines of the vertical/horizontal illusion appear unequal to us, but their physical lengths are the same. An hour spent waiting for a train seems endless, while an hour watching a play passes swiftly. The laws and facts of physics, independent experience, are not the same as those of psychology, which deals with dependent experience.

Introspection and Science   Titchener discussed the use of the word "introspection" in 1912 (p. 485), partly because of objections raised by many writers concerning the varied interpretations given to the word. What did it really mean, and was it necessary? Titchener did indeed believe that introspection was no different in kind from "inspection," and that it merely referred to a different object—consciousness rather than stimuli. That being the case, he asked "why do we need the word at all?" There were two reasons to retain it. First, the method of introspection was the only thing unique to psychology, at least as Titchener defined psychology. Without introspection, psychology could be carried out by physicists and biologists.

The second reason was that "introspection" was a better term for the beginner in psychology, the person who Titchener always fretted about. The professional may grasp the "subtle shift in attitude" that distinguishes the study of consciousness and the study of physical objects, but the beginner needs separate terms to label the two. Introspection is a poor term fraught with differences of usage, but it is thus necessary for practical reasons.

Wundt's Condemnation of Titchener's Program   Wundt did not approve of Titchener's program, as is apparent in the following passage, written in 1900. The method of introspection is a *"verfehlte Methode,"* and Wundt was exasperated at Titchener's backward step to introspection:

Introspective method (*introspective Methode*) relies either on arbitrary observations that go astray or on a withdrawal to a lonely sitting room where it becomes lost in self-absorption. The unreliability of this method is today rather universally recognized. Clearly Titchener has himself come under the influence of the deceptions of this method. (In Blumenthal 1985)

Elements before Function   Introspection is a difficult business, and it requires a lot of training to be proficient. Titchener knew, as have many writers before him, that conscious experience is a stream, a flux, a process, *not* a content that can be examined at leisure. He said of mental elements: their "essence is their processence" (Heidbreder 1933, p. 136). However, with effort—"hard introspective labor," he called it, elements of experience can be sorted out and the "what" can be categorized.

Titchener's labors led to the identification of three conscious elements, sensations, images, and affect. Sensations and images differ only in vividness, much as did Hume's "impressions and ideas." Affect, for Titchener, referred to feelings of pleasantness and unpleasantness. And sensations, images, and affect have certain attributes that define them. The first is *quality*, such as "red," "cold," "unpleasant," or "C-sharp."

They also have the attribute of *intensity*, as in "very loud" or "faint red." Quality and intensity were the attributes that Wundt had found ideas to have, with any others dependent on cultural factors. However, Titchener attributed *duration* to sensations, images, and affect, bearing in mind that this is psychological, and not physical, time!

Other attributes were matters of contention among Titchener and others. For example, Ebbinghaus held a very nativist position and gave to sensation attributes of extension in space, time, movement, likeness/difference, and quantity (Titchener 1910, p. 346). Titchener was more conservative, attributing extension in space only to vision and touch. Sights and touches can have the "original character of spatial outspread," since the retina and the skin are themselves extended in space, but that is not the case for smell and for hearing.

One can imagine easily how that opinion could be contested and then wonder how the contest could ever be decided. Does a shrill whistle seem to be more compressed in space than does the sound of rolling thunder or a bass note from a pipe organ? Don't odors seem spread in space, or is that spatiality derived from our movement as we follow the smell? If so, that would make touch the real basis for sensations of "olfactory" space.

Affect: Feelings Are Never Clear   Wundt had distinguished three dimensions of affect, but Titchener found only one—the dimension of pleasant to unpleasant. Wundt's excitation/depression and tension/relaxation were interpreted by Titchener as body responses, hence not pure mental content. Of course, Titchener used only introspective description, *not* the "method of impression," whereby bodily activities are monitored in the manner of modern psychophysiology. Instead, Titchener asked a lone subject to keep a record of affect revealed in introspection over a year's time. The subject reported only degrees of pleasantness and unpleasantness.[1]

Later experiments confirmed this finding, and the Cornell and Leipzig groups spent some years debating the dimensions of affect. Bear in mind that the dispute concerned affect as simple feelings and that no one disputed the existence of emotions, which are more complicated and dependent on experience and culture. "Happy," "sad," "disappointed," "ecstatic" and countless other states of emotion are certainly not simple feelings, not elements of experience as Wundt and Titchener described them.

Titchener and the Question of Attention[2] A very important attribute was variously called clarity, clearness, and attensity. This corresponds to what is usually called "attention," but it is treated as an attribute of sensations and images, much as James Mill had referred to the "vividness" of ideas. In treating attention thus, Titchener opposed Wundt's most fundamental belief—that apperception, the feeling of active attention, was a fundamental aspect of our experience. For Wundt, apperception was the agent of synthesis and analysis of consciousness and was in no way a property of ideas.

Titchener held that we do not experience attention as an active agent—feelings of attention are "not observed." Just as Hume could portray the self as derived, a construction, because "there is no impression of the self," Titchener could find no sensation identified with attention and so deemed it secondary, an attribute of sensation. What do we feel when we "attend" to something? Titchener (1910, p. 194) believed that body sensations are the source.

For example, we have a sensation of light, which alone has no meaning. We "attend," adding a feeling of strain around the eyes and a wrinkling of the forehead, until we have a perception of a light—"that bright something." The feelings of focusing, straining, attending, selecting, and the like may *feel* like an active attentional process—aren't we *trying* to attend? But, in fact, sensations and images run the show, and our feeling of attentional effort is no more real than the river's feeling that it has forcefully broken the logjam.

The Stimulus Error An illustration of Titchener's thinking lies in his conception of the stimulus error, the fundamental and fatal mistake to which introspecters were liable. It amounts to a description of *independent* experience that is mistaken for a description of *dependent* experience—we describe the *object*, not the experience of it. To use a crude example, if you are shown a plate sitting on a table several feet away from you, and you report "a round plate on a rectangular table," you have committed the stimulus error. Your previous experience has given you a theory of reality, according to which the plate would be round and the table rectangular *if* viewed from a particular "ideal" angle.

The Context Theory of Meaning[3]   Titchener (1910, p. 194) claimed originality for his theory of meaning, though it clearly derived from Berkeley's theory of matter of two centuries before, which was adopted by many, including Hume, Brown, John Stuart Mill, Helmholtz, Mach, and others. As Titchener described it, the core/context theory of meaning may have been original only in the fact that it did not specifically depend upon associations—at least, in his view.

When we speak of sensations, we exclude meaning. Percepts *mean*, and percepts always involve more than one sensation. There is a core that is consciously apprehended and a context which provides the meaning. Much of this context is not conscious, since it represents a residue of prior experience and even of experience that occurred in early childhood. And, perhaps curiously, much of that context arose in our behavior and the kinesthetic sensations that accompany behavior.

When we are first learning the meaning of "up," there is a turning of the head and eyes upward and the feelings that go with that behavior is a large part of the "meaning of up." "Out" is accompanied by thrusting of the arms away from the body, and "in" is understood by a withdrawing of the limbs toward the body. "Over," "through," "into," "around," and even "thing" occur with body movements. We denote "thing" by pointing. "Heavier" and "lighter," or "more and less" are likewise accompanied by body movements.

As we grow older, the words that we use to name objects and relations become independent of these bodily gestures and kinesthetic sensations. Where originally an "organism faces a situation by some bodily attitude" (Titchener 1910, p. 194), images take over meaning. And, since we are not taught to notice the kinesthetic sensations that go with movements and we do not assign words to identify them, they drop from consciousness.

We find ourselves in various "situations," a situation being the "meaningful experience of a conscious present" (Titchener 1910, chapter 13), and that meaning is now carried in a context that is no longer conscious. Hence, it is necessary, wrote Titchener, to study consciousness longitudinally, not just in transverse section, and so "trace meaning's degeneration." This cannot be done through the study of children's development, since children cannot be trained to introspect properly—it requires analysis by those who can be so trained, and that means that adults must do it. He called this a project of "extreme importance," but is it feasible?

Dealing with Würzburg's "Imageless Elements" Titchener had roomed with Külpe, and the two had collaborated in research and writing while Titchener was a student at Leipzig. He agreed with Külpe that Wundt was mistaken in denying that "higher mental processes" could be studied in the laboratory. However, the findings of Külpe's group seemed to corroborate Wundt's judgment! If simple processes like comparing lifted weights and producing associates to words were not carried in images, but only in *Bewüsstseinlagen*—conscious attitudes—how could the method of introspection have a future?

It was this problem that was the stimulus for Titchener's core-context theory of meaning and the proposal that meaning degenerates to unconsciousness. The kinesthetic and other sensations that accompanied the comparing of weights and the giving of associations were retrievable if introspective effort were applied. The Würzburgers were relatively inexperienced introspectionists, and they were not seeking sensations grounded in body movements. Titchener spent a good deal of time showing that the sensations existed and that "conscious attitudes," as he called them, could be analyzed to sensory components.

He offered many examples, noting that a given observer's report would differ from another's depending on their individual histories. The point was that any "meaning," or disposition, or conscious attitude is analyzable. In some cases, subjects were asked to identify the sensory meanings of enigmatic sentences that produce what seems an indefinable feeling. For example, "Infinity broods over all things" seems difficult to translate into sensations and images, but Titchener did manage it. For him, "infinity" took the form of a vast sky overhead and it palpitated, reflecting its "brooding."

That accounts for "infinity brooding over," and all that is left is "all things." "All" seemed to Titchener to be represented by the feelings one has when throwing one's arms widely out in front, as when preparing to hug an approaching loved one. That may have meant "all" to a barely verbal child, true enough. What of "things" or "thing?" A child points at a "thing," and the image of a hand with extended index finger—pointing—was Titchener's image of "thing." Imageless thoughts are not really imageless, if only the proper effort is applied in their analysis.

Examples from Titchener's Instructor's Manual, Part I

The Instructor's Manuals showed a human and sometimes a humorous side of Titchener. Part II dealt solely with psychophysics and methods employed therein and are thus of less interest. However, the first volume, part I, described actual experiments to be carried out in an undergraduate psychology laboratory course. They provide further insight into Titchener's psychology and his personality.

For example, the student's version begins with the statement that psychology is just beginning in America; hence, most of the research has been published in German or in French. The student is therefore expected to *learn* German and French, not well enough to be able to enjoy reading, but well enough to read technical articles in those languages!

Taste Contrast and Effects of Odors   Among the more easily describable experiments included is one on taste contrast (p. 107). The student finds that distilled water tastes sweet when contrasted with a taste of a fifty-percent salt solution and that it tastes salty when contrasted with a strong sweet solution. The effects of odor were demonstrated (p. 159) by asking the subject to hold a marker, with arm extended forward, against a moving roll of paper, and to avoid moving the marker, which traced a line as the paper moved.

While doing this, the subject is presented with a pleasant floral smell and the marker moves slightly laterally (outward). When an unpleasant smell, such as ammonia, is presented, the subject's arm and the marker move inward, toward the body. Subjects were unaware of any movement at first, until shown the deflection of the tracing.

That experiment illustrated the effects of pleasantness and unpleasantness—movement outward, or expansiveness, and movement inward, or contraction. The theory underlying that phenomenon was widely cited and first appeared in a German work of the nineteenth century.

The Attention Wave   Hugo Eckener was a student of Wundt's who later commanded the *Graf Zeppelin*, an airship that made dozens of transatlantic crossings and carried thousands of passengers, making him the most famous man in the world for a short time in the 1930s. His dissertation work concerned attention and the effects of irritating distractions. From that work came the phenomenon of the "attention wave," or cyclical fluctuations in attention that seemed to occur in six- to eight-second cycles (ibid., p. 195).

To experience this effect, a ticking watch was placed on the floor eight to ten meters from a subject seated in a chair in a quiet room. The distance of the watch was adjusted until its ticking was just audible. Then the subject attended to the periods during which the ticking could be heard and when it could not. Those on/off cycles tended to occur at six- to eight-second intervals.

Other exercises examined variations on the Müller–Lyer illusion, Stumpf's tests for unmusicalness, and dozens of other topics. The student's version of the manual also included what seems a humorous list of ten ways to fail the lab course; here is an example (1901, pp. xxviii, xix):

How to Fail in Laboratory Work

(3) See yourself in everything. If the Instructor begin an explanation, interrupt him with a story of your childhood which seems to illustrate the point that he is making. If he is formulating a law, interrupt him with an account of some exception that has occurred within your own or your friends' experience. Go into the minutest detail. If the Instructor incline to reject your anecdotes, argue the matter out with him in full.

The American Psychological Association was founded by G. Stanley Hall just before Titchener arrived in America, but he was never active in it. When it met in Ithaca, virtually across the street from his home, he declined to attend! Instead, he founded his own group in 1904 and called it the "Experimental Psychologists." It excluded animal, child, abnormal, and applied psychology—they were not "experimental," no matter how they may use experimentation. On his death, the organization became the Society of Experimental Psychologists, which added animal research to its meetings. That organization remains a group of "good old boys," so to speak, that offers membership by invitation only.

The End of Titchener's System

How Were Introspective Studies Done?   Beginning in 1910, the foundation upon which Titchener's system stood began to crumble—or at least, to change drastically. This was all due to the work of his own students and, most importantly, the dissertation of Cheves West Perky, published in 1910 as "An Experimental Study of Imagination." This report is interesting for at least two reasons. First, it clearly conveys the flavor of introspective research, which is otherwise difficult to conceive.

Second, Perky's research began the disintegration of the foundations of Titchener's model of mind as constituted of mental elements—sensation, image, and affect. Perky's intent was to distinguish types of imagery, but in so doing he found that the key distinction—between sensation and image—was impossible to maintain. This changed a way of thinking that went back to at least Reid and Stewart and perhaps to Aristotle. If sensation and image are not distinct, how do we know what is "real" and what is imaginary?

Can We Distinguish Sensation from Image? Perky's first experiment was an elaborate one, meant to create sensations that the observer would mistake for images—products of imagination. "The object of our first experiments was to build up, perceptual consciousness under conditions which should seem to the observer to be those of the formation of an imaginative consciousness" (Perky 1910, p. 428). Is it possible to present actual stimuli to a subject so that the subject honestly feels that they are imagined? If we have Reid's God-given power to distinguish sensation and imagination, then it should not be possible.

Margaret Floy Washburn, Titchener's first Ph.D. student and the first woman Ph.D. in the country, had written in 1899 (p. 32) that "perception and idea differ only in their manner of production" and that if peripheral stimulation is minimal, the conscious state is practically identical to that of central excitation—that is, sensations and images may be indistinguishable.

The procedure for Perky's experiments was elaborate and provides a picture of the way in which many introspective studies were done in Titchener's laboratory. A ground glass screen was installed in a dark room, and six colors were projected by lantern within outlines of forms meant to resemble objects. These included a (red) tomato, a (blue) book, a (deep yellow) banana, an (orange) orange, a (green) leaf, and a (light yellow) lemon.

Three experimenters were required for each subject/observer—one experimenter ran the projector and colored filters, and a second presented the form outlines, which were slowly oscillated so as to match a "subjective image" (Perky 1910, p. 430). The third experimenter was the only one present, as far as the observer was to know, and instructed the observer and recorded the data. Subjects were instructed to fixate on a white point in the middle of the glass screen to "image a tomato," for example. Initially there was nothing on the screen, and a second experimenter slowly turned up the projected tomato-form until the observer began to describe an image.

In Experiment 1, children were used as observers—girls thirteen and fourteen years old and a ten-year-old boy. Apparatus malfunction ruined the boy's data, but both girls described images and believed that they were products of imagination. Experiment 2 employed nineteen sophomores and eight other undergraduate students. Three undergraduates had to be dropped due to experimenter error in handling the equipment, "which was at once pounced upon and reported" (Perky 1910, p. 431).

The remaining twenty-four subjects "invariably took the percept for image" and were "surprised and indignant" when asked at the end if they were sure. Thus, when the lantern was turned up so that the subjects began describing an image, they testified that the image was just that and that there was nothing presented on the glass. This was Perky's most important finding, and one that the Titchener group took seriously. However, further experiments in the same series tell us more about the methods used by Titchener's group.

Do Images of Memory and of Imagination Differ?   The next set concerned the presence of kinesthetic elements—sensations of movement of body parts—in images of memory and in images of imagination.[4] It was hypothesized that memory images involve kinesthetic elements, particularly from the eyes, while imaginary images do not. However, how can such a possibility be assessed—purely through introspective reports?

Three male and three female graduate students participated, and all were familiar with the projects going on in the laboratory. A subject was seated in a dark room, with head steadied on a headrest and left eye screened. The right eye was to fixate on a luminous spot 1.5 meters away. Four other luminous spots formed a square that was positioned so as to fall on the blind spot on the retina. They were thus invisible, unless the head moved, at which time one or more could be seen. Subjects found it difficult to remain still so that the spots were not seen but were able to do so with practice.

They were then read individual words as stimulus items and instructed to use a hand signal to report the presence of imagery. In providing their introspective description, they also reported when they "saw the other lights," indicating that eye movement had occurred. In keeping with the thesis, images of memory, which could be referred to the subject's history, were accompanied by eye movements ("I saw the lights") ninety percent of the time. When the images were "imaginary," fantasied, eye movements occurred only thirty-two percent of the time.

The Aftermath of Perky's Findings   Evans (1972, pp. 170–174) described the fate of Titchener's structuralism after 1910. At the time that Perky worked, it was assumed that it was possible to examine experience as an "is," devoid of meaning, left as bare facts and essences. These bare facts were already defined as the three elements of experience—sensations, images, and affect. All three elements differed in quality, intensity, and protensity (duration), and some sensations and images varied in extensity and attensity (extension in space and clearness). Affect—feelings ranging from pleasant to unpleasant—were never clear.

Good-Bye to Images   However, Perky showed that it is easy to confuse sensations and images! If that is so, why are *two* names used—why not just say that sensations vary in intensity and we call faint ones "images?" Hence, it was time to say goodbye to images, leaving sensation and affect as mental elements.

Farewell to Sensations   In 1899 Mary Whiton Calkins had published a paper criticizing the definition of sensation used by an E. B. Talbot.[5] In 1913 the same argument was taken up by Carl Rahn in a doctoral thesis written for James Rowland Angell at Chicago. Calkins's argument was simple and compelling enough to convince Titchener.

Appealing to Titchener's positivistic views, Calkins and Rahn argued that conscious content must be restricted to that which exists, not to constructs or nonexperienced entities like "sensations." To this Titchener had to strongly agree, since that was indeed his credo. However, if that is the case, why do we even *talk* about sensations?

As Calkins had argued fourteen years before, Rahn pointed out that the conception of "sensations," as in "a sensation," is without meaning. Consider a deeply saturated red spot lasting ten seconds. It has attributes: red, saturation, duration, attensity (clearness), and that is all! Where is the "sensation?" Is that just a name for a nonsense classificatory term? We sense hues, like red, and intensities and extensities, and attensities, and protensities (spatial qualities, clearness, and duration), *but we do not sense sensations!*

Titchener responded to Rahn in 1915, where he seemed to shift sensation from "element" to mere classificatory term. However, by 1918 he had dropped all reference to "elements" of experience from his lecture course in "Systematic Psychology." The ultimate dimensions were the attributes: quality, intensity, protensity, extensity, and attensity. And even intensity was questionable by this time. For example, are different brightnesses of light different intensities, or are they different qualities (Evans 1972, pp. 172–173)?

Adieu to Affect   In 1924 J. P. Nafe published a dissertation on the experience of affect. For Titchener, the simple *feeling* of affect was restricted to the dimension pleasant–unpleasant, and that was the "element" of affect—all that is left, once the elemental status of image and sensation are gone. However, Nafe found that affect, as introspectively experienced, was reducible to feelings of *pressure*, with pleasure felt as "bright pressure" and unpleasantness felt as "dull pressure." Pressure is a variety of touch, and touch is a quality of sensation. So Nafe had reduced affect (pleasant and unpleasant simple feelings) to sensation, and sensation had *already* been jettisoned from systematic psychology.

Experience is only of attributes, and that is what Titchener wrote and taught in his last years. The attribute of protensity was changed from the simple conception of "time" to a process—"a pre-temporal welling forth." Extensity was characterized not as the extension of sensation in space, but as a "pre-spatial spread" (Evans, pp. 170–1740).

Stella Sharp and Mental Measurement   In 1898 Stella Emily Sharp received her Ph.D. with Titchener and published a careful study of mental testing the same year. Her findings bear on the worth of Galton's methods for the assessment of intellect and the similar methods used by others in Europe and in America.

In the 1890s there was great interest in the application of psychological methods to the assessment of mental deficiency and in the ranking of intellectual powers among individuals. The two competing views in this area were those of the German and the French schools, represented by Kraepelin and by Binet, respectively. Kraepelin had been a student of Wundt and was a pioneer in the classification of mental disorders.[6] He favored the examination of the simplest sensory and cognitive functions as estimates of intellect, while Binet and colleagues advocated tests of what could be called "higher mental functions."

For example, Emil Kraepelin examined perception by requiring subjects to count the number of specific letters in a piece of text, to search for particular letters, and to proofread texts. He assessed memory through the learning of lists of nonsense syllables and the learning of sets of figures. Association was measured through performance in addition, and motor skill was tested as success in writing from dictation and in writing as fast as possible. Other tests were of a similar elementary nature and were no doubt useful in the making of gross psychiatric diagnoses.

Similar "anthropometric" tests were popular in America in the 1890s, and Joseph Jastrow arranged a display of "mental tests" at the Chicago World's Fair in 1892. As described by Sharp (1898, p. 340), this consisted of five tests of touch sensitivity, five tests of coordination of touch and movement, twelve tests of visual discrimination, tests of memory for letters, lines, and forms, and assessment of simple reaction times. Along the same lines, James McKeen Cattell, Wundt's first assistant, published a paper titled "Mental Tests and Measurement" (1890, p. 373) in which he proposed tests such as the reproducing of intervals of time, memorizing alphabet letters, and simple reaction time.

Binet and Henri opposed the rationale for such mental tests and instead presented difficult tasks to different groups of subjects varying in age and education. For example, a very long sentence would be read to a subject, who was then to reproduce it. Other tests required abstraction and conceptualization rather than simple sensory judgments. Norms were established and subjects categorized relative to peer groups rather than according to a model of the "generalized human mind."

In fact, Titchener and his students were not favorably disposed toward any kind of mental testing nor toward applied psychology in general. Psychology had existed for less than twenty years by their reckoning and was in no position to assess something as vague as "intelligence," whatever the public demand for such tests. However, the "German" method, reflected also in the work of Galton, Jastrow, Cattell, and many others, was clearly more objectionable than was Binet's. This was probably because the former attempted to directly apply the methods of the laboratory and thus diminished the reputation of those methods.

Sharp evaluated a range of so-called "mental measures," comparing the performance of advanced students in the Sage School of Philosophy at Cornell with that of a "less advanced" group, Titchener's class of juniors during the 1897–1898 school year. Those tests that could be administered to groups were conducted by Titchener himself during the first ten minutes of his lecture periods. The many tests used included the following:

- Memory for sets of twelve letters or figures.
- Memory for words and for long sentences.
- Imagination assessed with ink blot interpretations.
- Literary imagination reflected in the number of sentences written in five minutes that included three words that were provided.

The remaining tests are less easily described. The "range of attention" test required subjects to first read a literary passage aloud and then to do so while simultaneously writing the letter "a" as many times as possible. Then reading was done while writing "ab," "abc," and so on through the alphabet if time allowed. "Observation tests" required the description of pictures after a brief viewing, and further tests assessed still more complicated abilities. Overall, the tests ranged from the elementary kind used by Kraepelin and others to tests of "higher functions" favored by Binet.

After this lengthy procedure, the data were analyzed in minute detail and presented in a number of tables. Some tests did show some differences between the groups of advanced and less advanced students, but the overall results were not encouraging. Sharp concluded that "the positive results have been wholly incommensurate with the labor required for the devising of tests and evaluation of results."

Nonetheless, it seemed clear to her that the "method of M. Binet is most productive of fruitful results," since the clearest differences appeared in the results of the tests of complex functions, not the simple ones. Later everyone would know that the methods of Galton, Kraepelin, and Cattell were not the methods of choice.

Titchener's Legacy

Almost half of Titchener's doctoral students were women—twenty-one of fifty-four—and his first was Margaret Floy Washburn, herself

Figure 12.3
Freud. Courtesy of the Archives of the History of American Psychology, University of Akron.

the first woman Ph.D. psychologist in America. She was, appropriately, one of the four editors of the *American Journal of Psychology* in 1927, the year that Titchener died suddenly of a brain tumor at the age of sixty. His brain remains preserved and on display at Cornell.

Freud and Psychoanalysis

Nun ist die Luft von solchem Spuk so voll,
Dass niemand weiss, wie er ihn meiden soll
[Now the air is so full of ghosts,
that no one knows how to avoid them]

(Freud 1910, cover sheet, German edition)

Freud (shown in figure 12.3) was a remarkable figure who always regarded himself as an outsider, was intensely antireligious, and never tired of criticizing philosophers as "players of games." His contempt for metaphysics of any kind was comparable to the attitudes of Francis

Bacon. He believed that psychoanalysis cannot create a new *Weltan-schauung* since it is already part of one—science.

Science is continually at war with religion, in Freud's view, and the side that he took was always science! It was the famous physiologist and positivist Ernst Brücke, materialist and opponent of occult forces, "who carried more weight with me than anyone else in my whole life," he wrote. Yet it was charged in the Europe of the late nineteenth century that his psychoanalysis was not science at all and that his theories were "a matter for the police rather than scientific congresses" (Gay 1989).

In 1923, the year that his jaw cancer was correctly diagnosed and two drastic operations were performed on his jaw and palate, the three intrapsychic forces familiar to countless millions of students and lay readers were added. Prior to that time, we will see that psychoanalysis bore striking and unexpected similarities to other views of the period, especially to Watson's behaviorism.

Freud's Life

Freud's work was largely complete prior to 1924 when, at age sixty-eight, he was asked to contribute to a collection of autobiographies of distinguished physicians. There he described his gymnasium education, where he excelled and received special privileges, and he recalled the early influences in his life. His father gave him free reign to follow whatever career he wished, and the political success of an older schoolmate briefly attracted him to the study of law. He was also "strongly attracted" by Darwinian theory, and that, along with the hearing of Goethe's essay on "Nature," led him to become a medical student.

During the first year of that schooling, he learned to behave as the "Opposition," when he experienced the discrimination against Jews, who were assumed "inferior and alien." However, in Ernst Brücke's physiological laboratory he found "rest and full satisfaction," along with scientists whom he could accept as models. He worked in Brücke's institute from 1876 to 1882, with short interruptions, and had hopes of gaining a post as assistant. He had no interest in the practice of medicine and would have continued in research following graduation in 1881 had Brücke not set him straight.

From Biological Research to "Quackery"   Brücke advised that, in view of his poverty, he should forget about a research career and become qualified in clinical medicine. Freud held Brücke in "the highest possible esteem" and so followed his advice, entering the Vienna General Hospital as a clinical assistant, and he soon became house physician. For more than six months he worked under the eminent Theodor Meynert, eminent professor of psychiatry. He had left Brücke working on the spinal cord of fishes and now began work on the tracts and nuclei of the human medulla.

Meynert allowed Freud access to the laboratory for his personal research and, according to Freud (Gay 1989, p. 5), proposed that he devote himself to brain anatomy. Further, he promised to hand over to Freud his lecturing work, since he felt himself too old to keep up with the newer methods. However, Freud declined the offer, "in alarm at the magnitude of the task; it is possible, too, that I had guessed already that this great man was by no means kindly disposed towards me" (Gay 1989, p. 5). Actually, it appears that by that time Freud had decided against a career in basic research, even though some of his work on the medulla had received favorable notice.

The fact was that it would be difficult to make a living in brain anatomy, just as it was in physiology, "and, with an eye to pecuniary considerations, I began to study nervous diseases" (ibid.). This was a desperate course to follow, since "neuropathology" did not exist as a specialty in Vienna, so a specialist had to be self-taught. Only Charcot, in Paris, was considered anything like an authority, so Freud planned to establish himself as a lecturer on nervous diseases in Vienna as a means to study with Charcot.

In the spring of 1885 a "traveling bursary of considerable value" allowed Freud to go to Paris in the fall and learn what he could from Charcot. At first he was paid little attention, but when he heard Charcot complain that he needed a translator to render his latest lectures into German, Freud volunteered and was from then on admitted to the circle of Charcot's acquaintances. He was later upset to hear that he had been accused of using his time in France to steal the ideas of Pierre Janet, whose name was never mentioned while Freud was at the Salpêtrière.

What impressed him was Charcot's work with hysteria, showing it genuine and observable in men as well as women. The affliction could be brought on by trauma or reproduced in faithful detail in hypnotized subjects. While not convinced that Charcot's interpretations were correct, the two agreed that the symptoms corresponded to popular ideas of what constituted a faculty or an anatomical member, but Charcot was less interested in the psychology of the disorder than in its neuro-pathology.

He published a number of papers on organic diseases of the nervous system and became adept at diagnosing lesions in the medulla. His diagnoses were accurate, as testified in autopsies, and American physicians came to hear his lectures. At that time he was familiar only with organic diseases—tumors, lesions, and inflammations. He presented on one occasion a neurotic suffering from constant headache as a case of localized inflammation of the covering of the brain (meningitis), and, as he put it, his audience "rose in revolt and deserted me" (Gay 1989, p. 6).

In 1886 he settled down in Vienna as a physician and "married the girl who had been waiting for me in a distant city for more than four years." It was her fault that he wasn't famous by then, or so he claimed, since when he visited her two years before, it interrupted his research on the anesthetic properties of cocaine, which he had obtained from the Darmstadt drug firm, Merck.

Rejection by the Medical Society   In 1886 Freud presented a lecture describing his experiences with Charcot. The audience was the Vienna Medical Society (*Gesellschaft der Arzte*). He was challenged by several listeners, including the president of the society and the powerful Theodur Meynert, in whose laboratory Freud had worked. What they questioned was evidence for hysteria in men, a preposterous notion in their view. Hysteria referred to conditions in which women showed symptoms in the absence of any discernible organic cause. Charcot was certain that it occurred in men, but the Germans were skeptical.

Freud finally found a male with hysterical hemi-anesthesia, who he presented before the society, but to no avail. Their minds were set, and Freud was again forced into what he called the Opposition. The existence of hysteria in men and the treatment of hysterical paralyses *through* suggestion were beyond the pale. Freud was excluded from Meynert's Institute and over time withdrew from academic circles—he no longer attended meetings of the Medical Society.

Hysterical illness could well render women dangerous, and even murder and arson were considered to be within their capabilities. This being the medical opinion of the time, it is easy to see why hysterical patients were considered undesirable and treated with suspicion and hostility by most physicians. But these were the patients treated by Freud from the moment he opened his practice.

Freud's Early Practice in Neurology

Anyone who wants to make a living from the treatment of nervous patients must clearly be able to do something to help them. My therapeutic arsenal contained only two weapons, electrotherapy and hypnotism, for prescribing a visit to a hydropathic establishment after a single consultation was an inadequate source of income. (Gay 1989, p. 9)

Sadly for Freud, the 1882 textbook of electrotherapy that he used was useless—equivalent to some "Egyptian dream-book," though the author, W. Erb, was the greatest German authority on neuropathology. This helped rid Freud of "innocent faith in authority" and prepared him to accept the conclusions of Moebius, who argued that any therapeutic effects of electrotherapy were due only to suggestion. Perhaps suggestion alone was enough, but electrotherapy was the treatment of choice for all manner of ailments, and it had been popular since the work of Volta and Galvani in the late eighteenth century.

Electrotherapy in the Treatment of Hysteria   Freud met Ida Bauer, a young woman whom he referred to as "Dora," in 1898—briefly—and in 1900 as a patient. She had experienced electrotherapy prior to her experience with Freud. Her case has been cited as an example of the misogyny of the time and of the practices of medicine common in the late nineteenth century. Freud mishandled her case, and his "Fragment of an Analysis of a Case of Hysteria" is sometimes used as an example of his forthrightness.

"Dora" had been a clinical case since childhood. Her loss of voice, coughing, and hoarseness had begun when she was eight, accompanied by migraine headaches through adolescence. When episodes of lost voice occurred, she was initially mute, with slow regaining of voice over three to five weeks. She also suffered from gastric pains, constipation, and irregular menstruation. Her family had the means to provide medical care, and many physicians had sought physical bases for her ailments, but nothing was found, and no treatments had helped. She was brought to Freud when almost eighteen with a strong antipathy toward physicians and a skepticism that their treatments would help her.

Freud had used electrotherapy only from 1886 to 1888 and substituted hypnosis and then psychoanalysis by the time that Dora was his patient. However, she had received electrotherapy previously, since the diagnosis of hysterical symptoms and the possession of money for the best treatment meant that electrotherapy was imperative. "Faradic treatment" was no pleasure (Erb, in Decker 1991, pp. 8–13).

The patient removed most of her clothing and sometimes wore a light gown. She sat on a chair with her bare feet on a flat, moistened electrode (or in a basin of water) connected to the negative end of a magnetic coil. The positive electrode was either a round, sponge-covered rod or the therapist's own hand, transmitting current from the electrode held in his other hand.

For ten- to twenty-minute sessions electric current would be applied over the body, beginning with the forehead, then the temples, the top of the head, the back of the head and neck, and slowly up and down the spinal column. The neck was stimulated separately, as were the chest and abdomen. The aim was to cause contraction of both the skeletal muscles and the visceral muscles, including those of the intestines. The peristalsis of the intestines was stimulated, so that waves of contractions could be felt and gurgling could be heard.

All varieties of patient reactions occurred—some felt refreshed and symptom free, while others were nauseous, dizzy, or faint. Repeated treatments usually left minor burns and redness of the skin, which sometimes peeled. Many patients benefited tremendously, with abatement of whatever symptoms brought them to the electrotherapist. Dora's speech problem was treated by direct electrical stimulation of the muscles of the larynx, a procedure that caused many to regain their voices. Patients often endured two to four treatments per week over periods ranging from two to six months.

The Change to Hypnosis Freud was more successful with hypnosis, which had impressed him since his student days, when he watched an exhibition by Hansen the "magnetist." The cataleptic rigidity, pallor, and other symptoms could be produced and removed, as he had seen done by Charcot in Paris. Even the use of suggestion alone seemed to work wonders in the hands of Liebeault and Bernheim—the "Nancy School" in France. Freud was now outside the medical establishment anyway, so the contempt for hypnosis and suggestion shown by the "professors of psychiatry" probably added to its appeal for him.

When he decided to use hypnotic suggestion, rather than the "haphazard and unsystematic psychotherapeutic methods" of his day, he was leaving what he had considered "real" medicine—the treatment of organic diseases. But that was no matter, since there were few patients with genuine organic nervous diseases and there were "crowds of neurotics, whose number seemed further multiplied by the way in which they hurried, with their troubles unsolved, from one physician to another" (Freud's autobiography, in Gay 1989, p. 9).

Hypnosis was also a lot of fun and provided the reputation of being a miracle worker. Nonetheless, Freud was not as good at it as he might have been and failed with some patients altogether. He went to Nancy, France, in 1889 and spent several weeks watching kindly old Auguste Liebeault working among the women and children of the lowest classes. Watching Hippolyte Bernheim's astonishing success with hospital patients, Freud was profoundly impressed with the possibility that powerful mental processes lay hidden from consciousness.

However, even these therapists had their limits. Freud had brought along a female patient "who had been handed over to me because no one else knew what to do with her." He had made her existence tolerable through "hypnotic influence," but she always relapsed, and he assumed that he had failed to hypnotize her deeply enough. Bernheim himself tried several times but achieved no more success than had Freud. He admitted to Freud that his success was much greater with hospital patients than with his private patients.

A Second Use for Hypnosis Liebeault, Bernheim, and others, including Freud, had used hypnosis to treat symptoms—to make the lame walk and the blind see—it was the suggestive influence that was important, with hypnosis merely increasing the effect. However, Freud had always used hypnosis in a second way, as an aid in questioning patients about the origin of symptoms, which otherwise seemed little known to the patient. The "monotonous procedure of suggestion" (Gay 1989, p. 11) was used to remove the symptoms, while hypnosis "satisfied the curiosity of the physician, who, after all, had a right to learn something of the origin of the phenomenon which he was striving to remove."

"Anna O." and the Beginnings of Psychoanalysis He began this method while still a worker in Brücke's laboratory and met Josef Breuer, formerly a distinguished researcher in physiology.[7] When Freud met him, he was a highly respected family physician in Vienna. Freud was impressed with Breuer's intelligence, and they soon became friends and collaborators. Breuer described a case of hysteria that he had treated in such a way as to penetrate to the real causes of hysteria.

When Freud later went to Paris he told Charcot of this case, but the "great man" showed no interest, and Freud forgot about it.

He later pressed Breuer for details of the case, involving a young girl of unusual intelligence who fell ill while nursing her father, to whom she was devoted. She suffered various paralyses and states of mental confusion, which, by chance, Breuer found were relieved when she described the fantasies she was currently experiencing. Breuer began a program of hypnosis and made her tell him what was bothering her whenever an attack occurred.

She could not connect life events and her symptoms when not hypnotized, but when she was, she immediately "discovered the missing connection." They always went back to events during her nursing of her father. While at her father's sickbed, some thought or impulse would come up and she would suppress it. Usually it required a number of such occurrences before she experienced a symptom, such as inability to speak German, paralysis of an arm, coughing, anesthesias, anorexia, and others. Under hypnosis, Breuer was able to bring to light the traumatic scenes responsible and the symptoms vanished. Breuer called the method catharsis, after Aristotle's term for the purging of emotions, and the patient, Bertha Pappenheim, called it "the talking cure." In fact, those were her words, since she was unable to speak German at that time!

Freud pressed Breuer for details of the case, known to him as "Anna O.," since Breuer wanted to preserve her anonymity. However, "over the final stage of this hypnotic treatment there rested a veil of obscurity, which Breuer never raised for me; and I could not understand why he had so long kept secret what seemed to me an invaluable discovery instead of making science the richer for it" (Gay 1989, p. 12). Nonetheless, Freud sought "Anna's" suppressed emotional episodes in his other patients, at first through hypnosis, and later through free association. He invariably found confirmation in every case and proposed to Breuer that they publish together. In 1893 they published a paper, "On the Psychical Mechanism of Hysterical Phenomena," and in 1895 their famous book, *Studies in Hysteria*, was published.

What Happened to Anna?   Carl Jung said in 1925 that Freud had told him privately that Anna had not actually been cured, and in the 1970s Henri Ellenberger completed the story. Ellenberger was a historian of psychiatry at the University of Montreal, who sought out the records on Bertha Pappenheim, Anna O.'s real name. Pappenheim had become a pioneer in social work in Germany during the 1930s, and the German government issued a stamp in her name decades later.

Ellenberger found records in a Swiss sanitarium showing that she was admitted there as a patient soon after ending her treatment under Breuer. The records showed that she had several relapses over the years, with the same symptoms that were assumed to have been cured (Goleman 1990, pp. 85–89). Pappenheim was Breuer's patient, not Freud's, and Breuer was clearly glad to be rid of her by the time that treatment ended. She had fallen in love with him, and the long periods he spent with her were greatly objected to by his wife. Pappenheim "objected too," in her typical hysterical physical manifestation, by appearing pregnant—presumably with Breuer's child—and was referred to the asylum discussed by Ellenberger.

The Founding of Psychoanalysis

If the account I have so far given has led the reader to expect that the *Studies in Hysteria* must, in all essentials of their material content, be the product of Breuer's mind, that is precisely what I myself have always maintained and what it has been my aim to repeat here. (Gay 1989, pp. 12–13)

Freud went on to point out that little was said of sexuality, though the case histories that he contributed mentioned sexual factors, but overall sexuality was attended to no more than were other emotional "excitations." When Breuer retired from this work, Freud wrote that "I became the sole administrator of his legacy" (Gay 1989, p. 13).

When Breuer and Freud separated, Freud interpreted it as due to Breuer's unwillingness to take the strong criticism that was directed at the *Studies*, as well as to demands of his normal work as a physician and family doctor. However, the most important factor was Breuer's disagreement with Freud's emphasis on sex as the basis for neurosis.

Freud became increasingly convinced that sexual factors were responsible for hysteria, and in 1914, while writing the "History of the Psycho-Analytic Movement," he thought back to remarks along those lines made by Breuer, Charcot, and others. They had told him "more than they knew themselves or were prepared to defend.... What I heard from them lay dormant and inactive within me, until the chance of my cathartic experiments brought it out as an apparently original discovery" (Gay 1989, p. 14). The deriving of hysteria from sexuality was actually a "going back to the very beginnings of medicine and following up a thought of Plato's," he learned later when reading an essay by Havelock Ellis.

Investigating the sexual life of his patients did not make Freud the most popular doctor in Vienna, but over time he became convinced that the neurasthenic patients that he saw were divisible into two forms of sexual malfunction—roughly abstinance and overindulgence—and the remedy of the sexual problem was necessary for the cure of the neurosis.

Out with Hypnosis   One day a female patient woke from a hypnotic session and threw her arms around Freud's neck, convincing him that hypnosis was an unwise practice that should be abandoned at once. Freud considered and rejected the possibility that he might have an "irresistible personal attraction." Hypnosis was not the method for him. But how to replace it? It had seemed essential as an aid in the recalling of repressed memories, necessary for cathartic treatment.

However, Freud remembered watching Bernheim at Nancy, whose patients claimed to have no memory of events that occurred during hypnotic sessions, which the French called "suggested sleep." Bernheim was sure that memory was there, and he insisted that the subject remember—the subject knew it all and only had to say it. When he said that and laid a hand on the subject's forehead, the forgotten memories returned in a flood.

Freud determined that this is the method he would use, insisting that the patients remember, using assurances and encouragement to force the forgotten facts to return. The new method allowed a closer view of the processes involved, and Freud was led to view the "forgotten" as the repressed that was retrievable only after overcoming resistance on the part of the patient.

Freudian Theory When It Made Sense
Based on what he knew by 1914, Freud offered a reconstruction of the process that leads to psychopathology, confining himself to a simple example. Suppose that an impulse arises in one's mind and that it is opposed by other powerful impulses—hatred toward a parent may be countered by impulses arising from the knowledge of social prohibitions against such feelings, for example. The two impulses, the "instinct" and the "resistance," would struggle briefly, and one would be conscious of this conflict. Soon the instinct would be defeated and driven out, and the energy that it held would be removed. Such a process happened many times in the lives of normal people, such as you and me, but was not the case in the experience of the neurotic.

For some reason, Freud knew not why, the ego withdrew from colliding with the instinct. It denied it access to consciousness and blocked its motor discharge, so that a hideous deed was prevented from occurring. However, the ego let the objectionable impulse keep its supply of energy—repressing it but not disarming it! Thereafter, the ego was required to protect itself against the ever-present threat of resurgence of the repressed impulse by allocating energy to keep it repressed. This was called an anticathexis, and it weakened the ego that kept it repressed.

Even so, the repressed impulse could still manifest itself in disguise, finding "means of discharge" via substitution and thus subverting the ego entirely. Freud's hysteria patients showed conversion reactions, whereby the repressed impulse expressed itself through somatic symptoms—the anesthesias and paralyses of hysteria. Such symptoms were a compromise, since the ego's resistance prevented their appearance in any but distorted form.

The "theory of repression" changed everything. Therapy was no longer concerned with just abreacting, or reexperiencing forgotten stressful events. Now the main effort was directed toward uncovering repressed acts and dealing with them. So different was this emphasis that the method of treatment was no longer called "catharsis" but became "psychoanalysis" (Gay 1989, p. 19).

Free Association   At first it was enough to overcome his patients' resistance by "insisting and encouraging," but that method was stressful for both patient and therapist and allowed too much possibility of "coaching" by the therapist. Therefore, the method of free association was substituted, in which the patient was to report whatever was thought, without consciously directing his or her thoughts and without withholding anything. However, Freud pointed out that this free association is not really free.

Resistance to expressing repressed material will still occur and will be expressed in two ways. First, the patient will object to telling everything, which is to violate the first rule—tell everything, so his reticence must be overcome. That done, the repression mechanism will ensure that the repressed material never comes to mind in pure form, only when disguised and apparently remote from its true identity. Hence, the analyst becomes an artist of interpretation and essential to the process. And the process becomes utterly uninterpretable to a spectator.

Bases of Motivation

All of our lives we seek peace and quiet. An increase in stimulation is always painful, or unpleasant, whether the increase be due to hunger and thirst or to anxiety and fear. The reduction in stimulation is always pleasant, as when we take in food or water and reduce hunger and thirst.

Instinctive urges have four characteristics that define them. Their aim (*Zeil*) is to reduce stimulation, to remove themselves, so to speak. To do this they refer to some external object (*Objekt*) that has been associated (cathected) with this instinct. The instinct has a source (*Quelle*) that must be a bodily process, such as that which signals hunger. Lastly, each instinct waxes and wanes in strength or impetus (*Drang*).

How many of these instincts are there? Freud saw many motives, like play and social motives, as derived from the fundamentals. The primal instincts are those of self-preservation (that is, ego instincts) and sexual instincts (at least, tentatively). After World War I Freud came to believe in an aggressive/self-destructive instinct, called thanatos by others.

What Is the Unconscious?

Now, too, we are in a position to state precisely what it is that repression denies to the rejected idea...namely, the translation of the idea into words which are to remain attached to the object. (In Gay 1989, pp. 562–568)

Freud's paper on the unconscious was published in 1915 when he was fifty-nine years old and possibly at the top of his form, a situation that would change radically over the next few years. He knew that the conception of an unconscious reservoir of ideas had been a key aspect of Herbart's philosophy of mind and that view had been opposed by virtually everyone. Leibniz stressed unconscious mentality, but that was long ago—Leibniz died in 1716. Only Fechner, among contemporaries, agreed that there is an active unconscious.

Freud noted that Fechner assumed that "the scene of action (*Schauplatz*) of dreams is different from that of waking...life" (Ellenberger 1956, pp. 201–214). Fechner concluded that after considering whether dreams may occur in the same landscape, but less intensely, so that they are below the threshold of waking consciousness. He decided against this, since occasionally the two or more scenes from dreams and waking alternate quickly or even occur simultaneously as in some cases of sleepwalking.

How Can We Know the Unconscious?   More than that—how can we justify the existence of the unconscious, where ideas go and remain? Wundt and his colleagues trenchantly argued against the existence of such a monstrosity, as did William James in 1890. Munsterberg said that the unconscious can be fully described in three words: "There is none." This was an idea that was not to be easily accepted, you may be sure.

Freud argued that the assumption of the unconscious was both necessary and legitimate and that numerous proofs of its existence are available. For instance, consider the gaps in consciousness and the ideas that "pop into our head" and the conclusions we reach without knowing how we did so. It is absurd to assume that every mental act is consciously experienced, yet those that are can be shown to be connected, if links are added, showing that unconscious links must exist. Much of the mind is unknown to consciousness.

Further, assuming a personal unconscious is doing no more than is done when we infer consciousness in other people. That assumption is an "inference by analogy," just as Romanes proposed, drawn on the evidence of observed utterances and actions. Or we could say that we spontaneously attribute our consciousness to others, and long ago this included animals, plants, stones, and so on. These days it extends only to animals, including other humans.

Freud proposed that we merely extend this process to ourselves, so that the dreams, "ideas out of the blue," misstatements, and the like that we notice in our own behavior are treated as the behavior of someone else—a second consciousness! Or so it seems. Actually, we find that this second "consciousness" is unlike the first; it contains alien and incredible things and is not really conscious at all. It is not "subconscious" either. It is unconscious and is only inferred by consciousness. Freud proposed that the perception of unconscious material may be as different from the actual psychic material as Kant viewed the phenomena of life to differ from the noumena that support them. "Like the physical, the psychical is not necessarily in reality what it appears to us to be." (In Gay 1989, p. 567)

How might we view the movement of ideas from unconscious to conscious? Is it better viewed as a real change in location, so that an idea is "freshly registered" in a new place? Or is it more likely a change in state of the idea, perhaps a heightening of clarity, as Titchener might put it. The choice is between topographical and functional, and Freud opts for topography only because it is easier to conceive and to talk about. The functional interpretation is probably more accurate, he wrote.

One support for the topographical, change-in-location view lies in the effects of telling a patient something that analysis has discovered to be repressed and unconscious. "You secretly hated your father," might be such an item. This has no effect on the patient, other than perhaps a quick and fresh repression of the item. It is as if ideas "go away," rather than change their function or status.

The Controversial Seduction Hypothesis During the 1980s and 1990s, a number of authors, having access to hitherto unavailable records, concluded that Freud was culpable in many instances in both his professional and private life. In particular, he was blamed for foolishness or fraud in his analysis of patients during the 1890s.

These patients suffered from obsessions or hysteria, and Freud determined that this was due to seduction in childhood, the memory of which was repressed and now producing symptoms. The patients strongly denied this, a reaction taken as confirmation, since denial frequently occurs when reference is made to repressed material. He came to view such seductions as almost a universal experience.

Later (1905) Freud would claim that the patients "told him" of the childhood sexual traumas, as they did, from his point of view. In 1914 he said that it was the influence of Charcot's theory of the traumatic origins of hysteria that led to the seduction hypothesis, though in 1895 and 1896 he objected to that theory. In any event, he abandoned the seduction theory since he came to find evidence that some subjects could not really have been seduced, and, further, he was certain that such an experience had never happened during his own childhood. His conclusion was that the patients had fantasized a seduction and repressed it—this means that repressed fantasy events are as effective in producing symptoms as are repressed memories of actual events.

Jeffrey Masson, author of *The Assault on Truth: Freud's Suppression of the Seduction Theory* (1984), argued that Freud's patients were indeed abused as children and that Freud changed to the fantasy interpretation solely to protect his friend Wilhelm Fliess from malpractice charges for his treatment of his patient, Emma Eckstein. She had complained of stomach pains and Freud had taken her to Fliess for nasal surgery, since Fliess had at the time convinced Freud of the psychic importance of that organ. He left a half-meter of gauze in her nasal cavity when he sewed her up and she hemorrhaged and nearly died.

Freud fled and was later revived with brandy. Amazingly, Eckstein remained his patient, now with stomach problems and a recurring nosebleed—even a year later. Masson claimed that Freud invented the fantasy interpretation of childhood seduction when he decided that Emma's complaints were wholly produced by fantasy. From that inauspicious beginning, fantasy gained a universal power in psychoanalytic theory.

Freud's Portrayal of the Childhood Seduction Theory   In view of the controversy that arose on the subject, it may be instructive to consult Freud's autobiography once again, where he discussed "an error into which I fell for a while and which might well have had fatal consequences for the whole of my work" (Gay 1989, pp. 3–41). He wrote that "under the influence of the technical procedure which I used at that time" most of his patients reported seductions by grown-up persons during their childhoods. For female patients, it was almost always the father who was the seducer.

Freud wrote that he believed these stories and thus felt that he had "discovered the roots of the subsequent neurosis," a conclusion that seemed supported by cases in which "relations of this kind with a father, uncle, or elder brother had continued up to an age at which memory was to be trusted" (Gay 1989, p. 20). He went on to say that "if the reader feels inclined to shake his head at my credulity, I cannot altogether blame him," though at that time Freud points out that he was encountering novelties daily and was trying to maintain a noncritical attitude. However, he then discovered that his patients' recollections were not trustworthy.

He was forced to recognize that these seductions had never taken place and that they were fantasies made up by his patients or "which I myself had perhaps forced on them." His confidence in his methods was shaken, since he still believed that the symptoms were related to childhood seductions. His conclusion, after "I had pulled myself together," was that the remembrances were fantasy and that whether real or fantasized, the neurosis was the same.[8] The seduction fantasies of his patients was, he felt, his first encounter with the Oedipus complex.

Whether his account here is truthful is the subject of late twentieth-century debate. As we will see, there is ample evidence that memories are not trustworthy, as Freud knew and as Munsterberg showed early in the twentieth century.

Later...

In 1923 Freud published *The Ego and the Id* (1923/1961), radically changing his conception of the psyche and launching the "ego psychologists." This is the origin of the popular structural conception of ego/superego/id, or "Ich," "Uber-Ich," and "Es," or "it." Now the ego itself has three levels of awareness—conscious, preconscious, and unconscious—and its work is to deal with the infantile desires of the id, the superego, existing as the constraints of conscience as internalized by the ego when it models the parents, and reality.

In this simplification, the ego reacts to threats of uncontrolled desires from the id, to the superego's unreasonable demands, and to reality's threats by manifesting anxiety. The psyche, thus simplified, becomes a battleground in which the ego reacts to anxiety by mobilizing defenses, including denial and repression, and "reason" is construed as a negotiator among battling forces of desire, self-deception, morals, and necessity. The preceding paragraphs are an edited rendition of Freud's view, with some value judgments added. In any event, Freudian theory was probably better before these "intrapsychic forces" were invented.

13 Pragmatism, Functionalism, Peirce, and James

The theory of evolution is beginning to do very good service by its reduction of all mentality to the type of reflex action. Cognition, in this view, is but a fleeting moment, a cross section at a certain point, of what in its totality is a motor phenomenon. (James, excerpted in Barrett and Aiken 1962, p. 164)

Origins of Functionalism

In 1907 James Rowland Angell of the University of Chicago defined functionalism. Angell called functional psychology "little more than a point of view, a program, an ambition" (p. 61). Its vitality came largely from its position as a protest against structural psychology and "it enjoys for the time being at least the peculiar vigor which attaches to Protestantism of any sort in its early stages before it has become respectable and orthodox" (p. 61).

He apologized for trying to characterize functional psychology, since there was nothing like unanimity among its members—but someone had to attempt to spell out what functionalists had in common. Part of what defined functionalism was "plainly discernible in the psychology of Aristotle" and in the writings of Spencer and Darwin—as well as in the name assigned to the group by Titchener. Angell's characterization of functionalism can be summarized as follows.

First, functionalism is concerned with operations, rather than contents. For example, the functionalists did not believe that mental states have the kind of permanence and stability, even momentary stability, that allows their examination. In particular, there is no storage and retrieval of thoughts.

Dewey and the Reflex Arc Concept: Aristotle in 1896

John Dewey, philosopher, psychologist, and educator at Chicago and Columbia, published a paper in 1896 entitled "The Reflex Arc Concept in Psychology." In 1942 the *Psychological Review* marked its fiftieth anniversary by asking "70 prominent psychologists" to report the twenty-five articles in the journal that they felt were the most important of the 1,434 that had been published. They were also to rank order the best five. Dewey's (1896) paper took first place (Langfeld 1943; Pronko and Herman 1982).

In that paper he attacked all those who held that we are mechanisms composed of discrete parts and those who viewed consciousness as the sum of discrete elements, such as sensations and ideas. He specifically criticized the Meynert scheme, then popular as a model for learning. (Theodur Meynert managed the Institute for Cerebral Physiology in Vienna, and Sigmund Freud worked there for a time.)

According to Meynert's theory, a child learns to avoid putting a hand into a flame because of a simple sequence of events. The sight of the flame leads to reaching, out of curiosity, and this is followed by the sensation of burning, followed by withdrawal of the hand. When the flame is next encountered, the sight calls up the idea of the burn, and the response is withdrawing rather than reaching. The sight of the flame and the sensation of the burn are associated, just as might be suggested by James Mill in the nineteenth century.

Dewey took an Aristotelian position and objected to the breaking up of the sequence into stimuli (the flame and the burn) and responses (reaching and withdrawing). He saw this as a clear instance of the error made by Plato, where mind (sensation) and body (muscular responding) are treated as separate. He proposed that the description be cast either in terms of sensation or in terms of responding, but not in terms of both sensation (or stimuli) and responses.

The sequence of events may be viewed differently in a dynamic or functional way. First, the flame is seen by the child as an attractive, shining, curiosity-arousing object, and the child reaches for it. "Seeing the flame" is not a passive thing—it is a "seeing for reaching." After the burn, it is not altogether true to say that the sight of the flame is associated with the pain of the burn. The experience actually has changed the flame. It is now an attractive, shining, curiosity-arousing, and painful thing. Our interchanges with objects give them their meanings, just as Aristotle saw sensation as actualization of potential. This view is compatible with the pragmatists' theory of meaning, stressing interactions with objects, rather than the reception of copies of them.

Thus, functionalism was concerned with *purpose*, adaptation, process, and activity—it dealt in verbs, rather than nouns. In a real sense,

Figure 13.1
James. Courtesy of the Archives of the History of American Psychology, University of Akron.

functionalism was a revival of Aristotle's thinking, a fact pointed out by many. That is why Dewey's paper on the reflex arc as a functional unit was popular. However, just because Titchener and others, including John B. Watson, gave them a name doesn't mean that they formed a coherent group. The functionalists were such a diverse group that it is pointless to trace their history in great detail.

However, the great promoter of the functional point of view was William James (shown in figure 13.1), and it is his views and those of Charles Peirce that warrant attention.

Pragmatism

...the scent of blood must be upon what you offer them, or else their interest does not wake up; the blood that is shed in our electives, fails to satisfy them very long...for them the three-year course is long enough.[1]

Charles Sanders Peirce was the son of Benjamin Peirce, Harvard mathematician, and was a physicist himself. Most of his life was spent working for the Coast and Geodetic Survey. Among his long-term

projects was the timing of pendulums at different locations and eleva-
tions in the world. This was done to precisely assess the force of gravity at these locations and so to better measure the shape of the earth.

Peirce was a difficult person and had many scrapes with his superiors. In part, this was due to the time he spent on projects unrelated to
physics. He was largely unappreciated during his lifetime, and his
temporary academic appointments were gained only because of the
influence of his kind and powerful friend, William James. He was an
intimidating man, and James wrote to his brother Henry with advice
on dealing with Peirce (Perry 1948, p. 143).

Peirce's chief achievement was the invention of *pragmatism*, the view
that formed the basis for much of the philosophy of the twentieth
century. Pragmatism in philosophy is functionalism in psychology, so
Peirce directly influenced not only James, but Dewey, Angell, and
many others. To understand pragmatism, we return to Descartes and
his attempt to determine how we can discern truth.

Peirce: How to Make Our Ideas Clear[2]

Recalling Descartes's insistence that we deal only with ideas that are
clear and distinct, Peirce (1877) asked how may logic help us to make
our ideas clear, freeing us from the vagaries of intuitions. The following excerpts may be viewed as the beginnings of pragmatism and
functionalism in philosophy and psychology, respectively. Or they
may constitute the beginnings of radical behaviorism as conceived by
Watson and later by Skinner:

> Descartes labored under the difficulty that we may seem to ourselves to have
> clear apprehensions of ideas which in truth are very hazy...no better remedy
> occurred to him than to require an abstract definition of every important
> term...and the books have ever since copied his words. There is no danger
> that his chimerical scheme will ever again be overvalued. Nothing new can
> ever be learned by analyzing definitions.
>
>   ...We have there found that the action of thought is excited by the irritation
> of doubt, and ceases when belief is attained; so that the production of belief is
> the sole function of thought. (In Barrett and Aiken 1962, p. 108)

Peirce's philosophy of pragmatism is actually a psychology of functionalism, no surprise. It defines belief, thought, and meaning in what
was then a novel manner—and a plausible one.

Peirce went on (ibid., pp. 115–117) applying the pragmatic criterion
to mechanics. He concluded with this passage:

In a recent, admired work on Analytic Mechanics (by Kirchhoff) it is stated that we understand precisely the effect of force, but what force itself is we do not understand! This is simply a self-contradiction. The idea which the word "force" excites in our minds has no other function than to affect our actions, and these actions can have no reference to force otherwise than through its effects. Consequently, if we know what the effects of force are, we are acquainted with every fact which is implied in saying that a force exists. (Ibid., p. 117)

William James did much for us, but it was he who scuttled pragmatism, redefining it so that Peirce could no longer endorse it.

William James

Professor Clifford calls it "guilt" and "sin" to believe even the truth without "scientific evidence." But what is the use of being a genius, unless with the same scientific evidence as other men, one can reach more truth than they? (In Barrett and Aiken 1962, p. 168)

James's Revision of Pragmatism
Unlike Peirce, James came to philosophy from biology and psychology, not from physical science. His treatment of pragmatism is therefore different, as signaled in his dedication of *Pragmatism* to John Stuart Mill. This is because of Mill's contributions to utilitarianism, which defines "good" action as that which promotes the greatest benefit and least suffering for the greatest number of people. James applied this to the definition of truth, such that a belief is true to the extent that its consequences are better than the consequences of lack of belief.

Hence, if my belief in Newton's laws of mechanics helps me build cannons that are accurate, Newton's laws are true. And if my belief in a religious practice has desirable consequences *for me*, that belief is justified. The communion is the literal body and blood of Christ if that belief helps me to lead my life. Despite the evidence for determinism in my conduct, if my belief in free will has benefits for me, then it is pragmatically true. Peirce would endorse the pragmatic truth of the first sentence of this paragraph, but he would surely not agree with the remaining examples!

Whether James's translation of pragmatism has therapeutic value or not, it was clearly a gross distortion of Peirce's criterion for meaning and truth in science. Furious that James had made pragmatism a mere matter of personal taste—of consequences of beliefs for individuals—

Peirce renamed his view "Pragmaticism," hoping that the name was "ugly enough to be safe from kidnappers."

The *Principles of Psychology*

James signed a contract in June of 1878 to write a book for Holt's American Science Series. The book was to be finished in two years, but Henry Holt felt misgivings about that optimistic schedule by fall of the same year.[1] The *Principles of Psychology* was finally published in 1890, twelve years after the contract was signed (Perry 1935, chapter 14). And, as James wrote the chapters, he published them as soon as each was finished (e.g., in *Popular Science Monthly*). This brought him money, but more importantly it strengthened his bid for a transfer from physiology to philosophy. He was also sick of working on one large project, writing to Stumpf in 1889, "a book hanging so long on one's hands at last gets outgrown, and even disgusting to one" (ibid., p. 71).

The *Principles* was supposed to be psychology, not metaphysics, so the mind/body question was shelved—for psychology, the commonsense notion of mind/body dualism was assumed to be true. When he subsequently considered the question again, radical empiricism resulted, and he felt forced to leave psychology and return to philosophy. He presented what was an overview of psychological thought, an overview that was influential for over a century.

What Was So Important in the *Principles*?   Virtually nothing in the book was original, and James claimed no originality (volume I, preface). All of the ideas that are normally attributed to James, from the stream of consciousness, to ideomotor action, to his analysis of the self, were taken from the writings of others, both predecessors and contemporaries. He almost always acknowledged those from whom he borrowed.

There is almost no coverage of the New Psychology of Wundt and Titchener, and the reader who searches for research results or data of any kind will not find much. Where descriptions of experimental work had to be included, as in chapter 17 ("Sensation"), James relied on a ghostwriter, and fourteen pages came "from the pen of my friend and pupil Mr. E. B. Delabarre" (1890, volume II, p. 13). James was never interested in research throughout his career—this book, like his other writings, was devoted to perceptive analyses of what were commonly considered the interesting phenomena of psychology. This was unlike other influential texts of the late nineteenth century. As one example, Bain's *The Senses and the Intellect* appeared in four editions from 1855 to 1879 and was so filled with data and "hard facts" that one wonders that anyone could be so diligent as to compile it all.

One biographer, the noted Harvard philosopher Ralph Barton Perry, excerpted letters that showed just how much James disliked research. And he strongly doubted that he could conduct it—he could not "torture my brain to devise new varieties of insipidity for publication...I was bowed down with weight of woe that I couldn't invent original investigations" (Perry 1935, p. 116). When a text did present much experimental research, James found it tedious: "Tedious not as really hard things, like physics and chemistry, are tedious, but tedious as the throwing of feathers hour after hour is tedious" (ibid., p. 119).

James's Positivism If James presented little data and if his conceptions were not original, why was his work so influential and enduring, while Bain's, though widely influential, did not endure nearly so long? James's strength comes from his unique viewpoint, which is still instructive to those of us living and working in the twenty-first century. For centuries there have been only two alternatives—the empiricist/ associationists and the rationalist/faculty positions, and he rejected both. He called his a "positivistic" view and included this in his preface of August 1890:

This book consequently rejects both the associationist and the spiritualist theories; and in this strictly positivistic point of view consists the only feature of it for which I feel tempted to claim originality.

Francis Bacon and August Comte could have contested that originality, of course, but neither was influential in 1890. James wrote as follows in the preface to the Italian translation:

We live at a time of transition and confusion in psychology as in many other things. The classic spiritualistic psychology using the soul and a number of distinct ready-made faculties as its principles of explanation, was long ago superseded by the school of association. But it still lingers...the older associationism itself retained a half scholastic character...it took the mind too statically. (Perry 1935, p. 52)

James referred frequently to both of these theories throughout the *Principles*, applying one or the other to specific cases. However, in the end, neither was acceptable.

James's positivism was described in a philosophical paper titled "What Pragmatism Means," (reprinted in Barrett and Aiken 1962), where he criticized all explanatory models fashioned in advance of what was to be explained—that is to say, rationalist models. He "turned his back" on abstraction, fixed principles, bad a priori reasons, verbal solutions, and closed systems. He turned toward concreteness, facts, action, and power. Pragmatism means "looking away from first things, principles, categories, supposed necessities; and of looking toward last things, fruits, consequences, facts" (Barrett and Aiken 1962, p. 183). Only thus can we escape the accumulation of conformity that is represented in the two classic alternatives.

James urged that we pass beyond these theories, and he wrote to Stumpf over a century ago (Perry 1935, p. 62) that we may turn from "psych-mythology and logicalism, and toward a truly empirical and sensationalistic point of view." He wanted psychology to become a "natural science," and, like all natural sciences, it must concentrate on "prediction and control" (1892, p. 149). Though he was personally no experimenter, James believed that it is facts, and not theories, that we need (ibid., p. 153). Such thoughts would be echoed by John B. Watson and B. F. Skinner, though neither saw that James was a kindred soul. However, he was one in main respects as evidenced in these excerpts from "The Sentiment of Rationality": not only is thought really activity, but meaning depends on actions (behavior) as well:

We are acquainted with a thing as soon as we have learned how to behave towards it, or how to meet the behavior which we expect from it. Up to that point it is still "strange" to us. (Barrett and Aiken 1962, p. 164)

Nine years before John B. Watson's (1913) first critique of the concept of consciousness, James wrote: "Consciousness . . . is the name of a non-entity. . . . It seems to me that the hour is ripe for it to be openly and universally discarded." James wrote that the "stream of thinking" is really the "stream of breathing" and that Kant's "I think" that accompanies experiences "is the 'I breathe' that actually does accompany them" (Barrett and Aiken 1962, p. 208). Watson believed that the introspectionist's mental life was a fiction, that seeing and hearing and remembering do not occur "inside" us. James agreed and quoted his colleague, Hugo Munsterberg:

The object of which I think, and of whose existence I take cognizance without now letting it work upon my senses, occupies its definite place in the outer world as much as does the object which I directly see. (Ibid., p. 214)

This positivist view, concentrating on phenomena, not theories, led him to some strange places. For example, he tried to communicate with the dead (Stevens 1989, pp. 76–81, 114–116) and instructed his wife to have his body photographed soon after his death, to facilitate possible communication from the beyond.

Nonetheless, the *Principles* left us with the best treatments of the major divisions of psychology that had been offered. Maybe it is the best ever offered—consider his treatment of one illustrative phenomenon.

Attention: Chapter 11 In James's opinion many theorists had ignored attention, since it interfered "with the smoothness of the tale" told by the associationist theories. However, without considering the importance of attention, we are left with a false notion of experience, which has us mentally mirroring an outer world, much as a video camera does. In fact, most of our experience is unattended, we select a minute part of it to call real and neglect the rest. That is to say, attention is selective and determines what we count as experience.

When we try to characterize attention further, we find that it is best defined with respect to its opposite, what the Germans called *Zerstreutheit*, or "scatterbrained absentmindedness." Attention is the opposite of that timeless, distracted feeling one has as one stares off into space after too many hours at the library:

Most people probably fall several times a day into a fit of something like this: The eyes are fixed on vacancy, the sounds of the world melt into confused unity, the attention is dispersed so that the whole body is felt, as it were, at once, and the foreground of consciousness is filled, if by anything, by a sort of solemn sense of surrender to the empty passing of time. In the dim background of our mind we know meanwhile what we ought to be doing: getting up, dressing ourselves, answering the person who has spoken to us, trying to make the next step in our reasoning. But somehow we cannot start; the *pensée de derrière la tête* [thought in the back of the head] fails to pierce the shell of lethargy that wraps our state about. Every moment we expect the spell to break, for we know no reason it should continue. But it does continue, pulse after pulse, and we float with it, until—also without reason that we can discover ... we wink our eyes, we shake our heads, the background-ideas become effective, and the wheels of life go round again. (James 1890, volume I, p. 405)

James described six varieties of attention defined by three characteristics. First, the object attended may be sensory or represented—that is, it may refer to a present object or a remembered one. Second, attention may be immediate or remote—as when an object is attended to for its own sake or because it represents something as does a word and its meaning. Third, attention may be passive or active—depending upon whether our attention is compelled or whether we make an "effort to attend." A loud sound that attracts attention independent of its meaning is an example of the simplest sort of attention; it is "passive-immediate-sensorial attention." Efforts to remember a name by picturing objects related to it serve as an example of "active-remote-represented attention."

Voluntary (active) attention is essentially what Wundt meant by apperception, and James believed that such attention can be maintained for no more than a second or so (Wundt would agree) unless the object changes. This, he suggested, tells us something of the difference between a dullard and a genius. The genius can attend to what seems to be an unchanging object, such as the riddle of the meaning of life, because the genius sees endless new features of the object and that effectively makes it an ever-changing object. The dullard sees the same "object" without embellishments and hence as an unchanging object. Such a person cannot attend long and seeks constantly changing situations—"a job where I meet new people every day," since otherwise, attention flags. The genius provides change, while the dullard must have it imposed from actual changes in the object.

Attention is the most important "activity of the mind," and it takes many forms. James's arrangement is the most complete and satisfying—and it illustrates the multitude forms that attention takes.

Bain's Law of Diffusion—Key to James's Thought   Chapter 23 of the *Principles* is indispensable introduction to the two famous chapters that follow—that deal with instinct and with emotion. Many later critics of those two chapters could have better understood James's rationale had they read it. It is titled "The Production of Movement" and presents the law of diffusion, as proposed by Bain. According to that law, every impression, be it produced by an external stimulus or by a train of ideas, produces movement of the whole organism. Bain referred to a "general agitation":

> ...*movement of the entire organism, and of each and all its parts.... A process set up anywhere in the centres reverberates everywhere, and in some way or other affects the organism throughout, making its activities greater or less.* (1890, volume 2, pp. 372, 381)

This effect can appear as an inhibition, but it is usually an augmenting. For example, *blood pulsing* from an open vein or artery can be made to flow faster if accompanied by a faster drumbeat. The sound and cadence of the drum obviously affects the viscera in ways unknown to consciousness. Along the same lines, when we are filled with fear, we might notice that it is *difficult to inhale* and when we are very angry, it is *hard to exhale*. When our attention is caught suddenly, we *hold our breath*. While we sleep, a sudden noise *makes our pupils dilate*, and rage constricts them. And emotion is reflected in the perspiration on our skin surface, hence the "psycho-galvanic" response as an index of agitation.[3] All of these facts support the proposition that all stimulation produces widespread bodily effects.

Those effects affect the viscera—the respiratory and cardiovascular systems and other body parts normally under autonomic nervous system control. However, the law of diffusion applies to the somatic (voluntary) nervous system as well, at least according to data James presented. In those cases the effect is called *dynamogeny*.

When we grip a hand dynamometer that measures the force that we can exert, we find that hearing high and loud musical notes increases our force and that hearing sad and low notes decreases it. Colored lights also have an effect, with red lights particularly effective in increasing the effort we can exert. A facilitory effect is also produced by tastes, especially sour, and by odors, especially musk.

These effects of dynamogeny affect the whole body and provide part of the tone of our experience. James cited Herr Schneider, who followed Avicenna and Aquinas in distinguishing the two basic reactions—moving toward, or expansion, and moving away, or contraction. Through every moment of every day our body reacts with facilitations and inhibitions to stimulation that we hardly notice or that we do not notice at all. This constant reaction of the whole body to constantly changing stimulation, from without or within, provides the framework for James's interpretation of instinct and of emotion.

Specifically Human Instincts William James did not hesitate to assign instincts to humans, and, in fact, his may be the longest list proposed by an authoritative writer. Like Darwin, James was very casual in his interpretations and seems to have accepted the premise that anything that "everyone seems to do" is instinctive. We saw in chapter 8 that his was not the only list and that rebellion arose in the 1920s, led by those who interpreted appeals to instinct as vacuous. Nonetheless, James's list is entertainingly presented and does include many insights worth considering. In addition, his list had great influence on his contemporaries and students. One, Edward Thorndike, even *expanded* James's list and devoted a volume of his three-volume *Educational Psychology* to instinct.

Recalling James's definition of instinct as purposive activity performed for the first time without knowledge of ends, we see that even digestion and respiration would be included. Therefore, James restricted his definition to cases in which action is directed toward an external object. At birth that includes sucking, biting, licking, chewing, spitting, pointing, clasping, carrying to mouth, crying, smiling, turning the head, and locomoting. Later instincts appear as the manifestations of "ripening," or maturation.

James and a Misunderstood Theory of Emotion

James (1884) first published what was later called the "James/Lange" theory of emotion in an article in a popular journal. It was reprinted in 1890 and in a much-abbreviated and confused form in *Psychology: Briefer Course*. The briefer course was not only briefer, but markedly inferior to the original. No wonder, since James was sick to death of the long version and only reluctantly wrote the condensation of 1892. I mention that because it is through reading the 1892 work that one can understand how James's theory of emotion could be misinterpreted so, as it was by Walter B. Cannon and scores of others. Let's begin by considering just what the theory *is* and to what it was opposed.

The Theory of Emotion of the Day   James was tired of the nineteenth-century treatment of emotions as mental—psychic entities that lead to actions that can be described. Descriptions were rife in his day, catalogs of divisions and subdivisions of emotional experience and expression.

For example, "grief" was interpreted as a mental state characterized by feelings of weariness and by pallor and cold owing to contraction of blood vessels. There may initially be an acute stage, accompanied by crying and moaning, a state accompanied by some pleasure. The chronic state that follows brings no pleasure, only feelings of sorrow and respiration that is dominated by exhaling, hence by frequent sighs.

"Hatred" was another unique mental state that produced external manifestations. It produces withdrawal of the head and trunk, projecting the hands forward, contraction of eyebrows, elevation of the upper lip and a general turning away—the face shows frowning, bared teeth and perhaps clenched jaws—and there may be foot stamping, deep breathing, and repetition of a word or syllable.

One could go on forever with descriptions of emotions as unique things, and there is virtue in doing so in literature, where the object is to share feelings. However, for psychology, the descriptions are "tedious" and their "subdivisions a sham." "I should as lief read descriptions of shapes of rocks on a New Hampshire farm." What, James asked, do emotions have in common? Or are they fundamental, eternal, and unique psychic entities, so that all we can do is describe them?

James knew of the theory of Carl Lange, a Danish physiologist who published in 1885 a work that was translated as *Über Gemustsbewegungen* (roughly, "production of emotion") in 1887. Lange proposed that the experience of emotion lies in the bodily response to objects, especially the vascular system. James wrote in 1890 that "Lange is generally right." That, along with the poorly done treatment in the 1892 book, ensured that the theory would be misinterpreted for decades and that a straw theory—a caricature of Lange's—would be attacked for decades.[4] Also to blame is the sad fact that even the best-known twentieth-century psychologists did not study primary sources.

The Actual James/Lange Theory   James proposed that all of the "coarser" emotions—fear, anger, sadness, joy, and the like—require bodily sensations for their normal experience. Unless one has been schooled in the opposite way, in the manner of the mentalists of then and now, this is obvious. What is fear without changes in breathing, a pounding heart, and cringing from the object of fear? *But* those bodily sensations are *not* the whole thing.

The mentalists say emotion is a mental thing, like a sensation, or a thought. For them, situations produce emotion as a mental state and that provokes the bodily expression. That is,

perception → emotion → bodily expression.

Recall that James believed in Bain's law of diffusion, which holds that all stimulation affects the whole body. Therefore, perceptions affect the whole body, and that effect is part of our normal experience. The sequence of events in the James/Lange theory is

perception → bodily expression → "feeling emotion."

How could it be otherwise, and why was there ever any fuss over it? Consider an example. I lose my fortune, I weep, and I am sad. Three things are involved as in any emotional experience. First comes the percept, whether it is the spectacle of my fortune seeping away or being stolen or just the idea of it. In other cases, the percept is an uncaged bear charging me or a fist raised in anger or the sight of a helpless child in danger. The second feature is the bodily reaction, which may be sobbing and wailing, running, striking out, bending to help, or whatever.

This includes *both skeletal muscles and the viscera*, of course. As I run from the bear, my heart is pounding and my pupils are dilated—both the skeletal/somatic and the autonomic nervous systems are working.

The combination of the percept, the sensations of muscles working, and the visceral feelings forms an experience that we call an emotion. "Fear" is impossible without cardiovascular feelings and muscle tensions, and joy is impossible without smiling and the tendency to laugh. There is no feeling of worry with a smooth brow and no feeling of embarrassment without feelings of pressure in the throat. These "instinctive reactions" are absolutely necessary for the normal experience of emotion. And, since bodies differ and the response of the "organic sounding board" takes many forms, *the number of emotions is infinite*, and conventional classifications are only approximations.

James on Will   A beginner in psychology might do well to read this long chapter to decide whether psychology is the major to choose. It is clear and profound and as interesting as psychology gets. If one dislikes it, change in major is warranted. The following is a brief summary, by no means a substitute for the original.

To begin with, voluntary (willed) action is always *secondary*—primary acts must occur before they can be willed. They happen either because they are reflexes, or instincts, or emotional reactions. The sensations of kinesthesia and proprioception that accompany movements are in fact the "memory images" of the movements, left behind as a supply of ideas of movements. Most importantly, these ideas are *aftereffects* of movement, feedback, rather than the feeling of the motor impulse itself.

Wundt had argued for the phenomenal existence of the *Innervationsgefühl*, or the feeling of the motor impuse sent from the brain via the spinal cord to the muscles. Many accepted the possibility of such a feeling, but James did not, and we know now that he was correct. There are no sensory receptors that could handle such input, only the kinesthetic and proprioceptive systems that signal muscular movement that has already occurred. Not only Wundt, but Bain, Mach, and even Helmholtz subscribed to the "motor feeling" position. Because of the prominence of Wundt's position, James was forced to argue against it "at tedious length."

James pointed out that motor feelings are unnecessary, since movements are often "knocked out of us," and even surprise us. Also, skilled performances are accomplished unconsciously—who can imagine the skilled pianist or marksman consciously controlling each movement. It is the *end* that is attended to. Even the seemingly powerful evidence in favor of a motor feeling is faulty. For example, the "feeling of exertion" when we make a fist is reported even by those paralyzed, for whom no feedback can occur because no movement occurs. Yet, that feeling can always be referred to other muscles that *are* tensing. The English physiologist Ferrier showed that these "feelings of effort" in a paralyzed limb evaporate when normal breathing is maintained, so that the respiratory muscles are not tensed.

On the other hand, when we are anesthetic, we cannot discriminate forces, weights, and the width of a grasped book. Feedback from movement and information on body position are necessary. Since there is no motor feeling, it can contribute nothing, and that is easily shown. When we grasp an unseen book and squeeze it, we can more or less accurately judge the number of pages or the width in inches of the book being grasped. However, we can do it as well even when a rubber band is wrapped around our fingers, adding to the force of the grip or when rubber bands pull outward, lessening that force. If such distortions of force make no difference, then force—motor feeling—cannot be important.

James described an example from his own experience that illustrates ideomotor action. The basic principle is that the idea of a movement, once dominant in consciousness, inevitably produces the movement, independent of any "feeling of motor innervation." He asked us to imagine getting "out of bed on a freezing morning" in a room without a fire and notice how the very vital principle within us opposes the act. We feel the warmth of the bed and the blankets and the cold on those parts of us uncovered.

These feelings lead to remaining in bed, of course. Opposed to those powerful feelings of warmth and cold and the motor effects they produce is the idea that we must get up, we have duties to perform and those will be harder to carry out the longer that we stay in bed. However, those ideas are weak and remote—no match for the feelings of warmth and cold that keep us in bed. Hence we stay in bed and never do get up.

However, we *do* get up, despite the domination of the powerful feelings of warmth and cold and their attendant motor effects. How does that happen? James, referring to what happens in "my own person," suggests that we doze off, so that the warmth and cold become less clear and those ideas of arising, the gains and penalties of arising and sleeping in, gain a hearing. We find that we are up. The ideas that would get us up needed only their chance, and they then do their work. He suggested that an aid to getting up lies in imagining as clearly as we can what it feels like to be standing by our bed, so that such ideas can produce motor effects when given a chance.

James noted that this applies to mind readers' methods. When the mind readers of his day (or ours) "read" the contents of a subject's mind by announcing the "thought of word," they received help from the facial expressions of the subject. Typically, the mind reader chatted with the subject, so as to "put the subject at ease." In the course of the chat, the performer would mention a number of words that could produce reactions from the subject. These would provide clues to the mind reader. Edward Thorndike, a graduate student of James's, originally planned a doctoral dissertation on this subject, using children as subjects.

Hedonism and Will   Hedonism is the doctrine that bases for all motivation are pleasures and pains. It was indeed Thomas Hobbes's view in the seventeenth century and, without worrying about it much, John Locke agreed. Subsequent British writers followed that path, and hedonism became synonymous with "British hedonism." During the nineteenth century, it was Spencer and Bain who most clearly espoused hedonism.[5]

James opposed this simpleminded doctrine, as he had to if he was to discuss will—hedonism had been *the* theory of will for some centuries.[6] He wrote that pleasure and pain might be the only comprehensible, reasonable, and ethical motives, but they are surely not the only psychological motives. It is not just that pleasure and pain are too vague and all-encompassing, James felt, but that many motives have nothing to do with them.

In the context of ideomotor action, pleasures and pains would be a prime source of the attention-getting power of ideas. According to this view, we act because ideas of pleasant outcomes guide us and ideas of painful outcomes repel us. That doctrine is a *great mistake*, and pleasures and pains are far from the only source of the power of ideas—

even if they really were motives. In fact, pleasures and pains play no part in our first acts—reflexes—nor in the last—habits. The most that they do is modify action that is already occurring for other reasons—as James noted, this view was earlier noted by Hume.

If there is to be one name for all the myriad sources of the power of ideas, James suggested that it be called *interest*. That includes things that are morbidly fascinating, tediously haunting, and mawkishly silly—such things may capture our attention whether we like it or not, and we find ourselves humming jingles promoting chewing gum or soft drinks. Are such things pleasant? Do we sniff a stink on purpose or seek danger or touch the wound to see whether it still hurts because they are pleasant? If the answer is yes, then pleasure loses whatever meaning it might have had. To say that ideas have "interest" is to confess our ignorance of all the contributors to the power of ideas.

Building a Strong Will If ideas prompt action, then free will would be the ability to determine what ideas are thought—to attend to them. That is true, but more difficult than it seems, due to the competition among ideas. For example, imagine the chance that is had for a good idea, such as acting prudently, when one is in the grip of an unwise passion, such as deciding to "make a fortune dealing in distressed real estate."

Herbart was wrong, and there is no literal "war of ideas," but it is true that the ability of an idea to have a hearing and to be attended to depends on its congruence with other ideas that are present. Reason has "a corpse-like finger" under such circumstances, and we find "cooling advice exasperating." We recoil from reason and push back the ideas that mean "halt," "go back," "forget it," "give up," "leave off," "sit down." All that a strong-willed person can do is exert a little more effort of attention and hold to the reasonable idea long enough to allow its reinforcements to enter. James wrote that if one can keep it from "flickering out" until it fills the mind, then the job is done and the wise "self-control" act is carried out. The relation is not that of mind to matter—rather, it is the self and its own states of mind. Train yourself to pay attention.

Is the Will Ever Free? This question boils down to the relation of the effort of attention and the object attended to. Is the effort always a function of the object—making will completely determined—or may it be free of it, at least, once in a while? Do we choose to believe that will is determined when it suits our purpose? For example, suppose that one spends weeks of thought beforehand and then commits a cowardly, dirty, and cruel act. Remorseful afterward, the miscreant decides that, after all, his will and thus his act is determined and blame need not be assigned. We feel that we act consciously and freely in daily situations and that we freely choose among alternatives. But often we see that our action was inevitable and that the feeling of free will was a delusion. Why isn't free will a delusion everywhere that it supposedly occurs? Is it all chimerical?

James knew that there is no answer to this question—the problem is insoluble on psychological grounds—forever beyond human reach. That said, he chose to believe in freedom of the will for esthetic and practical reasons. If we believe that will is not free, we are prone to a self-defeating fatalism, one that provides excuse for failure but that promotes our collapse to masses of yielding plaintiveness and fear. Belief in freedom allows us to be heroic, to face the world's tests and to be one of the lords and masters of the universe—a force to be reckoned with.[7] James ended the discussion of will by emphasizing that all of this—the most important topic in psychology—concerns our ideas, not mind and/or matter. "We call the more abundant mass of ideas ourselves," refer to our effort, and call the smaller mass of ideas "resistance." However, both the effort and resistance are ours "and to identify the self with *one* of them is an illusion and a trick of speech." That is surely something to think about.

Practical Realities   For most of us, the world of practical realities is the world of sense, and other worlds, like that of religion, are real, but with a "less real reality" (1890, volume II, p. 293). James agreed with Hume—belief is lively and active, an emotional reaction. When we find much that interests and excites us, we respond to many things as real. That which holds no interest is rubbishy and negligible. Do any of us care about the close acquaintances of Andrew Jackson? A few historians care very much, but for most of us such a topic has no reality at all.

Our sensations are real to us, and they depend upon our body, which has instincts that are very interesting to us. Certain things capture our attention and make us act—these things are real. Consider what is more and less real—a current ache and the cousin of Andy Jackson—and you will see that reality has a few simple characteristics. That is, here is what produces *belief* that what we are considering is real:

1. We believe in the reality of something that captures our attention and holds it.

2. We believe in things that are lively and vivid, especially when they are connected with pleasures and pains.

3. We believe in things that make us react, especially with instincts, like fear or revulsion or curiosity.

4. In other words, *real* things produce emotional interest, whether it be love, dread, or happiness.

5. Real things are congruent with our expectations.

Sometimes we believe in spirits conjured up by mediums, but we have to see and hear some manifestation of the lost soul. Our emotion and hopeful anticipation means that it does not take too much to convince us. Some churches use icons and relics from saints to aid in belief. Photos, chalk marks on the pavement, and being shown "the very knife" arouse the believing reaction, and all that we need is a suspect!

It was Renouvier, a favorite source for James, who referred to a "mental vertigo," the fostering of belief since passion is present. "Nothing false can feel like that!" Such an effect led to the atrocities committed by mobs who, in a passion, become convinced that "He did it!" or that "She is a witch." Give us something that makes us respond with our limbs and with our viscera and we believe it—thrust your hand into a fire and fire becomes more real than one could want. That applies to belief in the fire that burns us and to religious conversion. There is no "really real" reality, but there are things that we believe in, and they are as real as anything can be.

That seems unsatisfying, of course, but it's the truth.

Radical Empiricism

My thesis is that if we start with the supposition that there is only one primal stuff or material in the world, a stuff of which everything is composed, and if we call that stuff "pure experience," then knowing can easily be explained as a particular sort of relation towards one another into which portions of pure experience may enter. (James, in Wilshire 1971, p. 163)

Protagoras and Aristotle were epistemological monists, opposing the division between knower and known that was the trademark of the dualists, the Pythagoras/Plato position. As we have seen, virtually all subsequent thinkers followed Pythagoras and Plato, and the belief in a "mind" with faculties that operates the "machine of the body" is still the establishment viewpoint.

Radical empiricism is similar to the monism of Protagoras and
Aristotle and the empiricism of David Hume. Reality is our personal
experience, and that comes from our senses. The sum of empirical experience is the self—there is nothing more, and if there were, we can
never know it.

James wrote his pieces on radical empiricism during the last two
decades of his life. These works led, upon his death in 1910, to a movement at Harvard composed of a group of philosophers interested in
epistemology. They called themselves "the new realists" and argued
against the idealism of Oxford and of American universities. Following
James, they rejected dualism, both metaphysical and epistemological.
That is, they did not believe in a distinction between mind and body
and they did not believe in a distinction between subject and object. In
these ways they followed Protagoras and Aristotle against Plato and
his successors.

One member of the group was Edwin B. Holt, an important thinker
for many reasons, who was already discussed for his Aristotelian
views. He also co-edited a book composed of chapters written by him
and by his colleagues (Holt et al. 1912). The quote below gives the flavor of his writing style. Holt's title, "The Place for Illusory Perceptions
in a Realistic World," is descriptive. His thesis is difficult to describe
to a reader who does not accept radical empiricism but holds that there
is no illusory experience. This goes further than did Aristotle's view,
which asserted that there is no illusory sensation, but imagination
can produce fictions, just as Hume and others held many centuries
later. There is also no distinction between mind and body or between
knower and known:

The line that separates the existent and the nonexistent, or the false and the
true, or good and evil, or the real from the unreal, seldom coincides, and *never
significantly* coincides with the line that distinguishes mental and non-mental,
subject and object, knower and known. (p. 373)

14 Twentieth-Century Applied Psychology and Early Behaviorism

There are only two schools of psychology, one of them is Thorndike's and the other one isn't. (Joncich 1968, p. 527)

During the early decades of the twentieth century, American psychology was quickly and thoroughly dominated by behaviorist theories, originally those of Edward L. Thorndike and John B. Watson. In fact, their two views were profoundly different, but both emphasized the understanding of behavior, rather than conscious experience, and both denied that mental events "cause" our behavior. Beyond that similarity, they shared few features.

Thorndike's was a mediational theory—just as Locke had proposed that all of our knowledge is mediated by ideas, Thorndike's mediators were S-R connections. Learning was the strengthening of habits, and habits ultimately accounted for everything. This mediational view was carried on by other learning theorists, including Clark Hull. Just after the middle of the century it was translated into cognitive-sounding terms and became "cognitive science." In its many guises it has persisted as mainstream psychology. We first consider the progenitor of the mediational theories of the twentieth century. Thorndike's theory is still current in textbooks, unlike many theories that followed.

Thorndike's Connectionism

Play all you need to, rest all you need to, and work all the rest of the time.... coffee, cigarettes, and a black horse are all I want. (Joncich 1968, p. 575)

Edward Lee Thorndike was born in Williamsburg, Massachusetts, in 1874, the son of a Methodist minister. His experience as a "pathologically shy" youth convinced him that it is the period from eighteen to twenty-two that is the crucial formative period of life, not early child-hood, as conventionally believed. He attended Wesleyan University at a time when science was so poor in America that the texts in physics and chemistry were translations of the French originals.

As a graduate student at Harvard in 1885 he was converted from English to psychology by William James's course. By 1887 he was set on carrying out a dissertation on mind reading, using children as subjects and studying the subtle changes in facial expression that give away the "contents of the mind."

That project, on which he was to be assisted by Delabarre, was judged unacceptable, and he was urged to conduct animal research. Once he had obtained chickens as subjects, it appeared that Harvard had no space to house them, and they were kept for a time in William James's basement—until Alice James could stand them no longer. Seeking more hospitable surroundings, he left Harvard and enrolled at Columbia University.

He arrived at Seth Low Hall in New York, from which he was chased away, while resting with a basket he brought from Springfield, containing the "most educated hens in the world." He lived in a shanty at 159 West 108th Street with animals all around him. After graduation he spent a year on the faculty of Case Western Reserve and then joined the faculty at Teacher's College, Columbia University. It was there he spent the remainder of his forty-three-year career.

Thorndike's Career and Place in History

Thorndike is usually described as the advocate of the law of effect—the use of rewards and punishments—and as the one who showed that cats could learn to escape from puzzle boxes. While both of those statements are true, they are not especially significant, since many others had studied animal problem solving and the law of effect was certainly not news. We saw in chapter 8 that both Spencer and Bain had discussed trial-and-error learning, as had Lloyd Morgan—all decades before Thorndike's work. That being the case, why was Thorndike so famous? Why did his dissertation, *Animal Intelligence*, published as a monograph, draw such attention?

He was the first to argue against *mentalism*, the doctrine of the causal efficacy of ideas, while simultaneously showing that scientific methods can be applied to the whole subject matter of psychology. Not only learning, but memory, perception, wants, needs, attitudes, and the whole field of education were part of Thorndike's vision of psychology. And he cultivated that field like no one had before and like few have done since.

He published 102 items during the first twelve years of his marriage, including twelve books and monographs. Ultimately, over 450 books, monographs, and articles adorned his vitae—Thorndike was a man whose goal was to get to "the top of the heap" (Joncich 1968), and publishing was the way to do it. Most of his classroom notes, in fact, were written up and published right away. He wrote introductory psychology books, books on testing (1904) and educational psychology (1903), and textbooks for secondary schools.

When his son came home from school with a dictionary that routinely used obscure and difficult words to define simple ones, so that a candle might be defined as a "cylinder of tallow," he set about compiling a list of words and definitions that did not suffer such flaws. In 1921 he published the *Teacher's Wordbook* of 10,000 words, followed by a 20,000-word version in 1931.

He was critical of the arithmetic books of the day that were boring and abstract and so wrote books that were filled with practical problems. By 1918 the *Thorndike Arithmetics*, with less drill and more "hierarchical habit systems," had sold an estimated five million copies. At one point, they were adopted by the boards of education of every state in the union! Royalties from the sale of all of these books eased the pains of the Depression for the Thorndikes, since they exceeded his salary by several times.

He was an educator who believed that lectures were generally a waste of time for all concerned—the most and best learning comes from reading and doing. Though he is known for his application of the law of effect, a conception that is usually associated with environmentalism, he was a staunch hereditarian, who frequently suggested that eighty percent of what we call intelligence is inherited. He was also one of the first to define intelligence as "what intelligence tests measure" (Joncich 1968, p. 418).

When asked in the 1940s by the State of New York how they might best spend money in education, he replied that teachers should pick out the budding Darwins, Faradays, and Newtons who turn up in their classes and place all of their resources in them (Joncich 1968, p. 484). The rest will not benefit from education. He picked only the brightest graduate students and then left them alone. When he heard that an exceptionally bright graduate student was in the New York City area, he sought him out, attracted him to Columbia, and gave him his own office (Joncich 1968, p. 482)! The student, Abraham Maslow, was grateful for the rest of his life.

The Case against Mentalism
William James, Thorndike's own mentor and favorite teacher, was guilty of promoting the most egregious mentalism of the turn of the century. In 1890 James proposed, in his famous treatment of "Will," that mental entities produce bodily movements—that thoughts cause actions. This doctrine of ideomotor action was repugnant to Thorndike, and it was one of his first targets—in *Animal Intelligence* in 1898 and in his 1913 American Psychological Association presidential address. For Thorndike, this was nonsense, not because we don't have mental activity, but because that activity is activity, not "thoughts" that cause activity.

This means that our hopes, expectations, thoughts, moods, imaginations, and so forth are things that we do, just as we walk, talk, and write. Treating the mind as activity and doing research to study that activity was truly original with Thorndike. Aristotle's functioning was finally competing with Plato's being; psychology was activity, not content. The practical importance of this was plain—if we have methods to change behavior, so that we can adjust the hour that a student arises in the morning, we can change the same student's skill in geometry, if mathematical reasoning is also behavior. As he wrote:

Selective thinking, the management of abstractions and responsiveness to relations are are thus contrasted too sharply with memory, habit, and association by contiguity. As has been suggested, and as I shall try to prove later, the former also are matters of habit, due to the laws of readiness, exercise and effect. (Thorndike 1913, pp. 27–28)

Animal Intelligence
Borrowing the title of Romanes's popular book of a few decades before, Thorndike published his famous monograph in 1898, under the direction of the famous hereditarian and mental tester, James M. Cattell. His work began with the animals in "problem boxes."

Cats, dogs, and chicks were studied in twenty-seven problem situations—fifteen for cats, nine for dogs, and three for chicks. The cats and dogs were confronted with confinement in crude slatted boxes, where the object was to find a means of escape. That would be a lever, or string, or panel, depending on the box. The chicks' problems were confined to simple mazes, constructed of books stood on end. What did he find that made him so famous?

First, he attacked the "despised theory" that animals reason and that this is easily shown by observing them. His cats were clever New York City alley cats, placed in an enclosure that called for insight—spot the release mechanism and escape. However, the cats, though furious to escape, required minutes for the first escape, substantial time for the second and successive escapes, and an average of twenty trials to show "insight." After twenty trials, escapes occurred after six to eight seconds. If their behavior was "insightful," then insight is a slow process.

Second, Thorndike showed that selecting and connecting, the law of effect, could account for much more than had been anticipated by Herbert Spencer, Alexander Bain, and Conwy Lloyd Morgan when they proposed that trial-and-error learning occurred in animals.

Third, he elaborated on the law of effect, through his subsidiary laws, extending its power greatly. Here his associationism reached the subtlety of John Stuart Mill. In addition, Thorndike considered ways in which the law of effect—satisfiers and annoyers—might work. We will consider these contributions below, beginning with the law of effect, which, rightly or wrongly, is forever attached to Thorndike's name.

What Is the Law of Effect?   According to the law of effect, many behaviors are sensitive to their consequences; "satisfiers" following a behavior bond that behavior to the situation in which it occurred. When an "annoyer" follows a behavior, the connection between situation and behavior is weakened. Herbert Spencer, Alexander Bain, and Conwy Lloyd Morgan had made much of such trial-and-error learning. But what is a "trial?" A better description would be "success and error" learning, as Thorndike noted.

And then, what is "success?" Spencer, Bain, and Morgan had settled on adaptive action, represented by its ambassador, pleasure, as the criterion for success, and Thorndike seemed to accept this hedonistic interpretation. Why else would he have used "satisfiers and annoyers" to refer to the consequences of action? And who doubts that those terms are pretty much synonymous with pleasures and pains?

However, that was the thoughtless error of a twenty-four-year-old, and it was an error that was quickly righted. And it *was* a thoughtless error—Thorndike used variations of the word "right" as the most frequent satisfier to be used with people. Such a satisfier does not produce what we usually consider to be sensory pleasures and pains. The law of effect is not the "law of affect," as construed by some critics. Such criticism applies only to earlier conceptions of trial and error, such as Spencer's and Bain's. If satisfiers need not be pleasant, what must they be? What must they have in common?

In 1913 Thorndike proposed that some satisfiers and annoyers owe their power to heredity. For human beings, things like being with others, moving when refreshed, resting while tired, eating when hungry, and being partially covered when in bed are innate satisfiers. However, most satisfiers, from praise to money to fame, are not innately determined, as we see when we apply them to an infant or to adults under many conditions. Perhaps satisfiers and annoyers are better defined in terms of their effect on behavior. Thorndike wrote:

By a satisfying state of affairs is meant roughly one which the animal does nothing to avoid, often doing such things as will attain and preserve it. By an annoying state of affairs is meant roughly one which the animal avoids or changes. (1913, p. 2)

However, what do all the "states of affairs" that act as satisfiers at a given time have in common? Thorndike strove to answer this question by reference to what he called original behavior series. These were sequences of activities usually determined innately, such as pouncing on prey. But this also referred to an infant's grasping of a toy or the toy's withdrawal as satisfying and annoying, respectively. Successful operation means that a behavior series was not thwarted and the satisfying effect thus occurs.

Unless we can say more about successful operation, we are left with satisfaction defined as "ending with a satisfier." Thorndike never did solve the problem of independently defining satisfiers and annoyers, nor has anyone since.[1] However, one thing is certain—he did not mean to define them in hedonist terms.

The Range of the Law of Effect   Others noticed the importance of trial-and-error learning and thus the influence of the law of effect. However, Spencer and Bain were not about to apply that law as widely as would Thorndike. And Lloyd Morgan openly criticized Thorndike, calling for the "mind story" to complement the "body story" (Joncich 1968, p. 137). Thorndike was indeed an original.

Out with Faculty Psychology
Thorndike constantly emphasized the importance of the specifics of the teaching and learning process—natural, since learning is the selecting of specific behaviors and the connecting of them to specific stimuli

and situations. The prevailing mental discipline methods of the day derived from Scottish faculty psychology and advocated the exercising of mental faculties in the same way that muscles are exercised. This method promoted the forced memorization of poetry to strengthen the general faculty of memory and similar exercises to strengthen faculties of attention, logic, and so on.

Thorndike showed in an early paper (Thorndike and Woodworth 1901) that the discipline method was basically flawed. The forced memorizing of poetry was of no help in improving memory in general because there *is* no memory in general. There *are* memories for specific classes of things, such as poetry, faces, alphabet letters, words, and so on. However, practice memorizing one kind of material did not help memorizing other types of material.

By the same token, "attention" may be a single word, but it refers to a wide range of activities. Even "attention to words" may refer to the spelling, length, sound, or grammatical class of words. The point is that education must be specific about what is to be learned. What exactly is meant by words such as *patriotism, understanding of grammar,* and other vague goals of education?

Many of the terms we use are unsuitable—they either refer to faculties or powers of mind that are by no means single entities, such as "memory" and "attention." In addition, when we set out to deal with anger and aggression, we must distinguish among several varieties. There is anger due to restraint, to sudden pain, to combat in rivalry, and to many other causes. Only by remaining as specific as possible can we accurately describe behavior, and only then can we change it.

Readiness, Exercise, and Effect

Thorndike's writings prior to 1929 usually referred to three basic laws of learning, with the law of effect invariably third on the list. His law of exercise referred to his assumption that repetition alone could establish habits. This law was dropped in 1929. The law of readiness was first on the list and concerned the conditions under which a satisfier or annoyer is effective—the "successful operation" discussed above.

The law of readiness says that the effect of a putative satisfier depends on ongoing behavior, so that food acts as a satisfier in the context of preparatory eating behavior. Similarly, praise may be effective only when an individual's behavior is already oriented toward such a consequence. We now know, for example, that it is exceedingly difficult to train a pigeon to peck a disk to avoid shock. This is because pecking is preparatory behavior for eating and not for shock avoidance.

Subsidiary Laws

It is a fair wager that most applied psychologists of today who identify themselves as behavior therapists have no idea how comprehensive and sophisticated was Thorndike's theory. In addition to the laws of readiness, exercise, and effect, Thorndike proposed what could be called subsidiary laws, refinements of the basic three. They derive from the psychology of the late nineteenth century, and some were included in a book aimed at popular audiences, published in 1900. Five of the most frequently cited were the following:

• The *law of attitude, dispositions, or sets* showed Thorndike's awareness of and appreciation for the findings of the Würzburg School and of his colleague, Robert Woodworth, showing the importance of set and other terms that refer to the condition of the learner. What instructions has a person been given? Is a person reading for pleasure, or because an examination is coming up?

• The *law of multiple response* refers to a similar phenomenon, as our behavior in a new situation depends upon the behaviors we bring to it. Most of us cannot easily pronounce the German umlaut sound or do a smooth backstroke on the first try, so we do the best we can. As we continue, some behaviors are selected and connected by either natural or social consequences.

• The *law of piecemeal activity or selective attention* acknowledges that we never respond to all elements of a situation—some elements affect us strongly, while most others we ignore.

• The *law of response by analogy* is Thorndike's principle of transfer by identical elements—we act in a new situation as we did in a past similar situation. In education, this means that the effects of training may be expected to generalize to similar situations and that the more elements are shared by the training and the practical situations, the greater the benefit.

• Finally, the *law of associative shifting* explains how an originally insignificant item, such as a dollar bill or a rejection letter, can become a satisfier or annoyer. Similarly, it explains how other events that may act at one time as satisfiers—such as sports, the sound of children's merriment, and even daily life—may become annoyers. Associative shifting is actually a special case of the law of response by analogy. It occurs

when there is a change from an old to a new situation and the old response continues and is attached to the new situation. For example, a
therapist may treat a spider phobia by gradually introducing a spider
while maintaining relaxation in the patient. If properly done, the
patient's relaxation would persist from spider-absent through spider-
present conditions and become attached to the latter. In other cases,
continual defeat, the death of a child, or a long illness may turn sports,
children's laughter, and life itself into annoyers.

Actually, Practice Doesn't Make Perfect? By the late 1920s Thorndike had serious reservations about the law of exercise and about the
negative law of effect. Concerning the former, he carried out a long series of experiments testing the law of exercise, in some cases serving
as the principal subject himself. One experiment serves to convey the
flavor of this research.

His Experiment 5 included him as the main subject and a task
requiring the drawing of lines of specific lengths. Thorndike wrote:

Subject T (the writer), with eyes closed, drew a line to be as nearly as possible
2″ long, then one to be 4″ long, then one to be 6″ long, then one to be 8″ long.
This series of four acts he repeated 950 times. (1932a, p. 11)

He drew a total of 3,800 lines on sheets of paper, twelve lines to a
sheet. If the law of exercise were operating, one would expect that
the various lines drawn would become more similar in length. The
attempted four-inch lines would not more nearly approximate an
actual four inches, but those lengths more frequently drawn in the
early trials should become yet more frequent.

After careful analysis of these and other data, Thorndike concluded
that no such effect occurs and that there is no "law of exercise." Simple
repetition cannot establish habits—there must always be consequences, whether it is knowledge of results or other satisfiers and
annoyers.

Punishment Doesn't Work? Thorndike was renowned as an authority on education and as such his opinions on fundamental issues carried great weight. This was the case when the efficacy of punishment
came up. He had believed until the late 1920s that the effects of satisfiers and punishers were equal and opposite in direction—satisfiers
strengthen connections and annoyers weaken them.[2] However, by
1932 he had changed his mind and wrote,

Punishments...weaken the connection which produced them, when they do weaken it, by strengthening some competing connection. (1932b, p. 39)

His conclusion was based on research with both human and animal subjects—Experiment 71 was typical. "Nine subjects were given training in choosing the right meaning for a Spanish word from five in a series of two hundred." Responses were rewarded or punished by the experimenter, who announced right or wrong. After twelve or more repetitions of the list, Thorndike analyzed the effects of reward and punishment on the repetition of previous responses. He found that "right" produced a substantial effect on subsequent response choice but that "wrong" did not. In another experiment, subjects learned to match ten behaviors (e.g., open mouth wide, pull head back) with ten patterns drawn on cards. Again, the effect of being told "right" was substantial, whereas that of being told "wrong" was "approximately zero."

Having satisfied himself that punishment works only when it leads to new behaviors that may be followed by satisfiers, Thorndike vehemently criticized the use of punishment. He accused the family, the schools, and the church of overuse of punishment, even "inventing a hell after death to add more." This is especially egregious if punishment does not work, aside from provoking momentary disruption of activity. He recommended that if punishment must be used, at least make sure that it "belongs," that it is appropriate to the behavior being punished. Forestall its use altogether, if possible, and "shift to the comfort of other behavior." Above all, avoid the use of doctrinaire, fantastic, and perverted punishments! He was mistaken, as were many to follow.

Intelligence Is Eighty Percent Inherited

History records no career, war, or revolution that can compare in significance with the fact that the correlation between intellect and morality is approximately .3, a fact to which perhaps a fourth of the world's progress is due. (Joncich 1968, p. 310)

It is not a kindness to keep the public ignorant of the limited power of education. (Joncich 1968, p. 546)

Thorndike spent his career at Teachers College of Columbia University, yet his opinions regarding teaching were surprising. He felt that his own education, especially in college at Wesleyan University, would have been improved if unlimited cuts were allowed. As it was, he spent his time in the back of the classrooms doing other things. He was not known as a particularly good teacher himself and often commented that courses were a waste of time for all concerned. The "most and best" learning comes from reading books and doing things for oneself. It is "what the scholars do, not what the teacher does, (that) educates them" (ibid., p. 217).

Another strongly held opinion concerned the influence of heredity on intelligence and learning—as well as propensity to steal and other "traits." Despite the fact that he is often classified as a strong environmentalist, Thorndike viewed the power of education as severely limited by innate endowment. The laws of connectionism work within the bounds of some eighty percent domination by heredity. The first volume of his 1913 *Educational Psychology* was titled *The Original Nature of Man* and presented what was essentially William James's list of instincts. It also included passages such as this one:

The physician should know whether original nature lets a child eat too much and chew it not enough; the criminologist should know the relative shares of nature and nurture in the production of assault or theft. (Thorndike 1913)

Thorndike's biographer, Geraldine Joncich, referred to his "unmatched consistency in opposition to environmental theories" (1968, p. 317).

Thorndike and Applied Psychology

Thorndike (1949) believed that *The Psychology of Wants, Interests, and Attitudes*, published in 1935, was one of the best of the 450-some articles, monographs, and books that he published during a long career. This is because Thorndike believed his contribution to be the demonstration that the methods of science can be profitably applied to the difficult area of psychology, replacing the mysticism of the past. The 1935 book did so, he thought, and included a wide variety of applications.

For example, one study showed that interest in learning some facts is greater than that in learning others. For example, subjects learn birth dates of famous people better than those of unknowns. And the truth of a fact has little to do with whether it is easily learned. Learners remember birth dates of famous people, even when they are told that the dates are false. They even learn false biographies of famous people as well as—or better than—they learn the truth.

Some of his research involved questionnaires asking for people's "valuations of achievements, acts, and persons." For example, fourteen psychologists and forty-two unemployed professionals were asked to rate the goodness or badness of various activities performed by a forty-year-old chemist with three hours off on a Thursday. Some of the activities and ratings, on a scale ranging from −10 to +10, were as follows for the psychologists/unemployed:

Activity	Rating
Study chemistry	5.5/5.0
Read a detective story	1.5/2.0
Read literature issued by the Mormon Church	1.0/0.0
Writing and sending anonymous defamatory letters to several men about their wives	−10.0/−10.0
Teasing the monkeys in the zoo by holding out food and pulling it back when they reach for it	−4.0/−8.0

In a similar study, he asked sixty students and teachers of psychology, all under thirty years of age with thirty-nine of them unemployed, to provide "valuations of certain pains, deprivations, and frustrations." The question took the form, "For how much money would you suffer the following?" The dollar values—in 1930s Great Depression dollars—were as follows for the employed and unemployed:

Pains/Deprivations	Employed/Unemployed
Have one upper front tooth pulled	$5,000/$4,500
Become unable to smell	$300,000/$150,000
Fall into a trance or hibernating state throughout March of every year	$400,000/$200,000
Have to live all the rest of your life in Boston, Massachusetts	$100,000/$50,000
Lose all hope of life after death	$6,500/$50

We have since learned to be extremely skeptical of questionnaires, at least those that purport to assess "attitudes" and "opinions." Nonetheless, it is noteworthy that Thorndike's respondents seem to value the possibility of life after death very little, particularly when they are unemployed.

In a last example, the 1937 collection included ratings of "good" and "bad" words. Presumably, advertisers could take a tip and avoid words like "sylph" and "lushness" in their copy.

Good words: dawn, magnolia, gate, sailing, lilac, Lawrence, ozone, balance, tip, loud, flame, glow, Dorothy, vowel, genera, viola, fable, lease, avail, Hercules, Nancy.

Bad words: Katzenjammer, sylph, avouch, gladsomeness, succor, pellucid, tryst, pulchritude, bum, grot, brown, lushness.

This research has questionable value, of course, since even if subjects' ratings can be taken seriously, they are prone to all manner of variation among subgroups of a culture and surely among cultures. However, the point is that Thorndike succeeded in accomplishing his goal, showing that there is no aspect of human behavior or experience that cannot appear to be treated scientifically.

However, Thorndike was partly a creature of the nineteenth century, who endorsed the brain-as-switchboard conception of Spencer, Bain, James, and others. Instead of the sensations and images of the introspectionists, he referred to hypothetical "conduction units" and S-R connections in the brain. John Watson went further than that, charging that mediators are fit objects of belief only for savages.

Watson and Behaviorism

God knows I took enough philosophy to know something about it. But it wouldn't take hold. I passed my exams but the spark was not there. I got something out of the British School of Philosophers—mainly out of Hume, a little out of Locke, a bit out of Hartley, nothing out of Kant, and, strange to say, least of all out of John Dewey. I never knew what he was talking about then, and, unfortunately for me, I still don't know. (Watson 1936)

Biography

John Broadus Watson was born in 1878 on a farm a few miles from Greenville, South Carolina. After earning a master's degree at Furman University in Greenville in 1899, Watson became the youngest recipient of a Ph.D. at the University of Chicago. The director of his doctoral committee was James Angell, and the dissertation concerned the development of the rat's psyche (Watson 1903). That was 1903, and he spent several years as part-time janitor and as an instructor at Chicago. However, in 1908, the chance of a lifetime came, and he was offered a professorship and department chairmanship at Johns Hopkins, an offer he accepted.

Until 1915 his research was restricted to animal behavior, including several papers on kinesthesia and maze learning in rats, the behavior of noddy and sooty terns, and color vision and imitation in monkeys. After 1915 his interest centered on child development, an interest that remained after he left academics. A scandalous divorce cut short his academic career in 1920, leading to his forced resignation and a new career in advertising. Watson continued to lecture occasionally during the 1920s and published popular books and articles.

Behaviorism: Origin and Context

Although Watson often pointed out that he was not the founder of behaviorism, it is certain that he was its most vocal and effective advocate. He argued that the analysis of human consciousness, which had almost exclusively occupied psychologists, was misguided and extremely damaging to progress. If we treat humans objectively, we find that we can discover the factors that lead them to act as they do, and, knowing that, we can influence their actions.

Anticipating B. F. Skinner, Watson argued that a science of behavior can aid in the raising of our young and eventually lead to a world "fit for human habitation." This provoked strong opposition from his contemporaries, who mistakenly viewed behaviorism as a crass mechanical model of humanity, devoid of thoughts, hopes, dreams, and emotions. It was ironic that behaviorism was thought to favor mechanical explanations and to treat us as robots, since such a doctrine is precisely what behaviorism opposed. After Watson left academics, attacks on him were more successful than was warranted, since there was no way for him to respond.

Watson's Theory
In 1913 Watson published "Psychology as the Behaviorist Views It," a paper that blasted Titchener and the structuralists, as well as the functionalists. As Watson saw it, if mental content is slippery to deal with, how much more elusive are "functions"? And the functionalists were not averse to introspection as the method of choice, thus ensuring their condemnation. Though his friends and well-wishers urged him to refrain, he attacked vigorously and in language that was plain. He charged that the psychology of the time was a waste of time and that if it were continued we would still be arguing over whether auditory sensations were extended in space two hundred years hence.

Watson, clearly influenced by functionalist thought, argued that we can write a psychology that dispenses with terms such as consciousness, mind, sensations, and images, since such entities are pure inventions of the introspectionists, having no existence in fact. As he wrote in 1928, consciousness has never been seen, smelled, nor tasted, nor does it take part in any human reactions. Most were shocked when he denied the existence of consciousness, though James had done the same a few years before. What was Watson really questioning?

Watson was not denying that we see, hear, smell, hope, and remember. However, for him, as for Thorndike, these are activities, things that we *do*. Is there really a remainder—consciousness—after we subtract these activities from our experience? Is there really a thing called "mind," independent of these activities?

The goal for psychology was clear to Watson: We want to be able to predict with reasonable certainty what people will do in specific situations. Given a stimulus, defined as an object of inner or outer experience, what response may be expected? A stimulus might be a blow to the knee or an architect's education; a response could be a knee jerk or the building of a bridge. Similarly, we can determine what situations produce particular responses. Watson asked why do people yawn in crowded auditoriums, what conditions lead to crime, and what leads us to act and feel depressed?

In all such situations the discovery of the stimuli that call out one or another behavior should allow us to foresee their occurrence and influence them. Thus, the prediction and control of William James "Plea for a Scientific Psychology" found a strong backer in John Watson.

Learning, Motives, "S and R," Language, and Memory   Thorndike suggested that our actions depend upon the S-R connections that we are born with and the modifications in them that accrue with experience. Presumably, real connections among real neurons were involved. Watson would have none of this dependence on neural substrata—in 1919 he pointed out that he avoided illustrations of neural structures, since the reader must erroneously assume that the nervous system was important as a static structure.

What counts is the activity of the nervous system as part of a whole, only *one* part of an acting organism. He wrote, "one should strive to get the beginner to view the organism as a whole as rapidly as possible and to see in the working of all its parts an integrated personality" (Preface). The positing of S-R connections in the brain is not only needless but promotes the view that the brain is the initiator of action. We act as a whole, and we are not controlled merely by impulses sent from the brain. Rather, we are controlled by myriad external and internal stimuli and situations.

Watson wrote that we are "what we come with and what we have been through" (1919), and what we go through is by far the more important factor, at least, as far as psychology is concerned. Through life we are constantly adjusting—*adjustment* occurring when our actions remove a source of stimulation. Thus, we adjust to cold, to hunger, to a speck in the eye, to food in the alimentary tract, to a moving object in the visual field, or to a math problem. We adjust continuously while still in the womb, and we do not stop until we make the final adjustment, death.

A good many of the stimuli to which we adjust are due to bodily needs, such as hunger or sexual urges. Both produce movement that continues until the stimuli are abolished—the hunger is gone or the sexual urges gratified. In the future, movements that accompany such an effect will occur again, following the principles of frequency and recency. In addition, such successful adjustments may be accompanied by a decrease in emotional tension, as in the ending of great hunger. However, the emotional aspect is not essential, and if frequency and recency were not enough, what was necessary was definitely not Thorndike's satisfiers, which Watson interpreted as a hedonistic theory.

The "stimuli and responses" to which Watson referred were not synonymous with the S's and R's of later writers. When Watson (1930) wrote that the goal for psychology should be to predict the response, given the stimulus, and to discover the stimulus, given the response, he referred to both molar and molecular units. "S" was any object or state of affairs that was relevant, whether it be hunger pangs, a flash of light, one's family life, or an education in law. A response could be eating, building a house, swimming, talking, or arguing a case before the Supreme Court—we cannot expect that the appropriate units of description will always be on the same level.

Pattern Reactions   Watson classified our behavior into three kinds, *manual, verbal,* and *visceral,* all of which occur to some extent every instant of our lives. Manual behavior is any movement of our bodies caused by the contraction of striped muscles—it is what we ordinarily think of as "behavior." Verbal behavior was often called "laryngeal habits" and referred to any naming of things, whether by use of words or of gestures and other body movements. Watson pointed out in 1919 that there are many situations in life for which we have no organized reaction, and all that we can do is curl a lip, shrug, or utter "humpf." Visceral behavior is Watson's term for emotional reactions, which involve activity of the cardiovascular, respiratory, and digestive systems.

At any moment in our lives, all three systems are active, though one may be overshadowing another. As I write this, I notice verbal and manual activity, but the visceral part is hardly noticeable. At other times, as when trimming a hedge, the manual part overshadows the visceral and verbal portions. However, for Watson, all three forms of behavior occur simultaneously at every moment, though in different proportions.

Memory and Thinking

As far as *memory* goes, Watson denied its existence, at least as a conception of storage and retrieval of memories. Recall that this is no more than William James, James Angell, Munsterberg, Wundt, and many others taught and that the only proponents of "memory" as a storehouse were Herbart, in the early nineteenth century, and the faculty psychologists of the eighteenth and nineteenth centuries. When we speak of the storage and recall of memories, we delude ourselves into believing that we have explained something, while actually we have given one name to what is a multiplicity.

I meet a friend; I nod my recognition, shake his hand, and begin to speak with him of old times. Yet, I cannot for the life of me remember his name! What is it that I do remember? I "remember" the manual habits concerning him, so I shake hands. And I "remember" to feel glad, angry, or sad that I ran into him. Thus, *memory* is a word for the host of habits developed with respect to him in the past and which are active at this meeting. The point is, Watson felt, that too much emphasis is placed on verbal memory, the ability to "recall" and recite words and lists and to produce verbal descriptions of past events—memory is far more than that.

For Watson, *thinking* is part of what we do in the process of adjustment. It is talking to oneself, bearing in mind that "talking" includes much more than verbal behavior. We think with the whole body, just as we talk with the whole body. Thinking is a part of every adjustment, and it may include verbal elements, false starts, muscular tensions, emotional elements, and more. Imagine the manipulation of a Rubik's cube or other manual puzzle. Surely the solving of such

puzzles is "thinking," as much as is consciously solving a mental puzzle. Yet, it rarely involves any words and is independent of the rules of
grammar and syntax.

What of *consciousness*? Is that any more than a "pop" or literary term
that does not refer to any existent thing, but only to our naming activity? We name the universe of objects both inside and outside us, and
that is all that is meant by consciousness. It is all that we have reacted
to, labeled, and made a part of what we will respond to in the future.

Private Experience   Watson's critics have greatly misunderstood his
position on private experience. It is easy to conclude, as they have,
that when Watson denied mind, consciousness, and imagery, he was
denying experience in general. However, he was merely denying the
existence of mind, thoughts, images, and the like as actual things that
constitute mental content. In denying images, he was by no means
denying imagination as a name for something we do. But do we imagine images? We think, but do we think thoughts? Enough wasted effort
had been expended attempting to describe so-called "images" and
"thoughts"; behaviorists would study what people do, not what is supposed to be present in some mental realm.

Watson: Comparative Psychologist? Ethologist?

The climate is hell...the temperature of the sand...runs from 130–142F during the day. At night I am dog tired...This climate works havoc on your
mind. Your memory is not two hours long. (Samelson 1994, p. 13)

For many summers Watson was supported by government grants for
his study of the behavior of terns on the island of Tortuga in the Florida Keys. He caught some of the birds, observed their behavior, and
watched how they mated and how they raised their young. This led to
a fair understanding of terns, to which he referred in his 1913 paper.
He recommended the same strategy as the only key to understanding
more complicated life forms, such as preliterate humans or modern
Europeans. There is no shortcut; we must determine what we do, feel,
and think under specific circumstances. In spirit, his program was similar to that of naturalists of the late nineteenth and the twentieth centuries. And he did begin with animal behavior—was he an ethologist?

Despite contributing in many ways to the understanding of animal
behavior, Watson was "rejected by virtually all European ethologists":

Konrad Lorenz (1981, 1983) reported having been made critical of Watson's
alleged extreme environmentalism at the instigation of Karl Bühler.... In re-

sponse to a letter promoting Watson as a proto-ethologist, in 1982 Lorenz wrote me: "I begin with the confession that I am quite aware of having done some injustice to the behaviorists in general and to John Watson in particular. What I know about him, is only what Karl Bühler made me read of his works and this was calculated, I think, quite consciously to irritate me and raise my objections." (Dewsbury 1994)

Prior to 1920 or so Watson had concentrated on animal research, for reasons that he detailed in his 1913 pronouncement. He had worked with rats, three species of monkeys, and four species of birds. In 1915 F. M. Chapman, the editor of *Bird Lore,* wrote that "His papers should be examined by all serious students of birds" (in Dewsbury 1994).

On Bird Key, off the Florida coast, he spent four summers studying a colony of terns and examined nest building, mate and egg recognition, feeding, and daily activity rhythms, as well as food exchange during courtship, orientation, and homing. Unlike many later ethologists, Watson was careful to arrange his laboratory studies so that the apparatus was appropriate for the species involved.

Dewsbury (1994, p. 243) applauded Watson's work in developmental psychobiology, reflected in his Chicago doctoral dissertation on the development of nervous system and learning in rats. Watson also studied the development of body growth and behavior in rats and humans, a young monkey, and of two varieties of terns. He even observed imprinting, as had Spalding decades earlier.

His interests turned to sensation, and he was (Dewsbury 1994, p. 143) the first to study pheromonal communication in animals. He published on research methods in the study of vision and on the vision of rodents, monkeys, and birds.

Instincts and Innate Traits: Not Thorndike

The definition of instinct and "innate" has proven more complicated than was thought to be the case at the turn of the twentieth century. Watson (1928) proposed that the belief in instinct and traits—the "gifts" that are passed on from generation to generation—reflects only our desire to live forever, a desire that is fulfilled when we see our characteristics, both physical and "mental," in our children. "It is hard for most of us to believe that when we are dead we are dead all over, like Rover." Is that the whole story, or is there clear evidence that "intelligence" and "ambition" and "honesty" and "swordsmanship" and "personality" are passed on in the genes? Or is only the structure of the body inherited, along with a potential that may be actualized in many ways, depending on nurture?

Human Instincts   Watson carefully observed the development of hundreds of infants and concluded that we do come with a large set of instinctive reactions, but that they are much more elementary than is usually supposed (1919, 1930). We have instinctive fears, especially of loud noises and loss of support, and we sneeze, hiccup, have erections, cry, urinate, raise our heads, kick, and grasp, even in infancy and independent of environment.

We also come with inherited reactions to hundreds of objects, and most of these reactions are positive, like that to shining or moving objects. A few things produce hereditary negative reactions, such as pain or loud noises. During our lifetime, new stimuli become attached to those producing the original instinctive positive or negative reactions, and we live a life of attractions, aversions, and mixtures of attraction/aversion for reasons that elude us.

Watson's Real Argument against "Instinct"   Watson did not deny that heredity was a factor, but he stressed the almost wholly neglected effect of environment. The famous quotation below is virtually never published in any but the briefest version—the final brief paragraph. The pages that preceded this expanded version are worth reading but are too long for inclusion. See whether Watson was reasonable regarding nature and nurture, bearing in mind the cruel incompetence of the mental testing movement of the era:

Our conclusion, then, is that we have no real evidence of the inheritance of traits. I would feel perfectly confident in the ultimately favorable outcome of careful upbringing of a healthy, well-formed baby born of a long line of crooks, murderers and thieves and prostitutes. Who has any evidence to the contrary? Many, many thousands of children yearly, born from moral households and steadfast parents become wayward, steal, become prostitutes, through one mishap or another of nurture. (Watson 1930, pp. 103–104)

Watson's opinion was thoroughly against the grain of the time, and through the twentieth century the weight of conventional opinion has supported the hereditarian view. One area where heredity definitely does play a large part is in one of our most fundamental activities, the expressing of emotion.

Emotion

If all hearts were calm, the great artists of the world would have lived in vain...the world would be a sorry place indeed...if the distress of the child, of the weak and the downtrodden moved no eye to tears. (Watson 1919, p. 223)

The third class of innate reactions (after laryngeal and manual reactions) are those of the viscera, the heart of the emotions. The effects, both good and ill, of emotional learning were considered of vital importance by Watson, whose research was largely devoted to that subject while at Johns Hopkins. When he said that every reaction was a reaction of the whole body—a pattern reaction—he included the smooth muscles and glands that constitute the viscera.

Unlike manual and laryngeal responses, which are often discrete and specific, emotional reactions are the true pattern reactions, clearly involving the whole body. A bit of bad news may paralyze the striped muscles, stop digestion, and throw verbal habits into disarray. The cold sweat of fear, the head bowed in grief, and the weight of grief are not merely literary expressions; visceral or emotional reactions are reactions!

From 1915 into the 1920s, Watson and his students made countless observations of infants and children at the Phipps Clinic in Baltimore and later, in New York, at the Manhattan Day Nursery. Out of this came Watson's famous postulation of three basic emotions—the X, Y, and Z reactions, corresponding to fear, rage, and love. Soon after birth, the infant shows the innate fear reaction, characterized by closed eyes, a catching of the breath, spasmodic movements of both arms and legs, grasping with the hands, and puckered lips.

Such a reaction is reliably produced by a loud noise or loss of support but by nothing else except inflicted pain. Watson exposed six-month-old infants to every sort of zoo animal at close range, to pigeons flapping in a paper bag, to darkness, and to brightness. The infants never showed any sign of fear. Fears of such things appear later in childhood and are therefore present because they have been instilled by society or by the child's personal experience.

Watson and his colleagues spent much time studying acquired emotional reactions in a great many children. However, all of that seemed to have been crystallized by the textbooks into the case of Albert B., who was briefly experimented upon (see figure 14.1). "Little Albert's" case has acquired the status of a myth in many forms in many textbooks. Harris (1979) showed that many of the details of the case have been reported incorrectly in many of the texts, although all that the errant authors had to do was examine Watson's own account (1919, 1930; Watson and Rayner 1920).

Albert B. was "a wonderfully good child" of a wet nurse at the Lane Hospital in Baltimore who, at eleven months of age, feared only loud

Figure 14.1
Watson, Albert, and Rosalie. Courtesy of the Archives of the History of American Psychology, University of Akron.

noises and loss of support. He showed only curiosity when presented with a white rat. As he reached for it, a four-foot-long steel bar, 3/4 inch in diameter, was struck by a carpenter's hammer nearby but behind him and out of sight. He jumped violently and buried his face in the mattress, but he did not cry.

The rat was presented again, and, as Albert reached for it, the bar was struck again. Albert still did not cry, but he appeared so disturbed that no further trials were conducted. A week passed and the rat and loud noise were paired five more times—finally, Albert cried. The sight of the rat alone sent him crying and crawling away so rapidly that it was difficult to prevent him from falling off the bed. Albert had acquired a new fear.

Five days passed, and Albert was tested with blocks, a white rat, a rabbit, a dog, a sealskin coat, cotton wool, Watson's hair, and a Santa Claus mask with a white beard. The blocks had no effect, but all of the other objects produced a greater or lesser fear reaction, showing that the fear was not specific to the white rat but occurred to other objects that were white and/or hairy and furry.

Though Watson claimed that Albert was no longer available for research and that it was therefore impossible to investigate methods to remove this fear, Harris found that Watson was well aware that Albert would be leaving. In fact, Watson knew that Albert was to be adopted, and he knew the date of his departure. Why Watson would leave Albert in that state is unclear, since he must have had a good idea of how to effect a cure.

Watson[3] later described attempts to *remove* fears in seventy children, ages three months to seven years, who came with preestablished fears. Much of this work was done by Mary Cover Jones, a graduate student at Columbia University, for whom he was unofficial sponsor and for whom he had set up the Manhattan Day Nursery. One child's treatment was reported in 1930 in *Behaviorism* as the case of "Little Peter," a boy with a host of preestablished fears. He was afraid of rats, rabbits, fish, cotton, frogs, and mechanical toys. How might we remove such fears?

Watson described the methods used, including "disuse," or the preventing of exposure to the feared object, telling the child stories about the feared object, such as telling Peter Rabbit stories that portray the feared object—rabbits—as nondangerous, and forced exposure to the feared object, a method later called "emotional flooding." These proved ineffective, as did "social methods," such as pointing out that only "fraidy cats" are afraid of rabbits. Finally, an effective method, *reconditioning*, was tried and found to be effective in curing Peter of his fear of rabbits.

Reconditioning aims to connect a new reaction to the feared object, replacing the existing fear response. This was accomplished by presenting the feared object in such a way that it provoked no fear reaction; for example, the rabbit was presented at a great distance. Then, while Peter was engaged in incompatible behavior, eating crackers and milk, the rabbit was brought gradually nearer.

The rabbit was initially presented at a distance of forty feet and gradually brought nearer as Peter ate. Eventually, Peter petted the rabbit as he ate. This is the method later called systematic desensitization by Joseph Wolpe, who made it popular decades later. However, Watson failed to properly publicize what he had done, as Kurt Salzinger noted in discussing Watson's successful therapeutic techniques:

...one matter...has puzzled me for a long time, namely why, when there was some evidence in children, at least, that conditioning can explain the acquisition of a fear, it took some thirty years until someone like Wolpe (1958) used it to construct an actual therapeutic technique. Despite all the accusations of Watson as publicist, he failed to promote the application of the methods he had himself discovered. (In Todd and Morris 1994, pp. 151–158)

Salzinger concluded that in this and other cases Watson was more interested in research than in "applying the findings himself."

After Albert B.: Interpretations   The work done with Albert was hardly a carefully done piece of research, but it appeared in introductory textbooks within a year and became one of the classic studies of the century. In fact, only Pavlov's basic salivary conditioning in dogs has been mentioned more often in introductory textbooks (Todd 1994, pp. 75–107). Todd pointed out that the effect was far greater than Watson's 1913 "manifesto," which was virtually ignored at the time and has only been deemed important since the late twentieth century. The experiment was more a casual demonstration, as was admitted by the Watsons in 1921 (Watson and Watson 1921). The history of its recounting is odd and instructive (Todd 1994, pp. 94–95).

The Watson and Rayner experiment was replicated, and some data appeared to suggest that it was difficult to attach fears to inanimate and harmless objects, such as toys, and that live objects, such as rats or caterpillars, were required. This suggested that humans were innately prepared to learn to fear animals, and this possibility was promoted in a number of introductory texts, including one by Ruch in 1937. He proposed that "objects differ from each other in the amount of time required to condition an emotional response to them. Animals are not natively feared, but they can become conditioned fear stimuli very quickly" (Ruch 1937, p. 258, cited in Todd 1994, p. 95).

In fact, the replications were very poorly done, and even the best, Bregman's (1934), was so designed as to ensure that conditioned emotional responses would not occur to inanimate objects such as blocks (Todd 1994, p. 95). The evidence for innately prepared fear conditioning to living things was insubstantial. However, Ruch's book continued to carry the argument through the seventh edition in 1967, though other texts did not. In 1971 Seligman popularized the argument as a part of his campaign to establish "preparedness" as an aspect of learning. Seligman inaccurately described the Little Albert experiment, as well as the replications, and those errors remain in current textbooks that deal with the possibility of acquired fears (Todd 1994, p. 95). Watson and Rayner were right (Burns and Malone 1992).

Child Development and Personality

Between 1915 and 1920, Watson studied many infants over surprisingly protracted periods (that is, for months). He studied the development of simple reactions, such as blinking when an object rapidly approaches, to more complicated coordinations, such as learning to grasp a hanging candy or to avoid grasping a flame. After 1920, he relied on Mary Cover Jones's observations. When she left for California with her husband in 1926, Watson was left with only the two sons of his second marriage as subjects.

He was certain that children are greatly damaged by the average upbringing, and he made his views known in 1928 in *Psychological Care of Infant and Child*, a popular book that sold 100,000 copies within a few months. He described the ill effects that parents wreak when they stroke and pet their children and thus make them love their parents more than they should. On the other hand, the horrifying stories told to children, such as the Grimm's fairy tales, filled with witches that cook children, inculcate fears that cause problems for a lifetime.

Watson's opinions on child rearing have nothing necessary to do with behaviorism—rather, they reflect only his very idiosyncratic beliefs. Rosalie Rayner Watson, his wife from 1920 until the end of her life, described these methods in an article titled, "I am the Mother of a Behaviorist's Sons" (Watson 1930). The article begins,

THE WHOLE WORLD HAS HEARD FROM DR. JOHN B. WATSON, AUTHOR OF "BEHAVIORISM," BUT THIS IS THE FIRST TIME HIS WIFE HAS VENTURED TO TELL HOW THESE THEORIES WORK AT HOME.

Watson taught that a parent should "never hug or hit" a child; rather, he encouraged conditions that promote a healthy development, including varied experiences, taking responsibility, and treatment as an adult as early as possible. Rosalie Rayner Watson, his wife in 1920, appeared to come short of endorsing this doctrine entirely, but she endorsed it nonetheless:

I took care of the children myself when they were babies, and so their earliest responses were toward me. I bathed them, fed them, made them comfortable, and ... I am unanimously in favor of breaking the mother attachment as early as possible—or, better still, not allowing it to grow up.

She described the first time that their firstborn was left alone at the age of eight months. Rosalie felt that the baby would be upset were she to leave the house, so she told her husband to leave by the front door, past Billy, while she left through the back. Watson guessed her intention and forced her to leave by the front door with him.

...both my boys accept the fact that I go where and when I please, and their lives are organized so independently that they don't care. They don't rely upon one human being for their happiness. From their earliest moments, we taught them to play with objects instead of people, and one of the greatest struggles I had with nurses...was restraining them from entertaining the children.

This may seem to deny children their "childhood," but is a childhood as a pampered "pet" really a good preparation for life? Or does it just foster neurotic dependence? Is a child a doll/baby until it understands adult speech? It reduces to the old question of whether development reflects the unfolding of innate dispositions or the child is largely the product of its environment. The answer to this question varies, according to political climate, but Watson was pretty sure that the influence of the environment is important.

What is important is the shaping of the child's *personality*, a name given to the sum total of our behavioral "assets and liabilities," a cross-section of our current manual, visceral, and verbal habits. Watson mentioned the difference between a Ford and a Rolls Royce and drew a comparison:

He (John Doe) is as strong as a mule, can work at manual labor all day long. He is too stupid to lie.... He will work all right as a...digger of ditches.... William Wilkins...is good looking, educated, sophisticated, accustomed to good society, traveled, is good for work in many situations.... He, however, was a liar from infancy and could never be trusted in a responsible place. (Watson 1930, pp. 269–270)

Like Doe and Wilkins, we begin life fairly equal, but one of us is born to college-educated parents in Westport, Connecticut, and another is born to uneducated parents in Arkansas. It requires no gift of prophecy to know what is likely to happen to two such individuals.

Is there more to personality than that? What of the individual whose personality seems to fill the room, who is magnetic, and who easily dominates? What is a dominating personality? Watson believed that those qualities describe people whose appearance or behavior evokes our infantile reactions to authority. Such people usually resemble one of our parents and, like the parent, their behavior suggests that they expect swift and certain obedience. In addition, society teaches us in many ways, both formally and subtly, to recognize cues from those who demand our obedience and who can punish disobedience. If those cues are on the face on the billboard or television screen, they will at least draw our attention.

Dissociation, or splitting of personality, makes sense if personality is really the total of our habits at a given time. We are regularly in a few general kinds of situations—at home with the family, at work, at play, and so on. For each of those general situations, we have a stock of manual, verbal, and emotional habits, and they sometimes conflict. Everyone knows the conflict that arises when, as young adults, we visit our home and parents for a few days. The set of habits corresponding to "child" and those defining "adult" clash, leading to great discomfort. When a mental patient manifests different personalities, it is only an extreme case of what is true of all of us. If the subparts are given different names by the patient, it only shows the lack of awareness that this is so.

Mental Illness

Watson viewed mental illness as a perfectly normal phenomenon; it is the normal behavior for a specific pathological environment. Thomas Szasz is a psychiatrist who shared Watson's opinion that "mental illness" is a misnomer. There are physical diseases of the brain and nervous system that can produce insane behavior, but that is not "mental" illness—that is *physical* illness, due to an organic cause. Szasz wrote articles and books with titles like *The Myth of Mental Illness* (Szasz 1960) in which he denounced psychiatry as medical quackery when it should be an educational occupation for most patients. He clearly shared Watson's views.

Szasz compactly expressed his opinion in a Letter to the Editor of a magazine (1995, pp. 8–9). He first referred to the "fundamental fallacies on which modern psychiatry rests" and then went on:

In the bad old days of asylum psychiatry, insanity was synonymous with incompetence, and the route of admission to a public mental hospital was via a formal commitment by a court of law. Hence, psychiatrists resembled jailers and mental hospitals resembled prisons. After the second world war, psychiatrists embarked on an all-out effort to "medicalise" psychiatry's essentially non-medical functions ...

Here a problem arose, since diseases have accepted indicators that permit diagnosis. Fever, aches in the joints, coated tongue, headache, malaise, and blood in the stool are accompaniments of disease. How does one diagnose a "mental" illness? Szasz saw a conspiracy of psychiatrists:

There remained the problem that, unlike bodily diseases, so-called mental diseases lacked objectively demonstrable pathological markers. The solution was to replace the pathological criteria of disease with medical-political decision making—recasting, for instance, depression, idleness and lawlessness as illnesses. Miraculously, anti-psychotic drugs were promptly "discovered" that were said to cure, or at least ameliorate, severe mental diseases.

Psychiatrists then proved that the new drugs worked by declaring that patients need not be hospitalized, so long as they took their drugs. This "house of cards we call 'psychiatry'" is therefore, and unsurprisingly, in a "permanent state of economic and professional collapse." He asked what is really wrong with mental patients? And what do psychiatrists really do?

Watson's theory assumes that psychopathology is the result of learning, and one would think that it must therefore develop slowly. If that were the case, it should be feasible to detect impending derangement in advance, but that is notoriously not the case. Often it seems that a seemingly normal person suffers a "breakdown," as did Watson himself as a young adult. How can that happen? How does a set of manual, verbal, and emotional habits become deranged? It happens because the world changes and the old established habit patterns are no longer effective in maintaining adjustment to the demands of life:

Almost any event or happening might start a change; a flood might do it, a death in the family, an earthquake, a conversion to the church, a breakdown in health, a fist fight—anything that would break up your present habit patterns, throw you out of your routine and put you in such a position that you would have to learn to react to objects and situations different from those to which you have had to react in the past—such happenings might start the process of building a new personality for you. (Watson 1930, p. 301)

Regression In many cases, this "new personality" might be one you had at an earlier age—Watson describes the reversion to more primitive habit systems that occurs when we experience frustration. Who has not attempted some task that requires delicate coordinations, as in operating a demanding piece of machinery, like a sewing machine or an outboard motor? Repeated failure can make us "lose our head" and shake, hit, or otherwise revert to primitive behaviors. In cases where the frustration is greater, such as when we lose a job or when a person upon whom we rely betrays us or dies, the effect is magnified and we are "insane." Our old behaviors no longer provide adjustment.

How can this be remedied—how can "mental illness" be cured? It may be no easy matter to change the habits of a lifetime. Just as one does not learn chemistry or become a violin virtuoso in a week, one does not change a personality in a short time. However, it can be done, and Watson predicted that future mental hospitals would be devoted to just that. As Szasz said, psychiatry is an educational, not a medical specialty (1960).

Scandal in 1920

Several accounts, published in articles and textbooks . . . have alleged that Watson was dismissed because he was engaged in clandestine experiments on human sexual behavior. However, not only is there little evidence to support the story, but substantial documentary evidence exists in the court transcripts of Watson's divorce trial (Watson v. Watson, 1920), public and private correspondence of Johns Hopkins University officials and faculty, and interviews with family members that overwhelmingly refutes that assertion. (Buckley 1989)

Watson's divorce has become part of the folklore of psychology. It forced him into a line of work that he would not have otherwise chosen and cut short his academic career. In 1919 he was one of the best-known psychologists in America—a full professor at Johns Hopkins and editor of *Psychological Review*. He had spent years in animal research and studied children intensively for four years.

He had participated in many affairs over the years, but, according to one biographer (Cohen 1979), his wife of seventeen years, Mary Ickes Watson, had tolerated them for years. She was not unusually disturbed when he began an affair with Rosalie Rayner, a nineteen-year-old graduate student and Vassar graduate and daughter of a prominent Baltimore family. However, the affair persisted, and finally Mary procured more than a dozen love letters written to Rosalie by Watson. She gave them to her brother, who evidently attempted to blackmail Rosalie's father, Albert. In April of 1920 Watson and Mary were separated, and in September the letters fell into the hands of Johns Hopkins president Goodnow. It is not known whether Mary's blackguard brother or Albert Rayner turned the letters over.

Johns Hopkins was still smarting from a scandal involving James Mark Baldwin and a house of prostitution only a few years before. A faculty meeting produced no support for him from colleagues who must have viewed him as an arrogant upstart and he was called to President Goodnow's office and forced to resign. At age forty-two he moved to New York City, where a friend introduced him to people connected with J. Walter Thompson advertising agency, and was given a provisional job. He was probably hired to play "Dr. Watson, the famous scientist," rather than to actually participate as an ad man. However, by 1924 he was promoted to vice president and a salary of $60,000 a year, quite a sum at that time.

At J. Walter Thompson   His initial assignment was to conduct a survey of preferences for various types of rubber boots among users living along the Mississippi River, from Cairo, Illinois, to New Orleans. He was then sent to northern Ohio and western Pennsylvania to promote Yuban coffee in the grocery stores of that region. He must have done well because just thereafter he was made a vice-president of the company and was "Ad Rep" for these companies, among others.

Watson's Accounts at J. Walter Thompson[4]
- Baker, Associates, Co., Inc. (now General Foods) Franklin Baker's Chocolate and Coconut: 1925–1929
- General Motors (international): 1927–1930 (?)
- Johnson & Johnson Baby Powder: 1924–1926; Bovril: 1928
- Norwich Pharmacal—Swav Shaving Cream: 1928
- Pond's Extract Co.: 1928–1930

Because of his efforts, Johnson's baby powder became synonymous with purity, love, and being a good mother. Pond's became the cold cream of royalty, since Watson hired the queens of Spain and of Rumania to give testimonials. Watson applied the psychological strategy already popularized by Walter Dill Scott—rather than inform the public of the virtues of a product, inform the public which products it *wanted*.

Where Watson's particular psychology came in was in appealing to the customer through emotions—the basic fear, rage, and love reactions. He pointed out that those, along with sex, food, and shelter, represented six key elements that could be combined in 720 ways to sell a product. Johnson's baby powder ads showed happy, healthy babies being patted and stroked by a mother applying the powder. Rage can also be used to sell a product, provoked by restraint of movement, a condition experienced by motorists in traffic jams. What better advertising for a commuter train service than to show motorists snarled in traffic, while the fortunate train traveler has no worry about weather or traffic and is free to move about within the train?

Watson used fear in a campaign for Scott's toilet tissue in which ads showed an operating table surrounded by a group of surgeons. The operation looked serious and gruesome and the caption read, "and the problem began with harsh toilet tissue!"

Did Watson Really Apply Psychology in Advertising?   Coon (1994) showed that Watson did not originate the use of psychology in advertising. In fact, Watson himself denied that he used psychology in his advertising work, though this was when he was seventy-six years old and had harbored a bitterness for psychology for some decades.[5,6]

According to Coon, the use of testimonials and the practice of persuading the consumer that the product was desirable had its beginnings decades before. She claimed that Walter Dill Scott, if anyone, was responsible for applying psychology to advertising in the way ordinarily attributed to Watson. It was Scott who changed ads from rational and informative to emotional and persuasive.

Despite his disclaimer at age seventy-six, it seems clear that Watson believed, while working in advertising, that he *was* applying psychological methods, and his work during the 1920s and 1930s clearly shows that he was "doing psychology." Coon provided convincing evidence from the ads of the early twentieth century to support her claim that his contribution was to *increase the emphasis* on nonrational content—arousing emotion to gain the customer's attention—and almost eliminate the rational content of ads.

Examples of Speeches and Articles—From the Beginning   Through his career Watson wrote and spoke publicly on applications of psychology to business. The speeches and articles below are a few taken from a list supplied by the J. Walter Thompson Archives and cover the period from 1921, Watson's first year with the company, to 1935. If anything, the titles reflect an increased emphasis on the application of psychology fifteen years after Watson began his second career (from the J. Walter Thompson Archives):

• November 25, 1921. *How to Break Down Resistance to Life Insurance.* New York: J. Walter Thompson Company.

• January 3, 1922. "Can Science Determine Your Baby's Career Before It Can Talk?" *New York American Sunday Magazine.*

• July 1922. "What Cigarette Are You Smoking and Why?" *The J. Walter Thompson Bulletin*, No. 88.

• June 15, 1934. "Behavioristic Psychology Applied to Selling," *The Red Barrel* (Coca-cola publication).

• July 1934. "Our Fears: How They Develop," *The Red Barrel*.

• Oct 28, 1935. "The Psychology of the Consumer," speech before Advertising and Sales Club of Toronto.

Watson also gave radio talks that reflected his continued interest in psychology, for example:

• "Psychology as a Background Life." April 19, 1933, WEVD New York.

• "On Children." December 6, 1935, WEAF New York.

Watson was clearly a success in advertising, and he enjoyed the luxuries of a home on New York's Fifth Avenue and later a forty-acre farm in fashionable Westport, Connecticut. Through the 1920s he continued as an academic to the limited extent that he could. He supported Mary Cover Jones's work with children and wrote popular articles for *Harper's Magazine, Cosmopolitan*, and others.

For years he lectured weekly at the New School for Social Research and even publicly debated William McDougall in 1928. However, his

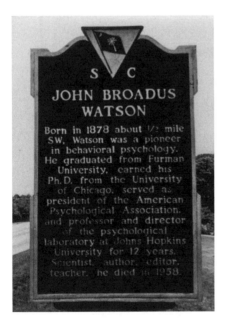

Figure 14.2
Historical marker placed on U.S. Highway 276, just northwest of Travelers Rest, South Carolina, near Greenville, John B. Watson's birthplace. Courtesy of the Archives of the History of American Psychology, University of Akron.

writing diminished after 1930, and, when Rosalie died in 1936, his writing ceased. He wrote that the lack of a laboratory and a ready reference library caused him to "dry up" (Watson 1936). After so long away from academics, he found that he had nothing more to say. (See figure 14.2.)

After having been shunned by the entire academic community (except for Edward Titchener, who remained a faithful friend until his death in 1927), Watson was belatedly honored by the American Psychological Association, which awarded him its gold medal in 1957. The award read that he had "initiated a revolution in psychological thought" and Watson initially seemed pleased. He backed out of accepting the award publicly at the last moment, however, and his psychiatrist son, Billy, accepted it in his stead. Watson died in 1958 at age eighty.

15   Gestalt Psychology and Kurt Lewin

Once in a conversation, the late Karl Lashley, one of the most important psychologists of the time, told me quietly, "Mr. Köhler, the work done by the Gestalt psychologists is surely most interesting. But sometimes I cannot help feeling that you have religion up your sleeves." (Köhler 1969, p. 48)

Gestalt psychology began in late nineteenth-century Germany in opposition to what was perceived as pervasive molecularism in psychology. The original Gestaltists were impressed with physics, not biology, and were perhaps inspired by the writings of the Scottish physicist James Clerk Maxwell. Many writers suggest that Gestalt views were actually absorbed into psychology and that the Gestaltist influence lies in whatever changes this caused in mainstream psychology (e.g., Bower and Hilgard 1981).

Kurt Lewin is often treated as a Gestaltist, though it is clear that he was no such thing. Gestalt psychologists were basic researchers earnestly attempting to understand the "physics of the mind." Lewin was an energetic applier and a student of topics that are often expressed in newspaper headlines—racial discrimination, industrial productivity, worker morale, and the like. He was responsible for many of the concepts that were used by social psychologists during the second half of the twentieth century.

Gestalt Psychology

For now the Gestalt psychologists discovered that this procedure made them neighbors of the most advanced natural scientists, the physicists. (Köhler 1969, pp. 48–49)

Wolfgang Köhler, last of the original Gestaltists, died in 1967, but the theory is still presented in a variety of textbooks and research papers.

Figure 15.1
Wertheimer. Courtesy of the Archives of the History of American Psychology, University of Akron.

Theirs was not only a psychological theory but a worldview and a philosophy of science (Ash 1985, pp. 295–344). Was their message relevant only in the early decades of the twentieth century, and has it been absorbed into mainstream psychology?

Beginnings of Gestalt Psychology

All three founders of Gestalt psychology were introduced to scientific research by Carl Stumpf. Interestingly, when Stumpf was first offered a professorship of philosophy at Berlin, the Prussian government included a laboratory as large as Wundt's, and a higher budget with more modern equipment. This was in 1893, and Stumpf turned it down! He did not favor psychology as a separate discipline involved in "big science." What he agreed to was a "Psychological Seminar," with lectures, exercises, and demonstrations.

His advanced workers included Max Wertheimer (see figure 15.1), Kurt Koffka (see figure 15.2), Wolfgang Köhler (see figure 15.3), Kurt Lewin, and others. Instruction in experimentation was given in Berlin by Hans Rupp and Friedrich Schumann, both of whom had been

Figure 15.2
Koffka. Courtesy of the Archives of the History of American Psychology, University of Akron.

Figure 15.3
Köhler. Courtesy of the Archives of the History of American Psychology, University of Akron.

trained by G. E. Müller. Stumpf taught his students to be guided by the loftiest ideals, reflected in a tribute from Wertheimer on Stumpf's seventieth birthday in 1918:

As much as you love and support work in specialized science, you have nonetheless taught us to keep our gaze directed to larger questions of principle, to work toward the fruitful cooperation of psychology and the theory of knowledge, with the highest problems of philosophy in view. None of us wishes to be locked up in the workroom of specialized science. (Ash 1985, p. 298)

The Beginnings: Wertheimer Attacks—the Wrong Enemy?

I remember Wertheimer at some of our New School seminars—a man of passionate convictions, who was extremely intolerant of all differences and who would shout at anyone who took issue with him. (Marrow 1969, p. 106)

The original outline of Gestalt Psychology was published by Max Wertheimer in 1922 as "Investigation of the Gestalt Doctrine." In it he criticized the prevailing psychology of his time, as he saw it. The Gestalt position rose in objection to the orthodox view, characterized by Wertheimer as resting on two hypotheses:

I. The mosaic or "bundle" hypothesis.—Every "complex" consists of a sum of elementary contents or pieces (e.g. sensations)
. . .
II. The association hypothesis.—If a certain content A has frequently occurred with B ("in spatio-temporal contiguity"), then there is a tendency for A to call up B. . . . This is the ground plan of associationism.

Wertheimer went on to characterize both hypotheses as instances of "and-summation, i.e. a construction from pieces . . . which, as primarily given fundaments, underlie all else."[1] From these there is no limit on the higher structures that may be erected, but, whatever they are, they depend on no intrinsic factors—organismic factors play no part in the construction of experience. In all, Wertheimer gave an adequate account of even the sophisticated associationism of Helmholtz and John Stuart Mill.

A Straw Man?   Were there such associationist ("and-summists") as Wertheimer described in 1922? Or was he flailing the corpse of Herbart, who had been gone for half a century? Wundt was not an and-summist, nor was G. E. Müller, who appeared to appreciate configurations at least as much as did some proto-Gestaltists, such as von Ehrenfels. In America, Titchener was still strong and he was an analyst, all right, but in a half decade he would be dead and his influence dispersed and diluted. Who was the object of criticism in 1922, and, similarly, who could be identified as the villains in the second half of the twentieth century?

The target was and is no straw man, that's certain, but it is also no individual or small group to whom we may easily point. Wertheimer was absolutely correct when he acknowledged this and pointed to the culprit:

But we are not examining "general doctrines"; the aim is to inquire what actually is done, what the positive content underlying the terminology of experimental reports really is... (Wertheimer 1922, p. 51, reproduced in Ellis 1939, p. 113)

No one in 1922 openly urged the strict associationist position that Wertheimer critiqued, and few did so during the following decades of the twentieth century. But it nonetheless existed as a tacit basis for much of the theory and research of the century.

What Are Gestalten? That is a very good question, and Wertheimer answered it in a more or less satisfying way:[2]

The given is itself in varying degrees "structured" ("gestaltet"), it consists of more or less definitely structured wholes and whole-processes with their whole-properties and laws, characteristic whole-tendencies and whole-determinations of parts.

Von Ehrenfels was promoting the doctrine of "form-qualities," or *Gestaltqualitäten*, during this period, and that view, like Mach's, makes a lot of sense. They emphasized form/structure/organization as an indispensable feature of percepts, perhaps more important than the elements themselves. The musician von Ehrenfels was constantly pointing to the melody that survives drastic transposition—changes in scale and key—so of course form qualities were important. However, Wertheimer would have none of that:

Nor are "Gestalten" the sums of aggregated contents erected subjectively upon primarily given pieces...not simply blind, additional, "Qualitäten," essentially as piecelike and intractable as "elements"...nor are they...merely "formal." (Wertheimer 1922, pp. 53–54; Ellis 1939, p. 15)

Wertheimer went on to predict that the study of perception "will not be grounded in a 'purely summative' point of view" (ibid). Physiology and stimulus constellations are what are important, so where does that leave psychology? In fact, Wertheimer wrote that this hypothesis permits "Psychological penetration of this problem" for the first time.

Gestalten are meaningful wholes, and "meaningful" is, as ever, difficult to define. It appears as "inner coherence," "an inner necessity," and, in general, "a whole is meaningful when concrete mutual dependency obtains among its parts." Others would try to clarify Wertheimer's characterization of Gestalt theory,[3] and are there Gestalten? Wertheimer concluded, "Whether there is such a thing as meaningfulness or not is simply a matter of fact" (Wertheimer 1922, p. 57; Ellis 1939, p. 16).

Fundamentals: Psychology as Physics

The words "Gestalt" and "Gestalt Psychology" have taken on an aura very unlike that meant by the founders of this viewpoint. Many psychologists and nonpsychologists take Gestalt theory to be a humanistic sentimentalism that deals with "the whole person," and takes "holistic viewpoints." Such stuff, whatever merits it might have, has no connection whatever with Gestalt Psychology.

Max Wertheimer grew up as a student of the violin and always appreciated music and auditory perception. He knew Albert Einstein later in life and understood physics well enough to understand Einstein's reconstruction of his thinking while devising relativity theory. Wolfgang Köhler had similar interests in audition and viewed mental life (and all life) as only an aspect of physics. The laws that govern the physical world govern the world of conscious experience as well. There was no "getting in touch with one's feelings" for these individuals. And we will see that Gestalt work in what could be called emotional well-being was far from therapeutic.

The Phi Phenomenon and Related Effects   Wertheimer first presented Gestalt theory in 1912, but not in his classic paper on apparent motion—the phi phenomenon—as is commonly thought. That paper was preceded by one on number concepts among primitive peoples (Wertheimer 1912a, pp. 321–378). Unlike what is supposed to be true of Western arithmetic, primitive peoples count units differently. One horse plus one horse is two horses, and one person plus one person is two persons. However, one horse plus one person is a rider.

That same year the phi paper was published, officially launching Gestalt psychology (Wertheimer 1912b). The phenomenon of apparent movement was known and had been studied for almost a century, since Plateau in the 1820s, so it was not a "discovery" that launched the movement. Ash pointed out that there existed a number of theories proposing to explain apparent motion as "motion sensations," "fused afterimages," and "illusions of judgment," by Mach, Marbe, and Schumann, respectively.

The psychophysicist Sigmund Exner had found that apparent motion can produce negative afterimages just as does real motion, and he proposed that some physiological process was involved rather than a judgment process (Ash 1985, p. 309). Wertheimer's experiments, using Koffka and Köhler as subjects and a tachistoscope[4] built by Schumann, refuted those theories while supporting Exner's physiological theory. When a vertical line is briefly presented, immediately followed by the presentation of a horizontal line, the perceived movement is not movement of anything; it is "pure phi," and it corresponds to the "cortical streak" brain process that underlies it. It is an example of a pure, dynamic phenomenon—motion in and of itself, not the motion of some thing and not the sum of a series of isolated events.

Koffka was "enthralled" and wrote in 1931,

Wertheimer did very much more: he joined the movement experience, the movement *phi*, to the psychology of pure simultaneity and of pure succession, the first corresponding to form or shape, the second to rhythm, melody, etc. This was the decisive step. (Ash 1985, p. 310)

The varieties of apparent motion were described in 1913 by Kenkel, a student of Koffka's who named alpha, beta, and gamma movement in 1913 and by Korte, also a Koffka student, who added delta movement in 1915. The main categories of apparent movement are as follows:[5]

phi mov't pure movement from pairs of flashing lights
beta mov't object moves from one to another position
alpha mov't size change w/successive presentation—Kenkel was working with the central line of the Müller/Lyer illusion as its two forms alternated successively.
gamma mov't expansion/contraction w/illumination change
delta mov't reversed mov't when second stimulus is much brighter—then the movement is in the direction opposite the order of presentation.

In 1915 Korte also worked out the laws of optimal movement, showing how it depends on the distance between the stimuli, the time between them, and their intensity. If the time interval is constant, the optimal distance for apparent movement varies directly with intensity. If the distance separating them is increased, intensity must be increased. The perception of phi depends also on expectations and attitude, so that an analytical attitude discourages it and a passive attitude promotes it. It is also easier to perceive movement of a meaningful unit, like an arm attached to a shoulder, than a line attached to another line.

In addition, it is clear that eye movements are unnecessary. Recall that this was the explanation endorsed by Wundt, though he did not originate it. When we see the apparent movement of the successively lit dots of light or of the vertical line that is succeeded quickly by a horizontal line, the apparent movement is no more than the movement of our eyes.

This is decidedly not the case, as is clear in the case of gamma movement, since the change is expansion and contraction, produced by changes in illumination, and it is unclear how the eyes could move to produce such an effect. Also, illusions of movement include the familiar spiral illusion of Plateau, introduced in 1850. Depending on direction of rotation, a spiral drawn on a disk appears to expand or to contract, an experience certainly not produced by eye movements.

Köhler and Koffka were impressed indeed with Wertheimer's findings. Fifty-four years later, in his final series of lectures, given at Princeton, Köhler began with a recounting of the 1912 phi experiment, complete with illustrations (Köhler 1969). Koffka, on the other hand, performed his own experiments and described them in 1930.

Three-Dimensional Motion Gestalten   Koffka described simple conditions that produce gestalt phenomena in three dimensions (Koffka 1930, in Murchison 1930, pp. 161–187). In the simplest case, the phi phenomenon is produced by successively exposing two parallel lines, so that movement is seen from left to right, for example. If a third parallel line is introduced between the two original lines and if the new line remains constantly visible, the movement appears behind the new permanent line. The observer describes the movement to appear to be passing through a tunnel. Koffka proposed that "the permanent line excludes the phi process from its own area without being capable of breaking it up. Thus the process is forced into the third dimension" (in Murchison 1930, p. 169).

The change from two- to three-dimensional movement also happens in other cases of phi. Benussi showed that if two dots, ten centimeters apart, are exposed in succession, we see at first the dot moving back and forth. However, after a while the "moving dot" appears to be moving in a circle in a horizontal plane, thus giving the appearance of depth. Koffka suggested that movement in a circular track cannot be in the vertical plane, since there are "no vectors upwards or downwards."

In yet another case, successive presentations of a V and an inverted V positioned above it result in movement as motion around the axis of symmetry. This resembles a spinning top—why does that appear, rather than a perception of movement from inverted V, to V, to inverted V, and so on? Koffka explained that this would require strong distortions in form—a V cannot flip back and forth vertically without change in appearance. The simpler organization, if movement is to be seen, is a spinning top.

Illusions and Laws of Grouping Since we live in an organized world, it is necessary to show how that organization occurs, and this is the function of the laws of Prägnanz. These laws describe the manner in which we tend to structure the world toward "good Gestalten," and many a Gestalt-sympathizing psychologist has difficulty in defining a "good Gestalt." One can say only that it is that toward which organization tends, and, since the Gestalt is the basic unit of experience, it is impossible to be more precise. We see a row of dots: . . . . . . and call it a line, showing the effects of proximity. We see the same number of dots arranged differently . . . . . . and call it three groups of dots, again because of proximity.

We tend to see objects as symmetrical, even when they are not; this follows the principle of symmetry. We see a circle with a small gap in it as closed, which follows the law of closure. We see the world as objects on backgrounds, which Edgar Rubin proposed as the principle of figure–ground. There are many more laws of organization, totaling well over one hundred (Helson 1925, pp. 342–370). The Gestaltists saw associationists overstressing the importance of contiguity in space and time, as well as similarity. These represent only two of the many laws of organization—proximity and similarity. And the law of effect reflects further misplaced emphasis, this time on the law of closure. When rewards act as such, it is because they provide closure by ending a preceding sequence of behavior, thus making a "unit" of that behavior. However, closure is no more important than contiguity/proximity, similarity, or other laws of organization. These laws are simply aspects of the behavior of physical forces.

Psychology *Is* Physics

For now the Gestalt psychologists discovered that this procedure made them neighbors of the most advanced natural scientists, the physicists.

The quotation above comes from Köhler's (1969) *The Task of Gestalt Psychology*[6] where, after a discussion of Wertheimer's principles of grouping according to proximity, similarity, and simplicity, Köhler drew the parallel with the physics of the turn of the century. This is not the mechanical physics of Newton, where particles in space and time individually act on one another—it is the physics of Pierre Curie, James Clerk Maxwell, Max Planck, and Ernst Mach. Here is the rationale behind Gestalt theory:[7]

Mach, for instance, asked this question: When a physical system approaches a state of equilibrium or a steady state, why is this change so often characterized by growing regularity, symmetry, and simplicity in the distribution of the material and the forces within the system?

Köhler also studied the writings of Clerk Maxwell, "the greatest figure in the development of field physics," and Max Planck, who introduced quantum physics. Maxwell described Faraday's earlier work, which made possible the electrical generator, as beginning with "wholes" and arriving at the parts by analysis, rather than the reverse, beginning with parts. He quoted Maxwell along these lines in a treatise published in 1873, noting that this was forty years before the Gestalt psychologists began:

We are accustomed to consider the universe as made up of parts.... To conceive of a particle, however, requires a process of abstraction, since all our perceptions are related to extended bodies, so that the idea of the *all* that is in our consciousness at a given instant is perhaps as primitive an idea as that of any individual thing. (Ibid., pp. 60–61)

Köhler's intention was to show by reference to the greats of physics that the Gestaltists were not preposterous—they were not "proceeding in a fantastic fashion." Far from it, in fact, since they were in agreement with the most natural of the natural sciences.

The physical analogy to which the Gestaltists turned was field theory, not Newton's mechanics or Descartes's geometry. To qualify as instances of Gestalt phenomena, physical processes had to meet what Köhler called "Ehrenfels's criteria." They had to be "suprasummative," so that qualities and effects were not derivable solely from properties of their parts, and they had to be transposable—so that their organization survived changes in the absolute values of their parts.

He pointed to electrostatics as an example. In an ellipsoidal conductor the density of charge is greatest at the points of greatest curvature and least where the curvature is least. It is the shape of the conductor, not its material or the quantity of charge. If charged particles are fed into one part of the conductor, the charge immediately redistributes itself to maintain the curvature/charge relationship.

Since the brain is a chemical/electrical entity, electrical fields there must correspond to perceptual Gestalten. To be isomorphic, brain processes need not mirror perceptions, they need only functionally correspond. It is easy to imagine how phenomena such as figure–ground and reversible figures, or even the Müller–Lyer illusion, could be produced by electrical fields and differences in charges on or in the cerebral cortex.

Köhler referred to Mach's findings in fluid dynamics as evidence that physical systems tend toward end states that are as simple and regular as possible. The tendency toward simplicity and regularity was called *Prägnanz* by Köhler. These principles apply to problem-solving behavior, as well as to perception, as Köhler tried to show in 1917.

Köhler and Insight?

I know that several psychologists will not easily believe that my description of intelligent behavior in apes is correct.... Therefore I have made moving pictures of some experiments of this type. They are much more convincing than all words and arguments which I might add in order to corroborate my statements; but we have no technique to give this strongest argument to the readers of a scientific journal. (Köhler 1926, pp. 145–161)

Wolfgang Köhler, the longest-lived and most influential of the Gestaltists, spent the years from 1913 to 1920 as director of the anthropoid research station of the Prussian Academy of Sciences on the island of Tenerife, in the Canary Islands off the west coast of Africa. He was twenty-six, seemingly young for a position of such responsibility, and he had no experience with apes or with any other animals. His doctoral dissertation at the Friedrich-Wilhelm University in Berlin in 1909 concerned hearing, and he continued his auditory research as assistant and instructor at the University of Frankfurt. Later he served as Wertheimer's subject in the famous phi experiments of 1912, when he became devoted to the Gestalt movement.

Why a young auditory researcher with no animal experience would be sent to a German research station on a Spanish island in the middle of the British shipping lanes just prior to World War I has become a subject for speculation (Ley 1990). The British quickly took control of the region when war broke out, and they saw no threat from German researchers studying apes on Tenerife. However, they might have wondered why the Germans had brought apes to the island—there were none there before 1913, and they were removed in 1920.

Inexperienced and perhaps distracted, Köhler nevertheless carried out a series of experiments on chimpanzees, chickens, and even children, published in translation as *The Mentality of Apes* in 1925. One line of research demonstrated *transposition learning* in chickens. He found that the birds could learn the concept of "degree of," so that after training to peck the lighter of two gray papers, they would choose the lighter of other presented pairs. They were responding to a relationship, not to the absolute values of the stimuli.

Even clearer results were obtained with apes and colors. Karl Lashley (1912) had found earlier that rats could learn to choose the larger of two circles. Over the next several decades, Lashley would side with the Gestaltists, stressing the importance of responding to relationships. This position was attacked more or less successfully by Clark Hull and his associates, who viewed Gestalt relationships as a "doctrine of despair" (1943, p. 26). Köhler was impressed with what seemed to be insightful problem solving by animals, and he saw this as damaging to psychological theories of the day, including Thorndike's connectionism.

In considering Köhler's findings, it is important to realize that he had little knowledge of the theories of the time, including Thorndike's (Ley 1990). He interpreted Thorndike's trial-and-error learning as no more than random and blind fumbling, with S-R connections mechanically stamped in by consequences. We have seen that this is not a fair representation of Thorndike's views, but Köhler was not alone in believing that it was.

Like other Gestaltists, Köhler believed that problem solving, perception, learning, and thinking involve the organism's regarding the relevant parts of its environment in a particular way. They stressed *Einsicht*, or "insight," which they saw as opposed to trial and error, as basis for learning. Köhler defined insight in 1925 as "the appearance of a complete solution with reference to the whole layout of the field." Let us examine Köhler's findings and assess just exactly what he found.

A typical problem for an ape required that two sticks be joined together to achieve the length necessary to retrieve a banana placed outside the bars of its cage. In another situation, an obstructing box had to be moved before the ape could reach the banana. A typical chimpanzee exhibited plenty of behaviors that Köhler described as "crude stupidities," but the moment of "Einsicht," or "insight," eventually came. Overall, the chimpanzees showed astonishing *stupidity*, not insight. In one case, Köhler wrote that "it did not dawn on Tschego for hours to push the obstructing box out of the way." Köhler judged errors as "good," when they were caused by "lack of comprehension of the conditions of the task." "Bad errors" were manifestations of "the crude stupidities arising from habit." These errors were extremely annoying to the experimenter; "It almost makes one angry," he wrote.

However, just as Watson's work with children was compressed into the story of Albert B., so Köhler's investigation of "ape mentality" was pretty much the story of *one* ape, Sultan. Only he could solve the most difficult problems without demonstration or assistance. When a banana was hung from the ceiling of a room and a wooden box was nearby on the floor, only he could move the box to use as a platform to reach the fruit. None of the others could do so without the assistance of demonstration. Chimpanzees are not adept at stacking boxes, and when they did manage to successfully stack them, it was often without regard for the location of the banana. Even Sultan failed here, so the "insight" shown was not striking.

Perception of Depth: Was Berkeley Mistaken?

Not only is tridimensional vision, as a result of organization, possible without binocular parallax and experience, but inasmuch as less articulate organization seems prior to more articulate organization, tridimensional vision must be the earlier form.... (Koffka 1930, p. 177)

Three-dimensional vision may be more basic and primitive than is two-dimensional vision, according to Koffka (1930, p. 216). But how can that be, since depth perception has been *explained*, and, as Koffka noted, the explanation is so widely accepted that no one bothers to do research on depth perception any longer? Not surprisingly, the Gestaltists did not accept the traditional account for depth perception, the theory proposed by Berkeley in 1709 and accepted as fact in the twentieth century. For example, Woodworth (1938) listed the many cues that transform the two-dimensional retinal image into a three-dimentional world.

That view begins with the fact that we have two eyes and specific retinal points that are disparately stimulated. Disparate images act as a cue for an inference of "outness"—therefore, we see depth, actually a compromise between seeing two objects and seeing one. It was Helmholtz who demonstrated conclusively that distance is the product of such "unconscious inferences."

Does that mean that our perception is really the sum of those stimulated points—the complex of sensations that result? That illustrates the complaint made first by Wertheimer and echoed by Köhler and then Koffka that psychology cannot be a matter of construction of wholes from pieces. After all, *physical science* no longer follows such a model, so why should psychology?

Koffka's argument was simple, though the evidence is difficult to summarize. First, he said that, according to Helmholtz's theory, we do not normally see double images because we interpret them as depth. It is only with effort that we can detect double images at all, as when we focus on a near object while attending to distant ones. However, Helmholtz knew well, Koffka contended, that double images may themselves be localized in space, an impossibility if they were the cue for space.

More convincingly, Koffka argued that depth perception occurs frequently in the absence of disparate retinal images. The depth perceived in the apparent movement demonstrations described above occur with monocular viewing. The Necker cube appears three-dimensional viewed with one eye, as do many other patterns that possess the structural properties required:

when simple symmetry is achievable in two dimensions, we shall see a plane figure; if it requires three dimensions, then we shall see a solid. But always the organization of the field resulting from retinal stimulation will show the greatest possible symmetry.

The most elementary case of space perception is the figure–ground relationship described by Edgar Rubin, since what is perceived as "figure" is perceived as in front of a "ground." However, this is true whether or not it really is closer than the background.

Even color brightness influences depth perception, since brighter colors seem more "surfacy" (Koffka 1930, p. 174) and are "thinner" than are dark, less bright colors which look "thicker," and show depth. "Brightness here does not mean simply the intensity of reflected light, but a quality that Koffka could only call "insistence." Titchener (1910) called it "self assertiveness," or "aggressiveness." Koffka suggested that when we look at a scale of shades of gray from white to black, there is more than an intensity difference. Compared with white, a dark gray is less aggressive, assertive, and "insistent." And it is thick and deep, compared with the white, which is "surfacy and thin."

Beyond Classic Gestalt Theory

Gunnar Johansson is familiar to students of developmental psychology because of his findings on the perception of "biological motion." In brief, Johansson showed that when a dozen or so lights are attached to a person's feet, knees, waist, elbows, wrists, and shoulders, observers instantly recognize "biological motion" when the configuration of lights is seen moving in the dark (Johansson 1975). Further, observers can distinguish male versus female models with fair accuracy, and even fairly young infants can distinguish biological from artificial motion. However, this later and more popular work derived from a broader basis in 1950 when Johansson extended Gestalt psychology beyond Wertheimer's laws of organization to include event perception (Johansson 1950).

Patterns of motions resolvable to horizontal and vertical components were described by Pierre Lissajous (1822–1880), a French physicist who reflected light from mirrors mounted on tuning forks held at right angles and created a variety of visual patterns, as may be more easily done with an oscilloscope. Ernst Mach, the German physicist already familiar to us, first considered such effects in psychology. Consider a simple example to see how resolution to vectors seems to explain phenomena.

Two spots move fairly slowly, at a rate of 0.7 centimeters per second, though frequency may be varied widely. One moves up and down vertically and the other back and forth horizontally. They briefly meet at the low point of the first spot and the extreme left of the second's path. Subjects may comprise a large audience, which looks at the two spots moving toward one another, fusing briefly, and moving apart. However, viewers clearly see the spots moving on an oblique path—the "vector resultant" of the vertical and horizontal motions. The two spots move toward one another, meet in the middle of the oblique "path," and retreat, sometimes appearing to collide and bounce away from one another.

Many more complex cases are possible, and some are described by Johansson. Effects occur even when motion is absent, as when the brightnesses of several lights are varied in such a way as to produce apparent motion. Imagine one light rhythmically changing intensity, as if "pumping," and you will see how it might seem to be approaching and retreating. These effects are "W-phenomena," or "wandering" phenomena, and Johansson was careful to show that they are not a subclass of gamma effects or stroboscopically produced apparent movement effects. Wertheimer's apparent movement effects disappeared if stimuli were separated by 200 milliseconds—simple succession was seen, rather than movement. W-effects occur within ranges of stimulus separation of 175 to 4,500 milliseconds and hence are a different order of event. These "motion Gestalts" (dropping the less-familiar German plural) are demonstrable with color changes, as "sound phantoms," and as "phantom air currents," (Johansson 1950, chapters 7, 8, and 9, respectively), but discussion of them is beyond the scope of this chapter.

Kurt Lewin: Gestaltist?

Motivation (which was Kurt Lewin's main interest) I will not discuss because we do not yet know how Lewin's important work is related to Gestalt psychology, the theme of my lectures. (Köhler 1969, p. 120)

Kurt Lewin (1890–1947) was not clearly a Gestalt psychologist, as Köhler's remark testifies, partly because he was not really a basic researcher, as Gestalt psychologists were and still are. He is particularly interesting and inspirational for those who see psychology as strictly applied, devoted to studying matters that are of popular interest, such as "insight" and the behavior of groups working under different kinds of leadership conditions.

In a real sense, Lewin was the model for the headline-grabbing forms of social psychology that show how subservient to authority people are and how a mock-jail setting can turn normal students into sadistic "guards" and cringing "prisoners." However, many students and colleagues remember him as an inspirational figure who first awakened their interest in psychology.[8]

Lewin[9] was born in Prussia on a date he often said was easy to remember—the ninth nine of ninety, referring to September 9, 1890 (Marrow 1969, p. 3). The family ran a store, over which the family lived. Kurt had an older sister, Hertha, and two younger brothers, Egon and Fritz. Even in childhood Kurt was an observer of social behavior. His brother Fritz was "tall, athletic, and high-spirited and excelled at sports" (Marrow 1969, p. 4), and he often came home late at night. But, however late he came, his mother, Recha, was waiting with motherly concern. Later Kurt's wife, Gertrud, believed that he gauged the depth of a woman's love or the affection of a friend by their willingness to wait for him, since he was always late for appointments and classes.

The Prussia of the turn of the twentieth century was strongly anti-Semitic; the aristocrats and army officers who were the cream of society would do business with Jews but would not have any social contact with them. Yet, oddly, Prussian law required religious education in elementary school, so Kurt and other Jewish children attended Jewish religious classes and underwent the Hebrew Bar Mitzvah ritual. The Lewin family still celebrated Christmas, however, and exchanged gifts as did other Prussians.

Berlin Education and Philosophical Interests

As an elementary school child, Kurt was sent to board with a family[10] that lived in Posen and later Berlin, since educational opportunities were much better away from Mogilno, their tiny home village. Kurt had not been a standout pupil thus far and was known for temper tantrums that led to the family nickname the "Furious Herring."[11] He was not suspected to be unusually intelligent until his last two years of gymnasium. Marrow noted a significant event that occurred when he was seventeen—one that is of utmost importance:

In 1907 he was introduced to Greek philosophy and fell in love with it. It was a love that lasted all his life. During this same period his scholastic record improved remarkably. (Marrow 1969, p. 5)

The fact is that a favorite paper contrasted Aristotle's doctrine of essences and natural law with Galileo's Enlightenment notions.[12] He argued for the status of opposites as extremes of continua, rather than as isolated "contrasts," and passionately argued against group-averaged data and for the intensive study of single cases. It may come as a surprise to those who know only Lewin's applied work, but he was always the philosopher. As his wife, Gertrud, said,

He never abandoned philosophy. In Berlin he lectured one year in psychology and had a seminar in philosophy; the next year he had a lecture in philosophy and a seminar in psychology. (Marrow 1969, p. 17)

An earlier philosophical/theoretical paper appeared in 1922 as an analysis of the concept of "identity" in the sciences (Lewin 1922). He believed that psychology had reached a turning point (*Wendepunkt*) comparable to that reached in physics in Galileo's time. He contrasted the ways in which physics and biology determine "genidentity," or the ways in which objects maintain identity over time and thus are treated as the "same" object. In physics, objects extend over time, and we can speak of the "same" star shining on the Roman Empire and on the Wrigley Building. And we can say that the material composing the star is essentially the same over the centuries.

However, in biology, we don't do that—the egg and the year-old chicken are structurally very different, yet we treat them as different stages of the same biological matter. The forty- and twenty-year-old are treated as "the same person," though few molecules may have survived the decades. Lewin concluded that physics and biology are therefore essentially different in their descriptive units and the two sciences are thus incommensurable—there is no translating one to the other.

As sciences mature, they purify and segregate themselves increasingly from other sciences. There may be some unity of the sciences, as Descartes hoped to establish, but that may be wishful thinking. Whether "physiological psychology" progresses or not, psychology is best served in segregating itself and developing an autonomous set of concepts, thus purifying itself as do all sciences that advance.

Lewin in Graduate School and as Soldier of Kaiser Wilhelm II

As a graduate student at Berlin he organized courses for the city's workers, whose powerlessness stemmed largely from their ignorance, and this enterprise was evidently successful. In 1914 World War I broke out, and, though he was about to finish his doctorate, he volunteered to serve in the German army, where he spent four years in combat and won the Iron Cross before being wounded in 1918. He volunteered as a private and left a lieutenant who had acquired the useful skill of being able to sleep while standing up and when walking or marching, a skill that he claimed he used later in life (Marrow 1969, p. 10). Lewin was wounded and hospitalized near the end of the war, and his youngest brother, Fritz, was killed in action.

Lewin's first, and perhaps most interesting, psychological work was published in 1917 and titled "War Landscape." He described how the "life space" of a soldier differed from that of a civilian, such that a lovely open field or a quiet spot beneath a cliff appears as inviting to the latter but dangerous to the soldier. More specifically, the landscape changes for the soldier as he approaches the front lines. When the soldier is still a great distance from the front, the landscape seems to stretch endlessly in all directions. However, as the front is approached, the landscape takes on boundaries, so that it has direction and a front and a back.

This structuring of the space is viewed as objective features of the landscape, though it is a function of "soldier needs" that influence perception. A soldier needs physical protection, food, a favorable position with respect to the enemy, and other things that structure his space. Even objects change character, from "peace things" to "war things," so that things become defined solely by their possible military application.

Lewin used the terms boundary, direction, zone, and topological theory in that paper and referred to the evil of the "dehumanizing of the enemy" as deplorable.[13] In 1918 Lewin returned to Berlin, where he found the research of Wertheimer, Köhler, and Koffka to be interesting but unappealing because of its lack of practical application.

He published two 1919 papers on workers in industry and in agriculture, pointing out the great differences in what is called "hard work." The agricultural worker must do many different things daily and according to season, where the industrial worker does more repetitive things and therefore receives less satisfaction.

He referred to the then-popular time-and-motion studies of industrial engineer F. W. Taylor, who promoted a stopwatch and clipboard approach to factory work. His advocacy of piecework pay[14] and efficiency through the elimination of inefficient motions earned him the nickname "Speedy" among workers. Lewin criticized Taylor, arguing for the "life value" of work over the exclusive emphasis on maximum efficiency (Lewin 1920).

Lewin joined the faculty at Berlin in 1921 and formed a group that met at the Swedish Cafe across the street from the Berlin Psychological Institute. There he noticed that waiters remembered their customers' bills only until they were paid, an observation that led to the later research of Bluma Zeigarnik.

Lewin's Theoretical Psychology

His work was so strongly focused on applied features of current culture that it is easy to forget that he did propose a field theory, about which he felt very strongly. He was influenced by the field physics that had grown in Germany during the early decades of the twentieth century, as were Wertheimer, Köhler, and Koffka, his companions at Berlin. He thought of people as systems of tensions that could be best seen as energy fields, constantly changing as they move in the life space, or psychological field.

The formula B = f(P,E) proposed that Behavior is a function of a Person operating in an Environment, all represented in ellipses called Jordan curves. This spatial representation came from topology, a geometry that represents things arranged in their relative positions, without precise, point-for-point duplication. These representations appeared all over Lewin's papers and became known as "Lewin's eggs" at the University of Berlin.[15]

Always there are spaces and forces and vectors and valences—it was almost psychoanalysis without concern for the history of the individual. Lewin's psychology was a psychology of the present, with no concern for the history that brought a person to the current situation. The 1920 book did not do well, and, as it received little notice, Lewin occupied himself with the founding of a psychological institute at Hebrew University in Jerusalem.

Lewin became known in America in 1929 when a student published a description of the experiments with Zeigarnik and portrayed Lewin as a Gestaltist dealing with psychic energies just as physicists had dealt with physical energies only a few decades before (Brown 1929). Lewin himself presented his ideas in the same year at the Ninth International Congress of Psychology at Yale. He presented his talk in German, but it didn't matter, since he showed films and communicated his enthusiasm to an audience which could not understand the language he spoke!

The film showed behavior of children that exemplified his views, such as the appearance of insight shown when an eighteen-month-old infant tries to sit on a spot on a stone. She managed to keep her eyes on the stone by looking down between her legs while backing over the stone—thus ensuring that she would sit on target. Gordon Allport, the Harvard social psychologist, was there and believed that a number of Americans were impressed with the film (again, Hothersall 2004, p. 235).

Real People, Not Statistical Myths
In 1931 Lewin contributed a piece in Murchison's *Handbook of Child Psychology* titled "Environmental Forces in Child Behavior and Devel-

opment," translated by Donald K. Adams.[16] In that chapter, which introduced Lewin to a wide audience, he argued for the study of the behavior of individual children. He proposed that it is imperative to understand well the life space of a single child rather than to collect data averaged over groups. The "average child," who exemplifies such research, has no existence in fact, only as a "statistical myth," to use Lewin's expression.[17]

It is Lewin's views, not those of the traditional Gestaltists, that lead psychologists to believe that the Gestaltists were advocating the study of "the whole person." That was pure Lewin, who did urge that the whole Gestalt of the child's life space be examined. You can rest assured that the result will not match the "statistical-average child."

Over the course of development, the child's life space changes from small and undifferentiated to large and differentiated—note that this is a view wholly in keeping with William James's views and with the tenets of the functionalism that had swept America in the first decades of the twentieth century. As Lewin cast it, the infant's concerns extend barely beyond the limits of its body, and a favorite toy may be removed from a few feet away with no protest. However, a two-year-old will react differently, as we all know.

In the 1931 chapter he also illustrated his method of representing fields and gradients of forces in the life space. He described detour problems, in which the child must move away from a highly valenced[18] goal object in order to eventually reach it. His methods and interpretations were identical to those of Köhler, whose subjects had been the apes brought to Tenerife.

Lewin also described conflict in terms of conflicting forces. A child may experience conflict between two attractive choices—an approach–approach conflict—or between other choices constituting approach–avoidance or avoidance–avoidance conflicts. Perhaps interestingly, he noted that once the choice is made in an approach–approach conflict, the rejected alternative looks mighty attractive.[19]

Perhaps the conception of psychological choice field that Lewin promoted is best illustrated in a strange case published as a very long monograph by one of his students at Berlin, a woman named Tamara Dembo.

A Demonstration of Induced Insanity

Tamara Dembo was a student of Kurt Lewin who reported[20] a fascinating demonstration of induced anger, interpreted as a Gestalt phenomenon. Her aim was to create a "field of forces" that would "transform a person's life space" in such a way as to produce strong emotion. In fact, the subjects were put into a situation where frustration produces anger, along with general disorganization of behavior. Dozens of subjects participated.

Each subject was seated in a chair within a rectangle marked on the floor and was asked to get a flower from a vase that was just out of reach, while keeping both feet within the rectangle. In that situation, the subject quickly finds a solution by leaning on the chair and thus reaching far enough to grasp the flower. Then the subject is asked to discover a second solution and confronts a "barrier," since there is no second solution and attempts to find one are frustrated.

The subject did not become aggressive at this point but merely informed the experimenters that there is no second solution. Attention to the task is diverted away, and readiness to leave is expressed. However, Dembo then created an "outer barrier" by insisting that there is indeed a second solution and that she is sure that the subject can discover it. To escape the field, the subject must repeatedly attempt to reach the impossible goal. Subjects frequently spent over an hour in this extremely unpleasant situation, before they fled it. However, strange things happened first.

Dembo's subjects reacted to the initial tension of the situation by "Moving up to a level of fantasy where barriers do not exist and wishes can come true" (de Rivera 1976, p. 372). This cannot be maintained and the subject returns to the impossible task, where tension accumulates. The tension acts to dissolve the various boundaries within the field, such as the real goal and an easy but unacceptable substitute—a flower within easy reach. That flower is rejected by the experimenters, and tension mounts. The boundary between reality and fantasy breaks down, along with the boundary separating public and private!

With a little effort, this progression toward insanity is easy to imagine—just picture yourself in a hopeless position, where you must act, but where there is no chance of success. As tension accumulates, your "objectivity" suffers, in a manner of speaking, as occurred with Dembo's subjects. At that point, her subjects engaged in "minor irrationalities—finding themselves holding the nearby flower, thinking that perhaps they really can do an impossible feat (such as hypnotizing the flower), telling the experimenter something that is really too personal to share, and so forth" (de Rivera 1976, p. 372). As the tension continues to mount, the boundaries of the field fade so completely that even the boundary defining the self versus the environment cannot be preserved. At this point the subject explodes in anger or, in many cases described by Koffka, the subject bolts from the room and is later found huddled in a corner, crying.

Including that experiment, sixty-four experiments were done between 1925 and 1928 with a total of twenty-seven subjects, each spending from one to two hours. The situations were designed to create tensions and generate anger as was the case in "fetch the flower." Other tasks were assigned that were also described as achievable, though they were not. For example, subjects were asked to throw rings over the necks of bottles fifteen feet away—until ten consecutive successes occurred. This was effectively impossible, but it seemed possible.

Dembo saw the effect of these experiments as a transformation of a person's life space, such that the situation becomes filled with tension, transforming the person. Emotion arises from a restructuring of the field, and the intensity of the emotion corresponds to the degree of transformation of the life space. Kurt Koffka endorsed the essentials of this view but preferred to interpret the dynamic organizations as states of tension within the ego (Koffka 1935, pp. 407–410).

Other Work at Berlin

Bluma Zeigarnik's dissertation work, a staple item in countless textbooks since it was published, showed the greater recall for uncompleted tasks (Zeigarnik 1927). This was the first corroboration of Lewin's notion of tension systems, with 164 subjects, child and adult, performing from eighteen to twenty-two tasks. These were simple, such as listing cities, solving riddles, counting backward, and stringing beads—half were completed and half interrupted. When subjects were later asked to recall the tasks, those interrupted were recalled twice as often; the ratio of recall of uncompleted to completed was 1.9 to 1. The first task recalled was three times as likely to be an uncompleted one.

Zeigarnik proposed that motivation for a "satisfying performance" arose from three sources: tension arising from a need to achieve completion as a goal in itself, personal ambition, and the "obligation" to follow the directions of the experimenter. The strength of these quasi-needs was manifested when, as often happened, the subject resisted the interruption. Subsequent experiments showed that it was not just the emotion aroused by interruption that was producing the effect. Subjects who were interrupted on one third of the tasks and subsequently allowed to finish them were no more likely to recall those tasks than the tasks that were uninterrupted. However, the third of the tasks that were interrupted and never finished were once again memorable.

Another Russian woman, Maria Ovsiankina, extended Zeigarnik's findings with 125 subjects who were usually interrupted "accidentally," rather than deliberately, and who were given a "free period" of eight to ten minutes immediately after the interruption. During that period, one hundred percent of the "accidentally" interrupted tasks were spontaneously resumed, and eighty-two percent of the deliberately interrupted tasks were resumed.

Ferdinand Hoppe used darts, ring tossing, puzzles, and arithmetic problems in a 1930 study of aspiration level. Subjects performed tasks of varying difficulty, including insoluble problems, and shifted their stated goals as a result of their experiences of success and failure. In 1928 Anitra Karsten studied psychical satiation, a term coined by Lewin to refer to a "decrease in tension level" due to repetition, but not to muscular fatigue. Her subjects repeatedly drew pencil patterns, read poems, or made pencil strokes until they wished to stop—"had no desire to continue." Tasks judged to be agreeable or disagreeable "sated" faster than did neutral tasks, and Lewin applied the results to the phenomenon of more frequent change in women's fashions than in men's.

It is noteworthy that in all of these experiments, which in many ways were the prototypes for the social psychology of the second half of the twentieth century, the actual behavior of many subjects was examined—no questionnaires were administered and no inferential statistics were used. You can rest assured that Lewin was later criticized for such practices, and he agreed that more subjects never hurt and that exact measurement is desirable in some cases. However, quantitative nicety was clearly of minor importance to him.

Lewin's "Action Research" at Iowa

The student explained this (his thesis topic) to Lewin and Lewin replied, "Ach, nonsense! Just nonsense!." To a student struggling with a thesis based on a new idea such as this, it's not very encouraging to hear your ideas called nonsense. Well, it turned out to be nonsense. (Roger Barker, in Marrow 1969, p. 94)

Lewin spent nine years at Iowa, from 1935–1944, as Research Professor of Child Psychology—he was able to bring Tamara Dembo, along with Roger Barker, who had just finished a doctorate at Stanford. It was there that Lewin began his "group dynamics action research," best known for its finding that groups of boys work more efficiently and harmoniously when organized democratically then when control is authoritarian or is largely absent—"laissez-faire." But that famous research was awfully crudely done, and Lewin's antipathy toward the Nazi authoritarian regime in Germany made it impossible for any other findings to emerge.

Other work was more substantial—for example, the "group decision" study done with anthropologist Margaret Mead to encourage the wartime eating of what were called "variety meats." Iowa wives claimed that their husbands specified what meats were to be served, but it was found that it was the wives who did the choosing and the husbands were stuck with that choice. A variety of other research had been published by 1940, and Lewin was becoming famous. And he was aware of the "publish or perish" policy that was conspicuous in America.

Work on level of aspiration that was begun in Berlin by a student named Hoppe was continued and is still recognizable in the studies of the kinds of goals that subjects high and low in need for achievement select. They select goals that are intermediate in difficulty, allowing perhaps a 50/50 chance of success. Those low in achievement need or high in fear of failure choose very easy or very difficult tasks.

The Zeigarnik effect, whereby subjects recall and resume interrupted tasks better than completed ones, and the frustration/dedifferentiation studies were widely known.

In one study, done by Barker, Dembo, and Lewin, children were allowed to play with ordinary toys for half an hour, at which time they were allowed access to a second room that had previously been blocked off with heavy wire mesh. The second room featured more attractive toys, and, after a period of access to them, the children were expelled from the room and access was prevented by the heavy wire screen and a conspicuous padlock. Blocking of goal-oriented behavior was designed to produce frustration, and it apparently did.

Subsequent play appeared regressive, so that a four-and-a-half-year-old became a babyish, thumb-sucking three-year-old. Play seemed less intellectual, unhappiness and restlessness were evident, and some aggression occurred. In a subsequent experiment by Wright, in which pairs of children served, there were actually attacks on the experimenter. The procedure thus appeared to produce regression, dedifferentiation of the life space so as to become more primitive.[21]

Lewin and Industrial Psychology: The Harwood Project
Lewin had become interested in industrial psychology as a young man
and published a critique of the Taylor system in 1920. He argued that
efficiency experts were not enough and that psychologists were needed
to ensure job satisfaction, an essential ingredient if high outputs are
to be achieved at low cost. It is not the hours worked but the "inner
value" of the work that is important (Marrow 1969, p. 17).

In 1939 the Harwood Manufacturing Corporation established an
operation in the mountains of rural Virginia, employing 300 local
women. After twelve weeks of training and the use of every known
method of incentive and pressure, their output was half that of the
company's plants in the Northeast, and Lewin was asked to intervene
(Lewin biographer Alfred Marrow was an officer of the company).

Lewin saw that the employees viewed the production quotas as
unattainable, so they had no "social reality" and the employees' failure
to attain them was not accompanied by feelings of failure. The quotas
were not really goals as far as the workers were concerned. The first
job, therefore, was to stop pressing individuals to improve and to convince them that the quotas could be met. Workers met in small groups,
since Lewin always believed that if group standards are set and group
attitudes exist, individuals do everything possible to conform to those
standards and attitudes.

The company also brought in sixty skilled workers from the North,
who immediately met and maintained production quotas. This had no
effect for the first two weeks, but then production of all workers
increased. Alex Bakelas was brought in to run things for Lewin, and
he began regular meetings with productive supervisors. A group of
workers was formed that was allowed to decide how to change to
increase production and to vote when and by how much to raise production quotas.

Having a hand in the production process raised quotas and production from seventy-five units a day to eighty-seven and then to ninety, a
level that was maintained for five months and that was matched by no
other group. In Lewin's words, "Deciding links motivation to action"
(Marrow 1969, p. 144), and discussion groups—or other kinds of
groups—were not enough.

Bakelas and J. R. P. French experimented further on methods of
increasing and maintaining production quotas without increasing "tension" in the participants' life spaces. Workers were allowed to plan
their days—when and how hard to work—as long as quotas were

met. Leadership training groups, later to be called T-groups, involved role playing and sensitivity training and were conducted by French in the early 1940s. French also persuaded the supervisors, all women, to accept the hiring of older workers. There was initial resistance, since the supervisors were sure that older workers—women over thirty—could not physically do the work, could not learn to do it, and would soon quit.

The war had brought on shortages of labor and older workers were themselves in short supply, so Harwood had to hire those that it could find. But how to convince the supervisors to accept them and give them a chance? French asked the supervisors themselves to form a group and look into the question, producing what data could be found to support their contentions. They found, of course, that older workers in fact performed better, learned faster, and stayed on the job longer than did younger workers, and, "these findings being their own, they trusted them."[22]

Group Dynamics at MIT

Lewin was a citizen by 1940, working part-time for the Office of Strategic Services, the precursor of the Central Intelligence Agency, and so was commuting between Iowa City and Washington. What he and his colleagues worked on is not specifically known, because of the veil of secrecy that shields wartime projects. However, it involved problems of boosting morale at home and lowering that of the enemy, choosing leaders, training them, increasing war production, and convincing civilians to change their diet to conform to wartime shortages.

Concerning the last category, Leon Festinger found that a newly introduced beverage was more readily accepted when the container in which it was distributed was also new (Marrow 1969, pp. 155–156). In 1944 Lewin was promised a million dollars' support from the American Jewish Council (AJC) to research racial and religious discrimination and to discover remedies for it. He also was promised support from the Field Foundation, and Iowa was pressing him to decide whether he would continue research and teaching there or go off on these new projects, since it was clear that no one could do both.

He contacted friends at Berkeley and at MIT, hoping that one could offer him a home—he preferred that it be Berkeley, because of the climate. As it happened, the MIT offer came first, and he moved to Newtonville, Massachusetts, in August of 1944. A year later an article was published that included the expression, "Nothing is as practical as a good theory" and described the goal of the new MIT center.[23] The key assumption of the center came from Lewin's experience at Harwood.

It seemed clear that the first thing to do was to set group norms and attitudes—individual members will then go to great lengths and through much suffering to conform to those norms. Hence, it is easier to change the group rather than the individuals comprising it! The center aimed to discover the forces that lead to group cohesiveness, the attractive and repellent forces that define groups. Homogeneity of individual members is not a factor, since members need not be similar, and the "whole is different from the sum of its parts," as Köhler would say.

Even at what was to be this late stage of his career, immersed in applied projects, his teaching was still philosophical and theoretical. Harold Kelley recalled the "exotic, specialized" subjects that Lewin covered—topological and vector analyses, as well as "Aristotelian versus Galilean modes of thought" (Marrow 1969, p. 188). John Thibaut, Lewin's assistant, was formerly a graduate student in philosophy at the University of North Carolina at Chapel Hill. Along with theory and philosophy, Lewin still drew diagrams in the snow, just as he had done decades earlier in Berlin.

Because of its generous funding, The AJC's Commission on Community Relations (CCI) in New York City demanded much of Lewin's time. The goal of the CCI was to better understand, and thus combat, prejudice. This was to be accomplished through long-term research on ways to train community leaders, to change environments, and to make minority groups feel that they belonged.

However, the AJC pressed for "fire fighting" responses to isolated acts of prejudice, the first occurring in 1946. Italian Catholic youths had disturbed Yom Kippur services at Coney Island—what could Lewin do about it? He had only two assistants at the time, and his chief assistant, Charles Hendry, had just quit because Lewin continually started new projects before old ones were complete. In many cases, the new projects interfered with or required abandoning of ongoing work.

Lewin met with local groups of Jews, Catholics, Protestants, and "Negroes" and immediately had the charges against the youths dropped—they were turned over to their priest and to the Catholic Big Brothers. It appeared that the miscreants were not really anti-Jewish but were generally hostile. After all manner of counseling they became substantially less aggressive, though their "attitudes" remained the same.[24] It was Lewin's view that "you can't legislate good will," and that objectionable behavior is best changed by withdrawing support from the local social group. As was true at Harwood, group norms work wonders.

In related work, Lewin and his assistants found that attitudes toward Negro sales clerks, as assessed by questionnaires, did not correspond with actions. People said that they would not shop at stores with black clerks—but observation showed that they did shop at such stores. Lewin planned to assess methods of integrating housing projects, and it was after his death that results clearly showed that mixing races and religious groups was superior to integration by separate building or area.

The Founding of T-Groups

In the summer of 1946 the state of Connecticut asked for help in training leaders to combat religious and racial prejudice, and Lewin's group held a two-week session at Teachers' College in New Britain. This was an important project both for Lewin, whose CCI was underfunded and understaffed, and for the Connecticut Interracial Commission, whose lack of success to date had called its competence into question. Frank Simpson, head of that commission, called Lewin.

Forty-one volunteers, mostly educators and social workers, half blacks and Jews, met daily in group discussions in which the staff and members of the group were treated as peers. The sessions were taped and reviewed in the evening by staff and then by "students." They spent time role playing and appraising their own behavior—this self-appraisal constituted about a fifth of their time.[25] Most participants, interviewed six months later, reported that they felt more competent working with groups and had more sensitivity to the feelings of others.

The Office of Naval Research awarded a grant to Lewin to establish the National Training Laboratories (NTL) in Bethel, Maine, but he died before the first meeting. The NTL was meant to deal with bigotry and raising the self-esteem of blacks and their children. Simple role-playing instances of bigotry were enacted and different responses tested. The most effective response to a bigot appeared to be a calm one, rather than a violent response or no response—at least this was the judgment of some 500 subjects who participated.

In Britain, the Tavistock Institute was founded by Eric Trist and A. T. M. Wilson, who had previously worked in the rehabilitation of returning British prisoners of war. Lewin published two papers in the first issue of *Human Relations*, a journal founded by Trist and Wilson and published jointly by Tavistock and Lewin's MIT group. He described his view of group dynamics as quasi-stationary equilibria, with forces promoting and resisting change and promoting and resisting discrimination. Change comes through methods that add to or diminish tension—in his view, decreases in tension are preferable.

On Tuesday, February 11, 1947, Kurt Lewin had a busy day and fell ill late in the evening. His family doctor determined that he had suffered a heart attack and should be hospitalized the next day. The fatal seizure came later that evening. He had seemed exhausted and almost frantic for some time—no longer playful and optimistic. In 1947 Donald Adams asked him when he would get back to *"vergleichenden Wissenschaftslehre,"* the comparative study of the sciences, as represented decades earlier in his Aristotle—Galileo paper and in lectures since. Adams remembered his answer:

I must do that. These things we are finding out will be discovered in five or ten years anyway, but this other might be fifty years away. (Marrow 1969, p. 235)

Or, never? Adams felt that the philosophy of "comparative sciences" was Lewin's real business in life. Maybe Lewin thought so too.

16 Science, Application, and Theory: Pavlov, Guthrie, and Hull

Ivan Petrovich Pavlov's venerable appearance at Yale's International Psychological Congress was no anticlimax to his visit at Harvard's International Physiological Congress (*Time*, Sept. 2)...though he spoke in Russian and in highly technical terms...they applauded him tremendously before and after he spoke. (Gerow 1988, p. 13)

Watson mentioned "conditioned responses" frequently in his writings promoting behaviorism, and he referred to Pavlov's research. However, he was not really familiar with Pavlovian conditioning. He had company—Horsley Gantt, a physician who translated Pavlov's lectures in 1927, estimated that fewer than a half dozen people understood Pavlov's work in the 1920s (Pavlov 1927).

However, by the late 1980s classical conditioning achieved what one writer (Turkkan 1989) called a "hegemony" in psychological and physiological research. In large part this was due to the success of conditioning methods in medicine and in other practical areas. During the 1930s, behavioral theories grew in popularity, particularly the S-R associationist behaviorisms that Skinner would later combat.[1] Edwin Guthrie's one-trial contiguity theory was almost a philosopher's behaviorism that began with a single, simple principle that could be applied to all psychological phenomena. Clark Hull's theory, though outwardly more complex and imposing, was in fact far simpler, and it dominated psychology for several decades of the middle twentieth century.

We begin with Pavlov (see figure 16.1), who was no behaviorist, though he was treated as one. He believed that Westerners never really understood him...but "they applauded nonetheless."

Figure 16.1
Pavlov. Courtesy of the Archives of the History of American Psychology, University of
Akron.

Pavlov

Pavloff. Ivan Petrovitch Pavloff (Pavlov or Pawlow—take your choice of Russian transliterations), physiologist, Nobel Prizewinner and indubitably the
most distinguished living scientist of Russia, sailed from New York for France,
July 14, on the *Majestic*, . . . he was robbed at the Grand Central Terminal of
$2,000—all his ready cash. . . . Commenting on his trying experiences, Dr. Pavl-
off said he was going back to Russia, where there is "law and order." . . . Pavloff
is 75 years old, tall, white haired, majestic, active. (Gerow 1988, p. 9)

Ivan Petrovich Pavlov was born the son of a priest in Ryazan, Russia,
in 1849 and began his higher education at a theological seminary. He
then attended Petersburg University and finally the Imperial Medical
Surgical Academy, where he earned a medical degree in 1883. His research on the physiology of digestion won him a Nobel Prize in 1904
and an international reputation that prepared an enthusiastic reception
for his psychological work.

Hence, he was well-known when his *Conditioned Reflexes*[2] appeared
in translation in 1927. Americans had heard news of the conditioned
reflex (CR), and some had made use of it in theoretical writings. How-

ever, few grasped its real significance, and even today it is rare when Pavlov is understood by American psychologists. He was not the "Pavlov" encountered in psychology textbooks.

Body as Living Machine

Soviet psychotherapy has developed under conditions entirely different from those in foreign countries and in pre-revolutionary Russia. It is being built on the basis of dialectical materialism, a materialist teaching of higher nervous activity, the unity of the mind and body, and the determination of consciousness by the conditions of life.[3]

The philosophy of the past several centuries had passed on the legacy of Descartes, a legacy that lives on in our commonsense views of the mind. According to this view, which is really the only one that we are taught, we each have (or we are) a mind trapped in the physical structure of a body. We are "ghosts in machines" (Ryle 1949).

Pavlov's views, and those of his colleagues, were quite different. For them, the body is also a machine and it is also marvelous, but it is a living machine, and that is all the difference. A body composed of living parts does not require a separate ghost/mind to guide it. There is mind, of course, but it is the product of the workings of the living body—it is not a separate entity. This was also Aristotle's view, and it implies, among other things, that there are no specific ailments that should be classed as psychosomatic.

Psychological and biological (somatic) factors are inseparable, so all disease is psychosomatic. Can any biological malfunction fail to influence the psyche? Can psychic influences fail to influence the body? Regarding bodily illness, Platonov wrote, "in light of the theory of the unity of mind and body any somatic disease is indissolubly connected with the state of the patient's higher nervous activity" (Platonov 1959, p. 12).

Given a mechanical (living) body and its functioning (the mind), how do we understand its workings? Pavlov believed that this was the business of physiology and that the psyche was best studied through investigation of the physiological activity of the cerebrum. Pavlov's work showed how the adjustments we make as the conditions of the world change around us can be understood as the workings of an integrative mechanism, controlled largely by the cerebral cortex.

Pavlov's Discovery

Pavlov had the insight to see the significance of a common and trivial occurrence. As recounted in countless textbooks, popular articles, and cartoons, Pavlov noticed that his dogs salivated when things that had previously accompanied food were present. Thus, the attendant's footsteps, the sight of a food dish, or the sight and smell of food provoked salivation and general agitation.

Pavlov had already won the Nobel Prize for his work in digestion, so it was natural that he would concentrate on salivation, rather than other food-anticipating behavior.[4] Such salivation represented a learned reflex, which Pavlov first called a "psychic reflex," and it was just that bare fact that was of such interest to Americans. At birth, or after a period of maturation, we have a set of reflexes that do not depend upon the conditions of our individual experience—they are "unconditional."

Instead of the sight of food, the sound of a bell, of bubbling water, or of the word "food" can become a signal, or conditioned stimulus (CS), as can electric shock. Thus, new cues can call out old reflexes. Is that all there was to it? Was that really news? Can we then account for all of our behavior and experience as the accumulation of CRs? If we decide that we can, we part company with Pavlov. Here is the real story.

The "Mind of the Glands"[5]

Pavlov was nominated for the Nobel Prize by the Finnish physiologist Robert Tigersteht for his showing of the "influence of psychic moment" on the digestive glands and the interdependence of mind and body. At that time Pavlov was besieged by dozens of physicians who were anxious to advance their careers by obtaining an academic doctorate. Their knowledge of physiology was superficial, but almost 100 of them spent more or less time in Pavlov's research group at the Military-Medical Academy in St. Petersberg. He assigned them projects in what was a "factory" research environment.

In late 1896 S. G. Vul'fson was assigned by Pavlov to work out the mechanisms controlling salivation, and it was Vul'fson who discovered the unusual "mind" of those glands. When edible food was introduced to the mouth, the secretion of the glands depended on the nature of the food and its dryness—dry food meant more salivation. This purposeful reaction also occurred in the stomach, where the gastric glands and the pancreas varied their secretion depending on the nature of the food introduced. All of these digestive glands reacted similarly to inedible substances, with little secretion that was the same in volume for different substances. *And in all cases, the reaction occurred only when the food or nonfood was in the digestive tract*; the reaction was entirely physiological.

However, Vul'fson found that the salivary glands reacted differently to different foods and to nonfood substances even when visually presented—when he "teased" the dogs. We have no direct control over the salivary glands, yet they react to things that we see and smell—they, alone among glands, have a "mind" in some sense! Vul'fson proposed that the salivary glands' psyche "sorts out," "arranges," and "judges" stimuli. Pavlov found a psychiatric expert to follow up this project and so recruited an expert neurologist/psychiatrist from the Alexander III Charity Home for the Mentally Ill to study the "mental life of the glands."

The CR in itself was not an end and Pavlov never believed that it might serve as a unit of analysis. That was preposterous.

Conditioning in America
American researchers and theorists adopted the vocabulary used by Pavlov and concentrated on the specific conditions that produce Pavlovian conditioning, later called classical conditioning, or simply conditioning. This led to endless parametric experiments carried out through the twentieth century. For example, Pavlov found that the CR developed faster if the CS slightly precedes the unconditioned stimulus (UCS) by a second or so, but it may still occur when far longer delays are used. However, Pavlov did not ask what is precisely the best delay between conditioned and unconditioned stimuli. Americans were very concerned, since the answer could provide clues concerning the minimum time for neural transmission in a nervous system conceived as a network of single associations. This was not Pavlov's nervous system.

Pavlov's irritation with those who failed to appreciate that brain physiology involves integration, not simple association, was plain in his attacks on them (Pavlov 1932). Razran (1965) detailed the objections that Pavlov and his followers raised against American interpretations of classical conditioning.

Sherrington and the Integrated Nervous System
In 1906 Sir Charles Sherrington published a book describing the workings of the spinal nervous system, *The Integrative Action of the Nervous System*. The book had two main effects: First, it established the reflex

as the basic unit of spinal physiology by showing the effects of the synapse on neural activity. Sherrington in fact named the synapse. Second, Sherrington showed how the spinal cord acts as a unit of integration, coordinating the activities of individual organs.

This process, which he called integrative action, cannot be understood simply by reference to individual reflexes or collections of them. Sherrington spent weeks considering the title for his Silliman Lectures at Yale and subsequent book, and he purposely left the term "reflex" out of the title (Swazey 1969). This was because he did not want to mislead readers into believing that individual S-R reflexes are important. Integrative action is important, and it depends on interactions between excitation and inhibition in the nervous system.

Inhibition in the Brain

Inhibitory action in the nervous system was a controversial issue during the nineteenth century, despite the 1846 demonstration by the Weber brothers of the inhibitory action of the vagus, the Xth cranial nerve, on the beating of the heart. Sherrington had made the case for inhibition in the spinal cord, and Pavlov was going to use the same behavioral/observational methods to show the interactions of excitation and inhibition in the brain.

Pavlov believed that his data showed that excitation and inhibition are brain processes aroused by UCSs that become attached to CSs. Thus, a reliable signal for food or for electric shock is very excitatory and might be called a strong CS+, noting that the "+" means that it is a strong signal, not that it signals something "good." A reliable signal for no food or shock would become strongly inhibitory and might be called a strong CS−, realizing that the "−" means that it signals "no UCS."

Konorski's Dog

Pavlov's evidences for inhibition are complex and difficult to describe, so we will consider only three interesting and easily summarized cases. The first was described by Jerzy Konorski (1967, pp. 325–326), a Pavlovian who ran a physiological institute in Warsaw. Imagine a hungry dog that is occasionally fed a small bit of food, and this always occurs just after a green light flashes. At other times a tone is sounded briefly and no food is ever delivered. When neither tone nor light is on, nothing happens, and during this period and during periods when the tone is on, the dog appears to be waiting for the light. Soon the light becomes a CS+ and the tone becomes a CS−. What of the no-tone-nor-light periods?

Is that interval also a CS−? There is no response from the dog, just as is the case during the tone, which explicitly signals "no food." The problem with the notion of inhibition is that it is not obvious whether lack of response means that inhibition is present or simply that excitation is absent. And inhibition means an actual *suppression* of responding that would otherwise occur.

When offered food during the light, the dog eats, and it eats when food is offered during the no-stimulus interval. However, when offered food just after the tone, the dog refuses—it turns away, and if food is forced on it, it spits it out. This indicated to Konorski that the tone elicited an "anti-eating" response, since it has become a reliable predictor of "no food"—inhibitory.

The Paradox of Inhibition

A second phenomenon associated with inhibition has been called the "paradox of inhibition." In delayed conditioning, a CS is presented and remains on during a delay period and a UCS is then presented. For example, Kimmel (1966) presented human subjects with tones that remained on for a few seconds until the painful electric shock that was the UCS was delivered. One component of the response to such a UCS is perspiration, which can be measured as a change in skin conductance, the galvanic skin response (GSR).[6] As trials continued, typically to a dozen or more, the GSR diminished and in some cases even decreased to levels below baseline. That is, the subjects appeared to be more relaxed than they were before the experiment began. How can that be?

Pavlov believed that stimuli present when no UCS ever occurs become inhibitory—the CR is suppressed. In delayed conditioning, the delay interval itself never features a UCS and it therefore becomes inhibitory, as does the CS present during its duration. You might wonder whether this can be, since the same tone is present through the delay and when the shock comes—doesn't that make it excitatory, since it is paired with shock? In fact, that is the case during early trials with food or shock or other UCSs, and the CR occurs throughout the interval. However, over a few trials, or more, depending on conditions, the CR diminishes in the early part of the interval, so that a "scallop" pattern of response appears—a pattern of increased responding through the interval.

Given that, it makes sense that if the interval is sufficiently brief, responding may be suppressed through the whole interval and even during the UCS itself, even when the UCS is painful shock. Kimmel found that when the shock was presented alone, a strong unconditioned response (UCR) occurred and the subjects reported pain. And they reported that it was painful even when their GSR had diminished. However, they also reported "organism-wide tranquility!"

Kimmel's findings are only one instance of this effect that was reported originally by Pavlov (1927, lecture 14). Humans show the effect when a noxious puff of air is the UCS and the CR eyeblink comes to be inhibited. Dogs show it when they refuse to eat when the interval between CS/UCS trials is reduced from ten minutes to ninety seconds. However, if a different CS+ was presented, they "ate avidly," as they did when no CS was present. In all of these cases, the CS specifically inhibited the CR and the UCR.

Real Experimental Neurosis

March 19, 1928
Physiologist Pavlov has reached the point where he can create a nervous system in animals similar to the nervous states of man which border on insanity. He is now applying his results to the reconditioning of the insane and the education of the mentally deficient. (Gerow 1988, p. 12)

A third inhibitory phenomenon played a large part in Soviet psychiatry and was interpreted as the result of conflict between excitation and inhibition. Experimental neurosis may be produced by presenting an impossible discrimination problem, the original involving a circle and an ellipse. Dogs were presented a circle with food and an ellipse without food, and their salivation to the CS+ and CS− was recorded. They quickly learned to salivate only during the CS+. Gradually, the stimuli were made more similar, as the ellipse was made more nearly circular, until the subject could no longer distinguish between the two shapes.

This should not be particularly upsetting, one would think. Food comes with the CS+ no matter what the dog does, and food does not come with the CS− no matter what the dog does. And the dog cannot make itself salivate, any more than we can.[7]

Perhaps there should be no ill effect, but there was one. When the forms can no longer be discriminated, the dog becomes agitated, barks, salivates, bites at its harness, and generally goes berserk. To prevent injury, the dog is removed and placed in a kennel, where it may remain "insane" for months or years. Are there parallels in human life?

Pavlov's Brain: Fields on the Surface of the Cortex

Mach Bands   Before briefly describing Pavlov's theory of brain function, consider the neural unit model proposed by the physicist Ernst Mach during the nineteenth century and recently adopted by researchers in sensory physiology. The latter include Bekesy (1967), Hubel and Wiesel (1959), and Ratliff (1965), all Nobel Prize winners. Mach had proposed in 1897 that the fundamental unit of sensation is not the point sensation but a "neural unit" composed of a center of excitation and an inhibitory surround. Hence, stimulation at a point on the skin, for example, produces sensation in a zone surrounding the stimulus and depressed responding surrounding that zone, acting to isolate the excitatory part, so to speak.

One reason for this proposal was to account for simultaneous brightness contrast and the accompanying Mach bands that occur. When you look at a surface of bright white that abuts a very black surface, the white is whitest and the black is blackest along the border—this is one version of Mach bands. Mach proposed that neural units spread across the retina viewing such a display would be capable of producing these bands. All units fire in proportion to the amount of light stimulation striking them, so the units viewing white fire far faster than those viewing black.

The inhibition surrounding each excitatory center affects that unit's neighbors and is proportional to firing rate. Hence, a unit in the midst of the white field is maximally inhibited by its neighbors and the counterpart in the black field is neither stimulated nor inhibited very much. Consider the units along the border, however. On the white side, the border units are inhibited by their neighboring white units, but not much by the black units, since their firing rate is low. This means that the white units can fire faster than neighbors on all sides and thus generate more inhibition on them, which lowers their firing rate and further releases the border white units from inhibition. That accounts for the bright band. The super inhibition from these units suppresses the firing of the black border units, and that accounts for the black band. That was Mach's theory in 1897. We will see that it was similar in general features to Pavlov's theory of 1927, a fact noted by Ratliff (1965).

Pavlov's Fields   Following Sherrington, Pavlov believed that the interaction of excitatory and inhibitory influences was basic to the working of the cortex. Years of research led to a summary model, based on cortical electrical fields, just as the Gestaltists were proposing at about the same time.[8]

The representations of CSs in the cortex may be excitatory or inhibitory, depending upon whether they explicitly predict UCS or no UCS. With repeated pairings or CS-alone presentations, the excitation and inhibition grow stronger, and three stages of development appear. In the first, weak excitation and inhibition spread, so that what we would call generalization occurs—a weak CS+ will increase responding to a weak CS− or CS+ that follows it. The same spreading of effects occurs very late in training, after many days or weeks of experience. The more interesting phase occurs in between these two.

With moderate excitation and inhibition, the spreading of effects is replaced by concentration; the concentrating of excitation around the cortical representation of a tone, for example, means that only tones very similar to it will be affected by generalization and thus elicit a CR. What also happens is that a presentation of a CS+ causes a decrease in the response to a CS− or CS+ that follows it, and the presentation of a CS− causes an increase in the CR to a CS+ or a CS− that follows it. In short, the aftereffects are opposite in direction to the effect of the CS. These sequential effects are Pavlovian induction and have been shown to occur in many conditioning situations (e.g., Catania and Gill 1964; Nevin and Shettleworth 1966; Malone 1976). It is seldom noted, but these effects occur when other CSs are presented simultaneously, as well.

Ratliff noted that the cortical representation proposed by Pavlov—excitatory centers/inhibitory surrounds, and the reverse—is the neural unit model! How comforting that Pavlov should reach the same conclusion that sensory physiologists would reach decades later.

Classical Conditioning in Medicine

Your feet, your muscles, your lungs, all your body has not yet forgotten and keeps saying to the brain, when the brain wants to lead it along the same hard path: No, I shall not come, I have suffered too much on this path. And the brain accepts the refusal, obeying without arguing the silent language of its comrades.[9]

Bykov used the quote from Guy de Maupassant to express the notion of the "living machine" that characterized Pavlov's thinking. Since 1928 the Russians studied interoceptive conditioning, or the conditioning of internal organs.[10] American researchers came to appreciate the medical applications of this work in the 1980s, when applications to diseases of the immune system were accidentally discovered. The treatment here must be brief, so we will consider only four cases of the thousands available.

First, Bykov (1957) showed that it is easy to classically condition basal metabolic rate, assessed by consumption of oxygen. Human subjects did stepups onto a stool forty times in two minutes, and oxygen consumption was assessed. The command "Get ready for the experiment" always was given two minutes before the command "Begin work" was given. The first command quickly became a CS, producing a CR increase in oxygen consumption of two hundred fifty percent during the first two days of training. Hence, the familiar effect of "get ready, get set..." is a conditioned response. The effect was not due to the "will" of the subject—other experiments showed that deep breathing and muscle tensing has negligible effects.

A practical application of conditioning of an internal organ was reported by Ince, Brucker, and Alba (1978), whose patient was a forty-year-old paraplegic man. His spinal cord had been completely severed a year before in an accident, and, among other things, he had lost control over urination and defecation. Ince et al. knew that a strong electric shock to the lower abdomen can elicit reflex urination, hence, it can act as a UCS.

A mild shock to the inner thigh was used as a CS paired with the intense shock to the abdomen. Remember, the patient was paralyzed and anesthetic, so the body parts involved were completely separated from the brain. However, the procedure worked, and the CS alone soon produced a strong urination CR. Thereafter, the patient was able to control urination by applying the CS. To maintain the effectiveness of the CS, it was necessary to pair the CS and UCS in occasional settings. However, the patient was able to apply the CS hundreds of times (over days and weeks) before extinction occurred and the CS lost its power. Other studies confirm the finding that interoceptive conditioning is long lasting.

Of the myriad applications of conditioning to medicine, none is more famous than that of Ader and Cohen's (1982) finding that the body's immune system can be conditioned. Diseases like AIDS, multiple sclerosis, allergies, and a host of others occur because of a lack of immune response or an overly strong response. Systemic lupus erythematosus, commonly called "lupus," occurs when the immune system reacts too strongly, so that healthy tissues are destroyed and death results.[11]

Ader and Cohen were using the drug cyclophosphamide to induce nausea in rats when they noticed their subjects succumbing to a variety of infections—the drug was depressing the immune systems![12] They then applied the drug to mice bred to contract lupus and found that it extended their lives. This benefit was due to suppression of the immune response, which they subsequently showed could be conditioned.

In brief, one group of mice (C100) received weekly pairings of a saccharine taste and an injection of the drug. A second group (C50) received the same treatment, except that on half the occasions the drug was replaced by saline solution. The third group (NC50) was treated as was the C50 group, except that the saccharine taste and injections occurred on different days. A final group recieved only saccharine and saline, unpaired.

Their genes ensured that all mice would die, but the longevity of the C50 group showed that the immune system suppression had become a CR. Both the C50 and the NC50 mice had the same amount of drug, saccharine, and saline. However, the taste/drug pairing for the C50 group meant that conditioning could occur. On average, the C50 group members outlived the NC50 mice by almost a month and a half—an increase of about twenty-five percent.

Ader and Cohen suggested that conditioning accounts for the placebo effects that have been reported for thousands of years. We are accustomed to CS (medicine/doctor) → feeling better, so that the "health response" becomes a CR. Turkkan (1989) surveyed many cases of placebo that fit this mold, as well as some nocebo effects that have been reported.

The Hegemony of Classical Conditioning

Pavlov had described drug CRs in 1927, but modern research was largely the work of Siegel (e.g., 1978), who demonstrated "opponent drug responses" that account for much drug tolerance and for some kinds of addiction. For example, if mice (or humans) are administered a fixed dose of morphine before they are placed on a hot plate, the anesthesia produced reduces the pain felt. Humans can tell us that, and mice demonstrate it by showing a longer latency before licking their paws, something that rodents do when placed on a hot surface.

When the same process is repeated forty-eight hours later, the anesthetic effect is less, and after another repetition or two the anesthetic effect is lost completely. That is the familiar effect called drug tolerance.

However, Siegel showed that this tolerance is caused by an opponent response that is tied to the contextual cues present—it is a CR opposite in direction to the UCR. Hence, the analgesia produced by morphine is a UCR and the CR is increased sensitivity to pain. This is shown to be the case when the mice are moved to a different room—then the full analgesic effect occurs (1978). Addiction to opiates and other drugs occurs when contextual cues evoke the opponent CR, which is unpleasant, since it is opposite to the effect of the drug. This is withdrawal and leads to seeking of the drug, to escape the aversive withdrawal CRs.

If the opponent CR process is clear, it should be evident why the taking of morphine or heroin in strange surroundings is often fatal. The usual dose produces a UCR that is countered by a compensating opponent CR attached to situational cues. In time, the dosage of the drug is increased to counter this tolerance effect. Then, in unfamiliar circumstances, the large dose is taken without the countering of the opponent CR, and the result is a lethal overdose. There are many references to this "enigmatic overdose" effect (e.g., Siegel 1991).[13]

Pavlov's Russian Rivals

Pavlov's method was to correlate gross behavioral functions with gross brain functions, unlike the traditional and rival neurophysiologists, who were concerned with nervous and synaptic conduction. Pavlov did not keep abreast of this literature and was out of touch by 1920. There was a lot of competition between the Pavlov School and the physiologists for research support (Smith 1992).

Until the 1920s, dominant positions in academic physiology were held by the neurophysiologists—the so-called Sechenov School. However, they were displaced in the 1920s by the Pavlov School. Inhibition was a key bone of contention.[14] The neurophysiologists claimed that the Pavlovians did not explain inhibition at all but only used it metaphorically. These people were sometimes called the Wedensky–Ukhtomsky school and were based at the Institute of Physiology at Saint Petersberg (Leningrad) University. Pavlov was at the Military-Medical Academy in the same city.

Pavlov's approach became dominant in Soviet science, from the 1920s until at least the early 1960s. His followers believed that his work was genuinely based on a dialectical conception of the human organism. In 1950 the Stalinists equated Pavlovian psychology with objective psychology and carried out a purge, led by Bykov and others, to eliminate offensive practices, such as the use of questionnaires and mental tests. They also had views on brain function and opposed the psychosurgery that was popular through the 1950s. For Pavlov and his school, the whole body is important in constituting the psyche. It took Western psychology most of the twentieth century to appreciate this (see Olson and Fazio 2001).

Edwin Guthrie's Practical and Homely Behaviorism

When we know that a man is head of a family, has been on relief for one year, has a high school education, for 15 years worked as a carpenter, has been living in southern Illinois, we have a much shrewder notion of his opinion on politics, art, religion, and morals...than we have by learning his extroversion index, his aggressiveness centile, or his honesty score. (Guthrie 1942, p. 52)

The popular and charming behaviorist Edwin Ray Guthrie (see figure 16.2) was born in 1886 in Lincoln, Nebraska, and graduated from the University of Nebraska with a degree in mathematics and philosophy. He taught high school mathematics for several years and then went to graduate school at the University of Pennsylvania.

Guthrie spent his career at the University of Washington, where he served both as professor of psychology and, for a time, dean of the graduate school. His theory is simple but powerful, at least in his hands. He produced only a small fraction of the published work of others—Thorndike published twenty-seven times the number of items. And he had few real followers, only Virginia Voeks and Fred Sheffield could really be called Guthrians.[15] However, he remains current, and it is the rare learning textbook that does not devote some space to discussion of his views (e.g., Bower and Hilgard 1981 and Malone 1990/ 2002). Guthrie's theory of "one-trial contiguity learning" can be summarized in the single noun "habit." In a real sense he represents a continuation of the practical associationist psychologies of the nineteenth century.

What Is Learned Is What Is Done

It seems too simple to be true, but life is a series of variations on a central theme: stereotypy. Whatever we do in a specific situation is what we will do when next in that situation. Since literal repetition of a situation is impossible, endless variation in behavior is possible. Consider an example.

"A boy enters a school in which there is on the playground little supervision and much bullying and fighting" (Guthrie 1942, p. 53). A

Figure 16.2
Guthrie. Courtesy of the Archives of the History of American Psychology, University of Akron.

bully attacks him, and his cries bring a teacher who rescues him. The following week, when the attack is repeated, he will do what he did last—cry—since that remains his reaction to the situation. But what if no teacher had rescued him, and his crying had occurred to no avail? He would have gone through a repertoire of other behaviors until each was exhausted, leaving only one, a violent attack on the bully that frightened him away. That would remain his response the next time that a bully appeared. What if the attack had not deterred the bully (Guthrie 1942, p. 54)?

To threatening or disturbing events in the world the individual continues to react so long as the disturbing situation continues or until exhausted. If exhaustion occurs and the disturbing situation is still present, we become habituated and learn to tolerate evils that were at first intolerable.

Once a habit is attached to a situation, the cues produced in the making of the movements may render the habit independent of the external situation. For example, a woman may be wearing a tight collar while giving her first speech, and she may pull at it while talking:

This mannerism may remain for years though all subsequent collars have been larger. The movement was originally started and guided by the pressure of collar on the neck. It now guides itself. (Guthrie 1942, p. 55)

Abnormal Psychology Is Normal

The possibility that psychopathology is normal in a pathological environment was not unique to Guthrie, of course, but he was unique in citing the unusual example. He first noted that we are made uncomfortable when our teeth are unbrushed, when a rug is out of place, when a faucet is dripping, when a problem in arithmetic is unsolved, when one's clothing is too different from that of one's peers, or when a word is mispronounced. Originally it may have been scolding from a parent or teacher or friend that caused the discomfort, but soon corrective actions occur to signs of the troublesome situation. We don't fail to brush our teeth or leave the faucet handle loose. The unfinished job, the unachieved result, is a substitute for the scolding, and we act to remove it. This may become compulsion.

The compulsive act in abnormal psychology is only a misplaced or embarrassing example of the same mechanism. When the sight of the hands instead of the sight of the dirt on the hands becomes a stimulus for anxiety which is relieved by washing them, we have a compulsion.

Guthrie on Reward and Punishment

Reward, punishment, purpose, motives, and intentions are all words that refer to higher-order behavior that is defined with respect to goals. For most psychologists that is fine, since it seems obvious that our activity is goal directed. Guthrie disputed this, pointing out that much that we do is not purposive, but aimless, useless, and often maladaptive.

No one denies that rewards and punishers are important and obvious determinants of what we do and think. What Guthrie denied was the primacy of rewards and punishers—he did not view them as primary and unanalyzable events.[16] When something acts to change a situation so as to preserve the association between the previous situation and the last act done, that is a case of "reward," or reinforcement. A rat turns right in a T-maze and comes into contact with a food dish. It begins to eat, leaving the "previous situation," the sights and smells of the maze, connected to turning right at the choice point. Someone asks me the date of the fall of the Byzantine Empire. I respond "1936?" and am told "no." So I continue proposing dates until I say "1453," followed by "right." The last thing that I said was the response most likely to recur the next time that the situation occurs.

Punishment, like reward, is also what Guthrie called a "mechanical arrangement" that is another variation on one-trial contiguity learning. Rewards end a series of activities, preserving the association between the situation and the last act before the situation changes—food may act as a reward for coming when called. However, the "reward" aspect does not lie in the object that is nominally the reward; rather, it lies in what it makes the subject do.

Eating is a behavior different from walking and pressing a lever, so it may serve as situation change and leave intact the relation "situation–coming when called." However, this is not because food is always rewarding! Food may act as a punisher, as when we are forced to eat when sated or when we are prepared to do something else. Rewards stop what we are doing and preserve its association to the situation. Punishers prod us to act.

To say that we do in a situation whatever we did last in the "same" situation is to say that our responses depend on context. This often means combinations of aspects of past situations, so that, for example, "walking on ice" is a combination of two classes of stimuli. There are those that have accompanied normal walking and another set that have accompanied falling. Thus, the altered pattern of walking is a mixture of normal walking and protective movements that occurred when we fell in the past. By the same token, when we "read while fatigued," we learn something new because the fatigue prevents us following as we read—we learn to read without following, as we discover when we try to recall what was read.

Intentions

Guthrie proposed that intentions, readinesses, and expectations were all fractional parts of complete reactions evoked because part of a stimulus complex was now present. This is pretty much what Thorndike meant by "readiness" and may be motor behaviors, vocalizations, imaginings, and so on. To appreciate what he meant, consider reading when we do it for pleasure versus when it is done in preparation for an examination an hour away. Or when we are called on to recite, isn't it easier when we expect it than when we are taken by surprise?[17] Part of the reason for this lies in the fact that when we expect something we are already "doing it," at least in part. Thus, we may be partially reciting, in the form of insignificant body movements, when we know that we will be called upon.

Perception, Imagery, and Memory

For Guthrie, perceiving is activity and percepts are habits. They are always evoked by some present cue, and they are specific. The associationists of the eighteenth and nineteenth centuries held the same view, and, in many ways, Guthrie's theory is the twentieth-century version of James Mill's *Analysis of the Phenomena of the Human Mind*, discussed in chapter 7.

Perception, imagery, memory, fantasy, and dreaming all depend upon present cues and upon redintegration, or the calling up of a compound by a cue which is part of the compound. Guthrie viewed this process as synonymous with conditioning. I sense the odor of food, stuffiness, perspiration, and urine and immediately am transported back to elementary school, where those odors dwelt. Briefly I can see the low water fountains and hear children's shrieks. Or, as Hutcheson said, the light through the church window brings up all kinds of religious associations.

Guthrie's treatment of memory was essentially correct, at least as later research suggested (Barnes and Underwood 1959; Tulving and Thompson 1973). Forgetting is not simply the fading away of memories—it is replacement by new memories. For example, I have a set of movements that allow me to type, but if I do not type for several months or years I lose my skill. That is because those movements are used in a host of other activities and thus become attached to new cues. On the other hand, I can ride a bicycle and play chess, activities that are not easily forgotten. The movements involved are shared by fewer other activities and are thus less likely to become attached to new cues.

Guthrie as Behavior Therapist: Changing Habits

Guthrie proposed several methods for changing habits, each of which has been used in behavior therapy. These are usually called the toleration method, the exhaustion method, and the method of incompatible stimuli, sometimes called counterconditioning. The last method is that used by Wolpe, discussed earlier. A stimulus provoking a phobic reaction, such as a spider, is gradually introduced, countered by stimulation producing muscular relaxation, whether through use of drugs or deep muscle relaxation.

The toleration method is actually a part of the method of incompatible stimuli and is comparable to training a horse to saddle by beginning with a light blanket placed on its back and gradually increasing the weight until the weight of saddle and rider is borne quietly. The same applies to elimination of a child's fear of the dark or a phobia connected with spiders. We want to change the behavior in the presence of the feared cues, but we are hampered by the violent reactions of the individual when the cues are presented. Hence, we introduce darkness and spiders in a slow and graded series, so that violent reactions do not occur.

The exhaustion method is comparable to the bronco-busting method of training horses—the rider mounts the horse, which bucks until exhausted or until the rider is thrown. The exhausted horse no longer bucks—it walks or stands with a rider and has learned a new habit to replace the old habit of bucking when weight is placed on its back.

To treat human problem habits, the procedure is straightforward. Place the child in darkness and the phobic in a cage filled with spiders. Eventually the agitation will cease, and something other than fear and violence will be learned. This technique is called emotional flooding today and must be used with caution, of course. Not only could a patient suffer a heart attack, but Guthrie would quickly point out that such treatment is bound to be strongly situation specific.

By the 1960s, behavior modification had become synonymous with the "analysis of behavior" of B. F. Skinner. However, as we saw above, the origin of the methods commonly used lies in Guthrie's writings (Malone 1978). This was clear in a government paper published in 1975 and authored by Stephanie Stoltz and two colleagues at the National Institute of Mental Health (1975). Among the methods they described were reinforcement and punishment, systematic desensitization (counterconditioning and toleration), overcorrection, and assertiveness training.

The overcorrection method entails forcing the author of a misdeed to atone by substituting the proper behavior for an improper one. A child or a mental patient may be required to repeatedly make a bed if the misdeed was messing up the bed, and a child who throws food may have to repeatedly clean it up. As ever, such practice ensures that whatever was the last act performed in a situation is the one that is preferred by society.

Assertiveness training is best done through role playing, so that in a sham situation where someone pushes ahead of you in line, you speak up and demand your rights. Such a method exemplifies Guthrie's emphasis on action done in situations where we want new behavior to occur. All of the verbal counseling in the world and all of the soliloquies on "rights" are without meaning unless behavior also changes.

Guthrie and Horton's Misinterpreted Experiment

Guthrie and a colleague, G. P. Horton, published the results of a famous set of experiments in 1946, though the data were collected in the 1930s (Guthrie and Horton 1946). *Cats in a Puzzle Box* was a kind of replication of Thorndike's 1898 experiments, but with a different aim. Thorndike was simply trying to show that ideas are not necessary for the mediation of what appears to be purposeful behavior—escape from a puzzle box. Guthrie and Horton, on the other hand, wanted to determine whether the details of the *whole sequences* of such behavior, perhaps fifteen minutes long, are as predictable as the end result. They were not concerned with the learning to get out of the box, but with precisely what went on during the whole episode inside the box.

Ironically, their work was criticized in 1979 by authors who misinterpreted their intent and their data. Moore and Stuttard (1979) provide an example of what has occurred repeatedly in the history of science: the misinterpretation of a position so that it becomes a straw man and the subsequent refuting of the "straw position." Let us consider what Guthrie and Horton actually did in their classic research and then see how the theoretical climate of the late 1970s predisposed many to accept Moore and Stuttard's critique as valid.

Guthrie and Horton used a box with a large glass front and a pole mounted vertically on the floor or, in some cases, hanging from the ceiling of the box. A total of 800 escapes by fifty cats were observed. In each case, the cat was inserted into the rear of the box by means of a smaller box, so that it was not touched by hand. After a wait of from ten seconds to a minute in the entry box, the cat was released into the large box. For the first three trials the glass front door was open and the cat could leave the box and eat from a saucer of salmon. On remaining trials, it was up to the cat to get out of the box on its own.

To open the door, the cat was required to apply pressure to the pole (or to the tube), leading subsequent writers to believe that it was the learning of this one act—any response that applied pressure to the pole—that was the focus of the experimenter's interest. They were wrong, as was clear in Guthrie and Horton's description of their procedure and results.

The cats were watched and sometimes filmed as they made their escapes. If the cat was not filmed, a written record of the cat's behavior was made. After an average of fifteen minutes of exploration, the cat usually hit the post and the glass door was raised. However, usually the post was the last feature of the box to be examined. First the cat spent a lot of time examining the barrier and the periphery of the box. After its escape, the cat was replaced in the box until it escaped again, at which time it was placed back in the box and so on.

What was surprising and difficult to convey to readers, as Guthrie noted, was the tremendous amount of stereotypy shown during the entire period that the cat was in the box. Each cat showed a "startling repetition of movements" during its whole stay in the box—a matter of minutes, usually. Stereotypy was not restricted to the movements that led to escape. For example, it was common for a cat to repeat a triple tour of the periphery, including frequent stops, in detail from one trial to the next. Further, the "unsuccessful" movements, those that did not contribute to escape, did not fade. In fact, they were often as frequent during the last trials as they were at the beginning.

Guthrie and Horton wrote that they were unable to predict the behavior of a given cat on the first trial, but "after watching the cat through one trial we can bet rather heavy odds that the second trial will repeat the routines of the first."

Hunger and Satiation

Gordon Allport, personality theorist (see figure 16.3), proposed (1937) that motives may become "functionally autonomous," so that scrimping and saving because of economic necessity may create misers, with scrimping continued during good times simply since it has become habitual. We saw in chapter 7 that John Gay proposed such a theory in the early eighteenth century, noting that people may come to value the having of money to the extent that they "sell their happiness for money." Both Gay and Allport were proposing that means may become ends simply because habits are established. That is very Guthrian.[18]

Figure 16.3
Allport. Courtesy of the Archives of the History of American Psychology, University of Akron.

Morgan (1974) and Mackintosh (1983) reviewed findings that provide strong support for functional autonomy and thus for Guthrie. The experiments reviewed show that behavior that was originally established and maintained by food or water rewards often persists, even when the "reward" is no longer of value to the subject. As Guthrie would say, behavior may become stereotyped and attached to the cues of the training situation. This has important implications for what we call "hunger" and "satiation."

Many others have found similar effects, often classified as the "contrafreeloading effect" or the "Protestant ethic" effect. For example, Davidson (1971) trained four rats to press a lever ten times for each food pellet received. After training, the rats were given all the food they wanted for eight days and placed back in the lever box, with free food present. The free food was ignored, and all four subjects pressed the lever and ate the resulting food "rewards." Why did they press? Evidently, because pressing, initially done only as a means to getting food, became autonomous, self-maintaining, stereotyped. Allport listed examples of what we call contrafreeloading dating back to 1917.

The stereotypy of behavior and its growing independent of rewards and needs and drives and whatever originally engendered it applies to human psychopathology, of course. William Hunt and his colleagues (1979) described effects similar to those described above but occurring in human patients, and they noted the relevance of Guthrie's theory to such data.

Clark L. Hull

Nothing is better evidence that Hull's influence remains than this indirect recognition by his detractors that it is still a force that could regain strength if the fashion of the moment were to fade or become less appealing. (Amsel and Rashotte 1984)

Clark Leonard Hull (see figure 16.4) wrote in his autobiography that he was born in a log house on a farm near Akron, New York, in 1884 (Hull 1952). He graduated from the University of Michigan and taught at a normal school in Richmond, Kentucky, where his load of twenty class meetings a week did not stop him from beginning the research that would constitute his doctoral thesis. His graduate work was at the University of Wisconsin, where he later joined the faculty. His most conspicuous characteristics were his ingenuity, adaptability, and ambition to become a leader in his field. That goal was certainly accomplished; although he died in 1952, his imprint is only too clear in psychology, as well as in many other areas where his students and their students carry on work that bears Hull's unmistakable mark.

His ingenuity was demonstrated early, when he first began doing his research at Wisconsin. He built what he called an "automatic memory machine" for the study of the evolution of concepts. Today any researcher would be helpless without a computer, and even the poorest of us seem better off than was Hull during his years at Wisconsin. He described his equipment:

I designed and constructed with the few hand tools there available an automatic memory machine which I used throughout most of my dissertation experiment. The drum was made from a tomato can fitted with wooden heads. (1952, pp. 148–149)

Hull was marvelously adaptive as well as ingenious. His first teaching at Wisconsin was in aptitude testing, a subject in which he was less

Figure 16.4
Hull. Courtesy of the Archives of the History of American Psychology, University of
Akron.

than expert—but Hull did nothing halfway. He wrote a book on the
subject, *Aptitude Testing*, in 1928, based on course materials. However,
aptitude testing was not the key to fame: "The survey leading to the
publication of *Aptitude Testing* left me with a fairly pessimistic view as
to the future of tests in this field, and I abandoned it permanently"
(1952, p. 151). He went on to write that he could always return to testing if other pursuits failed, since the field is suited to an older and less
creative person.

Hull was then asked to participate in an introductory course for
medical students. He felt that the general area of hypnosis and suggestibility was useful in medicine and so began learning what was
known in the field and teaching it to his students. Over a span of ten
years he and twenty students published thirty-two papers in that area,
and in 1933 his book *Hypnosis and Suggestibility* was published. By 1929
Hull's reputation was such that Yale invited him to New Haven as a

research scientist in their new Institute of Human Relations. That position meant that he had no teaching or administrative duties and that he was free to devote all of his time to research and writing.

When he arrived at Yale he planned to continue his work in hypnosis, but he was deterred from doing so by opposition from the medical authorities there. Irked, he attributed their opposition to superstitious fear that he had not encountered in the Midwest. It is likely that he also had not encountered the medical establishment in the Midwest.

He was encouraged to contribute toward the grand plan of the institute, which had gathered many psychologists, sociologists, anthropologists, and others in making a unified and integrated contribution to the social–behavioral sciences. He wrote that such an enterprise is best carried out with leadership in the form of a scientific Führer, but that such a system runs counter to our democratic policies and would hamper creativity by the individual members. Nonetheless, enough of the participating scientists were attracted by Hull's general point of view by attending his seminars that he became de facto director.

Deterred from studying hypnosis, he turned to animal behavior and outlined his plan in *Principles of Behavior*, published in 1943. This was revised and extended nine years later in 1952 in *A Behavior System*, and a third volume, intended to include human social behavior, was never written, owing to his death. However, he felt, as have many others, that the first two works included the framework of all that psychologists need to know.

A Sketch of Hull's Theory

Hull assumed three things concerning psychology and the way of doing science. First, he was convinced that we and other organisms must be viewed as biological machines, or automata. When we dispense with romantic illusions, we see that we are muscle, bone, blood, nerves, visceral organs, and similar stuff, and we must not lose sight of that fact.

Unlike Pavlov, whose thinking was always guided by biology and who saw mind as a property of the operation of biological systems, Hull was inclined toward physics and the view of the organism as a physical system. This may have owed to his undergraduate degree in engineering, but it rendered his viewpoint more like Descartes's than Aristotle's. In 1928 Hull considered possible titles for his analysis of the "higher mental processes," titles that provide a good idea of his intent (ibid., pp. 824–825):

Mechanisms of Thought

Mechanisms of Mind

Mental Mechanisms

Mechanisms of Mental Life

Psychology from the Standpoint of a Mechanist

Hull's second assumption was that it is absolutely essential to quantify, to measure and attach numbers, even if the basis for scaling is shaky. Much of his time was spent in assigning numbers to represent the degree of learning or the amount of motivation that is present under different conditions.

Third, Hull emphasized the importance of clearly stating basic assumptions in a way that permitted testing them. This was required both to give order to the field and to act as a guide to research. In 1943 he listed sixteen postulates, each followed by theorems and corollaries, in language meant to be unambiguous. A great many of Hull's followers were attracted because of the appeal of this hypothetico-deductive method. Psychological research often seems to lack direction, but in this case it seemed a systematic undertaking was under way. Guidelines were laid out in the *Principles of Behavior*, and one could turn to any page and find a postulate or corollary begging for experimental test. It was slow, but it was about time that psychology got on the sure path!

The Postulate System

It is believed that a clear formulation, even if later found incorrect, will ultimately lead more quickly and easily to a correct formulation than will a pussy-footing statement which might be more difficult to convict of falsity.

Hull wrote that in 1943 (p. 398), expressing his conviction that only through clear experimental tests of clear statements can we determine whether our assumptions are correct. The Gestalt "laws of organization" are too fuzzy to deal with, and that is why they are a "doctrine of despair." Hull's postulates were clear, and that, together with his reliance on the deductive method, parallels exactly Descartes's deductions from "clear and distinct ideas." According to his long-time collaborator, Kenneth Spence,[19] Hull adopted the hypothetico-deductive method after reading an impressive paper by Einstein in 1934.

The 1943 postulate set proved an influential guide for the research of the 1940s and 1950s; the set was altered somewhat in 1952, though not very drastically from the standpoint of an outsider, and the heart remained what it was in 1943. True followers of Hull ("Hullians," as they are still called) see the changes as far more fundamental. We will consider only an example, that is, postulate IV: primary reinforcement. This is Hull's most important postulate, but we will treat it only briefly. Hull viewed learning as the forming of habits, represented in his system as sHr, and they are learned S-R connections due to the action of the law of effect. The law of effect, "reinforcement" for Hull, always depends on the reduction of a need, just as ingestion of water reduces thirst, the sensation accompanying the need for water. To convey a sense of Hull's manner, the passage below presents this postulate in Hull's very words (1943, p. 178):

Whenever an effector activity ($r \rightarrow R$) and a receptor activity ($S \rightarrow s$) occur in close temporal contiguity...and this contiguity is closely associated with the diminution of a need...or with a stimulus which has been closely and consistently associated with the diminution of a need...there will result an increment to a tendency (Δ sHr) for that afferent impulse on that occasion to evoke that reaction. The increments from successive reactions summate in a manner which yields a combined habit strength (sHr) which is a simple positive growth function of the number of reinforcements.

The postulate says that whenever a response is made in the presence of stimuli and the reduction in a need occurs, a connection forms or is strengthened, linking the stimuli and responses involved. So every time that a dog comes, a child reads, or you study and that is followed by food, praise, or good grades, the tendency to repeat those behaviors in such situations increases—this is just Thorndike's law of effect. However, Hull was not Thorndike; he was little concerned with application and obsessed with quantification. Reinforcers strengthen S-R connections, but how much does each instance strengthen a connection, and what are effects of magnitude or delay of reinforcement?

Hull (1951) was serious when he proposed that habit strength increases in a simple manner:

$$\Delta sHr = F(M - sHr)$$

The increase in habit strength on a given trial is the product of a constant (F), which depends upon the situation, species, and so on, times the quantity M minus the current habit strength. M is the maximum habit strength and depends on the degree of need and the reinforcer used. As trials continue, the quantity (M − sHr) decreases, since sHr increases trial by trial. Thus, the increments added to habit strength become less and less as training progresses. For example, when we memorize a passage of poetry, the amount that we retain on the first reading is greater than that of the second, third, and fourth readings. As we approach M, the maximum, or asymptote, less is left to be learned, hence less of an increment is added.

Note that postulate IV, which defines reinforcement as drive reduction and requires reinforcement for learning to occur, conceives humans and other animals as drive-animated, satiation-seeking automata, and that is a very common view in psychology. Freud is probably the best-known exponent of such a view, and it is small wonder that Hull, who was gathering the accepted views of the psychology of the early twentieth century, would adopt it as well. For a complete discussion of the postulate system, see a good learning theories textbook.

About Intervening Variable Systems

More than a decade before Hull wrote *Principles of Behavior*, Edward Tolman, Hull's most vocal critic, proposed that we use intervening variables in psychology. Hull agreed fully with Tolman, and when his system was unveiled in 1943, it was composed almost wholly of intervening variables. What is an intervening variable? It is really easy to understand, but the question has given more than one graduate student trouble.

All that is necessary is to know that independent variables are what we usually call "causes"—I win the lottery or the Nobel Prize or have a checkup with "no cavities." Dependent variables are consequents, or what we usually call "effects"—I smile, say pleasant things, profess an optimistic attitude. John B. Watson and B. F. Skinner want our explanations to remain in those terms, and so did the positivists, like Ernst Mach, the turn-of-the-century physicist.

However, we seldom do that, since the list of independent and dependent variables that I listed cannot help but bring a conclusion to mind—"you mean happy." Of course I did, and other intervening variables are constantly used to summarize relationships between sets of causes and effects. Examples are hunger, thirst, anger, frustration, intelligence, moodiness, gravity, the electron, and many, many more. How could we communicate without intervening variables? How do we use intervening variables? We drink because we are thirsty, eat because we are hungry, work because we are industrious, study because we are studious, fight when we are angry, and so on? Are those explanations? Do I sleep because I am sleepy? Obviously, sometimes intervening variables constitute the nominal fallacy, the confusing of naming and explaining.

Knowledge, Purpose, and Foresight as Habit Mechanisms
I can find no evidence in Hull's writings that he realized how closely his theory corresponded to David Hartley's of 1750 (see chapter 7), but the resemblance is striking. That is not a criticism, since good ideas, as well as bad ones, are apt to endure or be resurrected. In this case, simple associationism based on hypothetical nervous system mechanisms again captured the mind of an able proponent. The question is how a biological machine might show knowledge, purpose, and foresight, which are usually construed as higher mental functions. In 1930 and 1931 Hull offered an answer, sketched only briefly here.

Hull began by making a few simplifying assumptions. First, the world affecting us may be simply represented, despite the protests of poets, writers, and philosophers, who have anguished over the question of the nature of reality, as a series of stimuli: S1, S2, ... and so on, ending with an Sg, or goal stimulus. The Sg represents some drive-reducing end of the sequence; perhaps food momentarily ends movement or we solve the anagram we have been working on. Whatever we are doing may be similarly simply represented as a series of responses: R1, R2, ..., ending with Rg, the goal response, which could be eating or producing the anagram solution.

As "high-grade organisms," we also have proprioceptors and thus receive feedback from movements. Muscle spindles and Golgi tendon organs let us know the position of our limbs, so the feedback from movement becomes an additional source of stimulation. For each movement, R, there is a specific feedback stimulus, s, so that the sequence appears as R1 → s1, R2 → s2, and so on. In a real sense, that sequence of feedback stimuli is a representation of the world sequence, since each was produced by a specific response that was produced by a specific stimulus in the world sequence. We thus transcribe, code, "know" the world through our actions in it, bearing in mind that this includes sights and smells and sounds as represented by the sequence of Ss. And, though Hull cited no sources, this conception is perfectly compatible with American pragmatic philosophy and functionalist psychology (see chapter 13).

Once we have knowledge, foresight is easily gained. If all sequences end in reinforcement, by definition, then stimuli are always becoming more or less strongly attached to responses, depending on the distance in time to reinforcement. That means that not only are the world stimuli attached to responses, but so are the feedback-produced stimuli. Thus, given an initiating "world stimulus," the first response sets off an old sequence that can maintain itself as a chain. That is, given S1, we have: $R1 \rightarrow s1 \rightarrow R2 \rightarrow s2 \rightarrow R3 \rightarrow s3 \ldots$ The first response produces its sensory feedback, which, via learned connection $s1 \rightarrow R2$, initiates a chain that rattles off independently of the world sequence stimuli. Thus, we recite the alphabet and button our shirts mindlessly, as chains that concern only our bodies. These chains can outrun the world sequence, of course, and that is the basis for foresight.

Finally, we build in purpose as a more potent form of foresight that arises from the effect of past goal attainment. Behavior with respect to goals is the goal response, RG, which is determined by the nature of the goal object. And it is evoked by the drive state (SD) that prevails, whether hunger, fear, or need for activity. The SG and SD are inseparable, of course, since a goal object is such only when a corresponding drive is present. The drive state evokes the consummatory response appropriate to it (RG), and those components that do not interfere with progress through the sequence constitute Hull's crowning achievement, in his view, the rg–sg mechanism.

This is a totally mechanical addition to Hull's totally mechanical theory, and it accounts for a variety of things, including the rationale for projective tests, such as the Rorschach or the Thematic Apperception Test (McClelland 1985). It treats anticipation and purpose as partial goal responses—fractional anticipatory goal responses. Since such responses occur at the end of goal sequences, they tend to predate goals, since stimuli are always present that were present at the time the goal response was made. The actual example that Hull used was premature ejaculation, but any example of what is commonly considered anticipation—thinking of food, receiving an award, or cringing in fear apply as well.

The fractional response itself, rg, has stimulus feedback, as do all responses, and this is sg. As a stimulus, sg becomes attached (conditioned) to responses, as do all stimuli. And the omission of anticipated goals can have effects, such as frustration. The many ramifications of this have been examined by a student and colleague of Spence, Abram Amsel (1962).

Hull and Gestalt Psychology

It should be no surprise to learn that Hull was contemptuous of Gestalt psychology; he called it a "doctrine of despair" in 1943. The Gestalt laws were too fuzzy to deal with from Hull's essentially Newtonian mechanical vision of science—field theory was incomprehensible.

Hull described a meeting with Köhler and others in a letter written to Kenneth Spence dated May 20, 1941. After a meeting of the psychological portion of the Philosophical Society in Philadelphia, the group went to a "beer joint" to talk. Hull managed to sit beside Köhler and suggested that psychology would be best served if they did less fighting and tried to clear up some of the "pseudo-differences" between them. After they debated who was fighting with whom,

Köhler then went on and made a remark something like this: "Also, I have heard it said that a professor in one of the prominent eastern universities is accustomed, when he refers to the Gestalt psychologists, to call them, 'those goddamned Gestalters.'" I must confess that my face was pretty red. The whole crowd gave me a good horse laugh, and of course I had it coming to me...it didn't occur to me to tell them that I always smile when I use that expression, which, it seems to me, does make a difference. (Amsel and Rashotte 1984, p. 22)

Hull told Köhler that scientific matters should be settled on a scientific and logical basis and not through warfare, to which Köhler replied that he was willing to discuss most things logically, but that when someone said that man was a slot machine, then he would fight. "And when he said the word 'fight,' he brought his fist down on the table with a resounding smack, and he did not smile when he said it, either." Hull was astonished by this attitude and pointed out that fighting would settle nothing—it was irrelevant to the scientific status of the thing.

Problems with the Self-Correcting System

Although others dispute his conclusion, Hull was convinced that Einstein had used the method of formal postulates and the deducing and testing of theorems in developing relativity theory. He also pointed to Isaac Newton's *Principia* as a model, with its "classical scientific system of the past." This despite Newton's famous "Hypothesis non fingo"—I make no hypotheses! Newton began his treatise with seven definitions (matter, motion, and so on) and continued with a set of postulates—his famous three laws of motion—followed by seventy-three formally proved theorems and many appended corollaries (Hull 1943, p. 7). And who can fault Newton's method?

It is easy to see why Hull's method was so appealing and why it converted so many to his point of view. Instead of the hodgepodge of theories, the uncertainty of the usefulness of one's particular research, and the never-ending debates among philosophers and humanists, we knew what we were doing and where we were going. We begin together with a clear set of postulates, make deductions from them, and test the deductions. We modify the theorems and postulates as necessary, so our self-correcting system cannot fail. Our postulates must become truer and truer as we learn more—who could argue with such a program? Many did not argue, and Hull's influence lay in large part on the promise that his method seemed to offer.

The necessary experiments cannot be done—they never come out absolutely, clearly, and unambiguously in favor of one hypothesis and against another. Such experiments—those that decide clearly and satisfy everyone—are called crucial experiments, and they are hard to come by. Hull was in a position to have the best research facilities and the best researchers available, in addition to having tremendous influence on the journals that publish research results. If the results of an experiment are not published, they do not exist. This means that a research finding must bear the scrutiny of journals' reviewers before one can be sure that the experiment was properly conducted and therefore that the data are interpretable.

Hull's opponents had their share of difficulties in getting their work published, and, once published, the authors could expect a counterattack from Hull's group. Many of his assistants and colleagues, such as Kenneth Spence and Neal Miller, were masters of research and could effectively point out deficiencies in findings critical of Hull's views and then show experimentally how Hull's was actually the correct view. Thus, the necessity for crucial experiments and the influential position that Hull enjoyed rendered the self-correcting system more a self-perpetuating system!

17 Radical Behaviorism and Cognitive Science: Contrasting Psychologies of the Twentieth Century?

Munsterberg and the Two Psychologies

The psychology of the late twentieth century was fragmented, but there was one fairly clear main division—that between radical behaviorism and cognitive psychology. Radical behaviorism, first promoted by B. F. Skinner (see figure 17.1), was far less popular—it didn't use the language of ordinary life, and so it seemed strange and difficult to understand. However, its basic tenets were present in social psychology, jurisprudence, educational psychology, and clinical psychology—whether workers in these areas realized it or not.[1] Cognitive psychology used ordinary language—the vocabulary of folk psychology—and so was more congenial to the general public. The situation was roughly the same at the turn of the century, as we can see by examining the works of Hugo Munsterberg.

Munsterberg had a "sense for the perspective and proportion of things," according to William James, who invited him to Harvard, where he spent the remainder of his life: 1892–1895 and 1897–1916 (Boring 1950, p. 128). When Munsterberg arrived, James changed his own title from "Professor of Psychology" to "Professor of Philosophy," implying that he had found a successor as a psychologist. Munsterberg *was* indeed a psychologist, as well as a physician and a philosopher. He could also be considered a founder of applied psychology, because of his research in psychotherapy, advertising, the psychology of law, and industrial psychology. And he certainly had "perspective."

He published twenty books in English and six in German, the best of which may be the 1914 *Psychology: General and Applied*, published by Appleton. The book is divided into two parts: causal psychology and purposive psychology. He believed that these two viewpoints must be kept separate, since he argued that they were as different as physics

Figure 17.1
Skinner. Personal collection.

and religion. "Causal psychology" is concerned with scientific explanation. "Purposive psychology" is wholly different—it is concerned with
a freely willing self with a personality and all kinds of stuff "inside" us,
as he put it.

In 284 pages Munsterberg presented "causal psychology" as associationism, but in the first thirty-two he was careful to make clear that
there is no unconscious store of memories, no images and words "lying
somewhere at the bottom of my mind" (Munsterberg 1914, p. 26). Earlier (1909) he had written that "the story of the subconscious mind can
be told in three words—there is none." In his view, the unconscious
was often employed to supply causes where there seemed to be gaps,
and, in fact, that was one of Freud's main reasons for postulating the
unconscious.

However, no "utterly fantastic" causes are needed, since our mental
life does indeed show regularity in its operations. *But it never features
anything that resembles causal necessity in the first place. If there is no necessity, there need be no causes.* Arguing against the cognitive psychology of

his day, Munsterberg wrote that it is childish to insist that ideas come, go to a storage place, and return as "remembered!" Those who do so insist must feel constantly aware of their "lap" as they walk around. They must be reassured when next they sit, just as the believer in the unconscious depository of ideas "recognizes" an old idea, come back again. Though thoughts do not really cause actions, they may accompany actions and are themselves produced by action. A person's thinking is as much a part of his actions as those are a product of his thought (p. 221).

Munsterberg's "causal psychology" is not the *only* kind of psychology. "Purpose-oriented" or functional psychology is very different but familiar to modern readers. It includes the world of beauty, understanding, love, faith, learning, and memory, where "our mental life is free," and immediate practical concerns are important. It is psychology as it is popularly construed. He wrote that we should let people have free will and memory and faith, but restrict those things to this viewpoint and see that it stays clear of the causal viewpoint.

Cognitive Psychology and Radical Behaviorism

Cognitive psychology, or "cognitive science," is not something that sprang up suddenly in the 1950s when psychologists "once again dared study the mind." "Cognitive psychology" really refers to nothing specific, though nonpsychologists and new students often suppose that it is a distinct field. An examination of textbooks in the area, summarized below, shows that cognitive psychology may have as many definitions as there are textbooks written about it.

Anyone interested in the conventional "faculties of mind" of popular psychology may be called a cognitive psychologist by default. Hence, researchers in sensation, perception, memory, attention, problem solving, imagination, language, and other cognitive-sounding areas may be called cognitive psychologists. If one follows the computer-induced "processing" view of cognition, then one is more likely to be called a "cognitive scientist," particularly if one emphasizes computer simulations rather than human-produced data. If writers make any reference to biological substrates, then "cognitive neuroscience" may be the fitting classification.

"Behaviorism" is also a nonspecific term, since so many variants exist. However, the only clear alternative to cognitive psychology is radical behaviorism, which contrasts strongly with *all* forms of cognitive psychology. This is so because it rejects the use of mediators, while *all* forms of cognitive psychology rely on mediation. But there are many views called "behavioral," and some of them do advocate the use of mediators, whether they be called habits, expectancies, S–R connections, associations, or something else. Those behaviorisms constitute what Skinner (1945) called "methodological behaviorism," and they are actually cognitive theories, as cognitive as a theory positing a set of processing stages.

Skinner's Radical Alternative

Critics might say that the problems are largely of his own making. Skinner's mode of psychological interpretation is countercultural; it is uncompromising and profoundly at odds with explanations of behavior that we learn in ordinary discourse. He has addressed broad as well as specialized audiences and has done so successfully in the sense of engaging many readers, but often at the cost of obscuring the subtlety and the foundations of his concepts. Thus we should not be surprised that many critics have not read his work in detail and that his position is often distorted through simplistic caricature. Furthermore, Skinner has seldom replied directly to his critics; in the absence of explicit correction, how can they be blamed for getting it wrong? (Hineline 1988)

The extraordinary appeal of inner causes...must be due to more than a linguistic practice. I suggest that it has the appeal of the arcane, the occult, the hermetic, the magical...beyond...the reach of reason. (Skinner 1974)

Skinner's operant conditioning theory and its applications presented in popular books and in the press have made him familiar to the general public. However, the public conception is a composite of media items that describe aspects of Pavlov, Watson, Thorndike, and Hull.

Skinner's Significance
John B. Watson "founded" behaviorism in 1913 and stressed that activity is the basic subject matter of psychology. And he said that our goal should be to discover the factors that influence that activity. His "theory" of learning was almost incidental.

However, behaviorism changed. Attention turned from the observation of the world and its effects on us—Hull and Tolman both postulated internal mechanisms "causing" our behavior. The dozens of intervening variables proposed by Hull made him a cognitive psychologist; if a theory emphasizes representations, then the theory is a cognitive theory. Skinner advocated a return to a strategy like Watson's, abandoning intervening variables and the theories that produced them.

Skinner proposed the intensive study of the behavior of simple organisms, like the rat and the pigeon. If we can discover the principles that govern their behavior, we will find applications to behavior in general, including human behavior and experience. We soon find, for example, that the method of systematically reinforcing successive approximations to an unusual and unlikely behavioral performance by a pigeon can also be used to shape the verbal behavior of a language-delayed child (Peterson 2004), that a schedule of reinforcement that keeps a rat steadily pressing a lever also keeps a gambler operating a slot machine, while another schedule affects rats and pigeons in exactly the same way that it affects humans on piecework pay schedules.[2]

In the 1950s there was a great deal of research on reinforcement schedules, and the findings quickly found application in education and mental health, not to mention commercial animal training. However, Skinner's point remained unclear to many as this passage shows:

There are, for example, the behaviorists, who follow psychologist B. F. Skinner in viewing the actions of animals as responses shaped by rewards and punishments rather than the result of internal decision making, emotions or intentions. (De Waal 1997, pp. 50–53)

De Waal clearly did not understand—behavior analysis applies as well to humans as to other animals. Skinner's message was that an analysis of contingencies, or the relations among stimuli, behavior, and patterns of consequences, is the proper strategy for psychology. An experimental analysis of behavior would account for observable behavior *and* for experience and mental activity. It would explain attention, remembering, perception, learning, dispositions, traits, and anything else we might include. By the end of the twentieth century, great progress was made, and many held Skinner personally responsible for advances in programmed instruction and behavior therapy. Although that is an exaggeration, his influence in these areas was undeniable.

Why Theories Are Unnecessary
In 1950 Skinner argued against theories not only in psychology but in all science. The puzzlement generated at the time continued for decades, and many readers were never able to understand that Skinner was simply arguing against the use of intervening variables, the mainstay of Hull, Tolman, and all psychological theories. Not only

did he argue against commonly reified intervening variables like perception, motivation, personality, industriousness, will, and the like, but he opposed the use of more innocuous terms, like "habit," and "association"!

The more obnoxious intervening variables are the staple explanations of everyday life, and they must have some virtue, since they have lasted a long time. For example, when someone behaves rudely toward you, you may seek the cause for this by asking someone who knows the offender better than you do. You are told that he or she is a nasty demon and that accounts for the rudeness toward you. For practical purposes, that might be all that you want to know—that the person often acts this way and that you might do well to avoid him or her in the future.

However, you learned only that names you had already assigned to the behavior—rudeness and aggressiveness—are appropriate names for that person's behavior much of the time. That is only naming, not explaining, that behavior. When we resort to such naming and say that someone is "aggressive, industrious, persistent, intelligent, and willful," and that she has a "great memory," we only name behaviors, and when we think we are explaining, we actually have only unfinished causal sequences, not explanations. These intervening variables are the main ingredient in virtually all psychological theories.

Real Explanations

Real explanations lie in the history of the individual and the species. Aggressive behavior may become strong because of the way one was raised, a history of failure, frequent disappointments, chronic pain, or thousands of other reasons. One salient possibility lies in the fact that aggressive action is often rewarded by deference or attention from others. We often don't care what the relevant history is, but Skinner wants us to know that naming it "aggressiveness" is no explanation.

In other cases we see that someone can recite a long list of words after a single reading and we refer to "a good memory." Is that an explanation? Are we further ahead when we commit this nominal fallacy than we were before? Might we better examine the individual's past practice with such lists or experience with mnemonic devices? In that history we will find the real explanations. There also we will find the explanations for what we now call "ambition," "willpower," "thirst," "perception," "memory," "learning," and all of the other names that now pass as explanations.

The Cognitive Revolution

> I was in graduate school at the University of Illinois from 1970 to 1974 and was always told by William F. Brewer that a revolution was going on. The present article started as a dissenting class paper that I wrote for him. (Leahey 1992, p. 315)

Where and when did the "cognitive revolution" begin, according to the revolutionary myth? Leahey wrote that the popularity of Kuhn's book, *The Structure of Scientific Revolutions*, meant that the thought of radical change—revolution—was in the air by 1970. And the protests of the 1960s tried to smash "the intellectual crockery of Western civilization," adding to the sense of great change in psychology, a discipline so fluid that it seems always changing. A revolution implies that some stable structure was replaced by a second stable structure. One can only wish that this were the case. Nonetheless, there are several landmarks to which various writers point when wistfully describing the beginnings of cognitive psychology.

In 1948 there was a meeting, the Hixon Symposium on Cerebral Mechanisms in Behavior, which included a much-cited presentation by the great neuroanatomist and physiologist Karl Lashley on the problem of serial order in behavior (Lashley 1951). He argued persuasively that chains of s-r or r-s or s-r-s units of the sort proposed by Hull and his followers could not operate quickly enough to account for sequences of actions that comprise a rapid set of key presses ordinarily performed by pianists. He also pointed to the necessity of contextual determinants of meaning, as in interpreting the heard word "right" and determining whether it was "right, rite, wright," or "write." Such arguments constituted a challenge to the s-r psychology of the day.

A second key date is September 11, 1956, at a Symposium on Information Theory at the Massachusetts Institute of Technology where Newell and Simon presented their ideas on computer simulation and Noam Chomsky criticized extant theories of language. Also, 1956 was the year of publication of George Miller's classic "The Magical Number Seven" paper that urged the application of information theory to psychology. The final stamp of "real existence" was applied in Ulric Neisser's 1967 book, *Cognitive Psychology*. That book emphasized information-processing interpretations of perception and attention (six chapters) and language, memory, and thought (four chapters). By 1990, the leading text was loaded differently, with a single chapter on perception and eleven on language, memory, and thought (Anderson, 2000). In 1970 the journal *Cognitive Psychology* was founded.

"Cognitive science" is a broader endeavor, including research from philosophy, linguistics, neuroscience, and artificial intelligence, and its existence may be traced to the founding of another journal, *Cognitive Science*, in 1976. Anderson (2000, p. 10) distinguished cognitive psychology/science in a manner that shows the continuity of cognitive psychology and the mainstream form of behaviorism:

It is not profitable to try to define precisely the differences, but cognitive science makes greater use of methods such as computer simulation of cognitive processes and logical analysis, while cognitive psychology relies heavily on experimental techniques that grew out of the behaviorist era for studying behavior.

And before all of this happened, in the 1940s and 1950s, there were signs of dissatisfaction, malaise, and unhappiness—"amorphous disquiet about psychological theory," a condition that seems perennial. The 1960s was the time of Kuhn's revolutions, and revolution is what many told us occurred. But did it?

No Revolutions in Psychology

The history of American psychology is a plausible but dangerous myth.... Save for Wundt's founding of psychology, revolution in psychology is a myth. But we need not assume that Kuhn is good philosophy of science. (Leahey 1992, p. 308)

Countless textbooks, articles, and graduate theses and dissertations accepted stories like Anderson's on faith, just as Anderson accepted it himself. Yet, it takes little investigation to find the truth—there was no cognitive revolution.

Leahey (1992, pp. 308–318) showed that no revolutions have occurred, partly because no real paradigms have existed to allow the conducting of "normal science." That is, the "study of mental life" of the 1890s was by no means a paradigm. "Introspection," for Wundt, was not the armchair examination of consciousness of William James —Wundt really meant the scientific study of sensation and perception, with verbal reports playing a very minor role. The Würzburg researchers, as well as Titchener, viewed introspection very differently, as the retrospective description of the "indescribable," the imageless thoughts/conscious attitudes they found. All studied "consciousness," but there was neither a shared paradigm nor a shared definition of basic terms used.

In fact, Leahey argued that no one defended the definition of psychology as "the study of consciousness" at the 1910 meeting of the American Psychological Association. And what the advent of behaviorism did shortly after was "revolutionary" only in its insistence that psychology be broadened to include animals, children, and the abnormal/clinical.[3] Thus, there was no behavioral revolution, but what of the cognitive revolution of the later twentieth century? Leahey quoted a French writer's opinion:[4] "The theme of a cognitive revolution in psychology, which borrows its terminology from the theory of scientific revolutions of Kuhn, has today become banal."

How can that be? Was there no cognitive revolution? Leahey's teachers told him that there was, leading him to construct a dissenting argument, a task that was not difficult. In Wundt's laboratory, the study of sensation, perception, and attention was effectively a behavioral enterprise as we found in chapter 11. Twentieth-century American behaviorists carried on this tradition, adding hypothetical mediating mechanisms by the 1940s and 1950s—Hull's internal r-s chains were the prototype of later mediational behavioral mechanisms.

Before and after this period, there were debates about the nature of these internal mechanisms. Are they intervening variables, like "honesty," useful in ordering data but having no real physical existence? Or are hypothetical constructs allowable, so that "cognitive maps" have real counterparts in the brain? Or was Skinner right, and are we better off without any mediating entities? Such squabbles may be seen as part of "normal science," but in Kuhn's original vision such debates occur when there is no paradigm, in the preparadigmatic stage of a science! That means that in the 1940s and 1950s there was no paradigm to topple, behavioral or other.

How Many Cognitive Psychologies?

Examination of late twentieth-century textbooks dealing with "cognitive psychology," "human cognition," "cognitive science," and the like quickly reveals that there are many, many varieties of cognitive psychology and very little agreement about exactly what may be its domain.

One might ask whether there even exists a coherent discipline that could be called "cognitive psychology." Examinations of textbooks on cognitive psychology are very instructive. White (1985) examined the studies cited in seven popular cognitive psychology textbooks. There were a total of 3,200 references, and only nineteen were included in all seven texts. What of those cited by four of the seven texts? That total was 144 items, again a small number. Two years before, he had examined the references in eight human memory textbooks, finding that of a total of 3,500 references, only ten were cited in all eight books. A "whopping 80%," or 2,800 references, were cited by only *one* of the books. White concluded that if less than one percent of the references appear in all the textbooks, there is far from unanimous agreement on the fundamentals of cognitive psychology.

How Many Behaviorisms?

While there are as many "cognitive psychologies" as there are textbook writers, there are really only two "behaviorisms." *Methodological* behaviorism is the kind most often described and criticized by outsiders —it has never been characteristic of B. F. Skinner's thinking. *Radical* behaviorism is very different, and that is the name of Skinner's view.

In 1945 Skinner published a piece on the operational analysis of terms in which he attacked the prevailing logical positivist philosophy of science, which had produced what he called methodological behaviorism. This is the view that there is a distinction between public and private events and that psychology (to remain scientific) can deal only with public events. This is the "arid philosophy of truth by agreement"; something is real if at least two observers agree. Methodological behaviorism leaves the mind to philosophers.

You will frequently read or be told that Skinner held the views of the methodological behaviorists and "wouldn't let us study the mind because it is unscientific." That is absolutely false. Indeed, Skinner presented his position, radical behaviorism, in contrast to methodological behaviorism! Radical behaviorism is Watsonian, in that it does not distinguish between private and public events. It treats "seeing" as an activity similar in kind to walking.

Skinner surely did not deny the existence of private experience, any more than did Watson, but he did deny the mind/body dualism of the mentalists and the methodological behaviorists. Thinking is something that we do, just as walking is something that we do, and we don't think mental thoughts any more than we walk mental steps. That part of the world within our bodies is difficult to describe because society has a difficult time teaching us to name it.

How can a parent who tells us that a ball is "blue" tell us that we have a stomachache? The parent must assess public accompaniments, such as swellings or wounds, collateral behavior, such as wincing or crying out, verbal reports established by past teaching, when questions like "where does it hurt?" are answered, and metaphors in verbal reports, such as sharp pains or dull aches.

There is no "inner world," any more than there is an "outer world." However, we are raised to believe that there are two worlds, and part of the cause of that is our language. That is why Skinner was so interested in etymology.

Skinner on Etymology

Skinner was very concerned with language throughout his career, particularly with the effect wrought by word usage in creating a nonexistant "inner world" as a surrogate for the world we actually inhabit. He pointed out that words and expressions that originally described things that we do came to refer instead to supposed inner states that "caused" behavior and experience. In a 1989 article he enumerated instances of such changes in usage that helped to create a false "inner world."

For example, to "grieve" originally meant to "bear a heavy burden." Over the years, people experiencing great losses were described as "grieving," or being "in grief," since they acted as though they were carrying a heavy burden. Eventually, grief and grieving became names for internal states. The list below includes other names for internal states that originated in descriptions of observable behaviors.

Word	Original Referent in Observable Activity
surprise	to seize or grasp
watch	to be awake
aware	wary, cautious
solve	loosen, set free
cogitate	shake up
emotion	movement, to be moved
happy	lucky ("hap" = luck; cf. hapless, mishap)
glad	shining, bright
sad	sated, as in filled with food and drink
angry	trouble(d), commotion

Figure 17.2
Baum. Personal collection.

Skinner's Direct Legacy

There are thousands of psychologists, educators, social workers, and businesspeople who consider themselves behavior analysts and who follow, more or less, the fundamental theses of Skinner. This is far from a homogeneous group; there is always much dissent among its members as is true of any large group whose members have different goals and hold different interpretations of their field. Part of the reason for disagreement stems from the inherent ambiguity in Skinner's writings.

For example, it is difficult to sort Skinner's views on radical behaviorism, the philosophy of a science of behavior, from operant conditioning, the theory that is used in practice. Skinner complained in 1977 that it was disappointing to have published nine books and to be seriously misunderstood by Richard Herrnstein, a former student and longtime colleague. William Baum (see figure 17.2) made a serious ef-

Figure 17.3
Rachlin. Personal collection.

fort to remedy this situation in 1994 by writing a book that was a frank attempt to present Skinner's ideas more clearly than had the master and thus to eliminate some of the misunderstandings that still prevail.

Mental as Molar: Aristotle Was Right
We saw in chapter 3 that Aristotle defined things like "love," "virtue," "bravery," and "springtime" as patterns of activities extending over time. There is no instantaneous "pang" of love that characterizes love in any meaningful way, and the concept of virtue can mean only a pattern of virtuous acts. Just as spring occurs over time, not with the sighting of a single swallow, love, virtue, and happiness are apprehensible only over time—perhaps a lifetime.

B. F. Skinner never saw how closely Aristotle's interpretation was to that of behavior analysis, but Howard Rachlin (see figure 17.3) surely did and had been pointing it out for decades before Baum wrote. Rachlin's (1994) *Behavior and Mind* shows convincingly that Aristotle was more a radical behaviorist than was Skinner himself. As Rachlin sees it, such "patterns of behavior over time" actually define what we treat as mental. In chapter 3 we saw how this view applies to love and virtue, and maybe to pain.

Freedom and Responsibility
The second half of Skinner's life was devoted to applying his vision of science to the large issues of freedom, praise, blame, and the design of cultures. His arguments were based on data gleaned from experiments in behavior analysis, and in most cases the subjects were animals. Sober and conservative researchers might counsel restraint and urge that basic research be encouraged and that the public be educated so as to respect fundamental research. However, that was not Skinner's way. In a series of popular books he extrapolated to the most vexing problems imaginable and proposed radical changes in the arrangement of cultures. Baum presented Skinner's case well, and we will consider it in outline before turning to a contemporary critique.

Freedom
"Freedom" can mean many things, and functional analyses of behavior often have to pin down the particular meaning of a word before more can be said or done. We can be free of restraint, whether political, social, or spiritual—free, at least, in principle, if not in fact. We are never really free, since that would mean that our activities were uncaused, undetermined by our genetic and personal history. We can feel free, in the sense that we feel our acts to be free of coercion. When we feel free, we feel happy, and Baum (1994, p. 155) quoted Amos Tversky, who pointed out that we gladly buy state lottery tickets but dislike paying the same tax when it is called a tax. We "choose" to buy the ticket, we say. Being free is illusion, but feeling free is happiness. Freedom is just a feeling.

Praise and Blame
Our justice system punishes crimes that are freely committed, though no one freely chooses to grow up in a ghetto, a condition that seems to encourage the "free" choice of crime. So goes Skinner's argument against punishment. He pointed out most clearly in 1971 that when it comes to giving credit, we commend ourselves, but when blame is to

be assigned, we blame extenuating circumstances, the environment, and other factors in our environment and our histories. However, all is determined by genes and personal history, and "credit" belongs there.

But so does blame! The more one believes in free will, wrote Skinner and later Baum, the more one advocates punishment. If the crime seems unrelated to the ordinary pattern of a person's life, as when a well-off person shoplifts, we call it "temporary insanity," or "kleptomania." Otherwise, crimes are punishable—subject to the retribution of society for breaking its rules. Yet, Skinner always argued, research has shown that punishment has undesired side effects and, as Baum points out, it makes people unhappy.

The alternative to the present vengeance-seeking judicial system is to coerce without aversive control, with positive reinforcers. If bribing students to stay in school and to do well works, then do it. Skinner has written so often on the evil effects of punishment that he may have started to believe it himself. However, punishment works.

Baum did a fine job in presenting Skinner's views, but his opinion is not universally shared. A second author presented a different picture, portraying Skinner as a rhetorical genius who parlayed basic research findings into a worldview that gained cult-like acceptance. Aspects of the basic research are firm and indisputable, but J. E. R. Staddon (see figure 17.4) argued that other data and interpretations are wrong, misrepresented, and productive of false conclusions. The popularity of these tainted views has spread to the humanities, which clearly alarmed Staddon, to whom we now turn.

Concerning Excesses of Behavior Analysis

Staddon (1993) published a brief but insightful book providing a history of behaviorism and a critique of Skinner's famous "superstition" experiment and of his extrapolation from basic laboratory findings to the problems of human societies. Staddon, a student of Richard Herrnstein, wrote from the insider's point of view, not from that of humanist or cognitive critics.

He argued that Skinner was mistaken regarding fundamentals of operant conditioning and that this is particularly unfortunate since he spent the second half of his life in a literary venture, extending operant fundamentals to all aspects of human life. One of Skinner's mistakes was his denial of the efficacy of punishment, the consequence of which was a boost for humanist "social constructionist" theories, described in chapter 1.

Figure 17.4
Staddon. Personal collection.

Skinner's version of such theory is the evolutionary analogy, which Staddon called "a match made in heaven" (p. 46). "Careless of details," with "audiences unaware," Skinner described the development of superstitions in pigeons as analogous to the selection of individuals in evolution, both of which form the basis of an evolutionary epistemology. This is simple stuff. In essence, behaviors, mutations, and beliefs are emitted, or generated, or proposed, or otherwise brought into being. Some are reinforced, selected, or accepted—these are analogous processes—and those survive and are strengthened.

Thus, just as the pigeon "thinks" that its superstitious behavior produced food, engendering the belief that a contiguous behavior brought it, all of our knowledge is illusory and subject to constant change and revision, depending upon the consequences that follow. Hence, we behave "as if" there is a God and "as if" there is scientific truth, though nothing can be relied upon and truth is a matter of convention. Skinner's "rhetorical genius, his "mays" and "must supposes," "expel from the reader's mind any questions," and the argument "slips seamlessly" from questionably interpreted pigeon data to the question of epistemology in general.

Worse, in Staddon's view, this relativistic view jibes with late-twentieth-century thought in literary theory, where many find the prospect of the "dissolution of knowledge...liberating" (pp. 55–56). Staddon cites Barbara Herrnstein-Smith (1988) as an example of this taking up of Skinner's ideas by the literary community. The relativistic theory of truth as no more than "consensually-agreed beliefs" is both unnecessary and unsatisfactory in Staddon's view.

Skinner's second error lies in his long-held but erroneous belief that punishment is ineffective, misused, and undesirable and that positive reinforcement is effective and good. In fact, Staddon contended, punishment is often better and quicker, and positive reinforcement is not "good," but is subject to misuse as readily as is punishment. Positive contingencies promote such things as vitae padding, stock market triumphs that cheat widows and orphans, flatterers, spoiled children, and workers' reactions to piecework pay.

The issue resolves to Skinner's argument for a scientific psychology. That argument pits the "autonomous man" of popular belief against a "scientific" view that allows no real autonomy but places the control of organisms wholly in the environment. The problem is that our knowledge of the environmental factors that determine action are not so advanced as to allow the extrapolations that Skinner was fond of making. Consider his treatment of praise and blame.

Autonomous Man and the Case against Punishment

Staddon criticized Skinner's arguments against "autonomous man," the assumption that we have free will and thus deserve rewards and punishments that come our way. Skinner believed, of course, that we are never free, though the causes may lie far in the past and very likely in patterns of behavior that were established over extended periods. Nonetheless, it is clear that actions always occur under coercion, and they thus warrant no merit or demerit. Hence, praise and blame are both unwarranted—Baum echoed this argument, and it is the theme of Skinner's (1971) book, *Beyond Freedom and Dignity*.

Skinner held that punishment thus serves only as vengeance, since phylogenic and ontogenic factors are actually "guilty." Only the primitive belief in free will justifies retribution, so punishment has no place in the justice system. It is important to note, as we did earlier in the chapter, that Skinner has questioned the effectiveness of punishment for decades after overwhelming evidence for that effectiveness was available.

However, does the use of punishment, which is relatively ineffective in Skinner's eyes, make sense only if free will is assumed? Staddon contended that the use of punishment is justified "precisely because people are sensitive to contingencies" (pp. 72–75). That is, our actions are indeed determined, and punishment is used to change actions. If the will were free and behavior uncaused, there would be no point in punishment or in any attempts to control.

Order in society is maintained largely by holding individuals responsible for their actions. "Holding responsible" means to make aware of aversive contingencies, especially long-term ones. Those serving prison sentences were not properly raised to understand that "if you do that, you'll spend 15 years in prison." In Staddon's view, Skinner's long-held opposition to punishment is an imposture—a device to make his theory seem unique. He turned to the philosopher W. V. O. Quine, quoted by a judge, for what must be the most cogent opinion on the use of punishment and the place of free will:[5]

> The division of acts into some for which a man is regarded as responsible, and others for which he is not, is part of the social apparatus of reward and punishment: responsibility is allocated where rewards and punishments have tended to work as incentives and deterrents. And being social rather than philosophical in purpose, the allocation of responsibility need not follow the division between free and coerced acts. A person who kills in self defense is excused from criminal liability, but not the killer who would not have killed had he not been raised in a poor home by harsh parents.

In summary, we know that punishment works and that Skinner's objections to its use were irrational. Those crimes that are treated as "freely willed" are those for which there are prescribed penalties. That is because society has found that penalties seem to work when applied to such actions, and that means that those actions are not actually free. When we refer to "freely willed actions," we are just referring to actions that are affected by their consequences. This is opposed to coerced actions, which will not be so affected and are therefore not considered free.

The metaphysical question of whether we are capable of free will is irrelevant to the question of whether punishment should be used, since two different domains are involved—philosophical and social/practical.

Skinner's Damage to Society and Its Repair

The horrible effect of Skinner's attacks on religion and traditional beliefs in general owes to his failure to substitute anything for them. Citing G. K. Chesterton, Staddon suggested that those who do not believe in God do not believe in "nothing," rather they believe in "anything." Their values are those of advertisers, who tell them what is good and bad, beautiful and ugly, moral and immoral, as well as what soft drink to buy and what jeans to wear. This is not Skinner's doing, but his popular writings lend support to other forces that seek to destroy traditional values.

Staddon emphasized that Skinner did make many contributions, from the invention of the Skinner box, "now the standard way of studying learned behavior in psychology and neurobiology" (p. 81), to showing that behavior need not be viewed only through the "dark glass" of inferential statistics. And he showed the amazing uniformity in behavior—among individuals and species—that occurs under various reinforcement schedules. He influenced education and, of course, clinical psychology, where behavior modification methods "are perhaps the only psychotherapeutic techniques whose efficacy (in a limited domain) has been conclusively proved."

His great contribution was the recognition of the importance of the environment and its effect on behavior over time rather than the "snapshots" captured in the attitude questionnaire. However, in works such as *Beyond Freedom and Dignity*, he extrapolated too far and attempted to answer questions where no satisfactory answer now exists. Staddon (1993) takes scant comfort in observing that Skinner's sin is no greater than

... social scientists—psychologists, psychiatrists, sociologists, economists—who continue to go beyond their narrow, particular, and often ideologically driven understandings of human nature in "expert" testimony of all kinds. They should keep silent, or at least show a decent modesty in the fact of our enormous ignorance. (p. 83)

However, if forbearance is shown, what should society do? How should we raise children and deal with crime? Who will tell us?

Human nature is stranger than we know—and stranger even than we can imagine. In vital matters like marriage, raising children, and the punishment of crime it will be many, many, years before the one-dimensional pronouncements of "experts" can be reliably trusted over traditional wisdom and personal experience. (Staddon 1993, p. 83)

I am certain that Helmholtz, Wundt, James, Titchener, and countless other of our predecessors would agree. But what would they think of the cognitive psychology of the late twentieth century? That was the heyday of information processing.

How Could Information Processing Have Been Popular?

there are addresses, readout rules, and holding mechanisms... our memories are filled with T-stacks, implicit associational responses, natural-language mediators, images, multiple traces, tags, kernel sentences, markers, relational rules, verbal loops, and one-buns. (Underwood 1972)

Watkins (1990) wrote a commentary on the proliferation of information-processing mechanisms in cognitive psychology, specifically, the study of memory. He was not alone, as his quotation from B. J. Underwood, dean of memory researchers, testifies. Watkins contended that so many theories have been offered by so many researchers "that we have entered an age of personalized theorizing."

There are a variety of reasons for this bizarre condition, ranging from the insistence by journal editors that data be "explained" in theoretical terms to the fact that criticized theories are usually "fine-tuned" to become new theories! Watkins argued persuasively that the number of hypothetical internal mechanisms that has been proposed is ludicrously excessive and stems from the emphasis of mediationism. Only by dispensing with some of these hypothetical internal mechanisms may we hope that "the number of theories would be reduced below the number of researchers."

Critics of Icons and Processing Stages

Ulric Neisser coined the term icon and devoted considerable space to it in his extremely influential text, *Cognitive Psychology*. Ralph Norman Haber has published more than a score of papers on iconic memory and processing stages. With this in view, it is interesting to examine their reconsiderations regarding what is in large part their creation.

Neisser's classic textbook was published in 1967 and was surely a landmark in cognitive psychology, but the Neisser of only nine years later was a very different person. In 1976 he published *Cognition and Reality*, where he turned against icons, processing stages, and the like and emphasized activity—one could almost say that he sounded like a behaviorist:[6] "[cognition] is something that organisms do... when perception is treated as something we do, rather than something thrust upon us, no internal mechanisms of selection are required at all." John

B. Watson would approve that, as well as Neisser's argument that too much emphasis has been placed on hypothetical models and not enough on environment. Neisser questioned the status of the icon and its relation to seeing—is that "copy" to be viewed as part of the world or of the subject? He compared the problem with the famed cyberneticist Norbert Weiner's problem of the man with an artificial arm working on a machine.

Where does the man begin and the machinery end? The icon is the first stage in processing, and, if we can best abandon it, can we abandon all of the other processing stages? That would be an abandoning of cognitive psychology itself as Neisser defined it in 1967. The point is precisely that made by B. F. Skinner in "Behaviorism at Fifty" (1963), and Neisser is the man who defined cognitive psychology as the study of processing stages only a few years earlier.

Many other cognitive scientists have criticized cognitive science since the 1970s shine wore off. Data are interpretable in many ways, and interpretations based on presuppositions about hypothetical processing mechanisms are especially apt to be wrong. Many disagree with Neisser and other critics, of course, but their leadership status lends extra force to their conclusions.

Memory and Forgetting
Research in long-term memory, or memory as we usually construe it, changed emphasis during the second half of the twentieth century. Before the 1960s, interest centered on factors that influenced forgetting; thereafter, more attention has been paid to the organization of memory, to memory in ordinary situations of life, and to the relation of awareness and memory. Consider what was known of memory at the turn of the century as presented by Hermann Ebbinghaus and by William James.

A German pioneer, Hermann Ebbinghaus, extended the domain of scientific psychology by showing that the mental faculty of memory could be objectively studied. Often neglected is the fact that, in so doing, he clarified the role of awareness in cognitive processes. And he wrote textbooks that popularized the New Psychology without pandering to popular tastes and preconceptions.

Ebbinghaus and Awareness
By 1897 Hermann Ebbinghaus had published the first volume of his immensely successful *Grundzuge der Psychologie*, a general text that has

been often compared to James's famous *Principles of Psychology*. This was immediately successful and was revised in 1905, followed by ninety-six pages of the second volume in 1908. He was asked to do a third edition of the first volume but died unexpectedly of pneumonia in 1909, at the age of fifty-nine, before that or the completion of the second volume could be accomplished.

Ebbinghaus's Contribution: Awareness and Implicit Memory

In 1885 Hermann Ebbinghaus published the results of investigations of the course of forgetting due just to the "influence of time or the daily events which fill it." Mimicking Fechner's psychophysical procedures, the inspiration for his work, he listed 2,300 CVC nonsense syllables.[7] These syllables were chosen so as to have no meaning in German (e.g., DUB, JIK, COZ).

You may notice that many products have since been given CVC names, making them more memorable than was the case in Ebbinghaus's day (e.g., BIZ, DUZ, JIF, FAB). He learned over 1,200 lists of three-letter nonsense syllables, with eight, twelve, or more syllables in each list. During each session, which lasted twenty minutes or so, he read through the lists one by one, at a rate of one syllable per two-fifths of a second, repeating each of the lists until he could recite it twice without error. Successive lists were separated by a pause of fifteen seconds, and his measure of memory retention was the savings in time when he relearned the same set (of eight or so) lists after a lapse of time.

This savings method is actually quite ingenious. Suppose that you learn some set of material for an exam and, when faced with the task of recalling it, you go blank. Are you indeed blank—is the effect of your study nil? Similarly, are your forgotten memories of last year or of ten years ago gone without a trace, or is something left? You recall nothing, so how can "what is left" be assessed? Suppose that you do not profit from hints ("begins with JIF"), and do not even recognize the material when presented? It seems forgotten—as if it were never known. Savings in relearning often shows that *something* is retained, even though no ordinary assessment of memory reveals it.

"Implicit" Memory and Unconscious Processes   Ebbinghaus's savings method was an early assessment of implicit memory, or "unconscious memory," a topic that became a focus of interest in the late twentieth century. Earlier, during the 1960s, controversy over "learning without awareness" and "subliminal perception" had raged, but the crude experiments presented by both sides in the controversy settled nothing and lent an aura of chicanery and foolishness to the field.

During the 1980s and 1990s, the methods had become refined, and the controversy was less coarsely conducted. By 1997, a major conference was even devoted to the topic of perceiving, learning, and remembering without conscious awareness. A topic that was of great interest to William James and to others of his time was once again interesting to researchers.[8] The methods used were new, but the interpretation of findings was as old and as controversial as ever. Since consciousness was never defined with any unanimity, matters must ever be murky and we mustn't be too quick to condemn.

One Method for Studying Implicit Perception and Memory: The Exclusive Stem Completion Method

Probably the simplest method to show implicit memory is the method of stem-word completion and the use of inclusive or exclusive instructions. A subject is shown a long list of words and later asked to complete word stems, such as TAB, which could be the stem for TABLE, or TABOO, or TABLEAU. In early experiments, subjects might be more apt to complete a stem with a word from the earlier set, and, if that word was not recognized as a set member, the use of it could be attributed to unconscious (implicit) processes. In a more sophisticated procedure, whether conscious or "unconscious" activity prevails can be assessed using a mask to limit the duration of a priming word to subthreshold values. That performance can then be compared with responding when the masking effect is removed.

Consider the procedure. Suppose that the prime word is presented just before the stem and masked by a bright or an obscuring field that occurs fifty milliseconds after the prime is presented. Assume also that it has been determined in advance that this subject cannot report having seen anything that is present for so brief a time. The subject has been told *not* to use the prime word, and these instructions will be followed if possible. But what if the subject claims to have seen no prime yet uses that word to complete the stem? Is that an unconscious priming effect, an instance of subliminal semantic activation? However, if the mask appears after the prime has been present longer, say for 240 milliseconds, the subject will explicitly avoid using the prime to complete the stem. Those who use the method claim that it separates explicit ("conscious") and implicit ("unconscious") processes.

This sounds close to Skinner's position—we are many "selves," some of which are conscious, in the sense that they can use language and describe private experience. However, others are not verbal and are shut off from the articulate, introspective self that we call "me." The infant's world is of this kind, and it remains so until society constructs a consciousness as it transmits its language. How many gradations might there be from the highest level of self-consciousness down to the lowest level of "implicit" memory?

Computer Simulation

The early modern idea that technology will lift from mankind the burdens of drudgery, allowing us to "become our essence"—to spend our time pondering lofty questions, thus reenacting the popularized Greek ideal of leisure—has in postmodernity reversed itself...it appears that "drudgery" is our essence...we have abdicated the throne of consciousness and pawned off the hardest questions to the new dogmas of computer science...(Tedrowe 1997)

During the late 1950s, Herbert Simon and Allen Newell of Carnegie-Mellon University and their associates at the RAND Corporation developed computer programs specifically designed to solve problems in the ways that humans solve problems. Newell, Simon, and Shaw (1957) designed such a program, the Logic Theorist, or LT, that could solve problems in symbolic logic. LT could "think!" and its ability to solve successive problems increased—it "learned!" Finally, it often arrived at sudden solutions—it showed "insight!"

Logic Theorist did this using only a few elementary operations; it read, wrote, stored, erased, and compared. It also used heuristics, or shortcut strategies to aid in the solution of problems. It broke complex problems into subparts, as Descartes advised, and it worked backward from the desired end states, and so on.

During the 1960s, LT was expanded to what was called General Problem Solver, or GPS, a series of programs developed over several years. It could solve problems in word algebra, as well as standards like the missionaries and cannibals and the Tower of Hanoi problem. The methods used came from simulations of human problem solving, and these resulted from an analysis of human performance.

Typically, a verbal protocol of human problem solving was obtained by posing problems of a given kind to human subjects who were required to verbalize every step they followed in solving the problem.

One common problem type was cryptoarithmetic, or "word algebra," as it was called above. Consider this simple example:

DONALD
+ GERALD
_____
ROBERT

Subjects are told that each letter corresponds to a digit and that D = 5. To what digits do the remaining letters correspond? One quickly notes that T must be zero, a conclusion that is verbalized, as is the result of examination of the other letters. A subject's verbal protocol might go like this:

"Since O + E = O, E must be 9, with 1 carried from N + R."

"Since D + G = R, D is 5 and R is 9 or less, G is 4 or less."

"R must be more than 5 and, since E is 9, R is 6, 7, or 8."

"But O + E + O, a 1 is carried and R is not 6, since D is 5."

"So R cannot be 6—it is 7 or 8."

This continues, letter by letter, until the problem is solved, using the rules of arithmetic learned in childhood.

However, we use more than the rules of arithmetic; as Simon and Newell pointed out we use heuristics, or rules of thumb, and typically the order of letters translated varies little from subject to subject. In this problem the order runs T, E, R, A, L, G, N, B, and O. The heuristic exemplified is to begin with the most constrained letters, such as E, which "must be" 9, and progress to less constrained letters, especially those that become constrained as successive letters are translated.

Could such problems be solved using an algorithm? An algorithm is a rule for solution that always works, unlike a heuristic, which might not. Thus, one could randomly try assignments of digits for letters and eventually succeed. However, "eventually" could be a long time, since there are 9 factorial (9!) ways in which to assign 9 digits to 9 letters, or 362,880 possible ways.

The Carnegie-Mellon group analyzed verbal protocols of problem solving by human subjects and incorporated the strategies in GPS. New problems were then presented to the program and to human subjects and performances compared. If the program behaved differently from the humans, GPS was revised; in the 1960s the goal was to simulate human performance, not merely to solve the problem. At that time, programs that did not simulate humans were categorized as artificial intelligence.

Simon and Newell passionately argued that GPS did simulate human problem solving and that the principles embodied in GPS are thus the principles of human thought. Clearly, this is one realization of Clark Hull's ideal, a theory of mind composed of clear principles embodied in a machine! Does this machine operate as did Hull's? Bower and Hilgard (1981) thought so, and their classic learning theories textbook presents Hull's main postulates in flowchart form, as a serial information processor. How does it work?

As it turns out, we are really very simple entities, at least if GPS and similar processors really operate as we do. We are merely serial processors, chugging along through a series of one-thing-at-a-time steps. We have only a few inputs and outputs, and we can retain a few symbolic inputs at a time in short-term storage, as in a buffer file. We have almost limitless long-term storage, though the storage process may be slow. Our retrieval is fast, though we may have accessibility problems. And we use heuristics.

GPS not only breaks problems into subparts but it uses "means–ends analysis," monitoring the discrepancy between the present state of a problem or subproblem and the desired end state. Operators were repeatedly applied to reduce the discrepancy, so that if one failed, another was applied and so on.

What Became of Computer Simulation?

We didn't hear much of computer simulation after the 1970s, partly because the breakthroughs promised in the 1960s clearly failed to materialize. Additionally, the range of problems that have been studied is extremely restricted. If you have ever written a computer program, you know that it is essential to be very specific, and this is no less true when one designs computer simulations. The initial features of the problem (the problem space) must be absolutely unambiguously specified, as must the goal or end state. And the operations that may be used to transform the initial state to the end state must be clearly specified.

Simulation was successful in the 1960s when problems were highly structured symbolic tasks—not bad, since even success with a narrow subset of problems is something. However, the limits of simulation by serial processors were recognized very early by critics, as well as by Allan Newell:

...information processing may well be an Alice in wonderland croquet game, with porcupine balls unrolling themselves and wandering off and flamingo mallets asking questions at inopportune times. (Newell 1962)

How can a program deal with the ambiguities of most of the situations that we call problems? Simulation with digital computers died out because the problems it could deal with were only those that humans were forced to solve as did digital computers.

Beyond Simulation

If Deep Blue does win, its victory will not represent the subjugation of man by machine. It will instead represent the victory of the combined efforts of the thousands of scientists, programmers, and engineers who created the machine and its programs over the singular effort of one man, Garry Kasparov. (Washington 1997)

One of the problems least amenable to simulation is the playing of chess. Even when simulation is tossed aside and the full power of the most advanced computers is applied, as represented by Deep Blue in 1997, human chess masters are usually victorious.[9] Simon and his associates gave up attempts to simulate chess; while the rules governing the game are specific enough, the ways of reaching end states are so numerous as to be effectively infinite. The analysis of verbal protocols and deriving of strategies stood no chance. A different strategy was used.

A Dutch investigator, de Groot (1966), pioneered this method with an examination of chess players ranging from internationally recognized masters to novices. He carried out two main forms of study. In the first, subjects were shown pictures of chess board layouts that might occur midway through a game. After fifteen seconds of viewing, they were asked to comment on the configuration of pieces and to suggest subsequent moves. Experts were able to evaluate the layouts much more skillfully than were the novices and they were able to comment on the likely history of the game to that point. They could evaluate the direction the game was taking and suggest specific (and good) next moves. Novices could often comment on the general direction of the game but were unable to describe the probable history of the game to that point or to suggest advantageous next moves.

In a second novice/master comparison, five-second presentations of middle-game configurations were presented and subjects were asked to reconstruct the layout of pieces on the board. Expert players had no difficulty with this and made few errors, while novices performed very poorly. Seven presentations were frequently necessary to enable the novice to reconstruct the boards as well as the expert could after one five-second presentation. Not surprisingly, when random arrangements of pieces were presented, the expert/novice difference disappeared.

Obviously, the experts' greater experience meant that they knew what the briefly presented boards "had to look like." Can more be said? Chase and Simon (1973) replicated de Groot's "reconstruction" experiment, finding what he had found. Further, they asked subjects to construct a board configuration matching one visible on another board. Eye movements were recorded and examined when board configurations differed in pieces, colors, proximities, and relations, such as "attack" and "defense."

Expert players consistently scanned in less time, as might be expected, and the experimenters concluded that thousands of hours playing chess leads to the "storing in LTM [long-term memory]" of many familiar configurations. They estimated the number to be somewhere between 10,000 and 100,000. Such research reflects emphasis on the problem of "representation"; in a real sense, the master "sees" differently from the novice, just as John Stuart Mill and Helmholtz told us happens.

Radical Behaviorism and Cognitive Psychology Blend in Modern Social Psychology?

Where's Awareness? The Hegemony of Mindlessness   Is cognitive science to remain a land of opportunity for every philosopher, engineer, computer expert, and other nonpsychologist who sees a market for apparent "breakthroughs?" Is our understanding of cognition to remain conceptually in the sixteenth and seventeenth centuries? Does the rapid rise and fall of symbolic information processing signal the end of psychology's participation in "cognitive science?" Can there be at least a psychology of cognition that accounts for common experience, even if it cannot routinely beat a chess master or solve anagrams?

Luckily, there is such a psychology, and it comes largely out of recent thought in social psychology, of all sources, and from odds and ends of research that has been done over the course of the twentieth century. While its origins were earlier—in the 1960s—the paper that really drew attention to social cognitive theory was published by

Figure 17.5
Nisbett. Personal collection.

Nisbett (see figure 17.5) and Wilson in 1977 with the catchy title "Telling More Than We Can Know: Verbal Reports on Mental Processes."

The Nature of Self Reports: Bem's Self-Perception

In a brilliant analysis of the nature of self reports, Daryl Bem (see figure 17.6) introduced the theory of "self-perception" in 1967. Bem is a social psychologist, but one familiar with radical behaviorism, who offered a compelling behavioral alternative to the cognitive mediational theory of cognitive dissonance, which was wildly popular at the time.

According to CD theory, dissonant cognitions having to do with our behavior, physiological states, and other beliefs may conflict, giving rise to an aversive drive similar to hunger. We then reduce this dissonance in various ways, often by changing our cognitions so that they do not conflict. For example, subjects induced to engage in counterattitudinal behavior, such as giving a pro–Fidel Castro speech, often show a change in "attitude" toward the disliked topic. In this case, Castro would be rated as less disliked, reducing the dissonance produced by giving the pro-Castro speech.

This is a prime example of a mediational theory, with imagined internal conflicts among imagined cognitions. Bem proposed that we

Figure 17.6
Bem. Personal collection.

examine the nature of self reports and reach a better understanding of so-called "attitude changes." Following Skinner's analysis, Bem (1967) argued that we learn to judge the "attitudes" of others through observations of their behavior, so we judge someone's "hunger" by how much we see him eat. Often we apply the same practice to ourselves, as when we conclude that "I was not as hungry as I thought."

In the majority of CD studies, subjects were asked questions for which they had no ready answer, and so assessed their "attitude" by considering their *own* behavior. I might give you a negative assessment of Castro if you ask me for one and I really have no firm opinion. But if you ask me again, after I have given a pro-Castro speech under coercion that I do not notice, I have more information to go on.

Bem emphasized that this was an account based on "radical behaviorism," but no one seemed to notice. Skinner learned of it at some time or other and wrote a note on it that appeared in his published notebooks. He knew that Bem saw self perception as a radical behavioral treatment, but for reasons I will never understand, Skinner wrote (in his *Notebooks*) that he didn't see the connection. Go figure.

Nisbett and Wilson: "Telling More Than We Can Know"

These authors surveyed data going back to the 1930s, as well as more recent findings by Bem, Schachter, Kelley, Jones, and others working in attribution theory. What may be surprising is their consistent finding that people have little knowledge of their "mental processes," though they commonly believe that they do.

We should remember that the Würzburg School had reached what seems to be the same conclusion, but even they might have been surprised at the extent of our oblivion regarding thinking. And Skinner and his followers should have recognized kindred doctrine in this latest form of attribution theory, just as Bem thought a decade before. Consider some of their findings, and then you will see the merit in their conclusions.

In one experiment, subjects were asked to judge the quality of clothes (four nightgowns or stockings) hanging on a rack. The 378 subjects chose the clothing hanging on the right end of the rack by a ratio of 4:1 over the other three positions. When asked why they chose what they did, subjects pointed to material, style, and workmanship to defend their choices. When told that the items' positions were randomly shuffled for each subject, but that the choice was still 4:1 for the right-hand item, subjects found it hard to believe. The subjects' choice behavior was easily explained as a position preference—what they thought determined their choice was irrelevant.

Ratings of "goodness," or esthetic judgments, are prone to all manner of spurious fluctuation, rendering such ratings of limited usefulness. Subjects watched a movie while a circular saw was loudly running just outside the viewing room. They rated the film and then were asked how they would have rated it were the saw not present. Of course, they said that they would have rated it higher, though a second group who watched the same film without the saw rated it just as did the first group.

Snake phobics were shown slides of snakes, followed by the word "shock" presented on a slide, while listening through headphones to false heartbeat sounds. The slide "shock" was followed by actual electric shock, and the false heartbeat sounds increased in rate, but the false heart rate never changed when a slide of a snake was shown. Subjects were later asked to approach and, if possible, to pet a live snake.

In this typical study of attribution, these subjects approached more closely and petted more often than did a group that had received different pretraining.

What has this to do with awareness? The subjects "learned" that their heart rate increased when shock was coming, but not when they saw a snake. Hence, they must not be as afraid of snakes as they had thought—their awareness of snake fear was faulty, as reflected in their approaching and touching. On the other hand, this was not the kind of "awareness" that is verbalized, since when asked directly about their fear of snakes, they reported that they were as fearful of them as ever.[10] In other attribution experiments, such as when subjects take fake "insomnia pills," changes in behavior are not correlated with changes in verbalization of motives and attitudes.

So, what does it mean to say that someone is aware of a state of mind or of the causes for action? In all the cases above, and in many more that Nisbett and Wilson described, outside observers knew why subjects did what they did better than did the subjects themselves. As Bem showed, if I see that you do not call your mother or eat brown bread over a six-month period, I know what you think of both mother and bread and I may know it better than you do! When you say that you "love mother," are you just mouthing a slogan learned in childhood that represents what people are supposed to say?

When can we say that a person is aware? Nisbett and Wilson suggested that we cannot take people's word for it and that the criterion for awareness should be instead verbal report which exceeds in accuracy that obtained from observers provided with a general description of the stimulus and response in question.

We typically don't know why we judge as we do. We are apt to think that President Kennedy's assassination was a conspiracy, because Oswald was too pitiful to cause such a mighty effect. One of our assumptions is that big effects have big causes, even though we constantly see exceptions to that rule. We like the police who help us change a tire in the rain, even though it is their job to do such things. When we stand in an elevator, we look up at the display showing the floors as we rise or fall, but we do not look at the other passengers, nor do we face the rear of the car.

What do people know? What is that content of consciousness that has been debated for so many centuries? These authors propose that there are three things that are known. First, we know personal historical facts, such as the name of our kindergarten teacher and the high school where we graduated. We know approximately what is the focus of our attention at any given time. I can tell whether I am listening to you or thinking about Christmas. And, finally, I can report my current sensations, more or less, and tell you something of my emotions, and sometimes I can do that better than can others who observe me. However, when I make a judgment, whether causal or esthetic, my report is often wrong, and when you explain your motives, you too are often wrong

Rationality Is Only Occasional

The psychophysics of value induce risk aversion in the domain of gains and risk seeking in the domain of losses. The psychophysics of chance induce over-weighting of sure things and of improbable events, relative to events of moderate probability. Decision problems can be described or framed in multiple ways that give rise to different preferences, contrary to the invariance criterion of rational choice. The process... explains some aspects of consumer behavior. (Kahneman and Tversky 1984, p. 341)

In 1984 Daniel Kahneman and Amos Tversky described their studies of the way we make choices—it is not a rational process. If we behaved as do rational decision makers, our choices would depend merely on expected utility, or the product of expected gain and utility. Utility is the value of something when presented as a choice. Five dollars has no utility unless it is compared with ten dollars or with nothing, which is usually the case. Expected utility takes into account the probability of the outcome's occurring. Hence, if I flip a fair coin, bet you ten dollars, and let you call it, the net expected utility for you would be as follows—say you called "heads":

$$P(\text{heads}) \times U(\text{heads}) + P(\text{tails}) \times U(\text{tails}) = (.5)\ (\$5)\ (.5)\ (-\$5).$$

Whether you choose heads or tails is immaterial for this one toss—you may win or lose. However, over the long run, if you continued betting, you would break even, of course. Curiously, when the odds are even over the long run, people are reluctant to bet on a single instance. You may see for yourself by offering an acquaintance a bet of five dollars on a coin toss—most will not take you up on it. Even when the odds are in their favor, people hesitate.

Daniel Bernoulli and Risky Choice

In 1738 Daniel Bernoulli, one member of a Swiss family of geniuses, published an essay that inspired Daniel Kahneman and Amos Tversky;

it concerned the reasons why people are averse to risk, unless they are very wealthy. For example, suppose that you have the chance to win $1,000, but it is an eighty-five-percent chance, with a fifteen-percent chance to win nothing. That is one alternative. The second choice is a sure $800. Which would you choose? The gamble has the higher net utility:

$$(.85 \times \$1000) + (.15 \times \$0) = \$850.$$

So why not take a chance on the $1,000, rather than settle for the $800—the expected utility of the gamble, considering probabilities of winning and losing, is $50 more. People choose the sure thing over the comparable gamble, showing risk aversion. Bernoulli showed that "value," or "subjective utility," is a nonlinear function that is concave, so that the difference between the value of $100 and $200 is greater than that between $1,100 and $1,200. Hence, a gain of $800 is more than eighty percent of the value of a gain of $1,000. This causes an "irrational" preference for the sure thing, since the smaller gain is seen to have more value than eighty percent of the larger.

Risk Seeking
Kahneman and Tversky also proposed that the function for losses is concave, so that the difference in subjective value between a loss of $100 and of $200 is greater than the difference between losses of $1,100 and $1,200. Risk seeking is a consequence of the convexity of the loss portion. Consider another example, presented as a pair of alternatives:

A. An eighty-five-percent chance to lose $1,000 (so fifteen-percent chance of no loss).

B. A sure loss of $800.

In this case, the large majority of people queried choose the gamble over the sure loss. This reflects risk seeking, since the expected value of the gamble is −$850, worse than the −$800 of the sure thing. Seeking risks when faced with losses occurs in cases other than monetary ones, such as cases where the "currency" is hours of pain, loss of lives, and other domains.

Compelling but Irrational
Bernoulli's function describes powerful effects on subjective valuations of gains and losses, and they belie the conventional canon that we are "rational animals" as Aristotle put it. Rational decision makers were

first described by von Neumann and Morgenstern (1947). They proposed that rational decision makers are guided by axioms, including transitivity (if we prefer A to B and B to C, then we prefer A to C), substitutability (if A is preferred to B, then an even chance to get A or C is preferred to an even chance to get B or C), and other less straightforward rules.

Two other simple rules are dominance and invariance. Dominance means that if two choices are equally attractive in all respects but one, the choice more attractive in that respect must be chosen. Invariance means that choice among alternatives should not change when the alternatives are presented or described in different manners. Kahneman and Tversky showed that the failure of invariance to hold is striking and pervasive. That subject is called the framing of alternatives.

The Framing Effect: A Failure of Invariance

The same choices can be framed in different ways, so as to appear to be prospects of gains or of losses, and this can radically influence our preferences. In a simple case, an oil company may offer a "discount for cash," or add a "surcharge for using a credit card." We may realize that the cost is the same, but the so-called "discount" is more appealing. Kahneman and Tversky carried out an experiment that is more impressive, clearly showing how strong are our biases. The following problem was posed to 152 subjects—the percentage of subjects who chose each of two alternatives is given in parentheses.

Imagine that the United States is preparing for the outbreak of an unusual Asian disease, which is expected to kill 600 people. Two alternative programs to combat the disease have been proposed. Assume that the exact scientific estimates of the consequences of the programs are as follows:

• If Program A is adopted, 200 people will be saved. (72%)
• If Program B is adopted, there is a one third probability that 600 people will be saved and a two thirds probability that no people will be saved. (28%)

The problem thus cast assumes a reference point in which the disease will kill 600 people and the programs refer to gains, the saving of people. Since we are risk averse when it comes to gains, subjects choose the sure thing over the risky alternative—better to save 200 for sure than to risk that none will be saved. Note that the expected value is 200 in both cases. What if the problem is rephrased slightly, as follows?

· If Program C is adopted, 400 people will die. (22%)
· If Program D is adopted, there is a one third probability that nobody will die and a two thirds probability that 600 people will die. (78%)

You can see that options C and D are precisely those of options A and B, but the second case is phrased in terms of losses, against a reference state in which no one dies. Since we tend to be risk seeking in cases of perceived losses, the majority of respondents chose D, since it includes a possibility that no one will die. However, that is exactly what Program B proposed, except in that case the risk appeared to apply to gains, not losses.

Programs A and C are identical and B and D are identical, yet A is chosen in the first case and C is not chosen in the second. Subjects may be given the two pairs of choices a few minutes apart and still choose A in the first case and D in the second. When they read the problems again they were often puzzled when the inconsistency in their choices was pointed out. Though they realized their contradictory choices, they still wanted to avoid risk in the "lives saved" version and risk seeking in the "lives lost" version. Kahneman and Tversky compare the paradox to a perceptual illusion rather than a computational error.

These considerations apply to the actual preferences both of physicians and of patients when considering alternative therapies. The preferences for hypothetical therapies for lung cancer differed greatly when their outcomes were described in terms of death or of survival. Since surgery always carries the risk of death, while radiation therapy does not, surgery was dispreferred when outcomes were described in terms of mortality rather than survival.

When we learn that surgery results in death for twenty percent of patients, we are less accepting of it than we we are told that there is an eighty percent survival rate. The principle is the same as the "lives saved" versus the "lives lost" options of the Asian disease problem. We are risk seeking when it comes to losses, but we prefer no risk of loss. We will take the safe radiation therapy over the risky surgery (McNeil, Pauker, Sox, and Tversky 1982).

Behavioral or Cognitive?

All of this research and this method of interpretation is behavioral, though many behaviorists don't know it. And most cognitive and social psychologists don't know it! Let's hope that things change someday and that both behaviorists and cognitivists read Aristotle, Francis Bacon, and Hume. And may they read William James, who summarized and distilled what was known of psychology in the late nineteenth century. Can we move past that century? Can we progress past the current trends in cognitive psychology and "cognitive neuroscience"?

Cognitive Psychology: The Nineteenth Century Continues?

In 1997, Clark Glymour, a worker in cognitive neuroscience, offered the following observation:

One January a few years ago, shortly after the governor of Arizona had been impeached and the Exxon Valdez had spilled its cargo around Port Arthur, I had one of those uncanny experiences reserved for the people who read old news. Paging through the San Jose Mercury for January 1917, I came upon an article describing the impeachment of the governor of Arizona and a report of a large oil spill at Valdez, Alaska. Nietzsche, it seems, was on to something, the Eternal Return, the no news under the sun, the history repeats itself sort of thing. I have had similar uncanny experiences over the last few years reading bits of the literature of cognitive science as it has emerged in our time, and reading in the same years the literature of physiology, psychology, and psychiatry in the closing years of the nineteenth century. (p. 377)

Perhaps that answers a question posed at the beginning of this book: "Why study the history of psychology?"

Notes

Chapter 1

1. The six volumes were published between 1830 and 1842. They were condensed to one volume by Harriet Martineau (1802–1876), a condensation enthusiastically approved by Comte.

2. Transit time refers to the time taken by a planet passing directly in front of the sun to traverse the face of the sun.

3. But heavier objects may fall faster in an atmosphere, where air resistance complicates things.

4. Born Claudius Ptolemy, in the city of Ptolemais on the Nile, Ptolemy defended Aristotle's model, which included fifty-five concentric translucent spheres, with the earth dead still in the middle.

5. Norwood Russell Hanson was an interesting man, a philosopher and historian of science at Cambridge, Yale, and Indiana Universities, who died attempting to break the world speed record for piston-driven aircraft, flying a Grumman Hellcat. His (1958/1965) book, *Patterns of Discovery*, illustrates his views on the progress of science.

6. See the review of Laudan's work in B. Batts and L. L. Crawford (1991). Problematic progress: A review of Laudan's *Progress and Its Problems* and *Science and Values. Journal of the Experimental Analysis of Behavior*, 55, 337–349.

Chapter 2

1. As far as I have seen, actual historical figures so named, like the tyrants of Syracuse, spelled their names *Dionysius*.

2. According to Zeller (1964), Dionysus was in the form of an ox at the time. This story appears in many, many forms, so that it is difficult to determine which is the "true myth."

3. This illustration assumes equal steps in determining fourths and fifths, as would be the case in Pythagorean tuning, where notes are determined by a scale of fifths—increasing by steps of 3/2. In modern equal-temperament tuning scales, where the ratios of frequencies of adjacent scale notes are always 1.06, a "b" may not be a "b." However, the fourths and fifths (i.e., ratios of 4:3 and 3:2) hold to thousandths of a percent.

4. Indeed, the theorem was not even an original contribution, since it had been used in surveying land since at least 1950 B.C. in Egypt and prior to 1000 B.C. in China.

5. When the ancients referred to "movement," they meant more than change of position in space. They included any change, including movement. Thus, the melting of ice is a movement.

6. Diogenes Laertius is an often-cited and sometimes unreliable historian who lived in the third century A.D.

7. In the ancient world, rhapsodists made a living reciting epic poems.

8. When an ancient figure is said to "flourish" in a given period, it means that she or he was forty years old or so.

9. This is similar to Plato's problem of participation, which he saw as a problem for his own theory of forms. Plato's theory shared salient flaws with the Pythagorean theories.

10. Soul, mind, and spirit are difficult to distinguish, even in Christianity. As Paul wrote (1 Thessalonians, 4:23), "May your spirit and soul and body be preserved entire, without blame at the coming of Christ" and (Hebrews 4:12) "For the word of God is living and active, and sharper than any two-edged sword, piercing even to the dividing of soul and spirit..."

11. Aristotle commenting on Democritus in Nahm, p. 186. Aristotle went on to criticize Democritus for failing to explain why breathing ceases in the first place—death is not a "chance event."

12. Aristotle wondered, "Why does Democritus assume this imprint, when in his discussion of forms he has supposed an emanation that conveys the object's form?" Other ancient authors do not attribute the "molded air" theory to Democritus (many are excerpted in Nahm, 1962, pp. 161–219).

13. Brett (1965). Aristotle criticized this view as "a most absurd blunder, for they make all sensible qualities tangible" (in Nahm, 1962, p. 188).

14. It is sometimes claimed that Protagoras was referring to "generic man," as the measure of reality, so that it is convention that is real. That is absolutely not the case and would make no sense, given his overall view. Nahm (1962, p. 221) agrees that Protagoras meant *individual* opinion as the measure of truth, and that was the opinion of ancient commentators.

15. The number of dialogues is more like thirty if only authenticated ones are counted.

16. Zeller (1964, p. 117). Eduard Zeller is one of the most frequently consulted and most highly regarded authorities on ancient philosophy. I have relied on him frequently in writing this and the previous chapter.

17. Poison hemlock, or *coniium maculata*, is a member of the *Apiaceae* (parsley) family, as are carrots, celery, coriander, fennel, and anise. It was long used by the Greeks as a means of avoiding caring for prisoners. Its effective ingredients are alkaloids that produce muscular weakness, paralysis of extremities, blindness, respiratory paralysis, and death. Leaves are most toxic when the plant is flowering. The effective ingredient, coniium was the first alkaloid to be synthesized—in 1886.

Chapter 3

1. Cyrenaics formed a school founded by Aristippus of Cyrene, a sometime student of Socrates. However, in opinions and practice the Cyrenaics were Sophists.

2. After Rouse, W. H. D. (Trans.) (1956). *Great Dialogues of Plato*. New York: New American Library, p. 309.

3. Especially valuable in showing the similarities is Donald Klein's 1970 textbook, *A History of Scientific Psychology*, New York: Basic Books.

4. The *Phaedrus*, especially parts IX, X, and XV.

5. Jowett, p. 330. See Philip Merlan (1944), "An Idea of Freud's in Plato," *The Personalist*, 25, pp. 54–63. Reference here is to p. 55.

6. Music had a wider meaning than later; it referred to all of the activities overseen by the nine muses. These goddesses were Calliope (epic poetry), Clio (history), Erato (erotic poetry), Euterpe (lyric poetry), Melpomene (tragedy), Polyhymnia (sacred song), Terpsichore (dancing), Thalia (comedy), Urania (astronomy).

7. Merlan, P. (1945). Brentano and Freud. *Journal of the History of Ideas, IV*, 5–377. A second paper with the same title and "a sequel," appeared in 1949, X, 451. Franz Brentano (1838–1917) was an Aristotelian philosopher also very familiar with Plato.

8. By Nahm, Zeller, and many other authors, but particularly by Russell, 1945.

9. Though he did apply it to artificial things, and the unfortunate example of the causes of the statue comes from his *Physics*, or *Natural Science*, Book II, part iii.

10. Metaphysical = having to do with the ultimate natures of things, such as distinguishing mind and body. Epistemological = having to do with knowledge as when considering the subject and object relation.

11. Aristotle's father and his son were both named Nicomachus. An earlier book, the *Eudemian Ethics*, is not comparable, based as it is on Aristotle's earlier and Platonic thought.

Chapter 4

1. Seneca, from Zeller, 1883, p. 235. It translates as "Fate leads the willing and drags the unwilling" (Kaufmann 1963, p. 569).

2. In 248 the thousand-year anniversary of Rome was celebrated with games ordered by Emperor Philippus, an Arab who became emperor under disgraceful circumstances. The traditional founding of Rome was in 753 B.C.

3. Porphyry (232–301?) was an interesting character himself, who published commentaries on Aristotle, Plato, and Theophrastus and on Aristotle's Categories. He wrote biographies of Pythagoras and Plotinus. His works were translated into many languages (Zeller, 1883).

4. This perfect entity is so unified that it cannot think or act in any other way, since this requires an actor and an acted-upon. God is One and above such plurality.

5. A Persian religion claiming authority from Jesus that interpreted all reality as a combat between good (light, vegetables) and evil (dark, meat). This was a heresy, needless to say.

6. Originally, "doctor" meant teacher, not physician.

7. Alan Turing (1912–1954) was a British mathematician who laid the foundation for the computer revolution, begun when he devised machines to break German codes during World War II. A Turing machine is a protypical computer that can conceivably read any code except that which serves as its operating system. It "cannot read its own tape." Turing's biography was published in 1959 by his mother and published by Cambridge University Press.

8. The year that marked the closing of the academy, the Lyceum, and other pagan schools by Justinian, as well as the founding of the Benedictine Order.

9. These are opposed to servile arts, the arts, crafts, trade, and other business traditionally done by slaves.

10. By 1354 they had provided 24 popes, 200 cardinals, 7,000 archbishops, 15,000 bishops, 1,560 canonized saints, and 5,000 candidates for sainthood. Beginning in the sixth century, the archbishops of Canterbury were Benedictines. Their motto, D.O.M., stands for "Domino Optimo Maximo."

11. Despite the kind intentions of St. Francis (1181–1226), the Franciscans were in charge of the inquisition in some countries.

12. This is a very long-lived idea, quoted in 1890 by William James, as the theory of Herr Schneider, assumed in laboratory exercises by Titchener in 1910.

Chapter 5

1. The earth must be the center of the universe, at least to the scholastics' way of thinking. The creation required a total of six days, five of which were devoted to earth and only one for the rest of the universe.

2. Bronowski, Jacob (1991). Black magic and white magic. In T. Ferris (Ed.), *The World Treasury of Physics, Astronomy, and Mathematics*. Boston: Little, Brown, pp. 810–820. As Bronowski pointed out, this is "white magic," as opposed to the older "black magic," which was intended to make nature work against her will.

3. Hobbes's original spellings referred to "Traynes" of "Reliques" that are not "casuall."

4. For Hobbes, this is found only in man, as a "lust of the mind . . . that . . . exceedeth the short vehemence of any carnal pleasure" (1651/1939, p. 152).

5. Russell, 1945, p. 560. According to Vrooman (1970, pp. 136–138), the mother of the child was a young Dutchwoman, Helen, or Helene, who may well have lived with Descartes during 1637–1640, though evidence is lacking. The child, Francine, died of scarlet fever in September of 1640.

6. "He so fatigued himself that his brain became fired, and he fell into a sort of rapture which had such an effect on his already-downcast spirit, that it was in a state to receive impressions of dreams and visions." Baillet, Vie de monsieur des Cartes, quoted by Jacques Maritain (1946), *The Dream of Descartes* (Trans. Mabelle L. Andison). London: Editions Poetry London, p. 151.

7. Russell (1945) notes that Descartes actually said that he spent the day *in* the stove. Vrooman (1970, p. 53) seems to think that Descartes treated the whole room as "my stove."

8. A society supposedly founded by the Catholic Rosenkranz in Germany in 1484 but which is referred to no earlier than 1614. The society was popular in the seventeenth and eighteenth centuries and claimed knowledge of alchemy, prolongation of life, and the gaining of power over spirits.

9. His "World," or "Cosmos," was suppressed or destroyed upon news of Galileo's persecution in 1632.

10. This Leiden company published the best-known edition of the *Meditations* and six editions of the *Principles of Philosophy*. It is no doubt the ancestor of Elsevier North Holland Publishing Company, a major publisher of technical and scholarly works.

11. As noted by Lao tse, sixth century B.C. philosopher and founder of Taoism, who dreamt that he was a butterfly. Later he wondered if in fact he was now a butterfly that dreams that it is Lao tse.

12. Though A. J. Ayer and Gilbert Ryle, among others, doubted that such conclusion was warranted; W. Doney, 1967, *Descartes: A Collection of Critical Essays*.

13. This is noted in a collection called *Cogitationes Privatae* (see Haldane, 1905, p. 48).

14. From *L'Homme Machine*, Leiden, 1748, Trans. by G. C. Bussey and Mary W. Calkins, Chicago: Open Court, 1927. Excerpted in Herrnstein and Boring (1965, pp. 272–278).

15. Ibid. Ironically, Emperor Friedrich Wilhelm reported that LaMettrie died as the consequence of overindulgence in a "pasty" of pheasant and truffles, this at the age of 42! See Boakes's (1984) excellent account.

Chapter 6

1. Readers familiar with Charleston, South Carolina, know that the city is bounded by the Ashley and the Cooper rivers. This shows the influence of Ashley and Locke on the Lords Proprietors of the Carolina colony, for whom Locke served as secretary.

2. "Epistle to the reader," an introduction to the *Essay*.

3. In his book *The Origin of Formes and Qualities*, published at Oxford in 1666.

4. No likeness of Damaris Cudworth appears to exist. There is a reference to a portrait of her in one of Locke's folios of papers, but when one examines the folio, there is no portrait.

5. In the view of Mary W. Calkins, in a 1929 biography in her edited collection of Berkeley's works.

6. Calkins, 1929, p. x. She also coined the term "radical behaviorism."

7. The same number of books was donated to Harvard University but later lost to fire.

8. In Kaufmann 1961, p. 317. Hume's last words, in a note written for him by his nephew and addressed to Smith, were "Adieu, etc."

9. Actually, Scotland's. In his autobiography he mentioned going to "another country" when he moved temporarily to London.

10. *Treatise*, Book III, part I, section II, reprinted in A. MacIntyre (Ed.), *Hume's Ethical Writings*. New York: Collier, 1965, pp. 196–197.

11. 1724–1804. In fact, all biographers agree that Kant believed himself to be Scottish. A discussion of this issue appears in Malone, J. C. (1995). Kant's Abstammung: Schottland? *Behavioural Processes, 34,* 1–2).

Chapter 7

1. The same principle was promoted in the twentieth century by the personality theorist Gordon Allport as the principle of the "functional autonomy of motives."

2. Concerning the fundamental principle of virtue or morality. In William King, An essay on the origin of evil. London, 1731, pp. xi–xxxiii, reproduced in Diamond, 1974, pp. 588–591.

3. Compare this with Clark Hull's postulate I in Hull, C. L. (1943) *Principles of Behavior*. New York: Appleton-Century-Crofts, and in chapter 14.

4. John Stuart Mill's *Autobiography*, reproduced in Max Lerner, *Essential Works of John Stuart Mill*, New York: Bantam, 1961, p. 12. Neither Mill could accept the concept of a God so evil that he preordained that most souls would spend eternity in hell. They believed that the original Hebrew god had been made more and more ferocious over the centuries and could warrant neither love nor belief.

5. I read the 1876 edition. According to Boring (1950, p. 245), the 1881 edition of *Mental Physiology* contains the first reference to the phrase "unconscious cerebration."

6. 1876, p. 351. William James used almost the same words in repeating Carpenter's argument in 1890.

Chapter 8

1. 7–1875, author of *Principles of Geology*, 1830–33. He was opposed by Georges Cuvier, founder of paleontology, reconstructor of fossil skeletons, and proponent of catastrophism (*Webster's Encyclopedia*, p. 241).

2. A brig, ninety feet long by twenty-four feet wide and rounded, so that it rolled and so provided Darwin with many episodes of seasickness during the five-year voyage.

3. Darwin's own words (in Ferris, 1988, p. 243).

4. From *Zoonomia*, reprinted in Charles Singer, *A History of Biology*. London: Abelard-Schuman, 1959, 3rd ed., p. 296.

5. 1744–1829, known better as the Chevalier de Lamarck.

6. According to Singer (p. 297), Lamarck was unlucky in mode of address, was arid in literary style, was personally eccentric, was married four times, supported a large family on a small salary, was overspeculative to the point of being a laughing stock, and was held in light esteem or in contempt by others.

7. On the positive side, he separated spiders from insects and emphasized the study of living things in general, inventing the term "biology." Lamarck coined that term in 1802, and its first use in the modern sense was by Sir William Lawrence in his *Lectures on Physiology* in 1818 (Singer 1959, p. 298).

8. In his autobiography he referred to a forced retired life, since social interaction always led to "violent shivering and vomiting attacks being thus brought on." G. de Beer (Ed.). (1983). *Autobiographies: Charles Darwin, Thomas Henry Huxley*. Oxford: Oxford University Press, p. 68.

9. Carbon-14 decays to nitrogen-14 with a half life of 5,570 years. This is a useful means for dating organic materials.

10. 1825–1895, grandfather of Julian Huxley, biologist and ecologist, Aldous Huxley, author of *Brave New World*, and Andrew Huxley, who shared the Nobel Prize in Physiology or Medicine in 1963 for his work on the chemical basis of neural transmission.

11. Ferris, 1988, p. 245. Details differ in accounts of this debate, and Ferris chose this version as the one preferred by Huxley himself as the most nearly accurate. It is taken from a book by his son, Julian.

12. 1848–1894. Romanes coined the term "comparative psychology."

13. That is to say, the genome is not affected by events during an individual lifetime—practicing the piano has no effect on genes, and so "musicality" is not heritable.

14. These and other experiments are described in *An Introduction to Comparative Psychology*, published in 1894.

15. The parallel with classical and instrumental learning, as stimulus–stimulus (S-S) and stimulus–response (S-R) association, is obvious. Morgan referred to findings such as the learned aversion to the sight of the cinnabar caterpillar and escape learning, by ducklings and by Tony, as instances of the two kinds of association.

16. Darwin's lack of influence in taxonomy during the nineteenth century is amazing. His lifelong friend, J. D. Hooker, died in 1911 at the age of ninety-four. He was an eminent botanical taxonomist who saw the drafts of the *Origin of Species* long before 1859 and who was an ardent Darwinist. His work spanned seventy-one years and was conducted as if Darwin had never lived (Singer 1959, pp. 558–559).

17. Plato also recommended such a practice and for the same reasons—in the *Republic*; see chapter 3.

18. This account in the last two paragraphs is taken from Boring (1957, pp. 478–479).

Chapter 9

1. Baron Wilhelm von Humboldt, philologist and statesman known for his analyses of languages as reflections of the cultures of their users.

2. *Nanna, oder der Seeleleben der Pflanzen*. Odd though this may seem, Alfred Binet, the founder of practical mental testing, published a piece on the mental life of microorganisms in 1881.

3. Only the first volume of the *Elemente* has been translated into English. Only two other books have been translated—a collection published under the title *Religion of a Scientist* in 1946 and *Life after Death* (*Büchlein vom Leben nach dem Tode*) in many editions—the newest in 1946. Scheerer noted that this is only five percent of the 25,223 pages he published in 176 items.

4. Despite the name, he was German, born and raised in Berlin. He was a pioneer in the study of the electrical, and then the chemical, bases for neural conduction.

5. Brücke was a teacher of Freud decades later and directed the Institute of Cerebral Physiology in Vienna.

6. Ernst Werner von Siemens (1816–1892) was a member of a family of technologists. He patented an electroplating process in 1842, a differential governor in 1844, and a steam engine. He was also a major participant, with his brother, Sir William, in the laying of the Atlantic cable in 1874, from the ship *Faraday*, by a company that he owned.

7. Reprinted in the Warrens (1968, p. 259).

8. Woodworth (1909, p. 255), cited by Roediger (1985, p. 523).

9. However, that seems unlikely, given H. L. Roediger's recent article—*Contemporary Psychology*, 1985, *30*, 519–523, Remembering Ebbinghaus. Ebbinghaus's copy of Fechner was an English edition.

10. "I got it only from you," quote from Boring (1950).

11. It was not translated into English until 1913 as *Memory: A Contribution to Experimental Psychology*, Teacher's College Press. A 1964 Dover edition also was published.

12. Hall had founded the *American Journal of Psychology* in 1887.

13. Do, re, mi, fa, sol, la, te...or, as he put it in Prop. VI, Prob. II of his *Optics*, 1730, 4th ed., "Sol, la, fa, sol, la, mi, fa, sol." Reproduced in W. S. Sahakian (Ed.). (1968). *History of Psychology: A Sourcebook in Systematic Psychology*. Itaska, IL: Peacock.

14. This is indeed the case. One major failing of the theory, as pointed out by Richard Gregory in *Eye and Brain*, is that no combination of three wavelengths can produce brown or metallic colors, such as silver and gold.

15. Details and supporting arguments may be found in Gregory, cited above, and in Turner, R. Steven (1994). *In the Eye's Mind: Vision and the Helmholtz–Hering Controversy*. Princeton, NJ: Princeton University Press.

16. In Helmholtz' *Wissenschaftliche Abhandlungen*, 3 volumes. Leipzig: J.A. Barth, 1895. Described in Turner (1995, pp. 95–99).

17. He actually called them two forms of *induction*, depending on the underlying cause—"*simultane Lichtinduction*" and "*successive Lichtinduction*."

18. For example, Marks, W. B., Dobelle, W. H., and MacNichol, E. F., Jr. (1964). Visual pigments of single primate cones. *Science, 143*, 1181–1182. Earlier work measured the light reflected from the retinas of living humans and showed a red and a green receptor—the reflection from the blue receptor was never strong enough. This was done by Rushton and colleagues in the 1950s. See Rushton, W. A. H. (1962). Visual pigments in man. In R. Held and W. Richards (Eds.), *Perception: Mechanisms and Models*. New York: Freeman.

19. Gregory (1978, chapter 8), Wandell (1994, chapter 9), Wasserman (1978, chapter 9. According to both Wasserman and Wandell, Land's findings were not really incredible to the real savants of vision research. But to most readers, there was an aura of magic about them.

20. See Wasserman's account or that provided by Land himself. Land, E. H. (1959). Experiments in color vision. *Scientific American, 200*, 84–89. Also Land, E. H. (1959). Color vision and the natural image. *Proceedings of the National Academy of Sciences, 45*, 116–129, and Land, E. H. (1986), Recent advances in retinex theory. *Vision Research, 26*, 7–22.

Chapter 10

1. There is no better source on the subject of brain function and localization than Oliver Sacks's *Awakenings* and his commentary on the making of the movie.

2. Ross Buck (1988), *Human Motivation and Emotion*, Wiley, p. 126. The hippocampus has been implicated in memory, emotion, memory consolidation, retrieval, attention, arousal, movement, inhibition, orienting, spatial mapping, and anxiety. And it probably is involved in even more than that.

3. A primary source for this section was Brazier, Mary A. B. (1959). The historical development of neurophysiology. In J. Field, H. W. Magoun, and V. E. Hall (Eds.), *Handbook of Physiology: Section 1: Neurophysiology* (volume 1). Washington, DC: American Physiological Society, pp. 1–58.

Chapter 11

1. This and other terms used by Herbart, such as fusions, assimilation, accommodation, apperception, and so on, were not his inventions. They had longer and shorter histories in German philosophy, particularly in the writings of Kant and of Leibniz. Herbart was original in gathering them together.

2. For a modern version of this approach, see Wegner & Pennebaker (1993), or visit Wegner's Harvard Web site.

3. The vagus is the tenth cranial nerve—it has both motor and sensory branches and serves the viscera.

4. *Lehre von den Muskelbewegungen.*

5. America's refusal to sell helium to the Germans contributed to the disastrous burning of the Hindenberg (LZ-129) at Lakehurst, New Jersey, in 1937. This diminished interest in airships.

6. When light dims, as at twilight, we become more sensitive to the higher frequency, short wavelength colors, such as the blues, and less sensitive to the long wavelength end of the spectrum, the reds. Hence, a red rose appears purplish at twilight. The effect is named after the Czech physiologist and pioneer of histology, Johannes Purkinje.

7. It is frequently translated as "social psychology," but that is misleading. A better translation is "racial psychology," since "*Völk*" means "a people," as in "German people" or "Western European people." "Cultural" seems a more apt adjective than does social.

8. Wundt's (1916) *Elements of Folk Psychology* is not to be confused with these volumes. It is oriented toward a popular audience, proposed stages of evolutions of culture, and is totally unlike the volumes of the *Völkerpsychologie*.

9. Wundt's *Grundriss*—Judd mistranslated just as had Titchener, but the passage here referred to seems honest enough.

10. The two major laws accompanying the law of creative synthesis, or resultants, were the laws of psychic contrast, referring to opposing pairs of emotions, and psychic relations, referring to the Fechner principle showing that sensory feelings depend on context.

11. B. F. Skinner devised a "verbal summator," as he called it, in the 1930s. It consisted of a recording of phonemes randomly arranged and listened to by subjects who took it to be

a "conversation in the next room." All that they heard was "ah...ooh...mmm...ehh..." and so on, and assimilation did the rest. Hermann Rorschach (1884–1922) used the same principle in his inkblot test, and David McClelland used Henry Murray's version of projective testing to assess need for achievement in the 1960s.

12. We later learned that binocular vision was not essential for the perception of depth. J. J. Gibson discovered that the best pilot in America had lost one eye in an industrial accident as an adolescent. Wiley Post piloted the airplane that crashed, killing Will Rogers.

13. Wundt, 1901, p. 427, emphasis added.

14. In the 1920s, when it was established that the electron (and proton) is essentially a wave phenomenon, Mach's skepticism seemed warranted. The particle/wave aspects of matter are particularly well described by Victor Weisskopf, 1989, *The Privilege of Being a Physicist*. New York: Freeman.

15. *"Das Radio einstellen"* means to tune the radio to a broadcasting station. *"Einstellung"* is the noun form of the verb.

16. *Regelbewusstseinslagen*—"rule-following conscious attitude"—though not verbalizable, since not carried in images.

17. 1928 letter to E. G. Boring, E. G. Boring papers, Department of Psychology and Social Relations, Harvard University. Cited in Blumenthal, 1985, p. 53, my chief source on Müller.

18. Blumenthal (1985, p. 55) points out that Jaensch was also inspired by the Nazi movement.

19. Katz distinguished surface colors as the hues that we see as lying on the surfaces of objects—what is ordinarily called "color." Volumic colors extend through three dimensions, as does colored fluid in a bottle or tank. Film color seems suspended in space, as when one views a deep blue sky through a tube or stares at a deeply saturated colored wall.

Chapter 12

1. The plausibility of that evidence is questionable, of course. This is especially true since the report was published only in German and referenced by Hilgard (1987). Titchener, E. B. (1899) Zur Kritik der Wundt'schen Gefuhlelehre. *Zeitschrift für Psychologie, 19,* 321–326.

2. Titchener's views on attention as an attribute were presented in lectures given at Columbia University in February of 1908—"Lectures on the Elementary Psychology of Feelings and Attention" (Boring, 1927, p. 499).

3. The context theory was first presented in lectures at the University of Illinois in 1909—"Lectures on the Experimental Psychology of the Thought Processes" (Boring, 1927, p. 499).

4. One might better say "memory" versus "fantasy," since the latter is what Perky meant by "imagination."

5. Attributes of sensation. *Psychological Review, 6,* 506–514. Mary Calkins also invented the method of paired-associates learning and coined the expression "radical behaviorism," the name later applied to B. F. Skinner's philosophy of behavior.

6. For example, he was the first to distinguish between manic–depressive psychosis and schizophrenia (*dementia praecox* as it was called then). His textbook of psychiatry was the standard for many years, just before and after the turn of the twentieth century.

7. Breuer demonstrated the effect of the tenth cranial nerve, the vagus, on respiration, along with Ewald Hering, and showed how the semicircular canals subserve balance.

8. A conclusion also reached in the late twentieth century by Freudian psychologist Michael Nash (1994). He plausibly argued that the therapeutic (or pathogenic) effect of traumatic "memories" may well be the same, whether they are accurate recollections or fantasies, perhaps produced by a therapist's questions.

Chapter 13

1. In 1891 James wrote an opinion for the *Harvard Monthly* concerning a proposal to shorten the period required for an A.B. from four to three years. James proposed that a longer diet of hay will not change a carnivore into a herbivore. In Perry (1948, p. 243).

2. Originally written in French for *Revue Philosophique* in 1877 and published in that journal with a translation in volumes 6 and 7, December 1878 and January 1879. Reprinted in W. Barrett and Henry D. Aiken (Eds.) (1962). *Philosophy in the Twentieth Century*, volume 1. New York: Random House, pp. 105–122.

3. The decrease in skin resistance to electric current when we perspire was first capitalized on by Féré in 1888, following work by Vigouroux in 1879.

4. Edward Titchener surely understood the James/Lange theory, which he criticized in his 1910 *Textbook*. And Edward Thorndike presented it accurately in his 1913 classic text. Few others did.

5. This neglects the utilitarians, like Bentham and Mill, but utilitarianism was a political philosophy, not psychology. Hutcheson's "greatest happiness for the greatest number" was irrelevant to psychological hedonism.

6. At least since Hobbes and some would say since Aristotle. Aristotle was not a hedonist for reasons given in chapter 3.

7. Locus of control people would refer to the same distinction between "sources" and "pawns," or inner versus outer control.

Chapter 14

1. David Premack made by far the most insightful contribution to understanding the law of effect, beginning in 1959—Toward empirical behavior laws: I. Positive reinforcement. *Psychological Review*, 66, 219–233. By the 1970s he had turned to the study of communication among subhuman primates.

2. As subsequent research showed, this original opinion was correct—see Catania (1992). *Learning*. Prentice-Hall.

3. For example, Mary Cover Jones (1924). The elimination of children's fears. *Journal of Experimental Psychology*, p. 382. John B. Watson's Powell Lecture in Psychological Theory at Clark University, January 17, 1925, Recent experiments on how we lose and change

our emotional equipment. In C. Murchison (Ed.). (1926). *Psychologies of 1924*. Worchester, MA: Clark University Press, pp. 59–81, and *Behaviorism*, 1930.

4. List received from Cynthia G. Swank, Archivist at J. Walter Thompson, November 20, 1984. The company archives concerning Watson have since been transferred to Duke University, Durham, North Carolina.

5. In an interview described by John C. Burnham, 1994, "John B. Watson: Interviewee, Professional Figure, Symbol." In Todd and Morris (pp. 65–73).

6. See also the doctoral dissertation of K. W. Buckley, presented as a paper at Old Dominion University in 1980 and published in 1982 as The selling of a psychologist: John Broadus Watson and the application of behavioral techniques to advertising. *Journal of the History of the Behavioral Sciences, 18*, 207–221. Buckley was also author of Watson's biography, *Mechanical Man*, already referred to.

Chapter 15

1. The German word for "construction" is "*Gebilde*," one of the names frequently used by Wundt (see chapter 11) and translated by Titchener and by Judd as "compound." Wertheimer never knew how Wundtian he was as he mistakenly attacked Wundtian psychology.

2. The unsatisfying common answer to that question is to point to examples—witness the textbooks crammed with Gestalt illustrations. Wertheimer's explanation comes from his 1922 paper (pp. 53–57, reproduced in Ellis, pp. 14–16).

3. Bower and Hilgard (1981) and Leahey (1992), authors of influential texts, confessed their bafflement concerning what the Gestaltists were trying to say.

4. A device for producing brief presentations of visual stimuli for precisely controlled durations. A few decades earlier Helmholtz was forced to use the spark generated by a Leyden jar to produce brief visual stimuli.

5. These are most of the varieties listed by Boring 1942, *Sensation and perception in the history of experimental psychology*, pp. 596–597.

6. See p. 59. His original writing on this subject was published in 1920 and in a second edition in 1924 as *Die physischen Gestalten in Ruhe und im stationären Zustand: Eine naturphilosophische Untersuchung*. Erlangen: Verlag der Philosophische Academie.

7. Ibid, pp. 58–59. Köhler was referring to Mach's 1897 *Die Mechanik in ihrer Entwicklung*, 3rd ed., pp. 389–390.

8. Those influenced by Lewin include Tamara Dembo, Roger Barker, John Thibaut, Harold Kelley, Kurt Back, Morton Deutsch, Edward Jones, Philip Zimbardo, Jerome Singer, Stanley Schachter, Leon Festinger, John Darley, Eliot Aronson, and others forming a "who's who" in social psychology. Perlman, D. (1984). Recent developments in personality and social psychology: A citation analysis. *Personality and Social Psychology Bulletin, 10*, 493–501.

9. "Leh-VEEN" is proper German pronunciation, but he changed it to "LEW-in" when his children were embarrassed by the German version.

10. This was his adoptive family, not his birth family, as some writers, such as Hothersall, suggest.

11. Marrow, p. 5. This no doubt translates to a better German form—or one might expect. My *Langenscheidt* specifies *wütend* and *Hering*, yielding the translation, "*Wütend-hering*," which seems no better than English.

12. Lewin, K. (1931). The conflict between Aristotelian and Galileian modes of thought in contemporary psychology. *Journal of Genetic Psychology, 5,* 141–177. Lewin only published a lifetime total of 101 items, including abstracts and pieces in church bulletins and clearly minor periodicals. Thus, he probably would not be considered top-rate at many modern universities, where status is defined as length of publication list.

13. A commentary on that article was written by Heider, F. (1959). On Lewin's methods and theory. *Journal of Social Issues*, No. 13.

14. A fixed-ratio schedule, in which pay directly depends upon number of units produced. Both humans and animals work very hard on such a schedule, but it has aversive aspects.

15. The students at Iowa would later call the diagrams "Lewin's potatoes," probably reflecting the greater familiarity with potatoes in Iowa.

16. C. Murchison (Ed.). (1931). *Handbook of Child Psychology*. Worcester, MA: Clark University Press. Don Adams later taught a course in animal behavior, and, thirty-nine years after the Lewin translation, I was the last psychology graduate student to take that course under him at Duke University. The other students were all in zoology.

17. Lewin's argument for the study of individual subjects jibes with the views of Freud, of course, and the views of very different people, such as Pavlov and Skinner. Astonishingly, however, researchers in child psychology continue to collect data averaged over groups.

18. "Valence" was the term coined by Donald Adams to refer to the attractive or repulsive power of objects. "Incentive" is a more commonly used term for such properties.

19. In the 1950s, long after Lewin's death, Leon Festinger would point to this as a source of cognitive dissonance and Jack Brehm would show that that dissonance is reduced by subsequently overvaluing the chosen alternative.

20. 1931/1976, originally in the journal *Psychologische Studien*, as an article of some 200 pages—in German. Her work is briefly described in Koffka'a (1935) *Principles of Gestalt Psychology*. New York: Harcourt-Brace (407–410).

21. Lewin always distinguished between regression and retrogression. The latter refers to reversion to an earlier state, but it need not be a more primitive state, as is the case with regression. For example, a retrogression from a state of age-induced senility would constitute a retrogression to a better state.

22. Marrow (p. 149). When Lewin heard of this finding—that participation in the discovery of facts about their beliefs greatly affects the attitudes of group members—he insisted that French write it up and publish it. In fact, he locked French in Marrow's New York office until the paper was dictated. It appeared as French, J. R. P., Jr., and Marrow, A. J. (1945). Changing a stereotype in industry. *Journal of Social Issues, 1,* 33–37.

23. Lewin, K. (1945). The research center for group dynamics at Massachusetts Institue of Technology. *Sociometry, 2,* 126–136.

24. It is now universally recognized that what people say are their opinions frequently do not jibe with their actions—attitudes and actions need not correlate. See chapter 16.

25. According to Marrow (1969, p. 213), it was eighteen percent of their time—ninety minutes every evening.

Chapter 16

1. To prepare the reader for what is often a surprise, we note that Skinner was never an S-R behaviorist and that he strongly disagreed with many of the assumptions of what is generally called "behaviorism."

2. *Conditioned Reflexes*. New York: Oxford University Press.

3. Platonov, K. (1959). *The Word as a Physiological and Therapeutic Factor*. Moscow: Foreign Languages Publishing House. This book presents Russian psychiatry, as practiced from the 1920s through the 1950s, complete with case histories. Interestingly, therapy was said to be firmly based on Pavlovian principles and may well have been, though treatment was largely suggestion and hypnosis, not classical conditioning as ordinarily construed.

4. A signal for food has wide-ranging effects on a hungry animal, whether it be dog or human. There is reflex orienting to the signal, salivation, increased peristalsis through-out the digestive tract, secretion of digestive enzymes by the stomach and small intestine, and so on. Together they are called the "cephalic relexes of digestion," since they are con-trolled by the brain.

5. The following section is taken from the article by Todes, D. P. (1997). From the ma-chine to the ghost within: Pavlov's transition from digestive physiology to conditional reflexes. *American Psychologist, 52,* 947–955.

6. Recall that this simple measure has gone by many names: the galvanic skin response, psychogalvanic reflex, electrodermal response, skin conductance level, and perhaps others that I have overlooked.

7. Without mediation, that is. We can work our tongues around in our mouth and mechanically stimulate salivation, or we can imagine a salivation-producing odor, like ammonia, or a taste, like steak. These cases represent somatic and cognitive mediation, respectively, though the "cognitive" method actually involves presenting ourselves with an effective CS.

8. Pavlov described the model in 1927. The Gestaltists were not aware of Pavlov's model at the time they were first speculating on isomorphism. Besides both being interested in electrical fields in the brain, both Pavlov's group and the Gestaltists believed their work to be a revolutionary achievement for psychology.

9. Bykov, K. M. (1957). *The Cerebral Cortex and the Internal Organs*. New York: Chemical Publishing. Bykov was the leader of the research on interoceptive conditioning and of the purges of anti-Pavlov academics during the 1950s. He pointed out that the mere discovery of the conditioned reflex had been made by Germans in the nineteenth century and even by earlier writers. By implication, the discovery in itself is of limited conse-quence without the view toward physiology that Pavlov added to it. You might say it is like a monkey discovering an automobile.

10. See the review by Razran (1961) and the summary by Bykov (1957), as well as the excellent account by Turkkan (1989). A more complete account than that given here appears in Malone (1990).

11. The newsman Charles Kuralt died of lupus on July 4, 1997.

12. In fact, cyclophosphamide was then used only to produce nausea—now it is commonly used to suppress the immune system in organ transplant cases. Ader and Cohen actually were trying to extinguish a learned aversion to the taste of saccharine that had been paired with cyclophosphamide injections. The suppression of the immune system was occurring to the saccharine taste alone.

13. There is a recent review of this sort of literature: Siegel, S. (1991). Feedforward processes in drug tolerance. In R. G. Lister and H. J. Weingartner (Eds.), *Perspectives in Cognitive Neuroscience* (pp. 405–416). New York: Oxford University Press.
   Siegel, S., Hinson, R. E., Krank, M. D., and McCully, J. (1982, April 23). Heroin "overdose" death: Contributions of drug-associated environmental cues. *Science, 216,* 436–437.

14. Roger Smith (1992). *Inhibition.* Berkeley: University of California Press.

15. W. K. Estes based his statistical theory of learning on Guthrie's theory, but Estes endorsed many "pop" cognitive features that Guthrie would have found repugnant.

16. It may seem curious to some readers to learn that Guthrie's interpretation of reinforcement and punishment was endorsed by Skinner, though not publicly. See Verplanck, W. S. (1994). Fifty-seven years of searching among behaviorisms: A memoir. Paper presented at the Third International Congress on Behaviorism and Behavioral Science, Palermo, Italy, October 4, 1994.

17. Both humans and rats prefer to receive signaled rather than unsignaled aversive events. Oddly, however, several lines of evidence suggest that signaled electric shock is judged more painful than unexpected shock. See Turkkan (1989).

18. The concept of functional autonomy has been attributed by Allport to Edward Tolman and by Tolman to William McDougall. We find it in the writings of John Gay and could probably trace it back further.

19. Preface to reprinting of Hull's 1943 book.

Chapter 17

1. As an additional example, a master's program in management (and later also in tourism) was established 20 years ago by Professor Giulio Bolacchi in Nuoro, Sardinia, Italy. A distinguished world-class Faculty composed of Professors of economics, sociology, and psychology from many American and other foreign universities participate with their specific contributions to the Ailun international graduate programs (see www.scienzesociali.ailun.it), which are grounded on a new paradigm for the integration of the social sciences founded on a strictly behavioristic perspective (G. Bolacchi, 2008, A new paradigm for the integration of the social sciences, in N. K. Innis, *Reflections on Adaptive Behavior*, MIT Press, pp. 315–354).

2. These are variable-ratio and fixed-ratio schedules, respectively.

3. Hilgard (1987) reached the same conclusion: Watson's behaviorism broadened psychology; it did not constrain it.

4. Leahey (1992, p. 313), quoting Legrand, M. (1990). Du behaviorisme au cognitivisme. *L'Annee Psychologique, 90,* 247–286. I present only the English translation.

5. Actually, quoted by Judge Richard Posner: Posner, R. A. (1990). *The Problems of Jurisprudence.* Harvard University Press, p. 176.

6. "Almost," since the label "behaviorist" means as little as does "cognitivist." There is a different version of cognitive psychology for every dozen or so cognitive psychologists, and I can think of at least fifteen distinctly different versions of behaviorism. Clark Hull is classified as a behaviorist, but the basics of his theory are identical with the symbolic information processing "cognitivists."

7. Though these were called nonsense syllables, some words appeared, as he noted.

8. And to granting agencies, who funded most of the participants at the 25th Carnegie Mellon Symposium on Cognition. The proceedings were published as J. D. Cohen and J. W. Schooler (Eds.) (1997), *Scientific Approaches to Consciousness*. Mahwah, NJ: Erlbaum.

9. In 1996 the chess master Boris Spassky soundly defeated an IBM-sponsored chess program, "Deep Blue," in a series of matches. Kasparov was defeated in 1997 in a grossly unfair contest, by a program specifically designed to beat him and no one else.

10. Described by Nisbett and Wilson, this is standard deceptive heart rate research from S. Valins and A. A. Ray (1967). Effects of cognitive desensitization on avoidance behavior. *Journal of Personality and Social Psychology, 1,* 345–350.

References

Aaron, R. I. (1931). Locke and Berkeley's Commonplace Book. *Mind*, New Series, *40*(160), 439–459.

Ader, R. & Cohen, H. (1982). Behaviorally conditioned immunosuppression and murine systemic lupus erythematosis. *Science, 215*, 1534–1536.

Allport, G. W. (1937). *Personality: A psychological interpretation*. New York: Holt.

Amsel, A. (1962). Frustrative nonreward in partial reinforcement and discrimination learning. *Psychological Review, 69*, 306–328.

Amsel, A., & Rashotte, M. (Eds.). (1984). *Mechanisms of adaptive behavior: Clark L. Hull's theoretical papers*. New York: Columbia University Press.

Anand, B. K., & Brobeck, J. R. (1951). Hypothalamic control of food intake in rats and cats. *Yale Journal of Biology and Medicine, 24*, 123–140.

Anderson, J. R. (2000). *Cognitive psychology and its implications* (5th ed.). New York: Worth Publishing.

Angell, J. R. (1907). The province of functional psychology. *Psychological Review, 14*, 61–91.

Angell, J. R., & Moore, A. W. (1896). Reaction time: A study in attention and habit. *Psychological Review, 3*, 245–258.

Aquinas, T. (1949). *On spiritual creatures* (Trans. M. Fitzpatrick & John Wellmuth). Milwaukee: Marquette University Press.

Aristotle (1961). *De Anima/On the soul* (Trans. W. D. Ross). Oxford, UK: Clarendon Press.

Asch, S. E. (1968). Wolfgang Köhler. *American Journal of Psychology, 81*, 110–119.

Ash, M. (1985). Gestalt psychology: Origins in Germany and reception in the United States. In Buxton, C. E. (Ed.), *Points of view in the modern history of psychology* (pp. 295–344). New York: Academic Press.

Ayer, A. J. (1934). Demonstration of the impossibility of metaphysics. *Mind*, New Series, *43*, 335–345.

Bacon, F. (1900). *The new Atlantis*. Cambridge, UK: Cambridge University Press.

Bacon, F. (1963). *The complete essays of Francis Bacon*. New York: Washington Square Press.

Bain, A. (1879). *The senses and the intellect* (3rd ed.). New York: Appleton.

Barker, R. G., Dembo, T., & Lewin, K. (1941). Frustration and regression. *University of Iowa Studies in Child Welfare, 18*(1).

Barnes, J. M., & Underwood, B. J. (1959). Fate of first list associations in transfer theory. *Journal of Experimental Psychology, 58,* 97–105.

Barrett, W., & Aiken, H. (Eds.). (1962). *Philosophy in the twentieth century* (Vol. 1). New York: Random House.

Batts, B., & Crawford, L. L. (1991). Problematic progress: A review of Laudan's *Progress and its problems* and *Science and values. Journal of the Experimental Analysis of Behavior, 55,* 337–349.

Baum, W. M. (1994). *Understanding behaviorism: Science, behavior, and culture.* New York: HarperCollins.

Bekesy, G. (1967). *Sensory inhibition.* Princeton, NJ: Princeton University Press.

Bem, D. J. (1967). Self-perception: An alternative interpretation of cognitive dissonance phenomena. *Psychological Review, 74,* 183–198.

Berlinski, D. (1995). *A tour of the calculus.* New York: Pantheon.

Binet, A., & Simon, K. (1916). *The development of intelligence in children* (Trans. E. S. Kite). Baltimore: Williams and Wilkins.

Blumenthal, A. L. (1970). *Language and psychology.* New York: Wiley.

Blumenthal, A. L. (1975). A reappraisal of Wilhelm Wundt. *The American Psychologist, 30,* 1081–1088.

Blumenthal, A. L. (1985). Wilhelm Wundt: Psychology as the propaedeutic science. In C. E. Buxton (Ed.), *Points of view in the modern history of psychology* (pp. 19–50). New York: Academic Press.

Boakes, R. A. (1984). *From Darwin to Behaviourism: Psychology and the minds of animals.* New York: Cambridge University Press.

Boring, E. G. (1927). Edward B. Titchener. *American Journal of Psychology, 38,* 489–506.

Boring, E. G. (1942). *Sensation and perception in the history of experimental psychology.* New York: Appleton-Century.

Boring, E. G. (1950). *A history of experimental psychology* (2nd ed.). New York: Appleton-Century-Crofts. (1st ed. 1929)

Bower, T. G. R. (1982). *Development in infancy* (2nd ed.). San Francisco: Freeman.

Bower, G. H., & Hilgard, E. R. (1981). *Theories of learning.* Englewod Cliffs, NJ: Prentice-Hall.

Brain, R. T. (1980). *Oxford dictionary of quotations* (3rd ed.). Oxford, UK: Oxford University Press.

Brazier, M. A. B. (1959). The historical development of neurophysiology. In J. Field, H. W. Magoun, & V. E. Hall (Eds.), *Handbook of physiology: Section 1: Neurophysiology* (Vol. 1, pp. 1–58). Washington, DC: American Physiological Society.

Brent, J. (1993). *Charles Sanders Peirce: A life*. Bloomington: Indiana University Press.

Brett, G. S., & Peters, R. S. (1965). *Brett's history of psychology* (2nd rev. ed.). Cambridge, MA: MIT Press.

Bridgeman, B. (1986). Relations between the physiology of attention and the physiology of consciousness. *Psychological Research, 48*, 259–266.

Bringmann, W. G., & Tweney, R. D. (1980). *Wundt studies: A centennial collection*. Toronto: Hogrefe.

Bronowski, J. (1991). Black magic and white magic. In T. Ferris (Ed.), *The world treasury of physics, astronomy, and mathematics* (pp. 810–820). Boston: Little, Brown.

Brown, J. F. (1929). The methods of Kurt Lewin in the psychology of action and affection. *Psychological Review, 36*, 200–221.

Brown, R. (1965). *Social psychology*. New York: Free Press.

Brown, T. (1820). *Lectures on the philosophy of the human mind*. Edinburgh: James Ballantyne & Co. for W. & C. Tait.

Buck, R. (1988). *Human motivation and emotion*. New York: Wiley.

Buckley, K. W. (1989). *Mechanical man and the beginnings of behaviorism*. New York: Guilford.

Buckley, K. W. (1982). The selling of a psychologist: John Broadus Watson and the application of behavioral techniques to advertising. *Journal of the History of the Behavioral Sciences, 18*, 207–221.

Burnham, J. C. (1994). John B. Watson: Interviewee, professional figure, symbol. In Todd, J. T. & E. K. Morris (Eds.), *Modern perspectives on John B. Watson and classical behaviorism* (pp. 65–73). Westport, CT: Greenwood.

Burns, J. D., & Malone, J. C., Jr. (1992). The influence of "preparedness" on autoshaping, schedule performance and choice. *Journal of the Experimental Analysis of Behavior, 58*, 399–413.

Burtt, E. A. (Ed.). (1939). *The English philosophers from Bacon to Mill*. New York: Modern Library.

Butterfield, H. (1965). *The origins of modern science*. New York: Free Press.

Bykov, K. M. (1957). *The cerebral cortex and the internal organs*. New York: Chemical Publishing.

Calkins, M. W. (1899). Attributes of sensation. *Psychological Review, 6*, 506–514.

Calkins, M. W. (1929). *Berkeley: Essay, principle, dialogues*. New York: Charles Scribner & Sons.

Carlson, N. R. (1991). *The physiology of behavior* (4th ed.). Boston: Allyn & Bacon.

Carpenter, W. B. (1855). *Principles of human physiology, with their chief applications to psychology, pathology, therapeutics, hygiene, and forensic medicine*. Philadelphia: Blanchard & Lea.

Carpenter, W. B. (1876). *Principles of mental physiology*. New York: Appleton.

Catania, A. C. (1992). *Learning*. Englewood Cliffs, NJ: Prentice-Hall.

Catania, A. C., & Gill, C. A. (1964). Inhibition and behavioral contrast. *Psychonomic Science, 1,* 257–258.

Cartmill, M. (1991). Science matters in the liberal arts. *Duke Faculty Newsletter,* November, 1–9.

Chase, W. G. & Simon, H. A. (1973). The mind's eye in chess. In W. G. Chase (Ed.), *Visual information processing* (pp. 215–281). New York: Academic Press.

Chow, K. L., & Leiman, A. L. (1970). Aspects of the structural and functional organization of the neocortex. *Neuroscience Research Program Bulletin, 8,* 157–220.

Cohen, D. (1979). *J. B. Watson: The founder of behaviorism.* London: Routledge & Kegan Paul.

Cohen, J. D., & Schooler, J. W. (Eds.). (1997). *Scientific approaches to consciousness.* Mahwah, NJ: Erlbaum.

Combe, G. (1834). *The constitution of man considered in relation to external objects* (3rd American ed.). Boston: Allen & Ticknor.

Coon, D. J. (1994). "Not a creature of reason": The alleged impact of Watsonian behaviorism on advertising in the 1920s. In J. T. Todd & E. K. Morris (Eds.), *Modern perspectives on John B. Watson and classical behaviorism* (pp. 37–63). Westport, CT: Greenwood.

Cooter, R. (1984). *The cultural meaning of popular science.* Cambridge, UK: Cambridge University Press.

Cornford, F. M. (1964). *The Republic of Plato.* New York: Oxford University Press.

Costall, A. (1993). How Lloyd Morgan's canon backfired. *Journal of the History of the Behavioral Sciences, 29,* 113–122.

Cranston, M. (1957). *John Locke: A biography.* London: Longmans, Green & Co., Ltd.

Danziger, K. (1980). The history of introspection reconsidered. *Journal of the History of the Behavioral Sciences, 16,* 241–262.

Darwin, C. (1871). *The descent of man, and selection in relation to sex.* London: J. Murray.

Darwin, E. (1794). *Zoonomia, or the laws of organic life* (2 vols.). London: J. Johnson.

Davis, J. D., & Hersh, R. (1981). *The mathematical experience.* Boston: Birkhauser.

Davidson, A. B. (1971). Factors affecting keypress responding by rats in the presence of free food. *Psychonomic Science, 24,* 135–137.

deBeer, G. (Ed.). (1983). *Autobiographies: Charles Darwin, Thomas Henry Huxley.* Oxford, UK: Oxford University Press.

de Groot, A. D. (1966). Perception and memory versus thought. In B. Kleinmuntz (Ed.), *Problem solving.* New York: Wiley.

Decker, H. S. (1991). *Freud, Dora, and Vienna 1900.* New York: Free Press.

Delgado, J. M. R. (1955). Evaluation of permanent implantation of electrodes within the brain. *Electroencephalography and Clinical Neurophysiology, 7,* 637–644.

Delgado, J. M. R. (1969). *Physical control of the mind.* New York: Harper & Row.

de Rivera, J. H. (Ed.) (1976). *Field theory as human science: Contributions by Lewin's Berlin group* (pp. 324–422). New York: Gardner Press.

Descartes, R. (1911). *Discourse on Method; The passions of the Soul; Meditations on First Philosophy; Rules for the direction of the mind.* In E. S. Haldane & G. R. T. Ross (Trans.), *The philosophical works of Descartes.* Cambridge, UK: Cambridge University Press.

De Waal, Frans (1997). Are we in anthropodenial? *Discover, 18,* 50–53.

Dewey, J. (1896). The reflex arc concept in psychology. *Psychological Review, 3,* 357–370.

Dewsbury, D. (1994). John B. Watson: Profile of a comparative psychologist and protoethologist. In J. T. Todd & E. K. Morris (Eds.), *Modern perspectives on classical and modern behaviorism* (pp. 169–178). Westport, CT: Greenwood.

Diamond, S. (1974). *The roots of psychology.* New York: Basic Books.

Doney, W. (1967). *Descartes: A collection of critical essays.* Garden City, NY: Anchor Books.

Downs, R. B. (1982). *Landmarks in science.* Littleton, CO: Libraries Unlimited, Inc.

Durant, W. (1926/1954). *The story of philosophy.* New York: Pocket Books.

Ebbinghaus, H. (1885). *Memory: A contribution to experimental psychology.* New York: Teachers College Press. (A 1964 Dover edition also was published.)

Egner, R. E. (1958). *Bertrand Russell's best.* New York: Mentor.

Eliot, C. W. (1909). *The Harvard classics.* New York: P. F. Collier & Son.

Ellenberger, H. F. (1956). The ancestry of dynamic therapy. *Bulletin of the Menninger Clinic, 20*(6), 288–299.

Ellenberger, H. F. (1956). Fechner and Freud. *Bulletin of the Menninger Clinic, 20,* 201–214.

Ellis, W. D. (1939). *A source book of gestalt psychology.* New York: Harcourt Brace.

Evans, R. (1972). E. B. Titchener and his lost system. *Journal of the History of the Behavioral Sciences, 8,* 168–180.

Fedio, P., & Van Buren, J. (1971). Cerebral mechanisms for perception and immediate memory under electrical stimulation in conscious man. Annual meeting of the American Psychological Association, Washington, DC.

Ferris, T. (1988). *Coming of age in the Milky Way.* New York: Morrow.

Ferris, T. (1991). *The world treasury of physics, astronomy, and mathematics.* Boston: Little, Brown.

Flourens, P. (1842). *Examen de phrenologie.* Paris: P. Paulin. English translation by D. de L. Meigs (1846). *Phrenology examined.* Philadelphia: Hogan & Thompson.

Fodor, J. A. (1983). *The modularity of mind.* Cambridge, UK: Cambridge University Press.

Fraser, A. C. (1901). *Berkeley.* Edinburgh: W. Blackwood.

Freeman, K. (1947). *Ancilla to the pre-Socratic philosophers: A complete translation of the fragments in Diels, Fragmente der Vorsokratiker.* Cambridge, MA: Harvard University Press.

Freeman, K. (1953). *The pre-Socratic philosophers: A companion to Diehls, fragmente der vorsokratiker* (3rd ed.). Oxford, UK: Basil Blackwell.

Freeman, R. B. 1977. *The works of Charles Darwin: An annotated bibliographical handlist* (2nd ed.). Folkstone: Dawson.

French, J. R. P., Jr., & Marrow, A. J. (1945). Changing a stereotype in industry. *Journal of Social Issues, 1*, 33–37.

Freud, S. (1913). *The interpretation of dreams* (3rd ed., p. 493; Trans. A. A. Brill). New York: Macmillan.

Freud, S. (1917). The history of the psychoanalytic movement (Trans. A. A. Brill). In *Nervous and mental disease monograph series (No. 25)*. New York: Nervous and Mental Disease Publishing Co.

Freud, S. (1923). *The ego and the id*. In *Standard edition* (Vol. 23).

Freud, S. (1935). *Autobiography* (Trans. J. Strachey). New York: Norton.

Fuller, B. A. G. (1945). *A history of philosophy*. New York: Henry Holt & Co.

Galanter, E. (1962). Contemporary psychophysics. In R. Brown, E. Galanter, E. H. Hess, & G. Mandler (Eds.), *New directions in psychology* (pp. 87–156). New York: Holt, Rinehart & Winston.

Gallie, R. D. (1989). *Thomas Reid and "the way of ideas."* Boston: Kluwer.

Galton, F. (1869). *Hereditary genius: An inquiry into its laws and consequences*. London: Macmillan.

Galton, F. (1883). *Inquiries into the human faculty and its development*. London: Macmillan. (Rerpinted, Bristol: Thoemmes Press, 1999.)

Garner, W. R. (1974). *The processing of information and structure*. Potomac, MD: Erlbaum.

Gay, P. (Ed.). (1989). *The Freud reader*. New York: Norton.

Gerow, J. R. (1988). *Psychology 1923–1988*. New York: Time Inc.

Gladwell, M. (1996). "My jaw dropped." *The New Yorker*, July 8.

Glymour, C. (1997). Deja Vu All Over Again? In J. D. Cohen & J. W. Schooler (Eds.), *Scientific approaches to consciousness* (pp. 373–377). Mahway, NJ: Erlbaum.

Glickman, S. E., & Schiff, B. B. (1967). A biological theory of reinforcement. *Psychological Review, 74*, 81–109.

Goldstein, E. B. (1989). *Sensation and perception*. Belmont, CA: Wadsworth.

Goleman, D. (1990, March 6). As a therapist, Freud fell short, scholars find. *New York Times*, pp. 85–89.

Gossett, T. F. (1963). *Race: The history of an idea in America*. Dallas, TX: Southern Methodist University Press.

Gould, S. J. (1993). *Eight little piggies: Reflections in natural history*. New York: Norton.

Graham, C. H., Sperling, H. G., Hsia, Y., & Coulson, A. H. (1961). The determination of some visual functions of a unilaterally color-blind subject: Methods and results. *Journal of Psychology, 51*, 3–32.

Green, D. M., & Swets, J. A. (1966). *Signal detection theory and psychophysics*. New York: Wiley.

Gregory, R. L. (1978). *Eye and brain* (4th ed). New York: McGraw-Hill.

Gregory, R. L. (1987). *The Oxford companion to the mind*. Oxford, UK: Oxford University Press.

Grene, M. (1963). *A portrait of Aristotle*. Chicago: University of Chicago Press.

Guthrie, E. R. (1942). *The psychology of human conflict*. New York: Harper & Brothers.

Guthrie, E. R. (1952). *The psychology of learning*. New York: Harper & Row. (Original work published 1935.)

Guthrie, E. R., & Horton, G. P. (1946). *Cats in a puzzle box*. New York: Rinehart.

Haldane, E. S. (1905). *Descartes: His life and times*. New York: E. P. Dutton & Co.

Haldane, E. S., & Ross, G. R. T. (1911). *The philosophical works of Descartes*. New York: Dover.

Handel, S. J. (1989). *Listening*. Cambridge, MA: MIT Press.

Hanson, N. R. (1958/1965). *Patterns of discovery: An inquiry into the conceptual foundations of science*. Cambridge, UK: Cambridge University Press.

Harris, B. (1979). What ever happened to little Albert? *American Psychologist, 34,* 151–160.

Hartley, D. (1749). *Observations on man, his frame, his duty, and his expectations*. London: Samuel Richardson.

Hebb, D. O. (1949). *The organization of behavior*. New York: Wiley.

Hebb, D. O. (1955). Drives and the C.N.S. *Psychological Review, 62,* 243–254.

Hebb, D. O. (1976). James Olds remembered. *APA Monitor, 7,* 5.

Heidbreder, E. (1933). *Seven psychologies*. New York: Appleton-Century-Crofts.

Heider, F. (1959). On Lewin's methods and theory. *Journal of Social Issues*, (13).

Held, R., & Rekosh, J. (1963). Motor–sensory feedback and the geometry of visual space. *Science, 141,* 722–723.

Helmholtz, H. (1866). *Handbook of physiological optics* (Trans. J. P. C. Southall). Rochester, NY: Optical Society of America.

Helson, H. (1925–1926). Psychology of Gestalt. *American Journal of Psychology, 36,* 342–370, 494–526, *37,* 25–62, 189–223.

Herbart, J. (1822). *Sämmtliche Werke* (Vol. 7), G. Hartenstein (Ed.) (1851, Leipzig: Voss, pp. 129–172). Reproduced in Diamond, S. (1974), *Roots of psychology* (pp. 673–678). New York: Basic Books.

Herrnstein, R., & Boring, E. G. (1965). *A source book in the history of psychology*. Cambridge, MA: Harvard University Press.

Hetherington, A. W., & Ranson, S. W. (1942). Hypothalamic lesions and adiposity in the rat. *Anatomical Record, 78,* 149–172.

Hilgard, E. R. (1987). *Psychology in America: A historical survey*. New York: Harcourt Brace Jovanovich.

Hineline, P. N. (1988). Getting Skinner straight. A review of A. C. Catania & S. Harnad (Eds.), *The selection of behavior: The operant behaviorism of B. F. Skinner: Comments and consequences. Contemporary Psychology, 35,* 225–226.

Hobbes, T. (1651/1939). *Leviathan, or the matter, forme, & power of a common-wealth, ecclesi-asticall and civil.* Oxford, UK: Basil Blackwell.

Holt, E. B., Marvin, W. T., Montague, W. P., Perry, R. B., Pitkin, W. B., & Spaulding, E. B. (1912). *The new realism.* New York: Macmillan.

Honzik, C. H. (1936). The role of kinesthesis in maze learning. *Science, 23,* 372–373.

Hothersall, D. (2004). *History of psychology* (4th ed.). New York: McGraw-Hill.

Hubel, D. H. & Wiesel, T. N. (1959). Receptive fields of single neurons in the cat's striate cortex. *Journal of Physiology, 140,* 574–591.

Hubel, D. H., & Wiesel, T. N. (1965). Receptive fields and functional architecture in two nonstriate visual areas (18 and 19) of the cat. *Journal of Neurophysiology, 28,* 229–289.

Hubel, D. H., & Wiesel, T. N. (1990). Brain mechanisms of vision. In I. Rock (Ed.), *The perceptual world* (pp. 3–24). New York: Freeman.

Hull, C. L. (1943). *Principles of behavior.* New York: Appleton-Century-Crofts.

Hull, C. L. (1951). *Essentials of behavior.* New Haven: Yale University Press.

Hull, C. L. (1952). Autobiography. In E. G. Boring, H. S. Langfeld, H. Werner, & R. M. Yerkes (Eds.), *A history of psychology in autobiography* (Vol. 4). Worcester, MA: Clark University Press.

Hunt, W. A., Matarazzo, J. D., Weiss, S. M., & Gentry, W. D. (1979). Associative learning, habit, and health behavior. *Journal of Behavioral Medicine, 2,* 111–124.

Hurvich, L. M., & Jameson, D. (1957). The opponent-process theory of color vision. *Psychological Review, 64,* 384–404.

Huxley, T. H. (1878). *Hume.* London: Macmillan.

Ince, L. P., Brucker, B. S., & Alba, A. (1978). Reflex conditioning in spinal man. *Journal of Comparative and Physiological Psychology, 92,* 796–802.

James, W. (1884). What is an emotion? *Mind, 9,* 188–205.

James, W. (1890). *Principles of psychology.* New York: Holt.

James, W. (1892). *Psychology, briefer course.* New York: Holt.

Johansson, G. (1950). *Configurations in visual event perception.* Uppsala: Almquist & Wiskel.

Johansson, G. (1975). Visual motion perception. *Scientific American, 232,* 76–89.

Johnson, C. S. (1956). The influence of Descartes on John Locke: A bibliographical study. *Revue International de Philosophie,* 1–21. (Published under her maiden name, C. S. Ware.)

Joncich, G. (1968). *The sane positivist.* Middletown, CT: Wesleyan University Press.

Jones, M. C. (1924). The elimination of children's fears. *Journal of Experimental Psychology,* 382–390.

Jowett, B. (1873). *Plato's The Republic.* New York: Scribner, Armstrong.

Kahneman, D. & Tversky, A. (1984). Choices, values, and frames. *American Psychologist, 39,* 341–350. (This was the text of their 1983 APA Award Address.)

Kalat, J. W. (1994). *Biological psychology* (4th ed.). Pacific Grove, CA: Brooks/Cole.

Kant, I. (1938). *The fundamental principles of the metaphysic of ethics* (Trans. O. Manthey-Zorn). New York, London: D. Appleton-Century.

Kaplan, J. (Ed.). (1992). *Bartlett's familiar quotations* (16th ed.). Boston: Little, Brown.

Katz, D. (1935). G. E. Müller. *Psychological Bulletin, 32,* 377–380.

Katz, D. (1948). *Psychological atlas.* New York: Philosophical Library.

Kaufman, W. A. (1961). *Philosophic classics.* Englewood Cliffs, NJ: Prentice-Hall.

Kersey, E. M. (1989). *Women philosophers.* New York: Greenwood.

Kimmel, H. D. (1966). Inhibition of the conditioned response in classical conditioning. *Psychological Review, 73,* 232–240.

King, W. (1731). *An essay on the origin of evil.* London. Reproduced in Diamond, 1974, pp. 588–591.

Klein, D. (1970). *A history of scientific psychology.* New York: Basic Books.

Kling, J. W., & Riggs, A. (1971). *Woodworth & Schlossberg's experimental psychology* (3rd ed.). New York: Holt, Rinehart & Winston.

Klüver, H., & Bucy, P. C. (1939). Preliminary analysis of functions of the temporal lobes in monkeys. *Archives of Neurology and Psychiatry, 42,* 979–1000.

Koffka, K. (1935). *Principles of Gestalt psychology.* New York: Harcourt Brace.

Köhler, W. (1917/1925). *The mentality of apes* (Trans. E. Winter). New York: Harcourt Brace.

Köhler, W. (1959). Gestalt psychology today. *American Psychologist, 14,* 727–734.

Köhler, W. (1969). *The task of Gestalt psychology.* Princeton, NJ: Princeton University Press.

Konorski, J. (1967). *Integrative activity of the brain.* Chicago: University of Chicago Press.

Kraepelin, E. (1883/1915). *Clinical psychiatry: A textbook for students and physicians* (7th ed., Trans. A. R. Diefendorf). New York: Macmillan.

Kuhn, T. S. (1962/1970). *The structure of scientific revolutions.* Chicago: University of Chicago Press.

Külpe, O. (1909). *Outlines of psychology* (Trans. E. B. Titchener). New York: Macmillan.

LaMettrie, J. (1748/1927). *L'Homme machine* (Trans. G. C. Bussey & M. W. Calkins). Chicago: Open Court.

Lacy, J. I. (1967). Somatic response patterning and stress: Some revisions of activation theory. In M. H. Appley & B. Trumbell (Eds.), *Physiological stress: Issues in research.* New York: Appleton-Century-Crofts.

Land, E. H. (1959). Experiments in color vision. *Scientific American, 200,* 84–89.

Land, E. H. (1959). Color vision and the natural image. *Proceedings of the National Academy of Sciences, 45,* 116–129.

Land, E. H. (1986). Recent advances in retinex theory. *Vision Research, 26,* 7–22.

Langfeld, H. S. (1943). Jubilee of the *Psychological Review:* Fifty volumes of the *Psychological Review. Psychological Review, 50,* 143–155.

Lashley, K. S. (1912). Visual discrimination of size and form in the albino rat. *Journal of Animal Behavior, 2,* 310–331.

Lashley, K. S. (1950). In search of the engram. *Symposia of the Society for Experimental Biology, 4,* 454–482.

Lashley, K. S. (1951). The problem of serial order in behavior. In L. A. Jeffress (Ed.), *Cerebral mechanisms in behavior: The Hixon Symposium* (pp. 112–146). New York: Wiley.

Leahey, T. H. (1992). *A history of psychology: Main currents in psychological thought* (3rd ed.). Englewood Cliffs, NJ: Prentice-Hall.

Lerner, M. (1961). *Essential works of John Stuart Mill.* New York: Bantam.

Lewin, K. (1920). Der Socialisierung des Taylorsystems. *Praktischer Sozialismus* (No. 4).

Lewin, K. (1922). *Der Begriff der Genese in Physik, Biologie und Entwicklungsgeschichte.* Berlin: Julius Springer.

Lewin, K. (1931). The conflict between Aristotelian and Galileian modes of thought in contemporary psychology. *Journal of Genetic Psychology, 5,* 141–177.

Lewin, K. (1945). The research center for group dynamics at Massachusetts Institute of Technology. *Sociometry, 2,* 126–136.

Ley, R. (1990). *A whisper of espionage.* Garden City, NY: Avery Publishing Group.

Littman R. A. (1979) Social and intellectual origins of experimental psychology. In E. Hearst (Ed.), *The first century of experimental psychology* (pp. 39–86). Hillsdale, NJ: Erlbaum.

Loomis, L. R. (1943). *Aristotle: On man in the universe.* Roslyn, NY: Walter J. Black, Inc.

Lorber, J. (1980). Is your brain really necessary? *Science, 210,* 1232–1234.

Mach, E. (1896/1959). *The analysis of sensations.* New York: Dover.

Machado, A. & Silva, F. J. (2007). Toward a richer view of the scientific method: The role of conceptual analysis. *American Psychologist, 62,* 671–681.

MacIntyre, A. (Ed.). (1965). *Hume's ethical writings.* New York: Collier.

Mackintosh, N. J. (1983). *Conditioning and associative learning.* New York: Oxford University Press.

Mahl, G. F., Rothenberg, A., Delgado, J. M. R., & Hamlin, H. (1964). Psychological responses in the human to intracerebral electric stimulation. *Psychosomatic Medicine, 26,* 337–368.

Malone, J. C. (1976). Local contrast and Pavlovian induction. *Journal of the Experimental Analysis of Behavior, 26,* 425–440.

Malone, J. C. (1978). Beyond the operant analysis of behavior. *Behavior Therapy, 9,* 584–591.

Malone, J. C. (1990). *Theories of learning: A historical approach.* Belmont, CA: Wadsworth (paperback version 2002).

Mandler, G., & Mandler, J. M. (1964). *Thinking: From association to gestalt*. New York: Wiley.

Marbe, K. (1936). Karl Marbe (Trans. M. Pilpel). In C. Murchison (Ed.), *History of psychology in autobiography* (pp. 181–213). Worchester, MA: Clark University Press.

Maritain, J. (1946). *The dream of Descartes* (Trans. Mabelle L. Andison). London: Editions Poetry London.

Marks, W. B., Dobelle, W. H., & E. F. MacNichol, Jr. (1964). Visual pigments of single primate cones. *Science, 143,* 1181–1182.

Marrow, A. F. (1969). *The practical theorist: The life and work of Kurt Lewin*. New York: Basic Books.

Martin, T. (1961). *The instructed vision: Scottish common sense philosophy and the origins of American fiction*. Bloomington: Indiana University Press.

Masson, J. (1984). *The assault on truth: Freud's suppression of the seduction theory*. New York: Farrar, Straus, & Giroux.

Matlin, M. (1994). *Cognition* (3rd ed.). Fort Worth, TX: Harcourt Brace.

McClelland, D. C. (1985). How motives, skills, and values determine what people do. *American Psychologist, 40,* 812–825.

McNeil, B., Pauker, S., Sox, H., Jr., & Tversky, A. (1982). On the elicitation of preferences for alternative therapies. *New England Journal of Medicine, 306,* 1259–1262.

Menage, G. (1690/1984). *The history of women philosophers* (Trans. B. Zedler). Lanham, MD: University Press of America.

Meringer, R., & Mayer, C. (1895). *Versprechen und verlesen: Eine psychologische studie.* Stuttgart: Goschen.

Merlan, P. (1944). An idea of Freud's in Plato. *The Personalist, 25,* 54–63.

Merlan, P. (1945). Brentano and Freud. *Journal of the History of Ideas, IV,* 375–377.

Merzenich, M. M., Nelson, R. J., Stryker, M. P., Cynader, M. S., Schoppman, A., & Zook, J. M. (1984). Somatosensory cortical map changes following digit amputation in adult monkeys. *The Journal of Comparative Neurology, 222,* 591–605.

Mill, J. (1829). *Analysis of the phenomena of the human mind*. London: Baldwin & Cradock.

Mill, J. S. (1843). *A system of logic, ratiocinative and inductive: Being a connected view of the principles of evidence, and methods of scientific investigation*. London: J. W. Parker.

Mill, J. S. (1865). *An examination of Sir William Hamilton's philosophy, and the principal philosophical questions discussed in his writings*. Boston: W. V. Spencer.

Miller, G. A. (1956). The magical number seven plus or minus two: Some limits on our capacity for processing information. *Psychological Review, 63,* 81–97.

Mitchell, R. W., Thompson, N. S., & Miles, H. L. (Eds.). (1997). *Anthropomorphism, anecdotes, and animals*. Albany: State University of New York Press.

Moore, B. R., & Stuttard, S. (1979). Dr. Guthrie and *felis domesticus,* or, tripping over the cat. *Science, 205,* 1031–1033.

Morgan, C. L. (1894). *An introduction to comparative psychology*. London: Walter Scott.

Morgan, M. J. (1974). Resistance to satiation. *Animal Behavior, 22,* 429–466.

Moruzzi, G., & Magoun, H. W. (1949). Brain stem reticular formation and activation of the EEG. *Electroencephalography and Clinical Neurophysiology, 1,* 455–473.

Munsterberg, H. (1914). *Psychology, general and applied*. New York: Appleton.

Munsterberg, H. (1914). *Psychology and social sanity*. London: T. F. Unwin.

Murchison, C. (Ed.). (1926). *Psychologies of 1924*. Worchester, MA: Clark University Press.

Murchison, C. (Ed.). *Psychologies of 1930*.Worchester, MA: Clark University Press.

Murchison, C. (Ed.). (1931). *Handbook of child psychology*. Worcester, MA: Clark University Press.

Nahm, M. C. (1962). *Selections from early Greek philosophy* (3rd ed.). New York: Appleton-Century-Crofts.

Nash, M. R. (1994). Memory distortion and sexual trauma: The problem of false negatives and false positives. *International Journal of Clinical and Experimental Hypnosis, 42,* 346–362.

Neisser, U. (1967). *Cognitive psychology*. New York: Appleton-Century- Crofts.

Neisser, U. (1976). *Cognition and reality*. San Francisco: Freeman.

Nevin, J. A., & Shettleworth, S. J. (1966). An analysis of contrast effects in multiple schedules. *Journal of the Experimental Analysis of Behavior, 9,* 305–315.

Newell, Allen. 1962. *Some problems of basic organization in problem-solving programs*. Santa Monica: Rand Corporation.

Newell, A., Simon, H. A., & Shaw, J. C. (1957). Empirical explorations of the logic theory machine: A case study in heuristic. *Proceedings of the Joint Western Computer Conference* (pp. 218–238). Institute of Radio Engineers (February).

Newton, I. (1730). *Optics* (Excerpt Prop. VI, Prob. II). Reproduced in W. S. Sahakian (Ed.) (1968), *History of psychology: A sourcebook in systematic psychology*. Itaska, IL: Peacock.

Nisbett, R. E., & Wilson, T. D. (1977). Telling more than we can know: Verbal reports on mental processes. *Psychological Review, 84,* 231– 259.

Olson, M. A., & Fazio, R. H. (2001). Implicit attitude formation through classical conditioning. *Psychological Science, 12,* 413–417.

Ogden, R. M. (1951). Oswald Külpe and the Würzburg School. *American Journal of Psychology, 64,* 4–19.

Papez, J. W. (1937). A proposed mechanism of emotion. *Archives of Neurological Psychiatry, 38,* 725–743.

Pattison, M. (1965). J. S. Mill on Hamilton. *The Reader, V,* 562.

Pavlov, I. P. (1927). *Lectures on conditioned reflexes* (Trans. W. H. Gantt & G. Volborth). New York: International.

Pavlov, I. P. (1932). The reply of a physiologist to psychologists. *Psychological Review, 39,* 91–127.

Peirce, C. S. (1878). How to make our ideas clear. *Popular Science Monthly, 12,* 286–302.

Penfield, W. (1958). *The excitable cortex in conscious man.* Springfield, IL: Charles C Thomas.

Penfield, W. (1977). *No man alone: A surgeon's story.* Boston: Little, Brown.

Perry, R. B. (1935). *The thought and character of William James* (Vols. 1–2). Boston: Little, Brown.

Perry, R. B. (1948). *The thought and character of William James: Briefer Version.* Cambridge, MA: Harvard University Press.

Perky, C. W. (1910). An experimental study of imagination. *American Journal of Psychology, 21,* 422–452.

Peters, R. S. (Ed.). (1965). *Brett's history of psychology.* Cambridge, MA: MIT Press.

Peterson, G. B. (2004). A day of great illumination: B. F. Skinner's discovery of shaping. *Journal of the Experimental Analysis of Behavior, 82,* 317–328.

Platonov, K. (1959). *The word as a physiological and therapeutic factor.* Moscow: Foreign Languages Publishing House.

Popper, K. (1963). *Conjectures and refutations: The growth of scientific knowledge.* London: Routledge & Kegen-Paul.

Posner, R. A. (1990). *The problems of jurisprudence.* Cambridge, MA: Harvard University Press.

Premack, D. (1959). Toward empirical behavior laws: I. Positive reinforcement. *Psychological Review, 66,* 219–233.

Pribram, K. H. (1971). *Languages of the brain: Experimental paradoxes and principles in neuropsychology.* Englewood Cliffs, NJ: Prentice-Hall.

Pronko, N. H. & Herman, D. T. (1982). From Dewey's reflex arc concept to transactionalism and beyond. *Behaviorism, 10,* 229–254.

Rachlin, H. (1994). *Behavior and mind: The roots of modern psychology.* Cambridge, UK: Cambridge University Press.

Rahn, C. (1913). The relation of sensation to other categories in contemporary psychology. *Psychological Monographs 21.* (Whole No. 67.)

Rand, A. (1982). *Philosophy: Who needs it?* Indianapolis, IN: Bobbs-Merrill Co.

Rand, B. (1912). *The classical psychologists.* Cambridge, MA: The Riverside Press.

Ratliff, F. (1965). *Mach bands: Quantitative studies of neural networks in the retina.* San Francisco: Holden-Day.

Razran, G. (1965). The observable unconscious and the inferable conscious in current Soviet psychology: Interoceptive conditioning, semantic conditioning, and the orienting reflex. *Psychological Review, 68,* 81–147.

Razran, G. (1965). Russian physiologists' psychology and American experimental psychology. *Psychological Bulletin, 63,* 42–64.

Reid, T. (1785). *Essays on the intellectual powers of man: Essay II.* In B. Rand (Ed.) (1912), *The classical psychologists.* Boston, MA: Houghton Mifflin.

Rescorla, R. A., & Wagner, A. R. (1972). A theory of Pavlovian conditioning: Variations on the effectiveness of reinforcement and nonreinforcement. In A. H. Black & W. F. Prokasy (Eds.), *Classical conditioning II*. New York: Appleton-Century-Crofts.

Roediger, H. L. (1985). Remembering Ebbinghaus. *Contemporary Psychology, 30*, 519–523.

Romanes, G. J. (1883). *Mental evolution in animals*. Westmead, Farnborough, UK: Gregg International Publishers.

Rorty, R. (1982). *Consequences of pragmatism: Essays*. Minneapolis: University of Minnesota Press.

Ross, J. B., & McLaughlin, M. M. (1949). *The portable medieval reader*. New York: Viking.

Ross, D. (1951). *Plato's theory of ideas*. Oxford, UK: Clarendon Press.

Rouse, W. H. D. (Trans.) (1956). *Great dialogues of Plato*. New York: New American Library.

Ruch, F. L. (1937). *Psychology and life*. Chicago: Scott, Foresman.

Rumelhart, D. E., McClelland, J. L., & the PDP Research Group. (1986). *Parallel distributed processing: Explorations in the microscructure of cognition*. Cambridge, MA: MIT Press.

Rushton, W. A. H. (1962). Visual pigments in man. In R. Held & W. Richards (Eds.), *Perception: Mechanisms and models*. New York: Freeman.

Russell, B. (1945). *The history of Western philosophy*. New York: Simon & Schuster.

Russell, B. (1959). *Wisdom of the west*. London: Crescent.

Ryle, G. (1949). *The concept of mind*. New York: Barnes & Noble.

Sacks, O. (1993, May 10). A neurologist's notebook: To see and not to see. *The New Yorker*, pp. 59–73.

Sahakian, W. S. (Ed.). (1968). *History of psychology: A sourcebook in systematic psychology*. Itaska, IL: Peacock.

Salzinger, K. (1994). On Watson. In Todd, J. T. & Morris, E. K. (Eds.), *Modern perspectives on John B. Watson and classical behaviorism* (pp. 151–158). Westport, CT: Greenwood.

Samelson, F. (1994). John B. Watson in 1913: Rhetoric and Practice. In Todd, J. T. & Morris, E. K. (Eds.), *Modern perspectives on John B. Watson and classical behaviorism* (pp. 3–18). Westport, CT: Greenwood.

Santayana, G. (1905). *Life of reason*. New York: C. Scribner's Sons.

Schachter, S. (1970). Some extraordinary facts about obese humans and rats. *American Psychologist, 26*, 129–144.

Scheerer, E. (1987). The unknown Fechner. *Psychological Research, 49*, 197–202.

Sechenov, I. M. (1863/1965). *Reflexes of the brain*. Cambridge, MA: MIT Press.

Sharp, S. E. (1898). Individual psychology: A study in psychological method. *American Journal of Psychology, 10*, 329–391.

Sherrington, C. S. (1906). *The integrative action of the nervous system*. New York: Schribner.

Siegel, S. (1978). Tolerance to the hyperthermic effect of morphine in the rat is a learned response. *Journal of Comparative and Physiological Psychology, 92*, 1137–1149.

Siegel, S. (1991). Feedforward processes in drug tolerance. In R. G. Lister & H. J. Weingartner (Eds.), *Perspectives in cognitive neuroscience* (pp. 405–416). New York: Oxford University Press.

Siegel, S., Hinson, R. E., Krank, M. D., & McCully, J. (1982). Heroin "overdose" death: Contributions of drug-associated environmental cues. *Science, 216*, 436–437.

Singer, C. (1959). *A history of biology* (3rd ed.). London: Abelard-Schuman.

Skinner, B. F. (1945). The operational analysis of psychological terms. *Psychological Review, 52*, 270–277.

Skinner, B. F. (1963). Behaviorism at fifty. *Science, 140*, 951–958.

Skinner, B. F. (1971). *Beyond freedom and dignity*. New York: Knopf.

Skinner, B. F. (1974). *About behaviorism*. New York: Random House.

Skinner, B. F. (1977). Herrnstein and the evolution of behaviorism. *American Psychologist, 32*, 1006–1012.

Skinner, B. F. (1989). The origins of cognitive thought. *American Psychologist, 44*, 13–18.

Smith, R. (1992). *Inhibition*. Berkeley: University of California Press.

Smith, T. V., & Grene, M. (1940). *From Descartes to Kant: Readings in the philosophy of the Renaissance and Enlightenment*. Chicago: University of Chicago Press.

Snow, C. P. (1961). *The two cultures and the scientific revolution*. Cambridge, UK: Cambridge University Press.

Sokolov, E. M. (1963). Higher nervous functions: The orienting reflex. *Annual Review of Physiology, 25*, 545–580.

Spurzheim, J. G. (1825). *A view of the philosophical principles of phrenology* (3rd ed.). London: Treuttel, Wurtz, & Richter.

Staddon, J. E. R. (1993). *Behaviorism*. London: Duckworth.

Staddon, J. E. R. (2001). *The new behaviorism: Mind, mechanism, and society*. Philadelphia: Psychology Press.

Stevens, J. (1989). When Hodgson spoke from the grave. *Yankee, 53*, 76–81, 114–116.

Stevens, S. S. (1936). A scale for the measurement of a psychological magnitude: Loudness. *Psychological Review, 43*, 405–416.

Stevens, S. S. (1967). The market for miracles, a review of C. E. M. Hansel (1966), *ESP: A scientific evaluation*. New York: Charles Scribner's Sons.

Stewart, D. (1793/1897). *Outlines of moral philosophy* (19th ed.). London: Sampson, Low, Marston & Co.

Stoltz, S. B., Wienkowski, L. A., & Brown, B. S. (1975). Behavior modification: A perspective on critical issues. *American Psychologist, 30*, 1027–1048.

Strachey, J. (1953–1975). *The complete psychological works of Sigmund Freud*. London: Hogarth Press.

Stratton, G. M. (1897). Vision without inversion of the retinal image. *Psychological Review, 4*, 341–360, 463–481.

Swazey, J. P. (1969). *Reflexes and motor integration: Sherrington's concept of integrative action.* Cambridge, MA: Harvard University Press.

Szasz, T. (1961). *The myth of mental illness: Foundations of a theory of personal conduct.* New York: Hoeber-Harper.

Szasz, T. (1995, September 30–October 6). [Letter to the editor]. *The Economist, 336,* 8–9.

Tedrowe, C. (1997, August). "Deep Blue Thoughts" [Letter to the editor]. *Harper's Magazine,* p. 6.

Thompson, R. F., & Robinson, D. N. (1979). Physiological psychology. In E. Hearst (Ed.), *The first century of experimental psychology.* Hillsdale, NJ: Erlbaum.

Thorndike, E. L. (1898). Animal intelligence: An experimental study of the associative processes in animals. *Psychological Review Monograph, 2* (Suppl. 8).

Thorndike, E. L. (1900). *Human nature club.* New York: Chautauqua Press.

Thorndike, E. L. (1913). *Educational psychology* (Vols. 1–3). New York: Teachers College.

Thorndike, E. L. (1932a). *The fundamentals of learning.* New York: Teachers College.

Thorndike, E. L. (1932b). Reward and punishment in animal learning. *Comparative Psychology Monographs, 8* (Whole 39).

Thorndike, E. L. (1937). Valuations of certain pains, deprivations, and frustrations. *Journal of General Psychology, 51,* 227–239.

Thorndike, E. L. (1949). *Selected writings from a connectionist's psychology.* New York: Appleton-Century-Crofts.

Thorndike, E. L., & Woodworth, R. S. (1901). Transfer of training: The influence of improvement in one mental function upon the efficiency of other functions. *Psychological Review, 8,* 247–261, 384–395, 553–564.

Titchener, E. B. (1896). *An outline of psychology.* New York: Macmillan.

Titchener, E. B. (1899). Zur Kritik der Wundt'schen Gefühlelehre. *Zeitschrift für Psychologie, 19,* 321–326.

Titchener, E. B. (1900). *A primer of psychology* (Rev. ed.). New York: Macmillan.

Titchener, E. B. (1901–1905). *Experimental psychology: A manual of laboratory practice* (2 vols. in 4). New York: Macmillan.

Titchener, E. B. (1910). *A textbook of psychology.* New York: Macmillan.

Titchener, E. B. (1912). The schema of introspection. *American Journal of Psychology, 23,* 485–508.

Titchener, E. B. (1925). Experimental psychology: A retrospect. *American Journal of Psychology, 36,* 313–323.

Todd, D. D. (1989). *The philosophical orations of Thomas Reid: Delivered at graduation ceremonies in King's College, Aberdeen, 1753, 1756, 1759, 1762.* Carbondale: Southern Illinois University Press.

Todd, J. T. (1994). What psychology has to say about John B. Watson: Classical behaviorism in psychology textbooks, 1920–1989. In J. T. Todd, & E. K. Morris (Eds.),

Modern perspectives on John B. Watson and classical behaviorism (pp. 75–107). Westport, CT: Greenwood.

Todes, D. P. (1997). From the machine to the ghost within: Pavlov's transition from digestive physiology to conditional reflexes. *American Psychologist, 52*, 947–955.

Tulving, E., & Thompson, D. M. (1973). Encoding specificity and retrieval process in episodic memory. *Psychological Review, 80*, 352–373.

Turkkan, J. S. (1989). Classical conditioning: The new hegemony. *Behavioral and Brain Sciences, 12*, 121–179.

Turner, R. S. (1994). *In the eye's mind: Vision and the Helmholtz–Hering controversy*. Princeton, NJ: Princeton University Press.

Underwood, B. J. (1972). Are we overloading memory? In A. W. Melton & E. Martin (Eds.), *Coding processes in human memory*. Washington, DC: Winston & Sons.

Valenstein, E. (1973). *Brain control: A critical examination of brain stimulation and psychosurgery*. New York: Wiley.

Valins, S., & Ray, A. A. (1967). Effects of cognitive desensitization on avoidance behavior. *Journal of Personality and Social Psychology, 1*, 345–350.

Verplanck, W. S. (1994, October). *Fifty-seven years of searching among behaviorisms: A memoir*. Paper presented at the Third International Congress on Behaviorism and Behavioral Science, Palermo, Italy.

von Neumann, J. & Morgenstern, O. (1947). *Theories of games and economic behavior* (2nd ed.). Princeton: Princeton University Press.

Vrooman, J. R. (1970). *René Descartes: A biography*. New York: Putnam.

Waithe, E. M. (1987). *A history of women philosophers, 600 B.C.–500 A.D.* Dordecht: Nijhoff; Hingham, MA. (Distr. by Kluwer).

Wandell, B. A. (1995). *Foundations of vision*. Sunderland, MA: Sinauer Associates, Inc.

Wansin, B. & Van Ittersum, K. (2003). Bottoms up! The influence of elongation on pouring and consumption of volume. *Journal of Consumer Research, Inc., 30*, 455–463.

Warren, R. M., & Warren, R. P. (1968). *Helmholtz on perception*. New York: Wiley.

Washburn, M. F. (1908). *The animal mind: A textbook of comparative psychology*. New York: Macmillan.

Washington, J. A. V. (1997, July). "Deep Blue" [Letter to the editor]. *Harper's Magazine*, p. 8.

Wasserman, G. S. (1978). *Color vision: An historical introduction*. New York: Wiley, 1978.

Watkins, M. J. (1990). Mediationism and the obfuscation of memory. *American Psychologist, 45*, 328–335.

Watson, J. B. (1903). *Animal education*. Chicago: University of Chicago Press.

Watson, J. B. (1913). Psychology as the behaviorist views it. *Psychological Review, 20*, 158–177.

Watson, J. B. (1919). *Psychology from the standpoint of a behaviorist*. Philadelphia: Lippincott.

Watson, J. B. (1928). *The ways of behaviorism.* New York: Harper & Brothers.

Watson, J. B. (1930). *Behaviorism.* (3rd ed.). New York: Norton.

Watson, J. B. (1936). John B. Watson. In C. Murchison (Ed.), *A history of psychology in autobiography.* Worcester, MA: Clark University Press.

Watson, J. B., & Rayner, R. (1920). Conditioned emotional reactions. *Journal of Experimental Psychology, 3,* 1–14.

Watson, J. B. & Watson, R. R. (1921). Studies in infant psychology. *Scientific Monthly, 13,* 493–515.

Weber, E. (1843). *De pulsu, resorptione, auditu, annotations, anatomicae et physiolologicae.* Reproduced in part in Herrnstein & Boring, pp. 64–66.

Wegner, D. M., & Pennebaker, J. W. (Eds.) (1993). *Handbook of mental control.* Englewood Cliffs, NJ: Prentice-Hall.

Weisskopf, V. (1989). *The privilege of being a physicist.* New York: Freeman.

Wertheimer, M. (1912a). Über das Denken der Naturvölker, I. Zahlen und Zahlgebilde. *Zeitschrift für Psychologie, 60,* 321–378.

Wertheimer, M. (1912b). Experimentelle Studien über das Sehen von Bewegung. *Zeitschrift für Psychologie, 60,* 161–265.

Wertheimer, M. (1922). Untersuchungen zur Lehre von der Gestalt: 1. Prinzipielle Bemerkungen. *Psychologische Forschung, 1,* 47–58.

Wheelwright, P. E. (Ed.). (1935). *Aristotle.* Garden City, NY: Doubleday.

White, M. J. (1985). On the status of cognitive psychology. *American Psychologist, 40,* 117–119.

Whorf, B. L. (1956). *Language, thought, and reality.* New York: John Wiley & Sons, and The Technology Press of MIT.

Wilshire, B. (1971). *William James: The essential writings.* New York: Harper & Row.

Woodworth, R. S. (1938). *Experimental psychology.* New York: Macmillan.

Wundt, W. M. (1900). *Völkerpsychologie: Eine untersuchung der entwicklung-gesetz von sprache, mythus, und sitte.* Leipzig: W. Englemann & Kroner.

Wundt, W. M. (1907). *Outlines of psychology.* (Trans. with cooperation of the author by C. H. Judd; 3rd rev. English ed., from German 7th ed.). Leipzig: Alfred Kröner Verlag.

Wundt, W. M. (1922). *Grundriss der Psychologie.* Leipzig: Alfred Kröner Verlag.

Zeigarnik, B. (1927). Das Behalten erledigter und underledigter Handlungen. *Psychologische Forschung, 9,* 1–85.

Zeller, E. (1883/1964). *Outlines of the history of Greek philosophy* (13th ed., Rev. by William Nestle, Trans. L. R. Palmer). Cleveland: Meridian.

Index